D1480923

THE
WISDOM
LITERATURE
AND
PSALMS

Old Testament Survey Series

THE
WISDOM
LITERATURE
AND
PSALMS

JAMES E. SMITH

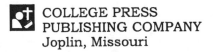 COLLEGE PRESS
PUBLISHING COMPANY
Joplin, Missouri

Library of Congress Cataloging-in-Publication Data

Smith, James E. (James Edward), 1939–
   The wisdom literature and Psalms / James E. Smith
   p. cm. — (Old Testament survey series)
   Includes bibliographical references.
   ISBN 0-89900-439-3
   1. Wisdom Literature—Criticism, interpretation, etc. 2. Wisdom
literature—History of Biblical events. 3. Wisdom literature—History
of contemporary events. 4. Bible. O.T. Psalms—Criticism, interpretation, etc.   I. Title. II. Series: Smith, James E. (James Edward),
1939– Old Testament survey series.
BS1455.S67 1996
223'.06—dc20   96-8511
                                             CIP

DEDICATED TO

Robert* & Wilma Authur
James & Sophie Pennington
Riley & Irene Prather
Vernon* & Thelma Simpson
Victor & Doloras Steger
George & Billie* Whitton

FOUNDING MEMBERS
SHERMAN (KY) CHURCH OF CHRIST

*Gone to be with the Lord

CONTENTS

THE BOOK OF ECCLESIASTES

THE SONG OF SOLOMON

CHARTS

PREFACE

As early as the fourth century AD Christian writers referred to the books of Job, Psalms, Proverbs, Ecclesiastes, and the Song of Solomon as the "poetic books." Perhaps more controversy swirls about these five books than any other division of the Old Testament. The canonicity of three of these books was questioned in ancient times. The interpretation of Ecclesiastes and Song of Solomon are notoriously difficult. Even among conservative scholars there is no unanimity regarding the date of Ecclesiastes and Job. The archaic poetry of some passages in these books make them virtually impossible to decipher at points.

In spite of these difficulties, the careful study of the poetic books is most rewarding. Job depicts faith under trial. Here the believer is assured that his suffering is not necessarily the result of grievous sin on his part, and that an all-wise and all-powerful God ultimately is in charge of the universe. In Psalms the believer can learn to express his faith in the various circumstances of life. This book is also full of direct messianic prophecies from the pen of the prophet David. Proverbs provides a collection of wise observations to guide the believer in his daily walk. Ecclesiastes stresses that faith is the key to meaning in this life, and that the enjoyment of life is a duty. The Song of Solomon places the divine seal of approval upon the human emotion of love and physical attraction. Lessons are taught in these books which help to place in proper perspective the message of the rest of the sacred word.

This present volume completes the Old Testament Survey Series. The author is indebted to College Press for the opportunity to make these notes available to the general public. As in the previous volumes of this series, Linda Stark, Librarian of Florida Christian College, has rendered invaluable service in securing research materials and in proof-reading the manuscript.

Unless otherwise indicated, the translation of the text is that of the author. Primary commentaries which have guided the author in the preparation of this material are these: For Job, A.B. Davidson, and H.C.O. Lanchester, *The Book of Job* in The Cambridge Bible for Schools and Colleges (1937); for Psalms, A.F. Kirkpatrick, *The Book of Psalms* in The Cambridge Bible for Schools and Colleges (1910); for Proverbs and Ecclesiastes, W.J. Deane, in *The Pulpit Commentary* (New York: Funk & Wagnalls, 1909); and for Song of Solomon, S.M. Lehrman, "The Song of Songs" in *The Five Megilloth* (1961).

CHAPTER ONE

Getting Acquainted with the Poetic Books
Aspiration for Christ

The poetic books have certain characteristics which set them apart from the other books of the Bible. First, these books are almost entirely written in Hebrew poetry. Second, they are not historically oriented. Except for the Book of Psalms, there are few historical allusions here. Third, these books deal with issues which are of universal concern to mankind. From the dawn of history human minds have grappled with such issues as suffering, love, and the brevity and meaning of human life. Fourth, direct divine speech is rare here. As a rule the writers are speaking for man to God rather than the reverse which is the essential characteristic of the prophetic books. Fifth, in treating these difficult topics these books exhibit boldness and honesty. Thus one could list a courageous spirit as one of the characteristics of this literature.

CANONICITY OF THE POETIC BOOKS

As to why these books were collected and preserved as part of the Israelite sacred literature, little knowledge exists. One can only speculate.

Three factors no doubt contributed to the preservation of the Book of Psalms. First, many of the psalms are connected with David, a man who claimed the gift of inspiration (2 Sam 23:2-3). Second, the prophetic emphasis of many of the psalms made this a valuable collection to preserve. Third, the use of the psalms for liturgical purposes in the temple no doubt would have made the truly religious among the Jews interested in preserving the collection for future generations.

Meredith Kline has argued that the Pentateuch was deliberately cast in the form of an ancient treaty. In his view the canonization of the rest of the books of the Old Testament can be explained in relationship to the ancient treaty components and concomitants. In that period a ceremony of ratification followed the acceptance of any treaty or covenant. So the record indicates that both at Sinai and in the plains of Moab when the covenant was renewed, such ceremonies were conducted. The Book of Psalms is in reality an amplification of the covenant ratification response described in the Pentateuch.

The wisdom books of Job, Proverbs, Ecclesiastes and Song of Solomon were preserved and collected because (1) wisdom was regarded as a gift of God (1 Kgs 3:28; 4:29); and (2) because these books—at least three of them—have Solomonic connections. The wisdom literature has at least five points of correspondence with the foundational books of the Pentateuch. First, they begin with the fear of God. Thus the way of wisdom is the way of the covenant which Israel received as a gift from Yahweh at Mt. Sinai. Israel manifested wisdom by keeping the covenant (Deut 4:6-8). Second, the wisdom books translated covenant stipulations into maxims and instructions which regulate conduct in different areas of life. Third, the wisdom books are concerned about explaining the covenant sanctions (penalties) which are set forth in the Pentateuch. Fourth, the wisdom books, as well as the Pentateuch, are concerned about the transmission of precepts to successive generations. Fifth, both the Law of Moses and the wisdom books emphasize wholehearted obedience to the Lord.

12

THE POETIC BOOKS IN JEWISH TRADITION

Even before the Christian age the Jews organized the holy books of Scripture into three divisions which came to be designated *Torah* ("Law"), *Nebhi'im* ("Prophets") and *Kethubhim* ("Writings"). The earliest testimony to the order of books in the third division is found in the Babylonian Talmud (*Baba Bathra* 14b): Ruth, Psalms, Job, Proverbs, Ecclesiastes, Song of Songs, Lamentations, Daniel, Esther, Ezra and Chronicles. Subsequently, Ecclesiastes and Song of Songs were segregated from Psalms, Job and Proverbs and placed with three others—Ruth, Lamentations, Esther—in a separate section of the *Kethubhim* called the *Megilloth* ("Rolls"). This was done for liturgical purposes. Each of the five books was read at one of the major Jewish festivals during the year.[1]

In Jewish circles Psalms, Job and Proverbs were always juxtaposed in the arrangement of Old Testament books. In the Middle Ages the scribes called Masoretes gave to this collection of three a special system of accentuation called mnemonically after the initial Hebrew letters of the books themselves, sometimes "Truth" (*'emeth*; reflecting the order Job, Proverbs, Psalms) and sometimes "Twins" (*te'om*; reflecting the order Psalms, Job, Proverbs). The principal Hebrew manuscripts have the three books in the order Psalms, Job, Proverbs. The first five editions of the Hebrew Bible have the books in this order. In the earliest Greek manuscripts, however, Psalms, Job and Proverbs are not inseparably linked.

THE POETIC BOOKS IN CHRISTIAN TRADITION

A. Recognition of the Group.

The first Church Father to recognize the five devotional books as a distinct group seems to have been Cyril of Jerusalem (d. AD 363). After "the historical books" he mentions the five books which are "written in verses": Job, Psalms, Proverbs, Ecclesiastes and Song of Solomon.[2] Apparently chronological considerations dictated the position of Job. Since Job was connected with the Patriarchal age, this book was placed before Psalms which was connected with David. Proverbs, Ecclesiastes and Song follow Psalms by virtue of their association with David's son Solomon.

Epiphanius speaks of the "five poetic works" and Gregory of Nazianzus the five "poetic books."[3] In the course of time the view that the five books were a distinct section of the Old Testament eventually prevailed in the church.[4]

B. Apocryphal Books.

Two other poetic/wisdom books circulated among the churches from the second century AD forward: the Wisdom of Jesus the son of Sirach [also called Ecclesiasticus], and the Wisdom of Solomon. These books are found in the three oldest Greek manuscripts of the Old Testament. The great Latin scholar Jerome (AD 346-420), after thorough investigation of the facts, discussed the status of Ecclesiasticus and Wisdom in the prologue to his commentary on "the three books of Solomon" (i.e., Proverbs, Ecclesiastes and Song). He acknowledged that these books circulated among the Christians. He labeled the Wisdom of Solomon as a "pseudepigraph," i.e., a book pretending to have been written by some hero of antiquity. He had seen a Hebrew copy of Ecclesiasticus, but affirms that Wisdom "is nowhere found among the Hebrews." He passes on the opinion of several ancient writers that Wisdom was actually written by the Jewish philosopher Philo. Jerome concluded his discussion of Ecclesiasticus and Wisdom with these words: "Therefore as the church indeed reads Judith, Tobit and the books of Maccabees, but does not receive them among the canonical books, so let it also read these two volumes for the edification of the people but not for establishing the authority of ecclesiastical dogmas." [5]

In AD 1546 the Council of Trent erased the distinction which Jerome made between books which are authoritative for doctrine and books which might be profitably read for edification. The Council decreed that no distinction should be made between the various books found in the Latin Vulgate Bible. All were equally authoritative. By decree of this council the Apocrypha had now officially become part of the Bible. The Vatican Council of 1869-70 reaffirmed and amplified the decree of Trent. In actual practice, however, Roman Catholic scholars refer to the fourteen books of the Apocrypha as "deuterocanonical," a term that in effect recognizes the distinction made by Jerome back in the fourth century.

Ecclesiasticus and Wisdom of Solomon were not part of the Bible Jesus knew, loved, and endorsed. These books were never received by the Jews as Scripture. According to Paul, the Jews were given the oracles of God (Rom 3:2). They had the privilege of guarding the sacred Scriptures through the centuries. Thus Christian theology requires the church to limit its Old Testament canon to those books received as Scripture by the Jews.

CHARACTERISTICS OF HEBREW POETRY

About one third of the Old Testament is written in poetic form; but the psalms are the prime example of Hebrew poetry. Much controversy surrounds the discussion of the nature of this poetry.

Discoveries in the ancient Near East have forced critics to reevaluate their position that biblical poetry was a late development—postexilic—in the history of Israel. Now it is clear that in neighboring cultures the hymnodical genre was being cultivated as early as the second millennium BC. Hymns from Egypt and Babylonia have surfaced as well as from the Canaanite culture. In terms of external data, there is no inherent difficulty with contending that biblical poetry was produced in written form in exactly the way the Bible portrays.

A. Poetic Parallelism.

Hebrew poetry is not primarily a poetry of rhyme and meter, although there is a certain rhythmic quality about it. To Robert Lowth in 1753 goes the credit for elucidating the primary characteristic of this kind of poetry, namely, parallelism.[6] Lowth identified three basic types of parallelism: synonymous, antithetic and synthetic.

In synonymous parallelism an initial line finds verbal parallels in the succeeding line. A good example is Ps 19:1.

"The heavens are telling the glory of God,
    and the expanse declares the work of his hands."

Here each of the key elements in line one has its parallel in the second line. Chiastic parallelism is a subtype of synonymous parallelism, but instead of giving the parallel ideas in the same order they are presented in the opposite order. Ps 51:1 is an example:

> "Have mercy on me, O God,
>> according to your lovingkindness,
>> according to the multitude of your mercies
> Blot out my transgression."

In antithetic parallelism the second line of a couplet expresses the opposite of the first. Ps 1:6, for example, places in contrast the way (lifestyle) of the righteous and the way of the wicked.

> "Because Yahweh knows a way of righteous ones,
>> but a way of wicked ones shall perish."

The term "synthetic" or "constructive" parallelism is used to describe all poetry which is not clearly synonymous or antithetic. Here the second line expands or amplifies the first line. In Ps 2:6, for example, the second line completes the first line:

> "But as for me, I have installed my king
> Upon Zion, my holy mountain."

Synthetic parallelism sometimes indicates a comparison. This is especially common in Proverbs, as in 15:17.

> "Better is a dish of vegetables where love is,
> Than a fattened ox and hatred with it."

In the reason type of synthetic parallelism the second line offers an explanation for what the first line affirms, as in Proverbs 26:4.

> "Do not answer a fool according to his folly,
>> Lest you also be like him."

Synthetic parallelism sometimes extends to more than two lines. In Ps 1:1, for example, the verbs "walk," "stand," and "sit" build to a climax.

"How blessed is the man who does not
walk in the counsel of the wicked,
nor stand in the path of sinners,
nor sit in the seat of scoffers."

Some authorities identify other types of parallelism in Hebrew poetry, but those illustrated above represent all the really significant types.

B. The Issue of Rhythm.

Does Hebrew poetry have an identifiable rhythmic pattern? That question has been hotly debated for years. A certain cadence is often observable in a selection, sometimes extending over several verses. For example, the opening verses of Ps 23 reflect a 2:2 pattern, i.e., each half-verse has two accentual stresses. Critics were convinced that where a given pattern broke down, they could emend (alter) the standard Hebrew text to restore the "original" rhythm. Liberal commentaries on the poetic books offer large numbers of conjectural emendations to accomplish this goal, emendations which often radically affect the meaning of the text.

The discovery of the Ras Shamra Tablets in 1928 shed great light on this issue. These poetic tablets are written in a Canaanite dialect (Ugaritic) closely related to Hebrew. The tablets date back to the time of Moses, and thus are contemporaneous with some of the oldest poetry in the Bible. A careful study of this literature has demonstrated that this ancient poetry displays no discernible metric pattern.[7] Parallelism requires lines of approximately equal length often with the same number of stressed syllables. This is what creates the impression at times that some rhythm was intended. In other words, what appears to be rhythm is really an accidental result of parallelism.[8]

C. Other Features.

Hebrew poetry has other features some of which are difficult, if not impossible, to display in English translation. These include:

1. Alliteration: the use of the same or similar sounds at the beginning of verses, or in stressed positions within a verse.

2. Paronomasia: a play on the sound and meaning of words.

3. Acrostic structure: verses (or sometimes half-verses, or stanzas) begin with successive letters of the Hebrew alphabet. In Psalm 119, for example, each of the eight verses in the first stanza begins with *Aleph*, the first letter of the Hebrew alphabet. The subsequent twenty-one stanzas display the same pattern, employing the remaining letters of the alphabet. In another example, the twenty-two verses in the poem concerning the virtuous woman (Prov 31:10-31) begin with successive letters of the Hebrew alphabet.

4. Terseness: The Hebrew poets said much in few words. The psalms consist for the most part of brief poetic phrases usually containing three Hebrew words, rarely more than four. Conjunctions are often omitted (e.g., Ps 23:1). In the technique of ellipsis the second line of a poetic verse assumes part of what appeared in the first line (e.g., Ps 88:6). Compactness of expression, however, sometimes makes difficult the interpretation of what the poets were trying to say.

5. Imagery: The use of imagery is not unique in poetic texts, but is particularly prominent there. Imagery is a concise way of writing because it simultaneously conveys information and evokes an emotional response. Pages of prose texts might be required to explain one simple line of poetic imagery such as "Yahweh is my shepherd." Imagery stimulates imagination.

AN INTRODUCTION TO BIBLICAL WISDOM

A. Backgrounds of Wisdom.

In the ancient Near East daily life was regulated by four classes of leaders: princes, priests, prophets, and pontificators or wise men. Practitioners of wisdom were quite prominent in Edom (Jer 49:7; Obad 8), Phoenicia (Ezek 28; Zech 9:2), Babylon (Isa 44:25; 47:10), Assyria (Isa 10:13), Egypt (Isa 19:11-13), and Persia (Esther 1:13).

At the time Israel's wisdom books were written, wisdom literature in neighboring cultures had been on scene for at least a millennium. Ancient Sumer and Babylonia, and especially Egypt, have contributed numerous compositions which fall into this category. From Egypt several collections of "instructions" designed for school boys or for royal trainees have come to light. Perhaps the most famous of these documents is "The Instruction of Amen-em-opet."[9] "The Babylonian

Theodicy" (ca. 1000 BC) is a dialogue between a sufferer and a friend concerning social injustice, a theme very similar to that of Job. Another Babylonian composition, "The Dialogue of Pessimism"[10] is a dialogue between a master and servant on the value of various human enterprises. This work, like Ecclesiastes, reflects upon the real meaning of life.

This brief survey suggests that the outward forms of biblical wisdom literature were well-known in the ancient Near East. The content of Hebrew wisdom, however, was grounded in her unique theology. Furthermore, New Testament teaching demands that biblical wisdom literature be regarded as the word of God. The Holy Spirit guided in the selection and/or production of the materials which appear in these books. Although revelational material is sparse here, one should not conclude that the Spirit was not active in the writing of these books.

B. Dimensions of Wisdom.

A survey of the Old Testament indicates the broad dimensions of "wisdom." First, skilled artisans were considered endowed with the gift of wisdom. Yahweh is said to have filled those craftsmen associated with the construction of the tabernacle (Bezalel, Oholiab) "with skill to perform every work of an engraver and of a designer and of an embroiderer" (Exod 35:35). Elsewhere the wisdom vocabulary is used of goldsmiths (Jer 10:9).

Second, those who are skilled in musical arts, either in composition (1 Kgs 4:31-32) or performance (Jer 9:17) are said to be endowed with wisdom. Third, military strategists and statesmen are called wise (Isa 10:13; 29:14; Jer 49:7). Fourth, magicians and soothsayers are considered wise men (Gen 41:8; Isa 44:25). Fifth, those who could make difficult judicial decisions are said to possess wisdom (2 Sam 14:17,20; 19:27). David, for example, was compared with the angel of God in respect to his judicial wisdom.

In Israel wise men ranked alongside priests and prophets as a legitimate source of national guidance. Wicked men plotted against the life of Jeremiah because his controversial preaching challenged the conventional thinking. They wanted Jeremiah removed from the scene so that "instruction may not perish from the priest, counsel from the wise or an oracle from the prophet" (Jer 18:18; cf. Ezek 7:26). Thus the priests were the official teachers of the law of God. The prophets delivered what were regarded as direct revelations from God. The wise men operated in the sphere of personal counsel and political advice.

ORIGINS OF BIBLICAL WISDOM LITERATURE

Biblical wisdom literature began to emerge during the period of the United Monarchy.

A. Solomon and Wisdom.[11]

God gave Solomon practical wisdom, understanding (ability to solve difficult problems), and "largeness of heart," i.e., comprehensive knowledge. The magnitude of his wisdom is indicated by four comparisons. His wisdom was like (1) "the sand of the seashore." (2) It exceeded that of the "children of the east," i.e., the various Arab tribes dwelling east of Canaan including the Edomites who were famous for their wisdom. (3) It exceeded that of Egypt which was famous for the knowledge of geometry, arithmetic, astronomy and medicine. (4) It exceeded that of the wise men of his own nation: Ethan, Heman, Calcol and Darda. Solomon's reputation as a polymath spread throughout all the surrounding nations (1 Kgs 4:29-31).

The Queen of Sheba traveled to Jerusalem to test the wisdom of the king himself. She observed that Solomon's servants were blessed because they had the opportunity to hear his wisdom continually (1 Kgs 10:8). Her comment may be evidence of a royal wisdom school for upper-class youth in the days of Solomon.

Only a small portion of the literary fruits of Solomon's wisdom has been incorporated into the Bible. During his reign this king spoke three thousand proverbs of which less than one third are preserved in the Book of Proverbs. Of his 1,005 songs, only three have survived: the beautiful Song of Songs, and two of the psalms (72, 127). In addition Solomon made observations based on his botanical and zoological studies. His great wisdom attracted the attention of the rulers throughout the Near East (1 Kgs 4:32-34).

The opening chapters of 1 Kings have as their major theme the wisdom of Solomon. His wisdom was not confined to writing clever verses or beautiful songs. The broad dimensions of ancient wisdom are revealed here. The sacred historian demonstrates Solomon's wisdom in political matters (1 Kgs 2:13-3:1), petition (1 Kgs 3:2-15), judgment (1 Kgs 3:16-28), administration (1 Kgs 4:1-6), economics (1 Kgs 4:7-28), negotiations (1 Kgs 5:1-12), and organization (1 Kgs 5:13-18).

Solomon's name is associated by text or tradition with three biblical wisdom books. As Moses was the mediator of the law, and David was chief contributor to Israel's psalmody, so Solomon is the father of biblical sapiential literature. He was Israel's wise man *par excellence.*

B. Wisdom and the Psalms.[12]

The psalmists frequently employ the language of wisdom. Four types of wisdom material are found in the Psalter. First, a psalm might incorporate a brief saying or proverb (Ps 127:1; 133:1). Ps 37 is largely made up of disconnected proverbs arranged in an acrostic format. Second, the wisdom poem focuses on the discussion of problems of life. For example, Ps 49 discusses the proper attitude toward earthly possessions. Third, the didactic psalms contain teaching about the "fear of God" (Ps 25) or contain admonitions to godliness based on the psalmist's experience (Pss 34; 62; 111). A fourth category of wisdom psalms are those which focus on religious doubt. The outstanding example is Ps 73 which wrestles with the problem of the prosperity of the wicked and the afflictions of the just. This psalm has affinity with the Book of Job.

C. Hezekiah and Wisdom.

In the days of good King Hezekiah the royal court was also active in wisdom activity. A major section of the Book of Proverbs has a superscription which ties the court of King Hezekiah to the wisdom schools: "These also are proverbs of Solomon which the men of Hezekiah king of Judah copied" (Prov 25:1). The immediate inference is that Hezekiah was a patron of literature. He was surrounded by scribes who were qualified to read and transcribe the proverbs which appeared in ancient manuscripts which had come down from the time of Solomon. In his efforts to recapture the glories of the reign of Solomon, Hezekiah endeavored to revive the ancient interest in wisdom.

D. Wisdom and the Prophets.

How did the prophets of Israel view wisdom? Were they totally at odds with the wise men? McKane[13] argued that the presuppositions of wise men and prophets were so different as to necessitate friction between the two groups. Certain passages might suggest that such was the case (e.g., Jer 8:8-9). What appears to have happened is that the practitioners of wisdom increasingly became secularized and politicized as time went on. Such individuals applied cold logic to political situations. The prophets brought God's revelation to bear on those same situations, a revelation which might be diametrically opposed to the course of action proposed by logic. Obviously wise men who had rejected the word of God would be at odds with the prophets. Prophets, however, attributed true wisdom to Yahweh (Isa 28:29; Jer 10:12). They borrowed from the practitioners of wisdom certain teaching techniques and vocabulary.[14] Therefore, the conclusion seems fully justified that the prophets would be supportive of wisdom which had not strayed from its core commitment to the fear of Yahweh.

CLASSIFICATION OF WISDOM BOOKS

At least two types of wisdom literature are represented in the poetic books. Philosophical wisdom, sometimes called higher or reflective wisdom, is illustrated in the books of Job and Ecclesiastes. The Book of Job is concerned about the issue of justice in the world. Ecclesiastes focuses on the meaning of life. Both books ask "Why?" In both books faith is grappling with serious issues. The "fear of Yahweh" undergirds all of the presuppositions and premises of these books.

Practical wisdom, sometimes called lower or prudential wisdom, is represented by the Book of Proverbs. This "home-spun" wisdom is also grounded in the the fear of Yahweh. Probably among the common people this type of wisdom was more popular than the reflective type.

Song of Songs also has been classified as wisdom literature, at least by some scholars. It is true that the core emphasis of the fear of

Yahweh is not present in this book. In fact, the name of God is not even mentioned. Yet the "song" was also one of the many manifestations of wisdom. Furthermore, the intention of this book also seems to be didactic.[15] It celebrates both virtue and fidelity, two qualities which certainly are prominent in wisdom literature. Furthermore, the ascription of this book to Solomon, the father of Israel's wisdom heritage, argues that this book should be regarded as a wisdom book. Viewed as such, "the Song is wisdom's reflection on the joyful and mysterious nature of love between a man and a woman within the institution of marriage."[16]

THE THEOLOGY OF WISDOM

Hebrew wisdom is built upon the foundation of the Law of Moses. In terms of emphasis, one reads little in the wisdom books of God as redeemer of his people. The mercy of God is also not particularly prominent, nor is the concept of repentance and restoration after sin. While the books make a few allusions to sacrifice (e.g., Job 1:5; Prov 21:27), this is not a major theme in this literature.

A. Foundational Principle.
Israel's wisdom was founded upon the fundamental concept of "the fear of Yahweh." The wisdom teachers seem to be concerned about translating the principles of the law of God into practical guidelines for everyday living. They did what the priests could not or would not do, namely, offer practical counsel for the life of the individual. The earliest wise men in Israel were deeply devout men who developed their teaching on a religious base.[17] Early wisdom schools may have been sponsored by the king rather than the temple. Nonetheless, godly priests could hardly have been opposed to the strong emphasis upon faithfulness to Yahweh and his law.

B. Major Tenets.
Besides the fear of the Lord, the key points in the theology of the wisdom teachers are these:
1. God is the creator of the universe (Job 28:23-27; 38:4–39:30; Prov 3:19-20; 8:22-34). Corollaries of this doctrine are these: (1)

23

Man is a moral creature responsible to the Creator for his conduct toward fellow creatures. The ethical content of this literature is built upon this doctrine.[18] (2) God is viewed in broad, universal terms rather than narrow nationalistic terms. He is God of all mankind, not just Israel.

2. God is the source of wisdom (Job 9:4; 11:6; 12:13; 32:8; Prov 2:6; 8:22-31). Wisdom is God's word written in nature and human experience illuminated by direct revelation in the law.[19] Parents and teachers are the custodians of this wisdom. They have the responsibility to pass it on; young people have the responsibility to receive it.

3. The individual has a moral responsibility to be a positive influence in society. He must not harm his neighbor in word or deed. He must provide for himself and his family. He must live up to his God-given potential.

4. The moral universe operates by the law of cause and effect. Righteousness is rewarded, and wickedness is punished (e.g., Prov 10:30). When this principle clashed with experience, the wisdom teachers explored and attempted to explain the contradiction.

The question of whether the biblical poetic books teach any concept of life after death has been debated through the years. Critical scholars generally do not allow for any thought of immortality before the exile. Any text which might express such a hope is forced to express a "this-world" expectation. On the surface this view seems questionable. The hope of life after death loomed large in the theology of surrounding nations (especially in Egypt) even before Israel became a nation. How is it that Israelites were incapable of expressing such a hope until it evolved in the closing decades of Old Testament history?

Recent studies among critical scholars such as Dahood[20] and Brichto[21] have reopened the issue about belief in life after death in the poetic books. Life and immortality were brought to light through the gospel (2 Tim 1:10). Though their hope was not as well-defined nor as firmly grounded as that of New Covenant believers, it now appears that the Old Testament saints also had an expectation of life beyond the grave.

ENDNOTES

1. The order of the five *Megilloth* follows the order of the festivals to which they are assigned: Song (Passover), Ruth (Pentecost), Lamentations (Fast of the Ninth of Ab commemorating the destruction of the temple), Ecclesiastes (Tabernacles), and Esther (Purim).

2. *Catechetical Lecture*, 4.35.

3. Cited by Edouard Dhorme, *A Commentary on the Book of Job* (Nashville: Nelson, 1984), x.

4. The location of Job seemed to present problems to some of the Fathers. Some placed Job after the prophets and before Esther (e.g., Origen; Hilary).

5. Cited by F.F. Bruce, *The Canon of Scripture* (Downers Grove, IL: InterVarsity, 1988), pp. 91f.

6. Robert Lowth, *Lectures on the Sacred Poetry of the Hebrews*, trans. G. Gregory, 2 vols. (1787; Reprint, New York: Garland, 1971).

7. G.D. Young, "Semitic Metrics and the Ugaritic Evidence," in *The Bible Today* (Feb 1949):150-155.

8. Franz Delitzsch, *Commentary on Psalms*, trans. Francis Bolton (Grand Rapids: Eerdmans, 1949), p. 28.

9. English translation can be found in *Ancient Near Eastern Texts Relating to the Old Testament*, ed. James Pritchard, pp. 421-424.

10. Ibid., pp. 600-601.

11. For a critical assessment of the role of Solomon in the wisdom tradition, see R.B.Y. Scott, "Solomon and the Beginnings of Wisdom in Israel" (pp. 84-101) and Albrecht Alt, "Solomonic Wisdom" (pp. 102-112), both in *Studies in Ancient Israelite Wisdom*, ed. James L. Crenshaw (New York: Ktav, 1976).

12. James Wood, *Wisdom Literature: An Introduction* (London: Duckworth, 1967), pp. 44-47.

13. William McKane, *Prophets and Wise Men* (Naperville, IL: Allenson, 1965), pp. 126-130.

14. J. Lindblom, "Wisdom in the Old Testament Prophets," in *Wisdom in Israel and in the Ancient Near East*, ed. M. Noth and D. Winton Thomas (Leiden: Brill, 1955), pp. 126-130.

15. Hassell Bullock, *An Introduction to the Old Testament Poetic Books* (Chicago: Moody, 1979), p. 27.

16. Brevard S. Childs, *Introduction to the Old Testament as Scripture* (Philadelphia: Fortress, 1979), p. 575.

17. On this point Gerhard von Rad (*Old Testament Theology*, 1:433f.) is surely correct. McKane (*Prophets*, p. 53) argues that the oldest wisdom in Israel was purely secular. Hassell Bullock (*Introduction*, p. 24) is correct when he argues: "a purely secular character for wisdom would seem out of keeping with a society where the secular and the sacred were so closely intertwined."

18. O.S. Rankin, *Israel's Wisdom Literature: Its Bearing on Theology and the History of Religion* (1936; Reprint, Edinburgh: T.&T. Clark, 1954), pp. 9-10.

19. Bullock, *Introduction,* p. 52.

20. Mitchell Dahood identified thirty-three passages in the Psalms, eight in Proverbs, and one in Ecclesiastes where he found evidence of belief in life after death. *Psalms* (Garden City, NJ: Doubleday, 1966-70), 3:xlvi-li.

21. Herbert C. Brichto, "Kin, Cult, Land and Afterlife—A Biblical Complex," *Hebrew Union College Annual* 44 (1973): 1-54.

BIBLIOGRAPHY

Baumgartner, W. "The Wisdom Literature." In *The Old Testament and Modern Study,* ed. H.H. Rowley, pp. 210-237. Oxford: Clarendon, 1951.

Bergant, Dianne. *What Are They Saying about Wisdom Literature?* New York: Paulist, 1984.

Blenkinsopp, Joseph. *Wisdom and Law in the Old Testament.* 2nd ed. Oxford University Press, 1995.

Bullock, C. Hassell. *An Introduction to the Old Testament Poetic Books.* Chicago: Moody, 1979.

Crenshaw, James L. *Old Testament Wisdom: An Introduction.* Atlanta: John Knox, 1981.

Gray, G.B. *The Forms of Hebrew Poetry.* 1915. New York: Ktav, 1972.

Kidner, Derek. "Wisdom Literature of the Old Testament" in *New Perspectives on the Old Testament,* ed. J. Barton Payne, pp. 157-171. Waco, TX: Word, 1970.

Lowth, Robert. *Lectures on the Sacred Poetry of the Hebrews.* 2 vols. 1787. New York: Garland, 1971.

Morgan, Donn F. *Wisdom in the Old Testament Traditions.* Atlanta: John Knox, 1981.

Murphy, Roland E. *Introduction to the Wisdom Literature of the Old Testament.* Old Testament Reading Guide. Collegeville, MN: Liturgical, 1965.

Noth, M., and D. Winton Thomas, eds. *Wisdom in Israel and in the*

Ancient Near East. Supplements to Vetus Testamentum, vol. 3. Leiden: Brill, 1955.

Rankin, O.S. *Israel's Wisdom Literature: Its Bearing on Theology and the History of Religion.* 1936. Reprint. Edinburgh: T. & T. Clark, 1954.

Robinson, T.H. *The Poetry of the Old Testament.* London: Duckworth, 1947.

Rylaarsdam, J. Cobert. *Revelation in Jewish Wisdom Literature.* Chicago: University of Chicago, 1946.

Scott, R.B.Y. *The Way of Wisdom.* New York: Macmillan, 1971.

Skehan, Patrick W. *Studies in Israelite Poetry and Wisdom.* Washington: Catholic Biblical Associations of America, 1971.

Wood, James. *Wisdom Literature: An Introduction.* London: Duckworth, 1967.

JOB

CHAPTER TWO

Getting Acquainted with Job
Faith under Fire

Perhaps the Book of Job is the best known of the sacred sixty-six in circles outside the immediate company of believers. Literature classes in high schools and colleges throughout the land invariably discuss this work. Thomas Carlyle, the nineteenth century Scottish essayist and historian, said concerning this book: "There is nothing written, I think, in the Bible or out of it, of equal literary merit." Few other compositions have such power to stretch minds, evoke sympathy, provoke inquiry, and expand vision. One who has eavesdropped on the discussions in the heavenly court, visited Job at the city dump, weighed the arguments of Job and his friends, and cowered before the thundering barrage of questions from the God of the whirlwind can never be the same again.

The book contains 10,102 words organized into forty-two chapters and 1,070 verses. The book is very moving, but it is incredibly complex. It is one of the most difficult books in the Bible to translate and interpret.[1]

31

NAME OF THE BOOK

The Book of Job, like several other Old Testament books, takes its title from the name of the principal character around whom the narrative revolves. The title "Job" is also found in the ancient Greek and Latin versions of the Old Testament.

The name Job (Heb., 'iyyobh) has been traced by some scholars to a root which means "to be an enemy." Those who accept this analysis suggest that the biblical name means either (1) opponent of Yahweh, or (2) one whom Yahweh has treated as an enemy. Others trace the name to an Arabic root which suggests the meaning "one who repents."[2]

W.F. Albright has offered the suggestion which is most widely accepted today. He interpreted the name as meaning "Where is (my) Father?" This name has been attested in the Egyptian texts as early as 2000 BC as well as in the famous Amarna letters (ca. 1350 BC). In both cases the name is that of tribal leaders in Palestine and its environs.[3] The fact that the name is attested in ancient literature and is not merely an artificial symbolic designation of the leading character supports the conclusion that the book records the actual experiences of an ancient tribal leader.

Job is mentioned three times in the Bible outside this book. In two of those occurrences (Ezek 14:14,20) he is mentioned alongside two other historical figures from the Old Testament, Noah and Daniel. James (5:11) commends Job's steadfastness during suffering as a model for Christians. These references indicate that later biblical writers viewed Job as a real person who lived in the past and who suffered.

INSPIRATION AND CANONICITY

The nature of the Book of Job raises interesting questions regarding the inspiration and authority of this book.

A. Inspiration.

The inspiration of Job, as part of a body of literature called "Scripture" is affirmed in 2 Tim 3:16. Though accolades may be heaped upon this book for its literary excellence, the Christian must never lose sight of the fact that this is God's word.

Explicit claims to inspiration are rare in the devotional books. A claim to inspiration is implicit, however, in the presentation of the heavenly council scene in chapters 1-2 and in the citation of the actual words of God in chs. 38-41. These chapters contain direct revelation which always requires inspiration to receive and to transmit accurately.

Chapters 3-37 contain the speeches of Job and four of his friends. In what sense are these chapters inspired? God himself pronounces Job's speeches to be "words without knowledge" (38:2). The Lord was angry with the sentiments expressed by Eliphaz, Bildad, and Zophar because they had not spoken what was right about him (42:7). In these chapters inspiration is working on the level of judicial selection and accurate narration, i.e., here God's Spirit has guided the author in the selection and accurate reporting of the materials. This is not to say that these wise men did not have certain true insights regarding God and life problems. Not every proposition generated by human wisdom and reason is false. Whatever truth these men spoke was offset by being set within a framework of a theology which was wrong headed.

What about the speeches of Elihu? His words are not explicitly repudiated in the epilogue. Should he be regarded as a prophet inspired to present the truth about God and life? Probably not. While Elihu's observations were closer to the truth, they too were based on human reason. Much of what he says is simply a restatement of the opinion of the older men.

B. Canonicity.

A key witness in the history of the Old Testament canon was Josephus (ca. AD 90). He indicates that the sacred books, which number only twenty-two,[4] were organized into three divisions: five books "which belong to Moses;" thirteen books by "the prophets who were after Moses;" and four books containing "hymns to God, and precepts for the conduct of human life" (*Against Apion* 1:8). An analysis of this statement about the breakdown of the books of Scripture indicates that in the first century AD Job must have been counted among the prophetic books.

33

The presence of the Book of Job in the collection of the Old Testament books has not been questioned either in the synagogue or in the church.[5] Citations in ancient Jewish sources make it clear that Job was part of the Scriptures recognized as divinely inspired by Jesus and the early Church. This is reason enough to view the canonicity of this book as settled forever.

PLACEMENT OF THE BOOK

Whereas the placement of Job in the Old Testament canon is secure enough, the position of the book in that collection has shifted over the years. Within a century of Josephus, Job's position had shifted from its placement among the "prophets" to an enlarged third division called by Jewish rabbis *Kethubhim* (Writings). The earliest testimony to this effect is found in a *baraitha* (a tradition from the period AD 70-200) quoted in the Babylonian Talmud (*Baba Bathra* 14b-15a). Jerome (ca. AD 405) seems to have been the first Christian writer to take note of the threefold arrangement of the Jewish tradition. He lists nine books among the Holy Writings (*Hagiographa*), including Job.

In the Hebrew tradition the Book of Job has been inseparably bound to the books of Psalms and Proverbs. Psalms stood first in the triad, while Proverbs and Job were interchangeable. This tripartite collection was given a special system of accentuation by the Masoretic scribes in the Middle Ages.

Septuagint (Greek) manuscripts differ widely in the placement of Job. One LXX manuscript places it at the very end of the Old Testament. The early lists of Old Testament books by Church Fathers also reflect great disparity in the placement of Job. Several place Job among the historical books (e.g., Augustine).

Jerome favored the order with Job as the first of the great poetic trilogy. This order was also favored by Cyril of Jerusalem and Gregory of Nazianzus. The Council of Trent ruled in favor of this order, and this has been generally accepted in modern versions. The basis of this order is not clear. Perhaps it is influenced by the tradition that this book antedates both Psalms and Proverbs. On the other hand, since the book begins and ends in historical prose perhaps it was viewed as an appropriate transition between the purely historical books and the purely poetical books.

In the ancient Syriac version the book of Job appears between Deuteronomy and Joshua. This placement may have been suggested by the patriarchal setting of the book and the belief that Moses was the author.[6]

AUTHORSHIP OF THE BOOK

The Book of Job itself names no author and claims no definite date for its composition. It is therefore an anonymous work; any assertion about the author or date must of necessity be deduced from contents of the book.

The Talmud tradition, followed by many early Christian writers, is that the book was written by Moses (*Baba Bathra* 14b). The time, nature, and theme of the book fit with this tradition. The great lawgiver may have compiled this work from records of the conversations made by Elihu.[7]

Certainly nothing about the style of the book points to Moses. The theory of Mosaic authorship, however, would explain (1) how this foreign book came to be possessed by the Hebrews; (2) how it attained a canonical status; (3) its patriarchal flavor and setting; and (4) the Aramaic flavor in some of the terminology of the book.[8] In addition, one might argue that an historical book is more likely to be reliable when it is written close to the events it describes. Since the book is set in an early period (see below), it is easier for some to believe that it was also written comparatively early.[9]

Critical scholars are of the opinion that the Book of Job was the result of an evolutionary process extending over centuries. In general they believe that the dialogues (chs. 3–31) form the original core of the book. At a much later time an old prose folk tale was divided and used as a frame for the poetic core. Some of these scholars would date the speeches of Elihu and Yahweh even later.[10]

DATE OF THE BOOK

The issue of the date of the writing of the book is separate from the issue of the date of the events described in the book. It is a mistake to try to infer the age of the *writer* from the circumstances of the *hero* of the book.

A. Date of the Events.

Because the book contains no references to historical events it is not easy to assign a probable date for the lifetime and career of Job. In addition, the book reflects a non-Israelite cultural background concerning which little or no information is available.[11]

The events seem to have taken place ca. 2000 BC during the Patriarchal period of Bible history. Several marks of antiquity appear in the prose sections. Some examples are: (1) Job performed his own sacrifice without priesthood or shrine (1:5); (2) Job's wealth is measured in flocks, herds and servants (1:3); (3) his land was subject to invasion by roving tribes (1:15-17); (4) Job's life span of 140 years is in harmony with the long lives of the patriarchs of Genesis (42:16); and (5) the names used in the book are authentic second millennium names.[12]

While these indications seem strong enough there is a problem. The locale of the book is Uz, not Palestine. A patriarchal/tribal society may well have persisted in that region even as late as the monarchy period in Israel. Nonetheless, in terms of the progress of redemption, Job is best understood as having lived before the Abrahamic covenant which narrowed the covenant to one particular family.[13]

B. Date of the Composition.

A survey of the scholarly discussions of Job indicates the widest divergence on the issue of the date for the composition of the book.

If the authorship is assigned to Moses, the book would have been written ca. 1450 BC; if to the age of Solomon, ca. 950 BC. Some would place the writing of Job even earlier. Baxter thinks that Job might be "the oldest book in the world."[14] Few modern scholars, however, would date the book as early as Moses. Other conservative scholars place the composition in the age of Solomon.[15] H.L. Ellison states that "a Solomonic date . . . is the earliest we can reasonably adopt."[16] Some conservative scholars believe that the internal evidence in the poetic sections points to the seventh century BC or later.[17]

Arguments based on the alleged lateness of the language is precarious. The book may have been editorially updated from time to time. Be that as it may, the linguistic evidence is so ambiguous that some scholars have reversed the argument. The language, they say, points to an early period of Israel's history.[18]

The writing of the book is best assigned to the age of Solomon, which was a time of literary flowering and interest in wisdom. There is nothing in the book, however, which conclusively refutes the ancient association of this book with Moses.

BACKGROUND OF THE BOOK

Job was a native of the land of Uz (1:1), a region somewhere northeast of Palestine. He was very wealthy (1:3,10). He was a respected judge and benefactor of his fellow citizens (29:7-25). He was a very righteous man (1:1,5,8). He was the father of seven sons and three daughters (1:2) at the outset of the book.

Is Job an historical book? Did the author intend this book to be a historical record of an actual event in the past and, if so, how precise did he intend it to be?

Most scholars today concede an historical "core" to this book. The author had before him an ancient tale of a patriarch who suffered. He has created ex imagino the poetic speeches which enable the major characters to discuss the theological issues pertaining to his suffering. Such is the view of many scholars who are considered conservative in their overall orientation.

So why are the speeches regarded as literary creations rather than actual orations? Primarily because they are in poetic form, and people did not normally speak to one another in poetic form, especially when in extreme distress.[19] The author has chosen to cast these speeches in poetry in order to elevate the book "from a specific historical event to a story with universal application."[20] Dillard and Longman pose a false dichotomy when they write: "The book of Job is not simply a historical chronicle; it is wisdom that is to be applied to all who hear it."[21] Could not the book at the same time be an accurate historical record and wisdom to be applied through the ages?

One would certainly have to concede that western people in the twentieth century do not ordinarily speak to one another in poetic verse, especially in times of distress. The main characters in Job, however, are wise men, living in the patriarchal world at least two thousand years before Christ. In oral societies speech tends to be more rhythmic and poetic.[22] One of the subplots in the book is the contest in wisdom between Job and the other speakers. This was not just a contest of logic and theology; wisdom required artistic expression. Wise men competing in the field of wisdom might well have communicated with one another in poetic form, even in a time of distress, especially if the distress was the very point under discussion.

The conclusion then is this: there is no good reason for not regarding the poetic sections in the book as transcriptions of what was actually said in a concrete historical situation.

The rabbinic sages were sharply divided in their interpretation of the man Job. Some regarded him as one of the few truly God-fearing men of the Bible, and certainly the most pious of Gentiles who ever lived. Others called him a blasphemer. Some said he served God out of love; others that fear alone motivated his godly service.

PURPOSE OF THE BOOK

In essence, Job challenged the sovereignty of God. Before his ordeal Job viewed God as mandated to always act in certain ordered and predictable ways. Job agreed with his friends that God was responsible for his sufferings. They argue from their orderly worldview that Job must have sinned else he would not be punished with suffering. Job argues from his personal experience of righteousness that his suffering cannot be punishment for sin for he has committed no sin worthy of such punishment. Nor will he accept that he is being tested. What he has experienced is torture, not testing. Therefore Job demands an explanation from God, although he realizes the hopelessness of any prospect of divine redress. For Job, it is not so much suffering which has become problematic; it is God himself. The challenge is: Can Job trust a God who is totally sovereign and whose activities cannot be circumscribed by the dictates of philosophy or theology?

God's response to Job accuses him only of one thing. He, a mere mortal, has interfered in God's affairs. God does not dismiss Job; he instructs him. The speeches of God at the conclusion of the book serve the purpose of bringing center stage both the majesty and mystery of the universe. All creation bears witness to God. Job's dilemma is resolved when he withdraws his challenge and acknowledges that he too is under the protection of the mysterious God who governs all creation.[23]

To be more specific, the Book of Job reveals who God is. It shows the kind of trust which God wants his children to have regarding him. Here is revealed God's favor toward his children and his absolute control over Satan.

STRUCTURE OF THE BOOK

The Book of Job may be described as a lengthy poem bracketed by two prose narratives (chs. 1-2; 42:7-17). The core of the book—the debate between Job and his friends—itself is bracketed by Job's lament (ch. 3) and his complaint (chs. 29-31). Hence in relation to his friends, Job is given the first and last words. The speeches of Elihu and Yahweh deliberately unbalance the symmetry of the book to call all the more attention to the inability of the major speakers to articulate a solution to the problem of the suffering of the righteous.

LITERARY CONSIDERATIONS

A. Genre.

Among the books of the Bible, Job is unique. Scholars have advanced a variety of proposals as to the genre of this book. No single genre classification, however, has gained widespread support. Some scholars have therefore suggested that the book is *sui generis,* i.e., a unique composition.[24] The designation "wisdom debate" seems to be as good as any for the book. Such a designation describes both its form as well as its content.[25]

One should not be surprised to find Near Eastern parallels to the Book of Job for two reasons. First, this is wisdom literature, and wisdom always has an international flavor. Second, the issue of the relationship of personal suffering and piety is one that challenges all religious systems.[26]

The literature of the ancient Near East contains several examples of tales of righteous sufferers.[27] None of these ancient stories is a true parallel to Job. Differences in theology, ethics, tone and mood clearly set apart the biblical account from its nearest competitors. Job's predicament "has a lengthy chain of precedent but no sign of direct ancestry."[28]

B. Style.

The Book of Job is mostly poetry. It contains examples of most of the various types of Hebrew parallelism. The author was a master of metaphor. He draws from flora, fauna, natural phenomena, and the human realm. Particularly noteworthy are the many botanical metaphors and similes used to depict the transience of human life (e.g., 14:2,7-12).

Quotations play a significant role in the book, though they sometimes are hard to identify. These include (1) direct quotations from a speaker's thoughts (e.g., 7:4); (2) quotations of a previous speaker's point of view (e.g., 31:1f.); and (3) proverbs (e.g., 32:6-8).[29]

The Book of Job contains examples of almost every kind of literature which appears in the Old Testament. The author has incorporated (1) laments (e.g., ch. 3), (2) complaints (e.g., chs. 6-7), (3) hymns (e.g., 9:4-10), (4) proverbs (e.g., 5:2), and (5) rhetorical questions (e.g., 4:7) in abundance.

C. Unity.

Critics have labeled large chunks of the Book of Job as later additions which add nothing to, or actually detract from, the message of the book. These include (1) the prose prologue and epilogue; (2) the wisdom poem (ch. 28); (3) Yahweh's second speech (40:1-41:34); and (4) the Elihu speeches (32:1-37:24). Even many conservative scholars concede that textual dislocation has occurred in the third cycle of the debate (chs. 22-27) because (supposedly) Bildad's speech is strangely short, and some of Job's speech sounds more like what Bildad had been saying. Some try to find the missing third speech of Zophar in the concluding words of Job's speech (27:13-23).

Discussions of the integrity of the Book of Job will no doubt continue. The tendency at the moment, however, is a commitment to grasp the message of the book in its present form. The opinion of Gordis indicates the direction of modern scholarship. He regards the book "as a superbly structured unity, the work of a single author of transcendental genius, both as a literary artist and as a religious thinker, with few peers, if any, in the history of mankind."[30]

SUFFERING IN JOB

Without question, suffering is the key issue discussed in this book. Specifically, why do righteous people like Job suffer?

A. Human Speculation.

The various characters who appear in the book reflect starkly different attitudes towards the issue of suffering. The three friends of Job all have essentially the same position regarding his suffering, namely, that he is being punished for some terrible sin, that only the acknowledgment of that sin would secure his restoration. Yet each of the three has his own way of arguing the point. Eliphaz was more of a mystic type. He based his argument on a vision of God which he claimed to have had. Bildad was a traditionalist who based his argument on time-honored concepts of justice. Zophar was the blustering dogmatist who stressed the consensus of human wisdom on the subject.

Elihu speaks at the conclusion of the third round of the debate. He was the youngest of the speakers. Though his view of suffering was also flawed, it certainly was more positive than that of the three older friends. He stressed that God refines people through suffering. Elihu saw in suffering a warning that has an educative function.

Job himself struggled with the issue of his suffering. In his worst moments he bitterly accused God of injustice toward him. In his better moments his faith soared, and he expressed confidence in something better beyond.

This can be summarized in three answers to the problem of pain presented in the book. (1) The bitter answer of Job. Suffering in my case is unwarranted, unjust and cruel. (2) The wrong answer of the friends: suffering is God's way of punishing specific sins. (3) The enlightened answer of Elihu: suffering is God's way to teach, discipline and refine.

41

B. Divine Response.

In the end Job is humbled by the realization that man cannot understand the ways of God in the natural order; so how can he begin to understand the principles of God's government in the spiritual realm? Suffering is one more manifestation of the mystery of providence.

The speeches of God indicate an interim solution to the problem at hand: suffering is a test of trusting God for who he is, not for what he does.[31] The term "interim solution" is appropriate because the book does not purport to give the final answer. The book reveals enough to permit the believer to cope with disaster. Suffering fulfills a divine purpose and exercises a gracious ministry in the godly. Behind the suffering of the godly is a loving Father with a high purpose, and beyond this veil of tears is a glorious "afterwards." Such suffering "is not judicial, but remedial; not punitive, but corrective; not retributive, but disciplinary; not a penalty, but a ministry."[32] This is the interim solution to the problem of suffering. The ultimate solution awaits that day when Christ comes to be glorified in his saints, and all the mysteries of life will be unlocked.

Some scholars argue that the book does in fact offer an answer to the problem of the suffering of the innocent. For M. Tsevat only the elimination of the principle of retribution can solve the problem of this book. He points to three passages in the God-speeches (38:12-15; 38:25-27; 40:8-14) suggesting that the natural world is not concerned with retribution. In this life God is not just or unjust but simply God.[33]

Obviously the God speeches at the conclusion of the book are supposed to offer some kind of answer to the issue of innocent suffering. Negatively, this material repudiates the old doctrine of a causal connection between suffering and moral evil. These points are made in the God-speeches: (1) the splendors of creation and providential sustainment (38:39-40) are proof of the justice of God. (2) The question of man's actual lot as contrasted with his rightful deserts is one on which God prefers to maintain silence. (3) Only if men could match God's wisdom and power could they grasp the working of God's providence.

THE TEACHING OF THE BOOK

A. Theology of the Book.

The Book of Job underscores the mysteries of God and the limitations of man's knowledge of him as perhaps no other book in the Bible. Certainly the book clearly presents the omniscience, omnipotence and justice of God. The attribute of God, however, which most baffled Job and his friends was his sovereignty, or freedom to act as he pleases. The God of this book does not operate by the books that men have written about him. He refuses to be bound by human concepts of him. He follows his own agenda, not one prescribed by theologians. He is free to keep secrets about himself, free to intervene or not intervene on man's behalf, free to answer man's objections about him or not. Job and his friends were frustrated because they were holding God to promises he had never made and setting forth rules for him which he would not follow.

The book also stress divine wisdom. The characters in the book all claim to possess wisdom. In the end, however, it is God alone who is the source of wisdom, and he distributes it as he sees fit. The proper human response to God's wisdom is repentance and submission, and that is exactly how Job responded (12:5f.). No matter how right his defense against his friends, before God the patriarch manifests heartfelt repentance of his own impatience toward the Lord. Thus the book encourages reverence.

B. Doctrine of Satan.

Job introduces Satan, "the adversary." His role in Job anticipates his role in the rest of the Bible. Satan had access to the presence of Yahweh, yet he was governed by his sovereignty. Satan fosters ill-will toward both God and man, who is made in God's image. His aim in this book is not so much to tempt Job to commit various sins, but to force him to the ultimate sin, the denial of God. Yet he is on a leash. He can do no more than he is permitted by his creator to do. In the end Satan is proved wrong about men and their relationship to God. He loses this skirmish. Believers can therefore take courage. Though Satan does his worst, Job proves that man can indeed remain faithful to the Lord.

C. Christological Content.

Like the other books of the Old Testament, Job looks forward to Christ. Questions are raised, great sobs of agony are heard, which Jesus alone can answer. The book takes its place in the testimony of the ages that there is a blank in the human heart which Jesus alone can fill.[34]

In this book Christ is anticipated in several ways. Job cries out for a mediator (9:33); he longs for a heavenly witness/advocate (16:19-21), a divine bondsman (17:3), and an interpreter (33:23-28). Job knows he needs someone who can unlock the mystery of suffering. Through his own suffering on the cross, Christ provided the victory over the plague of evil, pain and death itself.

The one passage in Job which may be regarded as predictive of Messiah is 19:23-27. Job here expresses confidence that his redeemer would one day stand upon the earth as "the last," i.e., he who survives the desolation of the present order. Job anticipated his personal resurrection to life in connection with the appearance of this redeemer.[35]

ENDNOTES

1. Raymond Dillard and Tremper Longman III, *An Introduction to the Old Testament* (Grand Rapids: Zondervan, 1994), p. 199.

2. G.L. Archer suggests another etymology: Job comes from an Arabic root meaning "to come back or repent." Hence Job may mean "one who turns back (to God). *A Survey of Old Testament Introduction* (Chicago: Moody, 1974), p. 462.

3. M.H. Pope, *Job*. Anchor Bible, 3rd. ed. (Garden City, NY: 1979), pp. 5f. Other possible parallels have been found in Akkadian texts from Mari and Alalakh.

4. The twenty-two books of Josephus are the same as the thirty-nine of the English Old Testament. Josephus counted Jeremiah-Lamentations as one book as he did Judges-Ruth and Ezra-Nehemiah. He counted the twelve Minor Prophets as one book.

5. The Second Council of Constantinople accused Theodore of Mopsuestia (ca. AD 350-428) of denying the inspiration of Job. He considered the author of the book to be a learned pagan, who assigned imaginary speeches to historical personages. Yet Theodore wrote a two-volume commentary on the book, and quotes from it in other writings. "His attitude seems therefore to have been one of drastic pruning, but to have fallen short of total rejection."

M.F. Wiles, "Theodore of Mopsuestia as Representative of the Antiochene School," in *The Cambridge History of the Bible*, ed. P.R. Ackroyd and C.F. Evans (London: Cambridge, 1970), 1:495.

   6. For a discussion of the various placements of Job in ancient manuscripts and lists, see Edouard Dhorme, *A Commentary on the Book of Job*, trans. Harold Knight (Nashville: Nelson, 1984), pp. vii-xii.

   7. N. Geisler, *A Popular Survey of the Old Testament* (Grand Rapids: Baker, 1977), p. 185. Geisler lists six arguments to support the Mosaic authorship.

   8. Archer, *Introduction*, p. 464.

   9. Ibid., p. 465.

   10. Dillard and Longman III, *Introduction*, p. 200.

   11. The comparative infrequent use of the name Yahweh (thirteen times) and preference for the name Shaddai, i.e., Almighty (at least thirty-one times), tends to confirm the non-Israelite background of the book.

   12. See W.F. Albright, "The Old Testament and Archaeology" in *Old Testament Commentary*, ed. Alleman and Flack (Philadelphia: Muhlenberg, 1948), p. 155. Evidence for the antiquity of the narrative of Job is discussed by M.H. Pope, "Book of Job" in *Interpreter's Dictionary of the Bible* (New York: Abingdon, 1962), 2:913f.

   13. Dillard and Longman III, *Introduction*, pp. 200f.

   14. J. Sidlow Baxter, *Explore the Book* (Grand Rapids: Zondervan, 1966), 3:25.

   15. E.J. Young, *An Introduction to the Old Testament*; rev. ed. (Grand Rapids: Eerdmans, 1960), p. 340.

   16. H.L. Ellison, "Job, Book of," *The New Bible Dictionary*, 2nd. ed. (Wheaton, IL: Tyndale, 1982), p. 636.

   17. W.S. LaSor, D.A. Hubbard and F. Bush believe that the untimely death of the godly Josiah at the hands of the Egyptians in 609 BC may have triggered a reevaluation of the standard beliefs about divine punishment and reward. *Old Testament Survey* (Grand Rapids: Eerdmans, 1982), p. 561.

   18. D.A. Robertson, *Linguistic Evidence in Dating Early Hebrew Poetry* (SBL Dissertation Series 3; Missoula: Society of Biblical Literature, 1972).

   19. Dillard and Longman III, *Introduction*, p. 207.

   20. Ibid.

   21. Ibid.

   22. Kevin Robb, *Literacy and Paideia in Ancient Greece* (New York: Oxford, 1944), 11. This reference was suggested to the author by his colleague Dr. Michael Chambers.

   23. G. von Rad, *Wisdom in Israel* (Nashville: Abingdon, 1972), pp. 207-225.

   24. Pope, *Job*, p. xxxi.

   25. P. Zerafa, *The Wisdom of God in the Book of Job* (Rome: Herder, 1978).

26. Dillard and Longman III, *Introduction*, pp. 205f.
27. For a concise discussion of related literature from the ancient Near East see R.K. Harrison, *Introduction to the Old Testament* (Grand Rapids: Eerdmans, 1969), pp. 1023-1027.
28. LaSor, Hubbard, Bush, *Survey*, p. 562; F.I. Andersen reaches a similar conclusion. He lists a number of factors pointing to the superiority of the Book of Job over its ancient Near Eastern counterparts. *Job, an Introduction and Commentary* in Tyndale Old Testament Commentary (Downers Grove: InterVarsity, 1976), p. 32.
29. See categorization of quotations in Robert Gordis, *The Book of God and Man* (Chicago: University of Chicago, 1965), pp. 174-189.
30. Robert Gordis, *The Book of Job: Commentary, New Translation and Special Studies* (New York: Jewish Theological Seminary 1978), p. 581.
31. Irving Jensen, *Jensen's Survey of the Old Testament* (Chicago: Moody, 1978), p. 269.
32. Baxter, *Explore*, 3:28.
33. M. Tsevat, "The Meaning of the Book of Job" in *Studies in Ancient Israelite Wisdom*, ed. James Crenshaw (New York: Ktav, 1976), pp. 341-376.
34. E. Heavenor, "Job" *The New Bible Commentary*, rev. ed. Ed. D. Guthrie (Grand Rapids: Eerdmans, 1970), p. 422.
35. James E. Smith, *What the Bible Teaches about the Promised Messiah* (Nashville: Nelson, 1993), pp. 216f.

BIBLIOGRAPHY

Andersen, Francis I. *Job, An Introduction and Commentary*. In Tyndale Old Testament Commentaries. Downers Grove, IL: InterVarsity, 1976.

Clines, D.J.A. *Job 1–20*. In Word Biblical Commentary. Waco: Word, 1989.

Driver, S.R. and G.B. Gray. *The Book of Job*. In International Critical Commentary. Edinburgh: Clark, 1921.

Dhorme, Edouard. *A Commentary on the Book of Job*. Nashville: Nelson, 1984.

Gibson, Edgar C.S. *The Book of Job*. 1899. Minneapolis: Klock & Klock, 1978.

Gordis, R. *The Book of Job: Commentary, New Translation, Special Studies*. New York: Jewish Theological Seminary, 1978.

Green, W.H. *The Argument of the Book of Job Unfolded*. New York: Robert Carter, 1874.

Habel, N.C. *The Book of Job*. In The Old Testament Library. Philadelphia: Westminster, 1985.

Hartley, J.E. *The Book of Job*. In New International Commentary on the Old Testament. Grand Rapids: Eerdmans, 1988.

Pope, M.H. *Job*. In Anchor Bible. Garden City, NY: Doubleday, 1965.

Reichert, Victor. *Job*. In Soncino Books of the Bible. London: Soncino, 1946.

Rowley, H.H. *Job*. In New Century Bible New Series. Greenwood, SC: Attic, 1970.

Zuck, Roy B. ed. *Sitting with Job*. Grand Rapids: Baker, 1992.

_____ . *Job*. In Everyman's Commentary. Chicago: Moody, 1978.

CHAPTER THREE

The Testing of Job
Job 1-3

The prologue to the book is designed to introduce the main characters and the setting. The author flashes before the reader pictures of Job's character and suffering, and Satan's accusations and attacks. The prologue initiates the plot by raising the problem that needs a resolution. It reveals to the reader circumstances of which the main characters are not aware throughout the book. The conflict in the prologue centers around the character of human devotion to God. Does anyone serve God unconditionally, without ulterior motive? This is the question on the human side. On the theological side, an even more profound issue is raised: What kind of God would allow his faithful servant to become a pawn in the hands of Satan? This is the problem of theodicy which has baffled believers and fueled atheism for centuries.

THE CIRCUMSTANCES OF JOB
Job 1:1-5

The opening paragraphs of the book set forth the place, person, piety and prosperity of the hero of this book.

A. His Name (1:1).

Those who regard the story of Job as fictional believe that the patriarch's name has been contrived by the author. The name seems to be derived from a root which carries the idea of "enmity, hostility." The vocalization of the Hebrew reflects a pattern which regularly designates a profession, or a habitual or characteristic activity. Thus Job would indicate one who is an implacable foe. Some take this idea of enmity in a passive sense, i.e., the name is intended to designate one who is the object of enmity or persecution. Job then would mean something like "the persecuted one."

As appealing as this explanation of the name may be, some strong arguments can be raised against it. First, there is no play on the name or allusion to its significance in the book. This is strange if the author coined the name. Second, though the name Job is unique to this man in the Bible, it appears to have been quite common in the second millennium BC.[1] The name *may* have been chosen for the hero of the story simply because it was an ordinary name. The position taken here, however, is that an ancient patriarch named Job actually experienced the trials set forth in this chapter.

B. His Place (1:1).

The setting of the book is in the "land of Uz." The exact location of Uz is uncertain. The name *Uz* appears several times in the Old Testament.[2] Uz was certainly outside Palestine as is indicated by the geographical references, customs and vocabulary reflected in the book. This land appears to have been east of Edom, in northern Arabia.[3] The narrative makes clear that Job lived near the desert (1:19); yet his land was fertile for agriculture and livestock (1:3,14; 42:12).

C. His Piety (1:1).

Four expressions describe the piety of Job. First, he was blameless (*tam*), i.e., whole, complete. He was a man without any obvious moral blemish, a man of integrity. The term *tam*, which is first used in Scripture of Noah (Gen 6:9), does not suggest that Job was sinless. Job's blamelessness is affirmed in heaven (1:8; 2:3), by Job's wife (2:9); and by Job himself (9:21). Even Job's antagonists concede the blamelessness of Job in a general way (e.g., 4:6), although they argued that he must have been guilty of some serious offense to account for his calamities.

Second, Job was "upright" (*yashar*), i.e., he did not deviate from God's standards. The combination of the terms "blameless" and "upright" indicate the peak of moral perfection.

Third, this patriarch is described as "fearing God," i.e., he reverenced the creator and humbly submitted to his will. The ancient sages viewed the fear of God as the foundation of wisdom as well as its goal.

Finally, Job "turned aside from evil," i.e., he avoided all that area which the Holy One had designated as sinful. The fear of God gives one the moral discernment to avoid evil.

D. His Prosperity (1:2-3).

Job was blessed with many children. He had seven sons and three daughters. In the Patriarchal period a large family was viewed as an asset. The children are mentioned directly following Job's piety to suggest that they were the reward of the Lord (cf. Ps 127:3). Seven children, especially sons, were considered the ideal blessing from the Lord (Ruth 4:15; cf. 1 Sam 2:5).

Job was a semi-nomadic chieftain whose wealth was measured in terms of livestock and servants. Seven thousand sheep provided clothing, food and wool for export. Three thousand camels and five hundred donkeys provided transportation of produce and merchandise to distant cities. Five hundred yoke of oxen provided meat, milk and plowing power for crops of wheat and barley (cf. 31:38-40) in Job's extensive fields. Job also had a very large number of servants.

Measured by the standards of his day, Job was "the greatest of all the men of the east" (1:3). His greatness did not lie in his wealth alone, but in the respect in which he was held and in his influence. Since the children of the east were noted for their wisdom (1 Kgs

4:30), the text may be suggesting that Job excelled in this respect as well as in his wealth.

E. His Priesthood (1:4-5).

Job's godly character is indicated in his concern for the spiritual well being of his grown children. He was faithful in his priestly ministry to his family. Each year the ten children of Job got together at one of their homes to celebrate birthdays.[4] That Job's sons each had their own house is another indication of the family wealth. The unmarried daughters probably stayed in their father's house (cf. 2 Sam 13:7,8,20). They were invited to share in the drinking feasts (1:4).

When the annual round of drinking feasts was concluded, Job performed a priestly ritual for his children. He first sent for his sons and "sanctified" them. This ritual probably consisted of washings and a change of garments (cf. Gen 35:2). Early the next morning he offered up burnt offerings "according to the number of them all." Perhaps he offered up the seven bulls and seven rams mentioned in 42:8.

Why these religious ceremonies? The old patriarch was concerned lest while under the influence of strong drink his children might have sinned by renouncing[5] God in their hearts. The text probably has in mind a momentary turning away of the heart from God in the midst of social merriment. This priestly sacrifice Job performed continually, i.e., after each year's round of feasting. This man of God was exemplary in his concern for his family (1:5).

THE CALAMITIES OF JOB
Job 1:6–2:13

The calamities of Job came in two stages: (1) his possessions were first assaulted (1:6-22), and then his person (2:1-10). In both stages the reader is permitted to know what Job could not know, namely, that these calamities were part of the testing of his faith orchestrated by Satan himself with the permission of Yahweh.

A. Satan's Slander of Job (1:6-12).

On a certain day the "sons of God" (angels)[6] presented themselves

52

(lit., stationed themselves) before the creator to report on their activities. A scene similar to this appears in 1 Kings 22:19-23 (cf. Ps 89:7). Satan[7] was among them. The term Satan means "the adversary" or "the opposer." Here, as in Zechariah 3:1, Satan stands before the Holy One to challenge the spiritual credentials of one of God's most noble servants (1:6).

Yahweh interrogated Satan about his activities. Satan responded that he had been traversing the earth. As he had walked back and forth in the earth he apparently was searching for those that he could accuse and devour (cf. 1 Pet 5:8). Yahweh asked Satan if he had considered the piety of Job "my servant."[8] Yahweh knows that Satan hates mankind and that he is convinced that every man has his price or breaking point. The Lord repeated the evaluation of the author of the book. Job was a man who was blameless and upright, who feared God and shunned evil. In Job Yahweh has a champion who will prove Satan wrong (1:7-8).

Satan responded to Yahweh's question with one of his own. "Does Job fear God for nought?" Thus the arch slanderer accused the patriarch of ulterior motives. Satan could not deny that Job was in fact a godly man. But *why* was he godly? The allegation is that Job is being paid by God through a life of ease and prosperity to be pious. Here is the fundamental issue in the book. Do men serve God for who he is? Or for what he does for them? Will a person worship God without personal gain? Is worship essentially selfish? (1:9).

Satan's second question accuses God of placing a thorny hedge around Job, his family and his possessions thereby protecting him from pain and hardship. Then Satan pointed out that God had blessed all the work of Job's hand thereby increasing (lit., causing to burst out) his substance in the land (1:10).

The stage was now set for Satan's challenge. "Put forth your hand now, and touch all that he has, and he will curse you to your face!" Yahweh then put all of Job's possessions into the power of the evil one. Satan was restricted, however, with regard to touching the person of Job. Armed with this warrant, Satan "went out from the presence of Yahweh" (1:11).

At least before the redemptive work of Christ, Satan had access to the heavenly throne room. Indeed he seems to have relished his role as the accuser of the brethren. The Scriptures say amazingly little about the origins and workings of Satan. He appears to have led a rebellion against God sometime before the fall of Adam in the garden (cf. 2 Pet 2:4; Jude 6). Here in Job he is seen as subordinate to God. His powers and sphere of influence are limited by the Lord. Yet the righteousness of God required, it would seem, a response to the criticism of Satan regarding Job.

The final book of the Bible suggests that at the ascension of Jesus Satan lost the right to appear in heaven. This one who accused the brethren day and night before God has now been "thrown down." Through the blood of the Lamb believers can overcome him (Rev 12:7-11). There is now no condemnation to those who are in Christ (Rom 8:1).

B. First Assault against Job (1:13-22).

The hammer blows of calamity began to fall almost immediately upon Job. The disasters fell on the day when Job's children were enjoying a feast at the home of the eldest brother (1:13).

A messenger came to Job with the news that the oxen and donkeys were seized by the Sabeans.[9] All the servants who attended these animals had been slain. Only the messenger had survived the attack (1:14-15).

Before the first messenger had finished his report, a second arrived. He notified Job that "the fire of God," i.e., lightning, had destroyed all the sheep and killed the servants who tended them. Again the messenger was the only survivor of the disaster (1:16).

While the second messenger was still speaking, a third arrived with more bad news. The Chaldeans had executed a well-planned three-pronged attack in which the camels had been captured and their keepers slain (1:17). The Chaldeans here are unsettled semi-nomadic marauders. Beginning in the ninth century they filtered into the civilized world and eventually took control of Babylon.

A fourth messenger brought the worst news of all. A blast of wind (a tornado?) off the desert had ripped through the house where Job's children were feasting. Job's sons—and presumably his daughters also—died in the disaster. The messenger alone had escaped the collapse of the house (1:18-19).

Job responded to these devastating reports by entering into a state of mourning. To demonstrate his agony he tore his robe and shaved his head.[10] Then he fell to the ground and did obeisance before God. The act probably consisted of touching the face to the ground a number of times (Gen 33:3; 1 Sam 20:41). In immortal words which still eloquently articulate human grief, Job cried out to God: "Naked came I out of my mother's womb, and naked shall I return thither. Yahweh gave, and Yahweh has taken away; blessed be the name of Yahweh" (1:20-21). Of course Job did not mean that he would return to his mother's womb, but to the earth which was the "womb" from which the original body of man was created.

In spite of these blows against him, Job "sinned not, nor charged God foolishly (tiphlah)," i.e., he did not consider that God had acted out of character (1:22). Satan is defeated, for he had predicted a curse.

C. Satan's Second Challenge (2:1-6).

The time lapse between the first and second assaults on Job cannot be determined. Jewish tradition assigns a year to the interval. On another day when the angelic hosts assembled before the Lord "Satan came also among them to station himself before Yahweh." These words suggest a distinction between Satan and those other spirit beings who were accustomed to report to the Lord (2:1).

The conversation between Yahweh and Satan follows the same pattern as in the first encounter. In response to a query by the Lord, Satan explained that he had been roaming about on the earth. Again Yahweh directed Satan's attention to the excellent character of Job. In spite of all that had happened to him the patriarch was holding fast to his integrity. Satan had incited Yahweh against this godly man "to destroy him without cause." Though Satan had instigated the experiment, Yahweh accepts responsibility for what happened to Job. The Lord seems indignant that Job should have been put through such torment (2:2-3).

Satan responded: "Skin for skin, yes, all that a man has will he give for his life." Obviously this is some ancient proverb, but there is no agreement as to what it means. Sometimes in Job the term "skin" means body (cf. 19:26). Perhaps the meaning here is "skin (or body) of others for one's own." In any case Satan was sure that if God touched this pious patriarch in his bone and flesh Job would curse the Lord to his face. Again Yahweh unleashed Satan. Job was placed in Satan's hands. The only restriction is that Job's life must be spared (2:4-6).

D. Job's Second Trial (2:7-13).

Immediately upon leaving the presence of Yahweh, Satan smote Job with "sore boils" from the sole of his feet unto the crown of his head. These skin ulcers must have itched, for Job scraped himself with a piece of broken pottery. He sat in the ashes, probably at the city garbage dump (2:7-8).[11]

Job's malady has received several diagnoses. The term "boils" (shechin) is connected with Egypt in Deut 28:27. For this reason Job's disease has been diagnosed as the leprosy called elephantiasis. The disease got its name from the swollen limbs and the black, corrugated skin which resembled that of an elephant. Ancient writers connected this disease with Egypt.[12]

The book describes Job's affliction in some detail, but the language is that of the poet, not the pathologist. The ulcers broke out within the body as well as without, making the breath loathsome (19:17). The sores bred worms (7:5). They alternately closed, having the appearance of clods of earth, and opened and ran. This means that the body was alternately swollen and emaciated (16:8). Job was haunted with horrible dreams (7:14), and unearthly terrors (3:25). He was harassed by a sensation of choking (7:15) which made his nights restless and frightful (7:4). His incessant pains made his days weary (7:1-4). His skin was black, his bones were filled with gnawing pains, as if a fire burned in them (30:30).

Job's wife broke under the strain of seeing her husband's suffering. She could not believe that her husband could "retain his integrity" in the face of such adversity. She urged Job to "curse God and die." Perhaps her actions here explain why Satan spared her in the first assault. Just as Eve in the garden became Satan's ally, so now Job's wife unknowingly is urging her husband to do the Devil's bidding. Her religion is represented as precisely the kind which Satan ascribed to Job (2:9).

Did Job's wife anticipate that renouncing God would bring an immediate and deadly stroke from heaven? Perhaps she only meant to suggest that one experiencing a terminal disease might as well give vent to his personal feelings and animosity toward God.[13]

Job rebuked his wife for her audacity. She was speaking as "foolish women,"[14] speak. He avoids calling his wife a "fool," i.e., godless person. Yet he implies that she had fallen into the snare of the Devil, and was attempting to use her influence to draw her husband after her. He pointed out that for many years they had received good things from the hand of God. Should they not expect from time to time to experience calamity?

Again Job passed the test. Satan was proved wrong. "In all this Job did not sin with his lips," i.e., he said nothing inappropriate about the justice of God. Some have taken the phrase "with his lips" to suggest that Job had inappropriate thoughts toward God but did not give voice to them. But thinking and speaking hardly differ in the East. The lips reveal what is in the heart (2:10).

Three friends of Job heard of his misfortune. How long a time intervened between Job's second affliction and the arrival of his friends cannot be ascertained. From various allusions (chs. 7, 19, 30), it is probable that a considerable time elapsed. The three friends who came to Job in his distress would have been semi-nomadic princes like himself, men who were all but his equals in rank, wealth, wisdom, and influence.

From Teman came Eliphaz. He may be the same Eliphaz who was the firstborn of Esau and the father of Teman (Gen 36:11,15,42; 1 Chr 1:36,53). Though the site has not been conclusively identified, Teman is thought to have been in the vicinity of Petra. Scripture represents Teman as one of the principal locations of Edom. The Temanites had a great reputation for wisdom (cf. Jer 49:7).

Less is known about the other two friends. Bildad came from Shuah, a site in Edom or Arabia perhaps named after one of the sons of Abraham and Keturah (cf. Gen 25:2). Zophar made his way to Job from Naamah, the location of which is unknown. These three men came with good intentions. The three friends had agreed among themselves to come to mourn with Job and to comfort him. This suggests that Eliphaz, Bildad and Zophar lived in the same general vicinity (2:11).

When they first laid eyes on Job, the three friends did not even recognize him. His disease had completely disfigured him. They joined Job in mourning. They lifted up their voices, tore their clothing, and threw dust into the air (a gesture of anger and disdain). For seven days and nights—the time normally allotted to mourning for the dead—the four friends sat upon the ground. No one spoke during that time because they could see that Job was in too much pain to engage in conversation. Comforters were not permitted to say a word until the mourner opened the conversation (2:12-13).

THE COMPLAINT OF JOB
Job 3:1-26

At the end of the seven days of silent mourning with his friends Job finally spoke. He broke out in a passionate cry that he might die.

A. He Prefers Nonexistence to Life (3:1-10).

Job cursed "his day," i.e. the day of his birth (cf. Jer 20:14-18). In this context the birthday stands for a life now so embittered that Job prefers nonexistence to life. This thought he expresses in a series of wishes.

First, Job curses the day of his birth and the night of his conception together. He wishes that the birthday would "perish," i.e., be stricken from history. Job next seems to go back in time before the birth to the conception. In poetry day and night can speak. The night knew the gender of the child before the actual birth. The night whispered the happy news that a male child had been born. In retrospect that conception announcement was really a sentence to a life of suffering. The language here (gebher) is consistent with other Scripture in recognizing the fetus as "a man" (3:1-3).

The next two verses focus on the day. Job wishes that "darkness" would seize that day. The Hebrew here uses several different words for darkness for which there is no equivalent English word. For the ancients darkness symbolized everything that was evil, fearsome and mysterious. Job wants that day so thoroughly to be hidden away that not even God would inquire after it. He requests that thick darkness and the shadow of death would claim that day as part of their domain. He wishes that clouds and anything else that blackens the

58

sky "terrify" that day, i.e., frighten it into not appearing. The point is, Job's birthday should never have happened (3:4-5).

The next four verses focus on the night. Job wants thick darkness to blacken the glittering desert night sky. That night, personified once again, should not express joy. Let that night "be barren," i.e., let no living thing date its birth to that night. Let there be no joyful birthday celebrations on that night (3:6-7).

That conception night should be cursed by those who, it was popularly believed, had the power to cast their spells on a day by making them dark with misfortune. These enchanters were skilled "to rouse up leviathan," i.e., the dragon. In poetic imagination a dark cloud that swallows up the lights of day or night is compared to a monster dragon. The enchanters were thought to have the power to set this dragon in motion (3:8).

Job asks that the "stars of the morning twilight" be darkened. Those stars normally herald the approach of day. That night of his conception should never be allowed to "behold the eyelids of the morning," i.e., the long streaming rays of morning light that come from the opening clouds which reveal the sun (3:9).

Why this bitter curse on that night of conception? Because that night personified should have shut up "the doors of my mother's womb" so as to prevent his conception. The night is under Job's curse for the crime of allowing his conception (3:10).

B. He Prefers Death to Survival (3:11-19).

If conception and birth had to be, Job asks why he had not died in infancy. A high incidence of infant mortality was the curse of the ancient world. Job considered himself unfortunate because he had survived to adulthood. He should have died as he came forth from the womb, or before they placed him on his father's knees,[15] or at least before he suckled at his mother's breasts for the first time (3:11-12).

Had he died in infancy he would have entered into rest. In death he would have joined the great kings and counselors of the past who were famous because of their building enterprises or their wealth. The point is, in death he would have been with honorable, even illustrious men. As it is, Job is viewed with contempt by even the lowliest of men (cf. ch. 30). Thus he wishes he had died in infancy (3:13-15).

The thought of dying in infancy triggers another thought. In view of his present anguish, it would have been better had he been stillborn and never had seen the light. Thus Job wishes he had never been conceived, never been born, was stillborn or had died in infancy. Any of those alternatives were better than the anguish which he was currently experiencing (3:16).

In Job's view death offered peace and quiet to men of all ranks and stations. In death the wicked are silenced as to their raging. Those who are weary with the burdens of life find rest there. Captives no longer are driven to forced labor. In death the small and great are alike. Job longs to be released from the suffering of the flesh. Yet he does not ever contemplate suicide. Godly men regard life as a precious gift which God gives and which only he can recall (3:17-19).

C. He Prefers the Grave to Misery (3:20-26).

In the final phase of his complaint, Job raises this question: Why does God not simply take the life of those who suffer rather than letting them continue in their miserable state? Job cannot understand why God gives light and life to those who live in "misery" and who are "bitter in soul." Though God is not directly named here, this constitutes an oblique criticism of the Lord. The term "bitter" is the plural of intensity. Job believes that many in this world are in the same miserable condition as he. The patriarch simply cannot understand why the Lord allows such miserable people to continue to live (3:20).

Job concludes that many, like himself, "long" (lit., wait) for death. Just as treasure hunters dig frantically until exhausted, so those who suffer intensely plead with God for death until they are weary in so doing. Such people actually rejoice at the moment when they are about to slip into the grave (3:21-22).

Job next turns from the general principle addressed in vv. 20-22, to the specific application to himself. He considers his way hidden or lost. God has shut him off from his former life by placing a hedge across his path. Job feels trapped in a miserable life. Not only does he refer to his physical condition, but also to his mental confusion as he tries to explain his fate rationally. He has no room to maneuver physically, emotionally, psychologically or theologically (3:23).

The complaint concludes in vv. 24-26 with further description of the suffering which Job was experiencing. Job complains that "my sighing comes before I eat," i.e., he cannot even think of eating. His condition has robbed him of all appetite. His groanings "are poured out like water," i.e., in a broad and constant stream. His worst fears come immediately upon him, everything that he imagines could happen actually happens. The affliction comes upon him like waves of the sea, but between each wave there is no respite. Before he can recover from one calamity, another falls upon him (3:24-26).

This frank and bitter complaint sets the stage for the discussion with his friends. Job's words and attitude shocked them into the response which appears in the following chapters.

ENDNOTES

1. See discussion under "Name of the Book" in the preceding chapter.

2. Aram had a son name Uz (Gen 10:23) as did Nahor, the brother of Abraham (Gen 22:21), and Dishan (Gen 36:28).

3. Others suggest that Uz was in Edom, southeast of the Dead Sea (cf. Lam 4:21), while still others locate the place in the region of Bashan, south of Damascus.

4. The text reads literally, "and his sons went and made a drinking feast each in a house on his day." Another view is that Job's children were celebrating a harvest festival at the end of the year. Less likely is the view that the author is describing a perpetual party on the part of the sons every day of every week.

5. Literally the Hebrew verb means "blessed." Translators regard this as a scribal euphemism. The thought that any person would curse God was too repugnant to record. The substitution of "blessed" for "cursed" has occurred in Job 1:11; 2:5,9; 1 Kgs 21:10,13; Ps 10:3. In the East when one greets or bids farewell to a friend he blesses him. From this custom the word "bless" may have taken on the meaning "to bid farewell," hence to renounce.

6. Angels are mentioned several times in the Book of Job. Thus men might appeal to angels for sympathy in times of severe persecution (5:1). Angels fulfill the office of interpreter between God and man (33:23). Angels form the council of God (15:8). Angels were present when the world was created (38:7). They are called holy ones because they attend God himself (5:1; 15:15). Though pure, in comparison to God himself they are impure (4:18; 15:15).

7. Here, as frequently in the Old Testament, the common noun plus the article forms a proper name.

8. The title "my servant" is used of Moses (Exod 14:31), Caleb (Num 14:24), David (2 Sam 7:5,8), Zerubbabel (Hag 2:23), Nebuchadnezzar (Jer 25:9) and of the prophets (e.g., 2 Kgs 9:7).

9. The Sabeans came from Sheba which appears to have been in the area of modern Medina in northern Arabia. For a discussion of the location of Sheba see M. Pope, *Job* in The Anchor Bible (Garden City, NY: Doubleday, 1965), p. 13.

10. Shaving the hair as a sign of mourning is expressly forbidden in the Law of Moses (Lev 19:27-28; Deut 14:1).

11. According to the Septuagint translation, the ashes were "on the dunghill outside the city." In the fourth century Chrysostom declared that pilgrims came from the ends of the earth to Arabia to visit Job's dunghill. See Pope, *Job*, pp. 21f.

12. Pliny, *Nat. Hist.* 25:7f. According to Deut 28:35 this disease is said to strike in the knees and legs, and to cover the entire body. Leprosy begins with *shechin* (Lev 13:18ff.). Others identify Job's malady as an especially severe case of a skin infection variously known in the Near East as "Bagdad Button" or "Jericho Rose," a boil, which becomes ulcerous and leaves a deep scar.

13. The LXX inserts a quite lengthy argument which the woman made to her husband in support of cursing God. She is portrayed as a bitter and despondent woman.

14. The occurrence of the word "foolish" (*nebhalah*) here and in Gen 34:7 suggested to some of the rabbis that Job's wife was Dinah, the daughter of Jacob.

15. The father received the newborn child on his knees as a token that he acknowledged paternity and accepted the responsibility of parentage.

CHAPTER FOUR

The Debate at the Dunghill
Job 4-14

The body of the Book of Job is a debate between Job and his three friends. The tone of Job's complaint and the implicit criticism of God's work in the world compelled them to speak up. The war of words focuses on the plight of the patriarch. Yet the discussion inevitably broadens to include the entire issue of theodicy, i.e., the question regarding the meaning of calamity in this life. In round one of this classic debate each of the friends speaks and Job responds to each in turn.

THE FIRST SPEECH OF ELIPHAZ
Swift Punishment to the Wicked
Job 4:1-5:27

Each of the friends of Job is a distinct personality. Eliphaz was a religious visionary. He claimed to have received his insights about suffering through revelation. He is the most contentious of the three, perhaps because he was the oldest. The speech of Eliphaz moves through five distinct phases.

A. Shock at Job's Despair (4:1-11).

Eliphaz began his speech with an apology for presuming to lecture his friend in such a time of personal anguish. Since Job, however, had broken the silence he now feels free to speak. Yet Eliphaz inquires whether his friend is able physically and emotionally to bear what he is about to say. Yet Eliphaz feels he cannot keep silent, (lit., hold back with words) (4:1-2).

In better times Job had "instructed" (*yissarta*) others. The word carries the connotations of chastisement, correction, discipline, and admonition. The patriarch had "strengthened" feeble hands, encouraged the faint, and provided support for tottering knees. Now it was time for Job to heed his own words (4:3-4).

Eliphaz was amazed that Job was now wilting under the calamity which he had experienced. The patriarch physically "faints" (*tele'*) and mentally is "perplexed" (*tibbahel*) (4:5).

Job, of all people, should be able to cope with adversity. Job's "fear" of the Lord, i.e., his piety, should be his confidence. His hope should be in the "perfect conduct" of his ways. Eliphaz seems to concede that Job's walk outwardly was beyond reproach. Thus the patriarch should have confidence that God would deal with him accordingly. Job needed to remember, however, that innocent people never perish. God never cuts off a righteous man in the prime of life. Therefore, Eliphaz's argument is that Job will either recover, in which case his outward righteousness would be confirmed, or he would die in which case men must conclude that there was some terrible hidden sin in his life (4:6-7).

Eliphaz bears testimony to his personal observation that "those who plow iniquity, and sow wickedness, reap the same." These sinners wilt when God merely breathes upon them. They "perish" in the "blast of God." God silences the voice of the most powerful lions. By this figure Eliphaz is suggesting that no sinner, however powerful, can escape divine wrath (4:8-11).

B. Warning against Job's Murmuring (4:12-21).

Eliphaz claims to have experienced an ominous dream or nightmare. What he saw in that dream caused his bones to shake, i.e., terrified him. He felt a "spirit" or "breath" pass near him. He sensed he was in the presence of some supernatural being. The hair of his flesh stood up. The figure stood still before him, but Eliphaz was not able to discern its form. He therefore cannot describe nor name this mysterious presence. Like Elijah on Mt. Horeb (cf. 1 Kgs 19:12), Eliphaz then heard a still voice (4:12-16).[1]

The visiting spirit—probably an angel—first asked two rhetorical questions: "Can mortal man be just before God? Can a man be pure before his Maker?"[2] Even angels and other heavenly servants fall far short of the glory of God. The Lord cannot put trust in his servants. His holy eye finds "folly" (error) in his angels. If these heavenly beings fall short of God's expectations, how much more "those that dwell in houses of clay," i.e., physical bodies. The foundation of man's house of clay is in the dust, not the heavenly places. Man is built on earth, derived from earth, and limited to earth. In this world man can be crushed as easily as a moth. Man's life span is but for a day compared to the heavenly beings. So insignificant is he that he passes away unobserved, like an insect. The death of man is like the collapse of a tent. When the supporting cord is pulled up, the tent collapses, and the inhabitant perishes from the earth. Worldly wisdom deserts man when he faces his mortality (4:17-21).

C. Application to Job's Situation (5:1-7).

Eliphaz thus far has addressed Job's complaint obliquely. He emphasizes the exalted purity of God, in order to rekindle reverence in Job's heart. He has pointed out that all creatures above and below have sinned against the Lord. Eliphaz now begins to apply these general principles to the case of Job.

First, Eliphaz, by means of two rhetorical commands, makes the point that Job has no one to whom he can appeal against God. Certainly "the holy ones" (angels), who are generally helpful to man, would not receive his complaint and come to his aid. They would view a complaint against God as utter folly. Thus Job's complaint is useless (5:1).

Second, Eliphaz warns that such complaint betrays a mind out of harmony with the Lord. Impatience with the chastisements of heaven and angry outbursts are the marks of a "fool" and a "silly person." Thus by such impatience Job will only bring increased calamity till he has perished from the earth (5:2).

Eliphaz now cites an example from his own experience to illustrate the truth of the observation in v. 2. He had observed a foolish man "taking root," i.e., giving evidence of permanence and prosperity. Suddenly God's judgment fell upon this man. Eliphaz, seeing the fall of this promising person, and knowing the significance of his fall, pronounced his habitation accursed (5:3).

The home of that fool who hardened himself against God became a desolation. His children were "crushed in the gate," i.e., they were powerless to defend themselves in the court which sat in the complex of buildings at the main gate of the city. No one stands up to deliver them in that venue. The abandoned lands of the fool are overrun by marauders. They break through the thorn-hedge which surrounds the field to eat the harvest. All of his substance falls prey to crafty schemers (5:4-5).

Eliphaz now sets forth a pithy observation about life. "Affliction does not come forth from the dust, neither does trouble spring out of the ground." The point is that affliction is not accidental. Men bring it on themselves by the choices which they make. "But man is born unto trouble, as the sparks fly upward." Man inclines toward sin which inevitably brings calamity upon himself. Evil desires flow from the heart of man as easily as sparks shoot up from a fire (5:6-7).

D. Exhortation to Seek the Lord (5:8-16).

Now Eliphaz begins to say what he would do if he were in Job's place: "I would seek unto God," i.e., he would turn his case over to the Lord. To support his suggestion to seek the Lord, Eliphaz paints a brilliant picture of God's power. He does "great things and unsearchable." He does "marvelous things" without number. Then follows a list of some of those wonderful acts (5:8-9).

First, the goodness of God is seen in that he sends rain upon the fields of the earth. Second, God "sets up on high those that be low." The Hebrew text allows that these words be connected to the sending of the rain in the previous verse giving this meaning: the abundant harvests resulting from the rains enable lowly people to prosper. The text can also stand on its own as a second beneficent act of God. This latter interpretation seems to be supported by the clause: "and those which mourn are exalted to safety," i.e., salvation. Such is the graciousness of God toward those who love and seek him (5:10-11).

When God deals with the arrogant and perverse, his power manifests itself in another way. First, "he frustrates the devices of the crafty." All of their schemes go awry so that they do not succeed. Second, "he takes the wise in their own craftiness." This is the only quotation from the Book of Job in the New Testament (cf. 1 Cor 3:19). The shrewd plans of the wicked are quickly thwarted. These worldly wise men are totally confused by the reversal of their counsels. Even in broad daylight they grope about in darkness, i.e., they have no clear insight as to how to cope with what has befallen them (5:12-14).

God rescues those against whom the wicked were scheming. The Lord is the champion of the "poor" and "needy." In the Lord is the hope of the world's downtrodden. Ultimately "iniquity must shut its mouth." The idea is that God has the last word (5:15-16).

E. Assurance of God's Goodness (5:17-27).

In view of the beneficent character of the Lord, Eliphaz can argue that those who experience affliction can be happy. God afflicts men only for the purpose of more abundantly blessing them. Therefore, affliction was a guarantee of greater blessing to follow. One, therefore should not "despise," i.e., take lightly, the chastening of the Almighty (5:17).

Eliphaz further amplifies his contention about the purpose of suffering. The Lord "makes sore" in order to bind up; he "wounds" in order to heal more perfectly. The Lord is like a surgeon who must inflict wounds in order to bring a sick man to sound health (5:18).

Eliphaz assures Job that God will deliver the one who trusts in him "in six troubles," yes even in "seven." This so-called X+1 formula appears frequently in the wisdom literature. It expresses the idea of completeness, i.e., in all troubles the Lord would deliver those who responded positively to his chastisement. Specific examples of how

God would deliver such a person are cited by Eliphaz: (1) in famine, (2) war, (3) the "scourge of the tongue," i.e., slander, and (4) the beasts of the earth. If he trusted in God, Job would be able to laugh in the face of "destruction and dearth" (5:19-22).

Once restored to the favor of the Lord, Job would "be in league with the stones of the field." The idea is that these stones would not impede him when he tilled his fields. The "beasts of the field" would be at peace with him, i.e., they would not be a menace to his flocks and herds. Job would have confidence in regard to his possessions. He would know peace in his "tent," i.e., homestead (5:23).

Eliphaz has described the blessings which Job would receive after restoration quite eloquently. Now he showed his insensitivity by a reference to the restoration of Job's "seed," i.e., progeny. His offspring would be numerous and powerful. Furthermore, Job would come to his grave "in a full age." In ancient culture this was the crowning blessing of man on earth, to live long and die old and full of years (5:25-26).

Eliphaz concludes his speech with an exclamation point. He acts as a spokesman for the other visitors when he says, "We have searched it, and so it is." Eliphaz and his companions believed in the health and wealth gospel. Serve God and prosper. Submit to God and be restored (5:27).

The speech of Eliphaz is a masterpiece. He certainly had a lofty conception of God. Yet he erred in two particulars. First, his speech showed little sympathy for Job's plight. Second, his theory that suffering is punishment for sin is not capable of universal application. Job certainly thought he was the exception. So in the final analysis, the speech of Eliphaz aggravated Job's misery rather than soothed it.

JOB'S RESPONSE TO ELIPHAZ
Job 6:1–7:21

Eliphaz had not mentioned any specific sin on Job's part. He had, however, painted dark pictures of the evil of human nature. Job saw the implication of what Eliphaz saw. He cannot believe that his friend really meant what his words suggested, namely, that Job was being punished for his evil nature.

A. Job Defends His Complaint (6:1-7).

Eliphaz had suggested that Job's complaint was inappropriate and disproportionate. Job counters by making four arguments. First, his "impatience" (*ka'as*), i.e., the attitude expressed in his initial complaint, would be outweighed in any balances by his calamities (*hayyah*). Job felt that it would take all the sand of the seashore to counterbalance the weight of his affliction in those balances. For this reason his initial words were "rash" (*la'ah*), i.e., wild or vain. Job admits a certain extravagance in his language, but he justifies it in view of the enormous burden of his affliction (6:1-3).

Second, the burden on Job's mind was as great as the affliction of his body. The physical pain alone was not what drove him to his complaint, but the fact that this affliction had come to him from God. He had been smitten by "the arrows of the Almighty," i.e., by the diseases and plagues with which God smites mankind. Job has concluded that God has become his enemy. God's arrows are poison-tipped. That poison has spread through Job's mind numbing his spiritual sensitivities and paralyzing his spirit.[3] If he has spoken inappropriately it is because of what God has done to him. The "terrors of God" have besieged Job, i.e., he fears even worse things to come (6:4).

Third, the depth of his agony is indicated by the fact that he wants no food. Lowly animals moan if they do not have the food they need. Job wants nothing to eat. He can no more eat his food than one can eat unsalted food. Food is loathsome to him. It has no more taste than the white of an egg. The lack of food might have caused a weakness which Job offers as another legitimate excuse for the tone of his complaint (6:5-7).

B. Job Laments His Condition (6:8-13).

Job's logical defense of his complaint is interrupted by an outburst of lamentation. He has one wish, one request of God. Job longs for death. He wishes that God would crush him, i.e., extinguish his life, that he would "cut me off," i.e., from the land of the living. The only comfort of which he can conceive is death. He is certain that nothing would mar his comfort in death, for he has never denied nor disobeyed the words of the Holy One. These are the words of a believer who is confident of his destiny in eternity (6:8-10).

Job describes the condition which has led him to prefer death to life. He feels he has no more strength to hold out any longer. He would need the strength of stones or brass to continue to hold out against the exhausting afflictions which oppress him. His disease has broken him, exhausted him. He has no inner resources left with which to cope with his affliction. Any thought of possible recovery is gone (6:11-13).

C. Job Derides His Comforters (6:14-30).

Job now feels that his friends are against him, that they do not appreciate his plight. To one who is "ready to faint," i.e., give up in despair, a friend should show "kindness" (*chesed*). The kindness should be shown "even if he forsake the fear of the Lord."[4] Job has received no such treatment from his friends. Though Eliphaz alone has spoken thus far, the others have indicated their agreement with his sentiments by gesture or facial expression (6:14).

Job accuses his "brethren" (is there a note of sarcasm here?) of being like a wadi which gushes with turbulent water produced by melting snow. Those same wadis wind their way toward the desert only to be consumed by the heat or lost in the sand. "They go into nothing and perish." Merchant caravans from Tema (in northern Arabia) or Sheba (in southern Arabia) could not find those brooks once they have reached the desert. Job's visitors are like that. When he needs them most they are nowhere to be found. They came and saw "a terror," the horrible appearance of Job, and they "were afraid." They were paralyzed at the sight of his calamity. Even worse, they judged his calamity to be an act of God, and therefore they were afraid to extend to him sympathy lest they also become a target for the wrath of the Almighty! (6:15-21).

Job had asked little of these friends. He had not asked them for a monetary gift. He had not asked them to deliver him from some adversary or ransom him from powerful robbers who might hold him captive. All he asks them to do is to point out to him the sins which they insinuate that he has committed, sins worthy of such severe punishment. If they will point these out to him, Job pledges to hold his peace (6:22-24).

Job points out that honest words are "powerful" (*marats*), or perhaps "painful" (NASB). Yet Job would welcome such forthrightness on their part. Their arguments, however, proved nothing for they were based on insinuations, *non sequiturs*, and faulting Job's language. Did these friends really intend to reprove Job's words? The words of one in despair like Job "are as wind," i.e., they should be overlooked as mere empty talk coming from a mind preoccupied with suffering (6:25-26).

Job accuses his friends of heartlessness. His words are quite severe. These three would "cast lots" for possession of an orphan. The situation envisioned here is that of ruthless creditors going after a potential young servant after a debtor has died (6:27).

Job requests that his friends please look him in the face. They should be able to judge by his countenance that he was not lying when he asserted his innocence. Job urges them to "turn" from their presuppositions about his problems. Let there be no injustice or wrong on the part of these friends in accusing him of guilt. Job boldly affirms: "My cause is righteous" (lit., "my right is in it"). The patriarch means that his plea against God in reference to his suffering has right on its side. He affirms that he has the ability to say whether or not he was innocent. He was able to discern the difference between right and wrong (6:28-30) [5]

D. Job Reflects on Life (7:1-10).

Job's complaint now takes a new direction. His own problems cause him to look at mankind in general.

1. The pain of life (7:1-5). Mankind is doomed to a short and hard life. His life is compared to "a time of service" or "the days of a hireling," i.e., a day laborer. In the heat of the day such a one "pants for" the shade, the shadows that signal the end of the day's work. He eagerly awaits the wages which the law required his employer to pay him at the conclusion of the working day (7:1-2).

Like the day laborer, Job longs for the end of his hard day of toil under the affliction which has decimated his body. He describes his time of toil as "months of vanity" and "wearisome nights," indicating that his disease had already endured a long time. He tosses and turns throughout the night longing for the sunrise which never seems to come (7:3).

Job's skin ulcers had bred worms. The hard, earth-like crusts which covered his sores were like lumps of dust. The sores would now and again break open and ooze pus (7:4-5).

2. *The brevity of life (7:6-10).* Job complains that his "days" (i.e., life) are "swifter than a weaver's shuttle." The point is not that each day was passing quickly, for he has already said that was not the case. Rather he means that his life is near its end. The "weaver's shuttle" moves rapidly across a loom in the making of cloth. What is worse, Job lives out his days "without hope," without any expectation of recovery or relief (7:6).

His hopeless condition drives Job to supplication. He asks the Lord to take note of the fact that his life is but "breath," i.e., brief. He is a mere mortal. Furthermore, Job asks God to remember that "my eye will not again see good," i.e., happiness or prosperity. Job has given up on this life. He will disappear from the earth.Then God may look for him among the living, but he shall be gone (7:7-8).

Like a cloud which soon disappears never to return, so a man who goes down to Sheol does not return to this world. Sheol is never the grave in the Old Testament but the abode of departed spirits. "He shall return no more to his house." The point is that if God does not deal with him soon it will be too late. He will be dead (7:9-10).

E. Job Reasons with God (7:11-21).

The thoughts of the brevity and bitterness of life trigger a new outburst on Job's part. Therefore he affirms that he will not restrain his mouth. He will speak out of the anguish of his spirit. He will lodge his complaint in the bitterness of his soul (7:11).

First, he argues that he is no threat or danger to anyone which might demand the attention of the Almighty. He is not the sea which must be confined lest it sweep over the land. Nor is he the mythological sea monster which threatened the universe. Job appears to allude to the Babylonian mythology in which the sea monster Tiamat had to be slain by the god Marduk at the creation of the world. A literary allusion to mythology does not imply that Job believed the myth any more than an allusion to Santa Claus means that one believes in the real existence of the jolly elf. To the ancients the tempestuous sea was viewed as a threat to the existence of civilization. God must watch

and control that "monster." Job's point is that he is no threat to anyone. So why is God focused on him to bring him down? (7:12).

Second, Job argues that he is too weak to deserve the continued
harassment from God. Normally a suffering person can find some
relief in sleep. Job could not. In his sleep he was terrified by dreams
and visions.[6] He experienced a choking sensation as part of his disease. Job declares that his terrifying nightmares drove him to long for
a choking episode which hopefully would be fatal. His affliction had
reduced him to nothing but bones. Thus he longed for death (7:13-
15).

Third, Job breaks out into a passionate cry that he loathes, i.e.,
hates, life. He does not wish to continue to live. He asks God to leave
him alone, i.e., cease afflicting him. Job thus agreed with his friends
that his disease came directly from the hand of God. If only the Lord
would desist from his attacks, his pains would cease. To support his
demand that God leave him alone, Job mentions the brevity of his
life: "For my days are vanity." Thus the patriarch seeks a respite from
his agony before his impending death (7:16).

Fourth, he argues that he is too insignificant to command the unrelenting attention of the Almighty. Why does God "magnify," i.e., consider as important, man by making him the object of such continued
affliction? Why would the omnipotent God set his "heart," i.e., his
mind, on an insignificant man? Does God have nothing better to do
than to "visit" a man with affliction every morning, and "try" him
every moment of the day? (7:17-18).

Fifth, Job argues that God could at least give him a moment's
respite. "How long will you not look away from me?" At least God
could suspend the agony long enough for Job to "swallow down my
spittle." The expression seems to be proverbial for a brief period of
time, long enough to at least swallow (7:19).

Sixth, Job argues that sin cannot affect God. So sin should not be
the reason for the afflictions which man must suffer. This point is
repeatedly raised in this book. God is too high to be affected by what
a person does in this world, whether his actions are sinful or righteous. Job calls God the "watcher" (notser) of men. The title here
bears an accusatory tone. This sufferer thinks of God constantly
watching for sin, watching for reasons to afflict men. At the moment

Job was his "target" (NASB). As a result Job has become a "burden" to himself, i.e., weary of his life (7:20-21).

Seventh, Job argues that God should simply forgive him of whatever sin he may have committed, not continue to punish him for some transgression of which he was unaware. The removal of sin would enable fellowship to be restored. The miserable patriarch was about to "lie down in the dust," i.e., die. Once that happens, it will be too late for God to seek after him. The sad implication is that the Lord will miss his old friend once he is gone (7:21).

THE SPEECH OF BILDAD
Just Discrimination
Job 8:1-22

Bildad ignored much of what Job had said in his long complaint. He comes directly to the point, namely, Job's complaint against God. Whereas Eliphaz had supported his argument with revelation and religious feeling, Bildad cites the moral traditions of the ancient sages.

A. Bildad's Argument (8:1-7).

Bildad began his speech by expressing his shock that any man could speak as Job had done to and about God. "How long will you speak these things?" He refers to the general tenor of the patriarch's speech which appears to him to be accusing God of injustice. Such words are "a mighty wind," i.e., violent and vain (8:1-2).

Bildad states his position in the form of a double question: "Will God pervert judgment? Will the Almighty pervert justice?" The Hebrew emphasizes the words "God" and "Almighty." Men may twist justice, but surely not God! The repetition of the word "pervert" (ye'avvet) adds to the force of the astonishment which Bildad expresses (8:3).

With insensitivity bordering on cruelty, Bildad recalls the death of Job's children. Bildad assumes that Job would agree that his children had been punished for sin against God. The Lord had "delivered them into the hand of their transgression," i.e., they were destroyed by the very sin they committed. The idea here is that wickedness carries its own retribution with it. Bildad's argument is built on the assumption

74

that all suffering is a punishment for sin (8:4). The ultimate teacher, Jesus of Nazareth, decisively rejected this notion in his explanation of a man's blindness (John 9:2-3) and his allusion to the accident in the tower of Siloam (Luke 13:4).

Bildad concluded that Job too had sinned, but not to the extent of his children. Their sin had been punished by instant death. Job, however, had been spared. Though his afflictions were severe, they were but chastisements meant for his correction. If Job would but make himself pure and upright, Bildad was certain that Yahweh would "awake" for him, i.e., hear his prayer and remove his affliction. The Lord would then restore the lost prosperity of Job's habitation. The patriarch's former estate, as great as it was, would be regarded as a small beginning compared to what God had in store for him after his affliction had passed (8:4-7).

B. Support for the Argument (8:8-19).

Bildad now supports his argument by citing the accumulated wisdom of the ages. He asks Job to consider "the former age" and "that which their fathers have searched out." Bildad is suggesting that the truth which he has just presented had been recognized through all antiquity backwards to the dawn of history. The patriarchs of those generations lived much longer than men in Job's day. Their long lives gave them a better opportunity to assess the truth about life. Compared to those patriarchs, Bildad says "we are but of yesterday," i.e., we have arrived on the scene of history just recently. Furthermore, whereas they lived enormously long lives, "our days upon earth are a shadow," i.e., our lives are transitory or fleeting. Therefore, the ancients can teach Job something, if he will listen. They will utter "words out of their heart," i.e., their true convictions based upon their long experience (8:8-10).

So what is the wisdom of the ancients? They referred to the papyrus plant and the rush—Egyptian plants—which in their proper environment, grow rapidly to great heights. Yet while those plants are still green, and before being cut down, the water is withdrawn from them and they suddenly wilt "before any other herb." So it is with godless men who forget the Lord. His sustaining grace is removed from their lives and they perish (8:11-13).

In a second figure from nature the ancients compared the confidence of men who forget God to a spider's web (lit., spider's house). When one leans on that flimsy house it falls (8:14-15).

In a third figure from nature a man is like a luxuriant plant which is suddenly destroyed leaving no trace of its former existence. Under the heat of the sun the plant becomes green. Its shoots spread over the garden. Its roots are entwined about a heap of rubble. They pierce the stony soil, and grip firmly the heart of the earth. Yet suddenly and wholly this plant is swept away. The place where once it grew denies ever having known the plant, i.e., there is no evidence that the plant was ever there. So ends the "joy" of his way, i.e., course of life of the man who rebels against God. "Out of the earth shall others spring," i.e., his place is occupied by others as if he had never existed (8:16-19).

C. Restatement of the Argument (8:20-22).

Bildad repeated his contention that "God will not cast off a perfect man." The word "perfect" (*tam*) describes Job in 1:1. Nor will God "uphold" (lit., hold the hand of) evildoers so as to help them. Bildad was confident that God would yet change the fortunes of Job. He would fill Job's mouth with laughter and jubilant shouts. Those who hate Job and rejoice in his suffering would be put to shame. Their "tent" or habitation would be destroyed. With these closing words Bildad clearly identifies himself and his two companions as friends of Job who wish him well. The friends apparently regarded Job as pious at heart. They concluded from calamities which befell him that he had committed some grievous sin against God.

JOB'S REPLY TO BILDAD
Job 9:1–10:22

Job's rambling response to Bildad is difficult to divide into paragraphs. The patriarch is giving vent to emotion which does not express itself in cold logic. At times in this speech Job takes up again matters discussed earlier by Eliphaz. A twofold analysis of this speech seems best. Job speaks of (1) the might of God which prohibits man from making a credible defense of his innocence; and (2) the mind of God which alone holds the key to the mystery of suffering.

The Might of God
Job 9:1-35

The speech begins with a conciliatory word. "Of a truth I know that it is so." Job agreed in principle with Bildad that God would not cast away the perfect man nor hold the hand of those who do evil. The problem, however, is that it is impossible for mere mortal man to defend his innocence before such an awesome being. Might makes right, and God is almighty. By these calamities the Lord has declared him guilty of something, while at the same time Job's conscience declared him innocent. He must therefore accept the verdict because he cannot contend with omnipotence which seemed resolved to hold him guilty (9:1-2).

If a man should desire to "contend," i.e., enter into a legal dispute, with God he could not succeed. A mere mortal could not answer even one of a thousand questions which the great Judge might ask him under cross examination. The Lord is as wise in heart as he is mighty in strength. No one has "hardened himself" against God with impunity (9:3-4).

A. God's Might in Creation (9:5-10).

God shakes the earth whenever he pleases, toppling mountains and shaking "the pillars of the earth," a poetic reference to the massive rock formations upon which the mountains rest (9:5-6).

When God wishes, the sun does not rise. The reference is probably to storms and darkness or to eclipses which make the sun seem not to rise. By those same mechanisms God "seals up the stars," i.e., blots out their light (9:7).

By himself alone God stretched out the heavens as a curtain, i.e., he placed each of the stars and planets in its proper place (9:8a).

God "treads upon the waves of the sea." The reference is probably to the storms which produce enormous waves which mount up to the heavens. They are but stepping stones for the feet of the Lord (9:8b).

The Lord created the great constellations of stars: the Bear, Orion, and the Pleiades as well as the "chambers of the south." The latter reference may be to the great spaces of the southern hemisphere of the heavens, with the constellations which they contain (9:10).

B. God's Might among the Creatures (9:11-24).

The power of God is invisible. It can be felt, but it is impossible to grasp. Yet the power of God is as irresistible as a ferocious beast carrying off its prey. Nobody dares to question that power when it is being displayed (9:11-12).

God does not withdraw his anger, i.e., his fury is persistent until it has accomplished its purpose. "The helpers of Rahab stoop under him." Rahab here is the monster of the sea, or perhaps just the sea itself.[7] The waves of the sea are the "helpers" of Rahab. Those monstrous waves are subdued before the Lord. If the mighty Rahab cannot stand before God, then Job certainly could not "answer" him, i.e., stand up to him. In a plea against the Lord one would need to choose his words very carefully. Because of the overbearing power of God, the calmness needed to choose those words would be destroyed. Even though he was righteous, yet he could not stand up to God. Thus he would "make supplication" to his "adversary," i.e., he would desert his own just plea and pray for mercy (9:13-15).

So what would happen if Job were to cite God to appear as a witness against divine injustice? Even if God should answer Job's complaint, he still could not hope for justice from his hand. Should he appear, Job would not believe that God would even listen to him (9:16).

Job next portrays what would happen if God did actually respond to Job's citation. He would not listen to Job's plea, but would crush him with his infinite power. Already God has sent a tempest of torment against Job. He had multiplied Job's wounds "without cause," i.e., for no reason. Job can hardly catch his breath. God has filled Job with "bitterness," i.e., made his life bitter. His present condition was another indication of the might of the Lord with which he would have to contend if he were to try to present his case to God (9:17-18).

Job feels the hopelessness of expecting legal justice in his plea against God. The might of God would intimidate him in any direct confrontation. Though he had right on his side, his own mouth would make him out wrong. Somehow God would twist his words into evidence against him. Were Job perfect, i.e., free from willful transgression, the effect of God's power would be that he would appear perverse or wicked (9:19-20).

The thought that he is helpless in the face of the might of the Lord who had no regard for his innocence, drives Job to a reckless outburst. Job declares: "I am perfect." He decides to take his life in his hands and plead his case before God. The phrase "I regard not myself" is literally, "I know not my soul." Job feels that the bold assertion of his innocence will provoke God to terminate his life instantly. That, however, no longer mattered. "It is all one," i.e., it does not matter whether or not he dies. He will have his say. God is a mighty crushing force which destroys both the perfect and the wicked, i.e., he destroys indiscriminately (9:21-22).

In Job's view God strikes suddenly with "the scourge," i.e., plague, pestilence, famine, war and the like. He then mocks at the "trial" or calamity of the innocent. God had permitted injustice to prevail throughout the earth. The wicked prevail in the earth; it is given into their hand. God "covers the faces of the judges" so that they cannot see the right to give the innocent justice. Thus, Job is charging that God does not just permit wrong, he causes wrong to have the upper hand. If God is not responsible for the prevailing wickedness, then who is? (9:23-24).

C. God's Might and Human Frailty (9:25-35).

This is Job's spiritual low point in the book. He thinks of God as the omnipotent power who prefers wickedness to righteousness. Job has generalized his own special situation. If he, being a "perfect" man, must suffer so much, then there is no justice in the world. In his mind God is the direct cause of all that transpires in the earth. Therefore, he cannot help but conclude that God is an unjust tyrant.

Job reflects again on the brevity of his life. He uses three new images to convey this thought. First, his days are "swifter than a runner," i.e., a courier. The days flee away, they result in nothing good for the patriarch. Second, the days are passed as "the swift ships," lit., the ships of reed. These two-man skiffs were constructed of a wooden keel and the rest of reeds. (cf. Isa 18:2). These vessels were light and extremely swift. Third, the days speed away "as the eagle that swoops on the prey" (9:25-26).

Job had contemplated putting his problems in the best possible light. He tried to forget his complaint, and change his sad face. He tried to "be of good cheer," lit. to brighten up. He was afraid, however, that such a show of cheerfulness might agitate God to intensify his sufferings. He was confident that God would not hold him to be innocent. Job's afflictions were the proof of his guilt in the estimation of God. Thus to hold him to be innocent would mean to remove his afflictions (9:27-28).

No matter what he does, Job feels that he will be condemned by God. That condemnation would reveal itself in his continued suffering. If he washed himself with snow, a symbol of the most perfect purity, still he would stand condemned. If he washed his hands with lye or potash, still God would plunge him into the ditch. He would be covered with such filth that his own clothes would refuse to cover him. The point here is Job's feeling that nothing he can do will enable him to regain good standing with God. In his view the Lord had predetermined to hold him guilty of something no matter what (9:29-31).

Why did Job feel that he could not establish his innocence before God? Because God is not a man like himself. Job felt the need for an intermediary, an arbiter, who would referee any confrontation which he might have with God. In his day, however, there was no such "umpire" (*mokhiach*) between the two of them. Such a mediator could put his hand on the two parties (God and Job), i.e., impose his authority over both, and force a just resolution of their differences. Here Job reflects the aspiration of Old Testament saints to see God as a man. In the incarnation the Lord fulfilled that aspiration (9:32-33).

If Job is to have any chance of pleading his cause to God, the "rod" of affliction must be removed from him. If God would lay aside his awful majesty, Job would assert his innocence and plead his own cause without fear. In his own consciousness he had no reason to fear God. Nevertheless, the might of God intimidated him. He feared even worse from God should he protest his plight (9:34-35).

The Mind of God
Job 10:1-22

Job now begins to make various suppositions as to why God has treated him so harshly. Each supposition is immediately refuted as being in contradiction to God's true nature. This part of the speech begins with another complaint about the weariness of life. He resolves to give free vent to his complaint, to let the bitterness of his confused soul express itself. He would plead once again that God not condemn him out of hand. He would insist that God reveal to him whatever it was that was causing the problem between them (10:1-2).

A. Does God Delight in Oppression? (10:3-7).

Job speculates about why God was treating him in this violent manner. Is it because God delights in oppression? Does he take pleasure in despising the work of his hands—a righteous man—in order to "shine" upon the "counsel of the wicked?" Is it possible, Job speculates, that God has eyes like a man? Maybe he has bad eyesight. Maybe he has seen some wickedness in the patriarch which is not there. Next Job asks if God is mortal, if his life be brief like human life. Is he afraid that Job will outlive him? Is he hastening to bring Job's sin to light by these crushing afflictions lest someone should rescue his victim? All of these speculations are vain. God knew that Job was guiltless. He knew that no one could rescue Job from his hand (10:3-7).

B. Did God Predestine Suffering? (10:8-13).

Job notes that he has been fashioned in all of his parts by the hands of the Almighty. The figure is that of a potter who has lavished infinite care upon his vessel. Now, however, the potter has chosen to crush that exquisite ornament into dust again (10:8-9).

Job next describes in poetic language the formation of the child in the womb, from conception to full growth. The "milk" which was poured out is his father's semen. The figure of being "curdled like cheese" refers to conception and the formation of the fetus. Flesh and bones began to appear. From the time of his birth God had granted "life and favor" to Job. Through God's "visitation" or care, his spirit, i.e., life, had been preserved to the present moment (10:10-12).

Job sees a contradiction between the treatment he had received in the womb and since his birth, and God's present treatment of him. He offers the theory that God must have determined this harsh treatment of Job from the very first. God had carefully fashioned him and cared for him in order the better to carry out his cruel purpose. "This [disaster] was with you," i.e., was your purpose, "and in your thoughts." The theme of the cruel purpose of God is further developed in the following verses (10:13).

C. Does God Mark Trivial Sins? (10:14-17).

Job accuses God of having marked every trivial sin which he had committed just so he could punish him. He cannot even imagine what would have been the outcome had he been wicked. Had he been absolutely righteous, it did not really matter. He would not have been allowed to lift up his head since he would have been filled with ignominy looking upon his affliction. If from time to time Job tried to lift up his head in some measure of human dignity, God would have hunted him as a lion. He would have shown himself "marvelous" against Job, i.e., marvelous in the variety and nature of his plagues and afflictions. God would have renewed his "witnesses," i.e., the afflictions which witnessed against him. The indignation against Job would only have increased. An ever-changing "host," i.e., army, of problems would have pursued him.

D. Conclusion (10:18-22).

Driven to despair by his conclusion about God's purpose regarding him, Job asks: Why did God ever give me existence at all? As in chapter 3 he wishes he had never been born, or that he had been carried straight from the womb to the tomb. It would have been better had he given up the spirit of life and no human eye had ever seen him (10:18-19).

Job concludes this speech by begging for a little respite from his pain before he departs to the land of deep darkness, i.e., the mysterious afterlife. Here Job reveals the Old Testament concept of Sheol. It was a land of darkness "without order," i.e., the kind of order which one observes in the physical creation (10:20-22).

THE SPEECH OF ZOPHAR
If a Man Could Meet God
Job 11:1-20

In his opening lament Job did not assert his innocence, but only bewailed his fate. Thus Eliphaz tacitly assumed his guilt without alluding to it. In his response to Eliphaz (chs. 6–7) Job only incidentally affirmed his innocence. Bildad overlooked these passing remarks. He regarded them as natural and not seriously intended. In his response to Bildad (chs. 9–10), however, Job had vigorously denied his guilt. Thus a new element is introduced into the debate. Job really *did* believe in his own innocence. Zophar addresses this issue head on.

A. Zophar's Wish (11:2-6).

After Job's last speech the friends sat in stunned silence for a time. Then Zophar spoke up. He felt compelled to reply lest Job think that by his many words he had proved his point. Zophar asks: "Should a man full of talk (lit., a man of lips) be justified?" The insinuation is that Job's words came merely from his lips. He had not spoken from the heart as had the ancients (cf. 8:10). His oration was so much hot air. Zophar accuses Job of "boastings." The reference is probably to the protestations of innocence. He also accused Job of mockery, i.e., of irreligious or skeptical talk. Someone had to stand up to this insolence. Someone had to make Job ashamed that he had ever uttered such words (11:2-3).

Specifically, Zophar accuses Job of having said: "My doctrine is pure." Though Job had never used precisely such words, Zophar is giving the gist of the patriarch's position. Job's doctrine is the shocking allegation that God afflicts a man whom he knows to be righteous. In addressing God, Job had said in effect: "I am clean in your eyes" (cf. 9:21; 10:7). He was the living proof of the truth of his "doctrine" about God. Zophar had never met a man with such a doctrine before. His irritation and lack of patience with such a novel idea are evident in the language he uses (11:4).

Job brashly had expressed his readiness to meet God face to face and plead his cause before him (cf. 9:16). Zophar wishes that such would transpire. He was quite sure, however, that the results of such a meeting would be very different from what Job imagined. The Lord would show Job "the secrets of wisdom," i.e., his omniscience. After all, sound wisdom has two sides, that which is obvious and that which is hidden. God knows both. Should the requested confrontation with God take place, Job might discover that he is actually being given less than he deserves from the hand of God (11:5-6).

B. God's Wisdom (11:7-12).

As Eliphaz focused on the holiness of God, Zophar now begins to describe the wisdom of God. By *wisdom*, Zophar refers to what theologians call the omniscience of God. He makes four points on this subject.

First, God's wisdom cannot be fathomed by man. The point is made by means of two questions: "Can you find out the deep things of God?" "Can you find the limits of the Almighty?" (11:7).

Second, God's wisdom fills all things. It is as high as the heavens and deeper than Sheol, the abode of the dead. It is longer than the earth and broader than the sea. Job cannot scale heaven nor penetrate Sheol. Job cannot travel across the earth nor span the sea. Thus his knowledge must be inferior to that of God (11:8-9).

Third, God's wisdom perceives hidden wickedness. No man can restrain the Lord when he "passes by" (cf. 9:11), or "shuts up," i.e., arrests people, or "calls an assembly" for judgment on a sinner. God is irresistible and accountable to no one. Why? Because he alone knows "false men." Without expending any effort to investigate, God "sees iniquity." His omniscience is immediate, absolute and beyond challenge (11:10-11).

Fourth, God's wisdom is the more glorious when compared to the stupidity of man. Empty-headed men will only get understanding when a wild donkey gives birth to a man. This proverbial statement suggests something which can never be. It is impossible for human beings to ever achieve anything like the wisdom of God (11:12).

C. Zophar's Exhortation (11:13-20).

Zophar appeals directly to Job. The second person pronoun in v. 13 is emphatic and serves to set Job apart from the "idiot" (NASB) of v. 12. First, he appeals to Job to set his heart right, i.e., bring his heart into a condition of right thought and feeling towards God. Second, Job needs to "stretch out" his hands in supplication to God. Third, he urges Job to put far away his personal "iniquity." Fourth, Zophar implores Job to remove "wickedness" from his "tents," i.e., his home (11:13-14).

Job had complained that he was not able to lift up his head before God (10:15). If Job will pursue the four-point plan outlined by Zophar then he would in fact be able to lift his head up "without spot," i.e., in conscious innocence. Job would then be "steadfast," i.e., would not experience those radical swings in feelings which he had displayed in his previous speeches. Gone will be the "fear" of which Job complained in 9:28. His misery then would be removed. He would forget his afflictions "as waters that are passed away." His life would be "clearer than the noonday," i.e., the confusion and perplexity would be gone. The "darkness" which he would experience in his life would only be a lesser light like that of the morning (11:15-17).

Zophar continues his litany of blessing which would follow Job's repentance. He would enjoy security. His despondency would be replaced by "hope." Before retiring at night he would look about for any potential dangers. There would be none. He would be able to rest in peace. His security and prosperity would draw to him the homage of many, who (as before) would seek his favor, lit., stroke your face (11:18-19).

On the other hand, Zophar sees a terrible fate for the wicked. Their eyes would fail, i.e., they would go blind. For them there is no escaping the righteous retribution of God. Their only hope is "to breathe their last," i.e., die. Eliphaz spoke of no cloud in the brightness which he anticipated for Job's future (cf. 5:19-26). Bildad spoke of perishing, but that would be the future of Job's enemies (cf. 8:22). Zophar threw out his warning in a more general way. Job may accept it if he feels it applies to him (11:20).

JOB'S RESPONSE TO ZOPHAR
Job 12:1–14:22

Zophar stressed the omniscient wisdom of God before which men should silence all complaint. This stung Job for it implied that he was ignorant of both himself and of God. He deeply resented these three men who because of his afflictions thought they were entitled to lecture him on the wisdom and the power of God. Job's reply to Zophar is full of sarcasm against their supposed superiority. Here also are further pathetic references to the lowness into which Job had sunk.

Job Defends His Wisdom
Job 12:1-25

Job first stresses that he has as much, if not more, knowledge about the workings of God than do his friends.

A. The Wisdom of His Friends (12:1-6).

Job begins with some cutting sarcasm aimed at demonstrating how inappropriate the remarks of his friends had been. He feigns admiration for their wisdom. "No doubt you are the people," i.e., the entire people, "and wisdom shall die with you!" Paraphrased Job is saying: You must be the only people in the world that know anything about wisdom! (12:1-2).

Job was not about to let these friends insinuate that he was stupid, or that they knew more about God than he. "I have understanding as well as you; I am not inferior to you!" The knowledge which Zophar thought was so profound was really common knowledge. Everybody knew what Zophar had said about God's wisdom to be true (12:3).

The facts of Job's situation, however, do not fit the theory of the friends that the righteous always prosper and the wicked are always punished. Look how far he had fallen. In former days he had called upon the Lord and had experienced answers to his prayers. Now Job has become a "joke" to his friends. This man who formerly was considered "just" and "blameless" is now considered to be a spiritual ignoramus. The three friends who were presently "at ease" had nothing but contempt for unfortunate sufferers whose feet had "slipped" (12:4-5).

On the other hand, "the tents of the destroyers prosper." Some actually "provoke" God by word and deed, yet they are secure. The last line of v. 6 is difficult. NASB "whom God brings into their power" does not fit well. The Hebrew reads literally "to whom God brings in his hand." Perhaps the NIV margin is the best translation: "secure in what God's hand brings them." In any case, the main point in the verse is clear. While godly men like Job suffer, grossly wicked men are blessed by God (12:6).

B. Wisdom through Observation (12:7-10).

The knowledge of God flaunted by the friends of Job was really not that profound. Anyone who had eyes to observe the life and fate of the lower creatures could have as much knowledge of God's wisdom and power as the three friends. In the beasts and birds, the earth and the fish of the sea one can see that the Lord rules with an absolute sway in this world. God moves among the living creatures upon the earth, dispensing life and death, in a way absolute and uncontrollable. Thus in nature one can see God's power and wisdom displayed.

C. Wisdom through Instruction (12:11-25).

One can also learn about the wisdom of God by listening to the elders discourse on this subject. Job does not despise the knowledge learned from the observations of others when it is pertinent. In the verses which follow Job refers to catastrophes both in nature and society which he could not have personally witnessed. He must have learned of these incidents from tradition.

Job respected the wisdom of the elders. Yet he does not advocate accepting as truth everything that one might hear from older people. The ear must "test words." Thus the ear here represents the reasoning faculty. Just as the palate instinctively tests the food men eat, so reason intuitively tests the truth of the words which enter the ear (12:11-12).

With him, i.e., God, is wisdom and might. The pronoun is emphatic in v. 13. "Might" is the power to execute what wisdom plans. The passage that follows to the end of the chapter describes God's operations in the world as they had been observed by men through the ages (12:13).

God breaks down walled cities, bringing them to ruins. He imprisons men and there is no escape. He withholds the waters, creating droughts. On other occasions, he sends cataclysmic floods upon the earth (12:14-15).

With God are "strength" and "wisdom" (*tushiyyah*).[8] Both he that

87

errs and he that leads into error are the same to God. They are both equally in his hand. Earthly distinctions mean nothing to him as far as his power is concerned. He leads powerful and wise counselors away "barefoot" (sholal), i.e., as slaves and captives. The greatest judges God turns into fools or shows to be fools. God "removes the bonds of kings," i.e., removes the authority of kings; and "binds their loins with a girdle," i.e., a common girdle of the laborer or the cord of the captive (12:16-18).[9]

The litany of earth's great ones continues. God can and does suddenly change their circumstances and humble them. Influential priests he also dispatches into captivity. "The mighty" (lit., the established) are overthrown by God's power. The word refers to those who occupied a high and permanent place among men. "The speech of the trusted men," i.e., eloquent men, he removes or silences. He removes "understanding" (sense, discretion) from the elders. He pours out "contempt" upon princes or nobles. He "loosens the belt of the strong." Garments were girt up for active endeavors. To loose the girdle means to incapacitate (12:19-21).

Other great transformations in life are attributed to God. He reveals "deep things" out of darkness. The idea is that the Lord sees into the most profound mysteries, and brings what is hidden to light. He brings to light "the shadow of death," the deepest darkness. God exposes and frustrates the deep and concealed plans of men. He also brings to light his own eternal counsels (cf. Rom 16:25) when the time is right (12:22).

Mighty nations are like putty in God's hand. He builds them up and tears them down. He scatters nations, and reassembles them. God removes the "heart," i.e., the understanding, of the leaders of men and thereby causes them to walk "in a wilderness," i.e., in perplexity. There they "grope in the dark without light," they stagger like drunkards in their confusion (12:23-25).

Job Rebukes His Friends
Job 13:1-12

Job has just painted a graphic picture of God's wisdom and might. He assures his friends that his knowledge of these things is not inferior in the least to theirs. Yet his theological knowledge has offered him no solution to the question which is haunting him, namely, Why am I suffering? (13:1-2).

In spite of his knowledge of God's wisdom and might, Job desires to speak directly to the Almighty, to reason with him. Surely God would understand him even if his friends did not. Job calls his friends "forgers of lies." Literally, they are falsehood plasterers. They smear their lies over God's government of the world so as to cover up all its hideous defects and give it a fair appearance.[10] They were "physicians of no value" for they were trying to deal with a problem which they were not competent to treat. Since the friends could not help Job, their silence would be the most helpful thing they could do. Job is hurling back at the friends the concluding words of Zophar's last speech: "Even a fool, when he holds his peace, is counted wise" (13:3-5).

Job now goes on the attack against his friends. He calls upon them to listen to his argument against them. First, he charges them with partiality for God. They are acting like advocates for God. In so doing they were speaking "unrighteously" and "deceitfully" in behalf of the Lord. In their partiality for God they were ignoring the facts in Job's case. They had no personal knowledge of any guilt in Job's life, yet they assumed that guilt. They took God's part in the argument, not because they had facts to back them, but because of superficial religiosity bordering on superstition (13:6-8).

What if God should search out the hearts of the three friends? Would they be able to deceive God as they had deceived their fellow man? God is so righteous and impartial that he would rebuke them for their misrepresentation of the facts even in his defense. These phony friends would stand paralyzed before God should their hearts come under scrutiny (13:9-11).

Job accuses the friends of using cliches—"memorable sayings"— which were nothing but "proverbs of ashes," i.e., worthless. The great arguments which they had used in defense of God turn out to be "defenses of clay" (13:12).

Job Challenges God's Wisdom
Job 13:13-22

Job senses that the friends were now anxious to jump back to the attack. He orders them to hold their peace so that he may have his say. In the Hebrew the first person pronoun is emphatic. He is willing to take whatever risk there may be to voice his complaint against God. He knows that what he is about to say will place his life in jeopardy (13:13-14).

Job 13:15 as translated in the KJV is one of the greatest statements of faith in the entire Bible: "Though he slay me, yet will I trust Him; even so I will defend my own ways before Him." As much as one might wish to cling to this rendering for sentimental reasons, the Hebrew rendering points in a different direction. Literally, the verse reads: "Behold, he shall slay me, I shall not wait; but my ways to his face I will defend." Job anticipated that God would slay him for what he was about to say. He would not wait for a death in the more distant future. He would speak his piece and accept his punishment.

The very fact that Job wishes to defend his life before God indicates that he is a righteous man. A godless man would not dare to go before God. His sense of innocence would be his "salvation," i.e., would secure him victory in his plea with God. To Job his consciousness of innocence was equivalent to innocence itself (13:16).

Job is certain of ultimate vindication. Therefore, he commands his friends to listen carefully to his cause. He declared: "I know that I shall be justified," i.e., found to be in the right (cf. 11:2). Who then would dare to stand up to oppose him? If anyone could produce a case against him, Job pledges that he would forever keep quiet, i.e., he would stop pleading his innocence. He would simply give up the effort of self-defense and die (13:17-19).

In his present condition Job did not feel capable of appearing before the Lord in his own defense. He therefore makes two petitions: (1) that God would withdraw his hand far from him; and (2) that God would not terrorize him. If those conditions are met, Job would certainly be willing to answer any summons to stand before God either as respondent or as appellant. The choice is left in God's hand.

The silence of heaven caused Job to conclude that he must present his case before God in his present condition (13:20-22).

Job Laments His Condition
Job 13:23-28

Job now confidently presents his case before God. His plea resembles that in chapters 7 and 10, but is more subdued and calm. Though he has not convinced his friends of his innocence, in his own mind he has settled the issue. In spite of the suspicions expressed by the friends, and in spite of the implications of his terrible suffering, he was convinced that he was innocent of any sin meriting such treatment. His boldness in presenting his case to God is viewed by Job as evidence of his innocence. A guilty man would have no inclination to plead his case before the righteous judge.

Job begins his plea with a demand to know the number of his sins. He wants to have heaven's indictment against him made clear. He is referring to great transgressions, to recent transgressions, to transgressions which would call forth such affliction from God. Job does not claim to be sinless (cf. v. 26); what he denies is that he was guilty of any sins of such magnitude as to account for his calamities (13:23).

Job cannot understand why one as great as God would pursue such an insignificant one as he. Why does God continue to hide his face from him thus making it appear that Job was a terrible enemy? Compared to the living God, Job felt he was nothing but a driven leaf or dry stubble, figures for that which is light and worthless. Can God take delight in assailing such an unequal opponent? (13:24-25).

The heavenly judge had written a bitter decision regarding Job. He was making the patriarch to "inherit" the sins of his youth. Job freely admitted the errors he had committed in his youth.[11] Job entertains the possibility that his present afflictions might be the punishment for his former sins which he had thought were forgiven long ago (13:26).

Again Job describes in three figures his physical plight. First, God had put his feet "in the stocks." The figure is derived from the practice of tying a log of wood to a prisoner's feet to make it difficult for him to move. Second, God watches all his paths. Job feels he is under constant surveillance. Third, God has drawn a line about the soles of his feet, i.e., he has prescribed his movements. Job is not permitted to overstep his bounds. His physical affliction and mental anguish restrict his ability to present an effective defense before God. Meanwhile, Job was like a worm-eaten object or a moth-eaten garment. He was slowly wasting away (13:27-28).[12]

Job Reflects on the Human Predicament
Job 14:1-12

In the last verse of chapter 13 Job thought of himself as one member of the human race. Now he begins to expound on the characteristics of this race. First, humankind experience a short and difficult life. Since woman was under the judgment of sorrow (Gen 3:16), one who is "born of woman" is of necessity weak and doomed to trouble. His days are few, like a flower which soon withers, or a shadow which quickly passes across a path. Flowers in the Bible nearly always suggest a beauty which is short-lived. Job expresses amazement that the great omnipotent God singled out such a creature for judgment (14:1-3).

Second, sin holds sway in the human race. He expresses this thought in a wish that one could bring forth something clean out of something unclean. Here Job expresses the same thought as Paul that "all have sinned and come short of the glory of God." To be human is to possess a tendency to sin. Job wishes it were otherwise. The point is this: since sinfulness is the universal lot of mankind, should not God show some forbearance? How can he single out certain individuals for such horrendous affliction? (14:4).

Third, the length of each person's life is predetermined by the Almighty. The Lord has "appointed his bounds that he cannot pass over." Therefore, Job pleads that God will "look away" from man, i.e., leave him alone, that they may have "rest." This will enable him to "fulfill his days like a hired man." Life at its best is hard. During the hot day the laborer has few joys. He looks forward to completing his day's work. Only at the end of the day does he have rest. So man will find no rest until the end of life's toilsome day (14:5-6).

Fourth, man's life inevitably terminates in death. His destiny is sadder than than of a tree. If a tree is cut down, it will sprout again. The roots may grow old, and the tree die from lack of moisture. The scent of water, however, causes the old dead stump to put forth sprigs like a plant. On the other hand, man dies and lies prostrate. He expires and disappears from the earth. His death is like that of a lake or river which dries up. The waters do not return. So man lies down and does not arise. The death sleep will continue until "the heavens be no more," i.e., throughout the duration of the present universe. Later Scripture (cf. Isa 26:19) will affirm that God will resurrect man from the grave at the end of the present age (14:7-12).

Job Contemplates the Here and the Hereafter
Job 14:13-22

Job did not believe that death ended personal existence. One continued to existence in the spirit world, in a place called Sheol. Job prayed that Sheol would be for him a place of refuge where he might hide until God's wrath had subsided. Should that happen, a resurrection might be possible in the future. Job frames this potential in a rhetorical question: "If a man die, shall he live?" If only he could be sure there was another life, then he could bear up under all the affliction which he was experiencing. When his rest in Sheol was over, and God called, Job would be most happy to respond (14:13 15).

The momentary contemplation of a future life is followed by a picture of the severity with which God deals with man in this present life. God had focused his attention on Job. He scrutinized every step the patriarch made. He made note of every sin. All of Job's transgressions were "sealed up in a bag" by the Lord, i.e., collected and preserved. Now God had brought down on Job the full force of his judgment. The present affliction is not due, then, to any one transgression, but is heaven's response to Job's sins collectively (14:16-17).

Man could not possibly survive this mighty outpouring of wrath. He must certainly perish. Even the greatest things in nature are eroded with the passing of time. Mountains eventually are shattered when their mighty rocks careen downhill. Turbulent waters eventually wear away the stones of the brook and wash away its banks. So God's visitations wear down the hope of man. The "hope" here envisioned is the hope of survival and recovery from affliction (14:18-19).

In his contest with man God must forever prevail with the result that man passes from the scene. Job graphically describes death when he says, "you change his countenance." At will God dispatches man to death. A father does not live to see his sons come to honor, nor brought low. Those in the abode of the dead know nothing of what is transpiring in the land of the living. Yet Job poetically depicts the dead man still suffering as his flesh rots away. In Sheol he knows only a mournful and dreary existence. Such was Job's concept of what would happen to him after his death (14:20-22).

Thus concludes the first cycle of speeches which was triggered by Job's first complaint in chapter 3. The three friends saw in Job's lament an implied indictment of God. Each in his own way, the friends have tried to defend God. Eliphaz emphasized the moral purity of God and his universal goodness. Bildad insisted on the justice of God in his rule of the world. Zophar stressed the omniscience of God as it impacts on his dealings with men.

At first Job answered the arguments of his friends, for the most part, indirectly. Since his suffering was the silent refutation of all they said, the patriarch dwelled mainly on those afflictions. The words and demeanor of Zophar, however, drove Job to respond directly to the argument against him. He was not terrified to meet God. In fact, he yearned to present himself before the Almighty. He called upon God to make clear the sins for which he was being punished.

Job's fearless defense of his integrity even in the face of their arguments concerning the nature of God caused the friends to look elsewhere for arguments to silence him.

ENDNOTES

1. In 4:16 the text literally reads: "stillness and a voice I heard." This could also be interpreted to mean that first there was an eerie silence, then the being spoke.

2. The translation "Shall mortal man be more just than God? Shall a man be more pure than his maker?" is possible but not likely. The charge against Job was that he made God unrighteous, not that he claimed to be more righteous than the Lord.

3. This is the only mention in the Bible of poisoned arrows.

4. The meaning of the second half of 6:14 is difficult to ascertain. NASB reads: "lest he forsake the fear of the Almighty," i.e., lack of a display of kindness might drive one's friend to the denial of God.

5. NASB renders 6:30b: "Cannot my palate discern calamities?" Job would then be affirming that he was able to discern the true nature of his calamities and perceive that they were undeserved.

6. Distressing dreams and terrors in sleep are said to be one of the symptoms of elephantiasis. A.B. Davidson and H.C.O. Lanchester, *The Book of Job* in "The Cambridge Bible for Schools and Colleges" (Cambridge: University Press, 1937), p. 64.

7. Elsewhere in the Old Testament *Rahab* may also represent (1) pride or arrogance; and (2) a name for Egypt (Ps 87:4; 89:10; Isa 30:7; 51:9).

8. Others prefer to translate *tushiyyah* as "victory" (Anchor Bible) or "power" (NIV) based on the use of the word in the Ugaritic myths.

9. Another view is that God sets captive kings free again and girds them once more for war.

10. Peake, cited by A.B. Davidson and H.C.O. Lanchester, *The Book of Job* in "The Cambridge Bible for Schools and Colleges," p. 112.

11. Job is not here looking back on gross youthful sins, but on such sins as youth are not free from. These are the kinds of sins he feared in the lives of his own children (cf. 1:5).

12. In 13:28 Job speaks of himself in the third person, perhaps because he thinks of himself as one of the human race in general. The thought would be that all human beings are in the process of wasting away.

CHAPTER FIVE

The Second Cycle of Speeches
Job 15-21

The visitors have thus far failed to get Job to acknowledge the heinous sins which have called forth this terrible affliction from God. Their theological arguments, based on the attributes of God, have made no impression on the patriarch. Job has staunchly defended his innocence. He has accused his friends of being insincere partisans for God (13:4f.). They concluded, therefore, that any further arguments in this direction would be equally fruitless.

If the first cycle of speeches focused on God, the second focuses on man, especially the wicked man. History and experience provided ample proof of how such a man is treated in the providence of God. The nature of the argument causes the accusations of the friends to become more pointed. At the same time, Job begins to realize more keenly his alienation from the friends. They regarded all of his protestations of innocence as clever obfuscations. In his three responses to the friends, Job fights his way through self-pity to finally tackle head on the arguments which the three had raised.

SECOND SPEECH OF ELIPHAZ
Job 15:1-35

As before, Eliphaz takes the lead. His speech sets the tone for the second round of the debate. His discourse builds on Job's last speech (chs. 12–14). Eliphaz first rebukes Job (vv. 2-16). Then he sets forth his understanding of the fate of a wicked man (vv. 17-35).

The Rebuke of Job
Job 15:1-16

The rebuke of Eliphaz alternates between accusing Job of pretentious boasting and charging him with irreverent reasoning.

A. Attack on Job's Attitude (15:2-6).
Eliphaz first attacks Job's contention (12:3; 13:2) that he had a wisdom beyond that of his friends. "Should a wise man make answer with knowledge of wind," i.e., empty and loud. A truly wise man should not need to "fill his belly with the east wind," i.e., puff himself up and then bring out of his mouth violent blasts of barren words. The east wind in the Near East was a figure for that which is violent and dry. A truly wise man would not attempt to reason with "unprofitable talk" or "speeches with which he can do no good" (15:2-3).

In the view of Eliphaz, Job had done worse than fill the debate with bluster. His words were impious. His conduct and logic tended to undercut the foundation of all devoutness and "fear," i.e., fear of the Lord. Job's outbursts hindered the quiet, scholarly and reverent meditation which normally characterized the interchange between scholars. Only a person who was inspired by deep evil within his own heart could speak in this fashion. Job had chosen to use the language of "the crafty." His protestations of innocence and complaints of unrighteousness in God were merely disingenuous pretenses put forward to divert attention from his own wickedness (15:4-5).

Job's utterances clearly proved his guilt. No other evidence was necessary. Eliphaz engages in a bit of circular reasoning regarding Job's wickedness. In v. 5 he argues that the patriarch's language and attitude are the result of his guilt. Then in v. 6 he argues that Job's guilt is proved by his language. Both verses support the contention of v. 4 that Job was undermining the foundations of religion (15:6).

B. Rebuke of Job's Claim (15:7-11).

Eliphaz returns to Job's claim of superior wisdom. He now interrogates the patriarch regarding the basis of that claim. Was Job the first man created? Such a man would naturally be endowed with preeminent wisdom as well as other superior attributes. Job, however, was not that man. Was Job that personified wisdom which was created before the earth? (cf. Prov 8:22ff.). Obviously not! Has Job been privy to the secret counsel of God? Was he a member of that divine council which surrounded God (Jer 23:22; Ps 89:7; Amos 3:7). Such a one would have full knowledge of the mysteries of God. Job obviously could not make a claim to this honor (15:7-8).

Eliphaz now abandons his biting sarcasm. In what specific respect did Job think that he knew more than his friends? Among those friends were men older than Job's father! Eliphaz probably is diplomatically referring to himself. Job has rejected the words of this graybeard even though his words contained "the consolations of God," i.e., comforting words from God. Eliphaz seems to be claiming that his first speech was inspired of God. He describes his previous words (ch. 4) as gentle and conciliatory. How can Job show such disrespect for the wisdom of one much older than he? (15:9-11).

C. Accusation of Job's Impertinence (15:12-16).

Eliphaz next rebukes what he considers to be Job's violent and irreverent behavior towards God. Again the accuser resorts to questions to make his points. Why had Job allowed his heart to carry him away? The "heart" is the excited mind and strong emotion. Why did his eyes "wink" or flash with signs of violent emotion? How could he allow his spirit (i.e., anger) to be turned against God? How could he allow such words to go forth out of his mouth? The reference is not so much to the content of the words, but to the passionate manner in which they were uttered (15:12-13).

What was there in man to justify Job's passionate defense of his innocence? "What is man that he should be clean?" One born of woman has no righteousness. Even the "holy ones" (i.e., angels) do not deserve God's trust. The heavens are not clean in God's sight. If that is true, how much less could a lowly human being stand before God? Man is abominable and corrupt. His lust for evil is like that of a thirsty man for water (15:14-16).

Defense of Traditional Theology
Job 15:17-35

Having concluded his personal attack, Eliphaz next takes up the principles which Job had set forth regarding God. Perhaps emboldened by the destitute condition of Job, the Temanite assumed a lofty tone.

A. The Source of His Theology (15:17-19).

"That which I have seen I will declare." Eliphaz attributed part of his first address to revelation (cf. 4:12ff.). It is not clear here whether the verb "see" refers to prophetic vision, or to natural observation. In any case, the doctrine set forth by Eliphaz was nothing new. What he has come to understand about God was the consistent theology of wise men throughout the generations. This theological tradition had never been corrupted by the inclusion of foreign philosophies. By rejecting such teaching, Job was showing disdain for the special tradition of his people, and he was espousing alien teaching (15:17-19).

B. The Essence of His Theology (15:20-24).

According to the tradition of the ages, "the wicked man travails in pain all of his days." The years of the "oppressor" are appointed by God, i.e., at the appropriate time such a one will be cut off from the land of the living. Eliphaz is suggesting that Job is being treated like a tyrant, one who strikes fear into the hearts of others. Divine justice, however, makes such oppressors imagine that they hear the sound of coming destruction. Eventually the day comes in the midst of his prosperity when "the spoiler" comes upon him and he is destroyed (15:20-21).

The wicked man anticipates a calamity from which he shall not escape. He feels that he is marked for the sword, i.e., the avenging sword of God. He anticipates the time when he shall be a hungry wanderer, roving about in search of bread. The shadow of calamity accompanies him wherever he goes ready at any moment to envelop him. "Distress and anguish" make the tyrant afraid. They prevail against him "as a king ready for battle," i.e., fully prepared and therefore irresistible. Such is the foreboding of the wicked. Eliphaz here articulates what he believes happens to the most wicked of men. At the same time he argues that even wicked men themselves recognize the principle that disaster will befall them because of their oppression (15:22-24).

C. Justification of His Theology (15:25-28).

Why do such terrible temporal judgments fall upon oppressors? First, because "he has stretched out his hand against God," i.e., he has defied God. He has acted arrogantly toward the Almighty. Like a warrior making an assault, he has run upon God with a massive shield. Whereas Job accused God of warring against him, Eliphaz accused Job of warring against God. Second, the wicked oppressor is cut down because he is guilty of self-indulgence. His face and thighs were fat. In the Old Testament a corpulent person symbolizes selfish luxury and spiritual insensitivity (15:25-27).

Third, the wicked would be cut off because he "dwelled in uninhabited cities." An uninhabited city was considered to be under the curse of God (cf. Josh 6:26; 1 Kgs 16:34). To occupy that which God had made desolate was considered extreme impiety (15:28).

D. The End of the Wicked (15:29-35).

The wicked will not be permitted to retain their wealth. Their crops will not bend down to the earth because of abundance. They will not "escape from darkness," i.e., the dreaded calamity which ultimately befalls such people. Their crops will be devastated by "the fire," i.e., drought. God's breath will blow him and his possessions away (15:29-30).

If a man trusts in "vanity," i.e., emptiness, then that is what he ultimately will experience. "It shall be accomplished before his time," i.e., his demise would come prematurely. His wealth would disappear like a flower dropping from an unripe olive tree or a grape falling from an unripe vine (15:31-33).

Eliphaz now drops the figures of speech to state in plain language

101

the final fate of the wicked. "The company (i.e., households) of the godless shall be barren," i.e., unfruitful. Under the curse of God they come to nothing. "Fire (i.e., judgment) shall consume the tents of bribery," i.e., households built up by injustice. The wicked "conceive mischief" and "bring forth calamity ('*aven*)." The point is that suffering and disaster inevitably follow evil and wrong.

JOB'S SECOND REPLY TO ELIPHAZ
Job 16:1–17:16

In the first cycle of speeches Job complained of God's enmity toward him. His appeal to the creator had been unanswered. God had abandoned him. In the second cycle of speeches a new realization weighs heavily on the mind of Job. Men have turned against him as well as God. Job longs for human sympathy. Yet he will not compromise on his conviction that he is innocent of any wrong which would merit such affliction as he was experiencing. In his response to Eliphaz, Job (1) expresses his exasperation with his friends; (2) pictures his sorrowful isolation; (3) appeals to God for vindication even after death; and (4) expresses his resignation to death.

A. His Continuing Disappointment (16:1-5).
Job begins his reply to Eliphaz by expressing his weariness with the monotonous speeches of his three friends. All three of his friends were "miserable comforters" (lit., comforters of trouble). Their "comfort" was based on the false assumption that he was guilty of some unconfessed sin. Their solution to his problem was to call upon him to repent. These words of "comfort" only increased his perplexity and misery (16:1-2).

Eliphaz had accused him of "windy knowledge" (cf. 15:2). Rhetorically Job asks, "Is there any end to words of wind?" The patriarch did not fear the empty harangues against him. Yet he cannot help but wonder aloud what provoked these friends to continue to answer him. Why do they not simply let the controversy drop? (16:3).

Job assures his friends that were their positions reversed, he would be able to speak as they do. He could "join words together" in formal and heartless speeches. He could shake his head at them in mocking astonishment that such pious men had fallen upon such hard times. In fact, were their positions reversed, he could do better than they, for he had the ability to strengthen people with his words (cf. 4:4). The point is, were their conditions reversed, Job would not do to his friends as they had done to him (16:4-5).

B. His Present Distress (16:6-17).

At this point Job seems to grasp clearly his isolation from men as well as God.

1. The isolation from man (16:7-11). Whether Job speaks out or restrains his speech, his condition has not changed. God has placed yet another burden upon him. The term "now" introduces the new situation which he finally had perceived. In the second person—prayer—he blames God for having "made desolate all my company." God's enmity toward Job has turned all his friends against him. All of those upon whom Job might depend for support had been turned into his enemies. He feels totally alone in this world. God has laid hold on Job. His afflictions were assumed by everyone to be witnesses of his guilt. His emaciated body rose up, as it were, and testified to his face that he was a sinner (16:7-8).

Job pictures the hostility of God toward him as a wild beast of prey with rending fury, flashing eyes and gnashing teeth. Since he has been so viciously treated by Yahweh, his friends have felt free to pounce upon him as well. Like a pack of wild dogs, they have snipped at him. Fearing no reprisal, they contemptuously have slapped, as it were, Job on the cheek. They have ganged up on him in his adversity. In his broken condition, God had delivered him to "the ungodly." He does not refer to his friends, but to the rabble of men which are further described in chapter 30 (16:9-11).

2. The brutality of God (16:12-14). Job now paints an even more graphic picture of the hostile attack of God. First, like some all-powerful wrestler, God seized him by the neck and dashed him to pieces. This attack came when Job was at ease and in security. He had not experienced any forebodings of conscience as Eliphaz had suggested (cf. 15:20ff.). Second, God had set him up like a target for his arrows. Arrow after arrow ripped into him, as it were, spilling his internal organs to the ground. Third, Job compares himself to a fort which has been breached and then stormed by enemy warriors.

3. The results of the hostility (16:15-17). Job next describes the result of these destructive attacks by God. First, he has put on sackcloth next to his skin as a sign of mourning. He "sewed" it on, i.e., it was his permanent garment. Second, he has thrust his "horn" in the dust. This was a sign of humiliation, the opposite of lifting up the horn (1 Sam 2:1). Third, he has wept until his face was flushed or inflamed and his eyes have become dim.[1] Yet Job could identify no misdeed in his life deserving of such suffering. His relations with his fellow man had not been characterized by "violence." His "prayer," i.e., his whole religious walk with God, was pure. Job thus repudiates the insinuations of Eliphaz (cf. 15:4,34) to the opposite effect.

C. His First Appeal to God (16:18-17:2).

The thought that he is suffering unjustly causes Job here, as elsewhere in the book, to lose self-control. He seems to have given up hope of any restoration in life. He longs now for vindication in the life to come.

God's destructive enmity will bring Job to death, though he had committed no sin worthy of such abuse. He therefore appeals to the earth not to cover his innocent blood. Even after death he wishes that his blood could lie on the surface of the earth unceasingly crying out to heaven for justice (cf. Gen 4:10). The "blood" here is a figure for violent and wrongful death (16:18).

Job's faith shines through the gloom at this point. He is convinced that even now he had a witness/advocate in heaven. In the Hebrew court the witness/advocate had the responsibility to testify in behalf of one, and to see justice done to him. The "witness" is not merely one who knows Job's innocence, but one who will testify to it in the court of public opinion (16:19).

Who is this heavenly witness? Not his friends! Does Job refer to God himself as his witness? Not likely, for he has just described God as his enemy. The context seems to connote that Job meant someone else. He was sure that in heaven he had a sponsor who would stand on his behalf and plead with God on his behalf.[2]

Job's friends are in fact mockers. No sympathy can be expected from that quarter. Therefore, Job "weeps to God," i.e., he appeals with tears to God himself. He longs that his heavenly witness would plead with God on his behalf, just as a person would do for his neighbor.[3] Job needed an advocate because his few years would soon come to an end. He would enter Sheol never to return to appear in the court of public opinion for self-vindication (16:20-22).

The first appeal concludes with further description of Job's plight. His spirit (life principle) was broken. His days were extinguished, i.e., had run their course. The grave was ready to receive him [lit., graves are mine]. Yet his friends still mock by holding out illusionary hopes of restoration. Through his tearful eyes he could only gaze on their "provocation" (lit., rebelliousnesses). The accusations of the friends revealed an attitude of rebellion against himself and God. Job gazes with incredulity on their audacity (17:1-2).

D. His Second Appeal to God (17:3-9).

Job now makes a new appeal to God. He asks God to put forth a pledge for him that at some point in the future he will cause his innocence to be recognized. Thus he is asking for God to be his defender as well as his judge. Such a request was necessary because there was no one else to stand up for him as his advocate at his trial. Literally Job asks, "Who is there who will strike hands with me?" Striking hands was a practice for ratifying an agreement or business transaction (17:3).

Job argues that if God will not stand up for him, no one will. The hearts of his three friends and all others have been blinded. They cannot make a true assessment of Job's cause. Therefore God would not "exalt them" by permitting some outcome which would meet their expectations. In fact, Job was so disgusted with his friends that he accused them of turning against him in order to seize some of his property. Such a despicable crime should bring upon their children the curse of blindness (17:4-5).

Again Job launches into a gloomy survey of his condition. Among the peoples of the surrounding tribes Job had become a byword. His calamity and the wickedness inferred from it would be widely known. He was treated like one upon whom people spit in contempt. His eyes had become dim through sorrow. His body was but a shadow of what it once was (17:6-7).

105

Religious people are appalled at seeing such afflictions inflicted upon a godly man. Such perversions of justice in the moral government of the world raise up moral indignation against the wicked who are prosperous. Yet Job is confident that righteous people would not allow themselves to be misled from the right path by the moral wrongs which God might permit in his world. They will cling to the life of righteousness. In fact, they will grow stronger and stronger in their commitment to purity. Though Job speaks here in the name of all upright people, he is expressing his own commitment. This verse is a brief but brilliant burst of light in the otherwise dark gloom of Job's present condition (17:8-9).

E. His Resignation to Death (17:10-16).

Job concludes his response to Eliphaz by rejecting the false hopes which his friends had held out to him. He challenges them to renew their attempts to solve his problem. Job, however, is confident that their renewed attempts would have no better success than their former efforts. They would be found by Job as foolish as before (17:10).

The friends held out hope that the bright day of restoration was about to dawn on the darkness of Job's calamity (cf. 11:17). The patriarch, however, was a realist. He views his days on earth as already past, his life with all its cherished purposes cut off. He has not been allowed to live long enough to fulfill the aspirations of his heart (17:11-12).

Job could only look forward to Sheol, and there was no light in Sheol! He was so close to death that he could call "the pit" (i.e., the grave) his father, and the worm, which would consume his body, his mother and sister. He is, as it were, a child of the grave! If he had any hope at this point it surely would go down to Sheol with him (17:11-16).

SECOND SPEECH OF BILDAD
Job 18:1-21

Several things in Job's last speech had offended Bildad the Shuhite. He resented the way Job spoke of his friends; he took offense at the way he spoke to and about God. The principal theme of this discourse is the destruction of the wicked. Eliphaz had suggested that the punishment of a sinner came largely from his own conscience. Bildad, however, argued that the punishment of sinners is part of the fixed order of the world and the moral instincts of mankind.

A. Bildad's Indignation (18:1-4).

Bildad begins with the same exclamation of impatient astonishment ("How long?") that he used in his earlier speech (cf. 8:2). What Job has done in his former speeches is to "lay snares for words," i.e., hunt for words to create specious arguments. He is suggesting that Job's remarks were unintelligent ramblings. Job had accused the friends of lacking understanding (cf. 17:4). It was not they, but he who was without wisdom. If any progress is to be made in the discussion, Job would have to admit some basic principles. In answering Job, Bildad uses the plural "you" possibly because the patriarch had identified himself with righteous sufferers (cf. 17:6ff.) who were persecuted by the wicked (18:1-2).

Bildad resented the implication that he and his friends were stupid beasts (cf. 12:7-9). What was worse, Job was treating his friends as "unclean" beasts (cf. 17:4,9-10). Much less should God be compared to a beast (cf. 16:9) who rips and tears. It is Job who tears himself in his self-righteous zeal. The earth is not going to be made desolate, nor is the rock to be removed from its place. The idea is that God is not about to overthrow the inextricable moral laws that govern the universe. God will not, Bildad argues, overturn the law that imputes wickedness to those who suffer (18:3-4).

B. The Principle of Retribution (18:5-11).

The rest of the speech of Bildad is devoted to his main theme: the destruction of the wicked. As in his first speech, Bildad employs graphic figures and proverbial sayings to argue his position. Bildad sets forth the moral principle that "the light of the wicked shall be put out." The beacon which marked his tent is extinguished, the flame in the hearth shines no more. His home is desolate (18:5-6).

Bildad employed a second figure to express the same thought. The firm, wide steps of prosperity become narrowed and hampered. Finally "his own counsel shall cast him down," i.e., the evil principles that guided his conduct ultimately lead to calamity (18:7).

The fall of the wicked is inevitable. The moral order of the world is such that wherever the wicked person turns he walks into a snare, a trap or a noose.[4] In the end he realizes his predicament. "Terrors shall make him afraid on every side." He tries to escape, but the terrors pursue close behind him (18:8-11).

C. The End of the Wicked (18:12-21).

The last days of a wicked person are next described by Bildad. First, his strength is weakened for lack of food. Second, the sinner's body is consumed by a terrible disease. That calamity here is called figuratively "the firstborn of death," i.e., the strongest child of death. The reference is to a fatal disease. Third, the wicked one is rooted out of his "tent," or home and is led away to "the king of terrors," i.e., to death (18:12-14).

Next Bildad speaks of the extinction of the name and race of the wicked person. First, he presents two pictures of the fate of the sinner's possessions. Either his possessions would pass into the hands of others, or be destroyed with a rain of brimstone from heaven. Second, the sinner's "branches shall wither." The tree is a figure for the family of the sinner. The sinner's family perishes with him.[5] Third, even the memory of the wicked man would perish from the land (18:15-17).

Bildad concludes his oratory with a description of the horror which people feel over the fate of the sinner. When the sinner was driven from the light of life to the darkness of death he would leave no offspring behind. Through the generations people would be horrified at the fate of that sinner. Bildad inscribes the picture which he has painted of the fate of the wicked with these words: "Surely such are the dwellings of the wicked, the place of one who does not know God" (18:18-21).

JOB'S SECOND RESPONSE TO BILDAD
Job 19:1-29

Although Bildad had attempted a theological discussion of the fate of the wicked in the abstract, many details in his description were borrowed from the circumstances of Job's case.[6] After preliminary words of a personal nature, Job develops the theme which occupies the rest of the chapter, namely, God's relationship to his suffering.

A. Job's Impatience with his Friends (19:2-6).

Job was weary with the tormenting and crushing words of his friends. "Ten times," i.e., over and over again, they had heaped their shameless reproach on Job. Even granted that Job may have "erred" (the mildest expression for sin), is it fair that this error abides constantly with him? (19:1-3).

If his friends mean to draw inferences from his calamities, then Job will tell them that it is God who had brought these on him unjustly. God had perverted his right. This, not his guilt, is the explanation of his afflictions. It was not his own feet which had led him into the net, as Bildad had alleged (cf. 18:8f.). Rather God had thrown his net about Job (19:4-6).

B. Job's Alienation from God (19:7-12).

Job begins to accuse God of hostile persecution. He feels that he has been entangled as a creature is snared. His cries for help in the face of the divine violence are not heard. From his ordeal there was no escape. God had "walled up" his way. He was trapped in "thick darkness," a symbol for perplexity and depression. These calamities were evidence that he was a transgressor. God took his "crown" of righteousness from his head, and stripped the glory of godliness from him (19:7-9).

God had broken Job down like one might dismantle a worthless building. Job declared: "I am gone!" He refers to his inevitable death from his disease which he regards as already upon him. His hope of life or recovery had been uprooted as a tree is torn down by a tornadic wind. God had kindled his wrath against him. He had treated Job as one of his adversaries. Job feels he is under attack by troops dispatched by God (19:10-12).

C. Job's Estrangement from Men (19:13-22).

Not only had God afflicted him with trouble, he had removed far from him all human sympathy. His relatives, outside his own immediate circle, and his acquaintances stood aloof from him. The menial servants within his house pay no respect to his calls for assistance. Even those most dear to him can no longer tolerate him. His breath is offensive to his wife. He was loathsome to his own brothers.[7] Little children, taking their cue from the attitude of their elders, mocked his feeble efforts to arise from the ground. Those who were his "associates" (lit., the men of my council) abhor him. Job had loved these men, had treasured the intellectual discourse which passed between them. Now they too had turned against him. This was the unkindest cut of all! (19:13-19).

In addition to facing the desertion and loathing of his fellow man, Job had to cope with the continuing deterioration of his body. He described his emaciated condition in these words: "My bone clings to my skin and my flesh." He is surviving the attack of disease "by the skin of my teeth." By this proverbial expression he means that there was next to nothing between him and death (19:20).

Overcome by his sense of the terrible enmity of God, Job cries out for the compassion of his fellows: "Have pity upon me, have pity upon me, O you my friends!" Only their sympathy can help him bear the thought that God has smitten him. He could not understand why they would join with God in persecuting him. Why could they not be satisfied with his flesh? In Near Eastern metaphor, to eat one's flesh is to attack someone verbally. Thus the question here is, Why do they not tire of making accusations against him? (19:21-22).

D. Job's Hope in the Future (19:23-27).

From the miserable present, Job turns to the future. He desires that his protestation of innocence be inscribed in a book, even chiseled into a rock. He wants future generations to realize that he suffered unjustly. Yet his faith soars to an even greater thought: "I know that my redeemer lives!" Job may die, but his redeemer lives on after him.

The term redeemer (go'el) is frequently used of God as the deliverer of his people out of captivity (e.g., Isa 49:7,26), and also as the deliverer of individuals from distress (e.g., Gen 48:16). Among men the go'el was the nearest blood-relation, who had certain duties to perform in connection with the deceased. Those duties included buying back lost property, caring for the widow of the deceased, and insuring justice be done if the relative had been unjustly slain (cf. Ruth 2:20; Num 35:19). Job here names God as his *go'el*. This divine *go'el* will vindicate his rights against the wrong done to him by both men and God. This passage is closely related to 16:18f. where Job alludes to a heavenly "witness" and "sponsor" or representative.

Concerning his redeemer (God) Job was confident of three facts. First, his redeemer would *arise*, i.e., he would appear, he would come forward. Heaven's inactivity would end in that great moment when God would intervene in human history. Second, his redeemer would arise *upon the dust*. The context here speaks of Job's body. The idea seems to be that there will be a coming of God to the soil in which Job's body lies buried. Third, his redeemer would appear on the earth as "the *last*."[8] The God of the Bible is the first and the last (Isa 44:6; 48:12). He existed before all things; he shall survive after the present order has been swept away (19:25).

Job here also expresses a strong confidence about himself. First, he is confident that he would survive death. After death he had hope that in the condition of a genuine human being he would have a favorable meeting with God. He would see God "after my awakening "[9] Even though his body be destroyed, yet Job was confident that from the standpoint of his flesh he would see God.[10]

Second, Job is confident that he will see God. Heretofore Job had indicated a need to *hear* God. In verses 26f. three times he speaks of *seeing* God. The reference to *skin, flesh*, and *eyes* make it clear that Job expected to have the experience of seeing God as a man would see him, not in a vision or as a disembodied spirit. Third, Job is confident that in that blessed day of sight, he would not see God as a stranger, i.e., God would no longer act as a stranger toward him (19:26-27).

E. A Final Threat (19:28-29).

Job's response to Bildad concludes with a threat to the three friends. God's future appearance which will bring joy to Job, will be terror to those who persecute him and charge him falsely. The three kept asserting that "the root of the matter," i.e., the real cause of Job's afflictions, was found in himself, in his transgressions. For such unfounded accusations these friends should fear the "wrath" of God and the "sword" of divine vengeance. They would thereby learn that God brings judgment on such injustice as they have heaped upon Job.

ZOPHAR'S SECOND SPEECH
Job 20:1-29

Zophar was angry with Job's threats against the three friends. After venting his anger against his host, Zophar developed his main point, namely, the brevity of the wicked person's prosperity. Like Bildad before him, he stressed that the wicked person is suddenly brought to destruction and destitution in the midst of his days. This speech is the most stinging speech of the friends thus far.

A. Reaction to Job's Reproach (20:1-11).
The Naamathite began his speech with "therefore," perhaps to indicate that what he had to say came in response to what had just been said. Zophar gives two reasons for his second speech. First, he was inwardly agitated by the reproaches and windy warnings of Job. Second, he had heard the insulting reproof of Job, and his "spirit of understanding" had formulated a rebuttal to what the patriarch had set forth. Perhaps Zophar put it this way to answer Job's earlier question, "What plagues you that you answer?" (20:1-3; cf. 16:3).

Zophar asserts that a principle of life had been observed since man was placed on earth, namely, "the triumphing of the wicked is short." The "joy" of the godless person is momentary. For a time he may rise to the heights of earthly glory where his head "touches the clouds." Yet he perishes like his own dung (20:4-7a). Zophar is not the most refined of the three friends.

Associates will be amazed at the sinner's quick demise. His moment of power and glory is as ephemeral as a dream or vision. Then those who knew him would see him no more. He will forever be missing from his place in society (20:7b-9).

In the midst of his years, when his bones are full of his youthful strength, the wicked man shall be cut off. His youth shall go down to the grave with him. The ill-gotten gain of the wicked person will be given away by the children of the deceased (20:10-11).

B. Divine Retribution of Sinners (20:12-22).

Zophar compares sin to a dainty morsel which tickles the palate. He will not swallow it hastily, but instead will turn it in his mouth with delight. Eventually he must swallow it, and in his bowels it will become deadly poison akin to the venom of cobras. A specific example of this principle is the ill-gotten gain which he amassed. That wealth does not abide with him. It must be disgorged. The figure is perhaps that of a food which the stomach cannot retain. "God shall cast them out of his belly" (20:12-15).

Whatever the sinner "sucks," i.e., indulges in, turns to the venom of cobras. He shall not look on "rivers of honey and curds," i.e., he would never enjoy life more abundant. He would be compelled to restore that for which he had labored. He shall not "swallow it down," i.e., enjoy it. However great the substance be which he has acquired, he shall not have the joy of it which he had promised himself. Why? Because he had oppressed and then abandoned the poor. He seized houses which he had not built (20:16-19).

The divine retribution upon the sinner is appropriate to his sin. He had felt and displayed a restless, insatiable greediness. "Nothing remains for him to devour." The greed of this person is recompensed by utter loss and want. In the moment of his greatest abundance his distress comes suddenly upon him. All those in destitution, and those he has oppressed shall rise up against him and make him their prey.

C. The Fullness of Judgment (20:23-29).

The belly of the sinner shall indeed be filled, but only by the judgments of the Almighty. The wrath of God comes upon him like rain. Seeking to escape from one death, he will flee into another. He faces an enemy, as it were, armed with a brass bow. That powerful weapon would send forth an arrow to pierce right through his body. Zophar depicts the sinner drawing out of his body the shaft of glittering steel, hoping to save himself. Soon, however, the terrors of death fall upon him (20:23-25).

Zophar piles up other figures for the judgment on the sinner. Complete darkness—a symbol for calamity—is reserved for the treasures of the sinner. An "unfanned fire," i.e., a supernatural fire, shall consume all that is left in his tent (20:26).

Heaven and earth conspire together against the sinner. There may be allusion here to Job's appeal to the earth (16:18) and his pretended assurance of having a witness in heaven (16:19; 19:25). The heavens "reveal" his iniquity in the chastisements which fall upon him. Earth rises up against him in the form of the hostility of his fellow man. In the day of God's wrath the possessions of the sinner shall be swept away with a flood (20:27-28).

Zophar concludes his speech by underscoring the picture he has drawn. Job should see himself in the picture. The insistence that such sudden reversal of fortunes as Job has experienced comes as judgment from God forces Job again to reply to his friend (20:29).

JOB'S SECOND RESPONSE TO ZOPHAR
Job 21:1-34

In the first round of the debate Job was overwhelmed with the thought that God had become his enemy; in the second with the thought that men had turned against him. In both rounds it took the caustic words of Zophar to focus his keen mind on the arguments of his friends. In his first response to Zophar, Job employed bitter sarcasm (ch. 12). Now the patriarch unleashes a barrage of facts which directly bear on the argument of the friends.

A. An Appeal for Attention (21:1-6).

To introduce his speech, Job offers four reasons why the friends should listen to him. First, the friends believed they were offering Job the consolations of God (15:11); the consolation he seeks from them is that they listen to him. Second, after he has spoken, Zophar (the verb is singular) may mock him if he wishes. Third, Job's complaint did not concern the friends, nor men in general for that matter. His complaint pertained to God. Because God was silent, Job felt he had reason to be impatient. Fourth, just a glance at the sufferer should astonish the friends into silence. Yet they gazed at him and just kept gabbing. Job himself was certainly horrified when he looked at himself.

B. The Prosperity of the Wicked (21:7-16).

Job now addresses the question, Why do the wicked prosper? Why under the moral government of God does he permit them to live? They not only live, they live to a ripe old age, and become mighty in the earth. Unlike Job, the wicked have the blessing of seeing their children grow up beside them. Not merely themselves and their children, but their homes and all in them are full of peace—another allusion to the rod of God which had fallen on all which belonged to Job. Their children dance and sing and play musical instruments (21:6-12).

The wicked spend their days in prosperity. Then in a moment, without the miseries of a prolonged illness, they die and go down to Sheol, the abode of dead spirits. Thus Job draws the picture of the peaceful end to a prosperous life (21:13). This is exactly opposite the picture presented by the friends. According to them, the wicked experience the pangs of conscience (15:20), an early death (20:11), a childless old age (18:19), and a disastrous end (20:24).

The wicked experienced all this joy and prosperity in spite of the fact that they had consciously excluded God from their lives. Their godlessness was not momentary and rash, but formal and reasoned. They did not wish to know his ways. They openly scoffed at the value of serving the Almighty or praying to him (21:14-15).

Finally, Job articulates the mystery. The prosperity of the wicked "is not in their hand," i.e., it does not depend upon them. It comes rather from God. Why does God so bless the faithless? Whatever the answer to that question—and Job certainly had no answer to offer—this suffering patriarch wanted no part of the counsel of the wicked. He repudiates the principles by which they live. His glowing description of the life of the wicked should not be interpreted to mean that he endorsed their lifestyle. Even though he does not understand the ways of God, he will not abandon God (21:16).

C. The Peace of the Wicked (21:17-21).

Job next argues that the wicked experience peace as well as prosperity. Sudden and disastrous visitations by God do not come upon them as the friends had repeatedly suggested. What examples can his opponents offer to support their assertion that the light of the wicked is put out (cf. 18:5-6), or that they experience calamity (cf. 18:12). What examples can his friends produce of the wicked being swept away like stubble or chaff before the wind? (21:17-18).

Perhaps his opponents will argue that though the wicked man personally may not suffer, his children certainly will. A dead man, however, does not know nor care what his children are experiencing. In a moral universe the wicked man personally should experience retribution. He should "drink of the wrath of the Almighty" (21:19-21).

D. The Audacity of the Friends (21:22-26).

The doctrine of providence articulated by the friends did not correspond to reality. By clinging to such a doctrine the friends were making themselves wiser than God. Will they then presume to teach God how to run the universe? The Almighty judges "those on high," i.e., heavenly beings. What man, then, can instruct him with regard to the affairs of earth? (21:22).

Job observed that death is the great leveler. Of those who die suddenly, one person is at the height of prosperity; another dies in bitterness, never having experienced the blessings of life. Though vastly different in life, both persons are together in the dust where the worm consumes their flesh. Job is arguing that one's character cannot be determined by his lot in life. Thus, the three friends should not presume to tell God to judge a person's life by his wealth or his health. All people die, and only God can be the accurate judge of their lives, regardless of the circumstances which they experienced in life (21:23-26).

E. The Ignorance of the Friends (21:27-34).

Job finally addresses the insinuations of his friends about himself. In describing the fate of the wicked they had Job in mind. When they asked in astonishment, "Where is the house of the prince?" they were speaking of him. The implication is that the dwelling of the wicked prince had been swept away (21:27-28).

Such insinuations reveal the gross ignorance of these antagonists. Have the three of them never asked for the witness of caravaneers who travel throughout the world? Such travelers tell a story quite different from that of the friends. What have these travelers observed? (21:29).

First, they observed that the wicked person was preserved in the day of destruction.[11] Second, they testified that the wicked man was allowed to continue in his evil ways without censure from any quarter. Third, they witness that the wicked man is buried in honor. He would be carried to his grave in solemn procession. His tomb would be guarded against desecration. Fourth, they observe that, far from being shunned by his fellow man, the wicked person is idolized. "All men shall draw after him," i.e., he shall have innumerable successors and imitators, just as he was preceded by countless others whom he resembled (21:30-33).

Job feels that he has refuted the theories of his friends in regard to the supposed calamities and misery of the wicked man, whether in life or death. Hence their attempts to comfort him by this line of thinking are vain. The suffering patriarch regards all their answers as falsehood. In spite of all their talk, the three friends had been of no help to him (21:34).

ENDNOTES

1. Those who think Job's disease was elephantiasis point to the involuntary weeping associated with that disease.

2. Roy Zuck, *Job* (Chicago: Moody, 1978), p. 78. Most commentators, however, think that Job refers to God himself as his witness.

3. NASB misses the point in 16:21. The wish is not that a man might plead with God, but that one might plead for man with God. The reference is probably to the "witness" of v. 19.

4. The Hebrew uses six different words in 18:8-10 for "snare," and it is difficult to find suitable variety of rendering in the English.

5. The figure of the tree here is reminiscent of Bildad's former plant-life lore in 8:11f;16f.

6. Examples of the allusions to Job's case are these: the brimstone from heaven (v. 15) points to the fire from heaven which fell on Job's cattle and their keepers (1:16); the withered tree (v. 16) reminded Job of his own wasted state; the horror of men (v. 20) is but a picture of what was transpiring in the disputation with the three friends.

7. The text reads literally "the sons of my womb." This phrase has been taken to be a reference to (1) his own children, perhaps children of concubines; (2) his brothers; and (3) his clan.

8. The term *"last"* in 19:25 is adjectival, not adverbial as recognized in the NASB margin.

9. Following J. Barton Payne in understanding 'ori (my skin) as an infinitive ('uri) meaning my awakening. The Encyclopedia of Bible Prophecy (New York: Harper & Row, 1973), p. 255.

10. The Hebrew preposition min (from) in 19:26 could signify "without my flesh" as in ASV. This would indicate spiritual immortality rather than bodily resurrection; but the resurrection concept better accords with the previous "awakening" and with Job's thought about hope for his body that began in 14:12-17.

11. Others interpret 21:30 as a quotation of the friends to which an appropriate introduction would be: "You say." It is best to understand the travelers as saying that the wicked are led away to safety from the destroying wrath of God.

CHAPTER SIX

The Final Round in the Debate
Job 22-31

In the first round of the debate Job's guests implied that he was a sinner, and they appealed to him to repent. In round two, they insinuated that he was guilty and stressed the terrible fate of the wicked, but they gave Job no opportunity to repent. In the last round of the debate, the friends attack Job with open accusations of specific sins. Job again stands his ground. He denies that the wicked always suffer; he emphatically rejects the contention that he is a deliberate trans gressor.

THIRD SPEECH OF ELIPHAZ
Job 22:1-30

Eliphaz takes up the argument made by Job that no moral principle could be detected in God's treatment of man (cf. 21:23-26). His speech moves through five phases.

119

A. God's Disinterest in Job (22:1-5).

As Eliphaz sees it, God's treatment of men cannot be due to any respect which he has to himself, for he is too lofty to be affected by anything human. Neither the "vigorous man" nor the "wise man" can be of any use to him. God receives no pleasure from man's righteousness, nor profit from his integrity. Eliphaz viewed God as largely disinterested in mankind (22:2-3).

God's treatment of men is for their sakes and according to what they are. Eliphaz did not think it possible that God would chastise men for their piety. Therefore, if Job has been afflicted, it must be for his sins. God's only concern was with justice. Therefore, he needed only to interact with man when retribution was required by man's sin (22:4-5).

B. Social Accusations against Job (22:6-11).

What specific sins had Job committed? Eliphaz now begins to enumerate them. They are such sins as a powerful Eastern ruler might naturally be expected to commit. First, he accused Job of inhumanity toward the poor. He had required collateral from destitute brothers who needed help, even taking their outer garments for such purposes (22:6).

Second, he had been inhospitable. He had not given water to the weary nor bread to the hungry. The duties of hospitality were very stringent in the ancient Near East. Job's stinginess was all the more inexcusable since he was a "mighty man" and highly respected.Third, Eliphaz accused Job of cruelty. When widows came seeking his help, he sent them away empty. The "strength" (lit. arms) of orphans had been crushed (22:7-9).

Because of his inhumanity and heartlessness, Job is surrounded by the snares and terrors of God. He finds himself in darkness, overwhelmed by a flood of affliction (22:10-11).

C. Spiritual Accusations against Job (22:12-20).

Eliphaz has suggested what Job's offenses must have been. Now he imagines what attitudes toward God were reflected in such actions. Job must believe that God is so far removed from earth that he could not possibly know what was happening here. From the perspective of the infinitely high heavens, how was it possible for him to distinguish the actions of one person from that of another? Furthermore, thick clouds block his view of earth as he walks about the circle of the heavens (22:12-14).[1]

According to Eliphaz, Job's attitude toward God resembled that of the great sinners before the Flood. Does Job wish to follow in those notorious footsteps? Those people were snatched away in judgment before their time. Their false foundation of beliefs was swept away by a river. The reference is probably to the Deluge (22:15-16).

Eliphaz next twisted Job's words. He turns the patriarch's sentences around to make it appear that he was a flagrant sinner who ordered God to depart from his life even though the Lord had caused him to prosper. Such was the attitude of those who lived before the Flood. So Eliphaz distanced himself from such arrogant defiance of deity and ingratitude. "The counsel of the wicked is far from me," he declared (22:17-18).

Righteous people see the judgment that comes to sinners "and are glad," Eliphaz asserts. The "innocent" mock them. The cutting off of those adversaries would be an occasion of great joy. To see their abundance destroyed in the fire of God's judgment would vindicate their belief in the justice of God (22:19-20).

D. Appeals and Incentives (22:21-25).

Eliphaz urges Job to reconcile himself with God, assuring him of restoration and peace if he will do so. Three exhortations, each accompanied by a promise, are directed to the sufferer. First, Eliphaz asked Job to "yield" to the Lord, and receive God's words into his heart. Should he do so, he would have peace and good would come to him (22:21-22).

Second, he should return to the Almighty by putting away his evil. Should he do so, he would be restored to his former state. Third, he should renounce his worldly wealth by flinging it to the dust or to the pebbles of a brook. If he should do so, the Almighty would be his gold and silver (22:23-25).

E. The Rewards of Repentance (22:26-30).

Following his appeals for repentance and accompanying incentives, Eliphaz lists four promises of what would follow upon Job's restoration. First, again Job would delight in the Almighty and lift up his face in confidence, unashamed by afflictions. Second, Job would be able to pray unto God with assurance of being heard. Since his prayers would be answered, he would have occasion to pay the vows which he made to the Lord (22:26-27).

Third, Job's plans for the future would stand and be realized, for the light of God would be on his ways. Fourth, any future casting down which he might experience would speedily be turned by God to an up-rising, because of his humility. Finally, Job's intercessory prayers on behalf of others who had sinned would be effective because of his own "clean hands," i.e., innocence. They would be delivered from judgment through his availing prayers (22:28-30).

The charges of unrighteousness (vv. 5-11) and ungodliness (vv. 12-17) illustrate how far men will go in the heat of debate to defend their religious theories. The concluding words of Eliphaz (vv. 21-30), however, are conciliatory and appropriate to one who is both aged and devout.

JOB'S THIRD RESPONSE TO ELIPHAZ
Job 23:1-24:25

Job is too absorbed with the painful mystery of God's providence to be able yet to give attention to the direct charges of wickedness which Eliphaz had made against him. In chapter 23 he speaks in reference to the injustice of what he has experienced. In chapter 24 he focuses on the injustice in the world in general.

Job Speaks Regarding Himself
Job 23:1-17

Job continues to be confident that he is experiencing an incredible wrong at the hands of God. He expresses again his desire to find God so as to present his case before him. Then Job lapses into discouragement as he contemplates his hopeless condition.

A. Job's Desire (23:1-7).

Job knew that his complaint against God was a rebellious act and would be so viewed by his friends. Though he tried to restrain his groaning, he could not. The text is properly translated: "My hand is heavy upon my groaning" (23:2).

Job ardently desires that he could come to God's judgment seat to plead his cause before him.There he eloquently would argue his case with irrefutable arguments. In that context he could demand plain answers. Faced with the facts of Job's case, God would be forced to admit the injustice which had been done to his servant. He was convinced that God would not take advantage of his great power. On this point Job has changed his opinion since his speech of 9:14-16. At that divine tribunal, Job was confident that he would be delivered forever from injustice at the hands of the heavenly judge (23:3-7).

B. Job's Defense (23:8-12).

Job suddenly returns to the reality of his isolation. God is everywhere, yet he can find him nowhere. The words "forward," "backward," "on the left hand," and "on the right hand" probably denote the four points of the compass. Job concluded that God must be avoiding him because he knew he was innocent. Should he encounter Job he would have to admit that a grave injustice had been done (23:8-10).

How could Job declare that if tried by God he would come forth as shining gold? Eliphaz had insinuated that Job was following the ancient path of wicked men (cf. 22:15). Not so. He had followed in the steps of the Lord and had never deviated therefrom. According to Eliphaz, Job needed to hear instruction from the mouth of God (cf. 22:22). In fact Job had never departed from the commandments of God. They were more precious to him than his daily bread (23:11-12).

C. Job's Discouragement (23:13-17).

Though he knows that Job is innocent, God is resolute in his determination to destroy the patriarch. Since God is omnipotent, he can do as he pleases. Eliphaz had argued that if Job repented he could have all his plans confirmed (cf. 22:28). Not so! God was carrying out in Job's life what *he* had decreed. All of this was a profound enigma to Job; but it was far from being a solitary one: "many such things are with him," i.e., this is but one out of many similar mysteries that happen under God's government of the world (23:13-14).

God's mysterious and irresistible ways trigger in Job a sense of dismay, terror and faintheartedness. By acting in what Job perceived to be an unjust way, the Lord had made the heart of the patriarch faint. The emphasis here is on what God had done. What dismays Job and renders him speechless is not the dark calamity which had overtaken him, and not the fact that his face had been marred and distorted by disease. What bothered him most was this: It was *God* who had inflicted the calamity upon him, and that for no just cause! (23:15-17).

Job Speaks Regarding the World around Him
Job 24:1-25

In chapter 24 Job cites several examples of the absence of any righteous rule of the world. The chapter begins with a question. Why does not the Almighty set aside times for sitting in judgment and dispensing justice to men? The question is in reality an accusation that God fails to exercise a righteous rule. They that "know" him, i.e., his people, wait in vain for some manifestation of his divine righteousness (24:1).

A. Complaint Regarding Public Crimes (24:2-12).

Job now proceeds to illustrate his complaint of the absence of righteousness in God's rule of the world. He mentions three crimes in particular: removing landmarks, stealing, and mistreatment of the needy. Boundary stones marked property lines. Disreputable men would move them in an attempt to enlarge their property. Stealing flocks of sheep and then pasturing them as one's own would be a brazen kind of theft in a pastoral society. Widows and orphans were deprived of the single ox or ass with which they might work their small fields. The needy were deprived of their rights (24:2-4a).

Job next paints a pitiful picture of the destitution of those he calls the "poor of the earth." Some think that Job is speaking in these verses of the plight of the aboriginal races of the regions east of the Jordan. Their land and homes had been seized by more powerful

tribes. They had fled the bitter oppressions to which they were subjected by their conquerors. They could only huddle together, like wild
donkeys, in obscure haunts to escape the violence of the oppressor.
The roots and herbage of the desert are the only nourishment they
can find for their children. For fruit they had to be content with the
neglected late gleanings of the vineyard of the wicked. The mountain
rains drench these thinly-clad outcasts as they "hug the rock," i.e.,
huddle closely under its ledge, for protection from the elements
(24:4b-8).

Wealthy men seized the nursing infants of bankrupt young widows
to raise as slaves in expectation of recouping financial loses. They
required as collaterial that which is upon the poor, i.e., their outer
garments. This class of destitute people would be forced by these
actions to go about "naked without clothing" (24:9-10a).

Though the slaves labored amidst the abundant harvest ("among
the sheaves") of their masters, these slaves were themselves faint with
hunger. Animals were treated more kindly (cf. Deut 25:4). Within the
walled vineyards and groves of the wealthy they pressed the olives for
oil and trod the wine presses. Though they produced an abundance of
wine by such labors, the slaves were not allowed to drink, thus they
"suffer thirst" (24:10b-11). The same injustice which was abundant in
the rural areas was also prevalent in the population centers. There
too men groaned under oppression. The wounded cried out for justice. Yet God takes no note of such wrongdoing. He appointed not
days (v. 1) for setting things right and thwarting the injustice (24:12).

B. Complaint Regarding Secret Sin (24:13-17).

The focus now shifts to those who "rebel against the light," i.e.,
they prefer to act under cloak of darkness. A murderer "arises with
the light," i.e., toward daybreak, while it is still partially dark. At that
early hour he waylays a solitary traveler. At night that same person
may act the part of a thief (24:13-14).

The adulterer waits for the twilight, i.e., of evening. Then he dis-
guises himself so that he may enter undetected into the house of his
neighbor. They "dig into houses," i.e., cut a hole through the mud
brick, as a secret entrance into the quarters of the woman with whom
they were committing sin. Since they are busy by night, the adulterers

shut themselves up in their own homes during the day. They fear the light of day as most men fear the dead of night. The "shadow of death," i.e., thick darkness of night, is where they are most comfortable (24:15-17).

C. Confidence in Final Judgment (24:18-25).

In the previous verses Job was upset because God did not do something to stop oppression and sin. Now he states that God *does* punish the wicked. Because commentators see a contradiction here, many try to circumvent what the patriarch plainly declares.[2] Job, however, never said that the wicked do *not* suffer. Instead, he argued that *both* the righteous and the wicked suffer, and *both* prosper.[3] The friends, on the other hand, argued that *only* the wicked suffered and *only* the righteous prospered.

To Job the wicked are as insignificant as a splinter on the surface of raging water. "Their portion," i.e., their fields and possessions, were under a curse, and consequently would become nonproductive. The day would come when that wicked person would no longer be able to "turn toward vineyards," i.e., enjoy the good life of which vineyards are a symbol. Sheol engulfs sinners. They disappear from earth as surely as the fierce heat melts winter snow. Even the one who gave birth to the sinner would forget him. None would take pleasure in him except the worm to which the decaying body would have a sweet taste. The wicked would be broken as suddenly as a tree that snaps in two in the throes of a storm (24:18-21).

This one who had taken advantage of defenseless women[4] would be dragged off by God. In that day the wicked would have "no assurance of life," i.e., that he would survive the judgment. Although it appears that he is giving the wicked security, God's eyes are upon them. For a time they are exalted because of their wealth and power. In judgment they will be debased, gathered up like heads of grain which have been cut off (24:22-25).

The friends had argued that the wicked were cut off immediately; Job argued that they were "exalted for a time." For this patriarch even a temporary exaltation of such people was an injustice. Job concludes his speech with a challenge to the three friends to prove him wrong (24:25).

THIRD SPEECH OF BILDAD
Job 25:1-6

Bildad perhaps felt himself unable to reply to Job's arguments. Yet he will not retire from the field without at least uttering one more protest against the spirit of his adversary. The facts of history and experience may support Job's contentions. Yet the spirit in which he has presented his arguments and the conclusions in respect to God which flowed from those arguments must be labeled false. Bildad repeats here the thoughts expressed earlier by Eliphaz and this is a sure indication that the controversy has exhausted itself.

To God belongs "dominion" and rule, and his majesty inspires terror. He dwells in the "high places," i.e., the heavens. There he "makes peace," i.e., brings calm to storms, through his awesome power. The armies which obey Yahweh's commands are innumerable. The reference here may be to the angelic host or to the stars themselves (cf. Isa 40:26). He commands the light of day as well. By the light which he sends forth, God reaches all, and brings all under his sway (25:1-3).

In view of the majesty and universal power of God, how can a man be righteous before him? Here Bildad is repeating the earlier words of Eliphaz (cf. 4:17a) and of Job himself (cf. 9:2b). Human beings are unclean by virtue of the sin they commit in their lives (cf. 4:17b; 15:14). Since Job was a member of the human race, he must be unclean before God (25:4).

Before the great creator, the moon and stars are only insignificant luminaries. Surely then, man—the Hebrew word points to man in his creaturely weakness—is puny before him. The "son of man," i.e., one born of man, is a weak and putrid maggot spiritually speaking. The moon "has no brightness," i.e., it only reflects light. The stars "are not pure in his sight," i.e., they are not bright in comparison with God. Eliphaz had contrasted man with the angels (cf. 4:18-19; 15:15-16), and here Bildad contrasts man with the moon and stars (25:5-6).

Bildad is aiming to get Job to face up to his worthlessness in the big scheme of things. The majesty of God, however, was not at issue in the debate. Therefore, Bildad's third speech was pointless. It offered no hope for the vindication which Job craved, and no hope for purification which Job already had said he did not need. This final word from Job's friends is disgusting in its evasiveness, heartlessness and hopelessness.

JOB'S THIRD RESPONSE TO BILDAD
Job 26:1-28:28

The poverty of the position of Job's adversaries is indicated by the brevity of Bildad's last speech. Zophar did not even rise to speak in this third round of the debate. Job had the last word. In chapter 26 he directly addressed the preceding speech of Bildad. In chapters 27-28 the patriarch begins his grand finale to all three opponents.

Response to Bildad
26:1-14

Job responds to Bildad by (1) rebuking his attitude; and (2) presenting his own portrait of the greatness of God.

A. Bildad's Weakness (26:1-4).

Bildad had argued that man, including Job, was puny and vile; Job responded by indicating that Bildad was the puny one. Job sarcastically expresses his admiration of Bildad's speech, and gratitude for the help it has been to him. The patriarch makes four accusations.

First, Bildad's brief speech had been no help to Job. If the patriarch was so weak and puny, why had not this friend "saved the arm without strength," i.e., supported, or helped Job. Second, Bildad had offered Job no wisdom or given any helpful insight regarding his plight. If Job was so stupid, why had not Bildad educated him? (26:2-3).

Third, Bildad had addressed his speech to one who was superior to him in wisdom: "To whom have you uttered words?" (12:3). Fourth, Bildad had spoken under his own inspiration, not that of the Holy Spirit, nor even that of the wise men of old. Bildad had been unable to help Job, and no one had helped him with his speech. Bildad was only speaking off the top of his head (26:4).

B. God's Greatness in the Underworld (26:5-6).

Bildad had stated that God was majestic; Job responded with statements about God's majesty that were far more majestic than Bildad's. God's power manifests itself in the underworld of departed spirits, and in the upper world of the earth and heavens.

Bildad had referred to the power of God as "making peace on high," i.e., in the heavens (25:2). Yet Job affirms that God's power is felt even in Sheol. The Rephaim (departed spirits) reside in Sheol. The word seems to mean "the elite among the dead."[5] That place of departed spirits is represented poetically as lying deep down under the waters of the sea, i.e., far removed from the scenes of earth. The dark and dreary Sheol is naked before the eyes of God. Abaddon[6] or Destruction (cf. 28:22) here is a synonym for Sheol (26:5-6).

C. God's Greatness in the Heavens (26:7-10).

In the heavens Job sees three evidences of the majesty of the Lord. First, God stretches out the brilliant constellations of the northern heavens as one would stretch out a tent on a pole. The heavens are stretched out "over empty space," i.e., the massive void between earth and heaven. He "hangs the earth on nothing." The earth is supported by nothing material. Therefore it must be supported by God himself (26:7).

Second, men bind up water in skins or bottles; God "binds up the waters in his thick clouds." Job was amazed at the thought that the clouds are floating reservoirs, which do not burst under the weight of torrential waters which they contain. God's power alone can account for this amazing thing. God can even use the clouds to obscure the full moon (26:8-9).

Third, God has "drawn a circle on the surface of the waters." The reference most likely is to the horizon which appears to be circular. The sun rises over the eastern horizon, moves across the arch of the heavens, and sets beyond the western horizon. Beyond this invisible circle lies the utter darkness of space (26:10).

D. God's Greatness in the Earth (26:11-14).

On earth Job sees three more evidences of God's majesty. First, the "pillars of heaven," i.e., the lofty mountains that reach into the clouds, "tremble" at the rebuke of the Lord. The reference is probably to thunder which in poetic literature is depicted as the voice of God. Another view is that when earthquakes shake the earth the mountains tremble with terror at his majesty (26:11).

Second, God stills the tempestuous sea. In Semitic thought the raging sea was personified and called Rahab (cf. 9:13). The God of the Bible smites this raging monster, i.e., he brings calm to the turbulent waters (26:12).

Third, by the breath of his mouth the Lord clears away the dreary skies so as to reveal the brightness of the heavens. Like a great dragon, the storm clouds swallowed up, as it were, the heavenly bodies. God, however, pierces and slays that swift serpent (26:13). In both this verse and the preceding there may be an allusion to the monsters which were deities in Canaanite theology. If so, the thought is that Yahweh is superior to all the imaginary gods of the heathen.

The power of God is surely illustrated in the mighty works described above. Yet what men can see of him in these works is but the "fringes" of his real operations. What men may hear of God is but a faint whisper. No man can comprehend the full unfolding of the thunderous power of the Almighty! (26:14). That Job's awareness of God's awesome power exceeded that of Bildad is clear from these words.

A Defense of His Innocence
27:1-23

Job paused to permit Zophar to speak, but this blustering friend had- exhausted his wisdom on the subject at hand. Therefore, Job resumes his own discourse. Here he addresses all three companions.[7]

A. Proclamation of Innocence (27:1-6).

With the solemnity of an oath by God, Job declares that he speaks in sincerity when affirming his innocence. "As God lives" was a traditional oath formula which indicated that what was about to be said was as certain as God's existence. Job senses the irony of swearing by God while at the same time accusing the Lord of gross injustice. By afflicting him, God has taken away Job's "right," i.e., his right standing before the Lord. By refusing to hear Job's case God had "embittered" his soul. From these words it is obvious that Job's mind has not changed. He still believes in God for he swears by him; but he charges God with injustice. An appeal to God stands side by side with an accusation against him (27:1-2).

As long as there was life (lit., breath) in his emaciated body, Job insisted that he would speak only the truth. He, therefore, could not concede that the friends were right in charging him with gross sin. Until his death Job declares that he would not "put away my integrity," i.e., refrain from asserting his innocence. Throughout his days he had held fast to righteousness, and he would not now let it go. His "heart," i.e., conscience, did not reproach him for his claims. This strongly worded oath of innocence is consistent with Job's earlier protestations of innocence (27:3-6).[8]

B. Imprecation Regarding His Enemies (27:7-11).

In the remaining verses of chapter 27 Job recounts the fate of the wicked man. He expresses the desire that his enemies share the fate of that wicked man. This is another way in which he affirms his own innocence. He did not consider himself among the wicked or guilty. In ancient justice one who made a false accusation against another had to suffer the penalty of the crime wrongly charged. The implication is that the three friends had falsely accused Job and thus deserved to suffer the punishment which they imagined that he should suffer (27:7).

In a series of three questions Job points out the dreary and desolate condition of the mind of the wicked person in affliction. The godless person has (1) no hope in the hour of death, (2) no answer when he cries for help in time of distress, and (3) no recourse to God throughout his life. The point is that the wicked have no place to turn when they need higher help. Since he had no fellowship with God, the wicked person cannot appeal to him. If Job was discouraged because of the silence of the heavens, at least he had someone to whom he could run in his plight. This fact alone would prove that he was not to be numbered among the wicked (27:8-10).

Eliphaz had urged Job to receive instruction from God (cf. 22:21-27). Job now reverses this suggestion. He will instruct the three

131

friends—the second person pronoun is plural—regarding God's power as it is revealed in his dealings with the wicked. Nonetheless, what he would tell them would only be reminders of what they already knew about God (27:10-11).

C. The Portion of the Wicked (27:12-23).

Job next begins to discourse on the fate of the wicked.[9] The utter destruction of the wicked is exhibited in five pictures. First, the wicked person loses his children. Though they be numerous, his children would be killed in war or would suffer in famine. Those who survived these fates would die of plague. The urgency of their burial would be such that customary funeral rites would be suspended (27:12-15). These words seem to contradict what Job asserted about the children of the wicked in 21:8-9. The earlier passage refutes the notion that the loss of children are proof of wickedness; this passage points to the ultimate fate of the wicked.

Second, the wicked person loses his wealth. Though he may pile up silver like dust and garments like clay, i.e., in plentiful amounts, he would not, however, be able to enjoy these material things. In the end his wealth would pass into the hands of the righteous and the innocent, who in this book are often equated with the poor (27:16-17). The ungodly are swept away. The righteous remain and enter into their possessions. The meek inherit the earth (Ps 37:29,34).

Third, the wicked person loses his home. His house would prove to be as unstable as a moth's cocoon or the temporary shelter erected by farmers as guard posts during the harvest. One day the wicked person is rich, but the next day he wakes up to poverty or worse. He "opens his eyes and he is not," i.e., he awakes just in time to view the coming destruction before being swept away (27:18-19).

Fourth, the wicked person himself would also be swept away. Overnight he would be overtaken by a terrifying flood. A windstorm off the eastern desert—known to natives as the sirocco—would snatch him away. This tempest would "hurl" at him its destructive arrows. Any attempt to escape would be futile (27:20-22).

Fifth, the fall of the wicked would produce glee in the hearts of those who hear of it. They would express their scorn and derision by hissing, or whistling (27:23).

A Discourse on Wisdom
28:1-28

Chapter 28 contains a single thought, namely, that wisdom cannot be reached by man. Though the wicked ultimately suffer a terrible fate (27:13-23), yet that does not solve all the riddles of providence. The three counselors had maintained that they knew God's ways. Job argues here that no man can discern the inscrutable mysteries of the majestic God.

A. Wisdom Cannot be Mined (28:1-14).

Job speaks of the various metals—silver, gold, iron, copper—and the precious stones[10] which are mined by man in the most ingenious ways. Miners were lowered by ropes through shafts into subterranean regions far below the sight of men on the surface. The digging beneath the ground produces rubble like that caused by fire on the surface (28:1-6).[11] Palestine had some minerals (cf. Deut 8:9), but no evidence exists that mining was practiced there. Important mines, however, did exist in the Sinai peninsula, in Egypt, and on the slopes of the Lebanon mountains.

The mines to which men go for their metals are inaccessible to animals. The birds of prey with their keen sight cannot find those places. The "proud beasts"—probably lions—which tread the earth have never had the courage to go where the miners go. Even the traditionally crafty serpent which lives in holes of the ground is unable to see or touch the underground treasures. Job seems to be expressing amazement at the ingenuity and boldness of man in securing the resources which he needs from beneath the earth (28:7-8).

If the place of mining is amazing, even more so is the mining operation itself. Man breaks through solid rock, overturns mountains at their base, cuts channels or tunnels in the rocks, and thus is able to reach the valuable metals. At times he must dam up underground streams so that they do not seep into the mine and hamper the work. All of this effort results in bringing to light that which was hidden in the darkness, namely, the precious metals (28:9-11).

In spite of man's technological sophistication, he cannot find wisdom. Nowhere in the "land of the living" (i.e., the inhabitable earth) has he been able to find this precious treasure. Even the mighty oceans must confess that wisdom is not to be found in them (28:12-14).

B. Wisdom Cannot Be Purchased (28:15-19).

Not only can man not find wisdom, he cannot even purchase it with the precious metals he has mined. Job uses a dozen different words for various valuable substances which were used as exchange in his day. Three of these words—"pure gold," "glass," and "crystal" in NASB—are used only here in the Old Testament, with the result that the meaning of them is far from certain. The main point, however, is clear. The most valuable substances known to man cannot purchase wisdom.

C. Wisdom Comes from God (28:20-28).

Where, then, is wisdom to be found? It is hidden from the eyes of all living creatures on earth. The keen-sighted birds do not know its location. Even Abaddon (Sheol, the abode of the dead) and death personified must confess that they have heard only rumors about wisdom, hence they know little about it (28:20-22).

God—the word is emphatic in the Hebrew—knows where wisdom can be found. He alone is omniscient. He sees in one effortless glance "to the ends of the earth" and "everything under the heavens" (28:23-24).

God is sovereign over his creation. In his providence he established regulations by which he governs the various aspects of nature. Storms appear to be without order; but they are determined by his wise and creative genius. He prescribed laws to govern the wind, waters, rain and lightning: the weight (i.e., force) of the wind, the measure (i.e., amount) of water, regularity of the rain, and the path followed by the thunderbolt (28:25-26).

At the very time when God established the laws of nature, he explored wisdom. He saw it, probed it, established it, and investigated it. While man cannot even *find* wisdom, these verbs suggest that God perfectly understands it. He has revealed a part of his wisdom to man. Although man cannot discover wisdom or purchase it, he can receive it from God. The essence of that wisdom is twofold: (1) fear God; and

(2) depart from evil (28:27-28). To fear God is to bring one's life into submission to him, to have confidence that he does all things right even when the rightness of his actions is not apparent to man. The "evil" from which man is to depart is determined by divine revelation. Thus the life of a truly wise person is God-centered, not self-centered (28:27-28).

Job 28 accomplishes several purposes in the book. First, it rebukes the shortsighted and superficial wisdom of his adversaries. It demonstrates that their limited theological outlook was false. Second, the chapter serves as a rebuttal to the friends' accusations that Job did not fear God, and needed to turn from evil. Third, the chapter underscores that God's earlier assessment of Job (1:1,8; 2:3) was correct, and the three friends were incorrect in their analysis of his life. Job had been fearing God and hating evil, but they had not. Truly the last verse of chapter 28 is one of the climactic moments in this book.

SUMMATION OF THE CASE
Job 29:1-31:40

The debate is now over; but as it was preceded in chapter 3 by a monologue of Job, so here it is followed by another of even greater literary beauty. The passage falls into three parts, corresponding to the separate chapters: (1) a picture of Job's former happiness; (2) a portrayal of his present condition; and (3) a protestation of innocence.

A Picture of Former Happiness
Job 29:1-25

Chapter 29 has four parts: (1) recollections of former happiness; (2) the reason for the adulation of men; (3) anticipation of continued prosperity; and (4) recapitulation of the respect which he had enjoyed.

A. Recollections of Former Happiness (29:1-10).

Job begins with a pathetic expression of regret as he remembers happier times. In those days he had experienced a different relationship with both God and men.

In former times God had watched over him, i.e., preserved him from harm. God's lamp shone above him and lighted his path illuminating the darkness before him. God's "lamp" is a figure for his favor, enlightenment and blessing. Job compares those former days to the "autumn" (NASB margin) of the year, the time of fruit-gathering and plenty, joy and thanksgiving. Those were the days when the "friendship" (lit., counsel, secret) of God watched over his tent (29:1-4).

As proof that God was with him in former days, Job cites two facts. First, he enjoyed his progeny: "My children were around me." Second, he experienced prosperity: "My steps were bathed in butter." This is a figure for the overflowing abundance amidst which he walked. The butter used in Palestine was often half liquid and could be drunk. Even the unfruitful "rock" seemed to pour out rivers of oil beside Job. The idea is that his blessings were so numerous that they came from the most unlikely sources (29:5-6).

Job's relationship with his fellow men was quite different in those former days. He had their respect; he enjoyed his association with them. From time to time Job left his estate to go to the city gate to transact some business. Such a "gate" was usually a building of considerable size where commercial and legal transactions were conducted. When Job entered the gate, the young men withdrew out of respect and the older men rose from their seats for the same reason. Job's arrival put a stop to speech and discussion already going on, which was not resumed until he had been heard (29:7-10).

B. Reasons for His Prestige (29:11-17).

Why did the leading citizens of the land show such respect for Job in those former days? Job's benevolence and kind treatment of the needy had earned him this respect. Even those who merely heard reports of his philanthropy "blessed" him, i.e., wished him happiness. The fatherless and widows are specific examples of the "poor" who needed kindness and help. Job even received the blessing of "the one ready to perish," i.e., the poorest of the poor (29:11-13).

In his dealings with his fellow man Job "put on righteousness," i.e., his life was wrapped up in doing what was right. He assisted the blind and the lame to do that which they were unable to do on their own. Job was "a father" to the needy. He even took up the case of strangers who came to him for assistance. As a great sheik, Job would often have to judge cases brought before him. In this work he acted with strict conscientiousness. Job "broke the jaws of the wicked." The figure is that of a beast of prey which has its booty already in its teeth. When an unjust oppressor seemed already to have triumphed and carried off his prey, it was torn from his jaws (29:14-17).

C. Anticipation of Continued Prosperity (29:18-20).

In the midst of that active and happy life Job anticipated length of days and continued prosperity. He thought that he would see death in his "nest," i.e., surrounded by those who belonged to him. He thought his days would be multiplied "as the sand," i.e., without number. His life was like a well-watered tree whose roots spread out to the waters and whose branches were kept fresh by the night dew. Job's "glory," i.e., the high respect and rank, would continue "fresh," i.e., new, not tarnished or diminished. His "bow," symbol of strength and power, would be "renewed" like a living tree, i.e., it would not lose its freshness and suppleness in his hand.

D. Recapitulation of His Previous Position (29:21-25).

Again Job mentions the prestigious position which he occupied in society prior to his affliction. People paid attention to him, i.e., they listened to his counsel. His wise words dropped like refreshing rain upon them. They anxiously waited for Job's pronouncements as a farmer might wait for the "latter rain," the spring showers. This rain was essential for a bountiful harvest. Job was superior in wisdom to those who came to him (29:21-23).

Job, with his broader insight and more capable counsel, smiled on those who were perplexed and despondent. What seemed insurmountable difficulty to them, seemed to Job a thing easy to overcome and nothing which should create anxiety. The despondency of others was never able to cloud the cheerfulness of his countenance. Job "chose out their way," i.e., he sought out their company. The perplexed recognized his leadership and set him as a king among them. Yet Job manifested no superior attitude toward them. He did his best to comfort those who mourned (29:24-25).

A PORTRAYAL OF PRESENT SUFFERING
Job 30:1-31

Chapter 30 forms a contrast to the previous chapter. The same subjects treated in the earlier chapter are repeated here, but in reverse order. The word "now" introduces three of the four paragraphs in this chapter.

A. Job's Present Ignominy (30:1-8).

In former days the young men retreated from court out of respect for Job. Now those young men hold Job in derision. The fathers of these youth had not been considered worthy of treatment which one might give his dogs. Those fathers were enfeebled and had fallen into premature decay. Yet the sons of these powerless men now look down on Job (30:1-2).

Job next describes an outcast race which were perhaps the aboriginals who once inhabited that land. Having had the respect of the most respectable, Job now had the contempt of the most contemptible (cf. 19:18), the very scum of the earth. These people had a shriveled appearance from lack of proper nourishment. They were reduced to devouring the roots which they gathered in the waste places.[12] When these wretched men tried to approach civilized dwellings, they were driven away and pursued with cries as men do a thief. They hid out in caves and bushes. Among the bushes they bray like the wild ass seeking for food. They throw themselves down like wild beasts under the bushes of the desert. These children of fools and the lowest of men had been crushed out of the land (30:3-8).

B. Job's Present Indignities (30:9-15).

The outcasts described in vv. 3-8 now treated Job with contempt. He was a subject for their taunt songs and bywords. They arrogantly stood aloof from Job. Some gave him the ultimate insult when they spat in his face. Earlier Job had spoken of this race of men with compassion (ch. 24); now he speaks of their conduct toward him with resentment. This race showed no appreciation for Job's feelings about them. They regarded Job as a member of the class that had dispossessed and oppressed them. So now they took a malicious delight in the calamities that had overtaken him (30:9-10).

138

God had loosed his bowstring and sent the arrow of affliction hurling into Job. So now the outcasts of society had "cast off the bridle" in respect to Job, i.e., they have cast off all restraint. They thrust aside the feet of Job as he tries to move from place to place. Like a besieging army, they had raised up their siege mounds from which to better attack him. They "break up" his path, i.e., the path of his life. They profit from Job's calamity, and no one is able to restrain them (30:11-13).

As soldiers charge through a breach in the wall of a besieged city, so these lowly rabble come at Job. The terrors continue to roll over the patriarch. The rabble pursue Job's honor as the wind blows away chaff. Job's prosperity has passed away like a cloud (30:14-15).

C. Job's Present Condition (30:16-24).

By his afflictions Job had been reduced to a condition of abject despondency: "My soul is poured out within me." In the night seasons he especially felt the gnawing pains of depression. His agony was so great that it seemed as though his bones had been pierced by a sword and his limbs wrenched from him. The great force of his disease had caused his garment to be disfigured, possibly by the discharge of his skin ulcers. His garment "binds" him, possibly because his writhing body has twisted them tightly about him (30:16-18).

God has indeed dealt severely with Job. He has plunged Job into the mire, dust and ashes. The reference may be to the custom of throwing dust over one's head to express lamentation. His garments are now covered with this filth. Job lifts his eyes heavenward and cries out to the Lord, but there is no answer. He tried to get God's attention by standing up. In spite of his importunity, God only seems to look upon him with silent indifference (30:19-21).

Job likens his afflictions to a roaring storm. God has not only cast him down into the mire (v. 19), he has tossed him to the wind. He has been carried away by that storm, destroyed by it. He knows that his afflictions can end in nothing but his death. Soon he will enter "the house of meeting for all living," i.e., Sheol, the place of the dead. Yet he instinctively cries out to God for help, even though he now has concluded that the effort is useless (30:22-24).

139

D. A Final Contrast (30:25-31).

The compassion which Job seeks in his affliction, was his practice to bestow in former days. He wept for those in trouble, and grieved for the needy. Since he had been so kindhearted, Job had expected that his own prosperity would continue. His afflictions were totally unexpected. He looked "for good" but he received "evil," i.e., calamity; he waited for "light" but experienced darkness (30:25-26).

Again Job describes his present state. He says that his "bowels," i.e., the seat of emotion, "boil." He is overcome by a tumult of mixed feelings, griefs, regrets and pains. He goes about "blackened" (NASB "mourning") but not by the sun. The reference is to the way his disease has affected his appearance: his color has turned black. He "stands up" in the assembly of desert creatures to cry for help. His cry was as mournful as that of the jackal (cf. Micah 1:8), as piercing as that of the ostrich. His blackened skin and burning fever silenced the joyous music which once filled his house. His harp and flute now played only funeral dirges to accompany the weeping of grief-stricken people (30:27-31).

A PROTESTATION OF INNOCENCE
Job 31:1-40

Chapter 31 consists of a series of protestations, accompanied by curses on himself if these protestations of innocence are not true. Here and there Job appeals to God to judge him. Fourteen times he employs the "if guilty" oath often followed by self-malediction ("let" thus and thus happen). The sins enumerated in this chapter are not monstrous crimes, but minute deviations from the loftiest standards of ethics and piety.

A. Not Guilty of Sensual Sin (31:1-12).

Job clears himself of cherishing or yielding to sensuous desires. Three different instances of sensual sin are cited. First, Job had not succumbed to the simple desire excited by the eye. He had made a "covenant" or agreement with his eyes, that they should obey his mind, or act always in harmony with his higher self. This contract with his eyes did not permit him to look upon a woman with lust (cf.

Matt 5:28). He knew that the look could lead to the desire, and the desire to sinful action. He had resolved to avoid the very source of potential sin. Job kept his eyes in check because he knew that God would take note of the smallest step in the direction of lust. A sinful glance at a woman might lead to "iniquity" and unrighteousness. The Almighty would bring calamity and disaster upon such sin. Hence, the fear of judgment caused Job to control his eyes (31:1-4).

Second, Job denies that he had ever yielded to sensual desire in word or deed. The patriarch denied that he had ever "walked with vanity" (falsehood) or "hasted to deceit." His feet were as innocent as his eyes. Here "vanity" and "deceit" are virtually personified. He has not kept company with these unsavory characters, nor allowed them to entice him to do some evil deed. Parenthetically he solemnly asserts before God that this denial is true. The "even" or fair "balance" of God's judgment would testify to his integrity. Never had Job turned out of the way of righteousness set before him by God (cf. 23:11). Never had his mind yielded to the lust of the eye. Never had his hands been stained by any sin resulting from lust (31:5-7).

To underscore this declaration of innocence Job pronounces a self-malediction. If what he had just claimed for himself is not true, then let another eat the fruit of his labor in the field, or even worse, simply uproot his crops (31:8).

Third, Job declares his innocence from the grossest form of sensual sin, adultery. He had never allowed his heart to be enticed by a woman. He had never laid wait at his neighbor's door for an opportunity to have illicit relations with another man's wife. Again Job seals the truthfulness of his assertion by pronouncing a self-malediction. If he has spoken untruth, then let his wife "grind" meal for another, i.e., be the slave of another, or let others "kneel down over her," i.e., degrade her sexually (31:9-10).

Adultery was a heinous crime punished "by the judges."[13] This is a sin which grows and destroys as a fire. Ultimately adultery brings one to "Abaddon," i.e., Sheol, the abode of the dead. This sin will "uproot" one's increase, i.e., lead to utter ruin (31:11-12).

B. Not Guilty of Abuse of Power (31:13-23).

Job next repudiates all misuse of the power which his rank gave him. First, he denies that he ever treated his servants contemptuously when they had a complaint against him. He treated them not as possessions, but as persons who had rights as well as he. And why so? Job understood that all men were fashioned by God in the womb. He also understood that one day God would "rise up" in judgment. In that day he would be required to give an account for the way he had treated his servants (31:13-15).

Second, Job denies that he was ever indifferent to the needs of the helpless. Earlier, Eliphaz had falsely accused Job of failing to help those in need (cf. 22:7-9). He did not withhold from the poor what they desired, namely, food. Widows did not look to him in vain for help. He shared his bread with the fatherless. Even from his youth he had assumed the role of the benefactor of the poor. From his mother's womb—a bit of a hyperbole—he had been a father to the fatherless and a guide to widows. He probably means that he had been taught by his mother to always assist the helpless. Job claims that he never saw a person perishing for want of clothing or covering that he did not supply them with wool from his sheep (31:16-20).

Third, Job denies that he had ever violently wronged anyone. He had not lifted up his hand against the fatherless because he saw his "help" in the gate. Because of his influence, Job could always have received a favorable verdict in court. Yet he did not oppress the helpless. To underscore the truth of his claim, Job again resorts to self-malediction. If he had ever used violence against another, then he wishes upon himself that the arm which he had used to injure others should be broken, that his shoulder should be dislodged from its socket (31:21-22).

Job concludes this unit by expressing the conviction by which his conduct was regulated. He stood in awe of the majesty of God and in fear of his judicial anger. Thus he was restrained from any of the sinful actions named in this unit (31:23).

C. Not Guilty of Dishonorable Attitude (31:24-34).

Job now repudiates another class of secret sins that would have dishonored him. First, he denies that he had a secret joy in the possession of wealth, that love of gain which is idolatry (Col 3:5). He had not put his hope or confidence in gold nor in the accumulation of wealth of other kinds (31:24-25).

Second, never had he been enticed to let his mouth kiss his hand in order to salute the rising sun or moon. The reference is to a gesture by which ancients symbolized the homage of the lips towards an object of veneration.[14] The worship of the heavenly bodies was widespread in the ancient Near East. Such adoration would have been an iniquity punishable by earthly judges. It would also be a denial of the existence of the living God who created the heavens and earth (31:26-28).

Third, Job denies that he ever felt secret joy at the misfortune of his enemy. He had never permitted himself, even in hasty anger, to throw out an imprecation against an enemy (31:29-30).

Fourth, the patriarch denies that he was stingy. The household servants wondered if there was anyone who had not yet been filled from Job's rich table. Job took in strangers who were traveling near his home (31:31-32).

Finally, Job denies hypocrisy. He did not try to conceal his transgressions like Adam[15] had done in the garden (cf. Hos 6:7). Had he been conscious of sins Job never would have ventured forth from the doors of his house. Fear of the contempt of men would have deterred him. A prominent person cannot play the role of a hypocrite long without facing exposure and humiliation. Job, however, was not deterred by any such fear; he frequented the assembly (29:7ff.). He knew he had nothing to hide. He lived in the broad daylight and without fear confronted all. The main charge made against Job by his friends was that he was a hypocrite. This charge is categorically repudiated in this unit (31:33-34).

D. Final Appeal to God (31:35-37).

Since the friends would not listen to him, Job desperately cried out to God to hear him. He puts his signature, as it were, to his plea of "Not guilty" which he has presented in the preceding verses. He desires his adversary—God—to submit his indictment against him in writing. The language is evidently taken from the judicial practice of the time, according to which both charge and defense were laid before the court in writing (31:35).

If Job but possessed the Almighty's indictment against him, he would not hide it as a thing that caused him shame. He would bear it

143

in triumph before the world as that which was his greatest honor. He would even wear it as a diadem upon his brow as that which would give him kingly dignity and adornment. The language expresses the strongest assurance that the indictment could in truth contain nothing against him. Job would declare to God "the number of my steps," i.e., every act of his life. He would approach God "as a prince," i.e., with the confident step and erect bearing of one who knows that nothing dishonoring can be laid to his charge (31:36-37).

E. Final Plea of Innocence (31:38-40).[16]

Job now renews his protestations of innocence by denying that he had been guilty of land seizure. Land unjustly seized would (so to speak) cry out against the thief. The land would join its rightful owner in mourning over the loss.[17] Job's land, however, did not cry out against him. He had not seized that land by doing violence to its rightful owners. If any of these assertions be untrue, then let that field produce briars instead of wheat, and stinkweed instead of barley. That would make the land utterly worthless.

ENDNOTES

1. In poetry the skies are considered the dome with which God covered the earth.

2. Some writers take 24:18-25 to be an interruption by Bildad, or Zophar. Others think Job is speaking ironically, at least in vv. 18-21. Still others think he is quoting one of his friends.

3. Francis I. Andersen, *Job: An Introduction and Commentary* (Downers Grove, IL: InterVarsity, 1976), pp. 213f.

4. Two types of defenseless women are named in 24:21: (1) widows; and (2) barren women. In both cases the allusion is to women who had no sons to uphold their rights.

5. Roy Zuck, *Job* (Chicago: Moody, 1978), p. 117.

6. The term *Abaddon* is used six times in the Old Testament: Job 26:6; 28:22; 31:12; Ps 88:11; Prov 15:11; 27:20.

7. The second person pronoun in 27:5,11,12 is plural, while in 26:2-4 it is singular.

8. Job asserted his innocence in response to Eliphaz (6:10,29-30; 16:17; 23:10-12); Bildad (9:35; 10:7), and Zophar (12:4; 13:18-19).

9. Several commentators argue that 27:13-23 are the words of Zophar, and represents the missing third speech of this friend. Several statements here are similar to Zophar's previous words. The passage, however, is consistent with Job's desire that his enemy (the three friends considered collectively) experience the same fate as the wicked. Job had never denied that the wicked would eventually be punished; he only questioned why they continued to prosper for such a long time.

10. The "sapphires" of 28:6 are lapis lazuli, the ore of which contains particles that look like gold. Zuck, *Job*, p. 124. Others think that the *place* where sapphires are found also contains the gold dust.

11. H.H. Rowley, *Job* in "The Century Bible" (Greenwood, SC: Attic, 1970), p. 228. The phrase "and underneath it is turned up as fire" (28:5) has received a variety of other interpretations: (1) the precious stones uncovered by digging glow like fire; (2) the ore-containing rocks had been produced by volcanic fire; or (3) mine blasting.

12. "Mallow" in 30:4 is a plant with sour-tasting leaves, growing in salty marshes. The broom-shrub roots were also very bitter. Only the poorest of the poor would resort to such plants for food.

13. In the Mosaic Law adultery was punishable by death (Deut 22:22).

14. A similar gesture was used in idolatrous worship in the kingdom of Israel. See 1 Kgs 19:18; Hos 13:2.

15. The words "like Adam" can be translated "like man." Thus some think Job is denying that he concealed sin in his heart as a hypocrite might do.

16. Many scholars feel that 31:38-40 is out of place and should be inserted elsewhere in the chapter. These verses, however, may be an example of an anticlimactic passage at the end of a speech creating a trailing-off effect (cf. e.g., 19:28-29).

17. Others think that the point in 31:38-39 is that Job had never misused his land as, for example, eating the produce of the land without paying the laborers.

CHAPTER SEVEN

An Angry Young Speaker
Job 32-37

The lengthy debate between Job and his three friends has now ended. The visitors argued that Job was being justly punished for some sin which he would not acknowledge. They have now been silenced by the patriarch's strong insistence that he did not deserve such suffering. Because the three considered Job's attitude to be self-righteous, they gave up (32:1).

At this point a fifth speaker enters the picture. Elihu was deeply angry with both sides of the debate. This young man's view of suffering is distinct from the three friends and his view of God is higher than theirs. In addition, Elihu makes an honest effort to respond to Job's complaints about God.[1] Whereas the three friends urged Job to repent of sins committed *before* the calamity, Elihu thought he needed to repent of pride which surfaced *during* the calamity. Whereas Eliphaz, Bildad and Zophar argued that Job was suffering because he had committed sin, Elihu suggests that Job has now sinned because he has been suffering. Job does not attempt to answer Elihu.

147

The Elihu speeches play a significant role in the movement of the book. They enhance the suspense by postponing the climax. They restate and reinforce the issues by reviewing Job's arguments (33:8-13), and the friends' answers, as well as introducing new ones. These speeches show that the younger wisdom was essentially no more effective than the older, despite its great verbosity. They amplify the theme stated briefly by Eliphaz (5:17) that suffering may have a disciplinary and refining role in God's providence (33:14-30; 36:8-12). These speeches prepare for the voice of God by chiding Job's arrogant ignorance of God's ways (35:16), and by placarding God's sovereignty over the whole creation as evidence of his trustworthiness in matters of justice. They give the final evidence of earthly inability to fathom heaven's mysteries.

INTRODUCTION TO ELIHU
Job 32:1-22

Chapter 32 contains an introduction to Elihu, first by the narrator, and then by Elihu himself.

A. The Narrator's Introduction (32:1-5).

The first five verses in chapter 32 are in prose, although, strange to say, the Hebrew is accented with the markings characteristic of poetic literature. Elihu appears to have been a listener during the progress of the debate between Job and his three friends. He is said to have been a Buzite. Buz was the brother of Uz (Gen 22:21) and son of Nahor. Later passages mention Buz along with Tema and reckon them among the Arab tribes (Jer 25:23). Elihu was of the family of Ram, and thus may have been an ancestor of David (32:2a; cf. Ruth 4:19-22).

The name Elihu means something like "my God is he." With a name like that it is little wonder that this young man presents himself as a champion of God's justice. Now he steps forward because his anger burned against Job "because he justified himself against God" (32:2b). The idea seems to be that he justified himself at the expense of God's justice (cf. 40:8). Three times in the opening five verses of the chapter the narrator makes reference to the anger of Elihu. He was definitely an angry young man!

In Job's view, and that of his time, God wrongly had passed a judgment of guilty upon him by smiting him with affliction. Scarcely mentioning the specifics of Job's case, as the three friends had done, Elihu addresses the question, Can God's justice be protested?

Elihu was angry with Eliphaz, Bildad and Zophar as well as Job. The three friends "had found no answer," yet they condemned the patriarch. Because they were his elders, the young man had waited in vain for them to produce an adequate answer to Job's perplexity concerning God. Elihu was angry because they had not been able with their logic to silence Job's charges against the Lord. The young man is not defending Job. Far from it. He blames the three for not producing good reasons to place upon Job's attitude a deserved condemnation (32:3-5).[2]

B. Elihu's Self-introduction (32:6-22).

In his self-introduction, Elihu presents a lengthy justification of his speaking. First, he indicates his respect for Job's three counselors. Elihu, being a youth, shrank from interfering in the discussion between the aged men. He was of the opinion that older and more experienced men should be those who teach wisdom to others. Now, however, Elihu perceived that wisdom did not always accompany gray hairs; it is a gift of God. In the beginning the Lord had placed his "spirit" or "breath" of life in man (Gen 2:7). This was a spirit of intelligence as well as life (cf. 33:4). Thus Elihu defends his right to speak on the basis of his God-given intellect. He implores the older men to listen to his opinion on the subject.[3] He is not here claiming some miraculous illumination for this moment as some have argued (32:6-10).

Second, Elihu evaluates what he had heard from the three friends of Job. He had hoped to hear them refute Job. He kept listening for further and different arguments from them. None of them, however, was able to convince Job or answer his arguments (32:11-12).

Elihu refuses to let the three friends excuse themselves for their failure to answer Job. They might try to say that they had found an unexpected wisdom in Job which only God could overcome. Job's wisdom, however, was not invincible. It remained to be seen how his wisdom would fare against another wisdom different from that of the three friends. Job had not yet matched his arguments against those of Elihu. In this angry young man, Job would face arguments much different from that of the three friends (32:13-14).

Third, Elihu expresses his desire to speak to the issue. The three friends had been embarrassed to silence before Job. Their silence, however, shall not have the effect of imposing silence on Elihu. He feels a crowd of arguments in his mind pressing for utterance with a force that cannot be resisted. He is, therefore, constrained to speak. He claims he is "full of words."[4] Elihu compares his speech to fermenting wine in a sealed wineskin. He is about to explode. He cannot restrain himself. He must speak that he might find relief (32:15-20).

Elihu closes out his introduction by insisting that he will speak without partiality. He will speak to the issue sincerely and fearlessly. He will not allow himself to be influenced by respect to the persons who sat before him, whether Job or the friends. Elihu is concerned only with the truth. Flattery is not part of his nature. His fear of God would prevent him from engaging in such a thing (32:21-22).

ELIHU'S FIRST ANSWER TO JOB
Does God Hear Man?
Job 33:1-33

The long introduction over, Elihu now begins to set forth his arguments. Chapter 33 addresses the issue: Does God hear man?

A. Request for Attention (33:1-7).

Elihu begins with an appeal that Job would hear him. Unlike the other speakers, he addresses Job by name. Elihu offers five reasons why Job should hear him. First, he promises the patriarch that he will speak candidly and sincerely. He possesses what Job had hoped to find in his three friends, namely, uprightness. Second, Elihu will set forth a conviction flowing from that spirit of God given to him in his creation. Because of his zeal for the Lord, Elihu feels that this spirit of God is within him in a powerful degree, and that gives him a higher wisdom than ordinary (33:1-4).

Third, Elihu will give Job an opportunity to respond. He offers, not a sermon, but a dialogue. Fourth, Elihu will not be condescending to

Job, nor take advantage of his physical weakness. Since both men had been "formed out of the clay" (Gen 2:7), both stood on equal footing before God. Thus Elihu considered himself to be equal with Job before God and not superior to him, as had the friends. Fifth, Elihu assures Job he will have no cause to be fearful in entering into this new discussion. Job had often complained that the terror and majesty of God overpowered him and made it impossible for him to plead his cause. He will feel no such pressure upon him from Elihu (33:5-7).

B. Summary of Job's Complaint (33:8-12).

Elihu summarizes what he has heard Job say in the preceding speeches, namely, that he was "clean," "without transgression," "innocent," and without "iniquity." Yet in spite of this, God had found, i.e., invented, grounds of enmity or hostility against him. The Lord now counted Job as an enemy to be shackled and guarded (cf. 13:27). Such was Job's feeling about how he had been treated by God (33:8-11).

Elihu now gives a general and preliminary answer to Job's charges against God. The patriarch cannot be in the right in such charges because God is greater than man. The three friends of Job had argued in the same way (cf. 8:3), though they hardly gave the idea the same importance that Elihu does. Elihu is suggesting that whatever concepts of justice may be prevalent among men, God's justice must of necessity be greater still. Hence charges of injustice must of necessity be ludicrous (33:12).

C. Divine Communications (33:13-28).

Job had interpreted the silence of heaven to be an indication that God acts in an arbitrary and hostile manner toward man (cf. e.g. 19:7; 30:20). To this charge Elihu responds that God speaks to man in many ways. He speaks in dreams and visions by which he instructs men and seeks to turn them away from doing evil. If man gives no heed to the warning, God speaks again to him in the same manner (33:13-15).

In dream revelations God "opens the ears of men," i.e., communicates clearly to them. He "seals their instruction," i.e., he confirms it, probably through the impressive circumstances and manner of the dream or vision. The recipient would have no doubt that God had spoken to him (33:16).

The purpose of such divine communication is to arrest men in their plans to do evil. God wishes to "turn man aside from his conduct," i.e., the prideful rebellious conduct to which he might be inclined. The effect of such revelation is that man is preserved from committing deadly sin, which would have brought destruction upon him "by the sword."[5] Five times in chapter 33 Elihu affirms that God saves men from "the pit," i.e., Sheol. Being frightened by nightmares (cf. 7:14), Job had missed the purpose of God's dream-warnings, namely, to preserve man from sin and death (33:17-18).

One who failed to learn from direct revelation through dreams would experience yet further discipline. He is chastened with pain which he felt even within his bones. In this condition he had no appetite for food. His body became emaciated. His flesh was consumed. If the words are to be interpreted literally, the description seems to point to leprosy. The life of this person gradually drew near "the pit," i.e., death. The "destroyers"—possibly the angels that bring death—were drawing near (33:19-22).

The afflicted man may have "an angel" who would interpret to him God's providential treatment of him. Such an angel would simply be "one among a thousand," i.e., one of the thousands of ministering spirits sent forth to do service on behalf of the people of God. This angel has the function of showing to a person what is right for him to do. Here Elihu contradicted Eliphaz, who had stated earlier that no angels could assist Job in his plight (cf. 5:1). In 9:33 Job too had bemoaned the absence of an arbiter to intercede on his behalf (33:23).

When the sufferer does what is right, then God is gracious to him. The Lord would order that the sufferer should be delivered from going down to the pit. He has been ransomed from death. The "ransom" might be the sinner's suffering or his repentance. On the other hand, the text might simply mean that God treats this man as ransomed and delivered (33:24).

As a consequence of the grace of God, the sufferer experiences restoration. His new-found health is like the freshness of a new childhood and the strength of a new youth. He is then restored to fellowship with God as well. His prayers are again answered. He again "may see his face with joy." One "sees" the invisible God in worship (cf. Heb 11:27). The point is that this man who once suffered is restored to his righteous standing before God. He therefore admits this man to all the blessings of righteousness (33:25-26).

The restored man would express thanksgiving for all that God had done for him. He will first confess his past sin. He would sing of the grace that did not deal with him as his sins deserved. He praises the Lord for having delivered his soul from going into the pit of death. Consequently he would see "the light" of life (33:27-28).

D. Summary and Challenge (33:29-33).

Elihu sums up his doctrine regarding the gracious purpose and effect of God's methods of speaking unto man. Again and again his graciousness is made obvious to men. He does whatever is necessary to bring back a soul from the pit of death so that he might see the light of life (33:28-29).

Elihu next challenges Job to continue to listen to his arguments. If he can reply to what has already been said, by all means he should do so. Elihu desires to do right by Job. If Job could give a satisfactory reply to his arguments he would be glad to acknowledge that the patriarch was in the right. If, on the other hand, he cannot reply to what has been said, then let him listen and learn wisdom from the young man (33:30-33).

Elihu viewed suffering as protective rather than retributive. Suffering was designed to preserve a person from death rather than a means of punishment leading to death as affirmed by the three counselors. The older men insisted that Job must take the initiative in repentance if he would be restored. Elihu urged Job to listen to an angel, and God would restore him.

Elihu may have been closer to the truth than the three older men. Like the three, however, he was wrong in assuming that Job's sickness had come upon him because of his sin. Also, when God spoke to Job he did so directly, not through an angel as Elihu had suggested. The young man was correct, however, in pointing out the pride which had grown in Job's heart as a result of his suffering.

ELIHU'S SECOND ANSWER TO JOB
Is God Unjust?
Job 34:1-37

In his second speech Elihu answered Job's accusation that God was unjust. At first (vv. 1-15) he addressed the bystanders. Then in v. 16 he spoke directly to Job.

A. Introduction (34:1-4).

Elihu invites the wise among those who listen to him to pay attention to what he further says, and to unite with him in seeking to discover the right in this cause between Job and God. The "wise men" are not the three friends, but bystanders. Elihu suggests that "the ear," i.e., the inner ear or understanding, tests words just like the palate is a judge of meats. In respect to Job's plea with God, Elihu pleads that all present will reach a just decision based upon common reason, i.e., the common reverent and just thoughts about God.

B. Job's Charges against God (34:5-9).

Elihu recites Job's statement of his cause against God. The patriarch had declared: "I am righteous," i.e., in the right, yet "God has taken away my right," i.e., what is rightly due to me. In other words, Job is saying that God has dealt with him unjustly. God's treatment of him seemed to undercut Job's claims of being in the right. Job had said that the "arrow" of divine affliction (NASB "my wound") is incurable even though he was without transgression (34:5-6).

Elihu cannot restrain his abhorrence of Job's sentiments. The patriarch has lapped up derision and scorn, i.e., impiety, like water. In expressing such opinions Job has gone over to the camp of the professed ungodly. Elihu concludes that Job did not think that being religious was of any benefit to a person. This idea Elihu will refute in the following chapter. Meanwhile, he directs his attention to the general charge that God is unjust (34:7-9).

C. Elihu's Response to Job's Charges (34:10-30).

Elihu first expresses his rejection of such sentiments as those of Job. They are contrary to right thoughts of God. Elihu rebuts the charge that God is unjust on the grounds of impiety. God cannot be thought of as acting in the way Job asserted (34:10-12).

Elihu argues that no motive for injustice in God, the creator of all, can be discovered. God of his own will made the world. He filled the creatures therein with his spirit of life. If God thought only of himself and withdrew his life-giving spirit, all flesh, including man, would perish immediately (34:13-15).

Elihu further argues that the foundation of government is justice. Injustice in the highest ruler is inconceivable. Partiality or injustice is not to be thought of in God, for all people, rich and poor, are alike the work of his hands. Suddenly and without anticipation ("at midnight") the people "are shaken and pass away." "Without hand," i.e., without human agency, the mighty ones of the earth are taken away (34:16-20).

God's strict justice may be seen in his government of the peoples and their princes alike. God's justice is unerring, for it is guided by omniscient insight. "His eyes are upon the ways of a person." No dark place can hide the sinner from the all-seeing eye of God. The supreme Judge needs no corroborating evidence or testimony in order to bring judgment on the wicked. God's observation of the sin is a sufficient basis of judgment. Mighty men are broken in pieces in ways which cannot be anticipated. Others are set in their place. Such is the way in which God manifests his just rule over peoples and princes (34:20-24).

Armed with such omniscient insight, God takes knowledge of men's works, and his judgment overtakes them without fail. He "overturns" the wicked in the night, thus destroying them. At other times he strikes them "in the open sight of others." Those who are swept away in judgment are (1) those who had turned aside from following the Lord; and (2) those who through oppression had caused the cry of the poor to come up to God (34:25-28).

Elihu upholds the sovereignty of God. Who can question him when he "gives quietness," i.e., rest or relief, to those who are oppressed? On the other hand, when he "hides his face," i.e., withdraws his favor or help in anger, who is able to "behold" him, i.e., obtain his favor? In either case, no one can condemn God's sovereign rule whether it be expressed with respect to individuals or with nations. God's operations

155

are directed by the great purpose of the good of men, that the nations be righteously and mercifully ruled (34:29-30).

D. Application to Job (34:31-37).

Elihu imagines a situation in which a complainer under affliction protests his innocence. He disclaims knowledge of any offense and desires to know what his sin was. He professes his readiness to desist from that sin when it is made clear to him. Elihu sees such a complaint as an effort to regulate the government of God, to dictate to him how he should act. Elihu distances himself from any such position: "You shall choose, and not I." Elihu encourages Job to specify what retribution he would regard as superior to that observed in God's rule of the world (34:31-33).

Elihu's second speech concludes with a verdict which all men of understanding must render regarding Job's demeanor. First, they would conclude that "Job speaks without knowledge, and his words are without wisdom." Second, they would desire that Job "were tried until the end," i.e., that his afflictions might be continued till he should desist answering in the manner of wicked men. Job's "answers" are his speeches in reply to the three friends, which are characterized as such as only ungodly men would utter (34:34-36).

Third, by his conduct Job had added "rebellion" to his "sin." His "rebellion" is his unsubmissive, defiant demeanor against God in his speeches; his "sin" is that of his former life, for which he has been cast into afflictions. Fourth, Job has shown his defiance against God openly ("among them") by "clapping his hands," a gesture of mockery and contempt (34:37).

Elihu here reveals his attitude toward Job. His judgment is that Job was a sinner in his former life, and a defiant rebel under his afflictions. Whereas Elihu had assured the three counselors that he would not use their kinds of arguments, yet in this speech he follows their lead. The language here exceeds in harshness almost anything that the three friends had said.

Was Elihu right? He certainly was right about God's authority, omniscience and power to judge sin. Elihu was right in reprimanding Job for demanding that God answer him by showing where he had sinned. However, in defending God's justice Elihu impugned Job's honesty about his innocence. None of the human speakers in the book knew anything about the contest between God and Satan. Consequently Elihu's assessment of the reason for Job's suffering was incorrect.

ELIHU'S THIRD ANSWER TO JOB
Does It Pay to Serve God?
Job 35:1-16

Job had argued that under God's government of the world it availed a person nothing to be righteous. This proposition, to which Elihu had earlier referred (34:9), is taken up in depth.

A. A Statement of Job's Position (35:1-4).

Elihu represents Job as maintaining that he has a just cause against God. Did he then have a right to assert this: That godliness profits nothing? If Job could successfully maintain this contention, his cause against God would be right. Elihu promised to rebut this position held by Job and "his companions," i.e., that circle of persons who cherished the same irreligious doubts in regard to God's providence as Job did.

B. A Statement of Elihu's Position (35:5-8).

To Elihu, one glance at the heavens, the infinitely exalted abode of God, must reveal that man's conduct, whether good or evil, cannot affect the Lord (cf. 22:12). He does not profit from man's righteousness, nor does he incur any loss from man's sin. It is in human life that the influence of righteousness or wickedness is seen. Since righteousness and wickedness are poles apart, they cannot have the same effect upon man.

C. Possible Exceptions Refuted (35:9-16).

So how does Elihu explain the anomaly that sometimes the righteous cry to God from under the heel of the oppressors? Why is it that such prayers for relief are not answered? The reason is that the cry is merely the natural voice of suffering; it is no true appeal to heaven. No one says, "Where is God?" This is the language of one who is devoutly seeking the Lord. True faith would recognize that God gives "songs in the night," i.e., sudden deliverances which cause one's mouth to be filled with praise (35:9-10).

God has given to men higher wisdom than he has given to the beasts. He communicates to them continuous instructions through his fellowship, his ways and his word. Their appeal to heaven, then, should not be the mere instinctive cry of suffering, but the voice of trust and submission. Man in his evil pride afflicts the beasts and fowl so that they cry out to heaven. They remain unheard, however, because their cry is "vanity," i.e., empty. When men address heaven their speech must be much more than the plaintive cry of a wounded beast! (35:11-13).

God will not hearken to the voice of one whose cries are empty, devoid of faith and devotion. How much less will he listen to one who, like Job, complains to him (1) that he cannot see him (as in 23:8); (2) that his government in the world is not righteous; and (3) that he refuses to receive a just appeal (35:14).

Because God does not bring judgment speedily upon the wicked, he seems as if he takes no knowledge of wrong and oppression. From this Job drew the futile conclusion that there was no advantage in being righteous more than in sinning. For this reason Job was opening his mouth in vain (35:15-16).

ELIHU'S FOURTH ANSWER TO JOB
Focus on the Greatness of God
Job 36:1-37:24

In his fourth and greatest speech Elihu is less philosophical and more practical. In his previous speeches he attempted to correct false theology. Here he presents his own more positive concepts of the creator.

A. Introduction (36:1-4).

Elihu desires Job to hear him still further. He offers four reasons why Job should continue to listen to him. First, he has still more to say in God's behalf. Second, what he is about to say is not trivial or commonplace. He claims that he will "fetch knowledge from afar," i.e., he will speak comprehensively by throwing light upon his subject from far-off regions. Third, his object again is to ascribe righteousness to his maker. All of Elihu's speeches are meant to be a defense of God against the charges of Job. Finally, Elihu claims complete truth for the teaching he is about to give.

B. God's Greatness in His Earthly Works (36:5-15).

Elihu argues that God is "mighty," especially in understanding. For this reason he does not despise anyone. He gives to the weakest his rights as much as to the most powerful, for they are all the work of his hand (cf. 34:19). His perfect "understanding" makes it impossible for him to "despise" any. Four times in chapter 36 Elihu uses the word "behold" to introduce a statement about God's power (36:5).

Elihu pointed out that although God is mighty, he does not lack mercy. Because of his perfect understanding, God gives to all men their due. He does not preserve the wicked, but he does give the afflicted their right. His careful providence especially keeps the righteous, whom he exalts to the loftiest stations, even kingship (36:6-7).

So how are the difficulties of life to be explained? That people are sometimes bound in the "fetters" of affliction cannot be denied. Such affliction is a discipline. It is a stimulus to rouse men out of their sinful lethargy; it is a warning to bring sin to their remembrance (36:8-10).

Affliction is graciously intended, but it may have different results depending on how people receive it. If people hearken to affliction, they shall spend their days "in prosperity." If they do not hearken, "they shall perish by the sword." As in 33:18, "the sword" is figurative for God's destructive judgments. That sinner would "die without knowledge" (cf. 4:21), i.e., he would die as a reprobate without any spiritual knowledge (36:11-12).

Sometimes afflictions are the means of revealing the true character of people. Those who are "godless in heart" will " lay up anger," i.e., become bitter and angry with man and God within their heart. They do not turn to God and cry out to him when they are bound with affliction. They perish in the midst of their days "among the unclean," lit., like the sodomizers. The reference seems to be to the male temple prostitutes (36:13-14).

Elihu argued that affliction was an instrument in the hands of God for deliverance. In the time of difficulty people generally are more open to hear the instruction of God and to bring their lives into harmony with his word (36:15).

C. Application to Job (36:16-25).

Elihu now applies the principles he has just enunciated to the case of Job. God was now attempting to lead Job out of "distress" into "a broad place" (a symbol of prosperity) where there is no "confinement" (a symbol of affliction). There his table would be full of "fatness," i.e., abundance. Job's present affliction is designed to save him from a worse evil (36:16).

Like the wicked, Job has expressed a negative judgment concerning the work of God in affliction. As long as Job acts in this way, then judgment and justice shall keep hold on him. God's condemnation of him will reveal itself in the continuance and increase of his chastisement (36:17).

Elihu warns Job not to allow his anger to entice him into rebellion against God. He also warns Job about being led astray by "the greatness of the ransom" by which he means the patriarch's severe affliction. No other ransom will avail—not riches nor all the power of wealth. Only the purification of suffering will cleanse him from his evil and deliver him from worse judgment (36:18-19).

Job had frequently expressed the desire to meet God in judgment. Elihu warns him that he should not desire "the night," here a figure of judgment. By the judgment of God nations are "taken away" in their place, i.e., on the spot, suddenly and without power of escape. Job is warned about desiring, (lit., panting after) such a judgment. He is further warned not to "turn to evil," i.e., a rebellious spirit. Job was more inclined to this attitude than toward submission to God's chastening hand (36:20-21).

Instead of murmuring, Job should bow under the mighty hand of God. God is supreme; through his providence he is a great teacher of men. No teacher can compare to him. None can pass judgment on his doings or accuse him of unrighteousness. Individuals should exalt the work of God which "men have sung," i.e., celebrated with praise. Men look on God's work, his operations, with wonder and awe, from a distance. His work is too great to be seen close at hand (36:22-25).

D. God's Greatness in Heavenly Works (36:26–37:13).

This section of the fourth speech begins (36:26) and ends with a statement of God's greatness (37:22-23). A similar statement is found in the middle of the unit (37:5).

God is so great as to transcend all knowledge of man. "The number of his years is unsearchable," i.e., he is eternal. A specific example of the greatness of God is seen in the formation of raindrops. He draws away from the great mass of waters the vapor which then condenses and falls in abundant rain upon the earth (36:26-28).

If the raindrops are wonderful, even more so the thunderstorm. The clouds accumulate and diffuse over the heavens. The dark clouds roar with thunder. These mighty clouds are here poetically called the "pavilion" of God. Though God is enveloped in the dark cloud, he is there encircled with his light. This light manifests itself to men's eyes in the lightning that shoots from the cloud and illumines it. He sits in the heavens enshrouded in the masses of water in the thunderclouds (36:29-30).

God judges peoples by the lightning and the rain cloud. By the former he scatters and confuses his enemies; by the latter he makes the earth fruitful. He holds in his hand, as it were, the lightning bolts and directs them to their mark. The noise of the thunder declares his presence. Even the cattle are alerted to what is about to happen by the thunder (36:31-33).

Elihu confesses that his heart trembles when he hears the thunder. The thunder is the voice of God, going forth out of his mouth. This thunderous voice and the accompanying lightning can be heard and seen to the ends of the earth. After each lightning bolt again the voice of thunder is heard. By the thunder and lightning God does wondrous things which are beyond the comprehension of man (37:1-5).

Snow is another wonder of God's power. He sends down the snow and the heavy winter rains. This winter weather "seals the hand of every man," i.e., forces labor in the fields to cease. All men by this enforced inactivity through the operations in nature may know his sovereign power. Also the beasts of the fields seek refuge from the winter storms in their dens (37:6-8).

Frost and ice are next cited as wonders of God's power. The cold wind blows from the north, the warm wind from the south. "By the breath of God," i.e., the wind, the ice is formed (37:9-10).

The movements of the clouds are directed by God over the face of the inhabited earth. These movements serve the purpose of correction or mercy in respect to men. Sometimes the movements are simply "for his earth," i.e., for the inanimate world (37:12-13).

E. Exhortation to Job (37:14-21).

Elihu concludes his speeches by exhorting Job to observe the wonders of God and to learn from them the unsearchableness of their creator. He uses a series of questions to humble Job and kindle awe in his soul (37:14).

Can Job explain how God establishes the clouds and causes the lightning to flash forth therefrom? Can he explain the marvelous way in which the clouds are poised in the heavens? Man has no part in causing these wonders, but only passively feels the effect of them. Beneath the sultry summer cloud when no wind is blowing, the clothing of a man gets warm. He is helpless to change the weather. The clear, dry summer skies of the land are compared to "a molten mirror" reflecting the bright rays of the sun upon the earth. Can Job "spread out" such a sky? (37:15-18).

The thought of the strong expanse of heaven stretched out by God suggests to Elihu his unspeakable greatness and unsearchableness. The young man demands that Job identify the words by which such a being can be addressed, if one sought to contend with him. "We cannot order our speech by reason of darkness," i.e., our ignorance in the presence of the unsearchableness of God. Elihu could not imagine that anyone would wish to enter into God's presence to strive with him. To do so would be to express a death wish, a wish "to be swallowed up" by disaster (37:19-20).

When the north wind has cleared the clouds from the sky, the light of the sun is too great to look upon. That golden splendor dazzles the beholder. Men cannot look upon the light when it shines in the cloudless heaven, much less look upon the majesty of God, surrounded as he is with awesome glory (37:21-22).

Elihu sums up his teaching regarding the greatness of God. The Lord is unsearchable. He is exalted in power. He will not do violence to justice. He would not unjustly afflict anyone. Elihu pleads with Job to join with mankind everywhere in showing reverence to God. The

Lord has no regard for those "who are wise of heart," i.e., those who are wise in their own eyes. Thus Elihu is calling upon Job to humble himself (37:23-24).

Elihu thus prepared the way for God to speak. Although he brought out aspects of the issue of suffering undeveloped by the three older friends of Job, he did not have total insight into Job's situation. Only a clear word from heaven can speak adequately to this problem.

ENDNOTES

1. Job's major complaints against God—innocent suffering, unjust persecutions, and refusal to hear—are answered in reverse order in 33:11-30, 34:1-30; 34:31-37.

2. According to Jewish tradition, 32:3 is one of the eighteen passages in the Old Testament where the scribes have ventured to emend the Hebrew text. The original reading is said to have been "they condemned God." This was altered from motives of reverence. The context, however, argues in favor of the standard reading of the text.

3. At least ten times in his speeches Elihu calls upon the older men to listen to him or to let him speak.

4. Elihu was certainly "full of words" as he claims in 32:18. The verses of his speeches total 156, longer than Job's final speech, or all the speeches of any one of the three friends.

5. NASB has opted for an emendation of the text in 33:18 by rendering: "Sheol" instead of "sword." The Hebrew text as it stands makes good sense. The "sword" is a figure here for God's destructive judgments. NIV offers yet another rendering in the notes: "from crossing the River."

CHAPTER EIGHT

The Voice from the Storm
Job 38-42

The Book of Job began with this question: *"Does Job serve God for nothing?"* Under challenge by Satan, the Lord had permitted the trial of Job. He has not renounced God as Satan had predicted. He has continued to cleave to God. His faith has soared to heights never experienced when he was healthy. Nonetheless, Job has not come out of the trial unscathed. His attitude toward God, especially in presuming to contend with him, has at times been blameworthy. Job had repeatedly requested that God answer him (e.g.,13:22; 31:35). That request is now granted.

The confrontation with God was not as Job imagined that it would be. The issue of Job's suffering was never addressed. The divine speech was not a lecture on theodicy. Nor does the Lord respond to the brash charges which the patriarch had made against his just rule of the world. Instead of answering questions from Job, God fired the questions—over seventy—at him! God was not on the witness stand. Job was, and he was subjected to intensive cross examination.

The Lord spoke "out of the storm" (38:1). When Yahweh condescends to speak with men he must veil himself in the storm cloud in which he descends and approaches the earth (cf. Exod 19:16f.; 1 Kgs 19:11ff.). Since part of the purpose here was to rebuke Job's attitude, he veils himself in terrors.

The object of God's answer to Job out of the storm is twofold: (1) to rebuke Job, and (2) to heal him, i.e., help him see the error of his accusations against the Lord. The speech of God is organized around two related questions: (1) Shall mortal man contend with God (38:1–40:5); and (2) Shall man charge God with wrong in his rule of the world? (40:6–42:6).

THE FIRST CHALLENGE
Shall Mortal Man Contend with God?
Job 38:1–40:5

The voice from the storm touches first on the presumption of a man seeking to contend with God. After reviewing the greatness of God as revealed in the inanimate world (38:1-38) and animate world (38:39–39:30), Job is humbled and brought to silence (40:1-5).

A. The Opening Challenge (38:2-3).

The speech of the Lord opens with a question expressing his astonishment and impatience with Job. "Who then is darkening counsel?" The word "counsel" suggests that the Lord has a plan or meaning in Job's afflictions. That purpose was being "darkened" or obscured by the perverse and ignorant construction put upon those afflictions by Job. His words were "without knowledge," i.e., without a true awareness of the facts, without an understanding of the controversy which had precipitated the trial (38:2).

God challenges the patriarch to "gird up" his loins, i.e., prepare for that contention which he had desired (cf. 9:35; 13:20). When undertaking a strenuous task a man in biblical times would gather up his flowing robe and tuck it into his waistband. Girding up the loins became a metaphor for preparation. Job had boasted that when God called to him, he would answer (13:22). The Lord is about to demonstrate that such a boast was empty (38:2-3).

B. Wonders of the Earth (38:4-18).

The questions began immediately. Dozens of inquiries are hurled at Job in rapid-fire with scarcely a moment allowed for reflection and response.

1. The creation (38:4-7). The examination begins in the area of cosmology. The smallness of man is indicated by his total ignorance regarding the creation of the earth. The creation is represented poetically as being like the construction of a building. "Were you there when I laid the foundations of the earth?" If so, let Job explain how this was done. For starters, God hurls four questions at him. (1) Who determined the measures of the earth? Of course Job knew the answer to this question. But the point is, Was he present to observe the creation? (2) Who stretched the line upon it [the earth], i.e., the construction line? If Job had firsthand knowledge of creation, then let him speak. (3). Upon what were the foundations [of the earth] sunk? (4) Who laid the cornerstone thereof? Here the earth is poetically compared to a great building with deep foundations. The cornerstone, as it were, was laid with great rejoicing among "the morning stars" and "the sons of God" (angels). The "morning stars" may be another name for the "sons of God" or the phrase may refer to the planets and stars. But was Job there at creation? (38:4-7).

2. The sea (38:8-11). Next the Lord turns to the sea. The poet used the language of childbirth to describe the origin of the oceans. The ocean here is represented as an infant giant, breaking forth from the "womb" at creation. The infant ocean was clothed in dark clouds (cf. Gen 1:2). That newborn monster had to be tamed by almighty power. An impassable boundary had to be set to restrain its fury. The earth's shorelines are presented as gates that hold back the proud waves as they try to advance against the earth (38:8-11).

3. The dawn (38:12-15). From the remote primeval origins, the Lord turns to an everyday occurrence. Since the day he was born had Job been able to "command" the morning, i.e., order it to appear? The poet depicts the dawn pouring forth its light along the whole horizon. It takes hold of the darkness which stretches as a covering over the earth. Seizing this covering by its extremities, the dawn shakes the wicked out of it. The idea here is that the wicked flee from the light (cf. John 3:19). The "light" of the wicked is really darkness (cf. 24:13-17). The "high arm" is the arm already uplifted to commit violence. With the dawning of a new day that arm is broken, i.e., the violent deed is not performed in the light. Thus the dawn is a moral as well as a physical agent (38:12-13,15).

Under the light of morning, the earth, which was formless in the darkness, takes shape like the clay under the impression of a seal. All things with clear-cut impression and vivid coloring stand forth under the light. Together they form a various, many-colored garment in which the earth is robed. Thus the blanket of darkness is removed daily, and the bright garment of light is put on (38:14).

4. *The depths (38:16-18).* Again the Lord resorts to the method of interrogation. Had Job explored the abysses of the deep? Had he entered the gates of Sheol, the abode of the dead? Sheol is poetically regarded as even lower than the abysses of the deep. Had Job surveyed the breadth of the earth? If he comprehends the vastness of the earth, let him declare it.

C. Wonders of the Heavens (38:19-38).

The divine examination now turns to meteorology and astronomy. Here again Job is humbled by his lack of knowledge.

1. *Light and darkness (38:19-21).* Here the poet imagines both light and darkness having dwelling places in the heavens. Can Job find his way to the abode of light, i.e., the place from which it streams forth over the earth? Does he know where the darkness resides? If he knows the way to the "house" or "boundary" of the territory of light let him take the light back to its abode! No doubt, the Lord says sarcastically, Job knows the way to the place of light, for he was on the scene when the light first was called forth out of darkness! He is as old as the dawn which morning by morning has overspread the earth since creation. The sarcasm is obvious. The point is that Job was not present at the creation (38:19-21).

2. *Meteorological phenomena (38:22-30).* The poet represents snow and hail as having been created and laid up in great storehouses in the heavens. The Lord brings them forth from his treasuries for use in his moral government of the earth. An example might be the hailstorm by which Yahweh defeated the Canaanites in the days of Joshua (Josh 10:11). Has Job inspected those trea-

suries? Was he present when God filled those storehouses at creation? (38:22-23).

Can Job explain the paths sought out by the lightning bolts, i.e., predict where the lightning will strike? Can he explain how the east wind spreads over the earth? Can he explain why the rain-flood seems to come down in channels from the heavens? Man is not, as he might think, the only object of God's regard. God's goodness is over all his works. He satisfies with rain the thirsty wilderness where no man is, that the tender grass may be refreshed (38:24-27).

Does the rain have a human father? Does Job, or any man, beget the rain or the drops of dew? No, they are marvels of God's creative power. What about the ice which was as hard as stone? Who generated ice? The phenomenon of ice, rare in that region, naturally appeared wonderful (38:28-30).

3. *The stars (38:31-33).* What control does Job have over the stars? Can he bind the stars of the constellation Pleiades together in their configuration? Can he loose the constellation Orion to make its way across the heavens? And what about the constellation Mazzaroth or the Bear?[1] Does Job know the "ordinances of the heavens," i.e., the laws which govern the movements of the heavenly bodies? Can Job in any way affect the way the heavenly bodies influence the earth? (38:31-33).

4. *The clouds (38:34-38).* Can Job lift up his voice and call down torrents of rain? Do the lightning bolts answer to the summons of Job? What about the inner man? Where does his wisdom come from? Yet even with that wisdom, who can count the clouds of the heavens? Who can pour out "the bottles of heaven," i.e., bring forth the rains which turn powdered earth to mud?

D. Wonders of Animal Life (38:39–39:30).

A series of brilliant pictures from the animal world have the same purpose as those given in the preceding section, i.e., they reveal the wisdom and power of God. Ten animals are mentioned, six beasts and four birds. They include the ferocious, the helpless, the shy, the strong, the bizarre, and the wild. The questions concerning these animals are grouped in twos. The list begins with the king of the beasts and concludes with the king of the birds.

1. The lion and the raven (38:39-41). First, the Lord points out the contrast between the lion and the raven in respect to the provision of food. The lioness is equipped with an instinct to hunt and catch her prey. She then returns to the den to feed her hungry young. Job cannot teach her anything about this skill. From the powerful lion the Lord turns to the lowly raven, one of the most common birds in Palestine. While the lion waits patiently and silently in his lair, the noisy raven surveys the terrain from her perch and wanders over the surface of the ground in search of food for her young. The cry of the young birds is considered an appeal to God (cf. Joel 1:20); the feeding of those chicks is proof of the providential care of the Almighty who does not overlook even the least of his creatures (38:39-41).

2. The goat and the hind (39:1-4). The goats and the hinds are next mentioned. The focus here is upon the birthing process of the two animals. Does Job know the time when the shy wild goat (or ibex) will bear its young? Does he know the gestation period for the hind? At the appointed time these animals "bow themselves" and "cast out their sorrows," i.e., get rid of their labor pains. These shy and solitary creatures, inhabiting the rocks, are without the care and help in bearing their young which domesticated creatures enjoy; yet their bearing is light and speedy. The young become strong and robust in the open field. Soon they leave their mothers to go forth and never return. God has equipped them to provide for themselves (39:1-4).

3. The wild donkey and ox (39:5-12). The questions concerning the next two animals have to do with freedom. The wild donkey has an indomitable love of liberty. Who gave this animal its freedom? It dwells in the desert, not under "bonds" (harnesses) like his domesticated cousin. He scorns the noise of the city and scoffs at the shouts of the driver which the tame donkey obeys. In the spring the wild donkey frequents the plains in which there are pools of water, and later the heights where grass is abundant. This animal is another marvel of God's creation (39:5-8).

The powerful wild ox (*rem*) cannot be bound by ropes to pull the plow through the fields. This wild creature will not abide by the grain crib like his domesticated brother. A farmer could not trust the wild ox to gather the grain to the threshing floor or to thresh it once it was there. The point here is the contrast between the wild ox and his tame brother.

The wild ox was fitted for all the labor performed by the domestic animal, but was untamable. Man can make use of the one; but who would dare to attempt to subdue the other. The Lord is the author of this diversity in these creatures which outwardly look so similar (39:9-12).

4. *The ostrich (39:13-18).* In several ways the ostrich is a strange bird. The female ostrich flaps her wings joyously "with pinion and plumage of a stork" (lit., a pious one). The point seems to be that there is an external similarity between the ostrich and the stork. The disposition of the two birds, however, is very different. She buries[2] her eggs and allows the earth to warm them (39:13-14).

The ostrich leaves some eggs outside the nest to serve as food for the newly hatched brood. To this practice the poet refers when he says: "she forgets that a foot may crush them, or that a wild beast may break them." She appears to treat her young "harshly." The reference is to another strange practice of this bird. When chased by hunters the adult birds will act as decoys, running hither and yon in an effort to draw off the intruders. From man's point of view, the ostrich shows no concern for her young (39:15-16).

The mother ostrich acts as she does because God has deprived her of wisdom. Yet he has granted to that bird a swiftness of foot. The "flying" of the ostrich consists of swift running, in which she maintains her balance by her outspread wings and tail. The bird has been clocked at up to forty miles per hour over short distances. With her head elevated to full height, she is able to laugh at the swiftness of the horse and its rider. This combination of questionable and admirable qualities illustrates the creative genius and sovereign ways of the Almighty. God has chosen to create this bizarre bird, and Job can do nothing about it (39:17-18).

5. *The horse (39:19-26).* The mention of the horse in contrast to the ostrich in v. 18 triggers the dramatic depiction of the war horse, another example of the creative diversity of God. Did Job, perhaps, give that animal his might? Did he clothe the neck of the horse with his mane? With a terrible snort the horse leaps effortlessly over obstacles like a locust. Did Job give the horse this strength? (39:19-20).

Anxious to enter the battle, the war horse paws the ground in anticipation. Fearlessly he goes out to meet an army of armed men. The movements of the rider's quiver, spear and javelin against the horse's side seems to spur the animal forward. The sound of the trumpet seems to instill in him fierceness and rage. The trumpet blast, thunderous commands of the officers and shouts of the troops cause the war horse to "smell" battle ahead. He says "Aha!" i.e., he impatiently neighs. He is anxious for action. The point is, Job had nothing to do with these wonders of beauty, courage and power which cause this animal to mingle in the conflicts of men with a fury which exceeds even their own (39:21-25).

6. *The hawk and the eagle (39:26-30)*. The last series of questions has to do with the subject of flight. Does Job have anything to do with the wisdom of the hawk which migrates southward when the cold weather sets in? What about the eagle?[3] Is it at Job's command that the eagle fixes her habitation fearlessly on the dizzy heights of the mountain cliff? Did he give to this bird her penetrating vision which scans the wide expanse and pierces into the deep ravine? Did he endow the eagle with her terrible instincts that show themselves at once in her young which "suck up blood"? The reference is to the scavenger habits of these birds which kill and rip apart their prey in order to take the bloody meat to their young (39:26-30).

E. The Reaction of Job (40:1-5).

The first speech of God ends as it began, with a challenge to Job. In the light of this awesome array of illustrations of divine power and wisdom, will the critic still persevere in his contention with Yahweh? The Lord directly appealed to the patriarch to respond to him (40:1-2).

Job, however, had been put in his place by the glory of God which has just been displayed to him verbally. He now sees himself as "insignificant." He declares: "I will lay my hand upon my mouth," i.e., restrain my speech. He had spoken his mind earlier ("once I have spoken . . . even twice"). Now he will be silent before God (40:3-5).

SECOND CHALLENGE TO JOB
Shall Man Charge God with Unrighteousness?
Job 40:6–42:6

Job had charged God with unrighteousness in his rule of the world. He regarded what had happened to himself as the prime illustration of that unrighteousness. God's second speech makes the point that any alleged superiority to God's justice must be accompanied by corresponding superiority in power. The speech demonstrates that Job does not even possess equality of power, not to mention superiority.

The second speech of God follows the pattern of the first. A challenge and interrogation of Job regarding nature is followed by a reply from Job. In the first speech two areas of nature were highlighted—the inanimate and animate. In this second speech two specific animals—Behemoth and Leviathan—are presented.

A. A Sarcastic Challenge to Job (40:6-14).

Again God speaks from the storm. Again Job is ordered to "gird up" his loins like a man, i.e., prepare to face God like a man (cf. 38:3). God has two questions which he demands that Job answer. First, will this feeble man "annul," i.e., make void or deny, God's "judgment," i.e., his rectitude as ruler of the world? Second, will Job condemn God's righteous rule of the world so as to make himself look more righteous? Such would be as much an offense against God as daring to contend with him (40:6-8).

God now sarcastically invites Job to "play God," and see if he could do any better. In order to play the role he would first need to deck himself with the thunder and majesty of the supreme Ruler. Let this man see if he is able to undertake the government of the world. Let Job humble all the proud ones on the earth. Let him tread down the wicked "where they stand," i.e., immediately after the wickedness has been committed. Though this is what Job would have, it is not God's method of government (40:9-12).

Let Job bring the wicked to "the dust," i.e., death. Let him "bind them," i.e., shut them up, in the "hidden place," i.e., Sheol. If he can do this, he will prove himself worthy of that place to which he aspires when he reproves the rule of God in the world. Then Yahweh himself will admit Job's independent might and will praise him as one who is able to save himself by his own "right hand," i.e., power (40:13-14).

In this challenge to Job there are two underlying assumptions. First, omnipotence is necessary in the ruler of the world; second, the government of the world involves keeping in check the forces of evil. God's rule is of this kind. It is a moral government. Exceptions to that

173

moral government there may *appear* to be from time to time. These, however, are not real exceptions.

B. The Monster Behemoth (40:15-24).

If Job is able to assume rule of the world and even contend with God, surely he would have no trouble subduing the mighty Behemoth and Leviathan. The point of introducing these monsters here is to impress on Job his puniness as over against God's power. If Job cannot enter into conflict with these creatures, he certainly could not stand up to the one who created them.

God first introduces the Behemoth. The exact identity of the Behemoth is not certain. Modern commentators assume that the hippopotamus is intended. The tail of the hippopotamus, however, is short and stumpy; it resembles in no way the description of the tail of Behemoth. Some scholars have proposed that some mythological monster is intended. In this context, however, it is more natural to regard both Behemoth and Leviathan as actual animals. Some have suggested that Behemoth was a brontosaurus dinosaur. Every interpretation presents difficulties. This author, however, believes that the hippopotamus is probably intended.

The Behemoth was as much a creation of God as was Job himself. This strange animal, though fitted by its size and strength to prey upon other creatures, feeds upon grass like the cattle. "He moves his tail like a cedar."⁴ If Behemoth is the hippopotamus, this description of its tail is an extreme exaggeration. The poet describes the bones of Behemoth as "tubes of bronze," i.e., very strong. His limbs are "like bars of iron" (40:15-18).

Behemoth is "the first of the ways of God," i.e., first in magnitude and power. The creator has given this creature teeth (or perhaps tusks) like a sword with which Behemoth shears the vegetation in front of him. To satisfy its hunger the animal depastures whole mountains where other beasts "play," i.e., they do not fear this grass-eating giant. His hunger satisfied, Behemoth lies down in thickets of lotus, reeds and willows (40:19-22).

Because of his size, Behemoth is not intimidated by raging rivers. He is confident though "Jordan rushes to his mouth," a specific example of a river in flood. When this creature is awake, no one can capture him (40:23-24).

174

C. The Monster Leviathan (41:1-34).

Leviathan has been identified as the whale, the dolphin, a marine dinosaur that survived the Flood, and the crocodile. The last view is the one this author accepts. The Lord first stresses the difficulty of capturing the animal through fishing or hunting techniques. Sandwiched between these two units is a lengthy description of the creature.

1. *Fishing for Leviathan (41:1-11).* One cannot snare this creature with a baited fish hook[5] or "press down his tongue with a cord." The idea seems to be to pass a cord round the lower jaw to lead the animal about. One cannot put a rope through the nose of Leviathan as one might put a stringer through the gills of fish. With sarcasm the poet points out that Leviathan would never beg to be spared or treated kindly by a would-be capturer (41:1-3).

Leviathan would never willingly bind himself to perpetual slavery as a Hebrew bondsman might do (cf. Deut 15:12-17). One cannot make a pet out of this creature. This beast cannot be found in the marketplace where traders and merchants (lit., Canaanites) haggle over its worth. One attempt to lay a hand on Leviathan will result in a battle which will never be repeated nor forgotten. The hope of any assailant to overcome this creature is vain. Most men would cower before the sight of this monster (41:4-9).

If none dare stir up Leviathan, who will stand before God who created him, or venture to contend with him? On the other hand, no one has any ground of contention with God. None has given anything to God, so as to have a claim against him, for all things under the heavens are his (41:10-11).

2. *Description of Leviathan (41:12-25).* The Lord now describes the mighty Leviathan: his limbs, strength, and graceful frame. He first focuses on the jaws of Leviathan. Who is able to strip off the outer garment, i.e., his coat of scales? Who is able to come with "his double bridle"? The term may refer particularly to the corners of the jaws. "Who can open the doors of his mouth," i.e., his mouth. "Around his teeth there is terror" (41:12-14).

Next the focus is on the scales of Leviathan. Each of his scales is like a shield. These shields are arranged in rows. These shields are "shut up as with a tight seal," i.e., they adhere closely to the body (41:15-17).

175

Leviathan breathes smoke and flame. The animal is said to inflate itself, as it lies basking in the sun, and then force the heated breath through its nostrils, which in the sun appears like a stream of light. The first parts of the animal that a person sees when it emerges from the water are the small eyes which are compared to the dawn's rays gradually appearing upon the horizon. The long-repressed hot breath is blown out along with water from his mouth; it shines in the sun like a fiery stream (41:18-21).

Leviathan is noted for his strength and hardness of muscle. His strength seems to reside in his neck. Wherever he appears, terror leaps up. The idea is that in the presence of Leviathan other creatures are startled and seek to escape. The "folds of his flesh" —the parts beneath the neck and belly—are firm and hard. His heart is as hard as the lower millstone which bears all the pressure upon it. When Leviathan arouses himself "the mighty are afraid" and bewildered (41:22-25).

3. *Hunting for Leviathan (41:26-34).* Leviathan can be subdued by no weapon known to man at that time. Sword, spear, dart or javelin have no effect upon him. Iron and bronze break before him like straw. He "laughs," as it were, at such weapons (41:26-29).

The scales on the underside of Leviathan, though smoother than those on the back, still are sharp. They leave an impression on the mire where he has lain as if a sharp threshing-sledge with teeth had gone over the area. As he glides through the water he leaves in his wake a shining track (41:30-32).

Leviathan has no rival on the earth. He is king among the proud beasts. He "looks on everything that is high," i.e., he looks them boldly in the face without terror (41:33-34).[6]

D. Job's Reply to the Challenge (42:1-6).

The Lord's words make Job feel more deeply than before that greatness which belongs to God alone. With deep compunction he retracts his past words and repents in dust and ashes. One "who cannot undertake God's works has no right to undermine God's ways."[7]

Job now realizes that God can do all things. There is no purpose which the Almighty cannot carry out. Job's reply reflects the great, general impression which God had made on him. The exhibition of the divine wisdom as it operates in nature has led him to feel that within his own history also there is a divine "thought" or "counsel" though he is unable to understand it (42:1-2).

Job repeats the words of the Almighty (38:2): "Who is this that hides counsel without knowledge?" He speaks of himself. As one that obscured counsel, Job had uttered that which he did not understand. The reference is to his former judgments regarding God's operations in the world, and the rashness of his own language. Job now admits the justice of the rebuke implied in this question (42:3).

Again Job repeats the words of the Lord (cf. 38:3; 40:7): "Hear, I beseech you, and I will speak; I will demand of you, and you declare unto me." Verse 5 reveals the spirit in which Job repeats the challenge. Now in the light of what he has learned about the Lord, he distances himself from that challenge to enter into a confrontation with the Almighty (42:4).

Job now disparages his former knowledge of God of which he had boasted in his previous speeches (chs. 12–13). That former knowledge now seems to him to be only such a knowledge as one gets by hearsay, i.e., it is confused and defective. Now his knowledge of God is that of eyesight, i.e., immediate and full (42:5).

Job's last word is the one he had resisted throughout the tense and tedious debate with his friends: "therefore I despise myself, and repent in dust and ashes" (42:6). This is not an admission that his suffering is deserved because of sin, but rather that his complaints against God stem from his ignorance of God. The answer to Job's questions lies not so much in a flood of new information as in a new relationship with the Lord. The "why" of suffering is not nearly so important as the "Who."

EPILOGUE
Job 42:7-17

The book closes as it began, in prose narrative. In the epilogue God rebukes Job's friends (vv. 7-9), and restores Job's fortunes (vv. 10-17).

A. Rebuke of Job's Friends (42:7-9).

The Lord now announces his opinion of the three friends. Eliphaz is directly addressed because he was the eldest and leader of the group. God's wrath had been kindled against Eliphaz and his two companions. They had not spoken that which was right concerning the Lord. The reference must be to the theories they put forth in regard to God's providence and the meaning of afflictions. In attacking the theories of the three friends, Job had spoken what was right on this matter (chs. 21, 23–24). This in no way endorses everything Job had said. He had in fact spoken many things that were both blameworthy and false, things for which he was rebuked by the Almighty (42:7).

The three friends had really impugned the providence of God in their professed defense of it. By covering up and ignoring the enigmas and seeming contradictions, they had cast more discredit upon God's providence than had Job, who had honestly held them up to the light.

The friends are directed to take seven bulls and seven rams and go to "my servant Job." He would pray for them, and the Lord promised to accept his intercession. Job was noted as a great intercessor (22:30; Ezek 14:14). Only by offering up these sacrifices and the accompanying intercessory prayer of Job would the three be spared from facing the wrath of God upon their folly. Again the Lord stresses that the three had not spoken the right thing about God's providence as had Job. The three friends did as they were told, "and the Lord accepted Job" (42:8-9).

B. Restoration of Job's Fortunes (42:10-17).

The Lord "turned the captivity of Job," i.e., reversed his fortunes, when he prayed for his friends. The expression means that Job's afflictions were removed and his prosperity restored. The patriarch was restored to a prosperity double that which he formerly enjoyed (42:10).

Earlier Job had lamented over the alienation of all his friends and acquaintances (cf. 19:13ff.). Now his former friends gathered about him. These guests each brought Job a piece of money and a gold ring. They comforted him concerning all the evil that the Lord had brought upon him (42:11).

178

Job's former prosperity was exactly doubled: fourteen thousand sheep, six thousand camels, a thousand yoke of oxen, and a thousand female donkeys. "So Yahweh blessed the latter end of Job more than his beginning" (42:12).

The former number of Job's children was restored to him. He had seven sons and three daughters. The daughters were particularly outstanding and they are given special emphasis. They were named Jemimah ("dove"), Keziah (cassia, the aromatic spice), and Keren-happuch ("horn of eye paint"). "In all the land were no women found so fair as the daughters of Job." Normally only sons received an inheritance. Job, however, gave these three daughters an inheritance among their brothers (42:13-16).

After his ordeal Job lived another 140 years. He saw his sons to the fourth generation. "So Job died, being old and full of days." James sums up the book: "You have heard of the patience of Job, and have seen the end of the Lord; that the Lord is very pitiful, and of tender mercy" (James 5:11).

ENDNOTES

1. The exact identities of Pleiades, Orion, Mazzaroth and the Bear are not known.

2. On the basis of Ugaritic studies scholars now propose to translate *'azabh* in 39:14 "put" rather than "abandon" (NASB). The mother ostrich does not abandon her eggs. She buries them in a shallow hole in the sand, covers them, and sits on them in order to protect them from predators.

3. In the Bible the term "eagle" embraces species of the vulture family. The so-called griffon-vulture is probably intended here.

4. On the basis of Ugaritic, Zuck proposes that the reference to the tail of Behemoth in 40:17 might read: "his tail stiffens like a cedar " Roy Zuck, *Job* (Chicago: Moody, 1978), p. 179.

5. In the Greek period Herodotus (2.70) describes the capture of a crocodile with a hook baited with pork. The author of Job, however, did not know of hooks that would be sufficiently large to catch such a monster.

6. One interesting interpretation of Behemoth and Leviathan in Job 40–41 is that they are symbols for Job himself. Early on in the book Job compared himself to Leviathan (3:8). Both animals struggle within their own habitat (like Job) but respond, in the midst of conflict with confidence and fidelity. John Gammie, "Behemoth and Leviathan: On the Didactic and Theological Significance of Job 40:15–41:26" in *Israelite Wisdom: Theological* and *Literary Essays in Honor of Samuel Terrien* ed. John Gammie, W. Brueggemann, et al. (Missoula, MT: Scholars Press, 1978), pp. 217-231.

7. Zuck, *Job*, p. 183.

PSALMS

CHAPTER NINE

Getting Acquainted with Psalms
Faith in Various Circumstances

The Book of Psalms is the largest book in the Bible. The 150 psalms which constitute this book are organized into 2,461 verses. The book contains 43,743 words. This book is unique in ancient literature. Although a variety of hymns from Egypt and Mesopotamia have been preserved, no comparable collection of songs from biblical times has come to light.

TITLE OF THE BOOK

The term *psalmos* was used in the Greek translation to render the Hebrew *mizmor*, the technical term for a song sung to the accompaniment of musical instruments.[1]

A. Hebrew Tradition.

The Hebrew Bible does not preserve any original title for the compilation of psalms as a whole. The closest one comes to finding a designation within the book itself is in 72:20, "The supplications (*tiphilloth*) of David the son of Jesse are ended." Not all the compositions of David prior to 72:20 are, strictly speaking, supplications. The term *tiphilloth* may therefore be used in a more generalized sense of any communication of man with God.

Building on the term *mizmor,* which occurs fifty-seven times in titles of individual psalms, some rabbis referred to all the psalms by the plural form *mizmoroth.*[2] That designation, however, never really "caught on." In Jewish literature the universally accepted Hebrew name for this book is *Sepher Tehillim,* "Book of Praises." *Tehillim* is frequently contracted to *Tillim* (*Baba Bathra* 14b).[3]

Tehillim and its singular form *tehillah* occur more than twenty times in the Psalter but only once to designate an individual psalm (Ps 145). The verb root from which this noun is derived, however, occurs at least seventy-one times in the book, predominately in the imperative form. The term "Hallelujah" ("Praise Yah") which occurs exclusively in the Book of Psalms in the Hebrew Bible was also, no doubt, a factor in name selection. That the name *Tehillim* ("Praises") emerged (or was selected) is thus appropriate, because (1) this book continuously calls upon men to praise the Lord; and (2) hymns play the dominant role among the various categories of psalms.

B. Greek Tradition.

Two traditions as to title are represented in Greek Old Testament manuscripts. Codex Vaticanus (4th century AD) titled this book *Psalmoi* (Psalms). This title follows the precedent of the New Testament. Jesus referred to "the book of Psalms" (Luke 20:42), and Peter did likewise (Acts 1:20).

The second Greek tradition is represented in Codex Alexandrinus (5th century) where this book is entitled *Psalteriou,* from which is derived the Latin *Psalterium,* and the English *Psalter.* This term refers to a stringed instrument which was normally used in psalm accompaniment.

BACKGROUND OF THE PSALMS

To appreciate the Book of Psalms one needs to be familiar with the backgrounds of psalmody and worship in Israel as well as the background of the individual psalms.

A. Backgrounds of Psalmody.

Biblical psalmody is traced back to Lamech in the Antediluvian period of biblical history (Gen 4:23-24). In the early history of Israel hymns were used to celebrate God's victory over his enemies, i.e., enemies of Israel. Moses and Miriam led the people in singing victory songs (Exod 15:18,21). Some time later Deborah the prophetess composed a hymn to celebrate Israel's victory over Canaanite oppressors (Judg 5).

The Old Testament record contains two allusions to ancient collections of poetic materials. The Book of the Wars of Yahweh (Num 21:14) appears to have been a collection of war songs celebrating Israel's conquest of the Transjordan area. The Book of Jashar apparently contained war songs from as early as the time of Joshua to at least the time of David. Fragments of this ancient book are quoted in Scripture (Josh 10:13; 2 Sam 1:18).

B. Backgrounds of Worship.

The growth of the Book of Psalms is directly related to interest in the temple of God. David gathered materials for that structure. He also organized the music program which would be used in the temple. Solomon began to build the temple in the fourth year of his reign (967 BC). The work was completed in the year 959 BC.

In the ancient Near East, guilds of singers and musicians connected with temples enjoyed official status and were highly organized. The Bible claims that David established similar guilds in Israel (1 Chr 6,15, et al.). That such singers existed during the first temple period is confirmed externally by a reference to male and female singers among the booty sent by King Hezekiah to Sennacherib in 701 BC.[4] Among the Israelites who returned from captivity in Babylon were two hundred singers of both sexes (Ezra 2:65,70) besides the Asaphites (Ezra 2:41; Neh 7:44) who were also connected with temple music (1 Chr 6:39).

Another group associated with temple music were the Korahites (1 Chr 6:31-33). They are not mentioned among those who returned from Babylon. This supports the biblical claims that the Korahites were singers and musicians in the first temple period. External evidence of the existence of such a group during the late monarchy was found among inscribed Hebrew ostraca discovered in the temple in Arad.[5]

Not all Israelite psalms found their way into the Book of Psalms. Many great hymns are found in the prophetic books. Two examples are the Song of the Vineyard in Isaiah 5:1-7 and the great hymn with which Habakkuk closed his prophecy.

C. Backgrounds of Individual Psalms.

For the most part the individual psalms are historically nonspecific. Widespread disagreement among scholars exists over the situation out of which each psalm originated. In the case of those who take the Hebrew psalm superscriptions seriously, the options are narrowed considerably. A psalm assigned to David, however, may be appropriate to several different events in his life. Only in thirteen cases do the superscriptions indicate a specific historical context for the psalm. Commentators often ignore the claims of the psalm superscriptions. (See below under "Psalm Title Claims"). They attempt to deduce from the contents of each psalm its historical background. Such attempts fall far short of compelling proof.[6]

Another factor with which the interpreter must reckon is that psalms written by David, for example, may have experienced editorial "updating" in the course of time in order to adapt the language to a new historical situation. This may be the case especially in Books Three-Five. (See below under "Organization of the Book"). Some scholars, therefore, speak of the "dynamic" quality of the psalms.[7]

Attempts to root individual psalms in one historical event may work against the intention of the psalms themselves. As instruments of worship, the psalms were meant to be historically generic. Perhaps this was a criterion used for determining which poems were included in these five collections. This might explain, for example, why some of those poems which appear in the historical books (e.g., Judg 5) were not included in the Psalter. It is true that the lack of historical specificity may at times make the precise meaning of a verse more difficult. On the whole, however, this characteristic of the psalms probably has enhanced rather than detracted from their value in worship.

CONTRIBUTORS TO THE BOOK

The texts of the psalms themselves do not indicate the author by name.[8] There are two sources of information regarding the authorship questions: (1) the psalm titles; and (2) Jewish and Christian tradition.

A. Psalm Title Claims.

The Hebrew superscriptions of one hundred psalms contain what appears to be a claim of authorship. A more or less prominent person is named, and to his name the preposition *lamed* is prefixed, what some have designated the *lamed auctoris*. Some scholars have argued that the expression does not in fact make an authorship claim, but merely indicates the name of an original collection from which an individual psalm was lifted. Others would claim that the expression indicates dedication of the composition to the memory of some worthy person in the mode of a modern book dedication.[9]

In support of the *lamed* formula as an authorship claim these points can be made: (1) In the psalm title of Habakkuk 3:1 the same formula is used in a manner which clearly indicates an authorship claim. (2) The Psalter is internally consistent in the use of the formula, i.e., it is used with names in addition to David where the concept of "dedication" or "collection" seems rather remote. (3) Very early the *lamed* formula was interpreted in terms of authorship as is indicated by the heading of Ps 18 and by the editorial insertion of 72:20.[10]

According to the superscriptions at least seven individuals wrote psalms which have been included in the biblical book. Seventy-three psalms are attributed to David, ten to the sons of Korah, twelve to Asaph, two to Solomon and one each to Ethan, Heman and Moses. Fifty psalms are anonymous. Probably a good portion of the anonymous psalms were also written by David.

David's skills as a musician are documented in the historical books of the Old Testament. The text of five poems composed by him have been incorporated by the biblical historians into their records.[11] In his youth David was known as a skillful player on the harp (1 Sam 16:16). He invented certain musical instruments (Amos 6:5).

Solomon must have inherited his father's love for music. He is said to have written 1,005 songs. One of these—the Song of Songs—appears in the Hebrew canon as a separate book. Korah, Asaph, Heman and Ethan were Levites who led the musical service of the temple in the days of David and Solomon.

Of those contributors known by name, only one is not associated with the period of David and Solomon. Psalm 90 is attributed to Moses. That Moses was musically inclined is indicated by the songs associated with him in the Pentateuch (Exod 15; Deut 31:22; 32:1-43).

B. Credibility of the Title Claims.

Critics, following the lead of Theodore of Mopsuestia (4th cent AD), generally regard the Hebrew titles which appear over many of the psalms to be of late date and unreliable as regards authorship. They point to the occasional discrepancies between the psalm titles in the standard Hebrew text, and those which appear in the Greek version. They further argue that the historical background reflected in the psalm itself sometimes seems to be at variance with that which is claimed in the title.

Several lines of argument can be put forward in support of the reliability of the Hebrew psalm titles.

1. Why would "later rabbis" attach titles to psalms whose texts clearly did not reflect the situations in David's life which they stipulated in the title?

2. Some of the titles allude to incidents in David's life which are mentioned nowhere else in the Old Testament (e.g., Ps 60). Would "later rabbis" manufacture historical incidents for David's life? If so, what possible motive could they have had?

3. Why did not "later rabbis" supply titles for the so-called "orphan psalms," i.e., titleless psalms, which often teem with historical details which might have been used to conjecture about the background of the poems?

4. Certainly the titles are much earlier than the Greek translation of the Old Testament. By the time this translation was made (ca. 150-

100 BC) the meaning of some of the technical terms which appear in the Hebrew titles had been completely forgotten.[12] This evidence would suggest that the titles are at least as old as Ezra.

5. Apparently it was customary for ancient poets to prefix titles to songs. This tendency can be seen in Isa 38:9; Hab 3:1; 2 Sam 1:17f.; 2 Sam 23:1 and Num 24:3.

6. The titles in the Hebrew Bible are counted as part of the text. Longer titles are numbered as separate verses. This reflects a tradition that the titles are very old, perhaps a part of the original text of the psalm.

The conclusion can only be that the Hebrew psalm titles were either part of the original text of the various psalms, or were added during the final collection of the psalms in the days of Ezra-Nehemiah.

C. Jewish Traditions.

In Jewish tradition three tendencies regarding authorship are worthy of note. First, there was a tendency to increase the number of individual contributors. The Septuagint translators were of the opinion that the prophets Haggai and Zechariah also contributed psalms to the book. Later rabbinic traditions spoke of ten contributors to the book, but the rabbis were not agreed on who the ten were (*Baba Bathra* 14b, 15a). Besides those named in the titles, they proposed the following additional contributors: Adam (4 psalms), Melchizedek, Abraham and/or Ezra.

A second tendency in Jewish tradition was to increase the individual contribution of some of the known authors of the book. In the Septuagint version thirteen additional psalms[13] are assigned to David. Another tradition expanded the contribution of Moses from one psalm to eleven (Pss 90–100). Because he was the dominant contributor, Jewish tradition often refers to David as the author of the book.[14] A curious reference in the Qumran Psalm Scroll 11QPsa ascribes to David a library of 3,600 "psalms" (*tehillim*) and 450 "songs" (*shirim*). These speculations carry little weight and are presented here only as curiosities in the discussions of psalm authorship.

CRITICISM AND DAVIDIC AUTHORSHIP

Critics have offered a number of arguments to contradict the biblical claim that David wrote psalms. Their arguments and the refutation offered by Archer[15] are summarized below.

1. Psalms attributed to David speak of the king in the third person rather than the first person (e.g., Ps 20, 21 etc.). Answer: A number of ancient writers (e.g., Xenophon, Julius Caesar) referred to themselves in the third person. First-person speeches attributed to Yahweh in the Old Testament frequently shift from first to third person.

2. Psalms attributed to David speak of the sanctuary as already standing (e.g., Ps 5, 27, etc.) when in fact the temple was not constructed until after David was dead. Answer: The terminology "temple," "house of Yahweh," and the like are used of the tabernacle long before the time of David (Josh 6:24; Judg 18:31; 1 Sam 1:9). Furthermore, David sometimes uses terminology like "booth" and "tent" (Ps 27). Such language would not be appropriate for Solomon's temple.

3. The psalms attributed to David reflect the influence of the Aramaic language, hence must come from the later period when Aramaic was the international language. Answer: The biblical text indicates that David had extensive contact with the Aramean states. Furthermore, even the Ras Shamra (Ugaritic) texts which are earlier than David, reflect the influence of the Aramaic language. Thus the presence of Aramaic influence in a psalm cannot disqualify David as the author.

4. David would not have the time nor the inclination to compose poetry. Answer: The psalm titles, and the historical and prophetic books testify to the importance of music and poetry in the career of David. Indeed he was called "the sweet psalmist of Israel" (2 Sam 23:1).

Psalm 18 is a virtual duplicate of David's Song of Thanksgiving when he had been delivered from all his enemies (2 Sam 22:2-51). Kirkpatrick comments on the creative genius reflected in this composition. He then remarks: "If such a Psalm could have been written by David, so might many others."[16]

Davidic authorship of many psalms is confirmed by New Testament usage. Some of those psalms which are anonymous in the

Psalter are specifically attributed to him. In no case, however, is any psalm attributed to David in the New Testament which the Hebrew title attributes to another writer. Some argue that "David" was simply the name assigned to the Book of Psalms in New Testament times. A survey of New Testament usage, however, indicates that both Jesus and his disciples assumed without question that David was the personal author of many of the psalms. Sometimes the very argument which is being made depends on Davidic authorship (cf. Matt 22:45).[17]

DATE OF THE BOOK

The issue of the date of the psalms is closely tied to that of authorship. The following discussion is based on the assumption that the authorship claims of the headings are reliable.

Psalm 90 by Moses is the earliest datable psalm. It was written about 1407 BC. The psalms of David and Asaph would have been composed between 1020 and 975 BC. Two psalms (Ps 72, 127) come from the period of Solomon's reign, about 950 BC. Dating the sons of Korah and the two Ezrahites who are mentioned as authors is difficult. Presumably they were preexilic. Of the psalms which carry no titles, some were undoubtedly Davidic (e.g., Ps 2 and 33) and the others date from a later period. A few are as late as the exile. Psalm 126 is the latest datable psalm. It comes from the period of restoration from captivity about 525 BC. No convincing argument has been made for dating any of the psalms later than about 400 BC.

The old liberal view that some of the psalms date to the Maccabean period between the Old and New Testaments has been discredited in recent years. The Ugaritic texts reveal an advanced poetic tradition in Canaan centuries before David. A large number of striking parallels between the biblical psalms and the Ugaritic poetry has been pointed out.[18] These parallels suggest that the Israelites adapted a poetic genre which they found already highly developed by the culture which surrounded them in Canaan.[19] Much of the phraseology of the psalms was current in Palestine long before the time of David. Hence one is hard pressed on linguistic grounds any longer to deny Davidic authorship of the psalms.

Nahum Sarna amasses abundant evidence against the Maccabean theory of authorship.[20] Among his more telling points are these: (1) The Psalter is free of Greek linguistic influence; (2) the theology of the Psalter is wholly devoid of Hellenistic concepts; and (3) psalms known to have been written during or shortly after the Maccabean period— those found in the Qumran library—indicate significant linguistic, stylistic, structural, thematic, and theological departures from the biblical psalms.

THE CANONICITY OF PSALMS

The canonicity of the Psalter has already been discussed in a general way in the first chapter of this study. Here a few other pertinent points need to be made.

A. Canonical Psalms.

The Book of Psalms was considered the most important book in the third division of the Old Testament canon, the so-called *Kethubhim* or *Hagiographa*. Though disputes arose over the organization of the book, no Jewish or Christian authority ever questioned the canonical status of this body of material.

Some discussion did arise in rabbinic circles as to the placement of the book within the third division of the canon. Some scholars thought it should follow the Book of Ruth. Since David was accepted as the author of (most of) Psalms, it was thought appropriate that his genealogy as reflected in the last chapter of Ruth should immediately precede this book. In Hebrew manuscripts Psalms either stands first in the *Kethubhim* or comes immediately after Ruth. In printed editions of the Hebrew Bible Psalms always heads the *Kethubhim*. Likely this is the oldest position as is suggested by Luke 24:44 (cf. 2 Macc 2:13). One can reasonably infer from this placement of the Psalter in the canon that the book was considered the most important in the *Kethubhim*.

The LXX locates Psalms at the beginning of the poetic books. The Latin and English order, where Job precedes Psalms, probably is based on the supposed antiquity of Job.

B. Apocryphal Psalms.

In Syriac (Syrian) manuscripts of this book five apocryphal psalms appear including one which is contained in Greek (Septuagint) manuscripts. The LXX adds Ps 151 with the notation "outside of the number," a recognition that the familiar 150 were the only psalms recognized as canonical. This is probably the earliest of the apocryphal psalms. The Hebrew original of this psalm has been discovered among the Dead Sea Scrolls. In 1962 three of the five Syrian apocryphal psalms were found in the Qumran library. This find confirmed the existence of an Hebrew original of (at least three) of the Syrian psalms. The Qumran Psalm Scroll (11QPsa) may not be a manuscript of the Book of Psalms, but a liturgical compilation used in religious services containing both canonical and noncanonical material.

A collection of eighteen apocryphal psalms attributed to Solomon appeared during the intertestamental period (ca. 68 BC). These psalms are modeled after the canonical Psalter. Many of the same themes appear: protests against man's injustice, petitions for God's deliverance, threats of punishment for sinners, and promises of reward for the righteous. Technical musical notes for musical settings suggest that the Psalms of Solomon may have been sung in some synagogue services. The book, however, was never considered part of the sacred canon either in Jewish or in Christian circles.

C. Canonical Intention.

Traditionally the psalms have been studied individually. More recently Brevard Childs has emphasized the question of the literary shape and theological intentionality of the Book of Psalms as a whole.[21] The work of Walter Brueggemann[22] illustrates where this line of study is leading. What follows summarizes his contributions to Psalm study.

Psalm 1 functions as an introduction to the entire book. The Psalter begins with a summons to obedience to the law and the confident assurance of the blessing to follow such obedience. The Psalter concludes with a psalm (150) which is absolutely unique. It urges praise, but offers no reason or motivations for the praise. The entire Psalter lives between the pious, trusting, confident boundaries of obedience and praise. Obedience is the launching pad for praise, and praise is the appropriate culmination of obedience. The structure of the Psalter would suggest that only the obedient can truly praise God.

The journey from dutiful obedience (Ps 1) to self-abandoning praise (Ps 150) is one that passes through the deep valley of candor about suffering in relationship to God's lovingkindness. The thesis of Ps 1 is sometimes questioned. Are the obedient always blessed, and the disobedient always punished? The faithful can only trust God and wait for his intervention.

Brueggemann sees Ps 73 as pivotal in the canonical structure of the Psalter. It is the theological center of the book. This psalm functions to introduce Books Three-Five just as Ps 1 introduced Books One-Two. Ps 73 begins with a reassertion of the thesis of Ps 1 that the obedient are blessed (v. 1). Then the psalmist immediately begins to suggest that the wicked in fact do prosper at times (vv. 2-13). Then he goes to the sanctuary where he realizes that the wicked will surely one day perish (vv. 17-20). The psalm then moves toward radical faith in which communion with God is the supreme good which dwarfs all other issues (vv. 23-26).

ORGANIZATION OF THE BOOK

As noted above, the individual psalms were written over a period of at least 850 years, from the time of Moses (Ps 90) to the exile (Ps 137) and beyond (Ps 126). The Psalter as it appears in the Hebrew Bible evolved in stages over centuries of time.

A. Small Groupings.

Within the Psalter are subordinate groupings of psalms. At some very early stage these smaller groups may have existed independently, but this is not certain. Attention has already been directed to the psalms of "the sons of Korah" (42-49), Asaph (73-83) and the Davidic groups (Book One; 138-145). Other groups include "the songs of ascents" (120-134), the "hallelujah" psalms (111-118; 146-150), the *maskil* groups (42-45, 52-55), *mikhtam* group (56-60), and the *hodu* psalms (105-107) which all begin with the Hebrew imperative for "give thanks."

B. The Development of Psalm Books.

From early times the psalms were grouped into five "books." The exact antiquity of the fivefold division of the Psalter cannot be determined. The earliest mention of this organization in Christian literature is in Hippolytus (ca. AD 200).

At the end of each "book" the editors inserted doxologies and other indications of the termination of a collection of psalms (cf. 72:20). That the first three "books" at one stage existed separately may be conceded. The first three doxologies (41:13; 72:18-19; 89:52) are clearly independent of the preceding psalm.

In the efforts to reconstruct the early history of the Psalter, Ps 72:20 is pivotal. This verse concludes the second "book" of the Psalter in this way: "This concludes the prayers of David son of Jesse." One would assume that at some point in the transmission of the Psalter that only Davidic psalms preceded this statement and that no Davidic psalms appeared after it. As a matter of fact, however, in the final edition of the Psalter several non-Davidic psalms precede Ps 72:20, and several Davidic psalms follow. This fact invites the conclusion that at some point psalms were editorially interwoven into an existing collection to create Book Two as it currently exists.[23]

The presence of duplicate psalms in the book also supports the contention that the five "books" represent independent and sequential collections. Ps 53 is a duplicate of Ps 14; Ps 70 repeats 40:13-17; and Ps 108 repeats material found in 57:7-11 and 60:5-12.

The division between Book Four and Book Five is another matter. Several factors indicate that these two "books" were originally one. (1) The doxology at the conclusion of Book Four is part of the Psalm 106, not an editorial addition as the doxologies at the end of the first three "books." (2) The two "books" have much in common. For example, eighteen of the sixty-one psalms in these two books have no superscription compared to only six psalms in the preceding eighty-nine. (3) No musical terms are found in these "books," in fact very few technical terms such as abound in the earlier psalms. (4) The term "Hallelujah" appears exclusively in books Four and Five. (5) The subject matter in both "books" is similar; praise and thanksgiving predominate here. (6) The Qumran Psalm Scroll intersperses into Book Five selections from Book Four. The impact of this Qumran scroll on the history of the Book of Psalms is difficult to assess. Perhaps it reflects a period before the division of Pss 90–150 into two "books."

At some point Book Four was separated into two separate books to make a total of five books. A psalmic tetrateuch became a pentateuch under the influence of the Torah which contains five books, Genesis through Deuteronomy. The connection of the five psalm "books" with Torah and worship may be indicated by the following points: (1) The doxologies indicate that the book divisions were fixed for the purposes of public worship. (2) Ps 1, which serves an an introduction to the entire Psalter, stresses the importance of Torah study. (3) The linkage between the two bodies of sacred literature was made in the tenth century rabbinic *midrash* to Ps 1 which states: "Moses gave the five books of the Torah to Israel, and David gave the five books of the Psalms to Israel."

C. Explanations of the Organization.

Various explanations have been offered for the fivefold organization of the Psalter. The fivefold arrangement cannot be attributed to subject matter, authorship, order of composition, or psalm form. The "books" do have certain distinctives associated with all these factors. Certainly there is no support for the fanciful suggestions that the five Psalter "books" were connected with the five great feasts of Judaism (like the five books of the *Megilloth*); or with five steps to moral perfection (Gregory of Nyssa).

NUMERATION OF PSALMS

Problems arise in the chapter and verse enumeration in the Psalter. This fact becomes very confusing to those who do research in this book.

A. Chapter Divisions.

Both the Hebrew text and the Greek text of Psalms contain 150 psalms. The division of the material into individual psalms, however, differs in these two major editions of the text. The LXX indicates a different tradition in five places: (1) it combines Pss 9–10 and (2) Pss 114–115. On the other hand, the LXX divides (3) Ps 116 and (4) Ps

147. The Latin Vulgate follows the numeration of the Greek version, and the Catholic English versions reflect that tradition. Protestant English versions have followed the numeration of the Hebrew Bible. Students must be aware of this difference in numbering when researching psalm references in Roman Catholic works.

The Talmud indicates that at some point Pss 1 and 2 were regarded as one chapter (*Berachoth* 9b). The New Testament, however, clearly quotes Ps 2:7 as coming from "the second psalm" (Acts 13:33).

Modern readers are familiar with a division of the Psalter into 150 chapters. Evidence indicates that various other arrangements were known. A Psalter of 148, 149, 151, 159 and even 170 chapters is mentioned in various rabbinic discussions.[24] The most frequently attested arrangement (other than the 150) is 147, according to tradition, one for each year of Jacob's life. Some Hebrew manuscripts and early printed editions of the Hebrew Bible have the Psalter divided into 147 chapters.

Perhaps it is no coincidence that the number of *sedarim* in the Torah (Pentateuch) is 147. These were the sections read in a three-year cycle in the Jewish synagogues. At one point there may have been an effort to have one psalm reading for each *sedar* from the Torah on sabbath days. Of the regular sabbath reading of Psalms, however, there is no certain evidence.

The chapter variations mentioned above have nothing to do with the content of the Psalter which remains the same in all editions. This evidence reflects differences in the divisions and combinations of the psalm units, a process which can be attested as early as the Septuagint (second century BC) as noted above. All in all, it is quite clear that no fixed and uniform system of chapter divisions of the Psalter existed in ancient times. Extant manuscripts suggest that early on scribes did not mark the transitions from one psalm to another, thus easily permitting variations in verse groupings.[25]

B. Verse Divisions.

In the oldest manuscript of Psalms—the Qumran Psalm Scroll—the psalms were written in prose form with nothing to indicate verse division, except in Ps 119 where the alphabetic arrangement provides a natural indication. Other Qumran scrolls, however, do indicate a rudimentary verse division. Thus verse division in the psalms must have come quite early.

Early (Tannaitic) rabbinic sources put the verse count of Psalms at 5,896, eight more than the Torah (*Kid.* 30a). Yet a Masoretic note at the conclusion of the Psalter lists the verse count as 2,527. Apparently the definition of what constituted a verse differed even among the Jewish scholars.

The English Bible differs somewhat from the Hebrew Bible in verse numeration. Though the Protestant English versions have followed the number of the individual psalms as found in the standard Hebrew text, they do not follow the verse numbering of the Hebrew. In the Hebrew Bible psalm titles consisting of three words or more are counted as one verse, sometimes two verses, in the Hebrew Bible. This means there may be a divergence in verse numbering between the Hebrew Bible and the English Bible when the psalm has a title. The Hebrew verse number will generally be one higher than the English number in this case. Some Bible commentaries cite the Hebrew verse numbers, and some cite the English numbers, and some indicate both in each citation.

THE PSALM TITLES

In the Hebrew Bible superscriptions or titles appear before 116 of the psalms, 125 if "Hallelujah" is regarded as a title in all the psalms which commence with it. The Talmud referred to those 34 (or 25) psalms without titles as "orphan psalms." The Greek version has assigned titles to all of the psalms except the first two.

A. Musical Notations.

A thorough study of the titles by J.W. Thirtle has indicated that the present arrangement of the psalm titles may not be original.[26] Using the psalm in Habakkuk 3 as a paradigm, Thirtle argued that many of the psalms originally possessed a postscript as well as a title. As time went on, a postscript of one psalm became confused with heading of the following psalm. This study assigned to the postscript the various musical notations which currently appear in the headings. When these elements appear in the English Bible in the beginning of a title, according to Thirtle, they have been incorrectly transferred from the original postscript at the end of the preceding psalm.

The most frequent (55 times) of the musical notations appearing in the book is *lamenatseach*, "to the choir leader." Perhaps this term was affixed to those psalms which were part of a special collection used in temple liturgy. It is interesting to note that one of the earliest English translations of the Psalter, that of Coverdale in 1535, arbitrarily omitted all the the technical terms from the titles.

B. Other Information.

If Thirtle is right—and his argument is persuasive—then the psalm title or prescript would contain any one or all three of these elements: (1) the technical classification of the psalm (e.g., *mizmor*); (2) the assignment of authorship; and (3) the occasion.

At least seven technical designations for psalm genres appear in the titles.[27] These are displayed in Chart No. 1.

Chart No. 1

TECHNICAL DESIGNATIONS OF PSALMS		
Term	**No. Psalms**	**Suggested Significance**
Mizmor	57	A song sung to the accompaniment of musical (stringed) instruments.
Shir	27	A general term for (vocal?) music.
Maskil	13	A didactic or contemplative poem.
Mikhtam	6	Uncertain. Perhaps a composition intended to record memorable thoughts, pithy sayings, or eloquent refrains.
Tephillah	5	A prayer.
Tehillah	5	A song of praise.
Shiggayon	1	An irregular or wandering song.

Thirteen titles contain information concerning the historical occasion of the compositions. All of these refer to events in the life of David. Critics generally dismiss these statements as unreliable. Conservative commentaries, however, are generally able to show rather convincing connections between what is said in the title and what is related in the psalm. Of course no one argues that these thirteen psalms were written immediately on the spot, but only after later reflection on the event.[28]

Three positions have been taken with regard to the psalm titles or superscriptions: (1) they are secondary additions which can afford no reliable information toward establishing the genuine historical setting of the psalms;[29] (2) they are authentic and infallible;[30] and (3) they are not original but reflect early reliable tradition.[31] Probably this third position is the most responsible.

CLASSIFICATION OF PSALMS

The literary appreciation of Psalms has a long history. The pioneer in this effort was Robert Lowth, an English professor at Oxford in the eighteenth century. His study of the poetry of the Psalms is still valuable. Even earlier, Jerome, Augustine and Josephus applied literary categories in their understanding of this material. In recent years psalm classification has become a major thrust of Old Testament study.

A. Form Criticism.

Hermann Gunkel (1904) pioneered the form critical approach to the psalms. His goal was to classify the psalms into various categories and then to identify the general situation in life which brought that category into existence. The great majority of psalms he was able to divide into five categories: (1) hymns intended for communal worship; (2) communal laments to express grief over some national disaster; (3) royal psalms which exalt the king as the servant of Yahweh; (4) individual laments over personal tragedy; and (5) individual songs of thanksgiving.

A few scholars have attempted to find significance in the consecutive groupings within the Psalter. Most scholars, however, follow the lead of Hermann Gunkel in categorizing the psalms into subgroups according to their literary form. No consensus exists among scholars regarding these categories because of differing conceptions about the function of the Psalter during Old Testament times.

B. Suggested Classification.

Classification of the psalms is made difficult by the fact that often two very different types of material have been fused into one psalm. The individual psalms are susceptible of diverse interpretation, and this makes uniformity in classification impossible. The tense system of the Hebrew language has a built in ambiguity (so it seems) which makes it difficult at times to decide when a psalm is a prayerful description of present trouble or when it is an enumeration of afflictions now happily past. Sarna sounds this caution: "Any attempt . . . to effect a systematic generic classification based on a commonality of theme, mood, occasion and style is bound to be more an exercise in convenience than precision."[32]

Though the psalms can be classified in various ways, the following patterns stand out.

1. Predictive psalms. Psalms 2, 16, 22, 45, 110, for example, are cited in the New Testament as personally predictive of events in the life of Jesus.

2. Praise hymns or hallelujah psalms such as 146–150 extol the wisdom, power and graciousness of God. Hymns are prominent in the Psalter. Some psalms extol God's greatness and providence (e.g., Ps 8, 100), while others extol his sovereignty over the universe (e.g., Pss 47, 96–99). Still others—the so-called Zion songs—praise the city which God had chosen for his habitation.

3. Petition or supplication psalms such as 6, 39, 86 pour out the needs of the human heart before God. Sometimes these supplications become psalms of confidence because of the absolute certainty that the prayers contained therein will be answered.

4. Penitential psalms such as 32, 38, 51, 102, 130, 143 confess sin and beg for reinstatement with God.

5. Perceptive or didactic or wisdom psalms such as 1, 19, and 119 discuss issues which perplex the human mind.

6. Profession or confession psalms such as 33, 103 and 107 set forth the psalmists' convictions about the mighty works of God.

7. Patriotic or historic psalms (e.g., 78, 105, 106) review the history of the relationship between Yahweh and his people.

8. Pilgrimage psalms (e.g., 120–134) were sung as worshipers made their way up the hill of Zion to celebrate the great festivals of the Mosaic dispensation.

PSALM STRUCTURE

The parallelism which is characteristic within individual verses of biblical poetry is also discernible in entire psalms. Older scholars referred to this phenomenon as alternation or inverted parallelism. In recent years the term "chiastic parallelism" has come into vogue. The word "chiasm" comes from the name of the Greek letter *chi*, which looks like the English letter X. An outline of a verse, a paragraph, or even a book which conforms to such a shape is called "chiastic." In its simplest form the chiastic outline could be diagrammed A-B-C-B-A, meaning that the first and fifth verses were parallel in thought as well as the second and fourth. The key verse in the psalm is represented by the letter C.

Robert Alden identified some forty-five psalms which reflected the chiastic structure in whole or in part. Alden likens a chiastic psalm to climbing a mountain, reaching its summit, and then descending the opposite side. One would discover on the reverse side the same climate zones, varieties of growth, temperature and barometric changes which he passed through on the climb to the summit. The recognition of chiastic structure in the psalms is an important advance. Conventional exegetical and homiletical outlines of the psalms, are appealing but artificial. The psalmists often appear to have organized their thoughts, whether consciously or unconsciously, according to this chiastic pattern. Discovery of the chiastic structure in these larger blocks of material can only enhance one's appreciation of the literary genius that produced the Hebrew Psalter.[33]

THE TEACHING OF THE PSALMS

The Book of Psalms stands virtually in the middle of the sixty-six books which comprise the Christian Bible. Athanasius, the fourth-century theologian, called the Psalter "an epitome of the whole Scriptures."[34] The Psalter's teaching is not presented systematically, but it is extensive. Some question this proposition on the grounds that the Psalter consists mostly of prayers offered to God, not oracles from God. Yet the book is part of the sacred canon, and that attests to this collection of (mostly) prayers as the word of God. These prayers were sanctioned for use in temple worship. In these two facts—canonicity and liturgical usage—the theology of the psalms is endorsed as normative teaching.

A. Theology.

The Psalter exhibits great diversity in terms of authorship, mood, occasion and use of the various psalms. Yet the Psalter reveals a unity of faith in Israel's covenant Lord and in covenant responsibility.[35] Whereas some psalms raise questions about God's actions in the world, there is no room in this collection for denial of faith.

The central figure in the psalms is God. Three names of God are prominent in this book: *'Elohim* (344), Yahweh (676) and *'Adonay* (53). The name *'Elohim* depicts God in his role as omnipotent creator. *Yahweh* is the self-existing God of covenant commitment. *'Adonay* depicts God as sovereign ruler. In certain sections of the Psalter one or the other of these names is used predominately. Thus scholars speak of Yahwistic and Elohistic psalms or sections of psalms.

Many of the psalms focus on Mount Zion, the center of the worship of Yahweh. Beginning with Psalm 90, most of the psalms are of a liturgical nature. These psalms constituted the hymnbook of the temple worshipers. They stress three responses to the grandeur of God's person. Submission is the appropriate response to the sovereignty of Yahweh. The power of God should evoke trust in those who come before him. Joy should characterize those who comprehend the grace of God.

Psalms makes a clear-cut distinction between sin and righteousness, the wicked and the righteous. The very first psalm emphasizes this contrast. The person who delights in the law of God is blessed. He is like a tree planted by plenteous waters. The wicked, however, are like the chaff which the wind drives away in the winnowing process.

B. Christology.

If one regards the New Testament as the final authority, then Psalms must be regarded as one of the most Christological books in the Old Testament. Sixteen psalms may be classified as personal messianic.[36] These are displayed with supporting New Testament references in Chart No. 2.

Chart No. 2

MESSIANIC PSALMS		
Psalm	Title	NT References
2	The Enthroned Son	Acts 4:25-27; 13:33
8	The Last Adam	Heb 2:6
16	Resurrection	Acts 2:25ff.; 13:35
22	Death & Resurrection	John 19:23f.; Matt 27:39ff.
40	Before Bethlehem	Heb 10:5ff.
45	Messiah's Deity	Heb 1:8
68	Advent & Ascension	Eph 4:8
69	Betrayer Punished	Acts 1:16f.; Matt 23:38; 27:34
72	Messiah's Reign	
78:1f.	Parable Teller	Matt 13:34f.
89	Promise to David	Acts 13:34
102	Externality of Christ	Heb 1:10ff.
109	Judgment on Judas	Acts 1:16f.
110	The Royal Priest	Heb 1:8f.; 5:6,10; 6:20; 7:17,21
118	Rejected Cornerstone	Matt 21:9,42; Acts 4:11
132	Promise to David	Acts 13:34

C. Imprecatory Psalms.

Imprecatory psalms are those in which the psalmist appeals to God to pour out his wrath upon enemies. Eighteen psalms include imprecatory language of some sort.[37] Of the 368 verses in these psalms, fewer than seventy contain imprecation, most of which are found in three psalms (35,69,109). These passages are jarring to the sensitivities of Christians who are taught in the school of Christ to turn the other cheek and pray for enemies.

Why are such violent sentiments expressed in the psalms? Some excuse this material on psychological grounds, i.e., the psalmist was under great stress. Others gloss over them on the grounds that the Old Testament sets forth a lower standard of morality. Others insist that these are inspired accounts of uninspired attitudes and utterances. These passages supposedly represent a low degree of morality or of revelation. Still others argue that David really did not write these psalms of imprecation; they were written during the Maccabean persecution which takes the personal vindictiveness out of these psalms. These explanations, however, ignore (1) the Old Testament condemnation of acts of revenge (Lev 19:18); and (2) the biblical claim that "all Scripture is inspired of God" (2 Tim 3:16).

So what can be said that might help a believer put the imprecatory psalms in proper perspective?

1. The psalmist was zealous to defend the righteousness of God wherever it was attacked or ignored. These are not expressions of a desire for *personal* revenge.

2. The psalmist was deeply concerned about defending God's representative, the king. Any action against this representative was viewed not simply as an act of treason, but as highhanded offense against God himself. Offending God's anointed was equivalent to offending God.

3. The psalmist's harsh cries of judgment were his way of expressing hatred for sin. This is poetry, and poetry tends to exaggerate passions. These exaggerated cries for destruction of sinners emphasize the writer's abhorrence of what God hates as well.

4. Old Testament believers did not have a clear view of judgment after death. Therefore, all judgment must be in this present life. Prior to the cross, the only tangible way in which the truth of God could be demonstrated to human observers was by the pragmatic test of disaster befalling those who were in error, and deliverance being granted to those who held to the truth. The cross was the supreme demonstration of God's displeasure over sin, and the empty tomb was the

demonstration of his power over evil. In the light of the cross and the empty tomb the believer today can wait patiently while God's longsuffering permits the wicked to enjoy his temporary success.[38]

5. Most of the imprecatory psalms were written by David, a man who did not possess a vengeful spirit. Frequently the Psalmist prayed for his enemies and tried to save them from their sins (e.g., Ps 35:13; 109:4,5).

6. Some of the questionable verses actually call for the destruction of sin, not the sinner.

7. Imprecations also appear in the New Testament.[39]

8. A harsh sentence does not necessarily imply a hateful spirit.

9. The Hebrew verbs can often be rendered in the future tense as simple prophecies, not wishes—the difference between "Let this happen" and "This will happen." In some instances these questionable verses (cf. 69:25) are quoted in the New Testament as prophecies of the fate of the wicked. Some of the imprecations are in messianic passages in which the language is prophetically put in the mouth of Messiah.

10. The culprits condemned in these passages persisted in sin. They were vicious, blasphemous, blood-thirsty men. The imprecations are against a class of sinners, not individuals. For the sake of the righteous and the advancement of God's kingdom evil must be rooted out.

11. Many of the imprecatory psalms are quoted in the New Testament.[40]

THE PURPOSE OF THE BOOK

The immediate purpose of the Book of Psalms was to provide for ancient worshipers a service hymnal which was the medium of prayer and praise for the Old Testament saints. The ultimate purpose was to reveal to saints of all the ages the appropriate ways to express their faith in various circumstances.

Psalms is a model for prayer and praise. The psalmists wrote with the expectation that others would use their compositions to express their own feelings before the Lord. They bared their souls. Sin, sorrow, shame, repentance, hope, faith, reverence and love are all forthrightly expressed here. Thus the book is one of the most practical books of the Bible. It is wondrously suited to the human heart in any generation. Believers through the centuries have found in this book the counterpart of every human experience.

Psalms has a polemical function. The psalmists were concerned to promote the exclusive worship of Yahweh over the nonexistent gods and goddesses of the ancient Near East. Ps 29 is particularly rich in this respect.

The Book of Psalms provides guidance for the believer's emotions just as the other books of Scripture provide guidance in the areas of faith and action. Here those who walk the path of persecution find solace in those saints who walked that same difficult path centuries ago. Here those who suffer can enter into a fellowship of sympathy which helps to remove the bitterness out of their tears. Here the penitent can find assurance of acceptance with God in the experiences of the psalmists. Here the Christian can discern the presence of the Savior in the prophetic sketches of his journey from glory to the cross and back to glory. In these inspired songs and sighs the believer can find consolation, confirmation and courage to face all the vicissitudes of life.

THE TEXT OF THE PSALMS

The consonantal text of the Book of Psalms is more reliable than earlier critical scholars had judged. Inscriptions and literature from the ancient Near East have opened up new vistas in understanding biblical idiom, ancient Hebrew orthography, lexicography, grammar, and syntax. Many of the alleged "corruptions" of the Hebrew text have melted away as each new discovery has been brought to light.

Some thirty manuscripts of the Book of Psalms were found among the Dead Sea Scrolls, more than any other book of the Bible. The remains of one scroll contain parts or all of thirty-seven of the canonical psalms.[41]

For the most part, the Qumran materials support the readings in the standard Hebrew text, the so-called Masoretic text. Some of these manuscripts are very small and in a poor state of preservation. Most of the numerous variations from the standard Hebrew text are merely orthographic in character. The variations very rarely require significant differences in interpretation. One interesting feature is that the name Yahweh—the so-called Tetragrammaton—is written in ancient Hebrew script. This has the effect of emphasizing the holy name and making it stand out on the pages which are written in the Aramaic script.

THE USE OF THE PSALMS

Without question the Book of Psalms has been the single most influential and widely used book of the Bible in both Jewish and Christian communities.

A. In the Temple.

The Book of Psalms was the hymn book of Mosaism, the proper name for the sacrificial worship of Old Testament times. Internal evidence suggests that this is so. Ps 33 apparently was sung as people approached the temple for worship. Ps 5:7 witnesses to the worship setting of that psalm. Similar references could be multiplied.

Psalm headings also point to the temple usage of the psalms. One psalm contains a specific liturgical note in the Hebrew title. Psalm 92 is entitled "A Psalm for the Sabbath Day." A few other less specific liturgical notations also appear, e.g., "to bring to remembrance" (Ps 38) and "a psalm of thanksgiving" (Ps 100). By the second century BC individual psalms were firmly anchored to the temple liturgy.

The Septuagint version includes titles which assign various psalms to be chanted in the temple on certain days of the week following the offering of the daily sacrifice. These notations may represent a tradition which was handed down from the times of Ezra-Nehemiah. The Mishnah (codified in late second century AD) accepted this same liturgy (*Tamid* 7.4).

Other psalms were chanted on special festivals. The *Hallel* (Pss 113–118)—the *Hallelujah* psalms—were chanted at virtually all the festivals. In addition, Ps 7 was used at Purim; Ps 12 was assigned to the eighth day of Tabernacles; Ps 30 for the Feast of Dedication; Ps 47 for New Year; Psalms 98 and 104 for New Moon, and the penitential psalms for the Day of Atonement.[42]

208

B. In the Synagogue.

The institution of the synagogue was the creation of the Pharisees during the intertestamental period. Whereas temple worship centered around the sacrificial altar, synagogue worship focused on the reading of Scripture and prayer. Over a three-year period the entire Pentateuch was read publicly. Selections from the *Nebhi'im* (Prophets) called the *Haphtarah* were also prescribed. While there is no evidence of a similar lectionary custom as regards the Psalter, it is clear that the psalms were prominent in the ancient synagogue.

Psalms were chanted antiphonally. The congregation often repeated after every verse chanted by the presenter the first verse of that psalm. At the conclusion the presenter added a doxology ending with "and say Amen," whereupon the congregation replied "Amen, Amen."[43]

C. In the Church.

Surprisingly little is known about worship in the New Testament church. Three times the epistles refer to the use of psalms by the early Christians (Eph 5.19, Col 3:16; Jas 5:13) without specifically linking that usage with the public assembly. Only in 1 Cor 14:26 is the term *psalmos* used specifically in the context of public worship. That the early Christians employed the Psalter in their public praise is probably a correct inference.

The delight of first century Christians in this book is indicated by the extensive quotations from it found in the New Testament. By one count, there are 283 direct quotes from the Old Testament in the New. Of these 116 (over 40%) are from Psalms.

In post-New Testament church history the Psalter seems to have become increasingly popular in the church. Church leaders prescribed the use of various psalms for Communion time, and for morning and evening worship. Some of the early Protestant leaders produced metrical arrangements of the Psalter designed for singing in the worship services of the church. The followers of John Calvin, for example, produced the Geneva Psalter in 1562. Some Protestants would use nothing but the Psalms in their public praise services.

ENDNOTES

1. Joseph H. Thayer, *A Greek-English Lexicon of the New Testament*, 4th ed. (Edinburgh: T. & T. Clark, 1901), p. 675.

2. See references from the Jerusalem Talmud in Nahum Sarna, *Encyclopaedia Judaica* (Jerusalem: Keter, 1972), s.v. "Psalms, Book of" 13:1303.

3. Older commentators explained the masculine plural ending on a feminine noun as due to the desire of the scribes to distinguish the collection of biblical psalms from all other song books. The Dead Sea Scrolls, however, produced examples of the so-called masculine plural form of this word indicating that it had no special "canonical" significance when used by the rabbis as a title for the Book of Psalms. The Medieval Hebrew writers Mishael b. Uziel and Abraham ibn Ezra refer to the book as *Sepher Tehilloth*, using the regular (biblical) feminine plural of *Tehillah*.

4. James Pritchard, *Ancient Near Eastern Texts Relating to the Old Testament*, 3rd. ed. (Princeton, NJ: University Press, 1969), p. 288.

5. Sarna, *Encyclopaedia*, 13:1315.

6. An extreme example is the dating of Ps 98 which has been assigned to the period of the Exodus by some scholars, and to the time of the restoration from Babylon by other scholars.

7. Raymond Dillard and Tremper Longman III, *An Introduction to the Old Testament* (Grand Rapids: Zondervan, 1994), p. 213.

8. Ps 72:20, which appears to be an exception, is probably an editorial addition to the original collection of all of the Davidic psalms of which Psalm 72 was the last unit.

9. The Septuagint translators seem on occasion to have used the equivalent Greek expression to denote dedication. For example, the heading of Ps 137 in the LXX reads "for David, of Jeremiah."

10. At least 56 of 73 occurrences of the *lamed* formula in reference to David occur in Books One and Two of Psalms, and 72:20 appears as the editorial note at the end of the second book. This is a sure indication of how the *lamed* formula was interpreted early on in scribal communities.

11. The five poems of David recorded in the historical books are: (1) the song of deliverance (2 Sam 22:2-51); (2) the song of the bow (2 Sam 1:19-27); (3) the lament over Abner (2 Sam 3:33-34); (4) the song of the ark (1 Chr 16:8-36); and (5) the last words of David (2 Sam 23:1-7).

12. G.L. Archer cites several examples. *A Survey of Old Testament Introduction,* pb. ed. (Chicago: Moody, 1985), p. 452.

13. In the LXX the following additional psalms are attributed to David: 33, 43, 71, 91, 93-99, 104, 137.

14. 2 Macc 2:13; *Mid. Pss.* 1:2; *Baba Bathra* 14b; 15a.

15. Archer, *Introduction*, pp. 448-450.

16. A.F. Kirkpatrick, *The Book of Psalms* in The Cambridge Bible for Schools and Colleges (Cambridge: University Press, 1910), p. xlii.

17. The New Testament evidence regarding Davidic authorship of the psalms is found in the following passages: Mark 12:36; Luke 20:42-44; Acts 2:25-28,34; Rom 4:6-8.

18. See footnotes to the Ugaritic portion of Pritchard's *Ancient Near Eastern Texts*. See also Mitchell Dahood, *Psalms, 3* vols, The Anchor Bible (Garden City, NY: Doubleday, 1966), 1:xxx.

19. Archer, *Introduction*, p. 453.

20. Sarna, *Encyclopaedia* , 13:1311.

21. Brevard Childs, *Introduction to the Old Testament as Scripture* (Philadelphia: Fortress, 1979), pp. 511-523. See also Gerald H. Wilson, *The Editing of the Hebrew Psalter*; SBL Dissertation Series, 76 (Chico, CA: Scholars Press, 1985; and James L. Mays, "The Place of the Torah-Psalms in the Psalter," *Journal of Biblical Literature* 106 (1987): 3-12.

22. Walter Brueggeman, "Bounded by Obedience and Praise: The Psalms as Canon," *Journal for the Study of the Old Testament* 50 (1991): 63-92.

23. David is the likely author of all the psalms in Book One. His name appears in the Hebrew title of all the psalms except 1, 2, 10, and 33. Ps 2 is attributed to David in the New Testament, and Ps 33 is attributed to him in the title which appears in the Greek version. Ps 10 has no title, probably because originally it formed a single composition with Ps 9. Pss 9–10 are regarded as a single composition in the LXX.

24. For references, see Sarna, *Encyclopaedia*, 13:1306.

25. Ibid.

26. J.W. Thirtle, *The Titles of the Psalms* (London: Frowde, 1904).

27. The psalm titles in the Septuagint have at least twenty-five divergencies from the Hebrew text. For example, seven have *psalmos* where the Hebrew does not read *mizmor*; seven have *ode* where the Hebrew lacks *shir*; and five have *allelouia* where the Hebrew has no *hulleluyah*. See Archer, *Introduction*, p. 457.

28. D. Kidner, *Psalms* in Tyndale Old Testament Commentaries (Downers Grove, IL: InterVarsity, 1973-76), pp. 43-46.

29. S. Mowinckel, *The Psalms in Israel's Worship*, tr. D.R. Ap-Thomas (Nashville: Abingdon, 1967), 2:100.

30. Kidner, *Psalms*, pp. 32-46.

31. E.J. Young, *An Introduction to the Old Testament*; rev. ed. (Grand Rapids: Eerdmans, 1960), pp. 316-326.

32. Sarna, *Encyclopaedia*, 13:1314.

33. R. Alden, "Chiastic Psalms,"*Journal of the Evangelical Theological Society* 17/1 (1974) 11-28; 19/3 (1976) 191-200; 21/3 (1978) 199-210.

34. Basil, bishop of Caesarea in the fourth century, called the Psalms a "compendium of all theology." Martin Luther referred to this book as "a little Bible, and the summary of the Old Testament." Cited by Tremper Longman III, "Psalms" in *A Complete Literary Guide to the Bible*, ed. Leland Ryken and Tremper Longman III (Grand Rapids: Zondervan, 1993), pp. 252f.

35. Hassell Bullock, *An Introduction to the Poetic Books of the Old Testament* (Chicago: Moody, 1979), p. 131.

36. For a discussion of the messianic psalms, see James E. Smith, *What the Bible Teaches about The Promised Messiah* (Nashville: Nelson, 1993).

37. These psalms contain imprecatory material: 5, 7, 10, 28, 31, 35, 40, 55, 58, 59, 69, 70, 71, 79, 109, 137, 139,140.

38. Archer, *Introduction,* p. 461.

39. 1 Cor 16:22; Gal 1:8f.; Rev 6:10.

40. E.g., these passages quote imprecatory psalms: Acts 1:20; Matt 23:38; Rom 11:7-10; John 15:25.

41. J.A. Sanders, *The Psalms Scroll of Qumran Cave 11*, Discoveries in the Judaean Desert of Jordan, vol. 4 (Oxford: Clarendon, 1965).

42. John A. Lamb, *The Psalms in Christian Worship* (London: Faith, 1962). On the use of instrumental music in the second temple, see Mishnah *Arakhin* 2:3-5.

43. Emil G. Hirsch, *The Jewish Encyclopedia* (New York: Ktav, n.d.) s.v. "Psalms." Psalms used in synagogue liturgy were: 105–107; 111–114; 116–118; 135–136; 146–150.

BIBLIOGRAPHY

Alexander, Joseph A. *The Psalms Translated and Explained.* 1873. Grand Rapids: Baker, 1975.

Alexander, William. *The Witness of the Psalms to Christ and Christianity.* New York: Dutton, 1877.

Clarke, Arthur G. *Analytical Studies in the Psalms.* Kilmarnock: John Ritchie, 1949.

Dahood, Mitchell. *Psalms.* The Anchor Bible. 3 vols. Garden City, NY: Doubleday, 1966, 1968, 1970.

Delitzsch, Franz. *The Psalms,* 1859-60. Keil and Delitzsch Commentaries. 3 vols. Grand Rapids: Eerdmans, n.d.

Dickson, David, *A Commentary on the Psalms.* 1655. 2 vols. Minneapolis: Klock & Klock, 1959.

Leupold, H.C. *Exposition of the Psalms.* 1959. Grand Rapids: Baker, 1969.

Lewis, C.S. *Reflections on the Psalms.* New York: Harcourt, Brace, 1958.

Perowne, J.J.S. *The Book of Psalms.* 1864. 2 vols. Grand Rapids: Zondervan, 1966.

Phillips, O.E. *Exploring the Messianic Psalms.* Philadelphia: Hebrew Christian Fellowship, 1967.

CHAPTER TEN

The Believer's Life
Psalms 1-15

Faith enables the believer to soar over the circumstances of life. After a two-psalm introduction to the entire Psalter, David sets forth the secret of living confidently, expectantly, and victoriously.

INTRODUCTORY PSALMS

Pss 1-2 form an appropriate prologue to the Psalter. They focus on two fundamental doctrines of the Old Testament, namely, (1) that the righteous ultimately prosper, and the wicked will finally face judgment; and (2) that ultimate victory for the righteous will occur with the coming of Messiah. Believers clung to these truths throughout the centuries of Old Testament history.

A. The Theme of the Psalter (Ps 1).

The first psalm is anonymous. David is most likely the author. Ps 1 has two main divisions: (1) The prosperity of the righteous (vv. 1-3); and (2) the insecurity of the wicked (vv. 4-6).

1:1. Sin takes a downward course. Adoption of the principles of the wicked ("walked in the counsel of wicked men") leads to persistence in the practices of notorious offenders ("stood in the way of sinners"). This in turn leads to deliberate association with those who openly mock at faith ("sit in the seat of the scorners").

1:2. True happiness is to be found not in ways of man's own devising, but in the revealed will of God.

1:3. The righteous person is like a well-watered and firmly-rooted tree, nourished by the supply of grace drawn from constant communion with God through the word.

1:4. The wicked are like chaff, i.e., worthless and liable to be swept away by every passing breeze.

1:5. The real character of the wicked shall be manifested in God's judgment. There the chaff shall be separated from the wheat (cf. Matt 3:12). Forever the wicked are separated from the people of God. The teaching of the psalm is grounded in the providence of God. Divine knowledge involves approval, care and guidance.

B. The Hope of the Psalter (Ps 2).

Psalm 2 is quoted seven times in the New Testament. In each instance it is applied to the Messiah.[1] The king, who in this psalm is the object of the fiercest hostility from man and the highest honor from God, is the Messiah.

Psalm 2 is attributed to David in the New Testament (Acts 2:30). What historical event, if any, prompted the writing of this psalm cannot be determined. At no time did David personally face rebellion from Gentile foes which once had been subject to him (vv. 1-3). Furthermore, David was anointed at Bethlehem and Hebron, not Mt. Zion (v. 6). David here is speaking strictly as a prophet.

Psalm 2 has four main divisons: (1) the revolt of men against God (vv. 1-3); (2) the response of God to the revolt (vv. 4-6); (3) the reign of Christ on Zion (vv. 7-9); and (4) the remarks of the psalmist (vv. 10-12).

2:1-3. A revolt by Gentile rulers against God and his anointed is doomed to failure. The early church took this to be a prophecy of the rejection and execution of Jesus (Acts 4:27f.).

2:4-5. God has but to speak, and those who arrogantly lifted themselves up against him are stricken with terror.

2:6. In spite of the rejection of his anointed one, God expresses his determination to install his earthly representative on Mt. Zion. Old Testament Zion is a type of the church of Christ (Heb 12:22). Here is predicted Messiah's enthronement as head over all things to the church (Acts 2:33).

2:7. God speaks directly to Messiah and declares him to be his Son. The words "today I have begotten you" refer to his installation in the royal office, not to his birth. The New Testament applies these words to the resurrection of Jesus (Acts 13:32f.; Heb 1:5; 5:5).

2:8. As a consequence of his elevation to royal rule, God bestows on the Son as an inheritance the Gentiles living throughout the world.

2:9. The enthroned Messiah smashes those who oppose him with an iron rod. The language of Rev 2:27 points to the fact that Christ has already received his rod of iron.

2:10-12. David pleads with his readers to "kiss the Son," i.e., kiss his feet in submission to his Lordship. The alternative is to face his fierce wrath.

LIVING CONFIDENTLY
Psalms 3–7

Ps 2 and Ps 8 reveal the hope of ultimate victory through the Messiah. Sandwiched between are five psalms which depict God's help to his people in the crises of life. The dominant theme in these psalms is that of the confidence with which the righteous can face life's problems.[2]

A. Guarded in Battle (Ps 3).

Ps 3 was written by David when he fled for his life from his son Absalom (2 Sam 15–18). It has four stanzas of two verses each: (1) the present distress (vv. 1-2); (2) the glorious deliverer (vv. 3-4); (3) the sublime confidence (vv. 5-6); and (4) the climactic petition (vv. 7-8).

3:1-2. David lays his need before Yahweh. He is threatened by a rebellion which hourly gathers fresh adherents. His cause is pronounced utterly desperate.

3:3. Men say that God has forsaken him, but David knows that it is not so. God is his "shield," and his "glory," and the one who had lifted him up from the depths of trouble on numerous occasions.

3:4. God had heard the previous prayers of David from "his holy hill," i.e., Mt. Zion, where the ark of the covenant was located. Though the ark was not with David during his flight from Absalom (2 Sam 15:25), still God would answer his prayers from that hill.

3:5-6. David's calmness on the eve of battle was a practical proof of his faith. The numbers were on the side of the rebellious son. But for divine intervention, David would have been defeated.

3:7-8. The concluding prayer for deliverance begins with the opening words of Israel's ancient marching song: "Arise, O Lord" (Num 10:35). This song was rich in memories of past deliverances of Israel.

B. Protected in Sleep (Ps 4).

Ps 4 is an evening hymn authored by David. It reflects the same crisis as the previous psalm. The psalm has a fourfold structure. An appeal to the rebels for repentance (vv. 2-5) is sandwiched between two short appeals to God for help (vv. 1,6). The psalm concludes with a final affirmation of trust in the Lord (vv. 7-8).

4:1. David addresses the Lord as "God of my righteousness." He was confident of the justice of his cause. To God alone he looks for help to vindicate his righteousness in the sight of men by making his cause to triumph.

4:2. David's "glory," i.e., his personal honor and royal dignity, was being assaulted. This rebellion, however, is vain. It cannot succeed any more than the rebellion against God and his anointed could succeed in Ps 2.

4:3. David is confident of victory because he is a godly man (chasid), i.e., one who is characterized by dutiful love to God and to his fellow men.

4:4-5. David warns the rebels to reflect on their course of action before it is too late. They should not allow their anger with his government to force them into sin. They needed to approach God in the right spirit and with "sacrifices of righteousness." They needed to "trust in Yahweh," not in revolution.

4:6. The masses had not yet made up their mind whether to follow the rebels or not. David prays that God would "lift up the light" of his countenence on both himself and his people, i.e., bless them.

4:7-8. David knows a joy and peace which are independent of outward circumstances. No anxieties would delay his sleep. In unshaken faith he claims Yahweh as his sole protector beside whom he needs no other.

C. Guided in Walk (Ps 5).

Like Ps 3, this psalm is a morning prayer. Just as David could face the night with confidence of anxiety-free slumber, so he could face each new day knowing that God would guide his steps. Ps 5 probably comes also from the period of Absalom's rebellion, but perhaps later than the preceding psalm. There David pled with the rebels; here he pleads against them because they have not responded to his loving appeals.

Ps 5 has a beautiful chiastic structure as has been pointed out by Scroggie.[3]

    A. The Devout Soul (vv. 1-3): singular.
       B. The Wicked (vv. 4-6).
          C. Personal (v. 7).
          C. Personal (v. 8).
       B. The Wicked (vv. 9-10).
    A. The Devout Soul (vv. 11-12): plural.

5:1-2. David asks Yahweh to hear his "meditation." The word, which is used elsewhere only in Ps 39:3, denotes either an unspoken prayer of the heart, or the low, murmuring utterance of brooding sorrow.

5:3. The first thought of David's day was prayer. When he prayed he would "look up," i.e., expect an answer.

5:4. The ground of David's confidence in an answer to prayer is the holiness of God ('*El*), who will tolerate no evil. An evil person cannot enjoy the hospitality and protection of heaven's king.

5:5-6. David mentions four classes of sinners: (1) the arrogant, who are guilty of blustering presumption; (2) workers of iniquity, those who make a practice of immorality; (3) those who speak lies; and (4) men of bloodshed and deceit, those who engage in murder by treachery.

5:7. While the wicked are banished from fellowship with God, David was confident that he had freedom of access by the grace of the Lord. In "fear," i.e., the spirit of awe and reverence, he would "worship toward" God's "holy temple," i.e., either the tabernacle or the heavenly temple (1 Kgs 8:22).

5:8. David prays that his path might be "straight," i.e., plain and level, so that he might not stumble or lose his way.

5:9. Such guidance is needed because his enemies plot rebellion and death while using deceitful words.

5:10. David prays that the plotting of the rebels might recoil upon themselves, that God might "cast them out" of their positions of power. Those who have rebelled against Yahweh's king have in effect rebelled against Yahweh.

5:11. The punishment of the wicked according to their deeds would be an occasion of rejoicing on the part of the godly. Such people love God's "name," i.e., everything he has revealed about himself.

5:12. The psalm concludes with an affirmation that God will indeed bless the righteous, protecting them as with a large shield from the insults and assaults of their enemies.

D. Sustained in Sickness (Ps 6).

Ps 6 is one of seven psalms in the Psalter known from ancient times in the church as the "penitential" psalms.[4] David composed this psalm probably some time after his sin with Bathsheba, but before Absalom's rebellion. It falls into three divisions: (1) earnest appeal (vv. 1-5); (2) extreme anguish (vv. 6-7); and (3) expected answer (vv. 8-10).

6:1. In his initial appeal, David pleads that his present suffering exceeds the measure of loving correction. He can interpret his suffering as a sign that the wrath of God was resting on him. David makes no confession of specific sin. Perhaps, like Job, he cannot think of any reason why God would treat him in this way.

6:2. David describes himself as "weak." He says his "bones" are "dismayed." In Hebrew poetry "bones" denote the whole physical organism of man. They are often depicted as the seat of health (Prov 16:24) or of pain, as here.

6:3. The inner self as well as the physical body is dismayed by the suffering. Jesus used the words of v. 3 in view of his approaching Passion (John 12:27). The appeal concludes with a haunting question: "How long?" He may refer to his suffering, or to the anger of God, or to the seeming refusal of God to hear his plea.

6:4. David appeals to God to "return," for Yahweh seems to have abandoned him. He entreats the Lord to be true to his nature as a God of "lovingkindness."

6:5. In Sheol, the abode of the dead, man would not be able to witness to others of the greatness of God as he does in this life. Old Testament saints were granted but a very partial revelation of the state after death. Nonetheless, this verse is misused when it is made to teach the doctrine of soul sleeping or annihilation.

6:6-7. David was weary with groaning and weeping. His sorrow was of long duration, and knew no respite. Malicious enemies aggravate his suffering by taunting him with being forsaken by God.

6:8-10. The cloud of gloom lifts. David suddenly realizes that his prayers have been heard. He therefore predicts the speedy confusion of his enemies. The dismay which he had felt in vv. 2-3 now rebounds on those who took malicious delight in his misfortunes.

E. Vindicated in Slander (Ps 7).

David wrote this psalm during the period when he was being pursued by Saul. A certain Benjamite named Cush[3]—one of Saul's partisans—had made slanderous insinuations against David (cf. 1 Sam 22:8) which inflamed the king's hatred toward his rival. This psalm has two principal divisions: (1) personal request for divine intervention (vv. 1-10); and (2) general reflections on divine righteousness (vv. 11-17).

7:1-2. David's cry for divine assistance is based on (1) his relationship to Yahweh: "my God" in whom "I put my trust;" and (2) the extremity of his need. His enemies are many, but one is conspicuous above all the others. This antagonist was as vicious as a lion. Cush, or perhaps Saul himself, is meant.

7:3-5. The appeal for help is supported by a strong assertion of innocence. If he is guilty of the crimes laid to his charge, may he be surrendered to the utmost fury of his enemies. Time and again David had "delivered" him who without cause had now become his enemy (1 Sam 24:4ff.; 26:8ff.). His conduct had been the exact opposite of that which was attributed to him.

7:6-7. David calls for Yahweh to convene an assembly, conduct an inquiry, and vindicate his innocence. The terms "arise" and "awake" simply invoke action on God's part (cf. 121:3f.). David requests that the peoples—both Israel and the Gentiles—stand around the tribunal. He asks God to "return on high," i.e., to the high throne of judgment from which for a time, it seemed, he had stepped down.

7:8. David asks for a favorable judgment from the divine judge based on his "righteousness" and his "integrity." He does not claim to be sinless, but he has a clear conscience. Specifically, he claims innocence of the charges of treachery which have been brought against him.

7:9. David now prays for the larger hope of the universal destruction of evil and the triumph of righteousness. This plea is grounded in these facts: (1) that God himself is righteous; (2) that he is a discerner of hearts, and (3) thus is able to render impartial judgment.

7:10. David recognizes that his "shield," i.e., defense, is "upon" God, i.e., it rests with God to defend him.

7:11-13. Whatever men may think, God's judicial wrath against evil never rests. God has already sharpened his sword and strung his bow with the arrow of punishment for evildoers.

7:14-16. The punishment of a wicked person is the inevitable result of his own actions. He falls into the snare which he has laid for others.

7:17. The psalm closes with a doxology. "Praise" in the Psalter is the acknowledgment due from man to God for his goodness. God's "righteousness" is manifested and vindicated in the judgment of the wicked. Because he is supreme governor, Yahweh is designated as "Most High," a title which is used some twenty-one times in the Psalter.

LIVING EXPECTANTLY
Psalms 8-10

The Old Testament believer anticipated a glorious future. He looked forward to the subjugation of all things, including enemies both within and without.

A. Ultimate Victory (Ps 8).

Ps 8 is messianic in some sense as is indicated by the fact that it is quoted four times in the New Testament and applied to Christ (Matt

21:16; Eph 1:20ff.; 1 Cor 15:27; Heb 2:6-9). David probably wrote this psalm in his mature years, but it contains meditations from his early shepherd days.

Ps 8 is organized around a basic proposition stated in identical words in the opening and closing verses. The intervening verses offer specific proofs or illustrations of the truth stated in the proposition. The psalm is organized in four units: (1) the proposition stated (v. 1); (2) the proof presented (vv. 2-4a); (3) the person anticipated (vv. 4b-8), and (4) the proposition repeated (v. 9).

8:1,9. Yahweh is sovereign ruler over all. His majestic "name"—his character, nature, personality—is recognized throughout the earth. The heavens bear witness to him.

8:2. Young children sang vigorous praises of Christ when he made his Palm Sunday entrance into Jerusalem (Matt 21:15f.). Their praise silenced the mouths of the enemies. The early disciples in childlike faith (cf. Matt 11:25; 18:1-6) embraced the Messiah and later bore powerful testimony to his identity.

8:3-4. God's condescension to "man" in his creaturely weakness ('enosh) points to his glory.

8:5. The ultimate manifestation of God's glory came when the Son of Man was made for a time to be lower than the angels. The correct interpretation of v. 5 is found in Heb 2:7. The incarnation and subsequent exaltation of Christ (Phil 2:6f.) are in view here.

8:6-8. Messiah was given universal authority at the time of his ascension. The original dominion over the earth given to Adam and subsequently lost is restored in the Messiah (Heb 2:8f.). During his earthly ministry the Son of Man on many occasions demonstrated his authority over nature.[6] All things now have been put under his feet. Christ now reigns from his throne on high (Heb 2:5; Eph 1:22; 1 Cor 15:25-27).

B. Judgment on External Enemies (Ps 9).

A close relationship exists between this Ps 9 and Ps 10. In some ancient versions they are reckoned as one. The absence of the title over Ps 10, the remnant of an acrostic structure, and similar language may indicate that at one time these two psalms were one also in the Hebrew text. The appropriateness of the separation, however, is indicated in the difference in tone and subject matter. Ps 9 focuses on the judgment of foreign enemies while in Ps 10 godless men within the nation are in view. On the whole, then, it is best to view Ps 10 as a companion piece to Ps 9, but not a continuation.

The occasion on which David penned Ps 9 cannot be determined. This psalm may celebrate his victories over foreign enemies (2 Sam 8). The psalm is a partial acrostic with segments beginning consecutively with nine of the first ten letters of the Hebrew alphabet.

The psalm has three main divisions: (1) praise for victories over national enemies in the past (vv. 1-12); (2) petition for personal victory in the present (vv. 13-16); and (3) prediction of universal victory in the future (vv. 17-20).

9:1-2. The psalmist resolves wholeheartedly to praise God for past deliverances even though he was faced with a current crisis.

9:3-4. In the defeat of his enemies David sees God's judicial intervention on his behalf. God has taken his seat upon the judgment throne, as it were, and he has pronounced and executed sentence in David's favor.

9:5-6. God has rebuked by defeat those wicked nations which had come against Israel. The very names of those enemies have been blotted off the roster of active nations.

9:7-10. The enemies of Israel are destroyed, but Yahweh sits forever enthroned as king and judge. His administration will be one of perfect righteousness. He is a "refuge" (lit., high tower) to those who trust in him.

9:11. Zion became the special abode of Yahweh from the time when the ark, the symbol of his presence, was placed there early in the reign of David. The psalmist calls upon his countrymen to declare among the peoples (foreign nations) the "doings" of Yahweh, i.e., his mighty works on behalf of his people. The first step toward their conversion is that they might know the evidences of his power and love.

9:12. The call to praise in v. 11 is based on the fact that Yahweh is the great *go'el*, the avenger of blood. He investigates all offenses against his sacred gift of human life, and demands satisfaction for "bloodshed," i.e., the wrongful taking of life. He does not forget the cry of the "humble," i.e., those whose condition calls for his special protection.

9:13-14. The psalmist had been brought down, as it were, to "gates of death" by those who hated him. He prays that he might be permitted to show forth anew the praises of the Lord "in the gates of the daughter of Zion," i.e., the most public places of Jerusalem. The citizens of Zion collectively are personified as a daughter of the place. This is the only place where this language appears in the Psalter.[7]

9:15-16. Wicked nations fall into the pit or net of their own making. *"Haggaion"* is a musical term which, in conjunction with *"Selah,"* here directs the musicians to produce a jubilant interlude to celebrate the divine triumph.

9:17. The experience of Yahweh's recent victory over the wicked gives the psalmist confidence that "the wicked shall be turned into Sheol," i.e., the career of the wicked in this world will be cut short by the judgment of God. The "wicked" are identified as the "nations that forget God." The implication here is that even heathen should know through nature the God of creation, even though they might not know of Yahweh through revelation.

9:18. Man forgets God; but God does not forget man.

9:19-20. The psalm ends with a prayer for further and still more complete judgment upon the wicked. "Strength" is a divine attribute which should not be given to mortal man (*'enosh*). The psalmist asks that the heathen nations be summoned to Yahweh's presence and taught a lesson about strength. He prays that some awe-inspiring demonstration of divine power might be displayed before them. The resulting terror would teach those nations that they are but mortal men.

C. Judgment on Internal Enemies (Ps 10).

The previous psalm focused on external enemies. Ps 10 points to the final overthrow of all enemies within Israel. The misgovernment of Saul's later years, and the civil war between David and Ishbosheth, may have created a climate of civil disorder in Israel at the time David began to rule over all Israel. The psalm has three divisions: (1) the opening complaint (v. 1-2); (2) the portrait of the wicked (vv. 3-11); and (3) the plea for divine intervention (vv. 12-18).

10:1. The opening question is in reality an accusation against the Lord for being an indifferent spectator when the poor one is taken in the devices of the wicked.[8]

10:3-4. The wicked one boasts that he obtains all that he wants without troubling himself about God. His lawless plundering of the poor indicates contempt for the Lord.

10:5-6. The wicked person feels secure. He fears neither man nor God. "His ways prosper at all times." He is never harassed by vicissitudes of fortune. He views God as too far away in heaven to interfere in his life. The possibility of retribution never crosses his mind. He "snorts," i.e., expresses scorn, at all his adversaries.

10:7. The wicked person is revealed in his speech. His mouth is full of "cursing," i.e., malicious imprecation; and all types of "deceits"; and "oppression," i.e., threatening words.

10:8-11. The crimes of the wicked person are ruthless. He lies in wait to rob as a lion lurking for its prey or a hunter snaring his game. His victims are the innocent and defenseless poor. The reference may be to (1) outlaw gangs; or (2) powerful nobles who plundered poorer neighbors.

10:12-13. The acrostic structure resumes in v. 12. Segments beginning consecutively with the last four letters of the Hebrew alphabet appear here. God is urged to "arise," i.e., get involved; to "lift up" his hand, i.e., assume the posture of action. The psalmist urges God not to forget the humble. Thus will the Lord vindicate his character against the blasphemous thoughts of the wicked.

10:14. God has seen all the oppression of the wicked one. His observation cannot fail to lead to action. The poor one can therefore commit his cause to God who will never abandon him. Experience teaches that God has always been a helper to the "fatherless."

10:15. The psalmist asks God to break the arm of the evildoer, i.e., render him powerless. He wants this judgment process to continue until God can find no wickedness to punish.

10:16. Yahweh is king forever. Just as the Canaanites were driven out before God's people, so the wicked must ultimately give place to the godly. Then Yahweh's land will become in truth the Holy Land.

10:17-18. God not only has seen the plight of the godly, he has heard their prayers. The prayer of faith will be answered. The day will come when oppression will cease from the land.

LIVING VICTORIOUSLY
Psalms 11-15

Pss 8-10 speak of the ultimate victory of the Lord in judgment over his enemies. Pss 11-15 speak of the daily victory which David experienced and which all believers can know.

A. Overcoming Fear (Ps 11).

David probably wrote this psalm during the period when he served in the court of King Saul (1 Sam 18-19). The psalm has three divisions: (1) the fearlessness of faith (vv. 1-3); (2) the foundation of faith (vv. 4-5); and (3) the fruit of faith (v. 7).[9]

11:1. David had taken refuge in Yahweh. To flee from the potential danger would be an act of unbelief as well as cowardice. David's friends who urged him to flee to the mountains were misguided.

11:2. The situation was desperate. David's life was in danger. The wicked are about to use the upright for target practice.

11:3. The state is compared to a building. The foundations upon which it rests are the fundamental principles of law and justice. The efforts of the righteous have done nothing to avert the general anarchy.

11:4. David is confident that "Yahweh is in his holy temple." Others judge by the appearance of the moment; his faith beholds the heavenly ruler exercising his sovereignty.

11:5-6. God's "soul" is his innermost, essential nature. He hates evil, and of necessity also the evil men who practice violence. The psalmist expresses the wish that the wicked might experience the fate of Sodom.

11:7. The character of Yahweh is the ground of the judgment which has been described. He not only punishes the wicked, he also rewards the righteous. If he hates violent deeds, he loves righteous acts. The righteous are admitted into the presence of the Lord. This theme will be further developed in Ps 15.

B. Overcoming Hypocrisy (Ps 12).

Ps 12 was probably written during David's period of service in Saul's court, or during the period of his flight from Saul. This was a

227

time when unscrupulous enemies were poisoning Saul's mind against David with slanderous accusations. This psalm has two main divisions: (1) a prayer (vv. 1-4); and (2) a prophecy (vv. 5-8).

12:1-2. David cries out for help because godly men are disappearing from the land. Hypocrisy and duplicity seem to be universal. Their words are "vanity" or falsehood, i.e., hollow and unreal. Their flatteries come from a double heart (lit., a heart and a heart) which thinks one thing and utters another.

12:3-4. David prays for the removal of these false-hearted braggarts. Unscrupulous courtiers appear to be meant. They deliberately propose to obtain their own ends by reckless disregard of truth, e.g., by flattery, slander, and false witness.

12:5. Because of the unjust oppression of the poor, Yahweh promises to "arise," i.e., get involved. The despised victim will be put beyond the reach of his tormentors.

12:6. In Yahweh's words there is no dross of flattery or falsehood. Unlike the words of men, they are wholly trustworthy.

12:7-8. David concludes with a final expression of confidence in Yahweh's protection, which is sorely needed when wickedness is unchecked.

C. Overcoming Anxiety (Ps 13).

Ps 13 reflects the anxiety of David when he was in flight from Saul. The language is general but one foe in particular stands out above the rest. This psalm has three divisions: (1) exasperation (vv. 1-2); (2) entreaty (vv. 3-4); and (3) exultation (vv. 5-6).

13:1-2. In the opening lines hope *despairs*. David feels that the Lord has forgotten him. Yet hope also *dares*. The question "How long?" implies a termination of the Lord's neglect of him.

13:3-4. David asks for divine intervention before he dies at the hands of his enemies. The implication is that the triumph of the enemies will cause the honor of God to suffer.

13:5-6. David begins to rejoice because he is certain that the deliverance will come.

D. Overcoming Corruption (Ps 14).

Ps 14 is also found in Book Two of the Psalter as Ps 53 with some variations. David wrote this psalm at some point between the capture of the stronghold of Jebus (1 Chr 11) and the transportation of the ark to Jerusalem (1 Chr 15–16). It has two equal stanzas with a concluding verse: (1) corruption of the world (vv. 1-3); (2) the oppression of the righteous (vv. 4-6); and (3) the aspiration of the psalmist (v. 7).

14:1. "The fool" is a class of people, not a particular individual. The word denotes moral depravity, not mere ignorance or weakness of reason. The fool conducts his life as if there is no God. This is not so much the philosophical denial of the atheist as the practical disregard of the immoral. Corrupt men give themselves over to practices which God abhors. Some think David is describing conditions before the Flood, at Babel, and in Sodom.

14:2. God "looked down" from heaven (cf. Gen 11:5; 18:21) with disapproval upon this corruption. He could find none who did "understand" and seek God. Note the use of *God*, not *Yahweh*. He speaks of mankind in general, not Israel.

14:3. The investigation showed that all had turned aside from the path of righteousness; all had become filthy. The first three verses of this psalm are quoted in Rom 3:10-12 to illustrate the principle that "All have sinned and come short of the glory of God."

14:4. God expresses amazement that the sons of men do not know the difference between right and wrong, do not call upon him, and oppress his people. The reference may be to the oppression of Israel by the Egyptians.

14:5. At some point, overwhelming calamity overtook "the workers of iniquity." If the previous verse refers to the oppression in Egypt, v. 5 would refer to the destruction of the Egyptians at the Red Sea. God is among "the generation of the righteous," i.e., his people.

14:6. The wicked mocked the trust which the poor put in Yahweh; but in the Lord the poor would find refuge.

14:7. David prays for the "salvation of Israel" to come out of Zion, the dwelling-place of Yahweh. The Lord will one day "restore the fortunes of his people" (NASB margin).[10]

E. Reward for Overcoming (Ps 15).

Ps 15 was composed by David, probably when he transported the ark to Jerusalem (2 Sam 6:12-19). This psalm begins with a question

(v. 1), and ends with a promise (v. 5b). The intervening verses answer the initial question.

15:1. The "tent" is that tent which David pitched for the ark of God on Mt. Zion. The question concerns who is worthy to be received as Yahweh's guest, to enjoy his protection and hospitality.

15:2. The conditions of access to God's presence are first stated positively and in general terms: one who (1) walks with integrity, i.e., blamelessly (*tamim*); (2) works righteousness; and (3) is committed to the truth.

15:3. He who would be God's guest (1) has no slander on his tongue; (2) does not do evil to his neighbor; nor (3) "takes up a reproach against his friend." He does not make his neighbor's faults or misfortunes the object of his ridicule or sarcasm.

15:4. The guest of God is one who (1) treats with contempt those who are reprobate, i.e., morally worthless; (2) honors those who fear Yahweh; and (3) performs his oaths without modification, even those that may have been made to his own disadvantage.

15:5. The guest of God would never lend money at interest to a brother in need (cf. Lev 25:36f.); nor would he take bribes to render judgments against the innocent (cf. Deut 27:25; Exod 23:7f.). The promise is that one who lives this lifestyle "shall never be moved." Such a person will not only be admitted to fellowship with Yahweh, but, under his protection, will also enjoy prosperity.

ENDNOTES

1. Ps 2 is quoted in Acts 4:24-28; 13:33; Heb 1:5; 5:5; Rev 2:27; 12:5; and 19:15.

2. G. Campbell Morgan suggests for this collection of psalms the theme "Authority Established." A.G. Clarke proposed the caption, "Revelation of the Divine Ruler."

3. W. Graham Scroggie, *The Psalms* (Old Tappan, NJ: Revell, 1965), 1:63.

4. The other six penitential psalms are: Pss 32, 38, 51, 102, 130 and 143. In Catholic ritual, these are read on Ash Wednesday.

5. Cush is a personal name not otherwise used in Scripture. There is no reason for taking it to mean a Cushite or Ethiopian (Jerome). An ancient Jewish interpretation is that Cush is a by-name for Saul himself as a "black-hearted man."

6. T. Earnest Wilson cites the following illustrations of Messiah's authority over creation: (1) the forces of nature (Mark 4:39-41; John 2:3-11; 6:5-14); (2) the wild beasts in the wilderness (Mark 1:13); (3) domesticated animals (Luke 19:30); (4) the fish of the sea (Matt 17:27); and (5) the fowl of the air (Luke 3:22). *Messianic Psalms* (Neptune, NJ: Louizeaux, 1978), p. 146.

7. The Psalter does, however, speak of the "daughter of Tyre" (45:12) and "daughter of Babylon" (137:8). The terminology "daughter of Zion" (Jerusalem) does occur frequently in the prophetic books.

8. The Hebrew in 10:2 can also be translated as a prayer: "Let [the wicked] be taken in the devices that they have imagined."

9. The outline of Ps 11 has been taken from A.G. Clarke, *Analytical Studies in the Psalms* (Grand Rapids: Kregel, 1979), p. 53.

10. KJV translates: "bring back the captivity of his people." That this phrase has a figurative sense is proved by Job 42:10; Zeph 2:7; Amos 9:14; Hosea 6:11.

CHAPTER ELEVEN

The Believer's Salvation
Psalms 16-29

God is the source of deliverance for the believer. In the next series of psalms, the focus is on what God does for his people. The psalmist then indicates how God's people can draw near to the Lord.

THE GOD OF LIFE
Psalm 16

Ps 16 is quoted twice in the New Testament and applied by apostolic inspiration to Jesus (Acts 2:25-28;13:35). Biblical authority, then, requires the personal messianic interpretation of at least v. 10. Since there is no change of subject indicated, one must conclude that the entire psalm speaks exclusively of Messiah. Such was the ancient view of the church.

David wrote Ps 16 (Acts 2:25ff.). The title refers to this psalm as a *mikhtam* of David. Six psalms have such a title.[1] The term is obscure, but it has been traced by some scholars to a root meaning "gold." A *mikhtam* then would be a precious psalm.[2] Though David is the writer, he is not the speaker in the psalm. The speaker is Christ (Acts 2:25-28).

Ps 16 consists of four thought divisions: (1) the cry (vv. 1-2); (2) the confession (vv. 3-4); (3) the commitment (vv. 5-8), and (4) the confidence (vv. 9-11) of Christ.

16:1-2. The opening verses of the psalm suggest that Messiah is in the depths of trouble. He refers to his Father as *'El*, the strong one, mighty to deliver in time of danger.

16:3. Messiah affirms his submission to the Father in that he calls him Lord (*'adhonay*). He acknowledges that doing the will of God is the priority of his life. Christ also confesses his high estimation of the *saints* of God. He delights in them, considers them the "excellent" ones, i.e., nobles.

16:4. Christ repudiates those who hasten after another god or messiah. Such will have multiplied sorrows. They will have no sacrifice for sin, for Messiah will not pour out on their behalf blood libations. Neither will he take their names upon his lips, i.e., he will make no intercession for them.

16:5-6. Christ regarded God's will as his portion and cup (sustenance). His "lot" (ministry) was in the hand of God. The Lord is to him as the choicest of possessions in the best of lands.

16:7-8. Christ received counsel, i.e., direction, from Yahweh. His goal was to always execute Yahweh's will.

16:9-10. Christ is confident that he would not be abandoned to the grave. He knew that his stay in the grave would not be of sufficient duration to produce corruption. He would be in that tomb only sufficient time to prove the reality of his death.

16:11. Christ expresses confidence that he would walk the path of life. He led the way out of the realm of death to become the firstfruits of the dead (1 Cor 15:20). He was confident that he would assume his rightful place at the right hand of the Father.

THE GOD OF DELIVERANCE
Psalms 17–18

Deliverance is the theme of Pss 17–18. In the first psalm the danger is clearly present; in the second the danger is past.

A. Prayer for Deliverance (Ps 17).

Ps 17 comes from the period of David's outlaw life. He is beset by proud and pitiless enemies bent on his destruction. One among those enemies—Saul—was particularly hostile (cf. 1 Sam 23:25-29). The psalm is one of five in the book to be called a "prayer." It contains three distinct petitions. David asks for deliverance on the grounds of (1) his personal integrity (vv. 1-5); (2) his relationship to God (vv. 6-12); and (3) his spiritual aspirations (vv. 13-15).

17:1. David comes before God with a righteous cause and a just appeal. He is confident of the integrity of his motives towards God and man. "A good conscience is an indispensable condition of earnest prayer."[3]

17:2. Yahweh's eyes "behold with equity," i.e., his discernment is complete and impartial.

17:3-5. David speaks boldly of his innocence of wrongdoing. In thought, word and deed he has nothing to fear from thorough scrutiny from Yahweh. He had followed the word of God and had shunned the ways of violent men. He had kept his feet steadfastly in the beaten path marked out by God.

17:7. David calls on the Lord to "make marvelous" his lovingkindness. The petition suggests a dramatic intervention on his behalf. The need was great, but the "right hand" (power) of his God was greater.

17:8-9. David asks (1) that God might guard him as one would guard the "apple" (pupil) of his eye; and (2) that God might "hide" him as a mother bird hides her chicks under her wings.

17:10-13. Those who attacked David are described as compassionless and contemptuous. They look for every opportunity of overthrowing David and his associates. One of their number—Saul—is compared to a lion, i.e., he is conspicuous by his ferocity and craftiness. David calls upon God to meet that lion as he is about to attack, to make him bow down in humble submission.

17:14. The enemies are described as "men of the world" who have their "portion" in this life only. By contrast, Yahweh himself is the portion of the righteous. Men of the world care only for the satisfaction of their lower appetites. God gives them their due in life, for example, treasure and children to whom to leave it.

17:15. David has higher aspirations than his attackers. Their prosperity is no problem to him, because his blessings are greater. To "behold" the face of God in worship is for him an incomparable joy. The phrase "when I awake" does not refer directly to resurrection from death, but to a renewal daily of his personal communion with God.

B. Praise for Deliverance (Ps 18).

Ps 18 is a thanksgiving hymn of David, the warrior king. It is a duplicate of 2 Sam 22. Such differences as appear between the two passages are due, no doubt, to revisions made by David himself as he prepared the psalm for use in the public services. The psalm seems to come from the middle of David's reign, when he was at the zenith of power (cf. 2 Sam 7:1). The king attributes his military success to the aid of Yahweh. In the title David is called "Yahweh's servant." Only a few who had a special relationship with the Lord are so designated, e.g., Moses, Joshua, Job, and especially Jesus. In using the title of himself David seems to be claiming divine authority for the words of this psalm.

Ps 18 has a chiastic structure which may displayed as follows:

    A. Praise to the Deliverer (vv. 1-3).

      B. Divine Power (vv. 4-19).

        C. Divine Procedure (vv. 20-24).

          D. Divine Principles (vv. 25-26).

        C. Divine Procedure (vv. 27-31).

      B. Divine Power (vv. 32-48).

    A. Praise to the Deliverer (vv. 49-50).

18:1-2. David uses nine titles for Yahweh to express all that he had found the Lord to be in his experience. Here occurs for the first time in the Psalter the title "rock" (*tsur*), so often used to describe the strength, faithfulness, and unchangeableness of Yahweh. The "horn" is a common symbol of irresistible strength, derived from horned animals, especially wild oxen.

18:3. "I will call upon Yahweh" expresses the conviction of God's faithfulness to answer prayer. Yahweh is the only object of Israel's praise.

18:4-6. In forceful figures David pictures the extremity of need in which he cried for help. The perils to which he had been exposed are described as waves which threatened to engulf him and sweep him away. Sheol and death are represented as hunters laying wait for his life with nets and snares.

18:7-15. David's prayer is answered forthwith. Yahweh comes to scatter his enemies. The Lord manifests himself in earthquake and storm. This awesome display of divine power in nature is probably an "ideal" theophany, i.e., visible manifestation of God. No record in the histories of David documents such an actual occurrence when God intervened through nature to rescue David. Yahweh is said to ride upon "a cherub" (v. 10). Cherubim in Scripture are depicted as attendants of God or guardians of sacred places. The cherubim depicted in the tabernacle and temple seem to have been winged human figures, representing the angelic attendants who minister in God's presence.

18:16-19. Yahweh reached forth from on high and rescued David from the floods of persecution. The "enemy" from whom David was delivered was Saul. From the narrow straits of peril, God had brought forth David into the "large place" of freedom. The reason Yahweh intervened was because he "delighted" in David.

18:20-23. David here does not claim sinlessness, but single-hearted devotion to the Lord. God (1 Kgs 14:8) and the sacred historian (1 Kgs 11:4; 15:5) testify to the essential integrity of this man. God's commandments were continually present to his mind as the rule of his life. He had carefully guarded himself against transgression. Obviously this psalm was written before David's great sin with Bathsheba.

18:24-27. Here is the law of God's moral government. His attitude towards men is conditioned by their attitude towards him. The person whose life is governed by the spirit of lovingkindness will himself experience the lovingkindness of the Lord. On the other hand, God is at cross purposes with the wicked, frustrating their plans, and punishing their wickedness. He permits such to follow their crooked ways till they bring them to destruction. God rewards humility, but crushes pride.

18:28-30. The general principles of God's dealing with men are confirmed by David in his own experience. The burning lamp is a natural metaphor for the continuance of life and prosperity. The figure is derived from the Oriental practice of keeping a light constantly burning in the tent or house. The allusion to the "troop" and the "wall" may refer specifically to David's pursuit of the Amalekites (1 Sam 30),[4] and the ease with which he captured the fortress of Zion (2 Sam 5:6-8).

18:31-34. David's strength in battle is attributed to Yahweh. He alone is *'Eloah*,[5] a God to be feared. God has made David's way "perfect," i.e., has enabled him to accomplish the goals of his life. God had made his feet like those of the hind. This animal was a type of the agility, swiftness, and surefootedness which were indispensable qualifications in ancient warfare. The "high places" where God had set him were the mountain fortresses of Judah. The ability to bend a metal bow was a sign of superior strength.

18:35-38. David gives Yahweh praise for his saving help. Yahweh's right hand supported him so that his feet would not slip. He enabled David to advance with firm, unwavering steps. Thus he had been able to consume his enemies. They had fallen wounded at his feet.

18:39-42. Thus girded with divine strength, David was able to subdue all his enemies. He had been able to place his feet upon their neck. In desperation these pagan enemies called upon Yahweh to save them from David. Yet he was able to crush them as dust, and cast them away as refuse.

18:43-45. David's dominion was established at home and abroad. Yahweh had brought David safely through the internal dissension which disturbed the early years of his reign while Saul's house still endeavored to maintain its position. He had enabled him to subjugate foreign nations as well. At the mere report of David's victories, other nations offered their allegiance (cf. 2 Sam 8:9ff.).

18:46-48. Yahweh is the *living* God, in contrast to the lifeless idols of the heathen. Vengeance is God's vindication of the righteousness and integrity of his servants. God had avenged David because of the cruel injustice of Saul. The "man of violence" from whom David was delivered is most likely Saul.

18:49. The praise of Yahweh for his faithfulness should be proclaimed among the nations. Thus someday these Gentiles may be brought to a saving knowledge of the Lord. These words are quoted by Paul in Rom 15:9 in proof that the Old Testament anticipated the admission of the Gentiles to the blessings of salvation.

18:50. David is God's anointed. The lovingkindness shown to David personally will be shown to his seed—including Christ Jesus—forever. "The words reach forward to the perfect life, and the world-wide victories, of the Christ, the Son of David."[6]

THE GOD OF REVELATION
Psalm 19

Psalm 19 comes from the pen of David. The exact occasion, how-ever, is not indicated. This psalm has three distinct parts: (1) God's revelation in nature (vv. 1-6); (2) God's revelation in the law (vv. 7-11); and (3) David's prayer for pardon (vv. 12-14). Some scholars believe that originally the first six verses were a separate psalm. If so, the two poems have been combined to make this point: Yahweh, the lawgiver of Israel, is 'El, the creator of the universe.

19:1. The "glory of God" is the unique majesty of Yahweh's being as it is revealed to man. It is that manifestation of his deity which the creature should recognize with reverent adoration. The heavens in their vastness, splendor, order and mystery are the most impressive reflection of his greatness and majesty. Simple men stand in awe of the starry skies; how much more those who are familiar with the probings of astronomy.

19:2. The proclamation of the heavenly bodies is continuous. The day and the night have been compared to the two parts of a choir, chanting forth alternately the praises of God.

19:3. The message of the heavenly bodies is real, but it is inarticu-late. Theirs is a silent eloquence. The Hebrew will not support the KJV rendering that states that the message of the heavens reaches all nations of every language alike.

19:4. The proclamation of the heavenly bodies is universal. Paul quotes these words in Rom 10:18 in making an analogy to the universal proclamation of the gospel. The poet singles out the sun as the chief wit-ness to God's glory. He personifies the sun as though it were a king or hero, for whose abode the creator has fixed a tent in the heavens.

19:5. The sun comes forth morning by morning like the bride-groom in all the splendor of his bridal attire, like the hero eager to put his strength to the test.

19:6. The beneficent influences of the sun's light and heat are universally felt.

19:7. The law of Yahweh—his special revelation through his word—is more glorious than the heavenly witness. That word revelation is "perfect," i.e., flawless, without defect or error; a guide which can neither mislead nor fail. The name *Yahweh* now replaces the name *'El* because the remainder of the psalm enters into the sphere of special revelation to Israel. Like food for the hungry, the law can refresh and restore the soul. The law is a "testimony" to God's will and man's duty. As such it is "sure," i.e., not variable or uncertain. The "simple" are those who have not closed their heart to instruction.

19:8. The "precepts" of the Lord are the various special injunctions in which man's obligations are set forth. These "make glad the heart" with the joy of moral satisfaction. To the psalmist the law was not a burdensome restriction of liberty, but a gracious reflection of the holiness of God, designed to lead man in the way of life and peace.

19:9. The "fear of Yahweh" is another synonym for the law, inasmuch as the aim of the law was to implant reverence for God in the hearts of men. It is "clean" or "pure" in contrast to the immoralities of heathenism.

19:10. The law in all its parts is a treasure to be coveted, a sweet treat to be savored.

19:11. As Yahweh's servant, David allows himself to be warned by God's law.

19:12-13. The contemplation of the holy law leads the psalmist to express his personal need of preservation and guidance. For sins committed in error and for hidden offenses the ceremonial law provided an atonement; but for sins committed "with a high hand," i.e., with a spirit of proud defiance, there was no atonement (Num 15:30f.). From such presumptuous sins he asks to be restrained.

19:14. Prayer uttered or unexpressed is a spiritual sacrifice. David asks that this sacrifice be accepted by the Lord. Yahweh is his "rock" and "redeemer," i.e., one who delivers David from the tyranny of enemies and the bondage of sin.

THE GOD OF BATTLE
Psalms 20–21

Psalms 20 and 21 are closely related in structure and contents. Both depict Yahweh as king of battle. The first is an intercession before the battle; the second is thanksgiving after the battle.

A. Intercession before Battle (Ps 20).

The writer is David; the occasion is uncertain. Most likely this psalm belongs to the period of David's wars recorded in 2 Sam 8–10. An ancient tradition assigned it to the time of David's war with the Ammonites (2 Sam 10:8; 12:26ff). This psalm was apparently intended to be sung as the sacrifice was being offered. It consists of two stanzas with a concluding verse: (1) the people's intercession for the king (vv. 1-5); (2) the king's anticipation of victory (vv. 6-8); and (3) concluding prayer of the whole congregation.

20:1. The prayer is that Yahweh would hear the king in the day of trouble The impending military campaign is in view. The people pray that God will prove himself to be all that his name implies that he is. They wish for God to protect the king as he protected Jacob.

20:2. The earthly sanctuary of Yahweh was located in Zion, the city of Jerusalem. From that sanctuary the congregation prayed that help would come to their king.

20:3. The prayer is that Yahweh might remember all the offerings by which in past time the king had expressed his devotion to the Lord. This would include the sacrifices presently being offered. Sacrifices were regularly offered before a war (1 Sam 7:9f.; 13:9-12).

20:4. The prayer continues that God might grant the counsel, i e , fulfill the battle plans, of David.

20:5. Yahweh was Israel's savior, and David was his chosen instrument for saving the people from their enemies. The citizens looked forward to waving the victory banners.

20:6. The voice of a priest, prophet or possibly the king himself expresses confidence that the pre-battle sacrifice had been accepted by Yahweh. To faith, the victory was already won. God's "anointed"—the king—most certainly would receive God's help.

20:7. The enemy puts its trust in horses and chariots; but Yahweh's name is the watchword and strength of his people.

20:8. Faith anticipates the entire subjugation of the enemy and the triumph of Israel.

20:9. The prayer for the earthly king is addressed to the heavenly king whose representative he is.

B. Thanksgiving after Battle (Ps 21).

David is the author of Ps 21, but the occasion is uncertain. Some think this may have been a national anthem which was used as a thanksgiving for victories granted in answer to prayer. The outline is similar to that of the preceding psalm: (1) thanksgiving for victory achieved; (2) anticipation of future victories; and (3) concluding prayer.

21:1-2. The prayers of Ps 20 have been answered. The victory has been won and the king rejoices in the strength of Yahweh which has been demonstrated on the battlefield. God has listened to the prayers for success of the expedition referred to in 20:3-5.

21:3. The victory is a divine confirmation of the sovereignty of the king. Once more, as it were, David has been crowned king. Some think an allusion to the confiscated crown of the king of Ammon is intended (2 Sam 12:30).

21:4-5. Long life was one of Yahweh's special blessings under the old covenant. David had been granted "length of days for ever and ever." To regard such language as fulfilled only in the sense that his posterity succeeded him on the throne is to rob this passage of its hint of immortality. Glory, honor and majesty are divine attributes. The victorious king shines with a reflection of these attributes.

21:6-7. The victorious king is the possessor and the medium of blessing. The victory is a pledge of divine favor and fellowship, an evidence that David walks in the light of Yahweh's smile. The blessing is grounded in two facts: David's trust in Yahweh, and the Lord's lovingkindness.

21:8-10. The king is addressed. He is promised triumph over all his enemies. They will all be consumed as fuel in a furnace. Even the "fruit," i.e., posterity, of the enemies would be destroyed. Some see here a direct reference to the terrible vengeance which David inflicted upon the Ammonites (2 Sam 12:31).

21:11-12. The enemies might come against David with evil intent. He would unleash against them a barrage of arrows which would cause them to turn their backs and flee.

21:13. The congregation's concluding prayer. Yahweh is exalted when he manifests his strength in mighty acts of salvation.

GOD AS SAVIOR
Psalm 22

Psalm 22 is the first and greatest of the passional psalms.[7] New Testament usage makes it clear that this Davidic psalm should be numbered among the messianic psalms. The description of the suffering here transcends anything which might have befallen David personally. So much of the language is inappropriate to David (cf. vv. 6,11,16,18). The truth is that this psalm reads as if it were composed at the foot of the cross. Ps 22 has two major divisions: (1) the gloom of the cross (vv. 1-21); and (2) the glory of the resurrection (vv. 22-31).

22:1. Christ has been forsaken by his Father. The forsaking was real. The opening utterance of the psalm furnished Jesus with the agonizing cry of his dying hour (Matt 27:45ff.). The word "groaning" is a strong word used of the shrieking of a person in intense pain.

22:2. The abandonment seemed permanent. The "night" here may refer to the darkness which covered the land at high noon during the crucifixion, or perhaps to the gloomy night spent in the garden.

22:3. The abandonment was necessary. The holy God cannot ignore sin. By punishing the sins of mankind on the cross God was demonstrating both his holiness and his compassion for lost humanity. Having been redeemed from sin's bondage by the suffering of Calvary, the true Israel of God raises up continuous praise to the Lord.

22:4-5. The abandonment does not suggest lack of power on God's part to deliver. History contains many examples of how God delivered those who trusted in him. The sufferer here trusted in the Lord. He knew that God could deliver him. In patient trust he accepted his lot as the will of God.

22:6-10. Another reason for the gloom of the speaker: he had become a reproach among men. He was regarded as a "worm"—a weak creature of the dust—and not a man. He was jeered by the people. The mocking priests used these words as they stood at the cross (Matt 27:39-44). They scoffed at Jesus' claim to be God's Son by urging him to cast himself upon Yahweh. Yet in spite of the cruel mockery, the sufferer remained firmly committed in faith to his Father.

22:12-18. The focus now is upon the physical agony of the sufferer. He likens his foes to strong bulls, lions, half-starved dogs, and wild oxen. He is utterly exhausted by the ordeal. His bones are disjointed. His heart is failing. His thirst is raging. He is near death. His hands and feet have been pierced.[8] His skin is so taut that he can count his bones. He watches helplessly as his persecutors gamble over custody of his garments (cf. John 19:23f.; Matt 27:35).

22:19-21. In spite of all his agony, the sufferer continues to trust God and pray to him for deliverance.

22:22. Here the mood of the psalm changes. Christ's victory over death is the occasion of great joy. After the suffering of the cross, Christ rejoined his "brethren," i.e., his faithful followers (Matt 28:10; John 20:17). Together the Redeemer and the redeemed praise the Father for the victory which has been won. The author of Hebrews applies this verse to the Savior. He identifies the assembly of this verse as the church (Heb 2:11f.).

22:23-24. Christ calls on all true descendants of Jacob to honor and praise the Father. Christ had not been permanently forsaken. The resurrection was the answer to Christ's cross petitions for deliverance. He was not delivered *from* death, but was triumphant *over* death.

22:25-27. Christ's victory over death is celebrated in worship. The "great assembly" consists of all those who fear the Lord. These "meek ones shall eat and be satisfied." They appropriate the benefits of his death by eating his body and blood (John 6:55). The believers pray for one another that each may remain faithful unto death. All the ends of the earth join in this worship.

22:28-29. Christ's victory over death ushers in his universal kingdom. All the wealthy will someday worship him (cf. Rev 21:24). Every mortal will one day yield to his sovereignty (cf. Phil 2:10).

22:30-31. Christ's victory over death demands evangelism. The true seed of Abraham (Gal 3:29) and Eve (Gen 3:15) will faithfully

render service to him through the years. God's plan for world
redemption involves the proclamation of God's "righteousness" as
revealed in the death, burial and resurrection of Jesus. "He has done
it" is one word in the Hebrew. God's work of redemption is finished.
Should the Lord tarry, generations yet unborn will learn of this great
truth and respond to it.

GOD AS SHEPHERD
Psalm 23

David is the writer of this "the pearl of psalms." It seems to be
based on recollections of his early shepherd life, and perhaps on his
gracious treatment by his friend Barzillai (2 Sam 17:27-29) late in his
reign. Ps 23 has two main divisions. God is presented as (1) good
shepherd (vv. 1-4) and (2) gracious host (vv. 5-6).

23:1. Yahweh is often presented as the shepherd of Israel. The
words "I shall not want" reflect both past experience and future confidence.

23:2. The shepherd makes his flock lie down in the noontime heat
in pastures of tender grass. He gently leads the flock beside "waters of
rest," i.e., streams where they may find rest and refreshment. The
eastern shepherd always leads and never drives his flock.

23:3. Yahweh renews and sustains the life of the psalmist. He
guides his people individually and collectively "in the paths of righteousness," i.e., in a way that is right with God and thus beneficial for
man. This Yahweh does "for his name's sake," i.e., in order to prove
himself to be what he has declared himself to be (Exod 34:5ff.).

23:4. Walking through the "valley of the shadow of death" or deep
gloom will not terrify the godly man. God's presence is the strength of
his people and their comfort. The shepherd's crook is poetically
described by two names. It is the *rod* or club with which he defends
his sheep from attack; and the *staff* with which he draws the straying
sheep back to safety.

23:5. The figure is changed. Yahweh is now described as the host
who bountifully entertains the psalmist at his table. This mark of favor
is public and unmistakable. Yahweh "anoints" the head. The reference is to the perfumes which were the regular accompaniment of an

Oriental banquet. The overflowing cup is the symbol of the generosity of the host. He provides for the joys as well as the necessities of life.

23:6. Though the wicked are hunted by calamity, the godly man anticipates nothing but goodness and mercy. He anticipates dwelling in the "house of Yahweh" forever. At the very least these words anticipate a long life spent in communion with God in his earthly dwelling, the tabernacle. Probably David is alluding to the hope of dwelling in the heavenly abode with the Lord.

GOD AS SOVEREIGN
Psalm 24

David wrote Ps 24 most probably for the inauguration of the newly captured fortress of Zion (2 Sam 6). The psalm is antiphonic, i.e., it consists of questions chanted by one part of the Levitical choir, and responses by another part of the choir. Ps 24 consists of three parts: (1) the conqueror's approach (vv. 1-2); (2) the conditions of access to Yahweh's sanctuary (vv. 3-6); (3) and the conqueror's arrival (vv. 7-10).

24:1. He who comes to take possession of Zion is Lord of all the earth. The word order of the Hebrew fixes attention on him whose approach is the theme of the psalm. This verse is cited by Paul (1 Cor 10:26) to confirm the intrinsic lawfulness of eating whatever is sold in the market.

24:2. The sovereignty of Yahweh is grounded in the fact that he is the creator of all that exists. He and no other laid the foundation of the world (cf. Job 38:4). The poetic imagery used here is derived from the observation of the land rising out of the seas.

24:3. The hill of Zion is Yahweh's holy place. Who can ascend that hill? Who can stand his ground in the presence of this awesome God?

24:4. To have clean hands is to be innocent of violence and wrongdoing. To be pure of heart is to be innocent even in thought and purpose as well as in deed. To "lift up the soul unto vanity" is to direct one's thoughts toward that which is transitory, false and unreal. It includes all that is unlike or opposed to the nature of God. To "swear deceitfully" is to misuse the name of God in false oaths so as to deceive one's fellow man.

24:5. The person who ascends that holy mount will receive a blessing from the Lord. "Righteousness" here is the vindication which comes by deliverance at the hand of "the God of his salvation."

24:6. The two previous verses describe the "generation," i.e., class of people, which seeks the Lord and seeks to be like their godly ancestor Jacob.

24:7. The procession has now reached the gates of Zion. The gates are summoned to open to admit the great king of glory. The ark was the symbol of Yahweh's majesty and the pledge of his presence among his people (2 Sam 6:2; Num 10:35f.). The "doors" of Zion are called "everlasting" because of their antiquity.

24:8. Those who guarded the gates are represented as challenging the comer's right to enter. The choir responds that Yahweh is the victor. He comes as he had purposed, to take his kingdom.

24:9-10. The challenge and response are repeated, with one important change. "Yahweh of hosts" is identified as the one who would enter the city. He claims to enter, not merely as a victorious warrior, but as the sovereign of the universe. This great title appears here for the first time in the Psalter. He is God of the armies of Israel (1 Sam 17:45), as well as the celestial bodies (Gen 2:1) and heavenly angels (1 Kgs 22:19). Hence the title came to mean: sovereign Lord of the universe.

DRAWING NEAR TO GOD
Psalms 25–29

The next series of psalms focuses on the redeemed as they seek to draw near to the redeemer. The psalms seem to be linked by key thoughts. The "integrity" of 25:21 is the main theme of Ps 26. David's love for God's house in 26:8 surfaces again in 27:4-5. The exhortation to wait on Yahweh in 27:14 becomes the victorious experience of 28:6-7. The predicted judgment of 28:4-5 reaches a climax in the description of the terrible thunderstorm of Ps 29.

A. In Simple Trust (Ps 25).

David wrote Ps 25, probably at the time of Absalom's rebellion. This is one of nine acrostic psalms,[9] but it is irregular. Two Hebrew letters are omitted, and two are doubled—the *aleph* and the *resh*. Perhaps the irregularity was intended by David to reflect the turbulent times in which the poem was written.

The psalm is built around three prayers: one at the beginning (vv. 1-7), one in the middle (v. 11), and one at the end (vv. 15-22). Sandwiched between these prayers are two reflections. One deals with the character of Yahweh (vv. 8-10), and one with his dealings with those who fear him (vv. 12-14).

25:1-2. David expresses a personal longing to approach God. Since his trust is in Yahweh alone, he asks that he would not be put to shame before his enemies.

25:3. David is confident that none who wait upon the Lord shall be put to shame. Those who "deal treacherously," i.e., desert Yahweh, will find themselves put to shame.

25:4. God's "ways" and "paths" are the purposes and methods of his providence; or more specifically, the course of life and conduct which he prescribes for men. David wants God to make those ways clear to him.

25:5. David wants to experience God's faithfulness because Yahweh is the "God of my salvation." He "waits" on the Lord all day.

25:6. David appeals to the unchangeableness of Yahweh. From ancient days he had shown himself to be a God of lovingkindness.

25:7. David asks God to overlook "the sins of my youth," i.e., the failures, errors, and lapses; the thoughtless transgressions of youth. Such forgiveness would make clear to all the essential "goodness" of God.

25:8-9. He who is simultaneously perfectly loving and perfectly upright must guide those who are prone to error. Those who are humble in spirit he will guide "in judgment," i.e., the practice of right.

25:10. In all his dealings, Yahweh shows his loving purpose and his faithfulness to his promises to those who on their part are faithful to him. The "covenant" is that system of law revealed at Mt. Sinai. The "testimonies" are the individual commandments of the Lord.

25:11. The thought of God's requirements makes David aware of his shortcomings. He prays for pardon and bases his petition on God's name, i.e., his revelation of himself as the God of mercy.

25:12-14. Yahweh will teach one who fears him "in the way he shall choose," i.e., what course to take in circumstances of doubt or difficulty. That man will prosper. His posterity after him shall inherit the land. "The secret of Yahweh" is with those who fear him, i.e., his intimate friendship and secret counsel (cf. Amos 3:7).

25:15. The psalmist's eyes are "ever towards Yahweh," i.e., in the attitude of expectant prayer. He was confident that the Lord would pluck his feet out of the net, i.e., release him from the entanglements and perplexities of life, whether due to his own mistakes or to the hostility of his enemies.

25:16-17. David asks that God turn his face of mercy unto him because he is "desolate," i.e., without other friend or helper. His troubles have multiplied. He needs deliverance from his distresses.

25:18. Sin is viewed as a burden which causes affliction and travail. He asks that this burden might be removed.

25:19-20. David's enemies are many and vicious. He calls upon the Lord to "keep" his soul and deliver him from these enemies. He asks that he not be put to shame because he trusts only in the Lord.

25:21. David asks that his single-hearted devotion to God and his honorable conduct toward men be as it were guardian angels at his side. He does not pray on the basis of his own merits, but on his total dependence upon God.

25:22. A concluding prayer for the nation may have been added to this psalm to make it more suitable for use in public worship.

B. In Godly Confidence (Ps 26).

At what time David penned these words cannot be determined with certainty. The psalm seems to have come from a period of national calamity. Some terrible fate is about to befall both the righteous and the wicked. In the previous psalm David contrasted his character with the character of God and he confessed his sin. Here he compares his character with that of the godless and he professes his sincerity.

This psalm consists of two prayers for vindication with reasons attached to support the petition. In the first (vv. 1-7) he grounds his request in his godly walk; in the second (vv. 8-12), in his devoted worship. The point of both petitions is to request that he may not share the premature fate of the wicked.

26:1. "Judge me" means "do me justice." David wants God to show him to be in the right, to vindicate his integrity by discriminating between him and wicked men. "Integrity" is sincerity of purpose and single-hearted devotion to the Lord. Such had been the rule of his life.

26:2. God already knows David, but he nonetheless offers himself fearlessly for a fresh scrutiny. His conscience is clear. If any sin remained in his heart, he was perfectly willing to have it purged away. Three verbs are used to express the thoroughness of the scrutiny: "examine me," "prove me," and "try me."

26:3. David's prayer is first of all grounded in the lovingkindness and faithfulness of Yahweh. These wonderful attributes were the object of his constant meditation, the daily experience of his life.

26:4-5. David offers proof of his integrity. He did not "sit with vain persons," i.e., he did not have prolonged involvement with them. "Men of vanity" live hollow lives based on unreality. David would have no association with hypocrites. He hated the congregation of evildoers and shunned it.

26:6-7. David would wash his hands to symbolize his innocence before taking his place in the ring of worshipers about the altar. There in public worship he would make known his thanksgiving to the Lord by declaring all his wondrous works.

26:8. David loved the house of God, the sanctuary where Yahweh dwelt among his people (Exod 25:8f.). Yahweh's "glory" is his manifested presence, of which the ark was the outward symbol.

26:9-10. Because of his genuine love of worship, David asks again that he might be spared from the fate of sinners. Such a prayer would be natural in a situation where some pestilence was striking down the righteous and the wicked indiscriminately. The sinners are described as "men of blood" because they do not hesitate to employ violence and murder to further their ends. "In whose hands is mischief" suggests that they deliberately plan and execute crime. Their right hand is full of bribes which they take to pervert justice. Nobles and men in authority are in view here.

26:11. With such evildoers David contrasts himself. Should his life be spared, his purpose will be to continue to walk in integrity. Therefore, he asks that Yahweh might "redeem" him from the fate of the wicked, and "be gracious" to him.

26:12. By faith David views his prayer as already granted. He has traversed the rough and gloomy path; now he stands in the open plain, where there is no more fear of stumbling or sudden assault. Hence he can render public thanksgiving to the Lord.

C. In Time of Attack (Ps 27).

David is the writer, but the occasion is not clear. An ancient tradition assigned this psalm to the turbulent period before David was anointed king over all Israel. Some modern scholars have suggested that this psalm comes from the time of Absalom's rebellion. The psalm contains (1) a testimony of faith (vv. 1-6); (2) the testing of faith (vv. 7-12); and (3) the triumph of faith (vv. 13-14). The radical change of mood following v. 6 has caused some to suggest that two separate psalms have here been combined into one.

27:1. With Yahweh on his side, David knows no fear. The Lord illuminates the darkness of trouble, anxiety, and danger. He is the psalmist's "salvation" and "stronghold," i.e., defense against all assaults.

27:2. David compares his enemies to wild beasts, eager to devour him. They stumble and fall in the effort.

27:3. Though he was often exposed to war, David was full of confidence. His faith banished fear.

27:4. David's chief desire in life was to be a guest in the house of Yahweh, i.e., the tabernacle which was God's temple or palace. There he could "behold," i.e., see with the eye of faith, "the beauty of Yahweh," i.e., his gracious kindness and loving character. David wished to "inquire" in Yahweh's temple, i.e., to seek the answers to spiritual mysteries.

27:5. One who abides in the house of God as his guest is secure from danger as one who is sheltered from heat and storm, or one who is safe from assault in some inaccessible rock fortress.

27:6. In the immediate future David anticipated not only protection, but victory over his enemies. In the "tabernacle" he would offer joyous sacrifices and sing praises to the Lord. The reference seems to be to the tent which David erected for the ark on Mt. Zion (2 Sam 6:17).

27:7-9. Here the psalm changes abruptly to plaintive and anxious supplication. While David had accepted the invitation to seek the face of the Lord, God seemed to be on the verge of hiding his face from him. Yahweh had been his help in past trials. Surely God cannot have changed.

27:10-11. Though he is friendless and forsaken as a deserted child, Yahweh would adopt him and care for him. God's love is stronger than that of the closest human relations. If David follows the course of life designed for him by God he will be safe. He prays that this way might be like a path along a level open plain, free from pitfalls and places where enemies may lurk in ambush.

27:12-14. David faced "false witnesses" who slandered him with cruel intent. He would have given up had he not had strong faith that he would continue to see "the goodness of Yahweh" in the land of the living. He refers here to this life on earth in contrast to Sheol, the abode of the dead. David encourages himself to be patient. Here faith rebukes faintheartedness.

D. In Time of Heavenly Silence (Ps 28).

Ps 28 was written by David, apparently during a time of national calamity. The flight from Absalom has been suggested as the occasion. The psalm consists of four strophes: (1) invocation (vv. 1-2); (2) supplication (vv. 3-5); (3) exultation (vv. 6-7); and (4) intercession (vv. 8-9).

28:1. David appeals to Yahweh as his "rock," the ground of his confidence. He asks the Lord not to turn aside from him as though he did not hear. If Yahweh remains silent, David believes that he will become "like those that go down into the pit," i.e., the dying or the dead. The "pit" is Sheol, the abode of the dead.

28:2. David uses a stronger word for "cry," one which means *to cry for help*. The gesture of lifting up the hands in prayer was the outward symbol of the uplifted heart. The exact posture of the hands in prayer (e.g., folded at the chest, or lifted over the head) remains uncertain. "The holy oracle" was the most sacred part of the tabernacle/temple where the ark was housed. The Old Testament worshiper faced the temple as he prayed to the Lord.

28:3. David prays that he may be distinguished from the wicked, and that they may be judged as they deserved. He asks that God might not "draw" him away as a criminal might be dragged off to execution. The "wicked" that he has in mind are those who profess "peace" with their neighbors, but who plot mischief in their hearts against them.

28:4. David prays that Yahweh might openly convict false and wicked men by manifesting his righteous judgments upon them, and punishing them as they deserve. This verse contains no vindictive craving for personal revenge.

28:5. The wicked are atheists in practice if not in profession. They deny that Yahweh governs the world. They refuse to discern his working in creation or in providence. Unbelief was the root sin in their lives. For this reason God will "break them down" rather than "build them up."

28:6-7. The psalmist breaks forth in thanksgiving. His prayer has been answered. He now knows by experience that Yahweh is his "strength" and "shield." David's trust in God was rewarded with help. He can now rejoice and sing.

28:8-9. The Lord is a strength unto his people. He is a "stronghold" of "salvation" (the Hebrew is plural, indicating manifold deliverance) to "his anointed," i.e., Israel's king. David calls upon Yahweh to "save" and "bless" his "inheritance," i.e., Israel (cf. Deut 4:20). He asks God to "feed" his people as a shepherd might care for his sheep. Finally, he asks that God might "lift up," i.e., carry them as a shepherd carries his sheep or a father carries his child.

E. The God of the Thunderstorm (Ps 29).

Ps 29 was written by David, but the specific occasion is uncertain. The placement of the psalm here is most appropriate. David raised his "voice" in supplication to Yahweh in 28:2; now the "voice" of God responds. Both psalms have similar conclusions.

The core of Ps 29 is a description of a terrible thunderstorm (vv. 3-9). This description is set between two stanzas of two verses each. The first of these (vv. 1-2) is an introductory call to worship; the last (vv. 10-11) is a concluding assurance of blessing.

29:1-2. David calls upon the "sons of God," i.e., angels (cf. Job 1:6; 2:2) to celebrate the glory of Yahweh. They are called upon to "give," i.e., ascribe or attribute, "glory and strength." The angels should confess and proclaim the glory which is due "his name," i.e., the glory which he reveals to the world. As the priests in the earthly temple are clothed in holy garments (Exod 28:2), so David calls upon these servants in the heavenly temple to so adorn themselves.

29:3-4. The particular occasion which is the basis of the opening call to praise is the exhibition of divine power in a thunderstorm. This "voice of Yahweh" is heard in the pealing of the thunder above the "many waters," i.e., the waters collected in the dense masses of storm-clouds. Not Yahweh's voice alone, but Yahweh himself is there upon those waters. Yahweh is thus depicted riding upon the clouds (cf. 18:9ff.).

29:5-6. In the storm the great cedars, symbols of that which is noblest and strongest in the forest, come crashing down. Mt. Lebanon and Mt. Sirion (i.e., Hermon; see Deut 3:9) seem to "skip about," i.e., shake, like a calf or wild ox.

29:7. The voice of Yahweh "divides the flames of fire." This is a poetical description of the forked lightnings darting from the cloud.

29:8. From the mountains of the far north, the storm sweeps down to the "wilderness of Kadesh" in the distant south.

29:9. The voice of Yahweh makes the hinds calve prematurely, in fear. The storm strips the forests bare of branches, leaves, and bark. Meanwhile in his heavenly temple the angelic worshipers (cf. vv. 1-2) are chanting praise as they witness this manifestation of Yahweh's glory.

29:10. The storm reminds David of that great Flood (*mabbul*) of Genesis. At that time God took his seat on his throne in order to execute that memorable judgment. If Yahweh was sovereign over that worldwide catastrophe, he is in control of all lesser storms since. He sits as king forever.

29:11. For his people Yahweh is not a God of terror. For them all ends in peace. The words "with peace" are like a rainbow of promise across the dark storm cloud of Ps 29. The psalm opened by revealing the throne of God in heaven surrounded by the praise of the angelic hosts. It ends on earth with God's people, blessed with peace even in the midst of the most awesome manifestations of his power.

ENDNOTES

1. The other *mikhtam* psalms have been grouped together in Pss 56–60.

2. Another explanation of *mikhtam* traces the word to a root which means "hidden." Thus a *mikhtam* would be a secret, mysterious psalm.

3. A.F. Kirkpatrick, *The Book of Psalms*, in The Cambridge Bible for Schools and Colleges (Cambridge: University Press, 1910), p. 79.

4. The term "troop" is used of the Amalekites three times in 1 Sam 30 (vv. 8,15,23).

5. *'Eloah* is the singular of the more common *'Elohim*. The singular is used frequently in Job, but in only three other passages in the Psalter: 50:22; 114:7; 139:19.

6. Kirkpatrick, *Psalms*, p. 100.

7. In a passional psalm there is extreme suffering. Other passional psalms are 35, 41, 55, 69, and 109.

8. The Hebrew text could be translated "like a lion, my hands and feet." Jewish commentators prefer this rendering which they take to mean that the enemies are mangling him as lions do their prey. The rendering *"pierced"* is supported by the ancient Septuagint, Vulgate and Syriac versions of the Old Testament.

9. The other eight acrostic psalms are 9–10, 25, 34, 37, 111, 112, 119, and 145.

CHAPTER TWELVE

The Experiences of the Redeemed
Psalms 30-41

The next series of psalms depicts the reaction of the people of God to the revelation of the deliverer in the preceding series. Here is the testimony of faith to the announcement of salvation. Here is a fuller appreciation of divine grace.

EXPRESSING GRATITUDE TO GOD
Psalms 30-34

Gratitude is the dominant element in Pss 30-34. The successful petition of heavenly grace can only result in thanksgiving.

A. For Deliverance (Ps 30).

David wrote Ps 30 on the occasion of the dedication of the "house of God." The reference is probably to the dedication of the site of the temple (1 Chr 21:26; 22:1). The psalm has four closely related parts: (1) praise (vv. 1-5); (2) confession (vv. 6-7); (3) supplication (vv. 11-12); and (4) testimony.

30:1. God had drawn up David from the depths of trouble. His death would have given his enemies occasion to rejoice; but that had not happened. So David expresses his determination to "exalt" Yahweh, i.e., extol his attributes.

30:2-3. Yahweh had "healed" David of some terrible sickness. His recovery was as life from the dead, a veritable resurrection from Sheol, the abode of the dead.

30:4. The godly are invited to join in thanksgiving, in view of those attributes of Yahweh which David recently had experienced. The thanksgiving would be "a memorial of his holiness" for the mercy and faithfulness in which Yahweh had manifested his holiness.

30:5. The adversity which results from God's anger lasts only for a moment, but his favor endures for length of days. The night of weeping inevitably gives way to the morning of singing for those who belong to him.

30:6. David confesses that carnal pride sprang up during the days of his good fortune. He forgot his dependence upon God and came perilously close to the godless man's self-confident boast: "I shall not be moved."

30:7-8. Yahweh had made David's "mountain" (Zion) to stand strong in the day of his prosperity. Because of David's pride, however, the Lord had hidden his face, i.e., withdrawn his favor. David therefore had become "troubled," a strong word expressing the confusion and helplessness of terror. In his trouble David learned the source of his strength. He turned to God in prayer.

30:9-10. The prayer begins with a rhetorical question. What advantage would it be to the Lord to permit his blood to be shed or to allow him to go down to the pit? Should that happen Yahweh would lose the praise of his devoted servant. The "dust," i.e., the grave, does not praise God's "truth," i.e., faithfulness. The point of the verse is not to describe the conditions which exist in the afterlife, but to stress that death would remove one voice from the choir of those who sing God's praises on earth. Since it is in the best interest of the Lord to preserve the life of David, he asks for divine mercy and help.

30:11-12. His prayer had now been answered. His life had been preserved. Sorrow had been turned to joy, the mourner's garb (sackcloth) replaced by festal clothing. David anticipates singing praise to the Lord "forever," i.e., for the rest of the days of his life. David's "glory" here is his soul or spirit.

B. For Lovingkindness (Ps 31).

Ps 31 was written by David most probably during the period of his persecution by Saul. The psalm may reflect his experience with the town of Keilah (1 Sam 23). It depicts the ebb and flow of faith during a period of deep distress. It has three main divisions: (1) sincere prayer of faith based on past experience (vv. 1-8); (2) urgent pleading because of present distress (vv. 9-18); and (3) grateful celebration of God's goodness (vv. 19-24).

31:1. David put his trust in God. He asks that he would never be "ashamed," i.e., be disappointed, by finding that his trust was vain. To desert his servant would be inconsistent with Yahweh's righteousness.

31:2-3. David asks that God might be his "strong rock" or "fortress-house" as he had been in the past. For the sake of "his name," i.e., his self-revelation, Yahweh would show himself to be all that he had revealed himself to be.

31:4. David compares his enemies to hunters or fowlers who would throw a net over him. He asks that God would rescue him from that net.

31:5. David commits his life spirit into God's care. He states a double ground for his act of trust: (1) his own past experience of God's redemption; and (2) the known character of Yahweh as God of faithfulness. To "redeem" here means primarily to deliver from temporal danger. The first line of this verse was uttered by Jesus just before his death (Luke 23:46).

31:6. David disclaims all sympathy and fellowship with those who worship false gods. The idols are "vanities of nothingness," i.e., they have no real existence, and delude their worshipers. David, however, knows Yahweh to be the "God of truth," i.e., the God who constantly proves his faithfulness.

31:7-8. An entreaty based on past experience. David asks that he might experience the joy that flows from the lovingkindness of God. In the past God had seen his affliction. He had not permitted David to be surrendered into the hand of his enemies. Yahweh had made

David's feet to stand "in a large place," i.e., had enabled him to move and act with freedom.

31:9-10. The tone of the psalm changes. David again finds himself in deep distress which has affected him soul and body. He is grief-stricken. He feels his pain in his "bones," which poetically represent the entire body. He attributes his weak physical condition to some unspecified sin which called for chastisement through suffering.

31:11-12. David feels totally isolated. His enemies hold him in disdain. His neighbors avoid him lest any sign of sympathy bring upon them similar divine retribution. As a dead man passes out of men's minds, so he has been forgotten. He is like a "broken" (lit., perishing) vessel, contemptuously flung aside and remembered no more.

31:13. David thinks he hears the enemies plotting against him on every side. Jeremiah used these very words to describe his plight (Jer 20:10).

31:14-15. When men turned from David, he turned to God. He recognized that his "times," i.e., the vicissitudes of his life, were under divine control. Thus he can appeal for deliverance from the hand of his enemies.

31:16. David asks that God might again let his face shine upon him, i.e., bless him. He pleads the lovingkindness of God as the ground of his appeal.

31:17-18. Again David asks that he not be made ashamed that he has placed his trust in God (cf. v. 1). Instead he asks that the wicked be put to shame, i.e., be shown to be totally wrong in their attitude toward God. Let those wicked ones who arrogantly speak against the righteous be silenced in the grave.

31:19-20. An interval has elapsed; David's prayer has been answered; the danger is past. God's goodness is like a treasure stored up, and at the proper time brought out and used for them that take refuge in him. This goodness is displayed "before the sons of men," i.e., publicly. Yahweh will hide the faithful in his presence. There the darkness of evil cannot penetrate.

31:21. David offers thanksgiving for deliverance which he has experienced. The Lord is praised because he had "made marvelous his lovingkindness" to David. The words "in a strong city" have been taken as a metaphorical reference to trouble generally. Those who take the words literally think the reference could be to David's escape from Keilah.

31:22. David admits that his faith had wavered during the hour of trial. Nonetheless, God had responded positively to his prayer.

31:23-24. David concludes by exhorting the faithful to love Yahweh because he "keeps faithfulness" and "rewards" the arrogant with judgment. Those who "hope in Yahweh" will be strengthened by him in the inner man. Therefore the faithful can be courageous.

C. For Forgiveness (Ps 32).

Ps 32 is the second of the seven so-called "penitential" psalms and the first of thirteen *"maskil"* psalms. A *"maskil"* is a psalm that gives instruction. The psalm was written by David almost certainly after his great sin with Bathsheba (2 Sam 11-12). Ps 51 was probably David's first prayer for pardon. This psalm fulfills the promise stated in 51:13 to instruct others about God's ways of forgiveness.

The main body of this psalm consists of two stanzas, one in which David addresses the Lord (vv. 3-7) and one in which the Lord speaks to David (vv. 8-9). An introduction (vv. 1-2) expresses the overflowing joy of realizing that sins have been forgiven. A conclusion (vv. 10-11) draws the stark contrast between the wicked and the trustful.

32:1-2. The person who experiences God's forgiveness is "blessed" or happy. This is the second beatitude of the Psalter (cf. Ps 1:1). Three words describe various aspects of sin. *Transgression*: rebellion, breaking away from God. *Sin*: missing the mark, wandering from the path. *Iniquity*: depravity, moral distortion. Forgiveness is also triply described as (1) the taking away of a burden; (2) covering, so that the foulness of sin no longer offends the eye of the holy God; and (3) the canceling of a debt, which is no longer held against the offender. The condition of God's forgiveness is absolute sincerity. There must be "no guile" in the spirit, no attempt to deceive self or God.

32:3-4. For a time David refused to acknowledge his sin to himself or to God. During that time the hand of the Lord was heavy upon him. He suffered a terrible illness. His "bones," i.e., his body seemed to grow old overnight. A fever burned up his vital body fluids. The term *"Selah"* indicates a musical interlude. This helped to underscore David's distress of mind.

32:5. Finally David acknowledged his sin to God, and he was pardoned. The form of the sentence emphasizes the immediateness of the pardon. The second person pronoun is emphatic. Another musical interlude (*Selah*) may have expressed the joy of forgiveness.

32:6. Based upon his experience, David exhorts sinners to call upon Yahweh "in a time of finding," i.e., in a time of acceptance. One who finds forgiveness will have nothing to fear when the flood of divine judgment is poured out. In that day the forgiven will find Yahweh to be a rock of refuge.

32:7. Forgiven David is now confident that Yahweh would be his hiding place in time of trouble. All about him the godly rejoice over his deliverance.

32:8. Surely God must here be the speaker, not the psalmist. Yahweh will now guide David. He will keep his ever-wakeful eye of providence upon him.

32:9. A warning is addressed to all not to resist God's will, nor neglect his instruction. Animals must be controlled and compelled by force to learn to submit to man's will. If man will not draw near to God and freely choose to obey his will he lowers himself to the level of a brute. God will treat him accordingly.

32:10-11. The wicked face "many sorrows," i.e., calamities and chastisements. Those who trust in Yahweh will be compassed about with his lovingkindness. For this reason the righteous can be glad and rejoice.

D. For Providence (Ps 33).

This congregational hymn of praise is closely related to the previous psalm. For this reason it has no title. That David is the writer is reflected in the Septuagint version. The historical occasion is not known, but it probably was written after some national deliverance. Following an introduction (vv. 1-2) the psalm focuses on (1) God in creation (vv. 4-9); and (2) God in history (vv. 10-19). The last three verses (vv. 20-22) form the conclusion which is a declaration of trust.

33:1-3. David exhorts all men to praise Yahweh. Similarity between v. 1 and the last verse of the preceding psalm indicates the connection between the two poems. The harp and psaltery were both stringed instruments, differing somewhat in form. Fresh mercies require new expressions of gratitude. The "loud voice" could refer to the music itself, or to the accompanying shouts of joy.

33:4-5. Yahweh's word and works are always in keeping with his character, namely, upright, righteous and just. The whole earth reflects the lovingkindness of Yahweh.

33:6. The "breath of his mouth" is synonymous with "the word of Yahweh." God had merely to will and the universe came into being. The "host" of the heavens are the heavenly bodies.

33:7. The separation of land and water (cf. Gen 1:9f.). The verb tense suggests that God continues to maintain the relationship between land and water. The "heap" probably refers to the appearance of the sea from the shore. The "storehouses" of the deep are the subterranean abysses where masses of water are stored (cf. Gen 7:11).

33:8-9. Man should stand in awe of the almighty creator. By simple divine fiat he created all that exists. He merely issued a command and the material universe stood before him ready to do his bidding. The third person pronoun is emphatic in v. 9.

33:10 11. Yahweh is sovereign over the earth. He frustrates the plans of the heathen. Yahweh's counsel, however, stands fast like his work of creation.

33:12. The psalmist now turns to Israel, the chosen people, Yahweh's inheritance among the nations. He pronounces a beatitude upon them (cf. Deut 33:29).

33:13-15. The God of Israel is omniscient. Since he created man, he must know man's heart. He continues to "form the hearts" of those who are born into this world. All are in some sense subservient to his plan and purpose.

33:16-19. Earthly resources—great armies, physical strength, a powerful horse—are deceptive. They cannot provide deliverance. True security is found in Yahweh's providential watch care. He aids those who "fear" him and "wait for his lovingkindness." He can deliver from violent death by war.

33:20-22. The people respond to the opening invitation to praise God. They "wait" on the Lord, "trust" in his holy name, i.e., his revelation of himself. They recognize him as their "help" and "shield." Therefore they can ask for his lovingkindness to be upon them.

E. For Salvation (Ps 34).

This acrostic psalm was written by David when he was a fugitive at the court of "Abimelech" of Gath. This must be a dynastic title (like Pharaoh) of the kings of Gath. The king's personal name was Achish. David discovered that he was in jeopardy in Gath, and so feigned madness so that his antagonists would leave him alone (1 Sam 21). Ps 34 has two main divisions. In the first the psalmist assumes the role of a joyous singer (vv. 1-10); in the second, that of a serious teacher (vv. 11-22).

34:1-2. David expresses his determination to praise God continually. "In Yahweh"—emphatic by position in the sentence—he will make his boast. He claims the sympathy of those who have learned humility in the school of suffering.

34:3-4. David invites the humble to join him in thanksgiving for deliverance. Man "magnifies" Yahweh by acknowledging and celebrating his greatness. He "exalts" God's name by confessing that he is supreme over all.

34:5-6. Such experience of Yahweh's help is not limited to the psalmist. Those who look unto him in earnest faith "are brightened," i.e., the light of the Lord illuminates their darkness. Their faces "shall not be put to blush" with disappointment. "This afflicted man" could refer to the poet himself, or to others who had been examples of God's protecting care.

34:7. The "angel of Yahweh" is a manifestation of God in the presence of his people (cf. Exod 23:20ff.). He is mentioned in only one other passage in the Psalter (cf. 35:5f.). He protects those who fear the Lord.

34:8. David invites everyone to "taste," i.e., put God to the test, and discover for themselves that he is "good." The strong man who takes refuge in him is "blessed" or happy.

34:9-10. The saints (holy ones) of God lack for nothing. The strongest beasts may lack food from time to time; not so God's people.

34:11. The fear of Yahweh includes reverence, and the conduct which reverence for God requires.

34:12-14. One who desires a long and happy life must guard his tongue from any evil, especially "guile" (deceit). He must depart from evil, and do good. He must "pursue" peace even when prolonged effort is required to apprehend it.

34:15-18. Yahweh watches over the righteous. He is attentive to their cries for help. "The face of Yahweh"—the manifestation of his presence—is against evildoers. In his wrath he will cut off even the name by which they might be remembered. The Lord is near those who have a contrite heart.

34:19-20. The righteous are not exempt from afflictions; but Yahweh sees them through each trial. He preserves the "bones," i.e., their whole being. Not one of his bones would be broken (John 19:36).

34:21-22. While the righteous are rescued out of all evils, evil brings the wicked to their death. Those who hate the righteous shall be held guilty by the Lord. Those who trust in the Lord shall be declared innocent.

DEALING WITH PROBLEMS
Psalms 35–39

The previous group of psalms celebrates the deliverance of the righteous out of difficulties. The next five psalms deal with specific problems which the righteous must face in their pilgrimage.

A. Attack by Ingrates (Ps 35).

Ps 35 was written by David, most probably during the period of Saul's persecution. Malicious courtiers stirred up the king against David. Against such men David directs his appeals to Yahweh. At the same time he solemnly protests his innocence of the charge of disloyalty. The psalm consists of three strophes, each ending on a vow of thanksgiving: (1) the intrigue (vv. 1-10), (2) ingratitude (vv. 11-18), and (3) inhumanity (vv. 19-28) of David's enemies.

35:1-3. David appeals to Yahweh to arm himself with "shield and buckler" as his champion. He should draw out his spear and "battle-axe" (NASB) and "stop the way" against his persecutors, i.e., stop them in their tracks.

35:4-6. David prays that those who pursued him might be disappointed in their aim, and that their attack might be repulsed. Then he prays that the enemies might be put to headlong flight as chaff is blown by the wind. He asks that these enemies be driven down a dark and slippery track, where they can neither see nor keep their footing. The angel of Yahweh (cf. 34:7) would then smite them down as they vainly tried to escape.

35:7-8. The enmity against David is not justified. A hunter's net and pitfalls are used as metaphors for the insidious character of their plots. David asks that their plans rebound upon them to their destruction. The plural "enemies" of v. 7 becomes focused on a single enemy in v. 8.

35:9-10. David rejoices over deliverance. The bodily frame ("all my bones") feels the joy. His experience has confirmed his faith that Yahweh is incomparable in power and goodness.

35:11-13. Enemies accused David of crimes of which he had no knowledge. Their treatment of him "bereaved" David's soul. The persecution of David is unjustified. He had showed sympathy when they were in trouble. He had prayed for their recovery, humbling himself before God with mourning and fasting. David says his prayer "kept returning" to his "bosom." This probably means that God rewarded him for his thoughtful prayer even though those he prayed for did not.

35:14-16. David had displayed the deepest grief for these enemies, a grief such as one might show for a friend or relative. These enemies, however, had rejoiced over his adversity. Like beasts of prey, they shredded his reputation with their vicious slander. With rage "they gnashed" on David "with their teeth," i.e., ripped him apart, "like godless jesters at a feast" (NASB).

35:17-18. David cannot understand how God can continue to look on his desperation and do nothing. He cries out for help. He pledges that he will give God public thanksgiving for this intervention.

35:19. David asks that his enemies not be able to rejoice over his misfortune, nor signal one another of their satisfaction with his fate by winking the eye. The words "They hate me without a cause" were quoted by Jesus as "fulfilled" in himself (John 15:25).

35:20-21. The enemies falsely had accused peaceful men of being troublers of Israel. With their open mouths they mocked the fall of the man whose skyrocketing fortunes had excited their envy.

35:22-24. Yahweh had seen the taunts of the enemies. He asks that God be not "silent," i.e., inactive, that God not make himself distant from him. He asks God to "awake" to his cause, to do him justice according to his righteousness.

35:25-26. David prays that the enemies might be frustrated in their wicked plans to "swallow" him, i.e., destroy all trace of his existence. Let those enemies be "clothed with shame."

35:27-28. David asks that those that welcomed the vindication of his innocence might be able to celebrate his deliverance. Those friends would magnify Yahweh who had shown delight in the welfare of his servant. David would join in the praise of Yahweh's righteousness "all the day long."

B. Attitudes of the Ungodly (Ps 36).

The occasion of this Davidic psalm is unknown. The only other psalm with the title "David the servant of Yahweh" is Ps 18. The three main divisions of Ps 36 focus on the sinner, the Savior, and the saint. The outline might be: (1) the wickedness of the wicked (vv. 1-4); (2) the graciousness of God (vv. 5-9); and (3) the confidence of the believer (vv. 10-12).

36:1-2. Transgression is personified and "utters its oracle" to the heart of the ungodly. The wicked person has made rebellion his god, and it is a lying spirit within him. Transgression persuades the wicked man that there is no need for him to dread God's judgments.

36:3-4. The fruits of reckless atheism are now indicated. The unbeliever's words are evil and deceitful. He has ceased to make any effort to follow the path of wisdom and goodness. He plans evil upon his bed at night. He has consciously chosen the wrong path; wrong excites no abhorrence in him.

36:5. For his part, David focuses on the character of God. Yahweh's lovingkindness and faithfulness reach to the heavens, i.e., they cannot be measured.

36:6. Yahweh's "righteousness"—his faithfulness to his character and covenant—is like the "the mountains of God," i.e., firm, unchanged, majestically conspicuous. God's judgment are "a great deep," i.e., mysterious, unfathomable, inexhaustible as the vast subterranean abyss of waters. The lower animals are the objects of God's care as well as man.

36:7. The lovingkindness of God is a precious treasure to David. The use of *God* rather than *Yahweh* here suggests that the love of God extends to all men, not just Israel. The "sons of man" take refuge in their loving creator.

36:8. God is gracious host as well as protector. He royally entertains his guests with "fatness" and "the river" of his delights. The metaphor is derived from the sacrificial meal, in which God receives the worshiper at his table.

36:9. God is the source of life and light. From him springs all that constitutes life, physical and spiritual—all that makes for true happiness.

36:10. David prays for the continuance of God's lovingkindness and righteousness, i.e., faithfulness, to those who "know" the Lord, i.e., have an intimate relationship with him. Such are also called "upright in heart."

36:11. He asks that he might not be trampled underfoot by proud oppressors, or driven from his home by wicked violence. The first four verses indicate that the psalmist was in danger of falling victim to these ruthless oppressors.

36:12. With the eye of faith David beholds the certain ruin of those who work iniquity. Such will be thrown down, and shall never be able to rise again.

C. Adversity of the Righteous (Ps 37).

David wrote this psalm, probably late in his life. It is acrostic in structure and didactic in tone. The acrostic is nearly perfect. Ps 37 grapples with the issue of theodicy, i.e., why do the wicked prosper and the righteous experience adversity. The psalm has four symmetrical divisions of 11,9,11,9 verses respectively: (1) counsel to troubled souls (vv. 1-11); (2) the fate of the wicked (vv. 12-20); (3) the future of the righteous (vv. 21-31); and (4) the final contrasts (vv. 32-40).

37:1-2. The psalm opens with an exhortation against discontent and envy over the prosperity of the wicked because their prosperity would be short-lived, like grass of the field.

37:3-4. The antidote to envious discontent is patient trust in Yahweh, and perseverance in the path of duty. The faithful should continue to "dwell in the land," i.e., the land of promise. It would seem that poor Israelites, driven from their homes by the powerful, were tempted to seek their fortunes in foreign lands. Thereby they would forfeit their national and religious privileges. To "delight" in the Lord is to take pleasure in his service, to enjoy his fellowship. Such as "delight" in the Lord shall be rewarded with their heart's desire, i.e., they will draw ever closer to their God.

37:5-6. David urges believers to "commit" (lit., roll) their way unto Yahweh. The believer should transfer all anxiety about life to the Lord "and he [emphatic] will do it," i.e., the Lord will take care of the situation. Whereas the just cause of the psalmist has been hidden, Yahweh would make it shine forth like the sun rising out of the darkness of the night. The rightness of his cause will become as clear as the full light of the noonday.

37:7-9. The remedy for impatience is to "rest in" or "be silent to" Yahweh in the calmness of faith. One should not be angry over the prosperity enjoyed by the wicked. Discontent is not only foolish and useless, but dangerous. It may lead one to deny God's providence and to cast his lot with the wicked. In the end, however, the evildoers will be "cut off," i.e., destroyed. The true Israel will then have undisturbed enjoyment of their inheritance in the Land of Promise.

37:10-11. The thought of the complete destruction of the wicked and the blessed inheritance of the meek is amplified. Here the inheritance of the land is equated with the enjoyment of abundant peace (cf. Matt 5:5).

37:12-13. Like a fierce beast the wicked gnashes his teeth in anticipation of seizing and devouring "the just." Yahweh, however, laughs, because he foresees the punishment of the wicked. "His day" is the day of appointed retribution for the sinner.

37:14-15. The poor, needy and "the upright of the way" were defenseless before the weapons of the wicked.

37:16-17. Better is "the little" possessed by a righteous person than the abundance (lit., tumults), i.e., ostentatious opulence, of the wicked. While Yahweh upholds the righteous, the "arms," i.e., power, of the wicked will finally be broken.

37:18-19. Yahweh cares for the godly. He knows "the days" of the upright, i.e., their lives are under his watchful care. Their posterity will continue in possession of the ancestral inheritance. In times of evil (calamity) such as famine, they will still find satisfaction in life.

37:20. In the end, the wicked perish. The enemies of Yahweh will fade away like "the glory," i.e., beautiful flowers, of the pastures. They shall disappear as completely as smoke.

37:21-22. The wicked are brought to poverty. They are forced to borrow what they can never repay. The righteous person, on the other hand, has enough and to spare. He is generous with his bounty. The former condition proceeds directly from the curse of God, the latter from his blessing.

37:23-24. If Yahweh directs the steps of a person then he will delight in his way. When he stumbles in life he will not be "cast down," for Yahweh will uphold him with his hand (power).

37:25-26. In support of the preceding verses, David offers a personal observation. He had never seen the righteous permanently deserted by God, or his children reduced to homeless beggary. Quite the contrary. The righteous not only have abundance, but they know how to use it.

37:27-29. One who departs from evil has the hope that he, in the person of his descendants, will dwell forever in the land. Yahweh loves justice. He will not forsake his saints (holy ones). The "seed" (descendants) of the wicked, however, will be "cut off" (destroyed).

37:30-31. The believer is secure because the "law of his God is in his heart." Without wavering he pursues the path of right.

37:32-33. The wicked constantly watch for opportunities to harm the righteous. Yahweh, however, will not leave the righteous in the power of the wicked, will not allow them to be unjustly condemned.

37:34. One who "waits on Yahweh" may be downtrodden, but ultimately he will be exalted. The wicked, on the other hand, will be cut off or destroyed.

37:35-36. The wicked are transitory. David had observed the wicked temporarily flourishing like a great tree. Shortly thereafter passersby could find no trace of that once proud tree.

37:37-38. The upright one is destined for peace. Those who rebel against God will be destroyed. Without posterity they would be annihilated.

37:39-40. Yahweh is the stronghold of the righteous in time of trouble. Because of their trust in him, he will deliver them from the wicked.

D. Afflictions of Sin (Ps 38).

The third of the so-called "penitential" psalms was written by David, probably during the period of Absalom's revolt. The sin to which he alludes may be the folly of indulging his children which led to disastrous consequences to David personally, and to his kingdom as well. The phrase "to bring to remembrance" in the title appears also in the title of Ps 70. This psalm consists of eleven double verses. These divide into three parts, each beginning with an appeal to Yahweh. This produces the outline: (1) the sufferings caused by sin (vv. 1-8); (2) the separation caused by sin (vv. 9-14); and (3) an appeal for deliverance (vv. 15-22).

38:1-2. David feels that he has experienced a chastisement of an angry judge, not a loving father. God's arrows of judgment had penetrated him. The reference is to some pain and sickness. Blow after blow from God's hand had fallen upon him.

38:3-4. David acknowledges that his own sin is the cause of the divine indignation. While God's wrath assaults him from without, the fever of sin consumes him from within. His sins are like a flood which overwhelms; like a burden which crushes.

38:5-6. David's festering and putrid "wounds" refer metaphorically to his scourging by God because of his "foolishness," i.e., sin. David is bent with pain. He goes about in the guise of a mourner.

38:7-10. His sickness has caused fever and inflammation. The inward moaning of his heart finds utterance in loud cries of distress. God knows the needs of David. His eyes are dim and dull with weakness and weeping.

38:11-12. David's friends stood aloof from him, treating him as if he were a leper. At the same time, pitiless enemies beset him with deadly snares and slanders.

38:13-14. Conscious of guilt David must keep silent and commit his cause to God. He had to exercise patience as though he had not heard the attacks on him. He could offer no arguments in his defense before God.

38:15-16. David could face the opposition of his enemies because his hope was in God. He was confident that God would answer his prayers for deliverance and thus refute the taunts of the enemies. The wicked always rejoice when the godly slip, for it confirms them in their ungodly lifestyle.

38:17-18. David is stumbling under the burden of his suffering. He confesses that sin is the cause of that suffering. He professes sorrow for that sin.

38:19-20. While he is weak, his enemies are vigorous. Their hatred of him is based on misrepresentations. He had endeavored to do good to these very men who now hate him. They were manifesting base ingratitude.

38:21-22. A final prayer. True repentance includes faith. David casts himself upon the mercy of God.

E. Agony of Unexpressed Grief (Ps 39).

This beautiful elegy was written by David, possibly during the period of Absalom's rebellion. It is definitely a sequel to the preceding psalm, and is related to Ps 62. David speaks throughout as one failing in strength. He expresses perplexity over the fact that ungodly men (e.g., Shimei) continue their evil with impunity. Ps 39 is organized in four thought movements: (1) the frustration of silence (vv. 1-3); (2) the brevity of life (vv. 4-6); (3) the comfort of hope (vv. 7-9); and (4) the cry for relief (vv. 10-13).

39:1-2. After meditation, David resolved to keep watch over thought, word and action. He fears that he may sin with his tongue by murmuring against God as he contrasts the prosperity of the wicked with his own circumstances. For this reason he kept absolutely silent, speaking neither good nor bad. The effort to suppress his feelings only aggravated his pain.

39:3. Silence proved impossible. The fire of passion could no longer be restrained from bursting into a flame of angry words.

39:4-5. David prays that he might realize how surely life must end, and how brief it must be at best. Thinking along these lines will cause him to know his frailty, i.e., his mortality. Life is but a "hand breadth," i.e., four fingers, half a span. Life is very short. Compared to the eternality of God, man's existence in the world amounts to nothing. At their very best, men are but a breath.

39:6. Man is an unsubstantial "phantom" (NASB) or shadow. Yet they are in constant turmoil over things which will not endure. He spends his days heaping up riches, but when he is dead someone else carries them off.

39:7. The Lord is the one stay in life. To him David turns. Nothing else was possible.

39:8-9. David prays to be delivered from the power of the sins which he regards as the cause of his present afflictions. The fool regards the sufferings of the godly as a mark of God's wrath, and taunts him accordingly. From this taunting David asks deliverance. He resigns himself to the will of God. He moves forward from the silence of bitterness to serene silence of the heart which submits to the will of God.

39:10-11. David asks that the "plague" of suffering might be removed because he is perishing under the blow of God's hand. Men are destroyed by God's chastisement as easily as the moth destroys a beautiful garment. Every man is only a transitory "breath."

39:12-13. David asks that Yahweh might take note of his tears and thus answer his prayers. Man is but a pilgrim passing through the earth which belongs to God. In this life man is God's guest, and David asks to be treated with the kindness extended to guests. Faced as he was with imminent death, David throws himself into the arms of God.

CONCLUSION
Psalms 40–41

Psalms 40–41 form an appropriate conclusion to Book One. Here the two major themes of the preceding psalms are displayed once again. In Ps 40 the heart of the redeemer is revealed; in Ps 41 the heart of men, both sinners and saints.

A. Past Deliverance and Present Distress (Ps 40).

Three verses from Ps 40 are quoted in Heb 10:5-7. According to the inspired apostle, in these verses Christ is speaking to the Father at the time he left heaven to come into the world. If Christ is the speaker in vv. 6-10—those quoted in Hebrews—then he probably should be regarded as the speaker throughout this psalm.[1]

David wrote this psalm either at the time of Absalom's rebellion, or the rebellion of Adonijah. Ps 40 speaks of a great (1) deliverance (vv. 1-4); (2) program (vv. 5-8); (3) message (vv. 9-10); (4) petition (vv. 11-13); (5) prediction (vv. 14-16); and (6) confidence (v. 17).

273

40:1. The Father inclined his ear and heard the cry of his Son. The image is that of one leaning forward to catch a faint or distant sound.

40:2. Messiah describes the ordeal which he had gone through as a horrible pit filled with clay in which there can be no firm footing. He was delivered from that experience, he regained his footing.

40:3-4. Messiah's joy after deliverance is expressed in song and praise. Many will take note of his victory and will come to fear Yahweh. A beautiful beatitude is pronounced on those who continue to trust Yahweh. Such do not look to arrogant rebels who spurn God.

40:5. Messiah praises the Father for his wonderful works. These acts are the product of God's incomparable wisdom respecting his people. Examples of divine beneficence are so numerous they cannot be counted.

40:6. On the eve of his descent into the world to provide the once-for-all sacrifice, Messiah indicates the attitude of God toward the hypocritical offerings being presented at the altar. Messiah speaks of his ears being "pierced" or "opened."[2] This is an allusion to submissive obedience to the Father (cf. Exod 21:1-6).

40:7-8. Messiah declares his intention to enter the world. He understood that in "the scroll of the book," i.e., the Old Covenant Scriptures, "it is written of me." The "book" specifically testified that Messiah would delight to do the will of the Father.

40:9-10. Christ proclaims the message of God in "the great congregation," either the whole of mankind, or among the people of God. He proclaims: (1) the righteousness, (2) faithfulness, (3) salvation, (4) lovingkindness, and (5) truth of God.

40:11. The unchangeableness of God's lovingkindness, and the truth of promises made to Messiah and through him are a solid ground of assurance that the Father would not withhold his tender mercies from the Son.

40:12. Since Messiah is the speaker, this verse should not be taken as a confession of sin but rather a description of what was done to the speaker. He is encompassed by evils. "My iniquities" are to be understood as "the iniquities done to me." The crimes committed against him had overwhelmed him: the unjust trials, the mockery, the buffeting, the scourging, the crown of thorns.

40:13-15. Messiah calls on the Father to aid him. He is confident regarding the fate of his enemies. On account of their shameful conduct with respect to Messiah, they would be desolate (cf. Matt 23:38).

40:16. While the enemies of Messiah face a bleak future, true worshipers rejoice and praise God.

40:17. Messiah describes himself in the midst of his suffering as afflicted and poor. Yet he knows the Father will remember him and make plans for his deliverance. He simply asks that God delay no longer in effecting the deliverance which he knows will be forthcoming.

B. Triumph over Trouble (Ps 41).

Ps 41 is another product of the pen of David, written probably during the rebellion by Absalom. This psalm has four divisions: (1) assurance of favor (vv. 1-3); (2) the sufferer's bed chamber (vv. 4-6); (3) the enemies' council chamber (vv. 7-9); and (4) appeal for restoration (vv. 10-12).

41:1-3. The last psalm in Book One begins like the first, with a beatitude. One is "blessed" who "considers" the poor (lit., the weak), i.e., shows compassion for them, in their day of calamity. David asks that the compassionate person not be given over to his enemies. Prayer becomes confidence that Yahweh would turn his sickness to health.

41:4-6. David presents his own case to the Lord. He asks for mercy. He regards his bodily ailment as the sign of spiritual disease. He wants healing of both. The enemies are anxiously awaiting his death and that of his posterity ("that his name perish"). Those who visit him feign friendship, but speak "vanity" or falsehood. During the visit they collect new information to turn against him in slander.

41:7-8. Outside the sickroom the enemies whisper their vicious speculations as to the cause of his illness. They speculate that David has a fatal disease caused by his wickedness. He will never leave his bed again.

41:9. His most trusted friend (lit. "the man of my peace"), who had eaten at the royal table, had "made great the heel" toward David, i.e., spurned him with brutal violence, exerted himself to trip up David and throw him down. The reference is probably to the betrayal of his trusted advisor Ahithophel who foreshadowed the treachery and fate of Judas (John 13:18).

41:10-12. David renews his prayer from v. 4. He is confident of God's favor and healing, that God would raise him up so that he, as the highest judicial official, might punish the traitor. His restoration will confirm his "integrity," i.e., his sincerity of purpose. He knows that he will be admitted to stand in the presence of the King of Kings "forever."

41:13. This doxology is not part of Ps 41, but stands here to mark the conclusion of Book One of the Psalter. For all of eternity let Yahweh be blessed. "Amen and Amen" means "so it is." This is the response of the congregation.

ENDNOTES

1. For a detailed discussion of the personal messianic interpretation of Ps 40, see James E. Smith, *What the Bible Teaches about the Promised Messiah* (Nashville: Nelson, 1993), pp. 113-121.

2. Hebrews 10:5, following the Septuagint, renders the clause: "a body you have prepared me." Where there is an ear, there is a body. The piercing of the ear was a token that a servant belonged wholly to his master. When the ears of the Messiah were pierced in love, God got his entire body.

CHAPTER THIRTEEN

Deliverance for the Estranged
Psalms 42-51

Book Two of the Psalter contains thirty-one psalms. In these psalms the name *'Elohim* (God) is used virtually to the exclusion of the name *Yahweh*. The overall theme of this second collection of psalms is "ruin and redemption." Sometimes Book Two is called the "Exodus" book of the Psalter because most of the illustrations are from Exodus, as those in Book One are from Genesis.

This second book of the Psalter is sometimes called the Korahitic book. The first eight psalms in this Book are attributed to the sons of Korah. Korah was the grandson of Kohath and great-grandson of Levi. He perished for his role in the rebellion against Moses at Kadesh-barnea. His family, however, escaped (Num 16; 26:11). The descendants of this infamous man came to hold important positions in Israel.

The Korahites were connected with temple music. Heman, one of David's three principal musicians, was a Korahite (1 Chr 6:31-33). His sons were leaders of fourteen out of the twenty-four courses of temple musicians (1 Chr 25:4ff.). In the days of Jehoshaphat they are mentioned as singers as well (2 Chr 20:19).

The Korahite psalms breathe a spirit of strong devotion to the temple, as one might expect. These psalms celebrate with enthusiastic pride the praise of Jerusalem as "the city of the Great King" which he had chosen for his own abode.

INTRODUCTION
Longing for Restoration
Psalms 42-43

As Book One began with a double psalm introduction, so also does Book Two. Pss 42-43 were originally one connected poem. The same circumstances appear to lie in the background of both. Both psalms have the same tone, spirit and language. The original poem probably was divided into two for devotional or liturgical purposes. Ps 42 emphasizes complaint; Ps 43 a prayer which supplements it. This division, however, was ancient. It appears in all the ancient versions of the Old Testament and in most Hebrew manuscripts.

Pss 42-43 were written by a Levite who had crossed the Jordan with David (v. 6). In the past he had been accustomed to conducting pilgrim companies up to Jerusalem for the great festivals. These psalms may be assigned to the time of Absalom's rebellion. They jointly constitute the second *"maskil"* psalm (cf. Ps 32).

Pss 42-43 consist of three stanzas of five verses, each ending with the same refrain: (1) the desire of his heart (42:1-5); (2) the description of his plight (42:6-10); and (3) the prayer for his deliverance (43:1-5).

42:1-2. The hind panting after water is a figure based on the sufferings of wild animals in a prolonged drought. The psalmist "thirsts" for the *living* God, as opposed to dead, impotent idols. This spiritual thirst is satisfied when the psalmist is able to "appear before God," i.e., visit the temple for worship.

42:3-4. Present sorrow is contrasted with past happiness. Tears take the place of his daily bread. The heathen taunt his plight, and the indifference or impotence of his God. In the past he had led pilgrims to Jerusalem for the festivals. The joyousness of these processions was proverbial. The God in whom he took such delight could not possibly have forsaken him in his personal exile.

42:5. Faith chides the despondent soul. To be "cast down" is to be bowed down like a mourner. He exhorts himself to "hope in God," i.e., to wait on him. He was confident that he would yet praise or thank God as in past times "for the help of his countenance." See also 42:11 and 43:5.

42:6. Overwhelmed with sorrow, the psalmist must turn to the Lord. He is cut off from the temple "in the land of Jordan and the Hermons." This would be in the vicinity of the town of Dan where the Jordan rises from the foothills of Mt. Hermon. The place is further pinpointed as "the hill Mizar," a spot otherwise unknown.

42:7. God is sending upon him one trouble after another. He is overwhelmed with a flood of misfortunes. The rushing waters nearby suggested this metaphor. The latter part of this verse was quoted by Jonah in his submarine prayer (Jonah 2:3).

42:8. The psalmist expresses the confidence that he will soon again experience the favor of God and give him thanks for his goodness. "Prayer" denotes any form of communion with God, but here predominantly thanksgiving. For one of the few times in Book Two the name Yahweh is used.

42:9-10. Though God has helped him in the past, he seems to have abandoned him in the present. God is still his "rock" (sela') or refuge. His enemies reproach him "with crushing in my bones," i.e., they stab him to the heart with their taunts. The "bones" in Hebrew poetry denote the whole physical organism. They are the seat of pain.

43:1. A prayer for deliverance grounded upon God's relation to him. "Judge me" is an appeal to the heavenly judge to do him justice and to vindicate his innocence by delivering him from the power of "a nation without lovingkindness," i.e., heathen without any feelings of humanity. The leader of these heathen is called "the deceitful and unjust man." Perhaps he had distinguished himself by his treachery.

43:2. The psalmist still views God as his "strength," his natural refuge and protector. Facts, however, seem to contradict faith. God seems to have cast him off. He goes about by himself in mourning.

43:3. He prays for restoration. God's "light and truth" are personified. "Light" symbolizes God's active presence. That "light" would prove God true to his character and promises. He asks that God's "light and truth" might lead him to the holy hill of Zion where the tabernacles of God are located. The plural indicates that Zion was God's preeminent earthly dwelling place.

43:4. God himself is the goal of pilgrimage. The altar is the means of approaching God and realizing his presence. There the psalmist will praise God through the music of his harp.

43:5. See on 42:5,11.

THE REVELATION OF GOD'S POWER
Psalms 44-45

Pss 44-45 are concerned about God's power. In the first of these two poems it is the failure to manifest divine power that bothered the psalmist. Ps 45 answers the perplexity of faith by pointing to the ultimate victories of Messiah.

A. The Perplexities of Faith (Ps 44).

The author was one of the Levitical sons of Korah. The psalm was written after an occasion of great national deliverance. The reference may be to the deliverance from the Assyrian attack against Judah in the days of good King Hezekiah. This is one of thirteen psalms called "maskil," which probably means a psalm intended to teach a lesson. The psalm has five main parts which can be summarized: (1) praise (vv. 1-3); (2) hope (vv. 4-8); (3) disappointment (vv. 9-16); (4) innocence (vv. 17-22); and (5) prayer (vv. 23-26).

44:1-2. Canaan was not captured through Israel's heroics, but through God's help. The "fathers" had passed down the reports of what God had done for his people "in the times of old," i.e., the days of the conquest under Joshua. By God's hand (power) the Canaanites were "cast out" and the Israelites were "planted" in the land. God made them "spread abroad" (NASB) in that land like a great tree which struck root and spread its branches in all directions.

44:3. The thought of the two previous verses is emphasized. It was not Israel's sword hand, but God's right hand which gave the victory. The "light" of God's countenance is his manifestation in human affairs. This God did for Israel as a favor, not as a reward for their national merit.

280

44:4. The recollection of the past gives fresh confidence in the present. God is Israel's king. It is his duty to defend his people. He has but to "command" and "Jacob" (the nation) would experience "deliverances," i.e., a full and complete deliverance.

44:5-8. Relying upon all that God had revealed about himself ("his name"), Israel would trample enemies as an ox might trample grain under its feet. Israel repudiates reliance upon deliverance by military prowess. Past experience justifies this confidence in the Lord. God has been the object of their praises in the past, and to him they are resolved to give thanks continually. "Selah" indicates a musical interlude which gives time for reflection.

44:9-11. Present circumstances seem to contradict the expressions of faith based on past experience. God had cast them off. He no longer went before the armies of Israel. (In ancient times the ark was carried into battle as the symbol of Yahweh's presence with the troops.) As a result, Israel had fled from the enemies, who had plundered the land at their will. Some of God's people had been butchered like sheep; others had been captured and sold as slaves.

44:12-14. God "sells" (delivers over) his people as though they were worthless. By so doing, God had gained nothing for himself. He had made his people an object of ridicule to neighboring nations. They shake their heads at Israel in derision. Among the heathen, Israel had become a "byword," i.e., they pointed to Israel's fate as a proverbial instance of a people abandoned by its God.

44:15-16. Disgrace stares the psalmist in the face all day long. Shame covers his face like a garment, inasmuch as the sense of shame betrays itself in one's countenance. The enemy "reproaches" Israel's impotence and "blasphemes" Yahweh by suggesting that he too is impotent. These two words are found in combination only in reference to Sennacherib's attitude during the Assyrian attack of 701 BC. (cf. 2 Kgs 19:6,22). The enemy is called "the avenger" because he is acting arrogantly in taking a role which belongs only to God (cf. Deut 32:35).

44:17-18. The calamity is unmerited. Israel had not "forgotten" Yahweh as their fathers often had done. They had not been unfaithful to God's covenant made at Sinai. They had not turned back from the Lord, neither inwardly nor outwardly (their "steps").

281

44:19. A "place of jackals" is a proverbial expression for a scene of ruin and desolation. The thought may be that God has reduced their land to a desert. God had covered them with "the shadow of death," i.e., the deep gloom which surrounds the time of death.

44:20-21. No apostasy could be concealed from the God who searches hearts. To "stretch out the hands" was a gesture of prayer in which the open palms symbolized the reception of blessing from the deity.

44:22. The claim here is that Israel was actually suffering as martyrs for the sake of their faith in Yahweh. Paul quoted this verse in Rom 8:36 to fortify Christians against the possibility that they too might have to face death for their faith.

44:23-24. God seemed to be asleep, though the psalmists knew that Yahweh never got weary as men do (121:3f.). He is urged to awake, i.e., to get involved in their plight, and not to leave them in a state of being "cast off."

44:25-26. To "hide the face" is the opposite of showing the light of his countenance. One might hide his face in anger or indifference. The psalmist asks that God no longer ignore the plight of his people since they lie crushed to the earth and helpless. The grounds of appeal is Yahweh's lovingkindness. The psalmist entreats God to be true to this central attribute of his character.

B. The Power of the King (Ps 45).

Ps 45 is a marriage song in which a mighty warrior and king is married to a beautiful princess. From the earliest times in Jewish and Christian circles Ps 45 has been understood to refer directly to Messiah. The most popular of many views is that this psalm was based on the marriage of Solomon to Pharaoh's daughter. A greater than Solomon, however, is here. This psalm has been called "the center and crown of the messianic psalms."[1] If this poem had any relation at all to a concrete historical situation, that is now lost.

Ps 45 is attributed to the sons of Korah. This is another *maskil* or teaching psalm. The nature of the psalm is described in the words "a song of beloved ones," i.e., a song of love. After a brief preface (v. 1) Ps 45 focuses on (1) the bridegroom (vv. 2-9a), (2) the bride (vv. 9b-12), and (3) the marriage (vv. 13-16).

45:1. The psalmist here states his theme: "I speak things I composed concerning a king." He then uses two figures to describe his eagerness to share his composition. His heart is a bubbling fountain; he cannot restrain himself. In the second figure he compares his tongue to the pen of a "ready writer," i.e., it is prompt to express and record the thoughts with which his mind is overflowing. He seems to realize that he is the instrument of a higher power.

45:2. The bridegroom was attractive to others because of the graciousness of his speech. These were blessings given forever to him by God.

45:3. The bridegroom is awesome in majesty. He is well-armed and capable of doing mighty things. He is called a mighty hero (gibbor). The terms "splendor" and "majesty" may refer to his armor.

45:4. The bridegroom is victorious in his cause. He rides forth on a warhorse or chariot to the conflict for which he is destined. He marches forth on behalf of truth, meekness, and righteousness. The bridegroom is triumphant over his enemies. The "right hand teaches" the king. This is a way of saying that the king shall demonstrate tremendous powers.

45:5. The battle is visualized. Arrows bring the king's enemies down under the advancing warrior.

45:6-7a. The bridegroom is a divine ruler. He is addressed as "God." He occupies an eternal throne. He is a righteous ruler who hates wickedness. His scepter would be the symbol of uprightness.

45:7b. The bridegroom is anointed by God and thus is elevated above his fellow kings. God anoints God! Hebrews 1:8-9 has these words spoken by God concerning the Son. The anointing oil is generally regarded as symbolic of the Holy Spirit. Jesus was anointed with the Holy Spirit (Luke 4:18).

45:8. The joy of the bridegroom is indicated. His garments are fragrant. He is made glad by the music of stringed instruments which are playing as he leaves the ivory palaces to attend his own wedding. Palace walls in antiquity frequently featured ivory inlays.

45:9a. In Oriental nuptial celebrations, virgin friends of the bride would greet and accompany the bridegroom to the marriage celebration. The fact that these friends of the bride are kings' daughters may serve to underscore the rank of the bride.

283

45:9b. The psalmist envisions the beautiful bride at the right hand of the divine king. Even before the marriage the bride is accorded royal dignity. She wears the title "queen" and is attired in gold. In God's eyes she is very precious. If the bridegroom in this psalm is Messiah, then the bride must be his people, the church of Christ (cf. Eph 5:22ff.).

45:10-11. The bride prepares to make the transition from the single to the married state. The psalmist advises the bride to sever the old ties and give Messiah wholehearted allegiance. She is encouraged to be submissive to him. Thus will she make herself most attractive to her divine husband.

45:12. The daughter of Tyre, i.e., the city personified as a woman, brings to the bride a gift. Prophetically this anticipates the conversion of Gentiles and the dedication of their possessions to the church, the bride of Christ. The "rich among the people" dedicate their wealth as well to the bride.

45:13-14. The bride is "all glorious within" her heart. Her outer garments are woven with gold. She is escorted to meet her husband by virgins, who here represent individual believers who are models of purity.

45:15. The bride and her maids enter the palace of the king in a mood of gay festivity. Weddings in biblical times were occasions of great happiness marked by music and dancing.

45:16. The king will have sons. The king's fathers according to the flesh are the patriarchs, prophets and priests of the Old Covenant. They will give way to the king's sons—the apostles and evangelists of the New Covenant. These sons will share the royal dignity. On the royal dignity of New Testament believers see 1 Pet 2:9; Rev 1:6; 5:10.

45:17. The writing of the psalmist will perpetuate the memory of the king throughout the generations. Other peoples besides Israel will praise the king throughout the ages.[2]

THE PRAISE FOR THE REDEEMER
Psalms 46-48

Psalms 46-48 form a trilogy of praise, in which a wondrous deliverance of Jerusalem from foreign enemies is celebrated. All three are designated as psalms of the sons of Korah. They may allude to the deliverance of Jerusalem in 701 BC from the armies of Sennacherib.

A. The Protection of the City (Ps 46).

Ps 46 has three parts: (1) Yahweh's protection (vv. 1-3); (2) Yahweh's presence (vv. 4-7); and (3) Yahweh's preeminence (vv. 8-11).

46:1-3. God's people are secure under his protection. They have nothing to fear, even though the solid earth were rent asunder and the mountains tumble into the sea. The raging sea depicts trouble on every side.

46:4. In contrast to the tumultuous sea threatening to engulf the solid mountain, is the gently flowing river which fertilized all the land over which it is distributed in channels and rivulets. This river is a symbol of the presence of Yahweh, blessing and gladdening his city (cf. Isa 8:6). God's people are likened unto a city. Yahweh is called "the Most High." By delivering his own city, he has proved himself the supreme ruler of the world.

46:5. Because God is in the midst of Jerusalem the city is more stable than the solid mountains of v. 3. God will help her "when morning dawns" (NASB). The dawn of deliverance follows the night of distress.

46:6. The same words which were used in vv. 2-3 of convulsion in the natural order are here applied to the commotions among the nations. God has but to speak with his voice of thunder and the earth melts in terror.

46:7. Here is a rare use of the name Yahweh in Book Two. The name "Yahweh of hosts" depicts God as commander of all the powers of earth and heaven, thus supreme sovereign. God had watched over Jacob their ancestor; now this God was the "refuge" (lit., high fortress) of Jacob's descendants. "Selah" suggests a musical interlude at this point.

46:8. The psalmist exhorts all nations to reflect upon this marvelous deliverance. They are invited to "behold," i.e., gaze, upon the sight. Yahweh has set "desolations" in the earth, namely, the total destruction of the enemy army.

46:9-10. Yahweh would one day bring about the final abolition of war. He would destroy the weapons of war. Yahweh admonishes the nations to desist from their vain endeavors to destroy his people. He bids them to recognize him as the true God who will one day manifest his absolute sovereignty.

46:11. The refrain of v. 7 is repeated with appropriate musical interlude.

B. The Preeminence of the Lord (Ps 47).

The second psalm in the triology of praise has three units: (1) Yahweh's exalted position (vv. 1-4); (2) recent deliverance (vv. 5-7); and (3) ultimate dominion (vv. 8-9).

47:1. All nations are called upon to acknowledge Yahweh as their king. On his accession to the throne a new king was saluted with clapping of hands and shouting. The "shout of triumph" is the joyous shouting which welcomes the victorious king.

47:2. Yahweh is not merely king of Israel, but king of all the earth. He is the Most High and should be respected for that.

47:3-4. The recent triumph by which Yahweh had once more driven out the enemies of his people from the land, proved that he had chosen that land for Israel's inheritance. The "pride of Jacob" is Canaan, the land on which Israel prided itself. Yahweh's love, not Israel's merit, was the ground of the choice.

47:5. Again the psalmist calls on the people to celebrate Yahweh's sovereignty. "God is gone up," i.e., returned to heaven, from the victory. Carrying the ark up the hill to the temple to the accompaniment of shouts and trumpets may have been the outward ceremony to celebrate God's return to heaven.

47:6-7. These verses contain five exhortations to sing praises to Yahweh for he is king over all the earth. The people are urged to sing a "maskil," a song that teaches others about the Lord.

47:8. Yahweh rules over the world. This verse declares not merely a fact, but an act. God has given fresh proof of his universal sovereignty. He has taken his seat upon his throne to judge and rule.

47:9. The psalmist foresees the day when the nations acknowledge Yahweh's sovereignty. He sees the "princes of the peoples" gathering to Jerusalem to pay homage. There they join the "people of the God of Abraham" in worship. Here is a prophecy of the union of Jews and Gentiles in the church of Christ. The "shields of the earth" are princes who are the protectors of their people. Yahweh is their overlord, and they come to acknowledge their dependence on him.

C. The Praise for the Redeemer (Ps 48).

The third psalm in the trilogy of praise has two main divisions: (1) Yahweh's actions on behalf of Zion (vv. 1-8); and (2) Zion's reactions to Yahweh's deliverance (vv. 9-14).

48:1. Yahweh has proved himself to be an *exceedingly* present help in trouble (46:1). By his triumph over the nations he is *exceedingly* exalted (47:9); and therefore he is *exceedingly* worthy to be praised. Zion in this psalm denotes the whole city of Jerusalem, not merely one of the hills on which it was built. As the place of the earthly abode of Yahweh, Zion is called his holy mountain.

48:2. In pagan mythology the uttermost part of the north was the home of the gods. The sacred city of Yahweh was not in the remote recesses of the north, but in the very midst of the city of his choice. Zion is in reality all that the pagans claimed for their fabled mount of the gods. The city of the great king Yahweh was beautiful in its elevation, and "the joy of the whole earth," i.e., the city which brought joy to all who visited it.

48:3. The enemy anticipated plundering the palaces of Zion. Yahweh, however, made himself known there as a high fortress.

48:4-7. The enemy joined together and crossed the border into Judah. When they came to Zion, they were smitten with terror and they retreated. They were as terrified as a woman in childbirth. God smashed the invaders just as he used the east wind to smash the merchant ships of Tarshish from time to time.

48:8. Experience had confirmed what tradition related of God's marvelous works on behalf of his people. Now God's people were confident that Yahweh would never cease to guard the city of his choice.

48:9-10. In temple worship Zion's citizens meditated on the significance of the deliverance. They realized that they had just experienced another manifestation of Yahweh's lovingkindness. God's revelation of power and lovingkindness receives worldwide celebration. To other nations besides Judah the destruction of the enemy was a cause of rejoicing. Now his people realized that Yahweh's "right hand is full of righteousness," i.e., ready to be exercised on behalf of his people in judgment on his enemies.

48:11. Mt. Zion should rejoice as well as "the daughters of Judah," i.e., the cities of Judah which had been captured by the enemy. Country towns were regarded as "daughters" of the capital.

48:12-13. The inhabitants of Jerusalem had been confined within its walls during the siege. Now they can freely walk around, and thankfully contemplate the safety of the walls, towers and palaces which had so recently been threatened by the enemy. They need to convince themselves that the city was intact so that they could bear accurate testimony to future generations.

48:14. Yahweh had proved himself the defender of his city and people. He will continue to be the same forever. His people confess their willingness to follow him until death.

THE REDEMPTION OF GOD'S PEOPLE
Psalms 49–51

The next three psalms are by different writers, but they share the common theme of redemption.

A. The Means of Redemption (Ps 49).

Ps 49 is another Korahite psalm. The author is a moralist who teaches that there are limits to what wealth can do. There is little to determine the date of this psalm. It may come from the eighth century BC when great wealth and great poverty existed side by side. The misuse of the power of wealth in this period is condemned by Isaiah, Micah, and Amos in particular. This psalm consists of an introduction (vv. 1-4) and two stanzas consisting of eight verses, each concluding with a refrain. Thus: (1) the false confidence of the wealthy (vv. 5-12); and (2) the final condition of the wealthy (vv. 13-20).

49:1-2. The problem of wealth is a universal one. Thus all people are called upon to pay attention to the words of this psalm. The word "world" is a peculiar word, found in this sense only in Ps 17:14. It denotes the lapse of time, the fleeting age, the world as uncertain and transitory. The "sons of mankind (*'adam*) and the sons of men (*'ish*)," i.e., those from the common multitude and those from the upper crust, are called upon to listen.

49:3. The words "wisdom" and "understanding" are both plural in Hebrew, denoting manifold wisdom and profound insight.

49:4. The poet claims to receive by revelation what he desires to teach. He will bend his ear to listen to the voice of God before he ventures himself to speak to men. The term "parable" (*mashal*) has a wide range of meanings. Here it refers to a didactic poem. The term "riddle" (*chidah*) also has a range of meanings. Here it refers to a profound or obscure utterance, a problem. The prosperity of the godless was one of the great enigmas of life to the pious Israelite. What the psalmist has learned through revelation on this subject he will "open upon the harp," i.e., set forth in a poem accompanied by music.

49:5-6. The psalmist has no need to fear "in the days of evil," i.e., when evil men have the upper hand. These wealthy and unscrupulous neighbors were eager to trip him up and get him into their power.

49:7-9. Those who worship wealth find their god powerless to deliver anyone from death, or ransom one whose death God requires. In some circumstances the sum to be paid by the man whose life was forfeit was to be assessed, probably in proportion to his culpability and his means (cf. Exod 21:30); but there is no ransom which can be paid to God. It is hopeless to think of attempting it (cf. Num 35:31). That man will die and see corruption regardless of his wealth.

49:10. Experience shows the rich man that all alike come to the grave. Even wisdom cannot deliver from death. The foolish (the self-confident braggart) and the senseless "perish," i.e., die in a similar way. Wealth can neither prolong life, nor be retained by its owner at death.

49:11-13. These godless ones do not consider that they must die. They comfort themselves with the delusion that their houses will last forever, and their names would be perpetuated in the names of their estates. Man's magnificence, however, must come to an end. In that sense he is like the beasts that perish. So it happens to these self-confident fools and their deluded followers. "*Selah*" indicates a musical interlude at this point.

49:14. The wicked are driven down to Sheol like a flock of sheep. Death (personified) is their shepherd. They shall perish in the night, and in the resurrection morning they shall find that the righteous have the rule over them. Their form or beauty will have been delivered up to Sheol, the abode of the dead, far from their exalted habitations.

49:15. The believer, however, is delivered from the power of Sheol. Does the psalmist look forward only to deliverance from the premature death of the wicked? Or does he anticipate a redemption after death? Verses 7-8 are offered in support of the former position, i.e., wealth is powerless to avert death, but God will deliver his servant. Verses 7-8, however, may be referring to the ravishing effects of death, not to the fact that men must die. Taken in this way, vv. 7-8 do not preclude the reference here to the believer's hope of victory over death.

49:16-17. The thought in v. 10 is resumed and amplified. The psalmist exhorts himself not to be afraid of the rich nor of the magnificence and splendor which accompany wealth. The rich man cannot take his wealth with him into Sheol.

49:18. The rich man congratulated himself on his good fortune. He flattered himself into thinking that he was beyond the reach of misfortune. The unthinking multitude worships success and wealth. They see nothing wrong in the selfish misuse of riches.

49:19. In the dark world of Sheol the rich man joins his ancestors, those whose lot had been fixed irrevocably, who will never see "light," i.e., eternal life in the qualitative sense.

49:20. The refrain of v. 12 is repeated with a significant variation. It is not the rich man, as such, who is no better than the cattle that perish, but the rich man who is destitute of discernment. He who has no hope after death is that person who knows no distinction between false and true riches, who reckons earthly and transitory wealth more precious than spiritual and eternal fellowship with God.

B. The Need for Redemption (Ps 50).

The writer is Asaph, one of three choral leaders among the Levites (1 Chr 15:17-19). He was chief minister before the ark (1 Chr 16:4-15), a seer (2 Chr 29:30), and poet. This is the only Asaphic psalm in Book Two of the Psalter; eleven others are found in Book Three. In all of Asaph's writings the holiness of God is a prominent theme. The historical occasion of this psalm may have been the great procession which brought the ark to Jerusalem (1 Chr 15–16). Like the preceding psalm, this is a didactic poem. It echoes the message of the prophets of Israel.

The psalm consists of four parts: (1) the arrival of the judge (vv. 1-6); (2) the judgment on dead works (vv. 7-15); (3) the judgment on despicable wickedness (vv. 16-21); and (4) a warning to the people (vv. 22-23).

50:1. Three names are used to point to various aspects of the character of the God with whom Israel must deal. *'El* is the mighty one; *'Elohim*, the awesome one; and *Yahweh*, the God of revelation and redemption. This exact threefold combination is found elsewhere only in Joshua 22:22. This great God summons all the earth to be witness to the trial of Israel.

50:2-3. Zion is now the abode of God. A dazzling blaze of light is the symbol of his presence. The poet is anxious for God to come near and declare his will. Lightnings and storm are the outward symbols which express his coming in judgment. He is a consuming fire (cf. Deut 4:24) devouring his enemies. He is an irresistible whirlwind sweeping them away like chaff.

50:4. The heavens and earth are summoned to be witnesses of the judgment of Israel because they are far older than man, and have watched the whole course of Israel's history. The concept is quite common in the Old Testament (e.g., Deut 4:26).

50:5. A command is given, perhaps to the angels, to gather "my saints," i.e., Israel, those who had entered into a covenant with the Lord. This covenant was inaugurated at Sinai by sacrifice (Exod 24:5ff.) and maintained through the generations by means of repeated sacrifices.

50:6. While the defendants are being gathered, the psalmist hears the heavens, which have been summoned to witness the trial, solemnly proclaiming the justice of the judge, as a guarantee of the impartiality of his judgment. *"Selah"* indicates a musical interlude during which worshipers could reflect on what was just said.

50:7-8. The trial begins. God acts as accuser as well as the judge. Because he is their God he has the right to give them law, and now to call them to account for their neglect of it. God's indictment does not relate to sacrifice; the stated offerings are duly presented "continually," i.e., daily, morning and evening (cf. Num 28:3ff.). In this section God is reproving those who offer sacrifices to him as a mere formality.

50:9-13. The owner of the vast herds of animals which roam the forests and range over a thousand mountains is not like some earthly king who comes and takes the choicest of his subjects' possessions at his will. If God had need of sustenance, he would not be dependent upon man for it. In heathen theology the gods had to be fed daily. Yahweh, however, needed no such sustenance. A spiritual being needs no material support.

50:14-15. What sacrifice then does God desire? Not the material sacrifices of the altar, but the offering of the heart. He desires spiritual sacrifices of thanksgiving. By such spiritual sacrifice the believer discharges his vows. Prayer also is proof of trust in God and commitment to him.

50:16-17. Yahweh now begins to reprove hypocrites. They pledged themselves to observe the law. They professed to fulfill their duty under God's covenant. Yet they hated "discipline," i.e., instruction in moral discipline. They cast God's words—his commandments—behind their back, i.e., they ignored them.

50:18-20. They gladly associated with thieves and adulterers. Their mouths spewed forth evil and falsehood. They deliberately slander even members of their own family.

50:21. These wicked people mistook the longsuffering of God for indifference. They degraded their conception of God into a reflection of themselves. They imagined that when Yahweh revealed himself he would prove to be only like a man. Instead, however, Yahweh was now listing the offenses of which they were guilty, bringing them under indictment in his court.

50:22. A final word is now given to the formalists who forget the spiritual character of worship, and the hypocrites who willfully ignored God's word. God threatens to come against them and tear them like a lion (cf. Hos 5:14).

50:23. This verse summarizes the teaching of the two main divisions of the psalm. God will show salvation to (1) those who offer the sacrifice of thanksgiving (as in v. 14); and (2) those who order their way aright, i.e., follow his commandments.

C. The Prerequisite of Redemption (Ps 51).

Ps 51 is the fourth of the so-called "penitential" psalms (the others being Pss 6, 32, 38). David wrote this psalm after the prophet Nathan had rebuked him for his sin with Bathsheba (2 Sam 11–12). This is the first of some eighteen psalms in Book Two bearing the name of David. Eight of these have titles connecting them with historical events in the life of the great king. The psalm has three main parts: (1) confession (vv. 1-6); (2) cleansing (vv. 7-12); and (3) consecration (vv. 13-19).

51:1-2. David prays for forgiveness and cleansing. The ground of this prayer is God's grace. "Lovingkindness" was the origin and the bond of the covenant between Yahweh and Israel. Sin is described in three aspects: (1) transgression, i.e., defection from God or rebellion against him; (2) iniquity, i.e., the perversion of right, depravity of conduct; and (3) sin, i.e., error, missing the mark. The removal of guilt is also triply described: (1) "blot out," i.e., sin is regarded as a debt recorded in God's book which needs to be erased and canceled; (2) "wash me," i.e., sin is regarded as an inward stain which only God can thoroughly cleanse; and (3) "cleanse me," i.e., as a leper might be cleansed of his disease.

51:3. The pronoun here is emphatic. His sins have been known to God all along. Now, however, David has come to know them himself; they are unceasingly present to his conscience, at least since Nathan had pricked his conscience with the word of God.

51:4. All sin ultimately is a sin against God, as a breach of his holy law. Moreover, the king, as Yahweh's representative, was in a special way responsible to him. David's admission of sin would make any sentence concerning him by God appear just. Man's sin brings out into a clearer light the justice and holiness of God.

51:5. David alludes to his sinful nature. He was born in sin, i.e., with a nature prone to do evil. The verse does not plead the sinfulness of his nature as an excuse for his conduct. Rather he is confessing that sin has infected his very nature. The verse furnishes no justification for the doctrine of *total* depravity.

51:6. God desires "truth," i.e., wholehearted devotion which is incapable of deceiving self, as David had done, or deceiving man as David had tried to do. Along with *truth*, God desires *wisdom* in the inner person, that spiritual discernment which is synonymous with the fear of Yahweh.

51:7. David calls for cleansing and restoration. The figurative language is borrowed from the ceremony of the law. A bunch of hyssop, a common herb which grew upon walls, was used as a sprinkler, especially in the rites for cleansing the leper and purifying the unclean (cf. Lev 14:4ff.). Washing and clothing of the body regularly formed part of the rites of purification. David here, however, is thinking of the inward and spiritual cleansing of which those outward rites were the symbol. He appeals to God himself to perform the office of the priest and cleanse him from his defilement.

51:8. Under the law the purification of the unclean was the prelude to his readmission to the gladness of sanctuary worship. So the inward cleansing of David will be the prelude to his restoration to that joy of God's salvation which he desires. God's displeasure had crushed his "bones," i.e., shattered his whole frame. Some prefer to read the verbs in this and the preceding verse as futures, thus indicating David's confidence in God's pardon.

51:9. David repeats his prayer for pardon, cleansing, and renewal. To hide the face from sin means to cease to look upon it in displeasure. "Blot out" again suggests a canceled debt (cf. v. 1).

51:10. David wants a radical change of heart and spirit, not a restoration of what was there before. A "steadfast spirit" is one that is fixed and resolute in its allegiance to God, unmoved by the assaults of temptation. Essentially here David is surrendering his heart to the Lord.

51:11. David prayed that he might not be cast away from God's presence. The Spirit of God came upon David when he departed from Saul (1 Sam 16:13f.). David apparently feared that, because of his sin, he might be deprived of God's favor and deserted by that Spirit which supplies comfort and guidance to believers.

51:12. Sin has destroyed the assurance of God's help which is ever a ground of rejoicing. He prays for that deliverance which he is confident (v. 8) God can and will grant him. He desires to be upheld from falling in the future by God's free or willing Spirit.

51:13. After he has experienced the joy of restoration to communion with God, he will endeavor to instruct transgressors in the ways of Yahweh. One of the most fitting fruits of repentance is the effort to keep others from falling into the same pitfall, and to guide back to the Lord those who have fallen.

51:14. David asks to be delivered from "bloodguiltiness," i.e., crimes for which the death penalty was appropriate. He refers to his crimes of adultery and murder (cf. 2 Sam 12:5,13). Should forgiveness be granted, David promises to sing of God's "righteousness," i.e., his faithfulness to his character and covenant. Pardon for the penitent is as much a manifestation of God's righteousness as judgment on the impenitent.

51:15-17. David asks for the power (ability) as well as the occasion to sing God's praise in the public assembly. He wants to praise God aright. Sin hinders genuine praise; pardon releases it. Such a thank offering he proposes to give because he knows that Yahweh does not desire a material offering so much as the sacrifice of a contrite heart. This is not a repudiation of all sacrificial worship but a recognition that the reality within is more desirable to God than the outward symbol. A "broken spirit and a contrite heart" are those in which the obstinacy of pride has been replaced by the humility of repentance. Some see here a reference to the fact that under the law no provision of sacrifice was made for deliberate transgression.

51:18-19. These verses may have been added by the exiles who adapted this psalm to their own situation. On the other hand, it is not impossible that the penitent David would utter this prayer on behalf of Zion, the city of God. To "build the walls of Jerusalem" may have been metaphorical for granting divine protection to the holy city. The "sacrifices of righteousness" are those offered in a right spirit and manner. In the whole burnt offering the worshiper symbolized his complete dedication to the Lord. A continued divine blessing on Zion would enable Yahweh's people to continue presenting to him these whole burnt offerings.

ENDNOTES

1. T. Earnest Wilson, *Messianic Psalms* (Neptune, NJ: Loulzeaux, 1978), p. 106.

2. On the messianic interpretation of Ps 45, see James E. Smith, *What the Bible Teaches about the Promised Messiah* (Nashville: Nelson, 1993), pp. 175-184.

CHAPTER FOURTEEN

The Faithful and the Faithless
Psalms 52-60

Nine Davidic psalms sketch a clear distinction between those who are faithful to God and those who are not.

THE FAITHLESS EXPOSED
Psalms 52–53

Pss 52–53 expose two types of faithless individuals, namely, the deceiver, and the fool.

A. The Deceiver Exposed (Ps 52).

The writer and occasion of this psalm are clearly indicated in the title (cf. 1 Sam 21-22). Doeg was chief of Saul's herdsmen. With malicious intent he reported facts to Saul which fueled his insane suspicion that David was plotting against his life. The results were disastrous to the priestly family of Ahimelech, and near disastrous to David himself. This is the first of four *"maskil"* (didactic) psalms in succession. The psalm falls into two divisions. Here David paints a portrait of: (1) the sinner (vv. 1-5); and (2) the saint (vv. 6-9).

52:1. The theme of the psalm is the contrast between man's wrongdoing, and God's lovingkindness. The two halves of this verse outline the psalm. The mighty man boasts of his success in evildoing. Such boasting is vain. The covenant love in which David trusts endures "all the day," i.e., long after the evildoer has faded from the scene. The word for God ('*El* = the mighty one) reminds the braggart that there is one stronger than he, who will call him to account.

52:2. The tongue of the mighty man "devises destruction." By falsehood, slander, false witness and the like Doeg hoped to bring about the destruction of David. His tongue is compared to a dangerous sharp razor which cuts before one is even aware. The mighty man is addressed as "worker of deceit."

52:3-4. This sinner chooses evil rather than good. He has no concern for "righteousness," i.e., truth which would lead to justice. The aim of his falsehoods is injustice. He loves "words of swallowing up," i.e., words which destroyed others. The mighty man again is addressed, this time as "deceitful tongue."

52:5. The punishment will correspond to the sin. The mighty man himself will be destroyed. God will pluck him out of his dwelling and drive him forth as a homeless wanderer. Though he be flourishing as a green tree, God will root him out of the land of the living, i.e., he will die suddenly and violently. "*Selah*"—a musical interlude—marks the conclusion of the first half of the psalm.

52:6. The sight of the fall of the mighty man fills the righteous with awe, i.e., a deeper respect for God's moral government. Malicious satisfaction at the calamity of the wicked is condemned (Job 31:29; Prov 24:17). Every vindication of God's righteousness, however, was greeted with joy. In this sense, the righteous laugh at the fall of the braggart.

52:7. The righteous sarcastically pronounce the epithet of the mighty man. As a matter of course he had not made God his stronghold. He trusted instead in his riches which were gained through wickedness.

52:8. The speaker compares himself to "a green olive tree in the house of God." Two common figures are here combined: the flourishing tree and the house guest. While the wicked man is rooted up, the psalmist flourishes. He is a guest in God's house, enjoying his favor and protection. God's "house" here may refer to the land of Israel from which the wicked are driven out (v. 5).

52:9. The speaker gives forever to God the sacrifice of thanksgiving because he has brought down the deceiver and braggart. In the presence of other godly people, i.e., publicly, he will continue to "wait" on Yahweh, i.e., his trust in the Lord would be a matter of public knowledge.

B. The Fool Exposed (Ps 53).

This psalm is a new rendition of Ps 14. In accordance with the usage of this section of the Psalter, *'Elohim* has been substituted for *Yahweh*. The earlier psalm appears to have been adapted by slight alterations to a second great deliverance which is, probably, the destruction of Sennacherib's army in 701 BC. For observations regarding the contents of this psalm, see on Ps 14.

THE FAITHFUL ENCOURAGED
Psalms 54–56

The next three psalms are designed to encourage the faithful when they are faced with the trials of life.

A. When Faced with Betrayal (Ps 54).

This psalm is another *"maskil"* (didactic) psalm of David. He wrote it when the Ziphites twice betrayed his whereabouts to Saul (1 Sam 23:14-15,19-24; 26:1-4). Ziph was a small town fifteen miles SE of Hebron in the territory of Judah. The psalm has a simple structure. It consists of (1) a prayer (vv. 1-3); and (2) the answer to prayer (vv. 4-7).

54:1-2. The "name of God" is the totality of his revealed attributes. David can appeal to the name because God has declared that it is his will to save those who put their trust in him. To "judge" means here "to do justice." David is confident that if justice is done, he will be delivered from his foes. The phrase "by your strength" indicates that God has not only the will, but the power to deliver his servant.

54:3. Those who oppose David are described as (1) "strangers," i.e., the Ziphites had not acted like fellow Judahites, but had betrayed David to the Benjamites who were seeking his life; (2) "violent men," i.e., Saul's men who were determined to destroy David; and (3) "they have not set God before them," i.e., they have no regard for God's will, nor do they fear his judgment. It was well known that God intended David to be Saul's successor. In attempting to deliver over David to Saul, the Ziphites were in fact fighting against God.

54:4-5. Based on past experience, David knew that God was on his side. Yahweh is the "upholder" of his soul. David's enemies lie in wait for him like a leopard for its prey. Yahweh would cause the evil which they were plotting to recoil upon their own heads. David asks God to "cut them off in your truth." God cannot be false to his promise to deliver David.

54:6-7. The deliverance from trouble will be effected by the overthrow of the enemies. David was confident that he would see what he desired to see, namely, their demise. For such salvation he would praise God's name (i.e., his nature, or attributes), and offer up free will sacrifices to him. It is not personal vindictiveness which brings David joy, but the vindication of God's faithfulness. The proof of this is found in the fact that no man was more gracious to his enemies than David.

B. When Overcome by Sorrow (Ps 55).

Ps 55 was written by David, most probably during the period of Absalom's rebellion (2 Sam 15-17). The psalm falls into three nearly equal divisions. It portrays David's (1) anguish (vv. 1-8); (2) anger (vv. 9-15); and (3) anticipation (vv. 16-23).

55:1-3a. David passionately appeals to God for a hearing in his distress. He asks God not to "hide" himself like an unmerciful man who turns away from misfortune which he does not want to relieve. The insulting, threatening "voice of the enemy" has caused him to be "restless," i.e., has distracted his mind. The wicked oppress, i.e, hem him in and crush him down.

55:3b-5. The enemy casts down "trouble" upon David, a metaphor from the practice of rolling stones down upon an enemy. Terrors such as only death alone can inspire have fallen upon him. He is overwhelmed with "horror."

55:6-8. David wishes he could be like the dove which wings its flight swiftly to its nest in the clefts of the inaccessible precipice, far from the haunts of men. Then he could find solace and safety in the isolation of the wilderness. There he would escape the storms of faction and party spirit raging within the city. *"Selah"* indicates a musical interlude.

55:9-11. David prays for the confusion of his enemies' counsels as the Lord confounded the language of all the earth at Babel. The city (Jerusalem) is full of violence and strife. "Iniquity" and "mischief" personified act as sentinels on the walls. Everywhere throughout the city, in the most public places of concourse, every form of evil and injustice was rampant, without check or intermission.

55:12. Foremost among David's enemies is one who had formerly been one of his most intimate and trusted friends. This is the most bitter ingredient in his cup of suffering. Ahithophel is doubtless the false friend here mentioned. Bathsheba was his granddaughter. He may have been resentful about what David had done to her and her husband. See 1 Chr 3:5; 2 Sam 11:3; 23:34,39.

55:13 14. David describes the chief enemy as "my equal," "my companion," and "my familiar friend," i.e., the very best of friends. The two had shared intimate secrets and worshiped together.

55:15. David asks for the destruction of his enemies by death. He asks that this fate may fall upon them suddenly so that they go down to Sheol alive like Korah and his company (cf. Num 16:30,33). Evil of every kind lodges in their homes and hearts. A sudden and premature death would be a visible judgment upon their crimes.

55:16-18. The trustful confidence of David begins to surface. He will continually offer up his prayers to his God. He is certain that his prayer will be answered. God will "redeem" his soul "in peace," i.e., will put him in a place of safety, from the "battle," i.e., the opposition which he was facing. This would be accomplished by "the many with me," which may refer to angels who watched over him. The name Yahweh here is significant. It is the God of covenant redemption to whom he can appeal, and under whose protection he can rest.

55:19. God will hear the raging of the enemies and answer them with judgment. God is designated as "he that sits enthroned eternally," i.e., as judge of the world. These enemies have as yet experienced no "changes," i.e., vicissitudes of fortune. God will humble those whose prosperity is uninterrupted, and who consequently do not fear God.

55:20-21. David reverts again to the treachery of his former friend. This man had "put forth his hands against such as be at peace with him," i.e., he had desecrated the sacred obligations of friendship. "The words of his mouth were smoother than butter," i.e., he was guilty of hypocritical flattery. All the while "war" was in his heart. His words were "softer than oil," yet behind those words were "drawn swords" ready to stab the victim to the heart.

55:22-23. David exhorts himself to cast his burden upon the Lord. God will not allow the righteous to be "shaken" forever. Their distress is but for a time. On the other hand, the enemies of the righteous will be brought down to the "pit of destruction," i.e., death. A premature death awaits "bloodthirsty and deceitful men." But the same God who destroys the wicked is the object of David's trust.

C. When Coping with Fear (Ps 56).

This *mikhtam* (see on Ps 16) of David is said to have been written when the Philistines took him at Gath (1 Sam 21:10-15). This psalm is closely related to Ps 34. The psalm consists of two stanzas and a concluding thanksgiving. Each of the stanzas ends with a refrain. Thus the psalm depicts (1) a prayer for deliverance (vv. 1-4); (2) the peril of death (vv. 5-11); and (3) the thanksgiving for deliverance (vv. 12-13).

56:1-2. David asks for divine mercy because "man would swallow me up," i.e., like a wild beast rushing upon its prey. He feels he is under the constant oppression of the enemy. The enemies are many; but God is the Most High (*marom*). David prays that God will prove his own supreme exaltation against these self-exalted braggarts.

56:3-4. David's sojourn in Gath is the only occasion on which he is recorded to have been afraid of man (1 Sam 21:12). Nonetheless David is determined—the pronoun is emphatic—to put his trust in God. Each day of peril disciplined his faith. David was confident that with the help of the Lord he would no longer fear what mere "flesh" could do to him.

56:5-6. From the heights of faith David returns to the urgent reality of present distress. All day long his enemies twist his words. Daily they tried to poison Saul's mind against him. The enemies lie in wait for David, i.e., try to ambush him. They mark his steps like hunters tracking their game. They watch for every opportunity to take his life.

56:7-8. Shall such wicked men escape punishment? David asks God to humble these people with judgment. The Lord knows all the days of David's fugitive life, when he was driven from his home to become a wanderer. David believes that God has put all his tears into a bottle, as though they were as precious as wine. His difficulties have all been noted in God's book of remembrance.

56:9-11. David is certain that God is on his side. His enemies, therefore, will be put to flight. David therefore repeats (essentially) the refrain of v. 4. He will praise God's word of promise.

56:12. David acknowledges his obligations before God. He will give thank offerings as well as votive offerings. He can speak of his deliverance from death as an accomplished fact. The Lord had delivered his feet from stumbling as the enemy attempted to thrust him down. David was permitted to "walk before God," i.e., serve him acceptably, here in the "light of the living," i.e., in the land of light as contrasted with the darkness of death.

THE FAITHFUL ENCOMPASSED
Psalms 57–60

The faithful have this consolation. No matter what their predicament may be in life, they know that they are compassed about by the all-powerful God. Nothing can befall them, save what he permits.

A. Protection from Pursuers (Ps 57).

Ps 57 is another *mikhtam* (see on Ps 16) of David written when he fled from Saul in the cave (1 Sam 24:1-8). This psalm has two main divisions: (1) a prayer for protection (vv. 1-5); and (2) a pledge to give thanks (vv. 6-11).

57:1. Beset by fierce and cruel enemies, David throws himself upon God's protection. "The shadow of your wings" is a beautiful metaphor taken from the care of the mother bird for her young. When danger threatens, the young run to her for shelter until the danger be past.

57:2-3. David resolves to call on "God Most High." The name implies that, as the supreme ruler of the world, God will be able to help him. God will send forth from heaven his "lovingkindness and truth" which are here personified as divine agents. By so doing God tramples those who attempt to trample David.

57:4. David depicts himself residing in the midst of vicious lions. He feels their hot breath and sharp teeth. They use their tongue against him like a sword. Yet David can lie down to rest in the midst of these savage beasts, knowing that God will protect him.

57:5. From his plight on earth, David looks up to heaven. He asks that God will manifest himself in majesty. What is needed is that he should manifest his supreme authority over the insolent rebels.

57:6. The enemies have tried to trap David in a net and a pit. For a time he was "bowed down," i.e., brought low, by their actions. In the end, however, David sees these enemies falling into their own traps.

57:7. David is firmly resolved to sing praise to the Lord. He exhorts himself ("my glory") to awake, to take up the instruments of music, and sing. By so doing he will "awake the dawn," i.e., bring on the day of deliverance.

57:8-11. David will praise the Lord even "among the nations," i.e., Gentiles. Mercy and truth which reach from earth to heaven demand worldwide praise. He concludes this psalm appropriately with the repetition of the refrain of v. 5.

B. Protection from Corrupt Judges (Ps 58).

David wrote Ps 58, probably during the period of Absalom's rebellion. The psalm has three main divisions: (1) A description of injustice (vv. 1-5); (2) a depiction of justice (vv. 6-9); and (3) a declaration of praise (vv. 10-11).

58:1. The judges are called "mighty ones" ('elim) because of their power over the lives of men.[1] Two rhetorical questions seem to accuse these judges of not rendering righteous and upright decisions.

58:2. Far from judging equitably, these judges were themselves the greatest offenders. Inwardly they were ever contriving some scheme of injustice. Instead of weighing decisions in the scales of justice (cf. Job 31:6), they weigh out violence "in the land," i.e., openly, and publicly they carry out the schemes they contrived in their hearts.

58:3. The judges belong to a class called the "wicked" who are estranged from God and his laws. From the day of their birth they seem to go astray, speaking lies.

58:4-5. The wicked are as insidious and venomous as serpents. They obstinately oppose all attempts to control them, like the poisonous deaf adder which resists the arts of the charmer. The ancients distinguished "the deaf" serpent from the one that answered the call of the charmer by hissing. The reference is to a class which manifests a diabolical aptitude for evil and opposition to good.

58:6. Since these enemies are obstinately and incurably evil, nothing remains but that they should be deprived of their power to hurt. The figure of the serpent is changed to that of the lion, typical of open ferocity. To "break" their teeth is equivalent to rendering them harmless.

58:7-8. David asks that these enemies be like a raging torrent which vanishes in the desert, or like broken arrows, i.e., he asks that they be rendered harmless. Let them be like a snail which seems to melt away and disappear as it leaves a slimy trail behind it;[2] or like the miscarriage of a woman which never comes to term.

58:9. The disrupted meal is another picture of sudden destruction of the wicked and their schemes. A traveler in the desert lights a fire of dry thorns under his cooking pot. It blazes up rapidly, but even so, before the pots are heated and the meat in them cooked, a sudden whirlwind sweeps away the fire. The whirlwind of divine judgment will sweep away their schemes before they can be implemented.

58:10. The righteous will rejoice over the punishment of the wicked. They regard the judgment as the vengeance of God on those who have willfully and obstinately resisted every effort for their reformation. A time comes in the moral government of the world when evil can no longer be tolerated; and the righteous cannot but rejoice at the triumph of good over evil and the proof that God is true to his revealed character as a just judge and sovereign ruler. The righteous man shall "wash his feet in the blood of the wicked," i.e., the wicked fall all about him.

58:11. The destruction of the wicked convinces men that (1) right living has its reward; and (2) God judges in the earth. The term "surely" used twice in the verse expresses the recognition of a truth which has been obscured or questioned in the past, but which has now been made clear.[3]

C. Protection from Enemies Within (Ps 59).

Ps 59 is another *mikhtam* (cf. Ps 16) of David, written at the time when he was threatened with arrest by Saul while in his own home (1 Sam 19:11-18). This psalm has two main divisions: (1) David's danger (vv. 1-9); and (2) David's deliverance (vv. 10-17).

59:1-4. David prays for deliverance from the enemies who are bent on taking his life. These enemies are described as "workers of iniquity," "men of blood," i.e., bloodthirsty men, and "strong ones." The tenses of the verbs indicate that secret plots have long been going on; now, however, the enemies are preparing a more open attack. Yet he has been guilty of no transgression, sin, or iniquity with respect to these men. Their hostility is unprovoked (cf. 1 Sam 20:1; 24:11). In this crisis he calls upon Yahweh to arouse himself from his apparent slumber of indifference and "meet him" as with an army of relief.

59:5. The second person pronoun here is emphatic. Yahweh is "God of hosts," i.e., he has power, and "God of Israel," i.e., he has obligations to his people. David calls on the Lord to "visit," i.e., punish, the nations. He asks that God be not gracious to them, the opposite of what he asks for himself. Since David's personal enemies were not in fact foreigners, one must conclude that (1) an original psalm of David has been altered by the editors of the Psalter for liturgical use; or (2) the prayer for judgment upon personal enemies is expanded into a prayer for judgment upon all the enemies of Israel.

59:6. David compares his enemies to a pack of savage and hungry dogs such as still infest the towns of that region. In the daytime they sleep in the sun, or slink lazily about; but at night they band together in search of food, howling dismally.

59:7-9. A flood of cursing and falsehood pours from the mouth of these enemies. They menace David with death or openly boast that he will soon be removed. The enemies sneer that there is no one to take David's part. The evil plans of David's enemies are as absurd as those of the heathen. Yahweh laughs at all of them because he knows their plans will never come to fruition. David's enemies are strong, but

God is stronger still. They watch his house (see psalm title), but he will "watch unto God." The Lord is his "high tower" of refuge in this time of attack.

59:10. David was confident that his prayer of v. 4 would be answered, that the Lord would "come to meet" him with lovingkindness. He believes that he will in fact live to see the demise of his attackers.

59:11. David does not want the enemies destroyed outright by some signal catastrophe, but visibly punished as a living example, until at last their own wickedness brings on their destruction. He wants God to "make them wander to and fro" like outcasts by means of his heavenly army (chayil). Yahweh is addressed here as "our shield." David is speaking as the representative of the nation.

59:12-13. David asks that his enemies be caught in their own snare, their plots recoiling upon themselves. Because of their prideful words, their cursing and lying, he asks that God might consume them in wrath "that they be no more." Thus will people unto the ends of the earth know that "God rules in Jacob," i.e., the nation Israel. Exhibitions of judgment upon wicked and violent men are evidence of God's sovereign reign.

59:14-15. A repetition of v. 6. The savage dogs prowl and growl all night in their efforts to get David in their teeth. They may tarry all night outside his doors. Yet David is confident that dawn will find him safe. The Hebrew suggests a strong contrast between the disappointed plots of the enemies (vv. 14-15) and the security of David (v. 16).

59:16-17. David is confident that "in the morning," after the night of anxiety, he will be singing joyous songs of praise. He will again know by experience that God was his strength and his high tower of refuge.

D. Protection from Enemies Without (Ps 60).

This psalm was written by David during the time of his wars. While David had been occupied in campaigns with the Arameans (Syrians), the Edomites apparently had seized the opportunity for invading the south of Judah. David quickly dispatched a force which routed the Edomites with great slaughter in the Valley of Salt south of the Dead Sea. This psalm was probably written just after David dispatched the

307

troops under Joab and before he knew the outcome of the battle. The poem has three stanzas of four verses each: (1) present defeat (vv. 1-4); (2) promised dominion (vv. 5-8); and (3) power for deliverance (vv. 9-12).

60:1. David complains that God has "cast off," i.e., abandoned, his people. He has "broken" them in some great calamity. It is a metaphor from the destruction of a wall or a building. It appeared that Yahweh was angry with Israel. David appeals for restoration of his favor.

60:2. The disaster is compared to an earthquake, which is often the symbol of great catastrophes and divine judgment. David asks that God "heal the breaches," i.e., repair, the damage which the calamity has caused.

60:3. Israel has been made to drink the "wine of staggering," i.e., the cup of God's wrath, a drugged potion which robs the drinker of reason. This metaphor expresses the confusion created by calamity, and the mockery which that confusion generates among bystanders.

60:4. Israel existed for one purpose: to display the glory of God among the nations. David believed that whenever an enemy came against his people, God would raise up a "banner" to represent his truth. Should Israel be defeated, that banner of truth was disgraced. David believed that God would not permit that to happen. "Selah" indicates a musical interlude at this point.

60:5. God's "beloved ones" (plural) are the Israelites. David asks for victory for those whom God loves. The "right hand" was the symbol of power.

60:6. "By his holiness" God had spoken, i.e., promised or sworn, to give certain lands to his people. God's holiness includes his whole essential nature in its moral aspect. His holiness makes it impossible for him to break his word. Here God is depicted as a victorious warrior, conquering the land and apportioning it out to his people. Shechem and Succoth, towns west and east of the Jordan, are both prominent in the history of Jacob (Gen 33:17-18). God will fulfill his promise to Jacob, apportioning to his people the land in which their great ancestor settled.

60:7. Gilead and Manasseh are territories east of Jordan. Ephraim and Judah are tribal areas west of Jordan. All are claimed by God and

have a right to his protection. Ephraim, the most powerful tribe and
the chief defense of the nation, is compared to a warrior's helmet.
Judah, as the tribe to which belonged the Davidic sovereignty, is compared to the royal scepter (cf. Gen 49:10).

60:8. In strong contrast to the honor assigned to Ephraim and
Judah is the disgrace of Moab and Edom. Moab, notorious for its
pride (Isa 16:6), is compared to the vessel which was brought to the
victorious warrior to wash his feet when he returned from battle. The
thought is that this ancient enemy of God's people would become a
vassal state, subject to the hegemony of Yahweh's vice-regent David.
Upon Edom Yahweh will cast his shoe, i.e., he would take possession
of Edom. Mighty Philistia must raise the "shout" (NASB) of homage
to its conqueror, Yahweh the God of Israel.

60:9. None but the Lord can give help to his people in the war
against Edom. The "strong city" here is probably Sela (later Petra),
the capital of Edom. Those who have visited the spot marvel with
Obadiah (v. 3) at its inaccessibility. The thought of a successful invasion of Edom is hopeless, unless Yahweh himself leads the army.[4]

60:10-12. Though God has for the moment deserted his people,
he will surely now give them aid. In bold faith David asks for divine
help against the adversary, for it is vain to look to human strength
for victory. He is confident that through the strength supplied by
God the armies of Israel will fight valiantly. God shall cast down the
adversaries.

ENDNOTES

1. The term *'elim* is not used elsewhere. Some want to change the vocalization of the consonants to produce *'Elohim*, as in Ps 82:1,6. The judges
would be called "gods" because they act as representatives of God in their
official office.

2. Another possibility is that the reference is to the way in which snails
dry up and perish in drought leaving their empty shells behind them.

3. The participle which is used with *'Elohim* in 58:11 is plural, suggesting that the term *'Elohim* should be rendered "divine powers," and not
"God." The ancient Septuagint and Syriac versions, however, take the final *m*
on the participle as a pronominal suffix and not a sign of the plural. Hence
the meaning would be: "There is a God that judges *them* in the earth."

4. The verb "lead" in 69:9 is in the perfect tense, which is sometimes used in questions to express a sense of difficulty or hopelessness. See A.F. Kirkpatrick, *The Book of Psalms*, in "The Cambridge Bible for Schools and Colleges" (Cambridge: University Press, 1910), p. 343.

CHAPTER FIFTEEN

David and the Great King
Psalms 61–72

Book Two concludes with twelve psalms which focus on the relationship between the earthly king and his God.

THE KING'S NEED
Psalms 61–64

The first four psalms depict the desperate straits in which David found himself. Though the king was in need, yet he trusted in the Lord and confidently expected his merciful intervention.

A. The King's Expectation (Ps 61).

This psalm was written by David probably when he was at Mahanaim in exile from Jerusalem and the temple. The revolt by Absalom has been put down (2 Sam 18). Though David's heart was crushed with the loss of his son, he must rejoice over the preservation of his crown. The psalm has two main divisions: (1) David's request for restoration (vv. 1-4); and (2) his expression of expectation (vv. 5-8).

311

61:1-2. The terms "cry" and "prayer" are often coupled to express the urgency of supplication. David cries "from the end of the land," i.e., from a place far distant from the capital (Jerusalem). He asks that God would lead him to a rock that is too high for him to climb alone. The "rock" represents asylum. God himself is the rock of refuge.

61:3-4. In past experience David had found Yahweh to be "a refuge" and "strong tower" from various enemies. In his exile he prays that he may once more "sojourn" as Yahweh's guest, enjoy his hospitality, and dwell in the place which he has consecrated by his presence. The term "tent" can refer to any dwelling, but it is natural to see here a reference to the tent which David erected in Jerusalem for the ark of God (2 Sam 6:17). David's trust would be "in the hiding place" of Yahweh's "wings." The reference is to the Holy of Holies where the wings of the cherubim were outspread to cover the mercy seat and the ark. This was viewed as God's earthly throne room.

61:5. David can offer the above prayers in confidence, for God has already heard his "vows." Prayers normally accompanied vows. God had given David "the heritage of those that fear" God's name. During the Absalom rebellion, true and faithful Israelites had supported David, the king of God's choice. Now these faithful ones have been restored to the possession of their rightful inheritance, from which they had been expelled by the circumstances of the rebellion.

61:6. David's life had been in danger, but now that danger was past. David here speaks in the third person because he is speaking of himself in his capacity as king, referring to the promises made to those who held that office. God promised faithful kings long life, and David here expresses confidence that the king's life will be "as many generations," i.e., he would be able to see more than one generation of his offspring.[1]

61:7. The king shall sit enthroned before God forever. This is an allusion to the promise of eternal dominion to the house of David. To reside in the presence of God means that one enjoys his favor and protection. God's covenant love and faithfulness to his promise are like guardian angels to the king. If reflected in the reign of the king, these attributes will be the safeguard of his throne.

61:8. The preservation of life demands lifelong thanksgiving. Fulfilling one's vows to God is a means of demonstrating thanksgiving. David is the speaker here.

B. The King's Trust (Ps 62).

David wrote this psalm, probably during the period of Absalom's rebellion. Ps 62 contains three equal stanzas: (1) a declaration of trust (vv. 1-4); (2) an exhortation to trust (vv. 5-8); and (3) an admonition concerning trust (vv. 9-12).

62:1-2. "Truly" or "only" (*'akh*) is characteristic of this psalm, appearing six times (vv. 1,2,4,5,6,9). To God alone David looks in patient calmness, waiting for the deliverance which will surely come. The three titles for God ("rock," "salvation," and "high tower") are also found in 18:2. The term *rock* conveys the strength, faithfulness, and unchangeableness of Yahweh. Nothing could move David from his reliance on the Lord.

62:3-4. Enemies kept hammering away at David with the intent of slaying him as if they were battering down a leaning wall. Such efforts are futile. The plot against the king is the result of gross hypocrisy and duplicity. The adversaries pronounce blessing on the king with their lips, but plot murder against him in their hearts.

62:5-6. It is only by constant self-exhortation that the calmness of v. 1 can be maintained. David repeats vv. 1-2 with slight variation which may reveal growing faith. Earlier he stated that he would not be *greatly* moved from his position of trust in God. Now he simply says: "I shall not be moved."

62:7-8. David exhorts his fainthearted followers, who were in danger of being carried away by the show of power on Absalom's side. He urges them to "pour out" their heart, i.e., all their anxiety, before the Lord. He reminds them that God is their refuge. *"Selah"* indicates a musical interlude at this point.

62:9. David admonishes his followers not to put their trust in man. Whatever their rank, wealth, or power, men are merely a breath which vanishes away. They have no weight or substance to tip the scales. Waverers would be influenced by seeing a number of leading men on Absalom's side.

62:10. David urges that they should not trust in wealth accumulated by oppression and robbery. Some were being tempted to covet the power which wealth brings, no matter what might be the means used for obtaining it.

62:11-12. "Once, yes twice," i.e., repeatedly, God has spoken and David has heard the double truth which supplies the answer to those who are tempted to trust in ill-gained wealth. Both power and lovingkindness belong to the Lord. He is both able and willing to "render to every man according to his work." The punishment of the wicked and the reward of the faithful attest God's power and love. Paul quotes these words in Rom 2:6ff.

C. The King's Satisfaction (Ps 63).

David wrote Ps 63 when he was in the wilderness of Judah during the Absalom revolt (2 Sam 15-18). Having been forced to leave Jerusalem, David and his followers took the Jericho road through the northern part of the wilderness of Judah. He lingered awhile at "the fords" before crossing the Jordan. The full extent of his danger from Absalom was not yet clear.

This psalm does not admit of clear division into stanzas. Scroggie[2] suggests: (1) the need for satisfaction (vv. 1-4); (2) the hope for satisfaction (vv. 5-7); and (3) the way of satisfaction (vv. 8-11)

63:1-2. David acknowledges *'Elohim* as his *'El*, i.e., the *strong one* to whom he can appeal with confidence in time of need. He longs for the Lord as a person might thirst for water in the midst of a dry and thirsty land. The wilderness where David found himself triggered this metaphor. He longs for the communion with deity which he had previously experienced at the sanctuary. There he had "gazed" upon (meditated) the power and glory of the creator. The ark was the symbol of God's presence, of his strength and glory. All the rituals of Old Covenant worship reinforced in his mind the greatness of God.

63:3. The lovingkindness of the Lord is better to him than life itself, for without it life would be nothing but a desert. It brings praise to his lips. Though his life was threatened, the danger faded out of sight in the consciousness of God's faithfulness.

63:4. As long as he had life in him he would fervently bless, i.e., praise, the Lord. The lifting up of the hands (turning palms up, rather than folding them) was the outward symbol of an uplifted heart.

314

63:5. God feeds the hungry soul with rich and bountiful food. That too led to joyous praise.

63:6-8. As he lies down at night he calls God to mind. He becomes so engrossed with the thought of his love that he meditates on it all night long. In Old Testament times the night was divided into three watches. He rejoices in "the shadow" of Yahweh's wings, i.e., in recollections of the ark with its cherubim of outstretched wings. He clings to the Lord and follows him. Because of that, God upholds him with his "right hand," i.e., power.

63:9. Those who seek David's life are emphatically contrasted with himself. While his path is upward toward God, theirs is downward to "the lower parts of the earth," i.e., to Sheol.

63:10-11. The enemies face an ignominious end, but the king emerges triumphant from the struggle. The enemies fall to the sword and are left unburied on the battlefield. Their corpses become a feast for packs of jackals. On the other hand, the king—David—shall rejoice in his God. Those who invoke the name of God in their oaths are those who are faithful worshipers. They share in the triumph of the king who is Yahweh's representative. Those who rebel against God and his king, who deluded men with false promises and lying accusations, shall be silenced.

D. The King's Confidence (Ps 64).

Ps 64 was composed by David, almost certainly during the period of Absalom's insurrection (2 Sam 15-18). The psalm has two main divisions: (1) David's complaint (vv. 1-6); and (2) David's champion (vv. 7-10).

64:1. David refers to his opening words as a "complaint." He asks that he might be preserved from the terror which the enemy inspires.

64:2-4. David was confident that Yahweh would hide him from the secret plans and open attack of the insurrectionists. Their tongue is like a sharpened sword; their words are like poisoned arrows which they shoot in secret places at those who are blameless before God. These men fear neither God nor the king.

64:5-6. The enemies spare no pains to make their plot successful. They say to themselves that there is no God who will take any account of their proceedings. They conceal their evil plans deep in their own hearts, but in vain. God knows their hearts.

64:7-8. When the rebels aim their arrows at the righteous, God shoots back. Swift retribution overtakes them unawares. Their tongue, the weapon with which they sought to destroy others, is turned against themselves. All who see their fate shall "wag the head" in scornful contempt.

64:9. Men in general who see the fate of the rebels are overcome by a wholesome fear (in contrast to the profane fearlessness of the ungodly in v. 4). These will publicly acknowledge that Yahweh rules the world. They will wisely apply to themselves the meaning of God's judgment.

64:10. For the righteous the judgment is an occasion of joy which stimulates even greater trust in the Lord.

THE KING'S RETURN
Psalms 65–66

The annual rains are one indication that God has returned to his people. Even more, the deliverance of his people from oppression signals that the Lord has again been merciful to them. These two manifestations of God's favor—the one natural, the other supernatural—are celebrated in the next two psalms.

A. Praise for Bountiful Harvests (Ps 65).

Ps 65 was composed by David, probably in connection with the Spring festival of firstfruits (Lev 23:10-14), in a period when his kingdom was established and peaceful. The psalm consists of three nearly equal stanzas: (1) the grace of God (vv. 1-4); (2) the greatness of God (vv. 5-8); and (3) the goodness of God (vv. 9-13).

65:1. It is the duty of grateful people to render thanks to God in the sanctuary. Praise is *silent* before God. The heart is so full that momentarily it can find no means of expression. Silence can be as full of praise as song and shout. In respectful silence the believers can perform their vows in offerings at the sanctuary.

65:2. Yahweh is the God who hears prayer. He is so addressed because once again he had demonstrated his willingness to respond to the cries of his people. David foresees the day when Yahweh's sanctuary would become a house of prayer for all nations.

65:3. The assembled congregation speaks of itself first as an individual ("against *me*"), then as an aggregate of individuals ("*our* transgressions"). The worshipers cannot defeat sin, but God can. He will "purge away" (cover, blot out) that sin.

65:4. A beatitude is pronounced on those fortunate enough to be chosen to approach God in the sanctuary. Visiting the sanctuary was a badge of membership in the Old Covenant Israel. True believers found satisfaction in that holy place.

65:5. In the future, as in the past, Yahweh will prove his righteousness by awe-inspiring deeds on behalf of his people in answer to their prayers. God's acts are "terrible" in that they strike fear into the hearts of his enemies, and fill his people with reverent awe. "Righteousness" is the principle of the divine government; it is closely related to "salvation." By righteousness, God's honor is pledged to answer prayer and deliver his people. Yahweh's mighty acts on behalf of his people in destroying their oppressors will lead all the oppressed and needy throughout the world to turn to him in trust.

65:6-8. Yahweh's power is demonstrated in that he created and sustains the mountains, the strongest and most solid parts of the earth. He controls the turbulent elements of nature and the tumultuous hosts of the nations which they symbolize. These mighty works impress distant people. From the furthest east to the furthest west he makes earth's inhabitants to shout for joy.

65:9-10. The special object of this psalm is now taken up. David wishes to express thanksgiving for the plenty of the year. He gratefully acknowledges that the rains which have fertilized the soil were God's gift. God's "stream" is the rain, with which he irrigates the land as out of a brimming aqueduct. The rains had prepared the ground for the seed and fostered its growth.

65:11-12. The Lord had crowned the year with his goodness, i.e., added fresh beauty and perfection to a year already marked by special bounty. Wherever he traverses on the earth he leaves rich blessings. This again is probably a reference to the latter rain which was more uncertain than the early rain, and was generally regarded as special blessing. The pastures of the uncultivated countryside and hills rejoice over the outpouring of the rain.

65:13. Sheep and wheat in abundance clothe the land because of the bountiful rains.

B. Praise for Awesome Works (Ps 66).

Ps 66 is anonymous, but the language appears to connect it with the deliverance of Judah from the host of Sennacherib in 701 BC (Isa 36–38). The psalm has two main divisions. The first twelve verses use the first person plural, as though a choir were singing; verses 13-20 are in the first person singular, as though it were intended for a soloist. Within these two main divisions four stanzas appear: (1) a summons to praise God (vv. 1-4); (2) the mighty works of God (vv. 5-7); (3) the marvelous ways of God (vv. 8-12); and (4) the exuberant worship of God (vv. 13-20).

66:1-4. All are summoned to worship God and acknowledge the greatness of his power. They should "make a joyful noise" or shout, i.e., greet him with the acclaim which befits a victorious king. They should "sing forth" the honor of God's name, i.e., his character. The praise should recognize the awesome works of God. It should contemplate the day when all enemies will become submissive to the Lord. It should acknowledge that one day all the earth will worship and praise God.

66:5. The nations are invited to contemplate some of God's awesome works for his people in the past. All men must fear God; but it depends on themselves whether they will reverence him as their God, or dread him as their enemy.

66:6. God turned the Red Sea and the Jordan River into dry land before his people. Identifying with the Israelites of ancient times, the psalmist regards the nation as possessing an unbroken continuity of life. Thus he can say: "there [at the Red Sea and Jordan] did we rejoice in him."

66:7-8. This God of awesome works past is still ruling in the present. He keeps watch lest any foe should injure Israel. The psalmist warns those who obstinately resist God's will to humble themselves. The psalmist calls upon the nations to praise God. He is conscious of Israel's mission to the world.

66:9. Israel was at the point of national death and ruin, but God preserved and upheld the nation. The particular deliverance will be described in the following verses.

66:10. Through the ordeal of the invasion, Israel had been purged of dross as impurities are smelted out of precious metals.

66:11. God had deliberately brought his people into the power of enemies to punish them for their sins. He had laid a crushing blow upon their "loins," i.e., an affliction which caused them to bow down under its weight.

66:12. As a vanquished people Israel had been flung down upon the ground, and trampled under the horse hoofs and chariot wheels of their conquerors. "Fire and water" are symbolic of extreme and varied dangers. God brought them through that adversity to "abundance," the opposite of the privations which had been endured.

66:13-15. The change to the singular pronoun indicates that the king enters the temple. He comes with burnt offerings expressing devotion, and peace offerings to fulfill his vows which he made in the hour of national distress. "Incense of rams" denotes the sweet savor of the sacrifice ascending as it was consumed by fire. Rams and he-goats were prescribed in the law for worship by the entire nation or its leaders, not by ordinary Israelites.

66:16. "All who fear God" are bidden to hear what he has done for the king who is speaking. In the light of the universal emphasis of this psalm, the phrase probably includes pious Gentiles who had been converted as well as Israelites.

66:17-19. Even while the king prayed, he had praises ready to offer up, so sure was he of a positive answer from the Lord. Hypocrisy would have disqualified the suppliant, but he was confident that he was no hypocrite. The answer to the prayer indicates that his assessment was correct. This is not self-righteousness, but the simplicity of a clear conscience.

66:20. The psalm concludes with praise to God for answered prayer and continued mercy.

THE KING'S KING
Psalms 67–69

The next three psalms extol the glories of heaven's king, and especially what he would do for his people through Messiah.

A. His Universal Reign (Ps 67).

Ps 67 is sometimes called Israel's Missionary Psalm. The writer is anonymous. Most likely it is to be assigned to the writer of the previous psalm. The background also is the same, namely, the miraculous rescue of Jerusalem from Sennacherib in 701 BC. Ps 67 consists of a core (vv. 3-5) which begins and ends with the same refrain. This core is sandwiched between an introduction (vv. 1-2) and a conclusion (vv. 6-7).

67:1. The psalm begins with words taken from the priestly blessing of Num 6:24ff., only *'Elohim* is substituted for *Yahweh*. For the face of God to shine "*with* us" would suggest the thought of God's favor *abiding with* his people.

67:2. The blessings which God bestows upon Israel will show the nations what a God he is and will make them desire to serve him. God's *way* is his gracious method of dealing with men which can be summed up in the word *salvation*.

67:3-4. The wish is expressed that all nations may soon acknowledge the God of Israel as their God. The Gentiles can rejoice for God shall "judge" or rule them with just and equitable government. He will "lead" those Gentiles as he led Israel through the wilderness. These verses clearly anticipate the messianic kingdom.

67:5-6. The refrain of v. 3 is repeated, but perhaps here it is more of an assertion of confidence than a wish. At least the Hebrew could be so rendered: "The peoples shall give thanks to you, O God." Under the rule of God the land will yield her increase, i.e., in God's kingdom there is abundance of food.

67:7. The thankful people declare that God is blessing them. They express their faith that he will continue to bless them. The result of this will be that the most remote nations will become worshipers of the only true God, the God of Israel.

B. His Mighty Conquest (Ps 68).

Ps 68 is notoriously difficult to translate and interpret. David wrote this psalm, perhaps at the time when the ark was transported from the home of Obed-edom to the tent in Jerusalem (2 Sam 6). The key to the meaning of the psalm is the citation by Paul in Eph 4:8 which sees in this psalm a prediction of the ascension of Christ. The messianic interpretation of Ps 68 suggests five divisions: (1) the advent (vv. 1-6); (2) accomplishments (vv. 7-17); (3) ascension (vv. 18-21); (4) announcement (vv. 22-31); and (5) appeal (vv. 32-35).

68:1-2. David anticipates a glorious coming of God. Before him the wicked flee like smoke before the wind, their powers of resistance to God melt like wax before a fire.

68:3-4. The righteous, on the other hand, stand before God and rejoice in his presence. God's advent is described under the figure of a journey of an oriental monarch before whose chariot engineers prepare the road. Through faith, obedience and godliness the righteous prepare for God's advent.

68:4-5. The coming one is *Yah*, shortened form of *Yahweh*. This name points to the Lord as the covenant-making, covenant-keeping God of redemption who shows himself mighty in the deliverance of his people. Yahweh is "the father of orphans," i.e., protector of the innocent and helpless. He is *judge* (vindicator) of widows. His *abode*, whether on earth or in heaven, is holy.

68:6. Only those who rebel against God never experience the spiritual transformation which may be likened to homecoming after a long journey or freedom after extended bondage. The rebels remain in the barren wastes of life.

68:7-10. David begins to set forth the history of Israel from the Exodus to the entry into Canaan. The thought here is that the past accomplishments of Yahweh are a key to his future actions. He pictures God leading his people through the wilderness to Sinai. A great thunderstorm and earthquake marked his presence there. During the forty years of wandering Yahweh showered upon them "rain," i.e., refreshing gifts such as manna, quail and water. These deeds prove that God will prepare a resting place for those who are poor and afflicted.

68:11-14. God led his people into Canaan. He merely spoke his word, and *kings of hosts* fled before Israel. Peaceful noncombatants were able to share in the distribution of the spoils of the routed enemy. Following the times of war, Israel enjoyed periods of peaceful prosperity which are likened to (1) the beautiful plumage of the dove; and (2) the dazzling whiteness of a patch of snow in the midst of dark terrain.

68:15-17. The hill of God (God's kingdom) is likened to a lofty mountain, i.e., his kingdom is invincible. The mountains (kingdoms) of the heathen world show envy or hostility toward Zion because Yahweh has chosen that place for his dwelling. Zion is protected by

321

the innumerable chariots of God as well as Yahweh's personal presence. That same glorious theophany (manifestation of God) which once took place on Sinai is now renewed on Zion.

68:18. Paul saw in this verse a prophecy of the ascension of Christ (Eph 4:8). The verse is in the second person. Thus it is a prayer. God is said to have ascended on high, i.e., to heaven, as a great conqueror. He has taken "captivity captive." All that once held men captive—Satan, sin, death—has been conquered. At his ascension Christ *received* gifts and then *gave* those gifts to those for whom they were intended. These spiritual gifts are given to men so that God might dwell among them. The reference is to the church of Christ which is the temple of the Holy Spirit (2 Cor 6:16).

68:19-20. The Lord daily loads down his people with salvation. He now makes possible escape even from death itself. On the other hand, this God smashes the heads of all his enemies. The "hairy scalp" refers to the unshorn hair of a warrior who had taken a vow not to cut his hair until victory was achieved. In spite of such zeal, the enemies of God will not succeed.

68:21-23. Yahweh speaks directly for the only time in the psalm. He confirms the confident acclaim of the victory expressed in the preceding verse. Even when the enemy seems to have escaped, God brings them back for punishment and destruction. The people of God will wade through the blood of those fallen foes. Though the language is unpleasant, the truth expressed here is essential. The judgment of the oppressor is in fact the necessary condition of the deliverance of the oppressed. Moreover such judgment is also an indispensable vindication of God's eternal justice.

68:24-28. The great victory over the forces of evil is celebrated in solemn worship. All men have been spectators of the conflict between God and his enemies. The *goings* refers to the festive procession celebrating God's victory. The victor returns to heaven to be hailed as king. The triumphant procession is accompanied by musicians. In the solemn assemblies of God's people the triumph over evil should be praised. The mention of the various tribes is a way of urging that *all* God's people should praise the victory.

68:29. David anticipates the day when Gentiles would pay tribute to the God of Jacob at his yet-to-be-built temple in Jerusalem.

68:30-31. David prays for God to "rebuke the wild beast of the reeds," i.e., the crocodile or hippopotamus, symbolic of Egypt, the most powerful of heathen states. The "crowd of bulls" may represent the leaders of the nations, the "calves" their subjects. Together these rulers and their subjects come to render tribute to the divine conqueror. Warlike enemies have been scattered by the hand of God. Princes of Egypt and Ethiopia submit to God's will. David is predicting the spread of Messiah's kingdom among the Gentiles.

68:32-34. In view of the conquests here foreseen, the whole world is summoned to acknowledge the God of Israel as universal sovereign. Yahweh rides as a conqueror in triumph through the heaven of heavens which existed long before the heavens as men know them. A voice from heaven urges people to acknowledge by the tribute of praise the power which is Yahweh's. He is entitled to such praise because of the greatness he displays in protecting Israel.

68:35. The nations seem to respond to the appeal of the preceding verse. They acknowledge the awesome might which God displays from his sanctuary in the midst of Israel. They recognize him as the source of Israel's preeminence. They bless his name, i.e., his revealed attributes.

C. His Innocent Suffering (Ps 69).

Ps 69 is quoted seven times in the New Testament. The manner in which this psalm is quoted seems to necessitate that the sufferer here is Messiah. Ps 69 claims to be Davidic in its heading. The psalm has three main divisions: (1) Messiah's prayer for deliverance (vv. 1-21); (2) his prophecy regarding his enemies (vv. 22-28); and (3) his profession of thanksgiving (vv. 29-36).

69:1-4. In his first petition, Messiah cries out for help. He was in serious danger, like that of drowning, and being stuck in deep mire in which there was no solid bottom. He had waited patiently on God. His throat is parched by excessive exertion, his eyes are exhausted from continued looking to God for help. He was facing numerous enemies who were out to destroy him. Though he was absolutely honest, they treated him like a thief.

69:5. He was confident that God knew the truth about his conduct. From one point of view, he was free from the charges laid against him by his antagonists. From another point of view, all the iniquities of mankind were charged upon him by imputation. Hence he was being chastised for his "sins" and his "foolishness," i.e., those sins which he had taken upon himself.

69:6. Should Messiah be left utterly to perish, those who put their trust in God will be put to scorn and confusion.

69:7-12. The second petition is that godly souls may not be hurt by the suffering which he experiences. This petition is strengthened by four reasons: (1) his sufferings were for God's sake; (2) his friends had abandoned him; (3) his zeal for the honor of God's house had brought reproach upon him;[3] and (4) his religious commitment had brought him mockery. The spiritual agony of Messiah is mentioned here, not in reference to his own suffering only, but to the sins of his people. One thinks of the tears shed by Jesus as he looked down upon the city of Jerusalem (Luke 19:41). People in positions of leadership ("those who sit in the gate") and those rascals who compose drunken ditties made light of Messiah's earnest concern for the salvation of his fellows.

69:13. In his third petition Messiah prays that God will hear him for three reasons: (1) he presents his petition "in an acceptable time," i.e., before it was too late; (2) he makes mention of the multitude of God's mercies; and (3) he speaks of the truth of God's promises of salvation.

69:14-15. The fourth petition is for deliverance. Messiah supports this petition by again vividly describing his plight in terms of drowning and entrapment in a pit.

69:16-17. To his fifth petition for deliverance Messiah adds three additional supporting thoughts: (1) he refers to the multitude of God's tender mercies; (2) he again refers to the trouble he experiences; and (3) he urges a swift response from God. Thus he implies that his situation was desperate.

69:18-21. In connection with his sixth petition for deliverance Messiah mentions four facts: (1) God knows the reproach which has been heaped upon him; (2) he is heavy hearted because of that reproach; (3) he was able to find no comfort on earth; and (4) tormentors had added affliction to affliction. Instead of meat they had given him *gall* (bitterness) and *vinegar* for drink.[4]

69:22-23. The beginning of ten plagues which would befall those who persecuted Messiah.[5] (1) God will curse all comforts of this life unto these adversaries. (2) All things will work for their woe and torment. (3) They shall not perceive the true intent of God's work. (4) They shall have no peace.

69:24-25. The plagues on the persecutors continue. (5) The wrath of God will be poured out on them. (6) The curse of God shall be on their houses and prosperity, and the place in which they have dwelled shall be abhorred. Peter regarded v. 25 as a prophecy regarding Judas. The prophecy does not merely apply to Judas as an individual, but to him as a representative of the Jewish people who rejected Christ.

69:26. The circumstances which justify these dire predictions are indicated. These adversaries have heaped abuse on the one that God had smitten.

69:27-28. The last four plagues on the adversaries are now listed. (7) The persecutors will go ever deeper into sin. (8) They become so hardened in sin that they shall not come into God's righteousness. (9) They shall meet with an untimely death. (10) These wicked enemies would not be numbered among the righteous.

69:29. The sufferer utters a confident prayer. He will not only be delivered, he will also be exalted. Messiah's salvation or deliverance is the resurrection.

69:30-31. Messiah praises the Father following his deliverance from suffering and death.

69:32-33. The "humble," i.e., true believers, shall rejoice over the victory of the sufferer (Messiah). They will experience a life more abundant because of his suffering. They can now have confidence that their prayers will be answered. The victory of the sufferer proves once and for all that God does not despise those who are imprisoned by affliction or oppression for his sake.

69:34. The psalm concludes with a prophecy of thanksgiving for blessings bestowed on God's people. The deliverance of the sufferer signals the salvation of Zion. The God who is faithful to the individual believer will also be faithful to the whole church.

69:35-36. The prophecy anticipates the destruction of the cities of Judah, and the subsequent rebuilding thereof after the Babylonian exile. So it was that after the exile the Jews once again possessed the Promised Land. The restored postexilic community is a type of the church enjoying the peace and security of Messiah's kingdom.

THE KING'S PLAN
Psalms 70–72

Heaven's king had a plan for world redemption. Ultimately his reign would be recognized to the ends of the earth. Meanwhile, believers must trust him and look to him for aid in times of difficulty.

A. An Urgent Call for Help (Ps 70).

What appears here is a repetition of Ps 40:13-17 which, with slight intentional variations, has been adapted for another occasion. The words "for a memorial" (NASB) also appear in the heading of Ps 38. This probably refers to the liturgical use of the psalm either in connection with the offering of incense (Lev 24:7), or at the offering of the *Azkara*, a special portion of the meal offering (Lev 2:2). The short psalm sets forth (1) a cry for help (v. 1); (2) a contrast in destinies (vv. 2-4); and (3) a confession of need (v. 5). For observations on this psalm, see notes on Ps 40:13-17.

B. A Testimony to Trust in God (Ps 71).

Ps 71 is anonymous. Some think that it originally was a continuation of the previous psalm. The close connection with the two preceding psalms, the absence of a title here, and the style, all suggest Davidic authorship. It probably belongs to the later period of David's life. The composition contains many quotations from other psalms, but the new combination has a significance all its own. In this psalm one thought grows out of another, and there is no marked division into stanzas; but in the first half (vv. 1-13) the emphasis is on prayer, and in the second half, praise (vv. 14-24).

71:1-3. The psalm begins with a prayer of faith in the midst of danger. These verses are taken, with but little change, from 31:1-3. See notes at that reference.

71:4-6. The ground of the psalmist's appeal for deliverance is now set forth. Those who threaten him are wicked, unrighteous and cruel.

He has trusted in God all his life. Verses 5-6 are a free adaptation of 22:9-10.

71:7-8. Those who saw his sufferings regarded the psalmist as a typical example of divine chastisement; but his faith remained unshaken. His mouth is filled with praises and honor for God all the day.

71:9-11. The psalmist asks God not to cast him away in his old age. Even though he is an old man, still the enemies speak and plot against him. They regarded him as abandoned by God.

71:12-13. Again the psalmist asks for God's swift help. He asks that those who oppose him would be confounded and consumed.

71:14-16. The psalmist contrasts his own future with that of his enemies. Salvation is coupled with righteousness, because the one is the outcome and visible manifestation of the other. The psalmist resolves to "come" with the mighty acts of God, i.e., he would use those mighty acts as the theme for his praise.

71:17-18. Past mercies are the ground of hope both for the psalmist and for the nation. He has been a lifelong disciple in the school of God. Through the years habitually he had been declaring God's "wondrous works" as they were manifested in nature and in his dealings with his people. He wishes still to be able to testify to God's strength and power in preserving him in his old age.

71:19-20. Yahweh is incomparable for power and goodness. His righteousness reaches to the height of heaven. The psalmist's hopes are not merely personal; he speaks on behalf of the nation whose representative he is. He looks for its restoration from its present state of humiliation. Israel is, as it were dead; but God can and will recall it to life.

71:21-22. The psalmist thinks of himself as sharing in the honor of the resuscitated nation. He can hardly be referring to personal dignity only. In response to this new proof of God's love he will praise God with "the psaltery," a stringed instrument, and the harp. The title "Holy One of Israel" signifies that God, in his character of a holy God, had entered into covenant with Israel. His holiness is pledged to redeem his people.

71:23-24. When he has been delivered from danger, the psalmist joyously will sing praises to the Lord. By faith he will speak constantly of God's righteousness which was manifested in the total confusion and shame of those that sought to hurt him.

C. Reign of a Glorious King (Ps 72).

Solomon is the author of this psalm. The imagery in the psalm is clearly borrowed from the peaceful and prosperous reign of this grand monarch. Solomon speaks here as a prophet. He anticipates the coming of the one who would be greater than himself (Matt 12:42). The reign of Messiah will be (1) righteous (vv. 1-7); (2) universal (vv. 8-11); (3) beneficent (vv. 12-14); and (4) perpetual (vv. 15-17). To these grand predictions Solomon appends his own doxology (vv. 18-19).

72:1-2. The king was the supreme court of the land. Messiah was expected to exercise judicial powers in perfection. His reign would be characterized by righteousness. Even the poor would be treated equitably by the glorious ruler here envisioned.

72:3-4. The result of the righteous rule would be a harvest of peace throughout the kingdom. Messiah would vindicate the rights of the afflicted. He would save the children of the needy from slavery, and crush those who oppress them.

72:5. Prayer and prediction are joined. Throughout all generations the name of God will be revered.

72:6-7. The coming of the messianic king is likened to "rain upon a mown field." He brings renewal and refreshment to a world scarred by war. Under this prince of peace the "righteous will flourish." His reign will continue so long as the moon endures and even beyond.

72:8. Messiah's kingdom stretches from sea to sea and "from the river [Euphrates] unto the ends of the earth." This is an obvious allusion to the boundaries of the Promised Land as defined in Exod 23:31.

72:9-11. Even those on the fringes of the civilized world will crouch in fear before him. In total humiliation and subjugation his enemies would "lick the dust." From distant lands men will come bringing their offerings. The Hebrew terminology used here indicates that worship offerings are in view. Tarshish on the coast of Spain represents the distant west; Sheba in Arabia represents the east. Seba appears to have been in Ethiopia. The verbs "bow" and "serve" can refer to either civil or religious subjugation.

72:12-14. Messiah's reign is beneficent. His justice is impartial. He would use his might on behalf of the unfortunate. He would not allow oppression and violence to be used against the humble.

72:15-16. The prosperity of Messiah's reign is depicted in terms of agricultural abundance. Zion, his capital, will "flourish like grass of the earth," i.e., the city has a flourishing population.

72:17. The name of Messiah will endure forever. Through him all nations of the earth would be blessed (cf. Gen 12:3). All nations will call him blessed because he is the source of their prosperity and salvation.

72:18-19. The psalm concludes with Solomon's personal praise for the God who would bring such a wonderful king into the world. Truly these are "wondrous things" which the prophet has been describing.

ENDNOTES

1. The language of 61:6 may express the conviction that the king would live on in his descendants. A.F. Kirkpatrick observes that "words which in their strict sense could apply to no human individual, become a prophecy of One greater than David." For this reason the Targum here interprets "king" by "King Messiah." *The Book of Psalms* in The Cambridge Bible for Schools and Colleges (Cambridge: University Press, 1910), p. 346.

2. W. Graham Scroggie, *The Psalms* (Old Tappan, NJ: Revell, 1965), 2:77-78.

3. The first half of 69:9 is applied to Jesus in John 2:17; the latter half is applied to him in Rom 15:3.

4. In the passion of Jesus circumstances were such that 69:21 received striking fulfillment. Romans usually gave those sentenced to the cross a sour wine with an infusion of myrrh for the purpose of deadening the pain. This practice was followed in the case of Jesus (Mark 15:23). On the part of the Roman soldiers this may have been an act of kindness; but considered as an act of the unbelieving Jews, it was adding anguish to one already overwhelmed with anguish. Matthew (27:34), therefore, suggests that the wine and myrrh offered to Christ are identical with the gall and vinegar of this prediction.

5. The imprecations contained in Ps 69:22-28 are not the outgrowth of a vengeful or selfish spirit. Jesus and Paul applied the words of these verses to the unbelieving Jews (Matt 23:38; Rom 11:9-10). These imprecations should be regarded as predictions.

CHAPTER SIXTEEN

The Mighty Help of God
Psalms 73-83

Book Three of the Psalter begins with Psalm 73. This is sometimes called the "Leviticus" book because of its emphasis on the sanctuary and holiness. The dominant name of God in the these psalms is still *'Elohim*.[1] The dominant theme in this Book is the worship of God under all circumstances.

The psalms here are all attributed to Asaph and the sons of Korah with the exception of Ps 86 which is assigned to David. For this reason Book Three is called the Asaphitic book. It is clear that all of the psalms which bear the name of Asaph could not have been written by David's musician, if indeed any of them were, for some unquestionably belong to the time of the Exile. The title may mean only that these psalms were taken from a collection preserved and used in the family or guild of Asaph. Yet these psalms are marked by distinctive characteristics. First, they have a prophetic character about them. Second, they are national rather than personal psalms.

INTRODUCTION
The Problem Presented
Psalms 73-74

Book Three begins with a double psalm introduction which sets forth the spiritual problem to be addressed in the psalms that follow.

A. Inequities of Life (Ps 73).

Ps 73 is the second of the psalms attributed to Asaph. On the identity of the author, see on Ps 50. The historical occasion of this psalm is unknown. It is the record of personal experience common to believers of any age. Like Pss 37 and 49 it treats the perennial problem of reconciling the theology of God's moral government of the world with experience and observation of the way things really are. This psalm has been dubbed the theological center of the Psalter. Following an introduction (vv. 1-2), the psalm is organized in two main divisions: (1) faith struggling (vv. 3-14); and (2) faith triumphant (vv. 15-26). Verses 27-28 form the conclusion.

73:1-2. The psalmist begins by stating the conclusion to which he had been led through the trial of his faith: "Truly God is good to Israel." Though he permits his people to suffer, he is essentially good to his people, such of them as are of "clean heart." Thus Asaph speaks throughout of the *true* Israel of God. Purity of heart and life is the condition of admission to his presence. At one point the psalmist had almost lost his faith in God's goodness. He had all but lost his footing in the slippery places of life's journey.

73:3-4. The reason why the psalmist nearly lost his footing is because he had become envious of the prosperity (lit., peace) of the "arrogant" and "wicked." The former term refers to those guilty of blustering presumption. Such men seem to have no pain in their death, i.e., they die a peaceful and quiet death. On the contrary, "their body is fat," i.e., healthy, when they die.

73:5-6.The wicked and arrogant seem to escape the misery which is the common lot of humanity. Consequently their pride and brutality go unchecked. Pride is their necklace and violence, their garment. The metaphor suggests that their attitude and action were clearly visible to all.

73:7-9. "Their eye bulges from fatness" describes the insolent look of these sleek-faced villains. Neither fear nor shame controls the utterance of their inward thoughts. Their own nefarious schemes are the subject of their conversation. They speak "from on high," i.e., they pontificate like they were deities speaking oracles. They blaspheme God, and browbeat their fellow men with their words.

73:10-11. The wicked are popular. The masses are carried away by the evil example of these arrogant men. They drink the waters of sinful pleasure with the wicked. These misled men begin to question God's omniscience. The names of God used here ('El = the mighty one; 'Elyon = supreme ruler) underscore the blasphemy of their skepticism.

73:12-14. The psalmist again frankly confesses the temptation which the prosperity of the wicked presents to him. If such evil men prosper, then the psalmist's pursuit of holiness had been in vain. He is not claiming sinlessness, but he does have a clear conscience about the life he had lived. He feels that the recompense of his piety had been chastisement. He had suffered continuously.

73:15-17. The psalmist was aware that if he continued to express his misgivings about the good fortune of the wicked, he would have been faithless to the interests of God's "children," i.e., Israel. Yet in his mind he could not reconcile the inequities of life with the revealed truth of God's character and promises. The pain of his perplexity continued to grow until he went to the temple, the place where God revealed his power and glory. There he began to reflect on the transitoriness of the prosperity of the wicked, and their nothingness in the sight of God.

73:18-20. The psalmist sets forth the awful fate of the wicked. They are set in dangerous places where they will stumble and fall to their ruin. They will be destroyed in a moment, swept away by sudden terrors. The dream would be over momentarily. When God arouses himself to judgment, he will have no particular regard for their "form," i.e., all their pretense and power.

73:21-22. The psalmist confesses his own errors, e.g., the folly of his former impatience. He had lowered himself to the level of a beast, for what distinguishes man from animals is his power of communion with God. He was worrying instead of worshiping.

73:23-24. The psalmist contrasts his present fellowship with God with his former period of depression. He knows that God will guide him with the very "counsel" which the wicked despise. After following that counsel through life's pilgrimage, the psalmist anticipated that God would "receive me to glory." At the very least, these words anticipate a visible demonstration that he is the object of God's loving favor. There may be much more here. He may anticipate reception into the glory of Yahweh's presence after death.

73:25-26. The psalmist now confesses that his relationship with God was completely satisfying. As long as he had God, there was no other in heaven or earth that he desired. God is the only source of happiness in the whole universe. Though bodily and mental powers fail, the psalmist claims "God is the rock of my heart," i.e., his sure refuge in every danger. Now that he has come to his spiritual senses, he will never look for any other refuge.

73:27-28. Desertion of God can lead only to ruin and death. To "whore" away from God is to be unfaithful to the terms of the covenant. The figure of marriage is used to express the closeness of Yahweh's relation to his people, and consequently apostasy is spoken of as infidelity to the marriage vow. For his part, the psalmist intends to "draw near" to God. Once he had been tempted to ask what profit there was in serving God; once he had openly spoken of his doubts. Now he finds in God's refuge a theme for endless praise.

B. Inactivity of God (Ps 74).

This psalm is the third attributed to Asaph. On the identity of this writer, see on Ps 50. This is the ninth in the series of thirteen *maskil* (instructional) psalms. A major disaster at Jerusalem is the background of this poem. Many commentators think the poem was written shortly after the destruction of Jerusalem by the Chaldeans in 586 BC. If this is the case, than "Asaph" would have to be a namesake of the famous Asaph, or else the family name rather than the personal name of the writer. The psalm contains three prayers (vv. 1-3; 10-11; 18-23) divided by two reflective meditations.

74:1. The psalmist appeals to God, who seems to have abandoned the people and city of his choice. God's rejection seemed permanent. "Smoke" is an evidence of the hot anger of God. As "the sheep" of God's pasture, Israel had a right to claim the love and protection of their divine shepherd.

74:2-3. Yahweh's relationship to Israel is ancient. He had "redeemed" or "purchased" this people out of slavery to be "the tribe" of his inheritance, i.e., the people who belonged especially to him. The psalmist asks God to remember Mt. Zion, his dwelling place, and to "lift up your feet," i.e., come in might and majesty to visit and deliver. The enemy has damaged the "sanctuary" (temple). The place appears to be perpetual ruins.

74:4. The psalmist begins to paint a vivid picture of the desecration of the temple by the heathen enemies. The temple courts were filled with shouting warriors instead of reverent worshipers. They had set up their military standards on those holy grounds, thus dramatizing the completeness of their triumph.

74:5-7. The enemy is compared to wood-cutters hewing down a forest. The beautiful artwork of the temple has been vandalized with hatchets and hammers. The sacred buildings have been burned and profaned.

74:8-9. By destroying the temple the enemy had done away with all the "solemn assemblies" in the land, i.e., the special occasions of worship and rejoicing. The "signs" or outward symbols of Israel's religion (e.g., festivals, sabbaths) were now forgotten. No prophet is on the scene to offer any encouragement.

74:10-11. The psalmist turns to God with the question "How long?" With this rhetorical question he entreats God to have pity on his people and to have regard to his own reputation. God's right hand which in days of old was stretched out to annihilate the Egyptians (Exod 15:12), is now, as it were, thrust idly into the folded garment. He asks God to take out that mighty hand, and use it on behalf of his people.

74:12. God's mighty works of redemption and creation attest his power to interpose for the deliverance of his people. In spite of his present seeming inactivity, he was still Israel's king. Yahweh works "salvations" (plural), i.e., manifold and great acts of deliverance. This he does "in the midst of the earth," i.e., in the sight of all the nations. He thereby asserts his claim to universal sovereignty.

74:13-14. The Exodus from Egypt is the classic example of the deliverances mentioned in v. 12. God parted the sea to permit the escape of his people. He smashed the heads of the "sea monsters" (NASB) and Leviathan, which here are symbolic of Egypt. Leviathan is probably the crocodile. These monsters are imagined as floating upon the surface of the water. The reference is to the destruction of Pharaoh's army in the Red Sea. The bodies were washed up on the shore to be devoured by the wild beasts of the desert.

74:15. Other examples of God's great power are cited. He broke open rocks and brought forth water from the rock (Exod 17:6; Num 20:8). He dried up the perennial stream of the Jordan to permit his people to cross over on dry land (Josh 4:23).

74:16-17. All the fixed laws of the natural world were established by God and are maintained by him. He established the pattern of day followed by night. The heavenly luminaries and even the sun were prepared by him. To him also are attributed the divisions of land and sea, and the apportionment of the land among the nations.

74:18-19. The psalmist returns to prayer. Yahweh, Israel's king, should remember that his name has been reproached. The term "foolish people" denotes the moral perversity of opposition to God. Israel is likened to a defenseless dove. They are "afflicted ones" who will be totally destroyed if their God forgets, i.e., ignores, them.

74:20. The psalmist asks God to remember "the covenant," i.e., the covenant with the patriarchs (Gen 17:2ff.); with the nation Israel (Exod 24:8); and with David (2 Sam 7:5-17). The people of God are desperate. They take refuge in "the dark places of the land," i.e., in caves and hiding places. In these places violence makes its home.

74:21. The psalmist asks that God not allow his poor and needy people to turn back from him unanswered and disappointed; that God will let the afflicted have cause to praise him for answered prayer.

74:22-23. Ps 74 concludes with an appeal for God to "plead," i.e., defend, his own cause, for his cause was the cause of Israel. The "fool" reproached God daily. His honor was at stake. The tumultuous voice of God's (and Israel's) adversaries was increasing. Delay in judgment was making matters worse by the day.

FAITH IN HIS HELP
Psalms 75–77

Though the situation was desperate for God's people, still they believed firmly that Yahweh would come to their aid.

A. The Certainty of Judgment (Ps 75).

Ps 75 is another work of Asaph (see on Ps 50), but whether the Asaph of David's day or a namesake is problematic. This psalm seems intended to serve as the divine answer to the appeal of the previous poem. It consists of three movements: (1) God's judgments in the past (vv. 1-3); the coming judgment upon the wicked (vv. 4-8); and (3) the ultimate vindication of the righteous (vv. 9-10).

75:1. The theme of the psalm is thanksgiving for a recent manifestation of God's presence and power among his people. God's "name," i.e., that which he has revealed of himself to men, was near. God is viewed as especially near when he manifests his presence. God's miracles of deliverance were on everyone's mouth.

75:2. God speaks. At the appropriate moment foreordained in the divine counsels, he manifests himself as judge of all the earth. The pronoun is emphatic in v. 2. Whatever men may do or think, God's intervention occurs right on schedule.

75:3. Though all the world is in terror and confusion, God has established a moral order in it. The first person pronoun is emphatic. Both the material and the spiritual world are often compared to a building with its foundations and pillars. The point is that God has established the fundamental laws which govern both the material and spiritual world.

75:4-5. The psalmist warns all presumptuous braggarts, based on the divine utterances of the preceding verses. The "fools" are warned not to "lift up the horn," a figure derived from animals tossing their heads in a display of strength. They should not continue to speak "with a stiff neck," i.e., arrogantly.

75:6-7. The psalmist sets forth the reason for the warning which he has just delivered to the foolish. True exaltation comes, not from earth, but from heaven, i.e., from God. He is the true judge or sovereign. He exalts one, and humbles another, according to his sovereign choice.

337

75:8. The judgment is described under the common figure of a cup of wine, which God gives the wicked to drink. The wine contains a "mixture" of herbs and spices to make it more seductive and intoxicating. The wicked must drink the cup to the last drop.

75:9. Forever—as long as life lasts (and beyond?)—the psalmist will praise the God of Jacob.

75:10. The speaker here is uncertain. Is it the psalmist? Or God? Probably God here answers the vow of praise of the preceding verse with a new promise. He will "cut off" all the horns of the wicked. On the other hand, the "horns" of the righteous one, i.e., Israel, will be exalted. Horns here are symbols of power.

B. The Overthrow of the Mighty (Ps 76).

Ps 76 is another psalm of Asaph (see on Ps 50). This is one of thirty psalms to also be designated a "song." The historical background is uncertain. The psalm has four stanzas of three verses each: (1) the deliverance of Zion (vv. 1-3); (2) the overthrow of the enemy (vv. 4-6); (3) the result of the mighty act (vv. 7-9); and (4) praise for the God of judgment (vv. 10-12).

76:1-3. God has once more shown his might in Zion by shattering the power of her assailants. By this recent deliverance he has once more "made himself known." The name "Israel" is the covenant name, denoting the people of God's choice. "Salem" here is either an old name for Jerusalem (Gen 14:18), or a poetical abbreviation. The name means "at peace," and it is used here as an allusion to the recent escape of Zion from destruction. At Zion Yahweh has "broken" the lightning-swift arrows of the enemy, as well as the other equipment which he might use in battle against the people of God.

76:4-6. In his destruction of the enemy, Yahweh shows himself to be more majestic than the "mountains of prey," i.e., the strongholds of the enemy, or metaphorical for the invaders themselves. The stouthearted enemies have allowed themselves to be spoiled. They have slumbered their last sleep, the sleep of death. They have not been able to find "their hands," i.e., their strength was paralyzed and they are unable to put forth effective resistance to the judgment of God. All the rush and roar of the battle—the chariot and horse—are now as silent as the grave.

76:7-9. The judgment of God is irresistible. Yahweh is to be feared. No one can stand before him when God is angry. God pronounced sentence upon the enemy when he intervened for the rescue of his people. This sentence was spoken "from heaven," the true abode of God and the seat of his judgment. The poet represents the earth watching in stunned silence as Yahweh arose from his heavenly throne to rescue "all the humble of the earth," i.e., idealized Israel in contrast to the wicked of the earth.

76:10. The psalmist begins to draw lessons from the judgment. "The wrath of man shall praise God," i.e., all rebellion against God's will must in the end redound to his glory; it serves to set his sovereignty in a clearer light. God girds on himself as an ornament the last futile efforts of human wrath, turning them to his own honor.[2]

76:11-12. Israel should pay the vows it made to the Lord in its hour of peril. The nations that dwell near God's city and people should now bring their tribute presents to the great king. Yahweh would cut off or destroy the plans of the enemy just as they are coming to maturity. The kings of the earth will meet their doom in his awesome power.

C. The Consolation of Recollection (Ps 77).

Ps 77 is another Asaph psalm, the occasion of which is difficult to fix. If the previous psalm depicted preservation from some mighty oppressor, this psalm depicts an oppression by some other oppressor. The psalm has two main divisions, the first presenting the present disaster (vv. 1-9), the second the past deliverance (vv. 10-20).

77:1-5. Faced with some terrible calamity, the psalmist resolved to cry aloud in prayer unto God. He was certain that the Lord would hear him. He sought God day and night with outstretched hands in the posture of prayer. He could not, however, find any consolation in prayer. In the agony of sorrow the psalmist was sleepless and speechless; it was God who withheld sleep from his eyes. He was perplexed and agitated by the mystery of Israel's present rejection and humiliation. He began to ponder the glorious record of God's mercies to his people in the days of old.

77:6-9. He recalled the songs of thanksgiving which he had once been able to sing in the night in contrast to his present cries of anguish or silent despair. He wonders if God has cast off his people forever. He wonders if God has forgotten or deliberately abandoned those attributes which he once proclaimed as the essence of his nature.

77:10-12. The psalmist rejects the implications of his own questions in the preceding verses. Such questions were prompted by his grief. Now he will recall "the years of the right hand of the most high," i.e., the times when Yahweh manifested his power on behalf of his people. He will recite the "deeds of Yah," i.e., Yahweh. This abbreviation "Yah" recalls the deliverance from Egypt (Exod 15:2), the greatest of all God's Old Covenant works.

77:13-15. God's way is holy. All the works of God in the world move in the sphere of holiness, separate from all sin and imperfection. No god (*'El*) can compare to God (*'Elohim*). The psalmist's God does wonders. Among the peoples of the earth he made known his strength. With a strong arm God had redeemed his people from bondage. The names "Jacob" (the tribes which left Canaan to live in Egypt) and "Joseph" (those tribes—Ephraim and Manasseh—which originated in Egypt) stand for the whole nation.

77:16-18. When he redeemed his people from Egyptian bondage, Yahweh manifested his sovereignty over nature. The waters of the Red Sea personified were conscious of the presence of their creator, and they were afraid. God came in storm perhaps reflecting the situation described in Exod 14:24-25. Thunder roared across the skies; lightning, like arrows, streaked toward the ground. The great noise seemed to shake the earth.

77:19-20. Once they had crossed the sea, the waters returned leaving no visible trace of God's victorious march. The convulsions of nature were the heralds of deliverance. The shepherd of Israel led forth his flock under the guidance of his chosen servants Moses and Aaron.

THE FACT OF HIS HELP
Psalm 78

Ps 78 is the seventh of the twelve Asaph psalms. This is also the first and longest of the so-called historical psalms as well as the twelfth of the *maskil* psalms which offer instruction. The psalm leads up to the choice of a site for the sanctuary. Asaph here functions as a prophet in interpreting Israel's past. In the outline of national history, the order is logical rather than chronological. Israel's misbehavior alternates with statements of Yahweh's mercy. The psalm begins with an introduction (vv. 1-11). The body of the poem has two main divisions: Israel's sin and God's grace (1) before the occupation of the land (vv. 12-55) and after (vv. 56-72).

A. Introduction (78:1-11).

78:1 2. Asaph calls upon his people to listen to his instruction. He refers to what follows as a "parable" or "dark saying," i.e., a record which has a deeper meaning. Jesus adopted the teaching methodology of the prophets of the old dispensation (Matt 13:34-35).

78:3-4.The trust of truth had been committed to the speakers by their ancestors to pass on to future generations. The "praises of Yahweh" are his praiseworthy acts, his "wonderful works."

78:5-6. Israelite parents were under a solemn commandment to teach their children the great facts of Israel's history, that the remembrance of them might be handed down from generation to generation (e.g., Deut 4:9).

78:7-8. Each generation should learn from the past to set their hope or confidence in God and not forget his mighty works. Evidence that they had not forgotten would be their obedience to the divine commands. They should learn not to be like their fathers who had proved to be stubborn and rebellious. The fathers did not "set their heart aright," i.e., they did not purpose to serve God. Their "spirit was not steadfast" or faithful. Fickleness, instability, and untrustworthiness were the characteristics of Israel's conduct.

78:9-11. Ephraim is singled out for special condemnation for cowardice in battle. The reference may be to the slackness of Ephraim in the conquest of Canaan (Judg 1). It seems better, however, to take the language figuratively. Like cowards who flee in battle, the Ephraimites failed to fight for the cause of God. They did not keep the covenant, nor obey the law. This came about because they forgot the wonders which God had showed them. The unfaithfulness of Ephraim after the entry into Canaan paved the way for the choice of Judah which is the climax of this psalm.

341

B. From Zoan (78:12-55).

78:12-16. Asaph reviews some of the mighty works of God in the land of Egypt and "the field (district) of Zoan," one of the great cities in the Nile delta. Yahweh divided the sea by causing the waters to stand in a heap. He led them by pillar of cloud and fire. He miraculously brought forth water from the rocks for them (Exod 17:6; Num 20:8ff.).

78:17-20. In spite of these miracles of mercy Israel sinned yet more. They "rebelled" against Yahweh in the wilderness by constant disobedience to his revealed will. They "tempted" God by their skeptical doubts of his goodness, and insolent demands that he should prove his presence in their midst. The specific example cited is the lust for meat in the wilderness and the open expression of doubt as to whether God could provide food for his people at all (Exod 16:2ff.).

78:21-24. Yahweh was angry at Israel because of their unbelief. A fire was kindled against his people at Taberah (Num 11:1ff.) before the giving of quail. His anger, like smoke, went up against Israel. Their unbelief and rebellion was inexcusable in view of the miracles he had wrought for them in the provision of the manna.

78:25-28. The manna is called "angels' food" because it came down from the heavens where the angels dwell. He also commanded the winds to bring in the quail which fell in abundance in the midst of their camp.

78:29-31. Yahweh gave them the food for which they lusted. Even while they were in the process of gorging themselves with the meat, judgment fell upon them (Num 11:33) and the plague broke out.

78:32-35. These judgments did not cause the people to repent. After the spies returned from Canaan, again they murmured in unbelief. For this they were condemned to wander in the wilderness (Num 14:22ff.). Punishments would result in temporary improvement. When under duress, they would cry out to the Lord. They would then remember that God Most High ('El 'Elyon) was their rock (refuge) and redeemer.

78:36. They treated God like a man who could be deceived by their hypocrisy. According to the reckoning of the Jewish scribes, this is the middle verse in the Psalter.

78:37-39. They lied to God because their heart was not right. The "heart" in Hebrew psychology is the seat of thought and will. While they pretended to serve God, they had not remained steadfastly loyal to their covenant obligations. Time and again Yahweh showed compassion to these hypocrites and did not destroy them. He took in account the frailty of their human nature.

78:40-48. An emphatic repetition of vv. 17-18. The Israelites "limited" God in that they did not believe that he could or would punish his special people. Israel limited God when they failed to remember his "hand" or power which had been exerted on their behalf, nor his mercy in redeeming them from the bondage of Egypt. They forgot the "signs" and "wonders" performed in the district of Zoan in northern Egypt. Of the ten plagues against Egypt the poet mentions (1) blood, (2) flies, (3) frogs, (4) locusts, and (5) hail. Cattle as well as crops were destroyed by the hail, being slain by the accompanying lightning.

78:49-51. The plagues against Egypt culminated in the death of the firstborn when Yahweh sent "a mission of evil angels" into the land, i.e., destroying angels, commissioned by God to execute his purposes of punishment (cf. Exod 12:23). He "leveled a path for his anger" through the land of Egypt. He delivered the firstborn, the chief of their strength, to the plague. The "tents of Ham" are the houses of Egypt, Ham being the ancestor of the Egyptians (Gen 10:6).

78:52-55. God led his flock out into the wilderness. They traveled safely through a harsh land, but their enemies were overwhelmed by the Red Sea. Yahweh brought his people to the border of his holy land, i.e., Canaan, that hill country where he would make his presence known. There he drove out the Gentiles and apportioned the land by lot to his people.

C. To Zion (78:56-72).

78:56-58. Once in the Promised Land Israel continued the pattern of rebellion. The name of God here "God Most High" ('Elohim 'Elyon) differs slightly from the title in v. 35. Israel rejected God's "testimonies," i.e., his commandments which bear witness to his will. They were unfaithful like their fathers. They were like a deceitful bow which looks good, but does not have the power to propel an arrow toward the target. By adopting Canaanite idolatries, they provoked the anger of the jealous God who can tolerate no rival.

343

78:59-64. Again God punished Israel for unfaithfulness. He abandoned them into the hands of their enemies. Yahweh abandoned his tabernacle, which was located in Shiloh in those days. The ark, the symbol of his strength and glory, he permitted to fall into the hands of the Philistines (1 Sam 4:17). Israelites fell by the sword in battle (1 Sam 4:2,10,17). The "fire" of war consumed the young men so that the maidens were forced to remain unmarried. The leading priests of the nation fell to the Philistine sword (1 Sam 4:11). In the universal distress the customary rites of mourning were not performed, even for a husband.

78:65-66. While they were at the mercy of their enemies, God seemed to be asleep. Suddenly he, as it were, awoke and rushed forward with the vigor of a mighty warrior refreshed by wine. He drove Israel's enemies backward to their perpetual shame. This is a general allusion to the victories over the Philistines and other enemies under Samuel, Saul and David.

78:67-69. After the victories over the Philistines, Yahweh "rejected the tabernacle of Joseph," i.e., Shiloh which was located in Ephraim, one of the two Joseph tribes. Shiloh apparently was destroyed by the Philistines. Never again did it serve as a sanctuary for Israel (cf. Jer 7:12,14; 26:6,9). Instead, Yahweh chose Mt. Zion in the tribe of Judah as the place of his dwelling. There he built his sanctuary which was as magnificent as the "heights" of the heavens or the earth which he had created.

78:70-72. God chose David "his servant" to be king. The title signifies one who stood in a special relationship with the Lord. It is bestowed on Abraham, Moses, Joshua, and Job as well as David. The shepherd boy was taken from being the keeper of Jesse's sheep to being the shepherd of God's flock. David performed that function with integrity, i.e., sincerity, of heart, and with "skillful hands," i.e., the discernment which was so necessary for effective governance.

SPECIAL MANIFESTATION OF HIS HELP
Psalms 79–81

The next three psalms focus on special manifestations of divine help to the distressed, the downtrodden and the faithful.

A. The Hope of the Distressed (Ps 79).

Ps 79 is attributed to Asaph. The occasion is not clear. Some think that the destruction of Jerusalem by the Chaldeans in 586 BC is in view. If the Asaph who wrote the psalm was the famous Levite of this name in the time of David, this psalm would have to be prophetic. It is better to view Asaph here as a latter namesake of the famous Asaph, i.e., a son of Asaph. The famous family name is used rather than that of the individual writer.

The psalm consists of three stanzas: (1) the problem (vv. 1-4); (2) the prayer for intervention (vv. 5-8); (3) a second prayer for pardon and vindication (vv. 9-13).

79:1-4. Gentiles have invaded God's "inheritance," i.e., the holy land. They have defiled the temple and laid Jerusalem in ruins (cf. Micah 3:12). Blood has flowed as freely as water around the city. Corpses of those who died in the defense of the city have been left unburied in accordance with the threats of the law (Deut 28:26) and prophets (e.g., Jer 7:33). The disaster has caused God's people to become the laughingstock of neighboring nations. The terms "servants" and "saints" stress Israel's covenant relationship to God.

79:5. The psalmist prays that God will cease to be angry with his own people. They recognize that by their infidelity they have offended the jealousy of Yahweh. Now they have experienced the fire of his wrath.

79:6-7. The psalmist asks that God's wrath be turned against the nations "which do not know" Yahweh, i.e., those who have made havoc of his people and who have mocked them (Jer 10:25).

79:8. Israel has been brought low by the destruction of its capital and temple. The people understand that this terrible disaster came in part because of the iniquities of the forefathers, i.e., sin has a cumulative effect. The psalmist prays that Yahweh would come to meet his people with mercy.

79:9-10. A new ground of appeal for God's intervention is offered. Yahweh is "the God of our salvation," i.e., the only savior of Israel. He urges God's pardon and deliverance "for the sake of the glory of your name," i.e., Yahweh's own glorious reputation. In the ancient Near East the fate of a nation reflected positively or negatively on the power of the deity worshiped by that nation. The psalmist

345

asks that God not defer vengeance against those who shed the blood of his servants until some future generation. He wants to live to see that judgment.

79:11. Those taken prisoner by the enemy are "the sons of death," i.e., they live a harsh existence in which they could die at any moment. The groans of these should move Yahweh as well as the shed blood of his servants. On their behalf the Lord is asked to exercise his great power (lit., arm).

79:12. Neighboring nations (e.g., Edom, Moab, Ammon) had mocked Yahweh because of what had happened in Jerusalem. In the view of the psalmist, such deserve a "sevenfold" recompense. "In their bosom" is a metaphor from the practice of carrying articles in the folds of the robe.

79:13. On the assumption that the Lord will respond to the preceding appeals for help, the "sheep" of Yahweh's pasture, the psalmist pledges thanksgiving forever. The nation will be able to resume its mission to set forth Yahweh's praise to all generations to come.

B. The Restorer of the Downtrodden (Ps 80).

Asaph again is the writer. The specific occasion is unknown. The poem has four divisions: (1) an appeal for divine intervention (vv. 1-3); (2) the need for Yahweh's intervention (vv. 4-7); (3) a metaphor for Yahweh's past care (vv. 8-13); and (4) an appeal for a new relationship with the Lord (vv. 14-19).

80:1. Yahweh is the "shepherd of Israel," hence the entire nation is entitled to his protective care (cf. 74:1). In the past he had led his flock Joseph (the northern tribes) through the wilderness. Yahweh sits enthroned "upon the cherubim." From the time of the wilderness wandering he had manifested himself from the "mercy seat" above the ark. That mercy seat was overshadowed by the wings of golden cherubim. Now the psalmist asks Yahweh to "shine forth," i.e., manifest himself anew in power and glory for the deliverance of his people.

80:2. The tribes of Ephraim, Benjamin, and Manasseh were united by the tie of common descent from Jacob's wife Rachel. The psalmist asks that Yahweh might march as a victorious champion "before" these tribes as he had marched before them through the wilderness.

These tribes needed a strong deliverance which only the strength of Yahweh could effect.

80:3-4. The words "turn us again" should probably be taken in a spiritual sense. These people need the help of God in coming back into his good graces. Then Yahweh would again cause his face to "shine" upon them, i.e., show his favor, and effect their deliverance from the oppressor. How long would the great and powerful Yahweh continue to be angry with his people? God's anger is so intense that even the prayers of his people are an offense to him.

80:5-6. Daily Yahweh's people are eating and drinking their own tears. Neighboring nations quarrel with one another over the territory which God's people can no longer defend. These enemies laugh at the helpless condition of God's people.

80:7. The refrain of v. 3 is repeated.

80:8-9. God had transplanted his precious vine Israel from Egypt to Canaan. As the vinedresser prepares the ground by clearing away the stones and thorns and all that would hinder growth, so God prepared Canaan for Israel by the expulsion of its old inhabitants. The vine struck deep roots and filled that land.

80:10-11. The vine Israel grew so that it overshadowed the mountainous country to the south, and the cedars of Lebanon to the north. The vine spread westward to the Mediterranean, and eastward to the Euphrates. These verses allude to the ideal boundaries of the Promised Land (Deut 11:24), boundaries realized in the time of David and Solomon (1 Kgs 4:24).

80:12-13. The hedge protecting the precious vine had been broken down. The relentless enemies of Israel are compared to wild boars and other beasts which ravage the vine and feed upon it. These circumstances are a riddle to Asaph.

80:14-15. The psalmist again appeals to the mighty God of hosts (i.e., universal sovereign) to turn his attention to the plight of his people. They are not only God's vine upon which he has expended so much effort; they are also "God's son" whom he has raised up.

80:16-17. The vine has been "cut down" as though it were fit for nothing. The Israelites perish, for God has not merely hidden his face, he has turned it upon them in anger. Asaph asks that Yahweh would put forth his power to protect the people which his hand had delivered

347

from Egypt and made into a nation. The phrase "son of man" underscores the present frailty of the nation which desperately needs divine aid. The figure of Israel as God's "son" undergirds this verse.

80:18-19. A fresh intervention of Yahweh on behalf of his vine/ son would evoke a fresh response of grateful praise. A revived people would cheerfully call upon Yahweh's name. The psalm concludes with a repetition of v. 7 with a significant change. "God of hosts" here becomes "Yahweh God of hosts." Asaph clinches his appeal by the use of the covenant name Yahweh, along with the title which expresses universal sovereignty.

C. The Strength of the Faithful (Ps 81).

Ps 81 is another Asaph psalm. Since it tells of the early history of Israel, Ps 81 is classified as an historical psalm. The psalm has three main divisions: (1) a call for celebration (vv. 1-5); (2) a stimulus for recollection (vv. 6-10); and (3) an expression of lamentation (vv. 11-16).

81:1-2. The psalmist calls upon his fellows to celebrate the "strength" of the God of Jacob, i.e., Yahweh. In so doing they are encouraged to make use of the "timbrel" (or tambourine), "harp" and "psaltery" (another stringed instrument).

81:3. In the Pentateuch the *shophar* or ram's horn is only prescribed for introducing the Jubilee year (Lev 25:9). Early Jewish tradition, however, stipulates that it was also used on the new moon of the month of Tishri, the civil New Year's day. If that is the case, the "solemn feast" mentioned here must be the Feast of Tabernacles, which began at the full moon on the fifteenth day of that seventh month. The blowing of the *shophar* at the beginning of the month is regarded as pointing forward to the feast.

81:4-5. The feast should be celebrated joyously because it is a continual witness to God's care for Israel. The festival ordinance had been established in the day when Yahweh "went out through the land of Egypt." Speaking as a representative of Israel at the time of the Exodus, the psalmist states: "I heard a language I did not know." This may be a way of underscoring the fact that the bondage suffered by Israel was in a foreign land. Another view is that the reference is to the "speech" of God, i.e., at the time of the Exodus God had not yet revealed himself as the God of redemption. Taken in this way, the following verse contains the substance of the words which Israel heard in Egypt from God.

81:6-7. Yahweh declares that he had set Israel apart from the bondage of Egypt. No more would they have to carry the baskets of bricks. He responded to their cries "in the secret place of thunder," i.e., in the thunder-cloud in which Yahweh conceals and reveals himself (Exod 14:10,24). He tested Israel's faith and obedience at the waters of Meribah (Exod 17:1ff.). The name Meribah ("Strife") was a reminder of unbelief and ingratitude (cf. Num 20:13). The libations of water at the Feast of Tabernacles were a commemoration of the supply of water in the wilderness at Meribah and elsewhere.

81:8-10. At Sinai Yahweh gave his people a solemn warning and exhortation. Absolute fidelity to him was the fundamental principle of the Sinaitic covenant. To Yahweh Israel owed its existence. The fact that he had redeemed them from Egypt constituted his claim upon their allegiance. God was ready liberally to satisfy all their needs. They but need to open their mouth, as it were, in expectation to him.

81:11-16. Israel did not hearken to Yahweh's voice. God punished them by leaving them to their own self-willed course of action. This eventually proved to be the ruin of the nation. Yahweh's mercy is inexhaustible. Even now if his people would obey him, he would subdue their enemies. The "hand" which had been turned against Israel would then be turned against their enemies. Those enemies would do homage to Israel. At that time God would bless his people with "wheat" and with "honey from the rock," i.e., he would fulfill his ancient promises to them (Deut 7:12-13).

THE SCOPE OF HIS HELP
Psalms 82–83

Yahweh comes to the aid of his people both at home and abroad. He destroys wicked judges who oppress the poor. He overthrows foreign enemies who have as their goal the overthrow of God's people.

A. At Home: The Judges (Ps 82).

Ps 82 is another Asaph psalm. It is a companion to Ps 50, the only Asaphic psalm in Book Two of the Psalter. In the latter all of Israel is gathered for judgment before the Lord; here the authorities of Israel are gathered for judgment. The psalm develops three thoughts: (1) the indictment of the judges (vv. 1-4); (2) the pronouncement against the judges (vv. 5-7); and (3) the exaltation of the supreme judge (v. 8).

82:1. The Lord "takes his stand" as supreme judge. He stands "in the assembly of God," i.e., an assembly summoned and presided over by God in his capacity of almighty ruler. The earthly judges are called "'Elohim," lit., gods or mighty ones, because of the power that they wield in the land.

82:2. The divine judge accuses the earthly judges of injustice and partiality to the rich and powerful. A musical interlude (Selah) gives the congregation time to reflect on the accusation, and builds expectation regarding what might follow.

82:3-4. The judges have no defense, so God proceeds to remind them of their duty. They are the agents of God to see that the weak and friendless have justice done them.

82:5. God is still the speaker; but instead of addressing the evil judges, he describes their incorrigible blindness and obstinacy. They do not have the knowledge which is a prerequisite for effective judgeship. What is worse, they walk on complacently self-satisfied in their ignorance and moral darkness. Their actions have resulted in shaking the foundations of the land, i.e., the foundational principles of moral order were imperiled by their actions.

82:6. The verse begins with an emphatic "I." It was by God's appointment that they have been invested with divine authority to execute judgment in his name. Jesus appealed to these words (John 10:34ff.) when the Jews accused him of blasphemy because he claimed to be one with God.

82:7-8. Though the judges bear these high titles, they will not be exempt from punishment. They would die like common men, and fall like any other prince whose ruin is recorded in history. Having witnessed the trial and condemnation of Israel's judges, Asaph is moved to appeal to God himself to assume the office of judge, not only for Israel, but for the entire world. The second person pronoun is emphatic. Yahweh must take possession of all the nations as their sovereign and their judge.

B. Abroad: The Enemies (Ps 83).

This is the last of the Asaphic psalms. The exact occasion is unknown. This is one of thirty psalms which also is identified as a "song." The psalm has four divisions: (1) a prayer that God will rescue his people from an enemy (vv. 1-4); (2) a description of the enemy gathered against Jerusalem (vv. 5-8); (3) an appeal that the enemy might meet the same fate as past enemies (vv. 9-12); and (4) a rationale for the destruction of the enemy (vv. 13-18).

83:1-2. This psalm begins with an urgent prayer that God would come to the rescue of his people. For the present, God seems to be indifferent to the danger of his people. Israel's enemies make a tumult, i.e., an uproar such as is produced by a throng of people. Their enemies need to be rebuked, and the heavens are silent. Yet God has only to speak a word and their schemes will be utterly frustrated. Israel's enemies are God's enemies. Their plot to destroy his people is a plot to frustrate the purposes of the Lord.

83:3-4. The enemy plots against Yahweh's "hidden ones," i.e., those the Lord protects in the day of trouble. The aim of the enemy is to obliterate the name of Israel from the map of the world.

83:5-8. The enemy is a confederacy of many nations. From the southeast come the nomadic Edomites and Ishmaelites. From the east come the Moabites and the Hagarenes who lived in the neighborhood of Hauran, east of Gilead. Gebal is either an area north of Tyre (Ezek 27:9) or a region in the northern part of the mountains of Edom. The Ammonites from the eastern desert and the Amalekites from the southern deserts were perennial enemies of Israel. Philistia and Tyre were on the Mediterranean coast. Assyria is mentioned here as an auxiliary of "the children of Lot" (Moab and Ammon), suggesting that it was not yet the world power it later would become.

83:9-10. Asaph prays that the confederation might be destroyed as the Midianites and Canaanites were destroyed in the period of the Judges. He takes these two historical examples in reverse order. The victory over the Canaanite forces of Jabin at the river Kishon by Deborah and Barak is narrated in Judges 4–5. In this case a storm contributed to the smashing defeat of Sisera's nine hundred iron chariots. A key spot in the defeat of the Canaanites was En-dor, which is not mentioned in the narrative of Judges, but was situated in the same area as Taanach and Megiddo which are mentioned (Judg 5:19). The unburied corpses of those Canaanites became "dung" upon the ground.

83:11. The Midianites and their allies were destroyed by Gideon (Judg 7,8). Oreb ("Raven") and Zeeb ("Wolf") were the princes, i.e., generals, of the Midianite forces; Zebah and Zalmunna were the kings of Midian. Isaiah also mentions this great victory (Isa 9:4; 10:26). These enemies fell by one another's hands.

83:12-13. The present enemies covet for themselves "the pastures of God," i.e., the land which he had given to his people Israel. Asaph prays that God will make the attacking confederacy "like whirling dust" (NASB) or stubble whirled away from the threshing floor.

83:14-18. Let the wrath of God come against the enemy as a forest fire. Let God pursue them with a destructive storm. Let that enemy experience defeat so that they may desire to seek the name of Yahweh, i.e., acknowledge him as true God, and submit themselves to his will. If they refuse to embrace Yahweh, let them experience the very ruin with which they currently threaten God's people. Repeated judgments would bring them eventually, albeit reluctantly, to recognize Yahweh as God over all the earth.

ENDNOTES

1. Statistics on the various names for God in Book Three are these: *'Elohim* = 60; *Yahweh* = 44; *'El* = 20; *'Adonay* = 15; and *Yah* = 2.

2. Another interpretation of 76:10: God girds on the wrath of his enemies as a sword, making the wrath of his enemies to minister to their final overthrow.

CHAPTER SEVENTEEN

The Hope of Divine Help
Psalms 84–89

The previous psalms in Book Three have stressed the fact of God's help for Israel, and the experience of his help. The last six psalms in this book stress the hope of his help.

THE CONFIDENCE IN DIVINE HELP
Psalms 84–85

Pss 84–85 express confidence that Yahweh will come to the aid of his people, who are depicted as pilgrims and wanderers in this world.

A. Strength for the Pilgrim (Ps 84).

Ps 84 is attributed to the sons of Korah. The date is uncertain. It probably belongs to the monarchy period when the temple was standing (v. 3). The psalm has the same structure as Pss 42–43 and may come from the same period. The former psalms stress the sadness of separation from God's sanctuary; this psalm emphasizes the gladness of access to that holy place. The psalm consists of three stanzas which are distinguished by the use of the musical interlude (*Selah*) inserted after verses 4 and 8. The stanzas indicate a chronological progression: (1) the pilgrim's ambition (vv. 1-4); (2) the pilgrim's approach (vv. 5-8); and (3) the pilgrim's arrival (vv. 9-12).

84:1-2. The psalmist expresses his delight in the house of God. The place is most lovely to him. He longs to set foot in that place again. Not the temple, but God himself is the final object of desire. The temple is only the means of realizing the presence of "the living God" (*'El chay* as in 42:2).

84:3-4. The psalmist envies the privilege of the birds which build their nests within the precincts of the temple. The birds nested, not in the actual altars, but in their vicinity. The actual ministers of the temple who reside in its precincts are regarded as most blessed because they constantly can be raising their praise to the Lord.

84:5-6. Happy are those whose minds are wholly set on pilgrimage to Zion. The "valley of Baca" was some waterless and barren valley through which pilgrims passed on their way to Jerusalem. Faith turns that place into a place of springs. Meanwhile God refreshes the pilgrims with showers of blessing from above. Instead of fainting on their toilsome journey the pilgrims gain fresh strength as they advance.

84:7-8. Finally the entire company arrives at the temple to "appear before God" at one of the major festivals in conformity with their covenant obligations. On the arrival, the leader of the group of pilgrims prays for a favorable audience with the Lord.

84:9. Now all the pilgrims join in prayer. They pray first for their king who is called "our shield" and "your anointed." The welfare of the whole nation was bound up with the welfare of the king. The prayer would be all the more appropriate if the king was godly, one who encouraged the pilgrimages to the temple.

84:10. A day spent in Yahweh's courts was better than a thousand others, and therefore the most opportune occasion for this prayer. The psalmist would rather perform the humblest service at the temple of the holy God than to be entertained as a guest where wickedness makes its home.

84:11. For this psalmist Yahweh was "a sun and shield," i.e., a source of light and protection. "Grace and glory" are the rewards of the upright, i.e., favor, honor and prosperity. The Lord would withhold no good thing from those who "walk uprightly," i.e., those who are devoted to God and are honest with their fellow men.

84:12. The psalm closes with a blessing upon those who put their trust in Yahweh.

B. Restoration of the Wanderer (Ps 85).

This psalm is attributed to the sons of Korah. The date of the composition is uncertain. Some scholars see here a reference to circumstances during the reign of King Hezekiah. The psalm has three unequal parts: (1) grateful recollection (vv. 1-3); (2) earnest supplication (vv. 4-7); and (3) glad anticipation (vv. 8-13).

85:1. God has forgiven and restored his people. He had "brought back the captivity of Jacob," i.e., reversed the fortunes of his people. He had received them back into his divine favor.

85:2. The Hebrew words here describe sin as (1) depravity or moral distortion; and (2) wandering from the way, or missing the mark. Forgiveness is represented as (1) the removal of a burden, and (2) the covering of the offense, which would otherwise meet the eye of the judge and call for punishment.

85:3. The wrath which had been unleashed against Israel had now been withdrawn. Yahweh now turned away from the fierceness of his anger which had been poured out upon Israel for its sin.

85:4. In spite of forgiveness and restoration, much is still lacking. The psalmist prays for assistance in turning even more completely to the Lord. He prays that God would cease to be provoked with this people.

85:5-7. Will God prolong his anger from one generation to another? Will Yahweh not now restore national life according to the promises of the prophets? The second person pronoun is emphatic. The prayer now turns to direct petition. The psalmist asks for mercy and salvation, i.e., deliverance.

85:8. The psalmist listens for Yahweh's answer to the prayer of his people. He was confident that the Lord would not always be angry. He would shortly speak "peace," i.e., words of reconciliation, with his saints, i.e., his holy ones. The assurance of a favorable response is based, not upon their merit, but on their relationship with the Lord. Yet the psalmist warns that this people must not "turn again to folly," i.e., the folly of self-confidence leading to unbelief and disobedience. This had been the cause of their past misfortunes.

85:9. The psalmist expands on the meaning of the word "peace" from the preceding verse. Yahweh's salvation is near to those that fear him, i.e., those who answer to their calling as "saints." That would mean that God's "glory," i.e., his presence, would be manifested in the land once again.

85:10. God's lovingkindness and truth—the love which moved him to enter into covenant with Israel, and the faithfulness which binds him to be true to his covenant—meet in Israel's redemption. "Righteousness" and "peace" meet one another with joyous welcome. Yahweh is a righteous God, and therefore a savior. Because salvation is his eternal purpose, and he cannot change his purpose. Therefore he reconciles his people to himself.

85:11-12. Truth springs up as a natural growth in response to God's manifestation of his saving righteousness. Thus harmony between earth and heaven is perfected. Material prosperity will go hand in hand with moral progress. Earth responds to the divine blessing.

85:13. Yahweh himself appears to lead his people forward. Before him as a herald goes the righteousness which moves him to the salvation of his people. His people will follow in his steps.

THE ATTITUDE TOWARD DIVINE HELP
Psalms 86-87

In the next two psalms the attitude toward Yahweh, the great helper is displayed first on the personal level, then on the national level. In Ps 86 an individual submits to the Lordship of Yahweh; in Ps 87 the whole nation recognizes him as Lord.

A. Personal Submission (Ps 86).

This is the only psalm in Book Three which is ascribed to David. The occasion may have been the time of Absalom's rebellion. This is one of five "prayer psalms." Ps 86 is not easily subdivided but a threefold breakdown may be helpful: (1) earnest petitions (vv. 1-5);

(2) the ground of confidence (vv. 6-10); and (3) prayer for guidance and protection (vv. 11-17).

86:1-4. The psalm begins with a series of petitions, each supported by the ground on which David pleads for a hearing. He asks (1) that God "bow down" his ear, i.e., hear him. The ground: he was afflicted and needy, and therefore one of those whom God has promised to help. (2) He asks that God would "preserve" his soul or life. The ground: he is a "godly man," i.e., a member of the covenant family. (3) He asks for mercy because he cries unto the Lord daily. (4) He asks for the restoration of joy for God alone is the object of his desires, his aspirations, and his prayers.

86:5-8. All of the above petitions are grounded in the nature of God. Yahweh is good; he is ready to forgive. He displays abundant mercy on all who call upon him. David is sure of an answer to his prayer, for Yahweh is the only true God. In v. 5 he mentioned God's *willingness* to answer prayer; here he comforts himself with the thought of his *ability* to do so. Among alleged gods none was like Yahweh. His power as manifested in his works is possessed by none of his would-be rivals.

86:9-11. All nations will one day come to worship Yahweh and glorify his name. He is great and performs marvelous works. He is the only true God. David quotes from one of his earlier psalms (27:11). Once he learns the way of God, he resolves to walk in it. He wants no divided allegiance. He wants all the powers of his heart to be focused on the Lord.

86:12-13. David will praise God with all his heart because he has been the recipient of abundant mercy from him. Yahweh had delivered his soul from the lowest Sheol. The reference here is to preservation from some premature death.

86:14-15. David is facing hostility from the "proud," i.e., those who place themselves above the law of both God and man, and from "violent men" who were seeking his life. These enemies gave no thought to God; they were irreligious men. With this proud and merciless opposition David contrasts the revealed character of God. He quotes from Exod 34:6, which reveals Yahweh to be a gracious and compassionate God. Though David may have deserved punishment, God cannot surely abandon him to his adversaries.

357

86:16-17. David prays that Yahweh would turn to him in mercy. He refers to himself as Yahweh's "servant" and "the son of your handmaid." David had been born to a godly woman, and was raised by her. Thus from his earliest days he had been a devout follower of the Lord. God had been his help and comfort in times past. David requests some visible and unmistakable sign of Yahweh's favor, a sign which his enemies could not mistake.

B. Formal Identification (Ps 87).

In its breadth of view and fullness of messianic hope, this psalm ranks with the grandest of prophetic utterances.[1] Ps 87 anticipates the day when Gentiles would be incorporated into the New Covenant Israel, the church of Christ (Eph 2:12f.).

Ps 87 is another psalm and "song" of the sons of Korah. An exact date cannot be assigned to it, but it seems to be connected with the transfer of the ark to Zion. This psalm has two main parts divided by *Selah*. To this a liturgical note has been appended. Thus the psalm points to: (1) the city of God (vv. 1-3); (2) the citizens of the city (vv. 4-6); and (3) the joy over Zion's prospects (v. 7).

87:1. Zion is a city founded by God himself. Its site is consecrated. The plural "mountains" may refer to the different hills upon which Jerusalem stood, or generally to the mountainous region in which the city was located.

87:2-3. Yahweh loves "the gates of Zion," i.e., the city itself, more than any of the other cities of Israel. This is the city of Yahweh's choice, his love, his care. "Glorious things" had been spoken about this city, promises which the psalmist now begins to enumerate.

87:4. God himself is the speaker. He publicly acknowledges "Rahab and Babylon" among them that recognize him as their God. "Rahab" ("arrogance") is a nickname for Egypt (Isa 30:7). God points the finger also to Philistia, Tyre and Ethiopia and in each case makes the shocking announcement: "This one was born there," i.e., in Zion. By divine edict each of these Gentile nations is invested with the full rights and privileges of citizenship as though they had been born in Zion. The divine utterance is introduced with "Behold!" which always introduces something that is shocking.

87:5. The psalmist speaks as a prophet. Not merely certain speci-fied nations but all the nations shall call Zion their mother city. Under the protection and blessing of Yahweh, Zion grows ever stronger and nobler as each fresh nation joins the universal kingdom of God.

87:6. Yahweh holds his census of the nations, and writes their names down in his book. One after another of them he registers as "born in Zion." This is the official confirmation of their rights of citizenship.

87:7. The psalm ends as abruptly as it began, with a brief verse which is far from clear. It is best explained as a snapshot of the universal rejoicing with which the citizens of the holy city greet their mother Zion. They dance and sing this refrain: "All my fountains are in you," i.e., in Zion. The holy city is the "fountain" of salvation. "All my fountains are in you" may be the name of some hymn which was to be sung at this point.

THE THEME OF GOD'S HELP SUMMARIZED
Psalms 88–89

Pss 88–89 summarize the previous psalms of Book Three. They point to the constant human need for deliverance, and the divine resources which are available to meet that need.

A. Human Need (Ps 88).

Ps 88 is an elegy, the saddest song in the Psalter. The writer is in deep, but not utter, despair. His prayer, however, indicates the presence of a lingering hope. Ps 88 has a composite title. First, it is said to be a song or psalm of the sons of Korah. This may mean that the psalm was taken from the Korahite collection. Second, the psalm is attributed to Heman the Ezrahite.

The designation of Heman here (and Ethan in the following psalm) as an "Ezrahite" is problematical. An Ezrahite is equivalent to a Zerahite, i.e., a descendant of Zerah of the tribe of Judah. Both Heman and Ethan are listed in 1 Chr 2:6 as sons of Zerah. Both are also listed among the wise men whose wisdom was exceeded by Solomon (1 Kgs 4:31). It is not clear whether or not these wise men were contemporary with Solomon.

The names Heman and Ethan also appear along with Asaph among the Levitical (Korahite) leaders of temple music (1 Chr 15:17,19). Heman also is called "the king's seer" or prophet (1 Chr

25:5). Is Heman the Ezrahite the same person as Heman the Korahite? Perhaps. The Korahite might be called an Ezrahite because he lived in the area of the Ezrahites. On the other hand, it is not impossible that this and the following psalm were actually written by the famous sages of the tribe of Judah.

The precise occasion which triggered this remorseful poem is not known. This psalm is the eleventh of the *maskil* (instruction) psalms. Organization in this elegy is not easy to discern. After the opening invocation (vv. 1-2) there appear to be three parts: (1) his desperate affliction (vv. 3-8); (2) his urgent appeal (vv. 9-14); and (3) a request for an explanation (vv. 15-18).

88:1-2. The psalmist appeals for a hearing before God. Though he feels that God has forsaken him, he still refers to him as "my God." He has cried night and day before the Lord. He asks God to incline his ear, i.e., listen, to his "cry." The word "cry" denotes a shrill piercing cry, frequently of joy, but sometimes, as here, of pain.

88:3-5. He pleads the urgency of his need as the ground for a hearing. He had drawn near to Sheol or "the pit," the abode of the dead. He was regarded as a dying man who had no strength left. He feels he is of no more worth than the dead who are slain in battle, whose corpses are hurled into a common grave. Those who are dead God "remembers" no more with his timely help and deliverance. They are "cut off" from Yahweh's gracious help and protection.

88:6-7. He feels God is already treating him as though he were dead. The "lowest pit," Sheol, that dark region beyond this present life, here is metaphorical for his depression and suffering. He describes his condition as "in the depths," i.e., of the sea of misery. Wave after wave of God's wrath seems to smash against him.

88:8. Like Job, the psalmist is deserted even by his closest friends. This is due to an act of God who has smitten him with a sickness which makes them loathe even the sight of him. His disease may have been leprosy, which was a living death in the ancient world. He was like a prisoner, shut away from all social contact.

88:9. He pleads that his prayers have been accompanied by the tears of mourning. His eyes have "wasted away," i.e., they are sunken and hollow looking. His hands have been stretched forth to God in the attitude of prayer.

88:10. He presses for an immediate answer to his appeals. If there is delay, he will be dead. He cannot believe that even God can reach beyond the grave to perform his wonders. And if he should, how could the dead arise to perform their duty of praising God for his wonderful works?

88:11-12. To proclaim God's lovingkindness and faithfulness is the delight of his people. In the grave, however, all praise as it is known in this world ceases. "Abaddon" (NASB) is a name for Sheol as the place of ruin.[2] God's wonders, as they are experienced in this life, will not be experienced in the land of darkness (death). Once dead, men are forgotten by their fellows. They are forgotten by God in the sense that he no longer performs his wondrous deliverances for them.

88:13-14. Unlike the dead, the psalmist can still pray, and in spite of all discouragement he will not cease to do so. His first thought each day will be a prayer. He cannot understand why the Lord seems to cast him aside, seems to hide his face (favor) from him.

88:15-18. The psalmist claims that his whole life has been spent at the point of death. Now and again he had suffered "terrors" brought on him by God. He probably refers to moments when he thought death was imminent. A flood of fiery streams of terror and calamity threatens to engulf him. There is none to stretch out a helping hand to this drowning man.

Thus does this song end in gloom. The psalmist obviously believes in God's love, though all he has experienced is understood to be signs of his wrath. He keeps on appealing to God, though God seems hostile to him. He knows that if he has any hope at all it is in God alone.

B. Divine Resource (Ps 89).

Ps 89 was written by Ethan the Ezrahite. On the identity of this Ethan, see the introduction to the previous psalm. Ethan is thought by some to be the same as Jeduthun (1 Chr 16:41f.; 25:6). The exact occasion of the psalm is unknown. It certainly was written after the delivery of the Nathan oracle to David (1 Sam 7), for he believed firmly in these promises. Yet Ethan foresaw the day when the Davidic dynasty would be humiliated, and men would question whether those promises could possibly be true. Ethan may have outlived Solomon. He may have seen the breakup of the kingdom. This psalm is the

361

twelfth of the *maskil* or instruction psalms. It sets forth Ethan's (1) theme (vv. 1-4); (2) praise (vv. 5-18); (3) confidence (vv. 19-37); (4) lament (vv. 38-45); and (5) appeal (vv. 46-51).

89:1-4. The theme of this psalm is the "lovingkindness" and "faithfulness" of Yahweh. Each of these terms occurs seven times in the psalm. Ethan has reached the conclusion that one stone after another will continue to be laid in the building of God's lovingkindness till it reaches to heaven itself. For Ethan the supreme illustration of the lovingkindness and faithfulness of God was the promise he made to David (2 Sam 7:5ff.). He was God's "servant," his "chosen one" to execute the divine program. With David, God had "ratified" a covenant. His descendants would be confirmed in permanent possession of the royal office in Israel. The "throne" of David would endure forever.

89:5-8. Ethan praises Yahweh by setting forth ten reasons why he believes in the fulfillment of the promises made to David. (1) The heavens are evidence of God's power to keep his promises and his faithfulness in so doing. (2) God is superior to any being in the heavenly realm. He has abundant resources for carrying out his promises. (3) God is held in reverence by his people because of his power and faithfulness. Therefore, Ethan has additional reason to believe what God promised concerning David.

89:9-10. (4) God is Lord of hosts, incomparable in strength and faithfulness by which he is, as it were, surrounded. Men can, therefore, believe the promise made concerning David. (5) He is Lord of the raging sea. He can suppress any tumults and troubles which arise against his people. (6) God has already displayed his power by crushing Rahab (Egypt) and scattering his enemies from time to time. What he hãs done in the past, he can and will do again.

89:11-14. (7) The entire universe and all it contains belongs to God. He who cares for the kingdom of nature will watch over the affairs of his people. (8) God is omnipotent. He will do even more for his people in the future than he has done in the past. (9) God's character underscores the certainty of his promises. Where he reigns there is perfect righteousness; mercy and truth are forerunners preparing the way before him.

89:15-18. (10) The blessedness of those who trust in God is another reason for continuing to maintain the faith. They walk in the

light of God's countenance and rejoice in God's name (his self-revelation). They can take special delight in God's righteousness which punishes the wicked and exalts the faithful. God is for his people a beautiful adornment and a mighty strength. Because of his favor, Israel can
triumph over enemies. God is the protector of his people. The holy
one of Israel is a king which believers can be proud to follow.

89:19-20. Through Nathan ("your holy one") and other prophets,
God revealed his purpose to send the Messiah into the world. The
revelation came in the form of a "vision." In describing the circumstances at the time God made this great revelation, Ethan makes five
points: (1) God had helped David to help his people. (2) In his
sovereign will, God had chosen David for exalted assignments among
the people. (3) Having made David his choice, God "found" David
through the mission of Samuel to Bethlehem. (4) David was God's
"servant." (5) David had been set apart to his office by the anointing
of holy oil administered by Samuel the prophet.

89:21-24. Ethan now begins to enumerate ten promises made to
David through Nathan the prophet. (1) David would be given divine
assistance in the administration of his kingdom. (2) David's subjects
would not be subdued, nor would wicked enemies succeed in making
them so miserable that they would renounce their rightful king.
(3) David's enemies both without and within would be destroyed,
beaten down suddenly or subjected to plague. (4) David would experience God's faithfulness and mercy for the benefit of his subjects. All
impediments to the growth of his kingdom would thus be removed.
(5) David's "horn" (i.e., power) would be exalted because his battles
would be fought in the name of God.

89:25-28. (6) David would have a special relationship to God. He
would be able to cry unto him in times of difficulty and call him "my
Father." (7) David would be exalted in rank over the kings of the
earth. He would be made (declared to be) God's firstborn. (8) God's
merciful covenant with David and his posterity would endure forever.

89:29-33. (9) The "throne" and "seed" of David would endure as
long as the world stands. Only in the everlasting kingdom of Christ
could such a promise find fulfillment. (10) God's promise to David
would not be disannulled by the unfaithfulness of some of his descendants. Any of his descendants who were disobedient to God would be

punished with multiple blows. Yet even in those moments God would not turn his back on the commitment to David. God is faithful to his word even when men are not.

89:34-37. God adds additional confirmation that the covenant made with David was immutable. He promises not to break nor in any way alter that covenant. God has sworn by his holiness, for there is nothing higher by which to swear. He cannot lie. The sun and moon bear eloquent testimony to the faithfulness of God in covenant keeping. The endurance of David's kingdom is likened to the permanence of the celestial bodies.

89:38-40. Ethan begins to describe conditions which seem to contradict what he confidently had affirmed. These verses should be understood as prophetic anticipation. Ethan foresees the dilapidated condition of the house of David. He uses seven concise strokes to paint the picture. (1) Times would come when it would appear that God had contemptuously rejected his anointed. (2) It would then appear that the covenant was dissolved and the kingdom and crown altogether ruined. (3) In those days Judah would be defenseless.

89:41-45. (4) Neighboring nations would take their fill of spoil, and in various other ways show their contempt for Judah. (5) The enemies of the house of David would be assisted by God, and the king himself would be put to flight. (6) All privileges and prerogatives of the Davidic kingdom would seem to be abolished. (7) The youthful vigor of the Davidic king would be cut short and he would be covered with shame.

89:46-48. The situation portrayed in the previous lament could not be allowed to continue. Ethan was convinced that God should give relief in those dark days. To this he offers seven arguments for speedy intervention. (1) The wrath of God against his people cannot last forever. (2) The Lord's people are of short life. If any relief is contemplated, it must be given before they pass from the scene. (3) The mercies which were part of God's promise to David, and the oath of God concerning those promises, compel his intervention.

89:49-52. (4) Zion should not be allowed to experience humiliation. (5) Zion bears in her bosom the nations of the world. She is their spiritual mother. This is a way of saying that Zion figures in the long-range plans of God for the world. (6) Israel's enemies are really God's enemies. (7) The enemies have reproached the footsteps of God's anointed, the Messiah. Although they have been told of Messiah's coming, yet they scoff at the delay in his coming. Nevertheless, the faithful cling to the promise of that coming and continue to praise God.

ENDNOTES

1. A.F. Kirkpatrick, *The Book of Psalms* in The Cambridge Bible for Schools and Colleges (Cambridge: University Press, 1910), p. 518.

2. Elsewhere Abaddon appears only in the wisdom literature: Job 26:6; 28:22; 31:12; Prov 15:11; 27:20. In Rev 9:11 Apollyon, "the destroyer" is the name of "the angel of the abyss."

CHAPTER EIGHTEEN

The Universal Rule of Yahweh
Psalms 90-106

Most of the psalms in Book Four (Pss 90–106) are anonymous, the exceptions being Ps 90 which is assigned to Moses, and Pss 101 and 103 which are Davidic. This is called the "Numbers" book because of the many allusions to the wilderness wandering of Israel. The dominant name of God in this book again is Yahweh. It occurs more than once in every psalm, and in some as many as eleven times. In addition, the abbreviated form *Yah* occurs seven times.[1] The dominant thought in these psalms is the universal worship rendered to Yahweh.

PRINCIPLES UNDERGIRDING HIS RULE
Psalms 90–92

Moulton has pointed out that the opening two psalms of Book Four answer to the two clauses in Moses' farewell blessing on Israel (Deut 33:27): "The eternal God is your dwelling place, and underneath are the everlasting arms."[2] Ps 90 develops the first of these lines, and Ps 91 develops the second.

A. Man's Failure (Ps 90).

Ps 90 is probably the oldest of all the psalms. It was written by Moses, no doubt during the thirty-eight years of wilderness wandering. The psalm falls naturally into three parts: (1) man's frailty before God (vv. 1-6); (2) man's sin against God (vv. 7-12); and (3) man's appeal to God (vv. 13-17).

90:1-2. The Lord (*'Adonay*), the sovereign ruler, has proved himself to be Israel's home "in generation and generation," i.e., in each successive generation. Even before the mountains or "world" (habitable part of the earth) were formed, God existed. From the infinite past to the infinite future he is *'El*, the God of sovereign power.

90:3-4. Man's life is at the disposal of the eternal God. He makes mortal man (*'enosh*) to return to the dust (lit., "pulverization") from which he came. God sweeps away one generation after another, for the longest span of human life is but a moment in his sight. A whole millennium to God, as he reviews it, is but as the past day when it draws towards its close, i.e., a brief space with all its events still present and familiar to the mind. Yea, to God a thousand years is as a "watch" of the night. Time no more exists for him than for the unconscious sleeper. The Hebrews divided each night into three watches.

90:5-6. Man is compared to a building swept away by a sudden burst of rain. He falls into the sleep of death. Man is like grass which grows up in the morning, but by evening it has withered.

90:7-8. Moses speaks of the current indignation of God which has "consumed" Israel. He has brought their sins into the light to deal with them, even the inward sin of the heart.

90:9-10. Man's life is as brief as a "sigh." Moses felt that life was drawing to a close under the cloud of God's judgment. Seventy or eighty years have been allotted to man. All upon which man prides himself brings only trouble; it has no real value.

90:11-12. A right understanding of the wrath of God is man's best safeguard against offending him. Learning to number the days of life—to recognize its brevity—will produce the kind of godly wisdom upon which God smiles.

90:13-14. Moses calls on God to return to his people, to "repent," i.e., have a change of attitude toward his servants. Israel was in a night of trouble. Moses asks that the joyous dawn may soon come.

90:15-17. Moses prays that the joy of restoration to God's favor be proportioned to the depth of Israel's humiliation. He asks that God might manifest his power on their behalf. He prays that the favor of the Lord might be upon them all that they might be successful in all their undertakings.

B. Man's Hope (Ps 91).

Ps 91 is anonymous, but there can be little doubt that it is by Moses. Like the previous psalm, it was probably composed at the beginning of the thirty-eight years of the wilderness wandering. Outlining this psalm is difficult. It seems to have two main divisions, both of which are introduced by professions of trust in Yahweh: (1) vv. 1-8; and (2) vv. 9-13. The psalm concludes with a divine assurance responding to the opening profession of trust.

91:1. Yahweh is a secure defense for those who take refuge in him. One who takes refuge in God will be treated as God's guest. His almighty power will be spread around him during the night of peril and trouble. The figure of the protective "shadow" is probably derived from the mother bird which hovers over her young.

91:2. The psalmist can and will address God in the language of faith. The Lord is his refuge and object of his trust.

91:3-4. The providential care of God is described in detail. Some think the second person singular here refers to Israel; others apply it to any individual godly Israelite. He will rescue from "the snare of the fowler," i.e., from insidious attempts against his life or welfare. He delivers as well from the deadly pestilence. As the mother bird covers her young with her wings, so God protects his people (cf. Deut 32:11). God's truth, i.e., his faithfulness to his promises, is a defense (shield) against these dangers.

91:5-8. Neither sudden assaults of enemies by night, nor open attacks by day shall have power to harm the believer. Not even plague and pestilence, here personified as destroying angels walking through the earth, shall have power over him. The wicked shall fall on all sides by the thousands, but the believer is safe, just as Israel was safe when the firstborn of Egypt were smitten (Exod 12:23). Unharmed, the believer will witness the punishment of the wicked, as Israel witnessed the destruction of the Egyptians at the Red Sea.

91:9-10. The Hebrew here is difficult, and various renderings have been proposed. The NASB understands v. 9 to be an explanation of the previous promises of security, namely, the believer has made the psalmist's God his refuge.

91:11-12. Angels watch over the godly one (Israel) to keep him from falling to his hurt. Satan quoted these verses in an effort to get Jesus to jump from the pinnacle of the temple (Matt 4:6; Luke 4:10-11).

91:13. The believer triumphantly shall overcome all obstacles and dangers, whether of fierce and open violence (the lion), or of secret and insidious treachery (the serpent).

91:14-16. God himself speaks, solemnly confirming the psalmist's faith. God "sets on high," i.e., in a place of safety, those who love him and know his name, i.e., understand his character. He grants to such a one "length of days" in fulfillment of the ancient promises (cf. Exod 20:12). The term "salvation" here refers to the visible manifestations of God's providence which prove his care for his people. Each such manifestation was a harbinger of the final messianic glory which is the goal of Old Testament hope.

C. Man's Restoration (Ps 92).

The writer and occasion of this psalm are unknown. The central thought is concisely stated in v. 8, namely, that Yahweh is enthroned on high. That key verse is surrounded by three thoughts: (1) the praise of the Lord (vv. 1-3); (2) the sovereignty of the Lord (vv. 4-8); and (3) the Lord and the righteous (vv. 9-15).

92:1-3. Praise for the Lord is deserved tribute for him, and joyous delight for man. The "name" of God is that which he has revealed about himself. The title "most high" points to God as supreme governor of the world. Morning and evening are natural times for prayer. "Lovingkindness" and "faithfulness" are the two key attributes which sum up God's relationship with his people. The praise may be verbal or instrumental.

92:4-6. Here the special ground for the praise of Yahweh is the manifestation of his sovereignty. The terms "work" and "doings" here refer to God's providence. It is the victory of righteousness which has gladdened this psalmist's heart. The grandeur and profundity of

Yahweh's designs for the government of the world stir his admiration. A "fool," i.e., someone who acts like a sensuous animal, does not discern spiritual things, and especially that which is mentioned in the following verses.

92:7-8. The wicked experience a rapid growth, but an equally rapid ruin. Their triumph is but the preparation for their fall. The wicked are transitory, but God is eternal sovereign.

92:9-10. Further confirmation of the sovereignty of Yahweh is offered. Yahweh's enemies will be scattered (lit., scatter themselves) and will perish. On the other hand, the "horn" of the godly will be exalted. The metaphor is derived from animals tossing their heads in the consciousness of their vigor and strength. The "unicorn" (KJV) is most likely the now extinct wild ox. The godly shall be anointed with oil as on occasions of festivity.

92:11. It is joyful news to godly people when those who threaten them are destroyed. The destruction of the wicked is the flip side of the deliverance of the godly. The one cannot take place without the other.

92:12-15. Though the wicked be but grass (v. 7), the righteous flourish like the fruitful palm and the fragrant cedar which apparently grew in the courts of God's temple. Such trees achieve great age and yet continue to bear fruit. The prosperity and happiness of the righteous are a witness to the faithfulness and justice of Yahweh.

ENTHRONEMENT OF THE KING
Psalms 93–96

Ps 93 is the first of seven "theocratic" psalms, the others being 95–100. The theme of these psalms is: Yahweh is king. Whereas this truth had been proclaimed in the days of Moses (Exod 15:18), in times of national difficulty God seemed to have abdicated his throne. These psalms celebrate some recent event in which Yahweh forcefully reasserted his sovereign rights.

A. The Fact of His Reign (Ps 93).

The writer of this psalm is anonymous and the occasion is unknown. Ps 93 has three thoughts: (1) the proclamation of Yahweh's

371

reign (vv. 1-2); (2) the security of his reign (vv. 3-4); and (3) the testimony of his reign (v. 5).

93:1-2. In some recent deliverance of Israel, Yahweh had asserted his sovereignty once again. He had put on his royal robes and girded himself "with strength" like a warrior for action. The result of his proclamation is that "the world," i.e., the moral world, had been reestablished. Though Yahweh has proclaimed his reign afresh, it is no novel thing. His sovereignty and his being are eternal.

93:3-4. The powers of the earth menace Yahweh's sovereignty in vain. Flooding rivers are here symbols of the great world powers which threaten to overspread the world (cf. Isa 8:7-8). The sea thundering against the shore as though it would engulf the dry land is a symbol of the heathen world menacing the kingdom of God. The Lord is above it all, untouched by those who would assert their sovereign will over the world.

93:5. The "testimonies" of God are his law which bears witness to his will and man's duty. The revelation in Scripture is the distinctive mark of Yahweh's kingdom. God's "house" here could be either the temple or the land of Israel. "Holiness," i.e., separation from sin and sinners, is appropriate for either. The psalm concludes with a wish that God's house will reflect that holiness forever (lit., for length of days). The language here suggests that the land has been rescued from being overrun by the heathen.

B. The Affirmation of His Reign (Ps 94).

Kingly power has as its first priority the subjugation of those who rebel against it. The occasion for this anonymous psalm is unknown. Ps 94 has two main divisions: (1) the psalmist's concern regarding the wicked (vv. 1-11); and (2) his confidence in Yahweh's righteousness (vv. 12-23).

94:1-2. An appeal to Yahweh as God ('El, the mighty one) to manifest himself as judge of the world and avenger of wrong. The word "vengeances" (plural) denotes the completeness of the retribution which he inflicts upon the wicked. To "shine forth" is to manifest himself in all the splendor of his presence. To "lift up" himself is to show himself to be the supremely exalted ruler. Yahweh is the "judge of the earth," i.e., the universal judge, who is needed to call the subordinate judges or rulers of the earth to account. The "proud" are those who are powerful in this world.

94:3-4. The psalmist wonders how long this great judge will tolerate the arrogant words and deeds of the wicked. Scholars disagree as to whether these wicked ones are foreign (Delitzsch; Kirkpatrick), or domestic (Maclaren; Rawlinson).

94:5-6. By brute force and extortion these wicked ones afflict God's "inheritance," i.e., his people. They murder the most defenseless people like widows, orphans, and "strangers," i.e., those whose lives, according to the traditions of Semitic hospitality, should have been inviolable.

94:7. The wicked proclaim their contempt for Israel's God as one who is either ignorant of the sufferings which they inflict, or indifferent to them.

94:8. From pleading with God, the psalmist turns to argue with those who might be tempted to agree with their oppressors about God. Such are "senseless" because they lack spiritual discernment. They are called "fools" or "stupid ones" (NASB) because they have given no intelligent consideration to the workings of God in the world.

94:9-10. A series of rhetorical questions makes the psalmist's point. It is absurd to suppose that the creator of the organs of sense does not himself have the ability to hear and see what is happening in this world. One who "chastens" the nations through disciplinary disasters must surely "rebuke" those who arrogantly oppress God's people.

94:11. Here is the positive answer to the self-delusion of the wicked and the doubters. Yahweh not only sees their works, he knows their very thoughts. "They" (masc. plural) refers to "man." The idea is that men are "vanity," i.e., feeble creatures. They certainly cannot escape the knowledge of God, nor entertain designs which he cannot fathom.

94:12-13. God educates his people through revelation. This gives the godly an insight into the ways of God's providence. It enables the godly person to endure calmly, without murmuring or losing heart, until the day of retribution overtakes the wicked. The figure of the "pit" is taken from the traps employed by hunters.

94:14-15. The day of retribution for the wicked will come because Yahweh cannot fully abandon his persecuted people. When those who pervert it are destroyed, judgment will again be administered upon principles of equity. The upright will then be supporters and adherents of that justice.

94:16-17. The psalmist has no champion but Yahweh. Without the help of the Lord, he already would have entered the silence of the grave.

94:18-19. At the very time the psalmist regarded himself as lost, the right hand of God's love had hold of him. While he was entertaining perplexing thoughts, God brought him comfort.

94:20-21. Though he may tolerate them for a time, it is inconceivable that Yahweh would let these wicked judges shelter themselves under his authority. The "throne of destruction" denotes the rulers or judges who were ready, like a yawning gulf, to swallow up the innocent. They cloak their "mischief" in legal garb. They unite in attacking the "righteous," i.e., the innocent, even condemning them to death.

94:22-23. The psalmist was confident that Yahweh would prove to be for him a "high tower" and a "rock of refuge." He would cause the wrongdoing of the wicked to recoil upon their own heads.

C. The Warning of His Reign (Ps 95).

The writer of Hebrews assigned this psalm to David. The psalm has two main divisions: (1) exultation in the Lord (vv. 1-7); and (2) admonition to the people of the Lord (vv. 8-11).

95:1-2. The psalm begins with a call to unite in worshiping Yahweh. The Lord should be greeted with loud shouts, with the acclamations which befit a victorious king. Worshipers should present themselves before him in his temple, bringing with them the sacrifices of thanksgiving.

95:3-5. The psalmist sets forth the reason for this worship service. Yahweh is a great king, superior to all the gods of the Gentiles. The depths of the earth and the soaring mountain peaks are all under his control. He (emphatic) made the raging seas and formed all the dry land.

95:6-7. The psalmist renews his call to worship Yahweh, on the ground of his relation to Israel. Worship of God should reflect the lowliest of homage, i.e., by bowing down and by kneeling. "Our maker" here probably refers to the formation of Israel as a nation, rather than to the creating of the heavens and earth. Yahweh is "our God." Israel is "his pasture," the flock which he shepherds. The psalmist expresses his desire that his generation, unlike their ancestors in the wilderness period, would listen to the voice of their God.

95:8-9. Yahweh now speaks a warning. Israel must not repeat the sins of obstinacy and unbelief by which their ancestors provoked him. Meribah ("Strife") and Massah ("Temptation") were symbolic names given to the spot of murmuring at the beginning (Exod 17:1-7) and end of the wilderness wandering (Num 20:1-13). At these sites the Israelites tempted and tried God by faithless doubts of his goodness and arbitrary demands that he should prove his power to them. This sin was committed in spite of the fact that they had just seen proof of God's power and goodwill in the Exodus and wilderness provisions.

95:10-11. God "loathed" that generation for forty years. Those people were prone to wander from the right way. They were incapable of recognizing the leadings of God's providence. God, therefore, swore that they should not enter into "my rest," i.e., the Promised Land (cf. Deut 12:9).

Verses 7b-11 are quoted in Hebrews 3:7-11, and applied as a warning to Christians who were in danger of unbelief, lest they too should fail to reach the rest promised to them.

D. The Response to His Reign (Ps 96).

Ps 96 is anonymous, but it is a substantial reproduction of the words written by David and handed over to Asaph on the occasion of the moving of the ark to the tent in Jerusalem (1 Chr 16:8-33). This psalm explores Yahweh's relationship to (1) the Israelites (vv. 1-3); (2) the Gentile gods (vv. 4-6); (3) the nations (vv. 7-9); and (4) the universe (vv. 10-13).

96:1-3. Fresh mercies demand fresh expressions of thanksgiving. All the earth is summoned to join in Israel's praise. Israel is urged to proclaim ceaselessly the good news of Yahweh's salvation. All the nations should hear of his marvelous works.

96:4-6. Yahweh is worthy to be praised. He is to be feared above all the so-called gods of men. Those idols are "things of nought," i.e., they do not really exist. Yahweh, however, is the creator of the heavens. The attributes of "honor" and "majesty" are perhaps personified and regarded as attendants standing in God's presence. In the sanctuary the psalmist can see the ark, the symbol of Yahweh's "strength" and "beauty" (cf. 78:61).

96:7-9. The psalmist appeals to the nations to acknowledge Yahweh. "The glory due his name" is given to the Lord when he is acknowledged as the one true and living God. The "offering" is that which subjects bring to their lord in token of their submission. The reference to the temple courts is one of the adaptations of the original poem by David written before the temple was built (cf. 1 Chr 16:29). As the priests were required to minister only in holy attire (Exod 28:2), so must the nations serve him in his temple clothed in holiness.

96:10-12. The message of Yahweh's reign should be proclaimed among the nations. He will establish the moral world so that it cannot be shaken by injustice. He shall judge the people with perfect equity. The psalmist appeals to nature to rejoice in the reign of Yahweh. God's righteous rule brings harmony and peace to all creation.

96:13. Yahweh comes to establish his righteous rule on earth. He comes to "judge," i.e., govern, the earth. Such government will, of course, inevitably require judicial judgment. Truth and righteousness characterize his government. Such passages must be classified as messianic.

GOVERNMENT OF THE KING
Psalms 97–100

The next four psalms focus on the government of the heavenly king and on the praise that is due him because of his righteous reign.

A. His Judgments (Ps 97).

The writer of this psalm was not an original poet. He skillfully combines here the language of earlier psalmists and prophets. Who he was and when he lived are not known. The psalm consists of four equal stanzas. The first two describe the coming of Yahweh to judgment, and the last two describe the consequences of this coming for Israel and for the nations.

97:1. The psalm begins with a proclamation of Yahweh's kingdom of power and righteousness. Even the distant islands and coastlands

376

of the Mediterranean Sea are called upon to join in the celebration of the manifestation of Yahweh's reign. Some recent overthrow of an international tyrant may be in view here.

97:2-3. Though Yahweh shrouds himself in mystery ("clouds and darkness") and comes with irresistible might, it is the consolation of his people to know that his kingdom is founded upon righteousness. Fire—symbolic of his wrath—goes before him to consume his enemies. The theophany at Sinai supplies the symbolism for this description.

97:4-6. The recent manifestation of Yahweh's power is described in terms of the great theophanies of the past. "His lightnings" illuminated the world as of old when he brought Israel out of Egypt. The earth trembled before him. The most solid and ancient parts of the earth are depicted as melting in his presence (cf. Micah 1:4). Yahweh's faithfulness to his people and his sovereign justice in the punishment of evil have been openly and visibly manifested in the sight of all the world.

97:7. Idolaters are dismayed at the impotence of their idols when Yahweh approaches in judgment. They discover their idols to be "things of nought," i.e., worthless. All supernatural beings, whether really existing or existing only in the minds of their worshipers, must do homage to Yahweh.

97:8-9. Zion and the "daughters" (cities) of Judah hear of Yahweh's great judgment in some distant place. The people of God are glad for the news. Yahweh had shown himself to be sovereign over the earth and superior to the gods worshiped any place thereon.

97:10-12. The people of God are exhorted to prove themselves in practice to be what they profess themselves to be. They must abhor all that is antagonistic to this holy God. God preserves those who are his godly ones by delivering them out of the hand of the wicked. "Light" is sown like seed, i.e., is broadly diffused, for the righteous. Light here symbolizes joy, gladness and victory. Thus the righteous should rejoice in every mention of the name of the Lord which brings to remembrance all that he is and does.

B. His Praise (Ps 98).

Nothing is known of the date and authorship of this psalm. This is the only psalm which bears the title *Mismor*, "A Psalm" without any addition. An ancient tradition reflected in the Greek version assigns this psalm to David. The psalm consists of three equal stanzas. It urges singing praise to the heavenly sovereign (1) by Israel (vv. 1-3); (2) all the earth (vv. 4-6); and (3) all nature (vv. 7-9).

98:1-3. Praise Yahweh for the glorious salvation which he has wrought. He has accomplished this deliverance by "his right hand, and his holy arm," i.e., he needed no help; his own might was all-sufficient. The deliverance of Israel was the outcome and the visible manifestation of Yahweh's faithfulness to his covenant. He had not forgotten his people. Even the distant parts of the earth had observed this marvelous deliverance.

98:4-9. The psalmist asks all the earth to salute its king with the glad shouts and music which are the proper greeting for a king upon his accession. Nature, too, should join the chorus of rejoicing. The sea, the rivers and the mountains should sing his praises.

C. His Reign (Ps 99).

The writer and occasion of this psalm are unknown. The psalm has three parts, each of which is marked by a refrain which declares the holiness of the Lord. The psalm celebrates (1) the sovereignty of Yahweh (vv. 1-3); (2) his righteous character (vv. 4-5); and (3) his faithfulness (vv. 6-9).

99:1-3. Yahweh has proclaimed himself king in Zion. All the earth should worship this holy God. The title "he who sits enthroned upon the cherubim" suggests that he who is supremely exalted in heaven has yet in time past condescended to dwell among his people on earth. The mercy seat of the ark, with the wings of the golden cherubim overshadowing, was considered God's earthly throne. Therefore, Zion is the seat of his universal sovereignty on earth. God's name, i.e., the revelation of his character, is "great and terrible," i.e., mighty deeds have been attributed to him. His highest claim to adoration, however, is his holiness, i.e., his absolute moral perfection.

99:4-5. Yahweh has established a kingdom of righteousness. The recent deliverance of Israel has given proof of the character of his reign. Believers are encouraged to worship "at his footstool," i.e., the ark (1 Chr 28:2). Again, it is his holiness which calls forth this worship.

99:6. The psalmist mentions three great intercessors of ancient Israel: Moses, Aaron and Samuel. The two brothers, Moses and Aaron, were "among the priests," i.e., they came from the priestly tribe. Moses interceded for Israel on numerous occasions. Aaron's most important moment of intercession is recorded in Num 16:46ff. Samuel also had a reputation as a great man of prayer (1 Sam 7:8-9).

99:7. Following intercession by Moses, Yahweh once more spoke to his people in the cloudy pillar (Exod 34:5). The reason for the efficacy of the prayers of Moses, Aaron and Samuel is that they were obedient to the Lord.

99:8. God pardoned his people in answer to intercessory prayer. Yet to vindicate his holiness he still brought chastisement, lest his people should imagine that sin can be taken lightly.

99:9. The psalm concludes with a final call to worship the God of Israel in Zion, in his holy mountain, for "holy is Yahweh our God."

D. His Worship (Ps 100).

Both the writer and the occasion of this psalm are unknown. This is the only psalm designated as "a psalm of thanksgiving." From ancient times this psalm has been used in the daily service of the synagoque. This brief psalm consists of two stanzas, each of which is a call to praise and a reason for so doing.

100:1-2. All lands are called upon to greet their sovereign with joyful praise. In the worship of the Lord all mankind regains its lost unity. The homage of worship takes the place of the homage of submission (2:12); now the nations can draw near with joy instead of fear.

100:3. Mankind should learn from the works of the Lord that he is the only true God. He "made" Israel of old to be a people for himself (Deut 32:6,18). Israel is his flock, the sheep of his pasture.

100:4-5. Yahweh's people are urged to enter the temple gates with thanksgiving and praise. The exhortation is based on the essential goodness of the Lord. His lovingkindness and faithfulness are experienced by generation after generation.

SUBMISSION OF THE KING
Psalm 101

Ps 101 has been the favorite psalm of rulers in many lands through the years. David wrote this poem in the early period of his reign, perhaps in connection with his efforts to move the ark to Jerusalem. This psalm sets forth David's desire to have a righteous court. Ps 101 has two major divisions. It focuses first on the king personally (vv. 1-4), and then on his kingdom (vv. 5-8).

101:1. "Lovingkindness and judgment" were characteristics of Yahweh's rule which should be reflected in the godly human monarch.

101:2-3. David was determined to pursue the way of integrity. He earnestly longs for closer fellowship with God. Even in the privacy of his own home he would walk the walk of the godly, for obedience to God's commands is a precondition of fellowship with him. He would entertain no wicked purpose; he would shake off any temptation to depravity like it was some accursed thing. Unfortunately, David was not able to maintain this standard to the end of his reign.

101:4. David is still speaking of himself. All crookedness and perversity shall be banished from his heart; he will not consciously tolerate evil there.

101:5-7. David resolves not to permit falsehood, pride and injustice around him; he will seek to fill his court with faithful ministers.

101:8. Day by day David would hold his court of justice in order that he might purge Jerusalem of evil and make it a holy city worthy of its title as "the city of Yahweh."

THE SHAPE OF PRAISE
Psalms 102–106

In the next five psalms, various aspects of God's character are singled out for praise.

A. The Eternal One (Ps 102).

Ps 102 is anonymous. Its historical background cannot be determined, although some take vv. 13-14 to refer to a time when Zion was in ruins. This is the fifth of the seven "penitential psalms." Actually the psalm is more the complaint of a sufferer than the confession of a sinner. The poem is called a "prayer" which an afflicted soul offers up to the Lord in the form of a complaint. The psalm contains three parts. The psalmist indicates (1) his complaint (vv. 1-11); (2) his consolation (vv. 12-22); and (3) his confidence (vv. 23-28).

102:1-3. The psalmist asks for a speedy hearing, pleading the extremity of his distress. He compares the brevity of his life to smoke. He likens himself to a sick man whose strength is being consumed by the burning heat of fever.

102:4-6. His heart—inner being—is dried up like a plant withered by the fierce heat of the sun. Sorrow and sickness have deprived him of all appetite for food. His continued sorrow reduced him to a state of emaciation in which his bones "cleave" to his skin. He compares himself to birds which haunt desolate places and ruins, uttering weird and mournful cries.

102:7-9. His nights are sleepless; he spends them like a solitary bird in mournful complaints. His enemies aggravate his sufferings by mocking him as one forsaken by God. They use his name in formulas for cursing others: "May God make you like that miserable soul." The ashes he has thrown over himself mingle with his food and his tears pollute his drink.

102:10-11. The psalmist believes that his suffering is punishment for sin. God has lifted him up as by some hurricane, and swept him away. He compares his life to the lengthening evening shadow, to the grass which fades so quickly.

102:12-13. The psalmist begins to focus his thoughts on the eternal sovereignty of the Lord. Yahweh's "name" is his memorial to one generation after another. It is the pledge of his sovereign rule. What he revealed himself to be at the Exodus, he must continue to be for all time to come. Since he rules, he must have compassion on Zion in accordance with his promise. The appointed time of Zion's restoration has come.

102:14-17. The psalmist offers another argument to move Yahweh's compassion on Zion. His servants look with yearning love towards Zion in its ruin. Zion's scattered stones and rubbish heaps— apparently all that is left of the place—are precious to them. The restoration of Zion will be a prelude to the conversion of the world.

Gentiles will pay homage to Yahweh when he has manifested his glory in the redemption of Zion, when he has answered the prayers of his faithful servants.

102:18-19. The good news of Yahweh's mercy will be recorded as the theme for the grateful praises of future generations. The restoration of Israel will be nothing short of a new creation. The praise will be justified because Yahweh will look down and hearken to the plight of his people.

102:20-21. Israel in exile is compared to a condemned captive languishing in prison and doomed to perish if Yahweh does not speedily intervene. God's intervention will result in the declaration of his praises in Zion.

102:22. Israel does not return to Zion alone. Israel's restoration sets the stage for a gathering of the nations to worship Yahweh there. The return of Old Covenant Israel was the prelude to the gathering of New Covenant Israel and the union of Jew and Gentile in the church of Christ.

102:23-24. The psalmist returns to the present. He takes up the thought of v. 11. Life has been a toilsome journey for him. He faces an untimely death. He prays that the eternal God would not cut short his life.

102:25-26. Compared with man's brief span of life, the natural world is an emblem of permanence; compared with God's eternity, it is seen to be transitory. He existed from all eternity; he called the earth into being. God will exist unchanged when the world has faded away. As one removes a worn-out garment, God will cast off the old heavens and earth for the new (Isa 65:17; 66:22).

102:27-28. Yahweh is unchanging; he does not wear down or wear out. The eternity of God is a pledge for the permanence of his people. Even if the psalmist and his contemporaries do not live to see the restoration of Israel, their descendants will have part in it. They shall "continue" (lit., dwell) in their land, restored to the favor of the Lord. In Hebrews 1:10-12 these words, which are addressed to Yahweh, are applied to Christ since he was the eternal Word who became flesh.

B. The Loving One (Ps 103).

David wrote this psalm, probably in his later life. This psalm is closely related to the preceding one. There the psalmist was filled with self-pity, but here that depression has been turned into joy. That psalm is petition, this one praise. The psalm has three divisions: (1) personal praise (vv. 1-5); (2) national praise (vv. 6-18); and (3) universal praise (vv. 19-22).

103:1-2. David exhorts all the faculties and powers of his being to praise God for his manifold mercies. Yahweh's "name" is holy in that he has revealed himself to be a holy God. David urges himself not to forget all the Lord has done for him.

103:3-5. David enumerates those things God has done for him as he continues to talk to himself. (1) He forgives all sins, and (2) heals all "diseases," i.e., the judgments with which Yahweh punished the guilty. The word includes all types of suffering. (3) He delivers from "the pit," i.e., death. (4) He crowns the believer's life with "lovingkindness and tender mercies." The goodness of the Lord renews the strength of the discouraged so that their spirits might soar like an eagle.

103:6-10. Yahweh's gracious dealing with men is illustrated from the experience of Israel. The Lord intervenes with righteous judgments whenever his people are oppressed. Yahweh made known his "ways," i.e., methods of dealing with men, to Moses (Exod 34:6). He proclaimed himself to be merciful and gracious. He is slow to anger, yet corrective punishment must surely come. Yet David admits that even in judgment God has punished Israel less than their iniquities deserved.

103:11-14. David compares the magnitude of the forgiving mercy of Yahweh to the height of the heaven. That mercy is extended to those that fear him, i.e., godly souls. Sins are completely removed from the penitent "as far as the east is from the west." Yahweh's attitude toward the shortcomings of his people is that of a father toward his young children. His mercy is motivated by the human condition. "He knows our frame," i.e., he understands that man is weak. His body ultimately returns to the dust from which it came.

103:15-18. Man passes from the scene like the grass of the field; but the mercy of God endures forever. His "righteousness," i.e., covenant faithfulness, will continue through the generations to those who remain true to the precepts of that covenant.

103:19-20. Yahweh has established his throne in heaven. It is unchanging and eternal. The mighty warrior angels who surround his throne are urged to praise the Lord. The perfect obedience of these angels is an example for mankind.

103:21-22. David next calls on Yahweh's "hosts" and "ministers" to praise him. These terms refer to lower ranking angels. Others take the term to refer metaphorically to the stars and the powers of nature which fulfill God's purposes. He next calls on all the created "works" of Yahweh to praise him. Lastly, he again exhorts himself to share in the universal praise of the Lord.

C. The Creator and Sustainer (Ps 104).

No more beautiful ode to creation has ever been written. The writer of this psalm is anonymous, but it is probably David. The occasion is unknown. The psalm pairs beautifully with the previous one. Here the stress is placed on the testimony of creation to the greatness of Yahweh. This psalm is difficult to outline. It begins with a brief call to praise (v. 1a), and concludes with a double call to praise (vv. 33-35). Any outline of the main body of the poem is somewhat arbitrary, but perhaps a twofold analysis is appropriate: (1) the forming of the earth (vv. 1b-18); and (2) the filling of the earth (vv. 19-32).

104:1-2. The greatness and majesty of Yahweh are exhibited in creation. In creation God robed himself, like a king, with "honor and majesty." Light, the first created element, is, as it were, God's robe, revealing while at the same time concealing him. The canopy of the sky is compared to a tent-curtain stretched out over the earth. By his simple fiat God spread out these heavens as easily as a man might pitch his tent.

104:3-4. God is depicted constructing his own dwelling above the waters that in the beginning surrounded the earth (Gen 1:2). The storm cloud and tempest are the symbols of his approach to earth. Even his spiritual agents are viewed as manifesting themselves in the physical phenomena of wind and lightning.

104:5-9. The earth is compared to a building erected upon solid foundations. Originally the entire surface of the earth was covered with water. God rebuked those waters and they retreated from the land masses. The mountains rose out of the sea. God set, as it were, boundaries for the sea to hold it in check.

104:10-13. Yahweh prepares the land by springs and rain, and makes bountiful provision for the wants of men and animals. The wild animals quench their thirst at these streams. Beside the springs and streams grow the trees which are the home of the birds, whose song of praise to their maker ever rises from the branches. The hills, watered by Yahweh, are satisfied and yield their produce which can truly be called Yahweh's "works."

104:14-18. The thought of the abundant produce of the land is further developed. Both beasts and man find sustenance and enjoyment in that which God brings forth from the earth. Grain, vintage and the oil of the olive were the chief products of Palestine. The trees with which God clothed the earth are also satisfied with the rains. In these trees the birds nest. In the lofty mountains God provided habitat for the wild goats and the rock badgers.

104:19-23. God filled the skies of the earth with sun and moon to mark the seasons and days. The daily sunsets lead to darkness which is a boon to many of the wild animals who search for their food by night. At sunrise these animals retreat to their dens, and man ventures forth for his day's work.

104:24-26. The psalmist expresses wonder and admiration at the variety and wisdom of God's works. He is amazed at the sight of the vast sea with living creatures large and small gathering their food both in the waters and around it. Thereon go the great ships. Therein "leviathan," the great sea monster, plays.

104:27-30. All the land and sea creatures depend upon Yahweh for life and food. He lends them their life breath for a time. When God recalls that breath, those creatures die and return to the dust from which they came. God, however, is continually sending forth his spirit to renew the face of the earth with fresh life.

104:31-32. The psalmist prays that this manifestation of God in nature may ever continue. He prays that God may continue to rejoice in his works as he did at the original creation (Gen 1:31). His look or touch is enough to remind the earth of the awful power of its creator. If he willed, he could annihilate it as easily as he created it.

104:34. The psalmist hopes that the creator will find this meditation "sweet," i.e., acceptable. As Yahweh rejoices in his works, so the psalmist rejoices in Yahweh.

104:35a. He prays that "sinners" might be removed from the earth so that the original harmony of creation might be restored. The Hebrew uses the intensive form of the word for "sinner" which implies obstinate, incorrigible and habitual sinners.

104:35b. The psalm concludes with the same self-exhortation with which it began. To this is added the general call to praise: *Hallelujah* ("praise Yahweh"). This word—according to Jewish tradition it should be rendered as one word—appears only in the Psalter, and it appears here for the first time.

D. The Mighty One (Ps 105).

Ps 105 is anonymous and the occasion is unknown, but the poet incorporates a large section (vv. 1-15) of the psalm of thanksgiving written by David when the ark was moved to Zion (1 Chr 16). The psalm consists of four nearly equal stanzas. Israelites are called upon to praise God for (1) his faithfulness to the covenant with the patriarchs (vv. 1-12); (2) his providential watch care over the patriarchs in their wanderings (vv. 13-24); (3) his judgments upon the Egyptian oppressors (vv. 25-36); and (4) his provision for his people after their release from Egypt (vv. 37-45).

105:1-4. The Israelites are summoned to proclaim to all the nations Yahweh's mighty deeds on behalf of his people. True devotion leads to deep inward joy which finds expression in thanksgiving. To "seek" Yahweh at his sanctuary and with one's whole heart is the duty and joy of his people. His strength and "face" (presence) are essential for the protection and blessing of Israel.

105:5-6. The Israelites should "remember" Yahweh's wonders, especially those connected with the Exodus. They should remember "the judgments of his mouth," i.e., the sentence pronounced and executed upon Pharaoh and the Egyptians. Such is the responsibility of Israelites because they are the "seed" of Abraham the servant of Yahweh. The children of Jacob have been chosen by the Lord for the purpose of making him known in the world.

105:7-12. Yahweh stands in a special relation to Israel; but he is no mere national deity. He exercises a universal rule over all nations as the judge of all the earth. Yet Yahweh never forgets the eternal covenant which he made with Abraham (Gen 17:2ff.), Isaac (Gen 26:3) and Jacob (Gen 28:13ff.). That covenant became "a law," i.e., a statute or decree. The promise of Israel's land inheritance was given when the patriarchs were but an insignificant clan living as "strangers" in the land of the Canaanites.

105:13-15. As the patriarchs traveled between the lands of the Canaanites, the Philistines and the Egyptians, Yahweh guarded them. He "reproved" kings, like Pharaoh (Gen 12:10ff.) and Abimelech (Gen 20; 26), for their sake. The patriarchs were regarded by God as his "anointed," i.e., men whose persons were sacred and inviolable. They were regarded as "prophets" because they were recipients of divine revelation.

105:16-22. Yahweh engineered the migration of Jacob to Egypt by means of a famine. Before the famine came, he had sent Joseph into Egypt to prepare the way for this migration. Joseph entered Egypt as a slave. When he was but a youth God had given him a word of promise about his destiny. That promise caused Joseph the suffering of exile and prison. Eventually, however, God's promise of exaltation over his brothers was fulfilled when Joseph was made the second ruler in the land of Egypt.

105:23-27. After Jacob and his sons entered "the land of Ham," i.e., Egypt, God multiplied his people and made them stronger than their oppressors. The Egyptians began to deal craftily in that they devised a plan to destroy Israel. At that time God sent Moses and Aaron who showed Yahweh's signs and wonders to the oppressors.

105:28-36. The psalmist enumerates the plagues against Egypt, but not in the familiar order. The ninth plague—darkness—broke the resistance of the Egyptians although it still took one last plague to convince Pharaoh. The psalmist then briefly mentions the plagues of (1) blood, (2) frogs, (3) flies, (4) lice, (5) hail accompanied by thunder and lightning, (6) locusts and (7) the death of the firstborn.

105:37-38. Israel marched forth from Egypt like a victorious army, with spoils which were virtually the reward of their long compulsory service (Exod 12:35f.), like a host of warriors in which none were weary. At that point the Egyptians were afraid of them, and were glad to see them leave the land.

105:39-41. Yahweh took care of his people while they wandered in the wilderness. He led them and protected them with a cloud canopy by day, and with a fiery cloud by night. He provided "the bread of heaven," i.e., manna, and quail as well. He brought forth a river of water from a rock for them (Exod 17:1ff.).

105:42-45. The joyous deliverance of the Exodus was but a manifestation of his faithfulness to the sacred promise which God had made to Abraham. Then Yahweh gave to his people "the lands of the nations," i.e., Canaan. There they inherited the fields, vineyards and cities which were the fruit of the labor of others. His purpose was that in that land Israel might follow the law of the Lord.

E. The Faithful and Patient One (Ps 106).

The writer and occasion of Ps 106 are unknown. This psalm is a companion of the previous poem. There the mighty deeds of Yahweh were remembered; here they are forgotten. The two psalms place in juxtaposition the faithfulness of Yahweh, and the lawlessness of Israel. The psalm has an introduction (vv. 1-5) and a conclusion (vv. 47-48), both of which contain praise, exhortation and prayer. Viewed geographically, the main body outlines the failings of Israel (1) in Egypt (vv. 6-12); (2) in the wilderness (vv. 13-33); and (3) in Canaan (vv. 34-46).

106:1-3. The psalmist urges praise for Yahweh because Israel's sin cannot exhaust his lovingkindness. No human voice can adequately celebrate Yahweh's mighty acts or worthily proclaim his praises. Those who are eligible to participate in the blessing to which the psalmist looks forward are those who obey his commandments.

106:4-5. The psalmist prays that he may share in the restoration of Israel to divine favor. He wants to see with satisfaction the good, gladness and glory of God's inheritance, Israel.

106:6. The main purpose of the psalm is now stated, namely, the confession of the constant sin of Israel throughout its history. The acknowledgement that the nation does not deserve the mercy for which it prays is the primary condition of forgiveness and restoration to God's favor. "We have sinned with our fathers" gives expression to the profound sense of national solidarity.

106:7-12. The first instance of Israel's sin was the unbelief and murmuring at the Red Sea. The marvelous works by which Yahweh had effected their deliverance from Egypt had failed to make them understand his character and will. At the first sign of danger, they rebelled against God's purpose to deliver them (Exod 14:11-12). Their conduct would have justified Yahweh causing them to return to Egypt. He acted, however, "for his name's sake," i.e., to uphold his character as a God of mercy, and to make known his might to the nations of the earth. He rebuked the sea and led them through the depths "as through a wilderness," i.e., on dry land. Then the waves returned to destroy totally their enemies. Momentarily their faith was rekindled. They sang praises to their deliverer.

106:13-15. The psalmist cites a second instance of Israel's sin. After the crossing of the sea, Israel refused to wait for God's plan of providing for their needs. They murmured against him more than once within a few weeks (Exod 15:22ff.; 16:2ff.; 17:2ff.). In the wilderness they "lusted" for meat and "tested" God by demanding proof that he was in their midst (Num 11:4). God punished them by giving them what they desired. Their self-willed lust brought sickness and death, not life and vigor.

106:16-18. Jealousy over the authority of Moses and Aaron was a third sin committed in the wilderness (Num 16:3-7). Aaron is called "the holy one of Yahweh" because he was set apart by the anointing oil to be the high priest. The leaders of the malcontents—Dathan and Abiram—were swallowed up by the earth (Deut 11:6). Those who were attempting to officiate as priests by offering incense were burned by fire from heaven (Num 16:35).

106:19-23. The worship of the calf at Horeb (Sinai) was a fourth sin of the wilderness period. In that idolatrous worship they exchanged "their glory," i.e., God, for the likeness of a dumb beast. They sinfully forgot all that Yahweh had done for them in Egypt and at the Red Sea. God would have destroyed them on the spot had not Moses "stood before him in the breach" like a warrior who stands in the gap of a city at the risk of his own life to repel the enemy.

106:24-27. When the spies returned from Canaan, Israel committed a fifth terrible sin, that of unbelief and cowardice. They rejected that delightful and desirable land of Canaan. They disbelieved Yahweh's promise to give that land to them. Instead of boldly preparing for the invasion, they sulked in their tents and murmured against God.

Yahweh then solemnly swore to them that they would all fall in that wilderness. He warned them that their descendants would be banished from the land of Canaan should they commit similar offenses against him (Lev 26:33; Deut 28:64).

106:28-31. The sixth instance of sin is the participation in the abominations of Moabite worship. They joined themselves as devotees to the Baal which was worshiped at Peor. "The sacrifices of the dead" were those sacrifices offered to lifeless gods. Their deeds provoked Yahweh to anger. A "plague" (lit., a smiting) broke out upon them. Decisive action by Phinehas, the grandson of Aaron, stayed the plague (Num 25:7f.). The zeal of Phinehas was rewarded with a covenant of everlasting priesthood.

106:32-33. The murmuring at Meribah (Num 20:1-13) is the seventh sin named. It is perhaps placed last as a climax, because here Moses himself was involved in the sin. The people's unbelief was the cause of the impatience and presumption for which Moses was punished by exclusion from Canaan.

106:34-39. Israel continued to disobey God even after entering Canaan. They did not destroy the Canaanites as they were ordered to do. Over the years they intermingled with the heathen which they had left in the land, and they learned their ways. They served the Canaanite idols, and this heathen worship became a snare to them. They even sacrificed their sons and daughters "unto demons," i.e., the false gods which were in reality demonic deceptions. The horror of human sacrifice is underscored by the tender age of the victims and their relation to the offerers. Thus was the land of Canaan polluted with innocent blood. The abandonment of Yahweh for other gods is described here, as frequently in the prophets, as infidelity to the marriage vow.

106:40-46. God's wrath was kindled against his unfaithful people. He delivered them into the power of their enemies. Time after time during the period of the Judges, God rescued his people from their oppressors. Still they refused to follow Yahweh's counsel, so he would bring them even lower. Each time, however, he would remember his covenant, and relent concerning his abandonment of them. He caused them to be pitied by their captors. The reference seems to be to the fairly humane treatment of the Jews once they were carried away to Babylon.

106:47. This prayer is the climax of the psalm. Confession of sin in effect throws Israel on the mercy of God. The psalmist wants to see this people return to their land where they can fulfill the purpose of their national calling. The praise of Yahweh is the end and object of Israel's existence.

106:48. The psalm closes with a doxology which also serves as the conclusion to Book Four. Thus this doxology differs from those of the first three books in that it is actually part of the psalm.

ENDNOTES

1. In Book Four *'Elohim* occurs in all eighteen times. It is absent altogether from five psalms. The name *'El* occurs nine times. The general term *'Adonay* occurs only twice.

2. Cited by W. Graham Scroggie, *The Psalms* (Old Tappan, NJ: Revell, 1965), 2:239.

CHAPTER NINETEEN

The Ways and the Word of God
Psalms 107-119

Book Five of the Psalter begins with Ps 107. Fifteen of the psalms found here are attributed to David, and one psalm (Ps 127) is assigned to Solomon. Again in this book the name Yahweh is predominant. It occurs in every psalm except two, in all some 236 times.[1] Some refer to Book Five as the "Deuteronomy" book of the Psalter because Israel appears here ready to take full possession of their land, and because here the nation takes a retrospective view of Yahweh's dealings with them over the centuries.

YAHWEH'S WAYS IN THE PAST
Psalms 107–108

The opening two psalms in Book Five look back to the works of Yahweh in the past. Yahweh had shown himself to be the redeemer and anchor of his people.

A. The Redeemer (Ps 107).

The writer and occasion of Ps 107 are unknown. It probably was composed during the early postexilic period, perhaps to accompany a national feast (vv. 22,32). The psalm is closely related to the two previous psalms. Ps 105 celebrates Israel's redemption from Egypt. Ps 106 is a confession of Israel's past failures. Ps 107 celebrates Israel's return from exile in foreign lands. The psalm has an introduction (vv. 1-3) and a conclusion (v. 43). The main body of the psalm has two main divisions: (1) Yahweh's goodness to his people (vv. 4-32); and (2) his government of the world (vv. 33-42).

107:1-3. Ps 107 begins with an invitation to those who have been redeemed from exile in Babylon to join in grateful confession of Yahweh's lovingkindness. Israelites from the four quarters of the earth returned to join the newly-founded community in Jerusalem.

107:4-9. Four pictures of Yahweh's lovingkindness to men are now developed. The first is that of travelers who had lost their way in the desert and were on the point of perishing, had God not provided for them.

107:10-16. The second picture of the lovingkindness of Yahweh is that of the liberation of captives languishing in exile. Such are described as sitting in "darkness" and in "the shadow of death," i.e., in unlighted vaults. This is a symbol of the misery of exile. Their suffering is a result of their sin. They had resisted the commands of God, and despised the wisdom of his purposes for them. They can now praise the Lord because Yahweh has broken down the "gates of brass" and "bars of iron" to set them free.

107:17-22. A third picture of Yahweh's lovingkindness is that of the restoration of those who have suffered sickness because of their sins. "Fools" are the morally perverse who persist in their transgression. The sickness envisioned removes appetite and brings the guilty to the gates of death. Yahweh sends forth "his word," which here is personified, to heal these desperately ill individuals. Such should render sacrifices of thanksgiving and bear public testimony to the wonderful works of Yahweh.

107:23-32. The fourth picture of Yahweh's lovingkindness is that of the rescue of sailors caught in a storm. Jonah may have been in the poet's mind. Merchant sailors are said to have seen the wonders of Yahweh in the deep. Yahweh sends the great ocean storms. The sailors' hearts melt as they ride their ships up and down on the gigantic waves. They are as confused as a drunk man when it comes to coping with the storm. They cry to Yahweh, and he calms the sea. Let such publicly praise the Lord in the temple when the congregation assembles for worship and when the rulers of the people sit in council.

107:33-38. The psalmist begins to enumerate proofs of Yahweh's providential government of the world. God punishes wickedness by making a fertile, well-watered land into a barren waste. That, in effect, is what had happened to Judah at the time of the exile. Now Yahweh has turned that wilderness into a fertile land again. The inhabitants can again grow their crops, raise their cattle and build their cities.

107:39-42. There is no change in subject. The psalmist continues to follow the fortunes of those whom Yahweh has blessed with prosperity. Temporary troubles may come, but Yahweh will not fail them in their need. The "princes" are any tyrannical oppressors. God humbles their pride and confounds their counsels. The psalmist may have in mind the troubles which were faced by those who returned from Babylon after the edict of Cyrus. When God comes to the aid of his people, all mockery of Israel and Israel's God are silenced. In such examples as these the wise man will discern the methods of Yahweh's providential dealings with men.

B. The Anchor (Ps 108).

This is the first of fifteen Davidic psalms collected in Book Five of the Psalter. It consists of parts of Ps 57 and Ps 60. Doubtless it was for liturgical purposes that these two fragments of older poems were combined into a new hymn. This was probably done after the return from Babylon to suit the new circumstances. The main thought here is that Yahweh is the anchor of the soul. The psalm consists of two parts: (1) praise for past help (vv. 1-5); and (2) prayer for present help (vv. 6-13). For observations, see comments on Ps 57:7-11 and Ps 60:5-12.

YAHWEH'S WAYS IN THE FUTURE
Psalms 109–110

Pss 109–110 are messianic, depicting the suffering of Christ and the glory which would follow.

A. Agony of Messiah (Ps 109).

According to New Testament authority, the betrayal of Christ by Judas is the subject of two prophetic psalms, Ps 69 and Ps 109. Both passages focus on the terrible judgment which would befall the betrayer.

Ps 109 was written by David during the period of Absalom's rebellion. The history of David's confrontation with various enemies uniquely qualified him to paint this picture of a betrayed saint. The psalm refers to many enemies, but the focus is on a single individual. In describing this archenemy David draws upon his own experiences with Saul who pursued him, Ahithophel who betrayed him, and Shemei who cursed him.[2] David here, however, writes as a prophet (Acts 1:16), and this necessitates that the speaker in this psalm is his greater descendant, Messiah.

Ps 109 consists of two cries for help (vv. 1-5; 20-31). Sandwiched between these two petitions is a pronouncement upon those who persecute the speaker (vv. 6-19).

109:1-5. God is the object of Messiah's praise, for the Father has never failed him in times past. Messiah's silence, however, is in stark contrast to the noisy clamor of the foe. His enemies are scheming to effect his ruin by groundless charges supported by false witnesses. These vicious foes surrounded him like a pack of wild dogs. They fought against him without cause. Messiah loved all men, even those who became his foes. His love was proved by his prayers on their behalf. Unfortunely, they had rewarded his intercession and compassion with evil and hatred.

109:6-7. God answers the prayer of Messiah by pronouncing the doom of his adversaries (Acts 1:16,20). One special adversary of Messiah is singled out for condemnation. Ten details of that judgment are indicated. (1) The enemy comes under the influence of Satan (cf. John 13:27). (2) He would be condemned in the judgment. (3) His prayer before God would be to no avail.

109:8-11. (4) His life would come to an end prematurely. (5) He would be succeeded in his office by another (cf. Acts 1:20). (6) His children will suffer by his death, for they would be fatherless. They would be forced to roam about begging as their home falls into ruin for lack of upkeep. (7) All that the betrayer had worked for would be taken from him by creditors.

109:12-15. (8) No one would extend compassion to the fatherless children of the betrayer. (9) The betrayer's sons would die childless. Eventually the family name would be removed from the register of citizens. (10) The punishment of the sins of his parents and ancestors, delayed and postponed in God's grace, would be brought to bear against the betrayer.

109:16-19. The terrible sentence against the betrayer is deserved. First, the betrayer showed no mercy toward that one who was preeminently "the poor, the needy, and the broken hearted." Second, the betrayer deliberately chose a policy of "cursing," i.e., bringing calamity on others. As a result, blessing would be removed far from him. His ill-will and negative conduct would be like a garment to him, and like substances taken into the body.

109:20. Messiah boldly announces the fate of all those who speak against him, those who make themselves his adversaries. Their fate would be like that of the betrayer.

109:21-22. Messiah enumerates the eight grounds upon which he implores the intervention of God on his behalf. (1) He asks God to act for the sake of his name, i.e., in his own best interest. Divine action on behalf of the agonizing savior would prove God to be all that he ever claimed to be. He mentions (2) God's good (i.e., abundant) mercy and (3) his own pitiful condition: he is "poor and needy." These words perhaps denote his physical condition. He is helpless in the flesh to resist his powerful adversaries. (4) The inward spiritual agony of the Messiah is reflected in the words "my heart is wounded within me."

109:23-25. The grounds for intervention continue. (5) He faces imminent death. His life is like a shadow when it stretches out towards evening. The dark hour of death is upon him. (6) Without God's help he is as helpless before his powerful adversaries as locusts driven about by wind. (7) In his distress Messiah had no appetite for food. Like a man in mourning he has abstained from the use of oil to soothe the skin in that harsh climate. (8) He has become an object of reproach. The enemies greet him with a gesture of contempt and abhorrence. He is treated as though he were an object of the wrath of God.

109:26-28. Again Messiah pleads for a deliverance which would be appropriate to the mercy of God, a deliverance so stupendous that even his enemies would have to recognize the hand (i.e., power) of God in it. He prays that the evil designs of his adversaries might fail. Even though they have cursed him with tongue and deed, let God override that curse with blessing. Let their moment of triumph be turned to their shame. At the same time, Messiah prays that he himself might know the joy that comes with victorious deliverance.

109:29-31. Messiah's prayer ends on a note of confidence that his enemies will be "clothed with shame." Their carefully designed plots will be turned to confusion. He anticipates the resumption of his former thanksgiving and praises. He knows that his Father stands at his right hand to aid him in court, as it were, against those who condemn him to death.

B. Exaltation of Messiah (Ps 110).

The New Testament supports the claim of the heading that Ps 110 was written by David (cf. Matt 22:42f.). No specific event is mentioned in the psalm which would furnish a clue as to its background. David here is functioning as a prophet. His attention is focused on Messiah.[3] Four thoughts regarding Messiah emerge in this psalm: (1) his enthronement (v. 1); (2) his government (vv. 2-3); (3) his priesthood (v. 4); and (4) his conquests (vv. 5-7).

110:1. The utterance in v. 1 is called an "oracle" (ne'um) of Yahweh. This terminology, common in the prophetic books, appears only here in the Psalter. What follows is a declaration of God concerning David's Lord.

With irresistible logic Jesus argued that the word "Lord" implied one superior to David. Of his successors only Messiah would be his superior. The authority of David's Lord is indicated here by two considerations. First, Messiah is at the "right hand of Yahweh," i.e., the place of honor and authority. Jesus indicated that he one day would sit in that position (Luke 22:69), and that enthronement took place after the ascension (Dan 7:13f.).[4] Second, Messiah's enemies have become his "footstool." The allusion is to the custom of conquerors placing their feet upon the necks of captured enemies as a symbolic token of total victory (cf. Josh 10:24).

110:2. Four aspects of Messiah's rule are brought out here. (1) The center of his rule is Zion. Physical Zion (Jerusalem) was a type of the true Zion, the kingdom of Christ (Heb 12:22). (2) The means of his rule is the shepherd's rod, a strong rod of iron (Ps 2:9) which God put in his hand on the day of his enthronement. The rod is the symbol of his power. (3) The commission under which he rules is suggested by the imperative "rule." He is active in the government of the kingdom. He has been delegated all authority in heaven and earth (Matt 28:18). (4) He rules "in the midst of his enemies," i.e., in spite of them.

110:3. This difficult verse presents seven essential ideas concerning the subjects of Messiah. (1) He would have a people who followed him. (2) This people would be in willing subjection to him. (3) The existence of this people would be a result of Messiah's power. (4) This people would appear before Messiah in great beauty—in robes of holy adorning or priestly garments. (5) From "the womb of the dawn," i.e., the very beginning of his reign Messiah would have such a group of followers. (6) The followers would display the vigor of youth, i.e., they would be filled with zeal for his cause. (7) The followers would bring refreshment to the barren world like the morning dew rejuvenates parched ground.

110:4. Five facts are stated regarding the priesthood of Messiah. (1) His priesthood is God-appointed, not inherited. (2) His priesthood is irrevocable, for it is underscored with a divine oath. God will not "relent" or change his purpose in this regard. (3) His priesthood is singular. The oath concerns one person, not a priestly dynasty. (4) His priesthood is eternal. He is a priest "forever." An eternal priesthood conferred on a single person can only be fulfilled in a person who lives forever. (5) His priesthood is unique, for it is "according to the manner of Melchizedek." Melchizedek was priest-king of the most high God in Gen 14. Since no priestly ancestors are mentioned one must conclude that he derived his priesthood from divine appointment.

110:5. The scene is one of battle. Yahweh stands at the right side of Messiah during the battle. Together they "strike through the adversaries." This day of wrath is the final showdown with the forces of evil.

110:6. Messiah shall judge (force into submission) Gentiles, those who reject his gracious priestly ministries. The corpses of those who attempt to withstand the conquering Messiah fill the land. The "head" (singular) of many countries will be mortally wounded. Perhaps this is an allusion to Satan who leads all opposition to Christ (cf. Gen 3:15). Ultimately Christ will destroy everything which opposes the universal spread of his kingdom.

110:7. While the enemies fall, Messiah presses on to total victory. The picture here is of a soldier chasing a fleeing enemy. He delays his pursuit only long enough to refresh himself at a stream. He then immediately continues the relentless chase. Complete victory is assured.

YAHWEH'S WAYS IN THE PRESENT
Psalms 111–112

Psalms 111 and 112 are closely connected in structure, content, and language. Both are regular acrostic psalms of twenty-two lines corresponding to the number of letters in the Hebrew alphabet. Ps 111 celebrates the power, goodness, and righteousness of Yahweh; Ps 112 describes the blessedness of those who serve him. Both psalms draw largely from older psalms and from Proverbs.

A. The Graciousness of God (Ps 111).

Ps 111 is anonymous and undated, but it probably belongs to the early postexilic period. The prefixed *"Hallelujah"* seems to indicate a liturgical use of the psalm. Outlines of acrostic poems are somewhat arbitrary, but the following may be helpful: (1) Yahweh's steadfast righteousness (vv. 1-4); (2) his ancient covenant (vv. 5-6); (3) his eternal precepts (vv. 7-8); and (4) his abiding purpose (vv. 9-10).[Hebrew initial letters in brackets.]

111:1. *[Aleph-Bet]* The congregation assembled for worship is called a "council" as being united by the sense of common fellowship.

Its members are described as "the upright," for it is presumed that they are motivated by true devotion. There the psalmist determines he will render public praise.

111:2-3. *[Gimel-Vav]* The grounds of praise for Yahweh are his "works." These should be studied with loving diligence by all who delight in learning to understand his revelation of himself. All of his works are a revelation of those attributes of royal dignity with which he clothes himself; at the same time they are the outcome of his eternal righteousness. With him there is no divorce between might and right.

111:4. *[Zayin-Chet]* Yahweh has made a memorial for his wonderful works, particularly the deliverance of his people from Egypt, (1) by the continuous tradition which they were charged to hand on from one generation to another; (2) and by the festivals and ordinances which commemorated that deliverance, especially the Passover. All his dealings with Israel illustrated that Yahweh was fundamentally "gracious and full of compassion."

111:5. *[Tet-Yod]* As Yahweh provided manna for Israel in the wilderness, so he provides for the wants of his people at all times. The deliverance from Egypt was a proof that Yahweh remembered his covenant with the patriarchs, and a pledge that he would never be unmindful of it.

111:6. *[Kaph-Lamed]* By dispossessing the Canaanites and giving Israel their land for its inheritance, Yahweh demonstrated his might. That gift was the pledge of a still wider sovereignty, to be fulfilled only in a spiritual way (Ps 2:8; Isa 60:14).

111:7a. *[Mem]* Yahweh's actions are manifestations of his eternal attributes of truth and justice (Deut 32:4). He is constantly true to his promises, unfailingly just in his moral government of the world. The gift of Canaan to Israel was the fulfillment of his promise to the patriarchs, while the expulsion of its former inhabitants was a just retribution for their sins.

111:7b-8. *[Nun-Ayin]* Memories of Sinai follow those of the Exodus. The commandments given there are as unchanging as the God who set them forth. They reflect his truth and uprightness.

111:9-10. *[Pey-Tav]* The "redemption" from Egypt gave proof of Yahweh's faithfulness to his covenant. By that great deliverance

401

Yahweh revealed himself as a God who is holy and must be feared. To fear him, therefore, is the starting point of all true wisdom. That wisdom manifests itself in obedience to Yahweh's commandments. In obedience one gains insight. All the attributes of God which demand man's praise are eternal. Therefore, people should praise God forever.

B. The Blessedness of the Godly (Ps 112).

This anonymous and undated psalm probably belongs to the early postexilic period. This psalm builds on the foundation of the final line of Ps 111: those who fear Yahweh should praise God for his blessing. Acrostic poems are hard to outline because each line is virtually a separate thought. A provisional outline for this psalm may be (1) the blessedness of the godly (vv. 1-4); (2) the blessedness of the gracious (vv. 5-9); and (3) the misery of the ungodly (v. 10).

112:1-3. [Aleph-Vav] The secret and source of all true happiness and prosperity is the fear of Yahweh, which leads to a cheerful and thorough obedience to his commandments. His posterity—"the generation of the upright"—shall be powerful and prosperous in the land. His "righteousness," i.e., the reward for his righteousness, is ongoing.

112:4-5. [Zayin-Yod] The godly person reflects the compassion of his God. "He arises as a light in the darkness for the upright ones," i.e., those who are poor but godly. Such people he befriends. He shows favor and lends to those in need. He takes care to injure no one in the conduct of his business.

112:6-8. [Kaph-Ayin] The godly person shall enjoy firm and unshaken prosperity. He will be remembered fondly for his acts of mercy. Since his conscience is clear, he has no fear of some terrible sin being exposed. His heart is steadfastly fixed on Yahweh. If he is attacked he is confident that in due time his cause, which is the cause of God and right, will triumph.

112:9. [Pey-Qoph] The godly person is generous with the poor. His "righteousness," i.e., the reward for his righteousness, endures forever. His "horn" shall be exalted with honor. The figure is taken from that of a proud beast who displays his vigor and power by waving his horns in the air.

112:10. [Resh-Tav] The wicked see the exaltation of the godly.

They are consumed with impotent rage. The gnashing of the teeth indicates frustration. That which the wicked desire comes to nothing.

YAHWEH'S WAYS CELEBRATED
Psalms 113–118

Pss 113–118 form the *Hallel*, or hymn of praise. This collection of psalms probably constituted the "hymn" which Jesus and the disciples sang as they left the upper room for the garden.

A. His Amazing Condescension (Ps 113).

This psalm is anonymous and undated. It seems to come from the postexilic period. The term *"Hallelujah"* indicates liturgical use. This call for praise consists of three equal stanzas: (1) a call for universal praise (vv. 1-3); (2) the ground of praise (vv. 4-6); and (3) the occasions of praise (vv. 7-9).

113:1-3. True Israelites are called "servants of Yahweh." Such are exhorted to praise "the name of Yahweh," i.e., the totality of that which God has revealed about himself. This praise of Yahweh should be perpetual and universal.

113:4-6. The praise of God is grounded in his exaltation and his condescension. He dwells on high above all nations. His glory is so great that it reaches to the heavens. Though he sits enthroned on high in heaven, yet he stoops to regard the earth.

113:7-8. Examples of Yahweh's gracious condescension are cited. These lines come from the ancient song of Hannah (1 Sam 2:8). To "sit in the dust" or "on the dunghill" is a metaphor for a condition of extreme degradation and misery. God lifts up his people from such a condition. "To dwell with princes" is a figure for elevation to the highest rank and dignity.

113:9. The psalmist cites a specific example of the way in which Yahweh gives sons to the barren housewife. Perhaps this is a further allusion to the experience of Hannah. Some see in the barren housewife here a picture of Zion whose sons were lost in the Babylonian captivity. Now her heart is gladdened by the restoration of her children to her.

B. His Awesome Presence (Ps 114).

The writer and occasion are unknown. Almost certainly this exquisite poem comes from the postexilic period. The poem consists of two main divisions: (1) a description of nature in tumult (vv. 1-4); and (2) an explanation of this tumult (vv. 5-8).

114:1-2. When Yahweh brought Israel out of Egypt—"from a people of strange language"—he separated them from all other nations to be a holy people over which he himself would rule. Israel would be his "sanctuary," i.e., his consecrated dwelling place. The whole nation is designated by its two principal divisions, namely, "Judah" and "Israel."

114:3-4. The Red Sea and the Jordan are personified. They are represented as hastening to withdraw the barriers they presented to Israel's Exodus from Egypt and entrance into Canaan. The "mountains skipped like rams" is a poetic description of the earthquake which accompanied the giving of the law at Sinai.

114:5-6. The poet challenges nature to explain her actions at the time of the Exodus.

114:7-8. It was Yahweh's presence that caused the earth to tremble at Sinai. The poet bids the earth tremble still at his presence. "The Lord" ('adon), denotes Yahweh as the Sovereign of the world, but he is also the God of Jacob (Israel). The God who made water flow from the rock at Rephidim and Kadesh (Exod 17:6; Num 20:8ff.) can still provide streams of blessing for his people. The Hebrew uses a timeless participle in this last sentence which suggests the continuing provision for his people.

C. His Exalted Glory (Ps 115).

Like the other psalms in this section, the writer and occasion are unknown. Ps 115 seems to come from the early postexilic period. This psalm is a response to the idolaters who taunted Israel during the time of her captivity. The psalm has five parts: (1) an appeal to God (vv. 1-3); (2) an evaluation of idols (vv. 4-8); (3) a call to trust (vv. 9-11); (4) assurance of blessing (vv. 12-15); and (5) a commitment to praise (vv. 16-18).

115:1-2. Here the psalmist appeals to God to vindicate his honor by ministering to his people. The captives know that they have no merits of their own on which to base their appeal. Rather he pleads that God might vindicate his honor, since the wretched condition of his people was a reflection on his deity. The heathen mocked the humiliating circumstances of Israel and questioned the power of their God. If Yahweh does not intervene on behalf of his people, it would then appear that his fundamental attributes of love and faithfulness had disappeared.

115:3. Though its outward circumstances may seem to justify the taunts of the heathen, Israel knows that Yahweh is supremely exalted and omnipotent. If his people suffer, it is because he wills it, not because he lacks power to help them.

115:4-8. The heathen who taunt captive Israel need to consider their own gods. Their idols are but their own handiwork. They cannot teach their worshipers nor see their needs; they cannot hear prayers nor smell the sweet savor of sacrifices. Such gods drag down their worshipers to the same level of senseless stupidity.

115:9-11. Here a leader would sing the first line of each verse addressed to God in the second person; then the congregation would respond with the second line in the third person. "Israel," "the house of Aaron," i.e., the priests, and "fearers of Yahweh" are called upon to trust in the Lord because he is the "help" and "shield" of his people.

115:12-13. By bringing his people back from captivity, Yahweh proved that he had not forgotten them. This deliverance is here viewed as a pledge that he would still further bless them. He would bless one and all without distinction.

115:14-16. The psalmist prays that the Lord would increase the numbers of the small postexilic community. This blessing is possible because he is the creator of the heaven and earth, i.e., he is omnipotent. The heavens belong to Yahweh, not to the astral deities of the Mesopotamian powers. He is therefore above and over the sons of men who inhabit the earth.

115:17-18. From heaven the psalmist passes to earth, and from earth to Sheol, the abode of the dead. The dead cannot praise God as they once did with the service of lip and life. It is not the purpose of the psalmist to discuss the status of those believers who are dead. He makes the obvious point that once a person is dead his lips are silent. On the other hand, "we" (emphatic) the living will continue to bless "Yah" forever, i.e., throughout the generations.

D. His Mighty Deliverance (Ps 116).

The anonymous poet of Ps 116 seems to have lived in the postexilic period. He had experienced a recent deliverance from deadly peril, the nature of which is uncertain. The psalmist speaks here of (1) his danger (vv. 1-4); (2) his deliverance (vv. 5-9); (3) his devotion (vv. 10-14); and (4) his delight (vv. 15-19).

116:1-2. The psalmist professes his love for Yahweh because the Lord has inclined his ear to his prayer. Answered prayer demands life-long love and gratitude.

116:3-4. The psalmist had been in great peril. He represents death and Sheol as hunters lying in wait for their prey with nooses and nets. In those circumstances he called on "the name of Yahweh," i.e., upon Yahweh as he has revealed himself to mankind.

116:5-6. In his own experience the psalmist had found Yahweh to be gracious, righteous, and merciful. Yahweh preserves "the simple," i.e., those whose lack of wisdom and experience exposes them to danger. In that category the psalmist included himself. When he was brought low by circumstances, Yahweh helped him.

116:7. The psalmist encourages himself with recollections of God's mercy. He urges himself to abandon anxiety and resume the perfect tranquility that springs from trust in God. The word "rest" is plural in the Hebrew, indicating full and complete rest. He reminds himself that God has dealt bountifully with him.

116:8-11. The psalmist drifts back into prayer. He recognizes that Yahweh had delivered him from death. He had dried up his tears, and prevented him from falling (before his enemies?). The psalmist pledges that he will render to Yahweh free and joyous service in the land of life and light. In his time of distress the psalmist had found human help unreliable. Yet he never lost his faith in God.

116:12-14. The psalmist asks himself how he might repay Yahweh for his benefits. He responds to his query with two affirmations. He pledges to "take the cup of salvations," i.e., the cup which was to be drunk as a part of the sacrifice of thanksgiving for great and manifold deliverance. He would call on Yahweh in recognition that he alone is the source of such blessing. He would publicly pay his vows to Yahweh. This normally would include certain sacrifices pledged to God during the emergency.

116:15-16. Through his experience the psalmist learned that the death of one of his "saints" (godly ones) is precious in the sight of Yahweh, i.e., their death is not a matter of indifference to him. He affirms that he is one of Yahweh's "servants." He is in fact the son of Yahweh's "handmaid," i.e., he had been raised by a godly mother from childhood to serve the Lord. For this reason, Yahweh had loosed his "bonds." He had been like a prisoner condemned to death before the Lord intervened.

116:17-19. In appreciation for what the Lord had done for him, the psalmist pledges to offer to him the sacrifice of thanksgiving (cf. Lev 7:11ff.). Verse 17, in essence, repeats v. 13. In the courts of the temple he would pay his vows to Yahweh. The emphasis here is on the *public* confession of gratitude.

E. His Universal Appeal (Ps 117).

The shortest of the psalms—seventeen words in the Hebrew—is anonymous. It is probably postexilic. The psalm presents two ideas: (1) the obligation of praise (v. 1); and (2) the occasion of praise (v. 2).

117:1. All nations are called upon to praise Yahweh. Two different words for praise are used here. Paul (Rom 15:11) quotes this verse as one of the Scriptures which foretold the extension of God's mercy to the Gentiles.

117:2. Mighty as Israel's transgressions were, God's mercy was mightier still. Lovingkindness and truth are fundamental attributes of Yahweh's character.

F. His Enduring Mercy (Ps 118).

That Ps 118 is messianic is attested by the citation of the psalm seven times in the New Testament.[5] Thirteen verses in the psalm are in the first person singular. If the rejected stone of v. 22 is Messiah—and that seems incontrovertible in the light of the New Testament evidence—then the sufferer in the first part of the psalm must also be Messiah.[6] The use of first person to refer to someone other than the author of a poem is not unknown in Christian hymnody.[7]

The last of the *Hallel* psalms is anonymous. Some think David is the writer; others assign it to the postexilic era. It appears to have been intended as a processional hymn, perhaps connected with the great celebration of Nehemiah 8. Antiphonal elements are present. The psalm has five movements. After an introductory call to praise (vv. 1-4), the poem describes deliverance from (1) distress (vv. 5-9); (2) danger (vv. 10-16); (3) death (vv. 17-21); and (4) disgrace (vv. 22-26).

118:1-4. All Israel is called upon to join in praising Yahweh for his unfailing goodness. The breakdown of the nation into "Israel," "the house of Aaron," i.e., the priests, and "those that fear Yahweh" has the effect of emphasis by enumeration (cf. 115:9-13).

118:5-7. Messiah begins to describe in general terms the distress from which his Father had delivered him. (1) The Father answered him "in a large place," i.e., he delivered him from the narrow place of distress. The Father answered the agonizing prayer of Gethsemane. He delivered Messiah, not *from* the ordeal, but *through* it. (2) Yahweh the Father was his great helper through the period of distress. He feared nothing which men could do to him. (3) Yahweh the Father took his part, i.e., actively aided him. This enabled Messiah to look in the face those who hated him.

118:8-9. Messiah pauses in the description of his distress to press home a great principle: It is better to trust in the Lord than to put confidence in man.

118:10-12. Three times in these verses Messiah describes himself as surrounded by enemies. They are identified as "all the Gentiles." The Romans and Jews acting like Gentiles taunted, mocked, and threatened him. Because of the countless numbers of assailants, and their furious desire to destroy him, the enemies are likened to vicious bees.

Three times in these verses Messiah expresses his confidence in ultimate victory: "I will cut them off." The raging fire of hatred against God's person and plan would be quenched. This will be done judicially, properly, circumspectly "in the name of Yahweh." Through the authority granted to him, Messiah will be the final judge of all, including those who with vengeance attacked him.

118:13-14. The leader of the foe is singled out here. Satan had emptied his arsenal in his attacks upon Jesus. With his death on the cross, Satan thought he had successfully destroyed Messiah. He, however, has more than adequate resources for dealing with this multitude of enemies. Yahweh the Father helped him. Messiah acknowledges his Father as his strength, song and salvation.

118:15-16. Messiah pauses anew to press home the application of what he has been saying. While Messiah's enemies are destroyed, there is "the sound of rejoicing and salvation in the tents of the righteous." The joyful song of salvation centers around "the right hand of Yahweh" which is exalted because he has fought valiantly.

118:17-18. Messiah expresses confidence in the ultimate victory over death when he declares: "I shall not die, but live." He was not abandoned to the power of death. He rose again to "declare the works of Yahweh."

The clause "Yahweh has chastened me sore" embraces all the suffering of Gethsemane and Calvary. Isaiah (ch. 53) indicates that Messiah would suffer vicariously for the sins of others. This suffering was part of God's grand plan, and in that sense the chastening can be attributed to the Father.

118:19-21. Returning triumphantly from his sacrificial mission, Messiah calls for "the gates of righteousness," i.e., the gates of the celestial city, to be opened to him. These gates open only to the just; they exclude all unrighteousness. Messiah returned to praise his Father. His prayers had been answered; his deliverance was complete. Through this same gate those who have been declared righteous through faith will follow their redeemer.

118:22. Messiah refers to himself as "the stone which the builders rejected." The leaders who were supposed to build up God's spiritual temple (Pharisees and Sadducees) refused to recognize Messiah as the rightful foundation upon which to build. That very stone, however, through the resurrection became "the head of the corner," i.e., the most important stone in the structure.

118:23-24. The saints of God can only marvel at the circumstances which led to the exaltation of the rejected stone. The resurrection of Jesus ushered in a new day for the human race. Believers can rejoice and be glad in this day. Death has been conquered.

118:25. The community of believers welcomes the triumphant Messiah. They cry out for Yahweh's salvation and prosperity to come. This is the Old Testament equivalent to praying: "Thy kingdom come!"

118:26. Messiah came "in the name of the Lord." In all that he did he was acting under a commission from his Father. The believing

409

community pronounced a blessing on this one who was in fact a blessing to all mankind. Out of the house of the Lord—the spiritual temple of 2 Pet 2:9—this worshipful blessing emanates.

118:27. Yahweh is God (*'El*, "the mighty one"). He has shown his power by delivering Messiah from death. In so doing he brought new light to those who sat in the darkness of sin (cf. Matt 4:16). Those who have been recipients of that gospel light cry out in earnest petition that the sacrifice made by Messiah might be a once-for-all-time offering. Sacrificial blood was smeared on the horns of the altar during the Old Covenant sacrificial ritual. For the sacrifice to be bound to the horns would make the effects of the offering perpetual.

118:28. Twice Messiah declares his submission to the Father. Twice he declares his desire to praise the Father. He is totally pleased with his earthly mission, with the grand deliverance which his sacrificial death and triumphant resurrection has made possible. The goodness of the Lord in sending Christ to be mankind's savior calls for everlasting praise. So the psalm ends as it began with an exhortation to express gratitude to God for his never-ending mercy.

YAHWEH'S INCOMPARABLE WORD
Psalm 119

The author and date of this unique psalm are uncertain. Coincidences between the language of the text and the history of Ezra's time hint that this great scribe may have been the writer. The composition is in the form of a perfect and regular alphabetic acrostic. The poem consists of twenty-two stanzas corresponding to the twenty-two letters of the Hebrew alphabet. Each stanza contains eight verses beginning with the same Hebrew letter. The theme of this poem is the excellence of the divine law.

The twenty-two sections seem to fall into three groups of seven, followed by the last section as a kind of appendix.

A. The Word and the Soul (119:1-56).

[Aleph] 1.The power of the word for blessing (119:1-8). Loyal obedience to Yahweh's law is the source of man's truest happiness. Integrity of life is defined as walking in Yahweh's law. To seek the

Lord with the whole heart includes worship, prayer and study of the word. These thoughts trigger a prayer that God's law might be the fixed rule of the psalmist's life. He is confident that no disgrace can befall one whose single aim is the observance of God's law in all its parts. He knows, however, that he has not yet attained to a complete knowledge of God's word. Yet he gives thanks for every advance in his understanding. He is determined to walk in the light of what he learns from that word. For that reason he asks that God might not forsake him as Israel in the Exile had been for a time forsaken by Yahweh as the punishment of its sin.

[Bet] 2. *The power of the word for cleansing (119:9-16).* A young man, who most needs help in keeping himself pure, can cleanse his way by taking heed to God's word. The psalmist prays that he might not err through ignorance or inadvertence. His intention is good, but his knowledge is small, and his strength is weak. He has treasured up the word in his heart as a safeguard from sin. Yet he prays for further instruction. He shares what he knows of God's word with others. He values the word more than riches. He will meditate on God's word, and not forget what he has learned.

[Gimel] 3. *The power of the word for knowledge (119:17-24).* The psalmist desires continued life so that he might have the opportunity for continued obedience. He prays that his eyes may be uncovered so that he might discern the mysteries of God's revelation. He compares himself to an alien in this world who must be taught his obligations to the Lord of the earth. His soul "is crushed," i.e., overwhelmed and consumed with longing for the fuller knowledge of God's "judgments," i.e., authoritative declarations of his will. He is confident that "the proud," i.e., those who sin willfully, who stray with respect to God's commands, are under his curse. Right now, however, he needs God to "strip off" from him the shame which those proud ones have heaped upon him. Even though those in authority plot against him, he continues to meditate on Yahweh's statutes.[8] The testimonies of God's word are his "counselors" in this time when others are plotting against him.

[Dalet] 4. *The power of the word for reviving (119:25-32).* The psalmist is in deep distress. He lies prostrate, crushed and unable to rise; but he can pray that God will revive him according to the

411

promises of the word (Deut 8:3). He has laid all the concerns of his life before the Lord. He prays for deeper insight into God's word so that he might meditate on those wonderful things. When tears would weigh him down, he asks that God would strengthen him according to the promises of the word. All conduct that is not governed by God's truth is called "the way of falsehood." The psalmist has chosen rather to follow "the way of faithfulness." The declarations of God's will are the rule of his life. He prays that God will keep him from disloyalty by granting him fresh instruction in his law. Since he cleaves to God's word, he prays that he will not be deprived of the blessings promised the obedient. When his heart is set free from the cramping constraint of trouble, the psalmist will use his liberty for an even more energetic service to the Lord.

[Hey] 5. *The power of the word for establishing (119:33-40).* The psalmist prays for a greater knowledge of God's statutes. He pledges to observe what he learns faithfully, wholeheartedly, and joyously. He asks for vigor to resist the temptations of covetousness and the pursuit of "vanity," i.e., all that is false, unreal, and worthless. He prays that God will perform for him the promises made to those who fear God. As he speaks, the psalmist is experiencing the scorn which he has to bear for his loyalty to God's law. The pronouncements of God are "good," and therefore he should not have to suffer for observing them. He needs fresh strength, for which he asks on the grounds of God's righteousness, i.e., that attribute which requires Yahweh to be true to his covenant promises.

[Vav] 6. *The power of the word for testimony (119:41-48).* The psalmist prays for the lovingkindness of the Lord to be manifested in deliverance, according to God's word. This will enable him to render a decisive answer to those who taunt him with the uselessness of serving God. If he fails to experience this deliverance, then he will be deprived of the power to bear witness to the truth before his tormentors. If God will give him this grace, he resolves to spend the rest of his life observing his law. In so doing he will be walking "in a broad place," i.e., he will know true freedom. Should the opportunity present itself, he is prepared to confess his love for God's word before rulers. He "lifts up his hands" to God's commandment, i.e., he shows them the utmost reverence.

412

[Zayin] 7. The power of the word for comfort (119:49-56).
God's word of promise has given the psalmist hope, and he pleads
that God will not forget it. Past experience of the sustaining power of
God's promise is his comfort in the present affliction. Though proud
scoffers ridicule his faith, he does not swerve from his adherence to
God's law. Divine ordinances handed down from ancient times are
true and sure in spite of all the ridicule of the scoffers. He becomes
extremely angry over those who forsake God's law. God's statutes
form the theme of his songs; they calm his mind and refresh his spirit
in this transitory life of trial. The constant recollection of the Lord and
all that he has revealed himself to be, is the most powerful motive to
observance of his laws. Whatever advantages others may have had
which the psalmist did not enjoy, this supreme privilege had been his,
namely, the keeping of God's precepts.

B. The Word and Society (119:57-112).

[Chet] 1. The power of the word for satisfaction (119:57-64).
God cannot be separated from his word. The proof that God is the
psalmist's "portion" is that he obeys his word. Because of this special
relationship, he asks Yahweh to be gracious to him. His introspection
from time to time led him quickly to order the course of his life in
accordance with God's laws. The wicked, like hunters, have laid
snares for him. Still he will not cast his lot with those who forget God.
In the night seasons he will awake from sleep to thank God for his
righteous ordinances. All those who fear the Lord share the psalmist's
love for God's word. Yahweh's universal lovingkindness makes him
long to know more of his will.

[Tet] 2. The power of the word for good (119:65-72). Yahweh
had kept his promises to the psalmist. He asks God to teach him
"good judgment" (lit., goodness of taste), i.e., the power to distinguish
promptly and surely between right and wrong. Prayer for further
instruction is grounded on past loyalty to the known will of God.
When he strayed from God's word, the psalmist experienced affliction
which brought him to repentance. Since God is fundamentally good,
he can appeal to him for further instruction. The "proud" have now
"forged a lie against me" (lit., plaster falsehood over me). Perhaps
they accused him of hypocrisy. His answer to their accusations was

413

more determination to obey God. These tormentors have hearts covered with fat, i.e., insensitive and incapable of receiving any spiritual impression. The psalmist, however, learns greater obedience through the affliction which he has experienced. In the furnace of affliction he has learned the inestimable preciousness of God's law.

[Yod] 3. *The power of the word for accomplishment (119:73-80)*. The psalmist acknowledges that God has created his body; he now asks that God will continue to enlighten his mind. He asks that other believers may see in him a joyous example of the reward of trustful patience. All God's laws are in conformity with the perfect standard of his righteousness; faithfulness to his covenant leads him to use chastisement to teach men obedience to those laws. Yet man needs to be comforted and revived lest he be overwhelmed by trouble. He prays that he may live so that he may continue to delight in God's laws. On the other hand, he asks that the proud be put to shame because they have dealt perversely with him for no cause. He asks that his experience of God's mercy show all the godly the blessedness of keeping God's testimonies.

[Kaph] 4. *The power of the word under testing (119:81-88)*. The psalmist describes his physical and mental strain while waiting for the Lord to fulfill his promises of deliverance. He was growing emaciated and disfigured by suffering and sorrow till he can scarcely be recognized, like a worn-out wineskin hanging above a fireplace is shriveled and blackened by smoke. He felt his days would be few if God did not hastily intervene. The proud, presumptuous sinners had dug pitfalls for him. His persecutors had almost succeeded in making an end of him, yet he still held fast to the law. If he was to continue glorifying God through the observance of his law, God must preserve his life.

[Lamed] 5. *The stability of the word (119:89-96)*. Yahweh's word is immutable; it belongs to that sphere which is above the ravages of time. The permanence of the earth which God has created is a symbol and guarantee of the permanence of his faithfulness. Heaven and earth obey the ordinances of God. If it had not been for the refreshment of God's law, the psalmist would have utterly lost heart because of his affliction. God's word had revived him. Because he belonged to God, he could ask for deliverance. In spite of the efforts of his enemies to destroy him, he found consolation in God's word. All earthly perfection has its limits; Yahweh's law is limitless.

[Mem] 6. *The power of the word to enlighten (119:97-104).* The psalmist loved God's word. It was the subject of his meditation all the day. Knowledge of God's word made him wiser than his enemies. It made him wiser than his teachers who derived their learning from other sources, and senior citizens who derive their wisdom from experience. The self-restraint which marked his conduct sprang from his desire to obey God. The Lord himself was his teacher, not men. God's words are sweeter than honey. The study of God's word gave him the power of discernment to reject all false teaching and laxity of conduct.

[Nun] 7. *The power of the word for guidance (119:105-112).* The psalmist sees God's word as a light to guide him safely amid the dangers which beset his path through the darkness of this world. Under oath he professes his determination to always observe that word. His resolute observance of the law, however, has exposed him to persecution; therefore he prays God to preserve his life according to his promise. He calls upon God to accept the sacrifice of prayer and praise, and his voluntary vows of devotion to the law. He claims that his soul is in his hand, i.e., his life is in danger. Yet he does not stray from the path of obedience. In the law he has an eternal inheritance which no one can take from him. Therefore, his heart is inclined to perform those statutes until the end of life.

C. The Word and the Sanctuary (119:113-168).

[Samech] 1. *The power of the word for holiness (119:113-120).* The psalmist hates the double-minded, i.e., unstable waverers who are half Israelites, half heathen; but he loves God's law. He regards the Lord as his "hiding place" and his "shield." His hope is in God's word. He wants no association with evildoers who might hinder him from keeping the law. In order to keep God's law, however, he needs sustaining grace. He prays that he might not be put to shame by the failure of his hope of deliverance. God removes the wicked, as the refiner of metals throws away the dross. The psalmist loves the testimonies of the Lord so that he might avoid their fate. The acts of judgment against the wicked and the laws in accordance with which they are punished cause the psalmist to tremble with fear.

[Ayin] 2. The power of the word in prayer (119:121-128). The psalmist is conscious of his own rectitude. He therefore prays that he might not be abandoned to his oppressors. He wants God to guarantee his welfare. His eyes fail watching for the deliverance which the righteous God had pledged to effect. This despondency triggers a hunger for a greater knowledge of God's word. As God's servant he must have more understanding. It is high time for Yahweh to interpose with an act of judgment upon the transgressors to vindicate his broken law. The more men break God's law, however, the more the psalmist values it. He holds in high esteem all of God's precepts, and hates every way which is contrary to those precepts.

[Pey] 3. The power of the word unto wisdom (119:129-136). The testimonies of the Lord are "wonderful," i.e., superhuman in their excellence. Their sublimity and mystery are what attracts the psalmist to them. The unfolding of that word equips the simple who need instruction to discern between right and wrong. He craved this wisdom food, and opened his mouth to receive it. He boldly suggests that those who love God's name are entitled to his mercy. He asks for guidance so that he might avoid both temptation from within and trial from without. He urges God to redeem him from oppressors so that he may freely practice his faith. He asks that God might illuminate the darkness that surrounds him with the light of his presence. The righteous indignation which he feels at one moment for the lawlessness of men (v. 53) is tempered here by profound sorrow and pity.

[Tsade] 4. The power of the word unto righteousness (119:137-144). The fundamental character of God is reflected in his law. His commandments express his absolute righteousness and faithfulness to his covenant. The psalmist's zeal for God has triggered animosity on the part of those who had forgotten God's word. He is especially drawn to God's word because it is pure, i.e., like pure gold without any impurities. Though he is insignificant in the eyes of men and despised for his strict adherence to the law, yet he cannot be moved from his allegiance to the Lord. He knows that Yahweh's righteousness is everlasting, and his law is truth. Yahweh's righteousness is reflected in the law. So even if trouble and anguish take hold of him, yet he will delight in God's commandments. The psalmist concludes this contemplation of the character of God's law with a prayer for fuller understanding of

416

it. Through the knowledge of that law and obedience to it, man really lives, i.e., truly realizes the purpose of his being.

[Qoph] 5. The power of the word unto hope (119:145-152). The psalmist prays to be kept faithful in the midst of faithlessness. Deliverance from his present predicament would give him the opportunity to continue observing God's testimonies. In the earliest twilight he cried for God's help. Through the night watches he mediates on God's word. He asks that God will hear him according to his lovingkindness and the principles set forth in his ordinances. When the adversaries draw near to assail him, he is confident that God is near to defend. Though these enemies had abandoned God's law, the psalmist knows that God's commandments are true. They may view God's laws as obsolete, but the psalmist had long before learned their eternal validity. His deeply rooted convictions cannot be shaken by the contempt or the threats of his enemies.

[Resh] 6. The power of the word for overcoming (119:153-160). Three times in this unit the psalmist makes an earnest appeal that God will revive him. He asks that the Lord consider his afflictions as he considered the afflictions of his people when they were in Egyptian bondage. He thinks of the dispute between himself and his enemies as a lawsuit, and he asks that God be his advocate. Such a request would not be in order if he were wicked; but he has sought after the divine statutes in spite of the pressure of his many enemies. Far from being attracted to the apostates in Israel, the psalmist felt disgust and loathing as he witnessed their transgressions. He asks God to consider that he loves the divine precepts. He adds up all God's commands and promises, and their sum total is truth.

[Shin] 7. The power of the word unto rest (119:161-168). This stanza like that of *Mem* contains no petition. The psalmist states that his loyalty to God's law has not been shaken by the unjust hostility of the authorities; rather he has feared to offend God. The holy awe which he feels toward the law is not inconsistent with holy joy. He hates "falsehood," i.e., anything connected with heathenism in contrast to the truth of God's law. "Seven times," i.e., repeatedly, each day he praises God for his righteous judgments. Those who love God's word find it a spring of constant inward peace, even in the midst of the most tumultuous times. Such walk firmly, i.e., confidently, without

stumbling into sin. The psalmist has put his hope in God; he has been diligent in observing his law. With the courage of a good conscience he appeals to God's omniscience in proof of the sincerity of his purpose.

D. The Word and the Shepherd (119:169-176).

[Tav] The final stanza contains concluding petitions. Once more the psalmist prays for fuller understanding or discernment, and for the freedom of outward circumstance which will enable him to use it. As a ground of both of these appeals he pleads God's word of promise. He prays for a spirit of joyous, exuberant thankfulness for God's continuous teaching, and for the character of the law which is the substance of that teaching. He asks for help on three grounds: (1) he has deliberately resolved to obey God's precepts; (2) he has long been waiting eagerly for deliverance from the hindrances to obedience which surround him; and (3) his devotion has been no grudging service, but his constant delight. The object of the revived life for which he has prayed so often in this psalm is that his whole self may praise God. At the moment he is as defenseless as a sheep which has wandered from the flock. Therefore he desperately needs for the good shepherd to "seek," i.e., rescue, him.

ENDNOTES

1. The name *'Elohim* occurs but thirty times, and *'El* but ten.

2. For a defense of the personal messianic interpretation of Ps 109 see James E. Smith, *What the Bible Teaches about the Promised Messiah* (Nashville: Nelson, 1993), pp. 138f.

3. For a defense of the personal messianic interpretation of Ps 110, see ibid., pp. 184f.

4. Four times the writer of Hebrews depicted Jesus Christ as sitting at the right hand of the Father: Heb 1:1-5; 8:1-2; 10:12; 12:1-3.

5. Ps 118 is cited in Matt 21:9,42; Mark 11:9f; 12:10f.; Luke 19:38; 20:17; and Acts 4:11.

6. For a defense of the personal messianic interpretation of Ps 118 see, J.E. Smith, *Promised Messiah*, pp. 122-128.

7. Frances Havergal penned the familiar words: "I gave my life for thee, my precious blood I shed." Believers understand that in this hymn Havergal has Christ speaking to the believer in the first person.

8. Some think the "princes" in 119:23 were foreign rulers, and that the psalmist must be speaking in the name of the nation and not as an individual. "Prince," however, was the title commonly given to Israelite nobility in the postexilic period. The psalmist was evidently persecuted by wealthy and powerful countrymen.

CHAPTER TWENTY

Songs of Pilgrimage
Psalms 120-134

Pss 120–134 is a special collection. Each of the fifteen psalms has at the head the words "A Song of Degrees" or "A Song of Ascents" (*shir ha-ma'aloth*). Ten of the psalms are anonymous; four are attributed to David, and one to Solomon. These psalms were designed for worship of the Lord. Frequent change of person suggests these songs were sung antiphonally.

Various explanations have been given to the title "Song of Degrees." Some think these fifteen psalms were sung on the fifteen steps leading to the temple. Others think the reference is musical, and signifies that the notes rose by degrees in succession. Still others link these songs with the degrees or steps which the shadow went back on the sundial of Ahaz (2 Kgs 20:8-11).[1] The view most widely accepted is that these psalms were sung by the Jews when they went up, three times a year, to the feasts in Jerusalem. With some modification, the organization of G. Campbell Morgan has been followed in this section.[2]

IN THE FAR COUNTRY
Psalms 120–121

In the first two of the songs of degrees the psalmist imagines himself in a distant land contemplating the return to Zion and the temple.

A. The Hope of the Pilgrim (Ps 120).

It is impossible to determine with any certainty the circumstances which called forth this anonymous psalm. The psalm appears primarily to refer to the sufferings of a pious Israelite among unsympathetic and hostile countrymen. As a pilgrim psalm, it received a national application to the circumstances of Israel during the Exile. The poem contains (1) the appeal (vv. 1-2); (2) the adversary (vv. 3-4); and (3) the affliction (vv. 5-7) of the psalmist.

120:1-2. The psalmist calls to mind past answers to prayer as an encouragement to fresh prayer in his present distress. He has been the victim of slander and misrepresentation. From this he asks deliverance.

120:3-4. A question is addressed to the tongue of the adversary. What will God do to such a wicked thing? The wicked one has shot arrows of slander at the innocent; so God will pierce him with arrows of his judgment. He has kindled a fire of strife by his falsehoods; but that wicked tongue would be scorched by the "glowing coals of the broom tree," i.e., the charcoal which makes the hottest fire and retains heat for the longest time.

120:5. The psalmist laments that he is compelled to live among neighbors who are so hostile. "Meshech" was a barbarous people living between the Black Sea and the Caspian Sea. "Kedar" was one of the wild tribes which roamed through the Arabian desert. The psalmist could not simultaneously be dwelling in the midst of these two peoples who were so far removed from one another. Therefore, he must be using these ethnic terms to describe his adversaries as the most ruthless and godless of men.

120:6-7. The psalmist has long endured the inhumanity of his adversaries. He has attempted to make peace with them, but every effort has been met with threats of greater hostility.

B. The Help of the Pilgrim (Ps 121).

This psalm is anonymous. It is especially adapted for antiphonal singing. The poem consists of two divisions: (1) anticipation of divine help (vv. 1-2); and (2) assurance of divine help (vv. 3-8).

121:1. The exile lifts up his eyes to the mountains upon which was built Zion, the seat of Yahweh's throne. From this place the Lord would send forth help to his people. The psalmist asks: "From whence comes my help?" The question does not express doubt or despondency, but is simply asked to introduce the answer which follows.

121:2. It is not from the mountain of Zion, but from Yahweh who has fixed his dwelling-place there that help comes. The fact that he was the maker of heavens and earth guarantees his power to help.

121:3. Another voice—perhaps a choir—sings these words back to the speaker of vv. 1-2. The Lord will not permit those who look to him to stumble. In his guardianship of his people Yahweh never slumbers.

121:4. Perhaps a third voice chimes in to underscore the thought that Israel's guardian never sleeps. Unlike a human sentinel, he is unceasing in his vigilance.

121:5-6. The comforting thought that Yahweh is the guardian of Israel is individualized. Yahweh is the believer's "shade" on his right hand. The basic idea here is "protection," but the exact significance of this metaphor is now lost. The "shade" protects his own from sunstroke, a metaphor for the dangers of the day. Neither would he allow his own to become moonstruck, a metaphor for the dangers of the night.

121:7-8. The metaphor of the preceding verses now becomes a forthright promise of preservation. The "going out" and the "coming in" refer to all of the believer's undertakings and occupations. Perhaps too these words refer specifically to the pilgrim's journey to Jerusalem. The watch care of the believer's guardian starts the moment he looks toward the hills of Zion, and it continues into the uncharted future.

THE START OF THE JOURNEY
Psalms 122-123

In the next two psalms the pilgrim has started his journey toward Jerusalem.

A. Anticipation of the Journey (Ps 122).

David wrote this psalm, probably soon after the ark was transported to Zion. The psalm has two main parts: (1) the prominence of Jerusalem (vv. 1-5); and (2) the peace of Jerusalem (vv. 6-9).

122:1. David recalls his joy when his neighbors summoned him to join in the pilgrimage to the sanctuary in Jerusalem.

122:2-4. The pilgrims anticipate standing within the gates of the Holy City. Jerusalem is "compact together," i.e., it is the epitome of mutual harmony of its inhabitants. Like a magnet the city draws all of the tribes to her. The practice of pilgrimage to Jerusalem is called a "testimony," i.e., law or institution which bore witness to Israel's relation to Yahweh as his people.

122:5. Jerusalem was the center of the nation's civil life as well as of its religious life. Here was located the supreme tribunal of the nation. This position was occupied by members of the house or family of David, i.e., the royal family.

122:6-7. The pilgrims are urged to pray for the peace of Jerusalem. Then David prays (1) for the prosperity of those who love the holy city; and (2) for the city itself, for her peace and prosperity.

122:8. The prayer for Jerusalem is uttered "for the sake of my brethren and companions," i.e., for the sake of those dwelling within the city to whom David feels himself attached in the bonds of the closest fellowship.

122:9. Again he prays for the peace of Jerusalem, the ground this time being the presence of the sanctuary of Yahweh there. Dear as the city is to him as the center of the nation's civil life, it is yet dearer as the center of her religious life.

B. Assurance in the Journey (Ps 123).

This psalm is anonymous. Some think Hezekiah was the writer. This short psalm speaks of (1) the commitment of God's people (vv. 1-2), and (2) their condition (vv. 3-4).

424

123:1. The eye of hope is turned toward Yahweh. Such has been the habit of the psalmist throughout his life. Yahweh is the supreme king and governor of the world.

123:2. Servants or slaves are dependent on the master of the household. They look to the "hand," i.e., power, of their master to supply all their needs. So Israel, which is Yahweh's household, acknowledges its dependence on him, and looks to him to relieve its present distress.

123:3-4. Suffering Israel, scorned and despised by insolent neighbors, pleads for divine mercy. The enemies of Israel are described as "those that are at ease," i.e., they live in careless security. They are also described as the "proud," i.e., those who have respect neither for God nor man.

THE JOURNEY
Psalms 124–125

In the next two psalms, the pilgrims are in the midst of their journey to the holy city.

A. Escape from Bondage (Ps 124).

Ps 124 is attributed to David. As in Pss 44 and 60 the background seems to be the time of the Syrian and Edomite wars. This song of thanksgiving employs the language and style of Davidic authorship. In the postexilic period the psalm may have been reinterpreted in terms of the deliverance from Babylonian captivity. The psalm can be organized under two heads: (1) a description of peril (vv. 1-5); (2) an ascription of praise (vv. 6-8).

124:1-3. Unless Yahweh had taken the part of Israel in this particular peril, the nation would have been destroyed by enemies. "Men" rose up against God's people; their anger was kindled against Israel. Without divine intervention, Israel would have been swallowed up as some monster swallows its prey.

124:4-5. The plight of Israel is likened to a drowning man. The "proud" waters swept over God's people. This term is especially appropriate as suggesting the insolence of the enemy.

425

124:6-7. The psalm now shifts to thanksgiving and confidence for the future. Yahweh has not permitted his people to become prey in the teeth of her enemies. Weak Israel is compared to a defenseless bird. God has broken the snare of the fowler. His people have escaped.

124:8. The escapees proclaim that their help is in God. He is the one who revealed himself to be a God of compassion, and this is memorialized in his name. He is the creator of heaven and earth. Thus Yahweh has the desire and the power to deliver his people from any trial.

B. First Glimpse of the City (Ps 125).

This psalm is anonymous. Some attribute it to Hezekiah and to the period just after the deliverance from the Assyrians in 701 BC. The psalm underscores (1) the protection of Yahweh (vv. 1-3); and (2) the righteousness of Yahweh (vv. 4-5).

125:1. To an Israelite, mountains were the symbol of all that was immovable and unchangeable. Mt. Zion is here named in particular because it was so intimately connected with divine purpose. To that rock-solid mount the pilgrims were making their way. No storms of trial could shake it.

125:2. All around Jerusalem are higher hills. This girdle of mountains to the psalmist was an ever-present symbol of Yahweh's guardianship of his people.

125:3. The wicked shall not always unjustly oppress Israel. The scepter is the symbol of rule and oppression. The "lot of the righteous" is the land of promise, so called with an allusion to its division by lot (Josh 18:10f.). Prolonged oppression might tempt Israelites in despair to deny their allegiance to Yahweh and make common cause with the enemy of their faith and nation.

125:4. The psalmist prays for "those that do good" and are "upright in their hearts," i.e., sincere in their commitment to him. He asks Yahweh to do good for these Israelites.

125:5. The psalmist issues a warning to those who might turn aside from the Lord to the tortuous courses of intrigue with enemies. Such would be led away to share the judgment of those whose hostility they have chosen to aid.

The words "peace be on Israel" are best taken as a concluding prayer or benediction (cf. Gal 6:16). "Peace" is the end of tyranny, hostility, division, disquiet and alarm; peace is freedom, harmony, security and blessedness.

APPROACHING THE CITY
Psalms 126–131

In the next six psalms the pilgrims are within sight of the sacred mount.

A. Joy and Repentance (Ps 126).

This psalm is anonymous. Some think Hezekiah is the writer; others assign it to the postexilic period. The psalm has two divisions: (1) praise for past help (vv. 1-3); and (2) prayer for further help (vv. 4-6).

126:1. Yahweh brought back the captives of Zion. The reference most likely is to the return from the Babylonian captivity. The redeemed Israelites could hardly believe that this deliverance was a reality rather than an illusion which would vanish like a dream.

126:2-3. Israel was filled with unspeakable joy over the deliverance. Even the Gentiles acknowledged the marvel of Israel's deliverance. The community of believers appropriates the language of the Gentiles: "Yahweh has done great things for us." That is the explanation of their joy.

126:4. The remnant prays for even greater blessing. "Turn again our captivity" means "restore our fortunes." "The South" or Negev was the arid district south of Judah where in summer all the brooks dry up. In the autumn they flow with water. Thus far the restoration of Israel had been only a trickle of water in the summer months. Now the feeble community asks that the blessings may come as the rushing water of autumn.

126:5-6. The efforts of the remnant to reestablish the nation had been carried on in the midst of hindrances and disappointments, anxieties and fears. In due time those efforts will bear fruit. The labor of sowing will shortly yield the joy of harvest.

B. Family Strength (Ps 127).

Solomon is the writer of this psalm. The psalm stresses two points which do not seem to be related: (1) the vanity of human effort (vv. 1-2); and (2) the value of divine endowment (vv. 3-5).

127:1. Without divine blessing human effort is futile whether it be in the efforts of a builder or the vigilance of the watchman. A man may build a house, but never dwell in it (Deut 28:30). The watchman may patrol the city or keep his watch on the wall, but he cannot secure the place from dangers such as fire or the assault by enemies.

127:2. Workaholics are addressed. They begin their labors early and continue them late; but through constant anxiety they may lose all the enjoyment of that which they earn. Those who are right with the Lord, however, enjoy their sleep. The point is, that God's blessing is necessary to prosper in one's toil.

127:3-5. Numerous children were considered a special blessing from the Lord. "Children of youth" are those who are born while the parents are young and vigorous. They will grow up in time to be a support for their parents' old age. Such children are like "arrows in the hand of a mighty man" in that they provide a defense against those who would take advantage of the elderly parents. A man with such a stalwart family to support him runs no risk of being wronged by powerful enemies through the perversion of justice in the courts.

C. Family Responsibility (Ps 128).

This anonymous psalm was probably composed during the postexilic period to encourage the members of the community at a time when there was much to dishearten. This is a companion psalm to the previous one. The psalm has two divisions: (1) a picture of the godly man (vv. 1-4); and (2) a prayer for the godly man (vv. 5-6).

128:1-2. To fear the Lord is to walk in his ways. Such a person is blessed or happy. This general principle is applied first to a father. He will enjoy the fruit of his labor.

128:3-4. The wife of a godly man would be a "fruitful vine." The fruitfulness, gracefulness, and preciousness of the vine are the obvious points of comparison. The vine's dependence and need of support may also be part of the comparison. The children are compared to "olive plants" fresh, full of promise and beautiful. Such will be the blessing of the person who loves the Lord.

128:5-6. The psalm concludes with a blessing pronounced on the god-fearing man. The desire is that God might bless such a man "out of Zion" where he sits enthroned as king. The psalmist desires that this man shall see "the good of Jerusalem" as he makes the annual pilgrimages there. May he live to a good old age and see his family perpetuated in his grandchildren.

D. A Backward Look (Ps 129).

This psalm was written by an anonymous poet of the postexilic period. It is modeled after Ps 124 which was by David. The psalm has two divisions: (1) the past afflictions of the righteous (vv. 1-4); and (2) the future judgment of the unrighteous (vv. 5-8).

129:1-2. The history of Israel is compared to the life of an individual. Israel's life began in Egypt. From the Egyptian bondage onward this people had been oppressed by enemies. "Let Israel say" suggests that the people should thankfully recall the lessons of their history. Though the enemies successfully had beaten Israel down again and again, they had not prevailed ultimately.

129:3. Israel is imagined as thrown prostrate, while the ruthless foe drives the plow up and down over him, brutally lacerating the back.

129:4. The same attribute of righteousness which compels Yahweh to punish, binds him to deliver, for it involves faithfulness to his covenant. He has broken the "cords of the wicked," i.e., plower's harness, so that they can no longer continue their work.

129:5. The psalmist expresses the wish that Israel's enemies would be foiled and repulsed in the present crisis as they had been in the past. In the postexilic period "those that hate Zion" were enemies like Sanballat and Tobiah who did all in their power to keep Nehemiah from reconstructing the walls of the city.

129:6-7. Let the enemies of Zion be "like grass on the housetops." This might include grains accidentally dropped on the roof. These plants might spring up on the mud-roof houses, but having no depth of soil, they wither prematurely and yield no joyous harvest. Let Zion's enemies perish before they can implement their destructive plans.

129:8. The fallen enemies will not receive the friendly greetings of those who pass by wishing Yahweh's blessing upon them. It will be very obvious that these enemies were under the curse of God.

E. Humility and Confidence (Ps 130).

Ps 130 is the sixth of the seven psalms designated by the early church "the penitential psalms." This anonymous psalm probably belongs to the period of Nehemiah. It has noticeable points of contact with the confession in Neh 9, as well as with Neh 1:4-11. The psalm has two divisions: (1) repentance expressed (vv. 1-4); and (2) redemption expected (vv. 5-8).

130:1-2. Deep waters are a common figure for distress and danger. National suffering as well as personal suffering is probably intended. Penitent Israel can plead for the audience with God which sin had made impossible.

130:3. If Yah [shortened form of Yahweh] should observe sins and keep them in remembrance who could stand before him in judgment? No one could maintain his innocence. All must stand condemned in that case. This verse is virtually a confession of sin and a plea for pardon.

130:4. In fact God does not remember iniquities, for he is a forgiving God. He forgives that men may fear him. The magnitude of God's forgiveness is truly as awesome as his works of creation or destruction.

130:5-6. In full confidence that Yahweh is a forgiving God, the psalmist can wait with patience and hope for God to act according to his word of promise on behalf of his people. He anxiously waits for the end of the night of trouble and the dawn of a happier day like a watchman watches for the first signs of the dawn which will release him from his duties.

130:7. The psalmist exhorts the people to wait in hope for the Lord. The grounds of this exhortation are (1) Yahweh's lovingkindness; and (2) his "plenteous redemption," i.e., manifold ways and means of effecting Israel's deliverance.

130:8. The psalm concludes with an emphatic declaration that Yahweh will redeem Israel from all iniquities. He removes both the penalty and guilt of sin.

F. Rest in God's Will (Ps 131).

This short psalm is attributed to David. It expresses David's (1) humility (vv. 1-2) and (2) his hope (v. 3).

131:1-2. A proud mind finds expression in haughty looks and ambitious schemes. David has determined to renounce such schemes. His soul is no longer disturbed by the storms of passion and the clamors of ambition. He compares himself to a child who has been through the troublesome process of weaning. He now can lie contentedly in its mother's arms without fretting or craving for the breast. The psalmist's soul has been weaned from worldly ambition. He can enjoy contentment in the absence of what was once considered indispensable.

131:3. David urges the entire nation to follow his example, to place their hope in Yahweh. In the spirit of resignation and contentment let Israel patiently wait for the further development of God's purposes.

THE ENTRANCE
David's Horn and Lamp
Psalm 132

Ps 132 is messianic by implication. It reflects the glorious promises which had been made to the house of David. The ultimate implications of the Davidic promises culminate in Messiah. The theme here is closely related to Ps 89 with this difference. Whereas the earlier psalm reveals a pessimistic outlook in places, this one rings with confidence.

Most commentators assign this psalm to the postexilic period. Some, however, assign Ps 132 to the united monarchy period. It may have been composed for the dedication of the temple. Solomon may have been the writer. Ps 132 has two main divisions. Verses 1-10 are a prayer by the people offered (perhaps) at the dedication of the temple. Verses 11-18 contain God's answer to that prayer.

132:1. The prayer of the people recalls the steps which led to the building of the temple. The petition is that all those things for which David yearned might be realized.

132:2-5. The building of God's house was the top priority of David's reign. The king vowed that he would not enter his house to sleep until he found a suitable sanctuary for his God.

132:6-7. The ark had all but been forgotten. In Ephrathah—another name for Bethlehem, David's ancestral home—the report was received that the ark had been located in the house of Abinadab (1 Sam 7:1f.) in "the fields of Jaar," i.e., Kirjath-jearim. David and like-minded friends set out for Kirjath-jearim to worship. The ark may have been housed in a humble tent at Abinadab's house, but to the true believer that was God's "exalted dwelling;" there was the footstool of his feet.

132:8-10. The words "Arise, O Yahweh" were an ancient formula which signaled the removal of the ark to a new site (Num 10:35). Here the transfer of the ark to Jerusalem is intended. The petition is that all of God's people might rejoice at the movement of the ark. The prayer concludes with a request that David's petitions might not be rejected.

132:11-12. God now answers the earnest prayer of his people. He elaborates on the promises he gave to David through the prophet Nathan (2 Sam 7:11ff.). God's zeal for the house of David is no less than David's zeal for God's house. God actually took an oath concerning David's dynasty[3] that he would set one of David's sons on the throne after him. The dynasty of David would continue uninterrupted so long as his descendants observed the law of Yahweh.

132:13. The permanence of the Davidic kingdom is based upon the divine choice of Zion. The magnificent temple erected there was a tangible proof that God had chosen the spot, and furthermore that he had made a divine commitment to David and his family.

132:14-15. The people had prayed that God would come to his "resting place" (v. 8). Now Yahweh assures them that Zion would be his eternal resting place and that this was so by his own choice. God would bless the very food and drink of his people. He would have special regard for the needs of the poor who lived there. Old Testament Zion is but the earthly preview of the New Covenant Zion (Heb 12:22) where the poor in spirit feast daily on the bread of life.

132:16. The people had prayed that their priests might be clothed in righteousness (v. 9). God now gives assurance that he will do even more than they ask. He will clothe the priests in "salvation," i.e., he will regard their priestly ministrations as effective to the salvation of the people. God will make the saints shout aloud for joy over their salvation. In the New Testament Zion administered by the greater David, all the citizens are priests who are clothed in salvation.

132:17. The people had prayed that God would grant blessings "for the sake of David" (v. 10). God will do more than that. He will "cause a horn to sprout for David." An animal horn in the Old Testament was the symbol of power. At the very least this figure points to the great prosperity and might which Yahweh would grant to the house of David. The verb "sprout," however, suggests a relationship to the prophecies of Jeremiah (23:5; 33:15) and Zechariah (3:8; 6:12) where *tsemach* (sprout) is used as a title for Messiah. Zacharias may have had this passage in mind when he said that the Lord has "visited and redeemed his people, and has raised up a horn of salvation for us in the house of his servant David" (Luke 1:68f.).

God will also make a "lamp" for David. The lamp indicates the continuance of the Davidic line which culminates in the one who called himself the light of the world. There may be an allusion here to the lamp which was kept burning continually in the tent of each family.

132:18. While his enemies are put to shame, the crown of David (in the person of his descendant and representative) would flourish. The word "crown" (*nezer*) was used not only of a king's crown, but of the high priest's diadem (Exod 29:6). David's greater son would have high priestly as well as royal status.

THE CITY AND WORSHIP
Psalms 133–134

In Pss 133–134 the pilgrims are within the temple engaging in glorious worship.

A. Unified Worship (Ps 133).

David is the writer of this brief psalm. The occasion may be the reunion of the whole nation after the civil discords of his early reign. The psalm consists of (1) a declaration regarding unity (v. 1); and (2) a description of its pleasantness (vv. 2-3).

133:1. David observes the outward expression of brotherhood of the various tribes as they gather for worship before the Lord. All Israelites were brothers, members of the family of God.

133:2. The brotherly conduct of the various tribes is compared to the sacred oil with which the high priest was anointed (Exod 30:23ff.).

433

This oil was poured on Aaron's head when he was consecrated to his office (Exod 29:7; Lev 8:12). It would flow down upon his beard and onto his shoulders and his breast, upon which he bore the names of the twelve tribes (Exod 28:9-12,17-21). This symbolized the consecration of the whole nation. The aromatic oil would diffuse its fragrance all around, symbolizing the holy influence which the life of Israel as consecrated people should have upon the world.

133:3. Dew is a symbol of what is refreshing, quickening, invigorating. The dew that falls on the slopes of Mt. Hermon is especially copious. Brotherly unity refreshes each individual just as the dew for much of the year brings refreshment and renewal to the dry mountains of Zion.

God had ordained that there in Jerusalem his blessing would be bestowed upon his people as they gathered in unified worship.

B. Conclusion of Worship (Ps 134).

This psalm was intended for use in temple worship. It was probably written during the postexilic period. No writer is indicated. This brief psalm consists of (1) an exhortation to the priests (vv. 1-2); and (2) an invocation by the priests (v. 3).

134:1. The phrase "stand before Yahweh" indicates priestly or Levitical ministration. This verse may suggest that praise services were held in the temple at night. Another view is that this exhortation was addressed to the ministers as the congregation exited the temple after the great public festivals.

134:2. Lifting up the hands was a gesture of prayer. The hands were lifted to the sanctuary, i.e., towards the most holy place, as the earthly dwelling-place of Yahweh.

134:3. The priests respond to the exhortation of the people with a blessing on the people. They invoke God's blessing on the worshipers "out of Zion," i.e., his abode. As they depart the sacred mount, the blessings of Yahweh will come to them from that mount. That he is the "maker of heaven and earth" implies his power to bless.

ENDNOTES

1. This view was first put forward by John Lightfoot, and further developed by J.W. Thirtle, *Old Testament Problems*, 1907. The ten anonymous psalms were written by Hezekiah in celebration of the ten degrees which the sun retreated on the sundial (cf. Isa 38:8,20). The five named psalms were added to the collection to make the total fifteen, the number of years added to Hezekiah's life.

2. G. Campbell Morgan, *The Analyzed Bible* (Old Tappen, NJ: Revell, 1964), p. 177.

3. No oath to David is mentioned in 2 Samuel 7, but God's solemn assurances there are equivalent to an oath. On this point compare Ps 89:3,35,49.

CHAPTER TWENTY-ONE

Songs of Final Praise
Psalms 135-150

Praise and worship are the focal points in the last sixteen psalms of the book. The journey from dutiful obedience of Ps 1, after passing through deep valleys of candor about suffering in relationship to God's lovingkindness, has now ascended the summit of self-abandoning praise to the Lord.

A CALL TO WORSHIP
Psalms 135-136

In Jewish circles these two psalms are sometimes called "the Great *Hallel*." The pair apparently were composed for worship in the second temple.

A. His Praiseworthiness (Ps 135).

The psalm is anonymous. A reasonable suggestion is that Ezra wrote this poem. Others date the psalm in the days of Hezekiah. This psalm is a mosaic of fragments of other psalms. The psalm consists of three divisions: (1) a call to praise (vv. 1-4); (2) an argument for praise (vv. 5-18); and (3) a second call to praise (vv. 19-21).

135:1-4. Those who minister in the temple are summoned to praise. It is appropriate and pleasant to sing praises to him for he is good. He is worthy of praise because he had chosen Israel to be his own people.

135:5-7. Yahweh's greatness and sovereignty is exhibited in nature. He is greater than all the so-called gods worshiped by the Gentiles. He exercises his sovereign will in heaven, in earth, in the seas and in the depths beneath the earth. Lightning, wind and rain are under his control.

135:8-12. Yahweh's sovereignty was exhibited in the deliverance of his people from Egypt and their establishment in the land of Canaan. He displayed tokens of his power against Pharaoh, ultimately destroying the firstborn of man and beast. Before Israel he smote Sihon and Og, mighty Amorite kings of the Transjordan region. He took their land and gave it as a heritage for Israel.

135:13-14. Yahweh is eternally the same. He will not forget his people. His name is called his "memorial" because it brings to mind all that he is and does. Such as he has revealed himself to be, he will continue to be forever. Because of his relationship with Israel, Yahweh would do them justice; he would not finally abandon them.

135:15-18. The gods of the heathen are only the work of men's hands. They cannot hear, see nor speak. They have no breath in them. They are lifeless. Those who worship such gods are equally senseless.

135:19-21. All Israel—the house of Aaron the priest, the Levites, and all who fear God—are called upon to praise the Lord. Yahweh's blessing goes forth out of his earthly habitation in Zion. From Zion where they meet to worship, his people's adoring praise must also ring out.

B. His Enduring Mercy (Ps 136).

This psalm was written at the same time as the previous one, possibly by the same person. It consists of a brief call to thanksgiving (vv. 1-3) followed by a description of the God to be thanked (vv. 4-25). The psalm concludes with another call to thanksgiving (v. 26).

136:1-9. Yahweh is the God of gods, and the Lord of lords. Even more precious, his lovingkindness endures forever. By wisdom Yahweh made the heavens and stretched out the earth upon the waters. He created the sun and moon to illuminate the heavens.

136:10-22. Yahweh is the deliverer of Israel. He smote the first-born of Egypt in order to bring out Israel. His mighty hand parted the waters of the Red Sea. He brought Israel through the waters, but destroyed the host of Pharaoh there. Yahweh led his people through the wilderness. The great kings Sihon and Og fell before him in Transjordan. Their lands were given to Israel as a heritage.

136:23-26. Yahweh is the deliverer of Israel and the supporter of all things living. He took note of the low estate of his people in the Exile. He redeemed them from their enemies. Yahweh also provides for all flesh. He, after all, is the God of heaven. This is the only occurrence of this title in the Psalter.

THE SUFFICIENCY OF YAHWEH
Psalms 137–139

Three psalms focus praise upon the sufficiency of Yahweh to meet all the needs of his people.

A. His Mighty Judgment (Ps 137).

This anonymous psalm was written in the early days after the return from the Babylonian captivity. It consists of three divisions: (1) painful recollection (vv. 1-3); (2) pure devotion (vv. 4-6); and (3) passionate imprecation (vv. 7-9).

137:1-3. The rivers of Babylon would include the Euphrates, its tributaries and numerous canals. There the captives sat down and wept as they remembered Zion, the city of God. On the willow trees they hung their harps because there was nothing about which to sing. Their harps were silent because of the heartless demands of their captors. They required the Jews to sing the sacred temple songs for their entertainment. Better not to sing at all than to be required to profane the sacred music.

137:4-6. The captives repudiate the idea of doing what would be treason to the memories of Zion. To have consented would have been an act of unfaithfulness to Zion. The psalmist pronounces imprecation upon himself should he forget Jerusalem. He asks that his right hand might forget its skill, his tongue stick to the roof of his mouth.

137:7-8. The psalmist's love for Jerusalem leads him to invoke vengeance on her enemies. He asks that God might punish the Edomites for their unbrotherly spite which rejoiced in the destruction of Jerusalem (cf. Lam 4:21). The "daughter of Babylon" is that city personified. The psalmist predicts the destruction of the place. The conquering enemy will be ruthless. They will enjoy inflicting upon the Babylonians the same treatment the Babylonians had dispensed to Israel. They would find sport in dashing little children against the rocks. Such is the prediction of this psalmist.

B. His Enabling Power (Ps 138).

David wrote this psalm. The historical occasion was the oracle delivered by Nathan pertaining to the permanence of the house of David (2 Sam 7). Ps 138 has three divisions: (1) acknowledgement of past blessings (vv. 1-3); (2) anticipation of universal praise (vv. 4-6); and (3) assurance in the divine purpose (vv. 7-8).

138:1-3. David resolves to praise God with all his heart. He faces enemies who are, in their own view, under the protection of powerful gods. This does not shake David's confidence in Yahweh. Therefore, he will publicly sing praises to his God. David would direct his worship toward the holy sanctuary. In his worship he would praise (1) the lovingkindness of God and (2) his truth or faithfulness. By the accomplishment of his promises Yahweh has surpassed all previous revelations of himself. David refers to some unspecified occasion when Yahweh answered his prayer and strengthened him in the inner man.

138:4-6. Yahweh's faithfulness to his promises will evoke the homage of the world. The kings of the earth will join David's thanksgiving. They will celebrate his providential methods of dealing with his people. His "glory" is revealed in the powerful deliverances of Israel. Exalted though he is, Yahweh never loses sight of the lowly. In due time he raises them up. As for the haughty, no distance hides them from his eye. They cannot escape the punishment they deserve.

138:7-8. Though fresh troubles may still await David, Yahweh will not fail to carry out his purposes for him. He will exert his power to save from the wrath of enemies. Yahweh will "perfect" or accomplish his promises and purposes for David because his lovingkindness is everlasting. The psalm concludes with a prayer that God will not forsake the "works" which he had undertaken for his people.

C. His Omniscience and Omnipotence (Ps 139).

This psalm of David is a companion to the preceding one. The same divine promise of an enduring house (2 Sam 7) is in view. The psalm focuses on the character of God. Yahweh is (1) omniscient (vv. 1-6); (2) omnipresent (vv. 7-12); (3) omnipotent (vv. 13-18); and (4) omnirighteous (vv. 19-24).

139:1-3. Yahweh has perfect knowledge of all David's life and thoughts. It is God alone who possesses such absolute knowledge of his creatures. He understands David's thoughts "afar off"; neither space nor time exist for God. The Lord had winnowed or sifted David, subjecting his life to the closest and most discriminating investigation.

139:4-6. God knows the spoken word which men can hear. He also knows the true meaning, and the secret thoughts which prompt its utterance. David feels that God has hemmed him in on all sides so that he cannot escape. God holds him in his grip, i.e., exercises authority over him. Such infinite knowledge baffles human thought. It is inaccessible to man.

139:7-12. God is everywhere present; man cannot escape nor hide himself from God. He fills heaven above and Sheol beneath. If David should fly across the sky with the swiftness of light from east ("the dawn") to west ("the sea"), still he would be under the authority and control of God. One cannot hide from God under cover of darkness.

139:13-16. God must know David perfectly for he "knit" him in the womb of his mother. He praises God because of the wondrous nature of his physical body and mental capacity. He had been fashioned with skill and care "in the lowest parts of the earth," i.e., the womb, which is so called because it is as dark and mysterious as Sheol. Even when he was in the form of an undeveloped embryo, God had his future mapped out in his "book" of providence. Here is clear expression of the belief that an ideal plan of life has been providentially marked out for every individual.

139:17-18. David delights to meditate upon the purposes of God's providence. He cannot even begin to count all the individual components of that theme. His last thoughts as he falls asleep are of God. When he awakes, he finds himself still in the Lord's presence, still occupied in contemplating the mystery of his being.

139:19-22. The problem of the existence of evil perplexes David. Why does God tolerate wicked men? Surely at some point God must slay such men. For this reason, David will have nothing to do with them. He does not wish to be tempted by their example and therefore be involved in their fate. The wicked are those who speak against God and take his name in vain. David loathed those that hate the Lord. He hates them with "perfect hatred," i.e., without any mental reservation.

139:23-24. David welcomes the continuance of the piercing scrutiny with which God examines him. He wants any wicked way which might be detected to be exposed. He wants God to lead him "in the way everlasting," i.e., a way of *life* as opposed to the way of ruin and death. He seems to perceive that such a way must lead on to fuller life after death as well as a more abundant life now.

THE HELPLESSNESS OF MAN
Psalms 140-143

The greatness of God can be appreciated when one reflects on the helplessness of man. This theme dominates the next four psalms.

A. Facing Persecution (Ps 140).

This psalm was written by David, but the specific occasion is uncertain. It may belong to the time of the persecution by Saul. A twofold breakdown is most useful. David (1) prays for deliverance (vv. 1-8); and (2) predicts destinies (vv. 9-13).

140:1-3. David prays for deliverance from the plots of his enemies who secretly and deliberately devised evil schemes against him. They were perpetually trying to pick a quarrel with him. The tongue of these enemies was both sharp (like a sword) and venomous (like a serpent's bite). "Adder's poison" was under their tongue, hidden like the poison gland of the asp. These words are quoted in Romans 3:13.

140:4-5. David repeats his prayer for deliverance from the plots of his enemies. They were trying to trip him up and overthrow him. Like hunters, the enemies were laying traps with lures and bait to attract him.

140:6-8. In his distress he appealed to Yahweh, pleading the relation which entitled him to expect protection. He was confident that the Lord would cover his head as with a helmet "in the day of armor," i.e., when armor is needed. He asks that God would frustrate the designs of the wicked lest they exalt themselves.

140:9-11. He asks that retribution might overtake the wicked. He asks that the mischief they are trying to do to him by slander recoil upon themselves, and overwhelm them. He asks that the fate of Sodom overtake these defiant offenders. If they try to escape the fiery storm, let them be swept away by torrents. Let their fall be final and irremediable. He prays that the evil designed for others might recoil upon the wicked.

140:12-13. The righteous have a very different destiny. Yahweh is the judge who maintains the cause of the weak and oppressed. In spite of present trials, the righteous shall survive to give thanks to the Lord. The upright shall dwell in his presence, i.e., in the land where Yahweh manifests himself in a special way.

B. Facing Peril (Ps 141).

This psalm of David was probably written during the period when Saul was persecuting. him. The fact that David was a prophet as well as a king is important to remember when interpreting any of the psalms attributed to him. The psalm consists of two divisions: (1) petitions (vv. 1-7); and (2) profession (vv. 8-10).

141:1-2. David asks for a favorable hearing. He has already been praying, and now he pleads for a speedy answer to his prayer for help. He asks that his prayer might be received as "incense," i.e., the sweet-smelling smoke from the altar of incense (Exod 30:7f.), or the sweet smoke of the sacrifice generally. The lifting of the hands was a gesture of prayer, the outward symbol of an uplifted heart. The "evening oblation" strictly speaking is the meal offering which accompanied the evening sacrifice, but the terminology here may include the whole of that sacrifice. The figure may have been suggested to David because he was accustomed to praying at that hour each afternoon.

141:3-4. David asks for grace to resist the temptation to sin in word, thought and deed. He wants to be guarded from adopting the profane language of the ungodly men by whom he was surrounded. He wishes to be fortified against the temptation to join powerful men in their wicked works and sensuous lifestyle.

141:5. David prays that he might willingly accept the correction and reproof of the godly. The rebuke of the righteous he would regard as refreshing oil which was poured out on heads at feasts. "Smite" here is a metaphor for severe correction. He prays that he will have the good sense not to reject that correction. On the other hand, he set his prayer power against the evil deeds of the wicked.

141:6-7. When the judges or leaders of the workers of iniquity have met with the fate they deserve, people would welcome David's advice and exhortation. Dispatching people from a cliff was one of the means of execution in ancient times. While these wicked ones are still in power the godly are the victims of persecution and oppression. The godly are murdered, and their dead bodies call for vengeance. Some take v. 5 to mean that the godly had been left without anything that makes life worth living. They were no better than skeletons ready to be swallowed up by Sheol.

141:8-10. David still looks to God in expectant prayer. He has put himself under Yahweh's protection. On the basis of that relationship, he appeals that God would not permit men to "pour out" his life blood on the ground. He prays that he might be delivered from the enticements of the wicked, which here are likened unto hunters' snares. He asks that the schemes of the wicked might recoil upon themselves.

C. Facing Despair (Ps 142).

The "cave" referred to in the heading is probably that of Adullam to which David retired when obliged to leave the land of Achish the Philistine. This is the last of the thirteen *"maskil"* or didactic psalms. It has two divisions: (1) the psalmist's desperate condition (vv. 1-4); and (2) his determined confidence (vv. 5-7).

142:1-2. David resolves to seek relief by laying his distress before Yahweh. He will cry "aloud," not merely in silent prayer. Such vocalization of distress gives relief to pent up feelings and expression of the intensity of the distress.

142:3-4. Yahweh knows David's peril and loneliness, even if he has no human sympathizers. David's spirit faints within him. He is in despair, but his comfort is that Yahweh knows the course which he must take, and the perils which beset him from treacherous enemies. On his right hand, where any protector would be standing, there is no one to take up his cause.

142:5-6. In the past David had cried out to God. He still continues to do so. God is his "refuge" and "portion" in the land of the living. He is confident that he will not die but live to declare the words of the Lord.

142:7. He now has been brought low. His persecutors were stronger than he. He is imprisoned, as it were, in distress. He prays that he may be released from that prison. Then he will praise Yahweh's name. Then the righteous—the loyal worshipers of Yahweh—will gather round him to share in his thanksgivings. He is confident that God will deal most bountifully with him.

D. Facing Darkness (Ps 143).

This psalm was written by David, in all probability during the flight from Absalom. The Septuagint supports this assessment. This is the last of the "penitential psalms" identified in the early church. It has two main divisions, separated by the musical interlude. In vv. 1-6 he presents his case, and in vv. 7-12 he makes his claim.

143:1-2. David appeals for mercy. His plea is based on God's "faithfulness" and his "righteousness," i.e., his unvarying conformity to his own character. He asks that God not put him on trial and pass sentence on him according to his just deserts. He is, after all, God's "servant," i.e., one who stands in a special relationship with the Lord. Without God's forgiveness, no human being can be considered "righteous" or innocent when standing before God.

143:3-4. David is undergoing severe persecution. He had been, as it were, buried alive in calamity which here is likened to the darkness of death. He feels appalled, stupefied and paralyzed at the apparent hopelessness of his position.

445

143:5-6. The thought of all that God had done in times past deepens David's despondency as he compares his present plight. He longs for a fresh manifestation of God's power as parched land longs for refreshing rain.

143:7-8. David prays for a speedy hearing before God. If God withdraws the light of his presence, he will be like the dying or the dead. He prays that the dawn might conclude this dark night of calamity, and bring the sunshine of Yahweh's lovingkindness to gladden his weary heart. He asks that God teach him to avoid the dangers which surround him and to order his conduct according to the divine will.

143:9-10. Since he has taken refuge in the Lord, David calls on Yahweh to deliver him from the enemies. He asks that the good spirit of the Lord lead him on "level ground," i.e., ground free of obstacles.

143:11-12. David is confident that Yahweh will deliver his servant if only for his name's sake, i.e., his reputation. God's "righteousness," i.e., faithful adherence to the terms of his covenant, will motivate him to bring David out of his distress. His deliverance would be effected when the Lord would cut off and destroy all those who tormented him. David's enemies are God's enemies too. They are traitors to his kingdom who have forfeited their right to live. For such hardened and impenitent offenders nothing remains but death.

THE APPROPRIATENESS OF PRAISE
Psalms 144-145

The next two psalms emphasize the appropriateness of praise.

A. The Rock of Strength (Ps 144).

David probably wrote this psalm in his later years. He seems to be recounting past mercies of the Lord for the benefit of his posterity. The psalm has three divisions: (1) the blessed Lord (vv. 1-2); (2) the concerned psalmist (vv. 3-11); and (3) the happy people (vv. 12-15).

144:1-2. David praises God for his ability to make war effectively. Five titles are given to the Lord. He is (1) my lovingkindness; (2) my fortress; (3) my high tower; (4) my deliverer; and (5) my shield. In this God David had taken refuge. Through the Lord he had been able to overcome his own people, i.e., internal dissensions.

144:3-4. Man's insignificance and transitoriness enhance the marvel of God's gracious care for him. Man is but a "breath," a mere
"shadow" that quickly passes away.

144:5-8. David prays that God will appear in his majesty and deliver him from his treacherous enemies. With lightning as his arrows,
Yahweh is asked to scatter and destroy those enemies. He requests
that God should put forth his hands to rescue him out of "many
waters," i.e., dangers at the hands of foreign enemies who swear to
falsehood; they cannot be trusted.

144:9-11. David promises to give thanks for the victory which he
is confident will be granted. Such a new manifestation of God's grace
will require a "new song." Yahweh is the God who gives "salvation"
or victory to kings, and to David his servant in particular. The "evil
sword" here is the calamity of war. Having expressed this confidence,
David repeats the prayer of vv. 7-8.

144:12. He expresses the wish that Israel's sons might become
stalwart plants, its daughters, stately pillars. The connection of these
verses to what precedes is difficult to ascertain. This may be a wish
concerning the well-being of God's people.

144:13-14. David expresses the wish that the barns may be full
and the livestock productive. He prays that the oxen may be laden
with the produce of the fields which they draw home in carts. He asks
that there be no hostile invasion of the country, nor a going forth to
surrender to an enemy. Let there be no outcry of mourning in the
streets of the land.

144:15. The poem concludes with an affirmation of the happiness
of God's people. The Lord is the source and sum of all true happiness, temporal and eternal.

B. Praise for the Holy One (Ps 145).

David is the writer of this final alphabetic psalm. The letters
appear in regular order except that the letter *nun* is omitted. There
is no indication of the particular occasion which called forth this
composition. This psalm speaks of (1) God's greatness (vv. 1-6);
(2) his goodness (vv. 7-10); (3) his glory (vv. 11-13); and (4) his grace
(vv. 14-21).

145:1-2. [Aleph-Bet] Israel's God is absolute, universal king. David resolves to praise his name "for ever and ever," i.e., throughout life and into eternity.

145:3-4. *[Gimel-Dalet]* There can be no more worthy object of praise than Yahweh. The greatness of this God is "unsearchable," i.e., beyond comprehension. One generation will praise the works of Yahweh to the next.

145:5-6. *[Hey-Vav]* Splendor, glory and majesty are the attributes of God as king. Such attributes will be praised along with all the marvelous works of the Lord. Yahweh manifests himself in terrible acts of judgment as well as mighty acts of deliverance. Such acts strike fear into the hearts of the enemies, and inspire his people with reverence.

145:7-8.*[Zayin-Chet]* Men will pour forth the praise for all that God is and does. He is the God of condescending grace and infinite compassion, whose will is love, and whose wrath is only manifested in the last resort against the hardened and impenitent.

145:9-10. *[Tet-Yod]* Yahweh is good to the whole creation. The works of creation respond to Yahweh's goodness and compassion. They bear witness to the sovereignty of their creator by their obedience to his laws. Certainly the "saints" or godly ones join in that praise.

145:11-13. *[Kaph-Mem]* God's people speak of the glory of Yahweh's kingdom, and of his power so that the sons of men will come to know of his mighty works and majesty. His kingdom is everlasting. He has ruled through generations past, and will continue to rule over generations yet future.

145:14-16. *[Samech-Pey]* Yahweh upholds those who are bowed down by the cares of life. He is the Father who distributes food to all his household. He opens his bountiful hand and satisfies the desire of every living thing.

145:17-18. *[Tsade-Qoph]* Yahweh is "righteous," i.e., true to his character. His lovingkindness is reflected in all his works. He is always just a prayer away from those who need his help. Those who call upon him must do so "in truth." The hypocrite finds no favor with him.

145:19-20. *[Resh-Shin]* Fear and love are the inseparable elements of true religion. Fear preserves love from degenerating into presumptuous familiarity; love prevents fear from becoming a servile and cringing dread. The victory of good must ultimately involve the defeat and destruction of evil.

145:21. *[Tav]* David has fixed his resolve. He will speak of the praise of the Lord. He, however, will never be satisfied until all flesh joins him in an unending chorus of praise for Yahweh.

THE HALLELUJAH CHORUS
Psalms 146–150

The Psalter closes with five *"Hallelujah"* psalms. All themes of praise peal forth here with mounting enthusiasm. All were prepared for liturgical use in the second temple. Petition is absent here; the focus is strictly on praise.

A. Praise for the Helper (Ps 146).

Ps 146 is anonymous. A tradition, reflected in the headings of the ancient versions, attributes the authorship to Haggai and Zechariah. The psalm is a chiasmus. It begins and ends with verses depicting the object of praise (vv. 1-2,10). Sandwiched between are sections suggesting whom not to trust (vv. 3-4), and whom to trust (vv. 5-9).

146:1-2. The worship of the congregation is individualized. The psalmist speaks for himself and offers to each worshiper words with which he can stir himself up to praise and to express his purpose.

146:3-4. Here is a warning against the temptation to rely upon the favor and protection of men, however powerful. Princes today will be dust tomorrow, and their loftiest schemes will crumble into dust with them. No doubt Gentile princes are in view. To use v. 4 as an argument that there is no conscious existence after death is truly a perversion of the point the psalmist is making. "Thoughts" here are equivalent to plans, or schemes.

146:5-6. The person who has his trust in the omnipotent creator is happy. Yahweh keeps truth forever, i.e., he is faithful to his promises and his covenant.

146:7. The psalmist now cites examples of Yahweh's beneficent action. The Lord judges the oppressed with equity. He feeds the hungry.

146:8-9. Five times the name Yahweh stands emphatically at the beginning of the line, to show that it is he and no other who does all these things. He looses prisoners. Prison may be a figure for exile, or for suffering generally. He opens blind eyes. Blindness may be a figure for moral and spiritual ignorance and helplessness in general. Yahweh raises up those who are bowed down. He loves the righteous or innocent. He watches over the defenseless, namely, strangers, orphans, and widows. On the other hand, he makes the way of the wicked crooked so as to frustrate their goals.

146:10. This wonderful God is Zion's God. His reign is eternal, not transitory like the dominion of earthly princes.

B. Praise for the Sovereign (Ps 147).

This psalm may have been written after a particularly cold winter (cf. vv. 16-17). It consists of three divisions, each beginning with a fresh call to praise. The psalmist urges worshipers to praise God for (1) his power (vv. 1-6); (2) his providence (vv. 7-11); and (3) his peace (vv. 12-20).

147:1-3. Praise Yahweh, for he is the restorer of Israel. He gathers Israel's outcasts, i.e., exiles, and builds up Jerusalem. The restoration and repeopling of the city are meant, not merely the physical reconstruction of houses and walls. He binds up the wounds and hurt of those exiles who had been crushed with grief and despair.

147:4-5. Yahweh's omniscience and omnipotence are partly a ground for praise, partly an encouragement to trust him. He who knows each separate star will not lose sight of one single Israelite. "To his understanding there is no number," i.e., it is incalculable.

147:6. Yahweh's power is manifested in his moral government of the world. Though the language is general, it has obviously a special reference to the restoration of Israel and the humiliation of their oppressors. The "meek" are those who have learned humility in the school of suffering. These he raises up; but he casts the wicked to the ground.

147:7-9. Yahweh sends the rains, which cause the grass to grow to feed the beasts and birds. For this he deserves praise.

147:10-11. Yahweh does not delight in physical strength, but in reverent trustfulness. Israel should not envy the military might of surrounding nations. The Lord takes pleasure in them that fear him and trust in his mercy.

147:12-14. The psalmist calls for praise because Yahweh had enabled his people to rebuild Jerusalem. He had blessed Zion's "children," i.e., citizens, within the restored city. The city now enjoys peace and prosperity.

147:15-18. God has manifested his power in the snow, frost and ice, phenomena which were somewhat uncommon in the Jerusalem area. At God's word the snows melt and flow over the ground to water the soil.

147:19-20. The Lord, whose word all nature obeys, has given Israel his word in the law, a privilege which distinguishes it from every other nation. Therefore, Israel should praise Yahweh.

C. The Praise of Creation (Ps 148).

This anonymous psalm certainly belongs to the period of the restoration of Jerusalem under Nehemiah. It consists of two divisions: (1) heavenly praise (vv. 1-6); and (2) earthly praise (vv. 7-14).

148:1-6. The psalmist calls for praise to ring out from the heavens. The angels and the "hosts"—here probably the stars—should join in that praise. "The heaven of heavens" is the highest heavens. The waters above the expanse in the clouds should praise God too. All that is in the heavens were created at the command of God. They owe their perpetual maintenance to his providence.

148:7-13. The earth should join the heavens in the praise of God. The sea monsters of the deep, the phenomena of weather, mountains, trees, beasts and fowl owe Yahweh their praise. Last of all man, as the crown of creation, is summoned to join the *Hallelujah* chorus without respect to station, age or sex.

148:14. Israel had special ground for praise. Yahweh had once more "lifted up the horn" of his people, i.e., given them dignity and power. Israel was a people near to Yahweh, i.e., they stood in a unique relationship to him. That relationship, which seemed to have been interrupted by the Exile, had now been restored. Yahweh once more dwelt in the midst of his people in the city of his choice.

D. The Praise of Saints (Ps 149).

Like the other four members of the *Hallelujah* chorus, this psalm comes from an anonymous writer of the postexilic period. It has two divisions: (1) praise for what God has done in the past (vv. 1-4); and (2) praise for what he will do in the future (vv. 5-9).

149:1-2. The psalmist urges praise for the Lord in "the congregation of the godly ones." Yahweh is Israel's maker; to him it owes its existence as a nation, and the present restoration of its national life. Though they now have no earthly king, Yahweh is still their sovereign as in days of old. The "children of Zion" are the citizens of restored Jerusalem.

149:3-4. Dancing was a natural expression of joy among the Israelites, as among other nations of antiquity. Musical instruments also express the believer's joy. This joy is occasioned by the fact that Yahweh "takes pleasure in his people." The deliverance which they have experienced is proof of the renewal of his favor. In captivity Israel had learned humility; and now Yahweh has "adorned" (beautified) his people with "salvation," i.e., with victory, welfare and prosperity.

149:5-6. The godly ones should exult in the "glory" of this renewed manifestation of God's presence. Songs of the night now take the place of tears and sorrow.

149:7-8. While they give God the highest praise, they should have ready "a sword of mouths," i.e., a devouring sword, to execute "vengeance" upon the Gentiles. These Gentiles will be made subject to Israel and to Israel's divine king (cf. Ps 2). Such predictions find their fulfillment in the militant advance of the soldiers of the cross.

149:9. Yahweh had pronounced and recorded in his book of remembrance the sentence against nations which refuse to embrace him and his people. The New Testament links the judgment upon those who do not obey God to the Second Coming of Christ (2 Thess 1:8-10). The defeat of the enemies brings honor to Yahweh's chosen people, the New Testament Israel.

E. Concluding Doxology (Ps 150).

The grand finale of the *Hallelujah* chorus is anonymous. No doubt it comes from the period of Ezra-Nehemiah. No outline is here discernible.

150:1-2. Yahweh is *'El*, the God of sovereign power. He should receive praise in his heavenly sanctuary, which is located in the "mighty expanse" which is his handiwork. He deserves to be praised for his "mighty acts" of creation, providence and redemption as well as for "his excellent greatness," i.e., his wondrous attributes.

150:3-5. Eight different musical instruments are named as appropriate to the praise of the Lord. The precise identification of some of these is uncertain. Praise through religious dance is also encouraged since that was common in ancient societies.

150:6. The psalmist calls on everything that has "breath" (*neshamah*) to praise God. The Hebrew term is used of that which was uniquely given to man at his creation (Gen 2:7). Not just priests and Levites only, but all Israel; not Israel only, but all mankind are called upon to join the *Hallelujah* chorus.

PROVERBS

CHAPTER TWENTY-TWO

Getting Acquainted with Proverbs
Faith the Foundation of Wisdom

Proverbs has its own special niche in the sacred canon. Unlike the law, Proverbs says next to nothing about sacrificial worship. Unlike the historical books, Proverbs does not allude to Israel's past or its popular heroes. Unlike the prophetic books, Proverbs has nothing to say of Israel's fate, good or bad. Unlike the Psalms, this book has no devotional material. All of these themes lie outside the province of this book. Prudent and moral behavior is the concern of Proverbs; it is God's how-to-do-it manual. It teaches the skill of getting along sensibly in life while at the same time pleasing God.[1]

This book of 15,043 words is organized into thirty-one chapters, 915 verses.

TITLE OF THE BOOK

The title of the third of the poetic books is "The proverbs of Solomon the son of David, king of Israel" (1:1). This was probably the

457

original title of the final edition of the book. The Septuagint rendering differs only slightly from the Hebrew. The Latin has simply "*Liber Proverbiorum*," i.e., The Book of Proverbs.

The term for "proverb" (*mashal*) comes from a root idea meaning "parallel" or "similar." The term thus signifies "a description by way of comparison." In Proverbs the term signifies an aphorism (as in 10:1–22:16) or a discourse (e.g., chs. 1–9).[2]

AUTHORSHIP OF THE BOOK

Proverbs itself testifies to multiple authors, although the bulk of the material was composed by Israel's wisest king, Solomon.

A. Solomonic Material.

Solomon's name is mentioned in the superscription over the book (1:1). It is also associated with two other major divisions of the book: 10:1–22:16; and 25:1–29:27. Contradicting this explicit claim, some modern scholars deny that anything in this book should be attributed to Solomon. According to these scholars, the attribution of major sections of the book to Solomon was only a "literary convention" on the part of the editor(s). Conservative scholars would accept the claims of Solomonic authorship within the book, and in addition would assign most of the other material in the book to him as well.[3] Others occupy a mediating position assigning 10:1–22:16 and 25:1–29:27 to Solomon, but nothing else.[4]

B. Hezekiah's Scribes.

According to 25:1 a group known as "the men of Hezekiah" contributed to the present Book of Proverbs. The Talmud contains an early Jewish tradition that "Hezekiah and his company wrote the Proverbs" (*Baba Bathra* 15a). Probably this tradition means that scribes in Hezekiah's court edited the final edition of the book, perhaps adding to it Solomonic proverbs which were not part of the original edition.

Only four proverbs which appear in the first Solomonic collection (10:1–22:16) reappear in identical form in the second or "Hezekiah" collection. Five others appear in slightly altered form. The scarcity of these duplications and near duplications may indicate that (1) Hezekiah's scribes knew of the earlier collection of proverbs; but (2) that they intended to produce a second volume of Solomonic proverbs to be placed alongside it without making it superfluous.[5] Since Solomon composed no less than three thousand proverbs (1 Kgs 4:32), there was ample material for later excerptors like Hezekiah's scribes.

C. Non-Solomonic Materials.

Various sections of Proverbs are attributed in the text to writers other than Solomon.

1. Sayings of the wise. Two headings in the book (22:17; 24:23) attribute the proverbs which follow to a group called "the wise." These may have been proverbs which already existed in Solomon's day. Guided by the Holy Spirit, Solomon incorporated them into the collections of his own creation.[6] That "the wise" antedated Solomon, however, is not certain.

2. The Agur material. Agur the son of Jakeh is mentioned only in 30:1. Nothing is known of him except what can be deduced from the material which he wrote. Some have suggested that the name Agur is a symbolic name for Solomon himself, but this is unlikely.[7] It may be, however, that Solomon was the one who selected this material to be appended to the works of his own creation; but this is not certain.

3. "The leech." Based on the Hebrew of 30:15, some rabbis took the term "leech" to be the proper name (Alukah) of another wise man. In view of the radical difference between this material and the preceding verses this old opinion may be of some weight.

4. The Lemuel material (31:1-9). The sayings of King Lemuel were actually passed down from his mother. These sayings concern the way kings should behave. Nothing is known of King Lemuel. As was the case with Agur some think this is a symbolic name for Solomon himself. This material, however, gives every appearance of being foreign in origin.

5. The anonymous poem (31:10-31). Proverbs concludes with a powerful acrostic poem on the virtuous woman, for which no authorship claim is made.

In summary, Solomon is responsible for producing or at least collecting the biggest part of this book (1:1-22:16; chs 25-29). The same king was probably responsible for collecting the material in 22:17–24:34 and chs. 30–31.

DATE OF THE BOOK

The issues of the authorship and date of the book are closely related. Older critics dated the bulk of the book to postexilic, even the intertestamental times. Toy, for example, held that nothing in the book dates earlier than 350 BC.[8] The criteria used for such dating (e.g., the influence of the Aramaic language upon the text) have now been recognized as inconclusive as to date.[9] In fact more recent scholars have demonstrated numerous parallels between Proverbs and the poetry which was being produced in the time of Solomon and even before.[10]

Scholars have generally viewed chapters 1–9 as a late composition, possibly even postexilic.[11] Their conclusion is based mainly on the personification—hypostatization—of wisdom in chs. 8–9. Such embodiment of abstract ideas, however, was not unknown in the ancient Near East centuries before the days of Solomon.[12] Certainly this material represents a more complex literary form than the sentence literature which dominates the rest of the book. Literary forms, however, do not move from simple to complex, as von Rad has demonstrated.[13] Kayatz has suggested that the differences between chs. 1–9 and the rest of the book have more to do with style than chronology.[14]

Some critical scholars are beginning to recognize a greater unity in the book than formerly was admitted. Using literary analysis, Patrick Skehan has argued that the author of chs 1–9 is also the editor of essentially the entire book.[15]

In terms of writing, all the material seems to date from the period of Solomon if not from his pen. A date of about 950 BC would not be far off. The book may have assumed its present form in the reign of Hezekiah about 700 BC.

BACKGROUND OF THE BOOK

Proverbial wisdom literature is attested in Egypt and Babylonia long before the time of Solomon. The Holy Spirit directed Solomon to employ this ancient literary form to communicate divine wisdom to his people. The age of Solomon was one of peace and tranquility such as would lend itself to the production of such wisdom books.

To what extent was the Book of Proverbs influenced by the wisdom schools of surrounding nations? Some scholars think that chs. 1–9 are modeled after Egyptian Instructions which served as textbooks in the schools.[16] In addition the wisdom admonition, which was quite common in Egypt, may have influenced the form of similar admonitions in Proverbs.

In 1924 A.W. Budge pointed out some similarities between one section of Proverbs and the Egyptian "Instruction of Amenemopet" which was discovered in 1888.[17] This work was originally dated to the Eighteenth Dynasty, which would be earlier than Solomon. Some scholars have concluded that Solomon adapted this work and incorporated it into the book of Proverbs as 22:17–24:34. Others have argued that the Egyptian writer copied from Proverbs.[18] Subsequent study of this problem has indicated these facts: (1) the Egyptian document is not nearly as old as once thought. At best it dates to the time of Solomon, and possibly is much more recent. (2) The similarities between the two documents is partly explained by the international character of wisdom (cf. 1 Kgs 4:29-34). (3) Certainly no direct "borrowing" took place between Amenemopet and Proverbs in either direction. One might concede that, guided by the Holy Spirit, Solomon has adapted and assimilated into the biblical worldview, the Egyptian material.[19] This concession, however, is not compelled by the data.

INSPIRATION OF THE BOOK

Wisdom literature does not make numerous explicit claims to inspiration such as one finds in the prophetic books of the Old Testament. Some regard 22:20-21 as a claim to inspiration: "Have I not written to you excellent things of counsels and knowledge, to make you know the certainty of the words of truth, that you may correctly answer him who sent you?" Chapters 30–31 each claim to be an "oracle" (ASV) or prophetic utterance communicated by God.

Scholars show a tendency to view the Book of Proverbs as being nothing more than a collection of aphorisms which hardly excel the sayings of Egyptian wise men. In this view the only authority behind a wisdom teaching is human experience. The proverbs, then, are fundamentally man-centered.[20] More recent scholarship has tended to view the proverbs as God-centered.[21] Throughout the ancient Near East the concept of divine order was of fundamental importance. Parallel to this concept was the belief that wisdom was a prerogative of the deity and could only be bestowed by God. In the Bible the counsel of the wise man is accorded the same force as the word of the prophet (Jer 18:18).

The authority for the proverbs derives, not from the personality of the counselor, nor from general experience, but ultimately from God. The biblical proverbs are not only tersely expressed deductions from daily experience, but also divine precepts (whether expressed or implied). Moreover, they grow out of, and point to, the fear of Yahweh as the basic principle of all true knowledge.

CANONICITY OF THE BOOK

Proverbs was preserved and revered by the people of God (1) because of its connection with Solomon who was considered a prophet because he had received a divine revelation; and (2) because the proverbs translate the principles of the law of Moses into simple and memorable sayings. Wisdom was of God, and Proverbs encapsulates God's wisdom pertaining to the everyday concerns of life.

A. In the Synagogue.

According to the Talmud, the canonicity of this book was discussed by the men of the Great Synagogue, an institution founded by Ezra, according to tradition (*Shab.* 30b). The basis of the opposition was what appears to be a contradiction between two successive verses. Prov 26:4 states: "Do not answer a fool according to his folly, lest you also be like him." The very next verse says: "Answer a fool as his folly deserves, lest he be wise in his own eyes." The rabbis found a reconciliation between the two verses: "the first refers to matters of learning; the other to general matters." From this passage it is clear that internal contradiction could not be tolerated in an inspired book. Should an apparent contradiction be discovered, it must be reconciled. In any case, Proverbs is cited with approval repeatedly in the Talmud.

Josephus (*Against Apion* 1.8) testifies to the structure of the Old Testament in first-century Palestine. He claimed that the Scriptures consisted of five books of law, thirteen books of prophets and four books "of hymns to God and precepts for the conduct of human life." Clearly Proverbs belongs in this third category. Josephus' twenty-two books are identical with the thirty-nine of the Old Testament, the differences being explained by a different method of counting.[22] His testimony establishes that Proverbs was part of the Scriptures in the first century AD.

B. In the Church.

That Jesus loved this book is clear. To Nicodemus he revealed the answer to the question posed by Agur the son of Jakeh (cf. Prov 30:4 with John 3:13). Furthermore, he reminded those who, like the undiscriminating "fools" of Proverbs, did not recognize him or his message that "wisdom is justified of her children" (Matt 11:19).

Some have argued that John's doctrine of the Logos (1:1-14) is based, at least in part, on the personification of Wisdom in Prov. 8.[23] Both Wisdom and the Logos exist from the beginning (8:22; John 1:1); are active in creation (8:30; John 1:3); and have a life-giving influence (8:35; John 1:4).

Some twenty quotations and allusions to Proverbs have been found in the New Testament, among which are these: 3:7a (Rom 12:16); 3:11f., (Heb 12:5f.); and 3:34 (Jas 4:6; 1 Pet 5:5b). In addition, the book was cited frequently as authoritative by the Church Fathers.

CHARACTERISTICS OF THE BOOK

A. The Nature of Proverbs.

The sentence literature which dominates the Book of Proverbs is amazing in several respects. First, the proverbs are extremely terse. They are the shortest poems of the Bible. The nature of the Hebrew language is such that five to eight carefully crafted Hebrew words do the work of a dozen or more in English. Each of these brief poems is a literary masterpiece. The proverbs have been likened to gems, cut and polished to the highest degree, so as to reveal their splendor.

Second, the biblical proverbs are profound. One scholar refers to individual proverbs as "compressed experience."[24] These tasty tidbits are meant to be savored, not swallowed whole. On the surface the meaning of a proverb may seem obvious. Only through prolonged contemplation, however, will the true dimensions of these carefully crafted sayings be discovered.

Third, the proverbs are timeless and time-tested, endorsed by the experience and observation of generations of wise men. Biblical proverbs, however, go beyond mere human experience and judgment. Biblical writers were guided by the Holy Spirit in the inclusion (or exclusion) of what appears in Scripture. They represent the mind of God as well as man.

Some scholars have expressed negative opinions about the proverbs in this book. Gottwald opines that they are "mediocre as literature, tedious as ethics, banal as religion." Their only purpose is to present God as "the Guardian of the system."[25] But given the date of their creation and the state of God's redemptive program, these proverbs represent a remarkable achievement.[26]

B. Classification of Proverbs.

The type of proverb which is most common in the book is the two-line (distich) proverb in which the second line builds upon the first by (1) repeating it in slightly different words; (2) contrasting it with an opposite point of view; (3) amplifying it; or (4) making a comparison with it. A few proverbs of four, six or eight lines can also be found here. R.B.Y. Scott[27] has identified seven proverbial patterns in which the author expresses the life principles which he advocates. In slightly modified form these are:

1. Congruity: "A man who flatters his neighbor is spreading a net for his steps" (29:5).

2. Contrast: "A sated man loathes honey, but to a famished man any bitter thing is sweet" (27:7).

3. Comparison: "Like cold water to a weary soul, so is good news from a distant land" (25:25).

4. Contrariety to proper order: "Why is there a price in the hand of a fool to buy wisdom, when he has no sense?" (17:16).

5. Classification: "The naive believes everything, but the prudent man considers his steps" (14:15).

6. Priority: "A good name is to be more desired than great riches, favor is better than silver and gold" (22:1).

7. Consequences: "The sluggard does not plow after the autumn, so he begs during the harvest and has nothing" (20:4).

THE STRUCTURE OF THE BOOK

A. Collections of Proverbs.

The Book of Proverbs has been described as a collection of collections.[28] Superscriptions in the text identify the various collections which make up the book. These are (1) "the proverbs of Solomon" (10:1–22:16); (2) "the words of the wise" (22:17–24:22); (3) "also these are by the wise" (24:23-34); (4) "also these are the proverbs of Solomon which the men of Hezekiah king of Judah transcribed" (25:1–29:27); (5) "the words of Agur" (30:1-33); and (6) "the words of Lemuel" (31:1-9). The book's heading in 1:1 probably serves also as the heading of the initial section of the book.

Certainly the writer or final editor never intended for these superscriptions to be an outlining device for the book. Proverbs displays a far more subtle structure.

B. Overall Structure.

The overall structure of the book is like an envelope. Chapters 1–9 open with the format of instruction from a father (or mother) to his son. This unit concludes with a personification of wisdom as a beautiful lady. The concluding chapter of the book begins (31:1-9) with the instruction of the queen mother to her son—the same genre as the bulk of chs. 1–9. Chapter 31 concludes with the poem of praise to the virtuous woman. Here is wisdom personalized in the form of a God-fearing wife. Thus in their similar structures, the opening chapters and the concluding chapter form the envelope in which the the shorter sayings of chs. 10–30 are packaged.

The structure of the book may also be likened to a trilevel ziggurat. At the base is the introduction (1:1-7) which supplies the foundation upon which the rest of the book is based. The second level, 1:8–9:18, serves as the hermeneutical guide to the interpretation of the rest of the book. Here are found the religious underpinnings of the maxims which follow.

C. Internal Cohesion.

A large portion of the book contains the short, sentence sayings which one generally associates with the title of the book. These sayings on cursory examination appear helter-skelter. They have been likened to a multistring necklace of mismatched gems and beads.[29] Proverbs about a particular subject are scattered throughout the collection.

Obviously these collections of sayings were brought together by ancient scribes who concluded that they were worthy of preservation as examples of Israel's wisdom. But what principles guided them? How do these isolated sayings and collections of sayings fit together?

Some sections of Proverbs are carefully organized, and some less so. Many modern writers have given up altogether on discovering any interrelatedness within the subsections of the book. Often commentaries on Proverbs opt for the topical approach which eliminates any obligation to suggest the connecting links within the book. Recent scholarship, however, has tended to find more cohesion in this part of the book than previously was recognized.[30]

THE TEACHING OF PROVERBS

Because a proverb compresses truth into a terse and striking statement, it catches on. It becomes easier to remember than to forget. A proverb does not argue; it assumes.[31] Its purpose is not to explain a matter, but to give pointed expression to it. Proverbs is considered didactive rather than reflective wisdom such as is exhibited in Job and Ecclesiastes.

A. Method of Teaching.

Learning life is like learning a language. One first must master the basic rules and patterns; the exceptions come later. So it is in Proverbs. The first subgrouping of sayings (chs. 10–15) focuses on the way things ought to be. In this section the neat antithesis between righteous and wicked is predominant. The proverb gives expression to realities that are usually true. Their brevity makes impossible the expression of qualifications or exceptions to the rules. This first group of proverbs teaches that blessings flow from godly living, that prosperity is a result of hard work, wisdom, and divine blessing.

The proverbs following chapter 15 recognize that things do not always work out this way. The "better . . . than" format of several of the proverbs indicates that the righteous are not always prosperous (16:8; 28:6), that the world is not always "either . . . or" nor "black . . . white." Shades of gray sometimes exist in the real world. The sequence of these collections is significant. Young people must first master the basic rules of life. They will learn soon enough that life also has its painful absurdities, injustices and irrational catastrophes.

B. Theological Teaching.

In Proverbs the Lord is understood to be the author of morality and justice. Monotheism is presupposed. The references to the law and prophecy (29:18), priesthood and sacrifice (15:8; 21:3,27), however, are scarce. The words of Solomon have inherent authority because wisdom is the gift of God.

Proverbs contains no direct prophecy of Christ. The wisdom, however, to which the wise man aspires is embodied in Christ. He exemplified without fail the ethical principles taught in Proverbs and in so doing left for his followers an example that they should follow in his steps (1 Pet 2:21).

C. Practical Teaching.

Proverbs is preoccupied with certain fundamental antagonisms: obedience vs. rebellion, industry vs. laziness, prudence vs. presumption, and so on. These are presented in such a way as to put a clearcut choice before the reader. Thus Solomon states his case so brilliantly that he leaves no room for compromise, vacillation or indecision.[32]

PURPOSE OF THE BOOK

Like other ancient Near Eastern wisdom books, Proverbs begins with a title, followed by a brief statement of its purposes. Solomon then sets forth the fundamental principle upon which all else rests.

467

A. Stated Objectives.

According to the author, his purpose in this book was to offer to his readers instruction in four areas. First, he desired his students to know (i.e., be intimately familiar with) two things: (1) wisdom (*chokhmah*), i.e., an understanding of what God requires of man, and what man owes to God; (2) "instruction" (*musar*), i.e., chastisement, correction, education and moral training. Instruction leads to godly wisdom. This familiarity with wisdom and instruction will demonstrate itself in ability to "perceive the words of understanding," i.e., to comprehend the utterances which proceed from wise men. "Understanding" (*binah*) refers to the ability to discern between good and bad, true and false, and between good and better. A student familiar with wisdom and instruction will demonstrate a mastery of those principles which will enable him to exercise proper discernment (1:2).

Second, Solomon wants his students "to receive the instruction of wisdom," i.e., discipline full of insight, discernment or thoughtfulness. This instruction in wisdom shows itself in three ways: (1) righteousness (*tsedeq*), i.e., that which is in accord with the will and ordinances of God; (2) judgment (*mishpat*), i.e., the delivery of a correct judgment on human actions; and (3) uprightness (*mesharim*), i.e., rectitude in thought and action, integrity (1:3).

Third, the author intends his work to be very helpful to vulnerable individuals. The "simple" (*petha'im*)—those who are susceptible to external impressions; the gullible and naive—need "prudence" (*'ormah*), i.e., the capacity for escaping the wiles of others. The "young man" (*na'ar*), i.e., a youth, needs "knowledge" (*da'ath*) and "discretion" (*mezimmah*). The former term refers to insight and knowledge of good and evil; the latter, to caution or discernment which puts the youth on his guard and prevents him being duped by others (1:4).

Fourth, the author intends to challenge the wise as well as aid the simple and the youth. From this book the wise man can increase "learning" (*leqach*) and "attain unto wise counsels" (*tachbuloth*), i.e., those maxims by which a person can direct his course through life. This latter term is derived from the navigational mechanism of a ship. The result will be that this wise person will be enabled to understand a "proverb," a "figure" (*melitzah*), and "riddles" (*chidah*) such as wise men put forward. The idea here is that the sages did not express their teachings in straightforward and plain language.

B. Fundamental Principle.

The introduction culminates in a theological declaration that serves as the fundamental point of orientation of the entire book: "The fear of Yahweh is the beginning of knowledge" (1:7a). The fear of God describes that reverential attitude or holy fear which man, when his heart is right, feels towards God. This is not servile fear, but filial fear, fear of offending the heavenly Father. It is hatred of evil and warm embracement of all that is holy and noble. One who would advance in knowledge must first be imbued with a reverence for the Lord. Faith here is seen as the foundation of reason, not its antagonist. It is faith that enables reason to connect with reality. Faith is the "beginning," the starting point of an exciting journey, the details of which will be elaborated in the rest of this book.

If the first half of 1:7 points to the levitational power of faith, the second half points to the gravitational pull of folly: "but fools despise wisdom and discipline" (1:7b). In eight Hebrew words this verse indicates the fundamental antithesis between the pull toward God and good and the pull toward evil and pseudo good. "Fools"—the incorrigibly perverse—who are unwilling to know God despise wisdom and discipline.

C. Observations.

When one's relationship with God is clear, all other relationships of life become clear. The student of wisdom comes to realize that, because he fears God, he has certain obligations with respect to his spouse, superiors, children, neighbors and friends. This book addresses the question of the "ought" of life: How ought one who professes faith in the Lord to live? Proverbs is a commentary on the basic law of love which was foundational to Old Covenant faith (Lev 19:18; Deut 6:5; cf. Mark 12:29-31).

The Book of Proverbs is intended to do for the believer's daily life what the Book of Psalms is intended to do for his devotional life.[33] While the psalms focus on the believer's worship, Proverbs focuses on his walk.[34]

Extrapolating from the wisdom of Proverbs one would conclude that the divine plan calls for a society in which people work hard, observe each other's rights, respect each other, and treat the less fortunate kindly. It is a society in which people are friendly, enjoy the pleasures of moderation, and love their families and homes. It is a society in which people are sincere, modest, self-controlled, temperate, reliable, chaste, willing to listen and learn. Those who live in this ideal society are forgiving, considerate, discreet, kind to animals, sweet-tempered, liberal, yet prudent. They keep an eye to their own welfare.

Some have suggested that Proverbs was to be a manual for use in the royal court to train future leaders. Such indeed does appear to be the purpose of much of the instruction material found in Egypt. Certain sections of Proverbs also reflect this emphasis (16:1–22:16; 25:2–7). Within the entire book, however, this is a minor thrust. In truth, all of God's people serve in the royal court of the King of kings. Thus the instruction of Proverbs is aimed for the most part at a general audience, not just those students who might one day stand in the presence of the earthly monarch.[35]

THE USE OF PROVERBS

This Solomonic book has been both praised and decried—praised as an anthology of the experiential wisdom of ancient Israel replete with artistic expressions of truth, and decried as a collection of propaganda intended to endorse and ensure the status quo. It has been quoted in support of quite divergent and sometimes opposing lifestyles.[36] Obviously, then, one must be very careful in how he approaches this book.

A. The Danger of Absolutizing.

Individual proverbs should not be absolutized.[37] The proverbs should be regarded as observations, not guarantees. Proverbs are not promises; they are generalizations of how things usually work out. Some of the proverbs are true only in certain situations. Only one who is wise will know the situation in which a particular proverb applies. Should one "answer a fool according to his folly" (26:5) or not (26:4)? A wise person will know when to apply each of these side-by-side verses.

Much harm is done when this principle is ignored. Many parents go to their grave thinking they have failed in parenting because they have heard Prov 22:6 absolutized: "Train up a child in the way he should go, and when he is old he will not depart from it." Are there no exceptions to this principle? Of course there are. Proverbs itself recognizes the exceptions in its numerous allusions to the foolish son.

B. The Principle of Greater Revelation.

Another principle which should help place the proverbs in proper perspective is to recognize that Jesus was the very embodiment of heavenly wisdom (Matt 12:19). This is not to say that Proverbs 8 is a prophecy of Christ; it is rather a poetic representation of God's attribute of wisdom. Yet all that divine wisdom entailed is embodied in Christ (1 Cor 1:30). In him are hidden all the treasures of wisdom and knowledge (Col 2:3). Thus the Christian must read Proverbs in the light of the continued revelation of God in Christ. If the Christian would exercise the wisdom which Solomon encouraged, he must mentally baptize this book into Christ and bring it into subjection to all that the Master taught.

ENDNOTES

1. S.H. Blank, "Proverbs, Book of" in *The Interpreter's Dictionary of the Bible*, ed. George Buttrick (Nashville: Abingdon, 1962), p. 940.

2. Crawford Toy, *A Critical and Exegetical Commentary on the Book of Proverbs*, The International Critical Commentary (New York: Scribner's, 1904), p. 4.

3. Gleason Archer, *A Survey of Old Testament Introduction*, pb. ed. (Chicago: Moody, 1985), pp. 476f.

4. Raymond B. Dillard and Tremper Longman II, *An Introduction to the Old Testament* (Grand Rapids: Zondervan, 1994), p. 236.

5. See Keil and Delitzsch, *Old Testament Commentaries: Psalm LXXVIII to Isaiah XIV* (Grand Rapids: Associated Publishers and Authors, n.d.), pp. 392f.

6. Such is the view of Archer, *Introduction*, pp. 476-477.

7. One of the latter rabbinic explanations is that Agur = "the compiler" and "son of Jakeh" = "one who spat out or despised" the word of God by taking many wives.

8. Toy, *Proverbs*, pp. xix-xxix.

9. E.J. Young, *An Introduction to the Old Testament*, rev. ed. (Grand Rapids: Eerdmans, 1960), p. 313.

10. W.F. Albright, "Some Canaanite-Phoenician Sources of Hebrew Wisdom," in *Wisdom in Israel and in the Ancient Near East*, ed. M. North and D. Winton Thomas (Leiden: Brill, 1955), pp. 1-15.

11. E.g., O. Essfeldt, *The Old Testament: An Introduction*, trans. Peter Ackroyd (New York: Harper and Row, 1965), p. 473.

12. K.A. Kitchen, *Ancient Orient and Old Testament* (Chicago: InterVarsity, 1966), pp. 126f.

13. G. von Rad, *Wisdom in Israel* (Nashville: Abingdon, 1972), pp. 27-28.

14. Cited by Dillard and Longman III, *Introduction*, p. 237.

15. Patrick Skehan "A Single Editor for the Whole Book of Proverbs," in *Studies in Ancient Israelite Wisdom* (Washington, DC: Catholic Biblical Association of America, 1971), 15-26. Skehan adds up the numerical value of the Hebrew letters in the headings and finds a correspondence in the number of proverbs in that section of the book.

16. R.N. Whybray, *The Intellectual Tradition of the Old Testament* (Berlin: Walter de Gruyter, 1974), pp. 57ff. Whybray, however, resists the notion that this material was composed in the royal court (as were the Egyptian forerunners). Proverbs was created, not by a professional scribe class, but by talented Israelite lay persons.

17. The text of this Egyptian document can be found in *Ancient Near Eastern Texts Relating to the Old Testament*, ed. James Pritchard, pp. 421-425.

18. The position that Proverbs was influenced by Amenemopet was argued by Erman, Gressmann, Sellin, and Humbert. The reverse position was argued by Oesterley, Kevin, Drioton, and Archer.

19. Such is the conclusion of G.E. Bryce, *A Legacy of Wisdom: The Egyptian Contribution to the Wisdom of Israel* (Lewisburg: Bucknell University Press, 1979).

20. Walther Zimmerli, "Concerning the Structure of Old Testament Wisdom," in *Studies in Ancient Israelite Wisdom*, ed. James Crenshaw (New York: Ktav, 1976), pp. 175-207.

21. Berend Gemser, "The Spiritual Structure of Biblical Aphoristic Wisdom" in *Studies in Ancient Israelite Wisdom*, ed. James Crenshaw, pp. 208-219.

22. Ruth was counted with Judges, and Lamentations with Jeremiah and Nehemiah with Ezra; the double books of Samuel, Kings and Chronicles were counted as one book each. The twelve Minor Prophets were counted as one book.

23. C.H. Dodd, *The Interpretation of the Fourth Gospel* (Cambridge: 1953), p. 275.

24. W.A.L. Elmslie, *Studies in Life from Jewish Proverbs* (London: Clarke, 1917), p. 16.

25. N.K. Gottwald, *A Light to the Nations* (New York: 1959), p. 472.

26. von Rad, *Wisdom*, p. 50.

27. R.B.Y. Scott, *Proverbs, Ecclesiastes* in The Anchor Bible (Garden City, NY: Doubleday, 1965), pp. 5-8.

28. W.S. LaSor, D.A. Hubbard, F.W. Bush, *Old Testament Survey* (Grand Rapids: Eerdmans, 1982), p. 547.

29. Raymond C. Van Leeuwen, "Proverbs," in *A Complete Literary Guide to the Bible*, ed. Leland Ryken and Tremper Longman III (Grand Rapids: Zondervan, 1993), p. 257.

30. R.N. Whybray, *The Composition of the Book of Proverbs*. Journal for the Study of the Old Testament Supplement Series 168 (Sheffield: JSOT, 1994).

31. G. Hassell Bullock, *An Introduction to the Old Testament Poetic Books* (Chicago: Moody, 1976), p. 159.

32. Archer, *Introduction*, p. 452.

33. W. Graham Scroggie, *Analytical Old Testament* (London: Pickering & Inglis, 1970), 1:140-141.

34. Irving Jensen, *Jensen's Old Testament Survey* (Chicago: Moody, 1978), p. 285.

35. W. Lee Humphries, "The Motif of the Wise Courtier in the Book of Proverbs," in *Israelite Wisdom: Theological and Literary Essays in Honor of Samuel Terrien*, ed. John Gammie, Walter Brueggemann et al. (Missoula, MT: Scholars Press, 1978), pp. 177-190.

36. Dianne Bergant, *What Are They Saying about Wisdom Literature?* (New York: Paulist, 1984), p. 31.

37. Dillard and Longman III (*Introduction*, 244) discuss the concept of "absolutizing the proverbs."

BIBLIOGRAPHY

Cohen, Abraham. *Proverbs*. Soncino Books of the Bible. London: Soncino, 1946.

Dahood, Mitchell. *Proverbs and Northwest Semitic Philology*. Rome: Pontificum Institutum Biblicum, 1963.

Delitzsch, Franz. *Commentary on the Proverbs of Solomon*. Trans. M.G. Easton (1874-75). 2 vols. Grand Rapids: Eerdmans, 1970.

Kidner, Derek. *Proverbs*. In Tyndale Old Testament Commentaries. Downers Grove, IL: InterVarsity, 1964.

McKane William. *Proverbs: A New Approach*. Old Testament Library. Philadelphia: Westminster, 1970.

Perowne, T.T. *The Proverbs*. The Cambridge Bible for Schools and Colleges. Cambridge: University Press, 1916.

Scott, R.B.Y. *Proverbs, Ecclesiastes*. Anchor Bible. Garden City, NY: Doubleday, 1965.

Toy, C.H. *The Book of Proverbs*. International Critical Commentary. New York: Scribners, 1916.

Whybray, R.N. *Wisdom in Proverbs: The Concept of Wisdom in Proverbs 1–9*. Napierville, IL: Allenson, 1968.

——————. *The Book of Proverbs*. The Cambridge Bible Commentary on the New English Bible. Cambridge: University Press, 1972.

——————. *The Composition of the Book of Proverbs*. Journal for the Study of the Old Testament Supplement series 168. Sheffield: JSOT, 1994.

Williams, J.G. *Those Who Ponder Proverbs: Aphoristic Thinking and Biblical Literature*. Sheffield: Almond, 1981.

CHAPTER TWENTY-THREE

The Call to Wisdom
Proverbs 1:10-3:35

The first main section of Proverbs consists of thirteen discourses addressed to young people by the teacher and by wisdom personified. Six of those discourses are treated in this chapter. The general purpose of these discourses is to exhibit the excellences of wisdom and illustrate the principle that "the fear of the Lord is the beginning of knowledge" or wisdom. Virtue is energetically promoted; vice is vigorously condemned. In this section the thesis is that godly wisdom is the aim of all moral effort.

Discourse One
WARNING AGAINST GANGSTERISM
Proverbs 1:10-19

The teacher first warns his "son" (pupil) against getting involved with gangs of thugs. He warns the young man of (1) the enticement of the gang; and (2) the punishment of gangsterism.

A. The Enticement of the Gang (1:10-14).

At some point in his life a young man might be enticed by "sinners" (*chatta'im*) to join a gang. The Hebrew term points to those habitually addicted to crime, i.e., thugs, gang members. The verb "entice" is a Hebrew form which expresses intensity. This enticement the young man must steadfastly reject (1:10).

The gang might offer four inducements to lure a young man into their number. First, they might offer excitement. "Let us lie in wait for blood," i.e., commit robbery even if it entails bloodshed. They would hide in unlikely places waiting for "the innocent"—a harmless traveler—to happen by. Such ambushes were "without cause," i.e., unjustified as acts of self-defense. The gang thrives on violence and revels in the loot acquired thereby. This passage gives the impression that gang violence was a major concern in the days of King Solomon (1:11).

Second, the gang offers the recruit empowerment. "Let us swallow them up alive as Sheol." Sheol (Gk. Hades)—the abode of departed spirits—and the grave utterly, suddenly and unexpectedly consume a person body and soul. So the gang intends to snatch away all property which its innocent victims may carry with them. Sheol silences all who enter therein. So the gang, to ensure its security, would silence all its victims. Gangsters display utter callousness about the value of human life (1:12).

Third, the gang offers the recruit enrichment. "All precious substance we will find. We will fill our houses with loot." The language points to a series of robberies. Those who join the gang will be enriched by a career of crime (1:13).

Fourth, the gang offers the recruit camaraderie. If the recruit will join the lawless band he will share in one purse. All would share equally in the resources of the group. The gang offers security, acceptance, and companionship (1:14).

B. The Punishment of the Gang (1:15-19).

The teacher urges his pupil not to "walk in the way" of the gang, not even to take the first step in that direction. The term "way" (*derek*) refers to the way of living and acting. The idea is, Do not associate with them nor have any dealings whatsoever! (1:15). In support of this admonition the teacher points to two characteristics of gangsterism.

First, gangsterism is rambunctious. While the recruit may "walk" in their way, they "run" to "evil" and "shed blood." "Evil" (ra') probably refers to robbery in particular.[1] Thus a youth who joins a gang for social or psychological reasons finds himself quickly caught up in the violation of the eighth and sixth commandments of the Decalogue. Fear of heaven's lawgiver is the ultimate deterrent to lawlessness.

Second, the teacher points to the stupidity of gangsterism. He utters this proverb: "For in vain the net is spread in the eyes of any bird." Even though birds see a net spread before them, they fly into it in an attempt to snatch the bait which has been put there. The spreading of the net does not deter the stupid bird. So gangsters while swooping down to steal the spoil from others, plunge to their own destruction with eyes wide open. They think that they lie in wait for the lives of others. In reality they find in this life of crime only death and destruction. "So are the ways of everyone that is greedy of gain." As surely as grain in a net lures birds, so are gangsters lured to their own destruction. Thus self-preservation is a motive for rejecting the enticement of the gang (1:17-19).

Discourse Two
WISDOM'S IMPASSIONED APPEAL.
Proverbs 1:20-33

In the second discourse godly wisdom is personified as a woman. In the streets of the city she lifts up her voice to all who will listen. From the earliest times a large number of expositors have seen in wisdom here a hypostasis or person, namely, the Lord Jesus. It is best, however, to view wisdom as a personification of an abstract concept rather than a person. Nevertheless, wisdom is divine, and the righteous person will give heed when she calls.

A. The Cry of Wisdom (1:20-23).

The poet begins by enumerating the five places where wisdom preaches, namely, (1) without, (2) in the streets, (3) in the broad places or chief places of concourse, (4) in the gates, and (5) in the city. Thus Lady Wisdom competes with Worldly Wisdom in the marketplace of ideas. The principles of godly conduct are not to be transmitted secretly to a small band of initiates. They are to be proclaimed at the busy crossroads of the noisy cities. In the entrances of the gates—the deep gateways where the elders sat to discuss community policy—there wisdom begs for a hearing. Wherever a crowd of people assembles, wisdom proclaims her message by prophets and teachers (1:20-21).

Wisdom appeals to three classes: the "simple" (*petayim*) are those who do not know, have never heard, and consequently never think about the divine standards of morality. The "scoffers" (*letsim*) are those who mock moral principles, willfully ignore them in their own conduct, and seek to corrupt others. "Fools" (*kesilim*) are those who "hate knowledge," i.e., they have no desire to inquire about the moral standards of the Lord (1:22).

Wisdom invites all to "return to my reproof," i.e, repent and submit to the correction of the divine word. To those who heed this exhortation, wisdom promises: "I will pour out (*'abbi'ah*) my spirit unto you." The verb used here means to stream forth or gush out. The outflow of the spirit of wisdom would be like the abundant and refreshing gushing of a spring of water. The spirit of wisdom here is parallel to "my words," i.e., the words of wisdom. The text does not say that it is through the spirit of wisdom that the words of wisdom are understood. Rather the idea is that the humble student is possessed of the spirit of wisdom when he comprehends and submits to the words of wisdom (1:23).

B. The Rejection of Wisdom (1:24-25).

The majority of people were deliberately deaf to the appeal of Lady Wisdom. When she called, they "refused," i.e., to listen. Yet she continues to "stretch out" her hand in a gesture of appeal (cf. Isa 65:2). Still virtually "no man regarded," (lit., perked up the ear). The context suggests that the appeal of Lady Wisdom had been of long duration (1:24).

In spite of the valiant efforts of Lady Wisdom to get a hearing for her message, the majority neglected or rejected (lit., let go) her advice. Wisdom's advice (*'etsah*) would be her recommendations for doing good. They were even less open to (lit., did not want or desire) wisdom's reproofs (*tokhachti*). Thus they wanted neither wisdom's positive direction nor her negative restraint (1:25).

C. The Results of Rejecting Wisdom (1:26-33).

The poet spells out four consequences of rejecting the appeal of Lady Wisdom.

1. *Calamity (1:26-27)*. Disaster (*'ed*) ultimately follows rejecting the appeal of Lady Wisdom. The Hebrew word points to a heavy and overwhelming misfortune which crushes its victims. The poet uses this term twice as he does also the term "fear" (*pachad*, that which causes fear). The terms "trouble" (*tsarah*) and "distress" (*tsuqah*) describe the results of that calamity. These words are an alliteration in Hebrew. They carry the idea of compression and narrowness, that feeling of being hemmed in, of having no room to maneuver, no place to turn. The swiftness and unexpectedness of that day of judgment is indicated by comparing the calamity to a storm (*sho'avah*)—a wasting, crushing tempest—or whirlwind (*suphah*)—a tornadic wind which carries everything before it.

2. *Mockery (1:26)*. When that distressful day arrives Lady Wisdom would have the last laugh (*sachaq*). She would mock (*la'ag*) those who had rejected her.

3. *Abandonment (1:28-30)*. The change from the second person to the third person in v. 28 may contain a subtle message. Those deemed fools by virtue of rejecting divine wisdom are no longer considered worthy to be addressed directly. When the destruction comes upon the land, the godless would cry out to Lady Wisdom, i.e., they would pray.

The intensity of the prayers of these wicked souls is stressed in the text. First, the verbs "they shall call," "they shall seek," and "they shall find" are unusual forms in the Hebrew which have the effect of intensifying the action. Second, the verb "they shall seek" carries the meaning "earnestly seek." It suggests one who rises early in the morning to commence a task, and thus indicates diligence and earnestness.

Lady Wisdom, however, would not respond to their appeals any more than they had responded to her appeals. The consistent teaching

479

of Scripture is that repentance is too late once the wheels of judgment are in motion. These sinners either pray too late or else they, having spurned the instruction of Lady Wisdom, do not know how to pray properly (1:28).

Why does Lady Wisdom turn a deaf ear to the desperate entreaties of the wicked? The wicked are without excuse. In the times of prosperity they "hated knowledge," i.e., the personal, experiential knowledge of God. They therefore did not choose (i.e., embrace with affection) a lifestyle which reflected the "fear of God," i.e., reverence for the creator. They neglected the counsel of Lady Wisdom. They despised, i.e., rejected with contempt, the reproof which godly wisdom brings to the life of the sinner. The doctrine of free will is implied in this passage. Each person chooses for himself the path of godly wisdom or the path of worldly wisdom (1:29-30).

4. *Nausea (1:31).* God's inexorable law of retribution requires that men will reap what they sow, and eat what they reap. Those who have rejected Lady Wisdom will "eat of the fruit of their own way," i.e., their manner of life. They will be filled (lit., satiated; nauseated) "with their own devices" (*mo'atsotehem*), i.e., ungodly counsels. This word almost always has a negative connotation. It refers to the evil schemes of the wicked.

D. Summary of the Argument (1:32-33).

Lady Wisdom now brings her message to a close by contrasting the fate of the foolish with the security of those who listen to her voice. The waywardness (*meshubhah*), i.e., apostasy, of the thoughtless (*petayim*) would lead to their destruction. The turning away is from the warnings and invitations of wisdom, and hence from God himself. The confidence (*shalavah*)—lit., quietness, condition of ease—of fools (*kesilim*) would destroy them. Worldly wisdom results in a false sense of security. A society not built upon a firm moral foundation is doomed to collapse (1:32).

Some would listen to Lady Wisdom. In contrast to the false security of the ungodly, these would "dwell securely," i.e., confidently, without danger, undisturbed among the distractions of this world. Like the psalmist, they will not fear "evil," i.e., calamity (Ps 23:4). This is no promise of a life free from trials. Lady Wisdom provides the principles which sustain one through good times and bad. Following Lady Wisdom enables one to avoid the ultimate calamity, i.e., eternal condemnation.

Discourse Three
THE FRUITS OF WISDOM
Proverbs 2:1-22

Lady Wisdom has just pointed out the disastrous consequences of rejecting her direction. Now the teacher[2] speaks for the second time to enumerate the happy results of choosing the path of wisdom. Several of the themes of the preceding discourse are reiterated.

A. The Search for Wisdom (2:1-4).

The third speech begins with a series of conditions upon which the promises of wisdom depend. First, the student must graciously acknowledge and accept the words of wisdom. He must "receive" the words of the teacher. Second, he must "lay up" *(titspon)* or treasure up the "commandments" of his mentor, i.e., principles for the conduct of life. The divine commandments are to be hidden away in the memory, in the understanding, in the conscience and in the heart. The teacher here calls upon his student to "hear *my* words" and treasure up "*my* commandments." The sages of Israel may have felt a divine compulsion to share godly wisdom, but they did not pretend to have a call to speak in God's name (2:1).

Third, the student must "incline" (*qashabh*) his ear to wisdom. The verb suggests the idea of sharpening the ear so as to give diligent attention to what is being spoken. Fourth, one must "stretch out" (*natah*) toward discernment (*tebhunah*), i.e., be eager to absorb what is being taught. The idea is to focus all the cognitive powers, in the spirit of humility and eagerness, on discernment. Biblical faith appeals to the intellect as well as to the emotions. "Discernment" refers to ethical sensitivities. Wisdom can be of no benefit unless people have first learned what it is. Thus outwardly ("the ear") and inwardly ("the heart") the student of wisdom must be focused if he is to possess the principles of godly living (2:2).

Fifth, the search for wisdom must be earnest as well as sincere.

481

The student must "call for" ethical understanding and discernment. He must "lift up the voice" in even greater intensity in order that his mind and heart might be filled with godly principles. The verbs used here frequently in Scripture indicate earnestness. Just as Lady Wisdom displays zeal in the pursuit of disciples (cf. 1:20f.), so the disciples must be zealous in the apprehension of wisdom. The term for "knowledge" (binah) here has virtually the same meaning as the term "discernment" in this and the preceding verse. This suggests that the emphasis in v. 3 is on the verbal action.

Sixth, the search for wisdom must be unrelenting. The student must pursue wisdom with that same unremitting labor with which men mine precious ore. The verb "seek" here is intensive in the original. The verb "search" (chaphas) has the connotation "to dig out." The thought here is similar to that in the parable of the hidden treasure and the pearl of great price (2:4; cf. Matt 13:44,46).

B. The Reward of Wisdom (2:5-9).

One who eagerly pursues moral perfection will ultimately come to "the fear of the Lord" and "the knowledge of God." The concept of the fear of the Lord embraces the whole range of religious emotion and affection which respond to the various attributes of God as revealed in Scripture. These feelings are expressed in worship. The "knowledge" of God includes cognitive knowledge, but much more. It is experiential knowledge of God or a life of communion and fellowship with him. The "fear of the Lord" and "the knowledge of God" are reciprocal. Without "fear" or reverence one cannot "know" him. At the same time, the more one knows God, the more he will reverence him (2:5).

The words of the teacher are not to be taken in some mystical sense as if by pursuing ethical discernment man can on his own find his way to God. The teacher points to God and revelation as the source of wisdom. The Lord does not leave his children groping in a moral morass for some point of reference. Yahweh gives wisdom to those who ask for it (cf. 1 Kgs 3:9,12). Out of the mouth of God comes knowledge and discernment. Only by submitting to the precepts revealed by God through the law and prophets does one come to wisdom and fellowship with God (2:6).

Two nouns describe those who follow godly wisdom. They are "the upright" (yesharim), i.e., the righteous; and "those who walk in integrity" (holekhe tom). To walk in integrity means to maintain a course of life regulated by godly principles. He who walks in integrity "lives with the fear of God as his principle, the word of God as his rule, and the glory of God as his end."[3]

That which God has laid up for the upright is called "sound wisdom" (tushiyyah). This term, common in Job and Proverbs, appears to mean something like "common sense that protects a person from stupid and dangerous mistakes." God makes this kind of wisdom available to all who seek it in the pages of the holy word. To those who "walk in integrity" in the path of that wisdom, Yahweh is a "shield."[4] He protects them in the midst of assaults by their enemies and from the fiery darts of the evil one (2:7).

Furthermore, the Lord "guards the paths of justice" i.e., the paths in which the just walk. He watches over all who walk therein, guides, superintends, and protects them. The Lord "preserves the paths of his godly ones" (chasidav), i.e., those who live by the principles of holiness and walk in paths of righteousness (2:8).

Those who pursue biblical wisdom will come to have a new perspective on four great concepts. They will understand righteousness (tsedeq), justice (mishpat), equity (mesharim) and "every good path," i.e., every course of action of which goodness is the goal. The latter term (ma'gal) literally means "wagon rut." The concept is the same as the straight and narrow path to which Jesus referred (2:9).

C. The Advantage of Wisdom (2:10-19).

Lady Wisdom takes up residence in the heart of those who pursue her. A believer finds the acquisition of biblical wisdom to be a pleasant experience with several practical advantages. "Discretion" (mezimmah) is the outward manifestation of wisdom. The word carries the connotation of wise choice following deliberation and reflection. "Discernment" (tebhunah) as in 2:11 is the intellectual power to discriminate between bad, good and better. Whereas Yahweh is said to function as guardian of the godly, here that function is transferred to wisdom personified. Those who welcome that wisdom into heart and mind are protected in their earthly pilgrimage in four areas (2:10-11).

First, biblical wisdom will deliver a believer "from an evil way," i.e., a course of conduct which is essentially wicked. The language points to any action or thought which is contrary to the holiness of God. Discretion within the heart will be a sufficient antidote for the allurements of this kind of lifestyle (2:12a).

Second, biblical wisdom delivers from a person who continues to speak "perverse things" (*tahpukhot*), lit., things which are upside down, the willful misrepresentation of that which is true and good. The reference is to those who champion some ethical system other than that which is based on reverence for God. These teachers have left "the paths of uprightness" in order to walk "in the ways of darkness." Scripture consistently depicts the path of faith and virtue as illuminated while the way of wickedness is shrouded in darkness. Darkness represents ignorance, error and wicked actions. These reprobates are further described as rejoicing to do evil and delighting in the convoluted morality of their hedonistic lifestyles and those of the sinners with whom they associate. They are "crooked in their ways and perverse [lit., turned aside] in their paths." Sinners are ever changing direction as impulse or fad dictates (2:12b-15).

Third, biblical wisdom will deliver a young man from the "strange" (*zarah*) or "alien" (*nokhriyyah*) woman. The reference is to one who today might be called a whore or prostitute. Such conduct was totally outside the covenant morality of ancient Israel. The Mosaic law contained stringent laws against prostitution (e.g., Lev 19:29). The law also prohibited intermarriage with women from surrounding nations where the sexual mores were not nearly so lofty. These "strange" or "alien" women originally may have come over to Israel through marriage. The man with biblical wisdom lodging in his heart would not be persuaded by the smooth, i.e., flattering, speech of such a woman. Sexual immorality is outside the bounds of biblical morality. A disciple of wisdom must be chaste in thought and deed (2:16).

The immoral woman is further described as one who had forsaken "the companion (*'alluph*) of her youth," i.e., her husband. By pursuing her adulterous lifestyle this woman suppressed all thought of "the covenant of her God." The seventh of the Ten Commandments prohibited adultery. The reference here, however, may be to the marriage covenant with her husband to which God was witness (cf. Mal

2:14). The author of Proverbs has a high view of marriage as a solemn commitment made in the presence of God, hence indissoluble except in the most extreme circumstances. The woman who commits adultery sins against God as well as her husband (2:17).[5]

By delivering her disciple from a life of immorality, Lady Wisdom spares him from ultimate destruction. The "house" (brothel?) of the adulteress "sinks down to death." Her house would include all who belong to her. She and they are all headed for the same fate. The paths of immorality are short cuts to the place of departed spirits (repha'im). The sin of adultery is deadly and leads to death, and from death there is no return (2:18-19; cf. Rev 21:8).

D. Encouragement and Warning (2:20-22).

The third discourse concludes with encouragement and warning. The ultimate purpose of godly wisdom is to lead a person "in the way of good men," i.e., "the paths of righteousness." The teacher wants his disciple "to keep" those paths, i.e., to carefully attend to the life of obedience which those paths follow (2:20).

Great reward comes to the person who chooses that way of life. First, they would enjoy security "in the land," i.e., the land of Israel. Occupation of Canaan was the fulfillment of a promise God made to Abraham, Isaac and Jacob. Continued residence there was conditional. To dwell in the land was always put forward as the reward for obedience to God's commands (e.g., Lev 25:18). The "perfect" or wholehearted (temimim) are those steadfast in loyalty to the Lord. These would remain permanently in that land. Jesus (Matt 5:5) enlarged on this promise when he stated that "the meek shall inherit the earth" (2:21).

On the other hand, those who do not follow wisdom have nothing in which to hope. The "wicked" (resha'im) would be "cut off" from the land, i.e., expelled. They would lose all the blessings of that relationship with the Lord. The same is true of the "faithless" (bogedim), those who secretly and treacherously walk away from the Lord. These will be "plucked up," i.e., rooted up, like a worthless tree. The point in both verbs is that the destruction of those who lack wisdom will be complete (2:22).

Discourse Four
THE BLESSING OF WISDOM
Proverbs 3:1-18

The fourth discourse of Proverbs is in a sense a continuation of the third. The same themes of the spiritual and moral benefits of pursuing wisdom appear here.

A. Exhortations (3:1-12).

The speech begins with six exhortations, each accompanied by a promise.

1. Obey God (3:1-2). The teacher appeals to his student not to forget his "teaching" and "commandments." The verb here does not refer to inadvertent memory lapse, but to willful disregard and neglect of the admonitions of the teacher. Since the teacher is presenting the way and words of God, to obey his instruction is to obey God (3:1).

The inducements to godly obedience are three. First, the obedient student would find "length of days," i.e., the prolongation of life, its duration to the appointed limit.[6] As a general principle, living a godly life tends toward good health, and hence longer life. Second, the obedient one would find "years of life" (lit., lives). The life which God promises is measured by quality as well as quantity. The godly life is an abundant life, a life of true happiness and enjoyment. Third, the godly life is one of "peace" (*shalom*), total well-being. He who follows biblical wisdom will experience contentment and tranquility (3:2).

2. Remember God (3:3-4). The student should not permit "kindness" and "truth" to slip away from him. These two virtues are frequently combined in Proverbs and Psalms. "Kindness" (*chesed*) is that obligatory love which displays itself in such matters as extending a helping hand, forgiving offenses, and sympathizing with those in trouble. This term excludes all selfishness and hate. "Truth" (*'emet*) is keeping one's commitments, honoring one's word. This virtue excludes all hypocrisy. The disciple of wisdom should "write" the godly instructions of the teacher "upon the table" of his heart, i.e., he should internalize them and make them the mainspring of life. He should bind them about the neck either as ornaments or as treasures to be preserved from loss (3:3).

One who follows "truth" and "kindness" will find, i.e., obtain or attain, two wonderful blessings. First, he will obtain "grace" (*khen*), i.e., he will be viewed favorably. Second, he will attain a "good reputation" (*sekhel tobh*) in the sight of both God and man, i.e., be viewed favorably and spoken of favorably (3:4).

3. *Trust God (3:5-6).* The teacher calls upon his disciple to "trust Yahweh," i.e., to set one's hope and confidence in him. His trust in God should be with "all his heart," i.e., complete. The tendency is to follow divine guidance only when it agrees with human logic or fleshly inclinations. The believer must not "lean upon," i.e., find support in, his own understanding. At best, man's understanding of life is fallible, wavering and uncertain. It offers no support (3:5).

One must therefore "acknowledge" (lit., know) God in all his ways, i.e., in all the various activities and pursuits of life. The idea is that in every aspect of life one should focus on God and walk in the spiritual light which he has provided. The admonition guards against the tendency of acknowledging God only in formal worship or in the crises of life. To acknowledge God is to consult his will, seek his direction and recognize his sovereignty over all life. When the believer does this, the Lord will "direct" (lit., make straight) his paths. The idea is that he will remove the obstacles which impede progress. Thus the believer's walk will be virtuous, happy and prosperous (3:6).

4. *Reverence God (3:7-8).* The teacher urges his disciple to avoid arrogance: "Be not wise in your own eyes," i.e., in your own estimation. Life offers many paths the final destiny of which is destruction. Godly reverence, which is the foundation of knowledge (cf. 1:7), guides a person to a virtuous life. The "fear of the Lord" is the best corrective to one's own wisdom. On the other hand, arrogance and conceit cause people to ignore all the warning signs of both revelation and social convention. Self-trust is "unwisdom" and it is dangerous (cf. Isa 5:21). The "fear of the Lord" also has this advantage: it leads to the departure from evil (3:7).

The advice of the teacher is imminently practical. Fearing the Lord and departing from evil leads to a happy and wholesome life. The "navel" stands here for the entire body. Thus "health to your navel" is an idiom expressing physical well-being. A godly lifestyle promotes respect for the body. The same idea is conveyed in the words

487

"marrow for your bones." Just as marrow keeps bones alive and strong, so wisdom gives vigor and vitality to life (3:8).

5. *Honor God (3:9-10).* One who follows divine wisdom honors God with his substance. He has an obligation to use God's bounty in ways of which God approves. This would include tithing, free-will offerings and charitable giving. Money dispensed in the honor of God is never ill-spent. As a specific example of this general principle, the teacher mentions the firstfruits of the harvest (Deut 18:4; 26:2). The law required that a token portion of the harvest be presented to the Lord in recognition that the entire harvest belonged to him. The term "firstfruits" also carried with it the idea of the best. Thus one honors God when he gives him the best of what he has (3:9).

To those who honored God with their substance, Proverbs holds out the prospects of packed barns and overflowing vats. The "new wine" promised is grape juice which has not become completely fermented. The general principle here is that adherence to God's precepts results in material reward (Deut 28:1-8). In this respect the Old Covenant differs from the spiritual blessings of far greater value promised in the New Covenant.[7] On the surface this appears to be a selfish motive for encouraging believers to give back to God their substance. In reality, this is a faith challenge. Worldly wisdom would never conclude that one could increase his wealth by giving it away.

6. *Submit to God (3:11-12).* Attached to the promise of material reward is a an admonition to submit to the "chastening" (*musar*) and "correction" (*tokhachah*) of the Lord. The two terms are virtually synonymous pointing to correction by reproof and, when necessary, by punishment. God should be forgotten neither in times of prosperity, nor in times of adversity. The believer will not "despise," i.e., reject, occasions of difficulty. They despise the chastening of the Lord who do not humbly submit to it, but resist and become angry with God, man and life in general. To "spurn" (*quts*) indicates an even stronger aversion to divine chastening. The word literally means "to feel loathing or nausea; to abhor." To loathe the correction of the Lord is to allow it to estrange one from God completely (3:11).

The believer knows that occasions of adversity have a beneficent purpose. He who follows wisdom will try to grow through such experiences. Thus the teacher recognizes that material reward does not in fact always follow fidelity to wisdom. Misfortune tends either to draw people closer to the Lord, or to make them resolute in evil. The teacher is urging the former reaction. He would have his disciple to understand that adversity actually is a tool of a loving heavenly Father. He uses that tool to shape man's attitudes and actions (3:12; cf. Deut 8:5; Heb 12:5f.).[8]

B. Blessing (3:13-18).

The teacher continues to enumerate the advantages of acquiring wisdom. He declares "Happy is the man" (lit., blessings of the man) who has found wisdom. The plural of excellence is used here. Thus supreme blessing belongs to this person who "has found" (Heb. perfect tense) wisdom. The blessing extends also to the person who continues to derive (imperfect tense) his "understanding" from God. The verb (yaphiq) has the idea of drawing out from another for one's own use. In this case God himself is the well from which a man continues to draw out spiritual understanding. Most likely the teacher has in mind the spiritual joy and tranquility which result from a life of trusting God. To find wisdom means to learn her ways, to appreciate her worth, and to practice her walk (3:13).

Why is he who acquires wisdom happy? Because the merchandising, i.e., the profit which accrues from it, is greater than that of silver or fine gold. Wisdom is more precious than rubies, or as some modern scholars prefer, corals. These were obtained from the Red Sea and from India. No material thing which a person might desire can be compared to the value of wisdom (3:14-15).

In what respects is wisdom incomparable in value? Wisdom confers upon her disciples handfuls of blessing. In her right hand—the superior position—she offers the blessing of blessings, namely, "length of days," i.e., long life. In her left hand she offers "riches and honor." The term "honor" when combined with the term "riches" always signifies the splendor of luxury. There are material advantages to be gained by following wisdom (3:16).

The paths of wisdom lead to a life of "pleasantness" and "peace." These words describe a life of satisfaction, free of worries. Wisdom is "a tree of life" for she imparts to those who "take hold" of her a life more abundant.[9] All those who continue to "hold fast" (tamakh is a plural participle) to wisdom share equally in the same "blessing" (*me'usshar*). Perhaps the idea here is that wisdom restores the life which was lost through Adam's transgression. Those who take hold of wisdom and hold on tenaciously have in their hand the key to true happiness, i.e., spiritual blessing (3:17-18).

Discourse Five
WISDOM AND CREATION
Proverbs 3:19-26

Reference to the tree of life (v. 18) may have triggered the following discussion of wisdom as the power by which God created the world and by which he governs it. The thought here is that wisdom makes order out of chaos in the individual life as well as in the cosmos.

A. The Power of God (3:19-20).

By wisdom God "founded" (*yasadh*), i.e., created, the earth.[10] By "understanding"—identical with wisdom—he "established" (*konen*), i.e., set up or erected, the heavens. The combination "heavens and earth" is equivalent to the modern term *universe*. The idea of wisdom being present at the creation will be discussed in chapter 8 (3:19).

The Lord's "knowledge"—another synonym for wisdom—is the controlling force of the physical universe. By his knowledge the Lord has broken up "the depths" where the subterranean waters are stored. The reference may be to the Great Flood (cf. Gen 7:11). At the same time, that "knowledge" regularly produces the dew from "the clouds." Palestine was totally dependent upon dew for moisture during the dry season. Thus whether in the great and unique catastrophes of the past or the gentle and ordinary occurrences of the physical world, the hand of the Lord is in them all (3:20).

B. The Provision of God (3:21-22).

Since wisdom is so powerful, the teacher urges his student not to let "them," i.e., God's wisdom, understanding and knowledge of the preceding verses, "depart from your eyes," i.e., fade from the mind. He should guard "sound wisdom" (cf. 2:7) and "discretion" (cf. 1:4) like one who guards a treasure (3:21).

Why should one be so focused on wisdom and discretion? More abundant life and life eternal belong to those who walk the paths of wisdom (cf. 3:18). At the same time wisdom, understanding and knowledge shall be "grace" to the "neck." The soul and neck in this verse stand for the whole person, both his inner and outer aspect. The idea is that following God's wisdom causes one to hold his head erect, and consequently gives him a noble and attractive appearance. Another view is that wisdom is like the adornment of the outer life which procures the praise of both man and God (3:22).

C. The Protection of God (3:23-26).

Several promises of protection are offered to one who clings to wisdom. First, he will walk "securely," i.e., free from anxiety and danger (cf. 1:33). In that path there would be no danger one would "dash" the foot, i.e., trip over something. Second, the practitioner of wisdom will lie down without fear. His sleep will be "sweet," i.e., undisturbed by worry and guilt (3:23-24).

Third, one who walks in wisdom's paths should have no fear of "sudden terror," i.e., unexpected calamity. He can fearlessly face "the destruction of the wicked." This could be taken to be (1) the devastation caused by wicked men when they persecute the righteous; or (2) the devastation which God eventually brings on the wicked. Fourth, throughout life the Lord is the believer's "confidence." Those who rely on God will have no feeling of helplessness. The Lord would keep that one's foot from being caught in the snares set by evildoers (3:25-26).

Discourse Six
THE DUTIES OF WISDOM
Proverbs 3:27-35

Wisdom must be translated into action and lifestyle. The teacher wants his disciple to realize that there are obligations associated with godly wisdom. This he accomplishes through an exhortation and a warning.

A. Exhortation Regarding Benevolence (3:27-30).

Four negative proverbs urge the disciple of wisdom to be generous to his fellows. First, he should not "withhold good from him to whom

491

it is due" (lit., "to its owners"). "Good" refers to any good deed or act of beneficence. The limitation on this command is this: "when it is in the power of your hand to do it," i.e., when you are in a position to do so and when you have the opportunity to do so (cf. Gal 6:10). The allusion may be to a charity upon which the poor have a claim under the law of Moses. The implication here is that man owns nothing. He is but a steward of that with which God has blessed him (3:27).

Second, when one came seeking help, the disciple of wisdom should not send that person away with promises that help would be forthcoming "tomorrow." That only adds to a person's worry. At the same time being forced to ask for help a second time is demeaning. Third, never should a disciple of wisdom devise evil against a neighbor "who dwells securely." Such a one is unsuspecting; he therefore takes no measures for self-protection. To violate the trust of someone is an act of treachery which is an outrage to all law, human and divine. Fourth, one who follows wisdom should not deliberately pick a quarrel and stir up contention when there is no cause for it. This admonition is aimed at those who through jealousy or envy create an occasion to fight with those who are peaceful and quiet (3:28-30).

B. Warning Regarding the Wicked (3:31-35).

The disciple of wisdom should not only avoid oppression against a neighbor; he should not even associate with those who practice violence. He should not "envy" those who have gained riches by illegal means. Envy is the first step in imitation. "Choose none of his ways," the teacher admonishes (3:31). Four reasons are advanced for avoiding association with the wicked.

First, the "perverse" person (naloz) is one who had turned aside from the straight and narrow path. Such a one is an "abomination" (to'ebhah) to the Lord, i.e., something repugnant to him. These words indicate that worldly success and wealth are not always a sign of God's favor. On the other hand the "counsel" (sod) of the Lord is with those who are upright. The word refers to that special favor in which the Lord reveals to some what he conceals from others. The upright enjoy this intimate friendship with God (3:32).

Second, "the curse of the Lord," i.e., sentence or pronouncement, is on the house of the wicked. Those who gain riches by violence or fraud will not be allowed by God to enjoy the fruits of their wickedness. The "curse" includes the infliction of temporal misfortune (cf. Deut 28:20) ending with the "cutting off" of the wicked (Ps 37:22). On the other hand, God "blesses," i.e., pronounces good, the habitation of the righteousness. The "blessing" is both physical and spiritual (3:33).

Third, "scorners" (cf. 1:22) would be repaid in kind by the Lord. "Scorners" (*letsim*) are those who mock the precepts and truths of God. The Lord repays their arrogant scorn with scorn. He frustrates all their plans. He resists them. On the other hand, the "humble" (*'anayim*) are those who submit to the will of God. To the humble God gives "grace," i.e., he shows favor to them (3:34; cf. Jas 4:6).

Fourth, those who follow wisdom, i.e., pursue a godly lifestyle, "inherit honor" or "glory" (*kabhodh*). That is the birthright of the sons of God. The glory which they receive is not merely that of men, but of God as well. Fools (*kesilim*), on the other hand, "carry away" (lit., "lift up, exalt") shame as their portion.[11] They earn the contempt of their neighbors (3:35).

ENDNOTES

1. Some respected rabbinic commentators think that "evil" in 1:16 refers to the "harm" which the life of crime brings to the gang member. Likewise they opine that the bloodshed in this verse is not murder (as in v. 11), but the death sentence passed upon gang members by the court.

2. That wisdom personified is no longer the speaker seems clear enough from the use of the terms "wisdom and understanding" in v. 2 without the possessive suffix "my" which characterized the previous discourse.

3. Wardlaw, quoted by W.J. Deane, "Proverbs" in *The Pulpit Commentary* (New York: Funk & Wagnalls, 1909), p. 36.

4. Another view is that it is the biblical common sense in 2:7 which is a shield against temptation to those who walk in integrity.

5. Proverbs always represents monogamy as the rule. It condemns illicit intercourse, and discountenances divorce. Though Solomon was a polygamist of the worst sort, he understood the divine intention regarding marriage.

6. This same promise is appended to honoring parents in the fifth commandment (cf. Exod 20:12). Solomon was promised length of days if he walked in the way of the Lord (1 Kgs 3:14), a condition which he did not keep all of his life.

7. Others point out that this is the Book of Proverbs, not the Book of Guarantees. Proverbs states principles that are generally, but not inevitably, true. Thus material reward for honoring God with one's substance generally is the case. Another view of such promises is that adherence to the law of God would produce a godly society in which a secure, happy and contented life for all members of the community is possible.

8. Commentators have observed that 3:11 expresses the problem of the Book of Job, and 3:12 its solution.

9. The expression "tree of life" appears three other places in the book: 11:30; 13:12; 15:4.

10. The verb *yasadh* is also used of the creation of the earth by God in Job 38:4 and Ps 24:2; 78:69. The primary meaning of the verb is "to give fixity to," "to lay fast."

11. Others interpret the last half of 3:35: fools exalt shame, prize what others despise; or shame lifts fools up in order to sweep them away to destroy them.

CHAPTER TWENTY-FOUR

The Warnings of the Teacher
Proverbs 4-6

A new group of discourses begins in chapter 4 as is indicated by the first use of the plural "my sons" in the address. This address appears again in 5:7 and 7:24. The prevailing tone in these discourses is that of warning rather than positive exhortation which has characterized the first six discourses in the book.

Discourse Seven
THE DISCIPLINE OF WISDOM
Proverbs 4:1-27

The general aim of the seventh discourse is similar to those which preceded, namely, to exalt wisdom. Here, however, the teacher introduces a new mode of instruction. Previously he has spoken in his own authority, and he has summoned wisdom personified to make her appeal. Here he transports his readers into an Israelite home and permits them to hear the earnest and loving advice of a father to his children.[1] The father's advice (vv. 4-19) is bracketed by the teacher's own admonition (in vv. 1-3 and vv. 20-27). The aspect of wisdom which is most in evidence here is that of discipline which leads to obedience.

A. The Father's Exhortation (4:1-4a).

The seventh discourse begins with the exhortation to "sons" to hear "instruction" (*musar*) and to give earnest attention (*qashabh*) "to know," i.e., acquire, "understanding" (*binah*). The speaker then indicates four reasons why the children should listen to what follows.

First, this is the instruction of "a father," not "your father." The language suggests that the father is seeking to impart to his children the family values which had been handed down to him. This conclusion is further reinforced in v. 2 by the term "teaching" (*leqach*). The Hebrew term suggests that which has been received from another. Hence the teaching about to be transmitted to the children is that which had been handed down from previous generations, i.e., traditional family values. If the writer here is Solomon, then the "father" would be David (4:1).

Second, the children should pay close attention because their father is about to give them "good" teaching. This direction is intrinsically good. It is also good in the source from which it was derived, and good in the effects upon the lives of the children. Therefore this "teaching" (*torah*) or direction should not be forsaken. This passage underscores the principle that attention to parental advice is incumbent on children. The disregard of such advice is the mark of ingratitude and depravity (4:2).

Third, the children should give heed because of the example of their father. He had been "a son unto my father." The implication is that more than a biological relationship existed between the father and his father before him. He had been a respectful and obedient son. His father had taught him, and he had listened to that instruction (v. 4a). This is indicated by the fact that he is now passing on that instruction (3:3a).

Fourth, the children should listen to the forthcoming instruction because it was dictated by affection. The speaker insists that he was the object of tender care or love from his mother. He was "the only one" (*yachidh*) in the sight of his mother. The Hebrew term does not necessarily point to an only child. Rather it suggests that he had been the focus of his mother's affection.[2] The mother dispensed the love, and the father the discipline (*musar* in v. 1) in both its positive and negative connotations (4:3b). Thus both the father and mother have a vital role in producing well-rounded children.

B. The Grandfather's Appeal (4:4b-9).
At this point and through v. 19 the father is passing on to his children what his father before had thought. The grandfather had first appealed to his son, on the basis of the special relationship which existed between them, to let his "heart" (i.e., mind) "hold fast" the words which were being communicated. He promised his son (Solomon) that he would "live," i.e., have a long and happy life, if he obeyed the commandments of his father (4:4).

The grandfather appealed to his son to "acquire" (*qanah*, lit., "purchase") wisdom and understanding. The verb is repeated for emphasis, i.e., "purchase at any price." The son should not "forget" the words of his father, nor "turn aside," i.e., spurn, them (4:5).

Again wisdom (and understanding) is compared to a beautiful woman to whom one should be faithful throughout life. Fidelity to her would pay great dividends. Wisdom would "preserve" and "keep" those who hold her close (4:6).

"Wisdom is the principal thing, therefore get wisdom" (KJV). Paraphrased, the father is saying that wisdom is the highest good, and therefore ought to be obtained. Wisdom should be acquired with all one's "acquiring," i.e., with all one has acquired or gotten. The idea is that no price is too high to be paid for wisdom, no sacrifice is too great. Once one realizes how essential wisdom is to a productive life, he will spare no effort to acquire her (4:7).

If one will "extol" wisdom, i.e., esteem her highly, she will "exalt" him, i.e., in the estimation of his fellows. Those who warmly "embrace" wisdom receive honor. Wisdom will place on the head of those who seek her "a garland of praise" and "a crown of glory."[3] The idea here is that wisdom shall confer true dignity on those who seek her (4:8-9).

C. The Grandfather's Promise (4:10-13).

The grandfather now buttresses his appeal for consideration of his sayings with several incentives. First, he promises to the attentive son that "the years of your lives (plural) shall be multiplied" (cf. 3:2). These words suggest not only the prolongation of life, but a life of prosperity and enjoyment. Second, the words of the grandfather should be heeded because he had directed his son in the way of wisdom, in "upright paths," i.e., straight or even paths. The course of rectitude is one that goes straight or unswervingly to its destination. A crooked road is a long road; a hilly road is a tiring road. Such is the path of sin (4:10-11).[4]

Third, if the son walked in the paths outlined by his father he would find no obstacle. To "walk" here may indicate the ordinary affairs of life. To "run" points to emergency situations. In either case there would be no stumbling. The Lord would remove all stumbling-blocks from the way. Fourth, "instruction" (*musar*), i.e., wisdom, brings "life" to those who "take hold" of her. Life more abundant depends upon the observance of the precepts of wisdom. To the extent that wisdom is retained and guarded, so is life secured (4:12-13).

D. The Grandfather's Warning (4:14-19).

The grandfather pled with his son not to imitate the lifestyle of the "wicked" or "evil men" as described in 1:10ff. The terms "path" or "way" here as throughout Proverbs indicates manner of life, or lifestyle. He used six strong imperatives in this warning. (1) One should not enter that path. If he does, however, (2) he should not walk therein, i.e., persevere in it. It is much better to (3) avoid it, i.e., leave it alone, (4) pass not by it, i.e., do not even go near those who pursue this course of action; (5) turn from it, and (6) pass on, i.e., put the greatest possible distance between you and that evil life (4:14-15).

Why does the grandfather want his son to avoid the path of the wicked? First, they are consumed with a craving for sin and violence. They are unable to sleep at night if their day has passed without some shady deal or act of violence. Sin is like a narcotic which enables them to sleep. Second, the wicked "eat the bread of wickedness," i.e., the bread which is derived from wickedness. They "drink the wine of violence," i.e., the wine procured by violent deeds. The idea is that they derive their livelihood from wickedness and injustice (4:16-17).

Third, thick darkness (*'aphelah*), i.e., confusion, unholiness, misery and gloom, is the lot of those who choose the path of wicked men. The term used here is the same used in the account of the plague against Egypt (Exod 10:21-23). Sooner or later they stumble in that darkness to their own destruction. Whereas the wicked go ever deeper into darkness, those who start down the path of righteousness experience illumination (lit., "light of brightness") which grows ever more brilliant the further one walks. Eventually they arrive at the "full day," lit., "the standing firm of the day." The reference is to the full splendor of noontime, which here seems to represent that eternal day into which the righteous enter at the conclusion of life. The verse illustrates the gradual growth and increase of the righteous in knowledge, holiness and joy as they proceed along the path of wisdom (4:18-19).

E. The Father's Appeal (4:20-27).

Whether the father continues to transmit the teachings of his father, or speaks directly to his son in these verses is not clear.[5] Since the father's teaching is built on that of his father before him, the message is the same in either case.

Again there is an appeal to the son for attentiveness to the words which follow. He should keep those words before his eyes, i.e., use them as the guide for all conduct. He should implant them deep in the heart (i.e., mind) where they are less likely to be removed (cf. 3:21). The expression implies cherishing them with an internal affection (cf. Deut 6:6-8). Those words remembered and applied would produce life (the word is plural as usual in Proverbs) in the fullest sense of that word. They would be "health to all their health," i.e., the key to a healthy life. An immoral life is regarded by Proverbs as unhealthy, a moral life as sound health (4:21-22).

1. The inward life (4:23). The supreme thing that the son should guard is the heart, "for out of it are the issues of life." In modern terms the "heart" might be called the soul, the personality, the psyche. The text assumes that one can and should control that upon which his mind dwells. Evil thoughts must be barred or expelled. The "issues of life" are the impulses, the choices, the decisions that affect the nature of man's existence in this world. If the heart is pure, the life will be pure. Conversely, if the heart is corrupt, the life will be corrupt. In Hebrew psychology the heart is the center of moral consciousness and the seat of the affections.[6]

2. *The outward life (4:24-27).* The son is urged to guard his lips and eyes as well as his heart. He should put away "crookedness of mouth" and "perverse lips." This is a mouth that falsifies the truth. The admonition has a twofold application. First, he should not indulge in this kind of speech himself. When evil thoughts are allowed to crystallize into words, wickedness has reached an advanced level. Second, he should not associate with those who are guilty of perverse speech (4:24).

He should let his eyes "look right on." Shifty eyes indicate hypocrisy and falsehood. A student of wisdom fixes his gaze on a goal. This admonition promotes simplicity of aim or principle, singleness of motive. The moral gaze must be firmly fixed, for when it wanders, the purity of the soul is imperiled (4:25).

The son is urged to watch the course of his feet as well. He must avoid every false step. He should "make plain" (lit., "weigh") the path of his feet. The sense of the passage is this: weigh the options, choose the right course, and persevere in that course of action. The son is urged to make sure that all of his ways are "established," i.e., well considered. From this path he should not turn to the right hand or to the left. Nothing should be permitted to draw him off the right way, neither adversity, nor prosperity, nor temptation of any kind. By staying on this right path the son would remove his foot from evil, i.e., avoid wrong conduct and foolish extremes (4:26-27).

Discourse Eight
WISDOM IN SEXUAL MATTERS
Proverbs 5:1-23

One of the hardest areas of life for a young man to follow the path of wisdom is in that of sexual morality. The teacher glanced at this topic in 2:15-19. He now develops at length his teaching on the evils of adultery and the beauty of marriage. After an appeal for attention

(vv. 1-6), the teacher issues warnings against adultery (vv. 7-14), exhortations to enjoy marriage (vv. 15-20), and a final warning against adultery (vv. 21-23).

A. Deception of the Adulteress (5:1-6).

The appeal in the eighth wisdom discourse seems to be addressed to older youth, perhaps even married men. The teacher again addresses his pupil as "my son." The perceived filial relationship between a teacher and his student is often what keeps the latter on the straight and narrow path. The teacher here uses the possessive "my" to define the wisdom for which he begs attention. It is not merely wisdom in the abstract which he begs his son (pupil) to hear, but that which the teacher, by personal experience, knows to be true wisdom (5:1).

Two reasons are set forth as to why attentiveness to wisdom is in order. First, the teacher's wisdom would aid the student to preserve "discretion" (*mezimmot*), i.e., reflection. The word is plural to indicate intensification. Wisdom would put restraints upon the thought processes and would result in resolutions which would display themselves in prudent behavior. Second, wisdom would also help the student's lips to preserve "knowledge." The idea here is that one who possesses the knowledge of wisdom will not permit to escape from his lips anything at odds with godliness (5:2).

In life one must cope with competing voices which appeal for attention and allegiance. The teacher knows that his competition is formidable. The lips of a "strange woman" (an adulteress) "drip honey," i.e., her words are enticing, flattering, pleasant to hear. Her "mouth" (lit., "palate") "is smoother than oil." The reference is again to what comes out of her mouth. Her words are both plausible and persuasive. Only wisdom will enable a young man to correctly evaluate the true and deadly character of her seductive speech (5:3).

The adulteress promises pleasure, freedom from danger, excitement never before experienced. In the end, however, the association with her would be as bitter as "wormwood." "Wormwood" is a bitter and deadly plant of which several species grow in Palestine. It is used throughout the Old Testament as a symbol of the painful and distasteful consequences of adultery. The adulteress promises what she cannot deliver. Her honey-coated words turn to wormwood. Her smooth enticements become a sharp two-edged sword, lit., "a sword of mouths," i.e., a sword of extreme sharpness (5:4).

The feet of the adulteress "go down to death." The idea is that her immoral lifestyle hastens her demise. Those who get involved with her share her fate in a premature trip to Sheol, the abode of the dead. The adulteress leads her victims to ruin because "she walks not in the path of life." The Hebrew seems to emphasize that the adulteress is far removed from even entering the "way of life," i.e., the safe course which has life more abundant as its goal. Her ways are "unstable," lit., go to and fro, like the uncertain and dangerous steps of the drunk or the blind. Yet she does not perceive the danger in her lifestyle (5:5-6).

B. Dangers of Adultery (5:7-14).

Again the teacher asks for attentiveness to his words. He addresses this appeal to his "children," using the plural as in 4:1. The following verses, however, use the singular. This has the effect of personalizing his remarks (5:7).

The adulteress and her house are to be avoided as if they were infected with some mortal disease. Why should the student stay far removed from the house of the adulteress? The teacher offers five reasons (5:8; cf. 1 Cor 6:18).

First, in pursuing the harlot the young man will waste his youth. In her house he would lose his "vigor" and his "years," i.e., the most useful and valuable years of life. The thought may also be that his years would be cut short through the immoral lifestyle. In the harlot's house he might also confront "the cruel." This has been taken to refer to (1) the harlot herself who has no love for the youth and no concern about his well being; (2) the husband of the harlot who would deal mercilessly with his wife's lover; and (3) the associates of the harlot who might fall upon the young man and strip him of his possessions. The term "cruel" is masculine singular, but it may here be used in a collective sense. By hanging around such rough places the youth would surely have his days cut short (5:9).

Second, in the harlot's house the youth would squander his wealth. There "strangers" would be filled with his "strength," i.e., that which he had earned by the sweat of his brow. Such profligate actions might deprive his own family of food and clothing. The "strangers" and "aliens" would be the panderers who share the woman's immoral earnings. These "strangers" would be indifferent to the ruin of the young man (5:10).

Third, the immoral lifestyle would cause the young man to lose his health as well as his wealth. In the end his "flesh" and "body" would be consumed, i.e., his physical powers would be exhausted through the dissolute living. Perhaps there is an allusion here to venereal diseases which most often are contracted by those who sleep in the harlot's bed. At the end when the body has wasted away, the profligate will "moan" (naham), lit., "groan." This is the loud wail which reveals the mental anguish of a hopeless soul who sees no remedy for his misspent life (5:11).

Fourth, the immoral lifestyle leads to self-reproach. He would lament the day when he hated "instruction" (musar), those stern warnings intended to dissuade him from approaching a harlot. He would one day painfully remember how he had despised in his heart the "reproof" which followed his earlier flirtations with the adulteress. He would chastise himself for not having listened to his godly teachers (5:12-13).

Fifth, the immoral lifestyle jeopardizes one's standing in the congregation of the Lord. Illicit sexual activity was an "evil" worthy of death under the Old Testament law. Only thus could the "evil" be removed from Israel (cf. Deut 22:22). On reflection it will be brought home to the philanderer that he had committed such an "evil" in the midst of the congregation. He thus had placed his very life in danger by judicial execution. To be cut off from God's people is to place one's eternal destiny in jeopardy (5:14).

C. Delights of Marriage (5:15-19).

The teacher now outlines several reasons why the godly man should confine his sexual energies to the marriage relationship. First, the teacher reminds his pupil that he has chosen a wife. In this passage "well," "cistern" and "fountain" (v. 18) are metaphorical for one's wife. This figure emphasizes the value of the wife (cf. Song 4:15). In a region starved for water, the cistern or well was one of the most valuable possessions and adjuncts of the Eastern house. The passage is not indicating that a wife is a mere possession. She is the "cistern" of her husband because he had chosen her as his spouse, his companion for life.

Second, the wife is the God-ordained and socially sanctioned source of satisfaction for the sexual urges. "Drinking water" from one's cistern is metaphorical for sexual intercourse. The idea is: one should find contentment and satisfaction of natural impulses with his own wife. The figure points to the pure, innocent, and chaste nature of the physical pleasures of marriage. Just as water of the cistern and well are pure and suitable for drinking, so marital sex is wholesome. Just as water quenches thirst, so marital intercourse is designed to satisfy the "thirst" for physical intimacy which most human beings experience (5:15; cf.1 Cor 7:9).

Third, in legitimate marriage one may make a contribution to society through the children which he generates. If the "well" and "cistern" in the previous verse refer to one's wife, the "fountains" and "rivers of waters" here refer to children, the legitimate issue of lawful marriage.[7] While procreation is a worry in an illegitimate relationship, in lawful marriage one need not fear if conception takes place. On the contrary, a lawful marriage is blessed with many children who may go forth into the streets for the public good (5:16).

Fourth, in chaste intercourse with a lawful wife one can insure that offspring are one's own. Promiscuous and unlawful intercourse throws paternity into doubt. To underscore the importance of legitimate birth the Hebrew reads literally, "Let them [the children] belong to you, to you alone." The last clause in verse 17 points to the repugnant situation to be avoided: "and not to strangers with you." The multiple sex partners of the harlot bring into question the paternity of any children born to her (5:17).

Fifth, in marital intercourse a wife can and will be blessed. "Let your fountain [wife] be blessed." She is his "fountain" because she is the source of his legitimate children. An Israelite wife regarded herself, and was regarded by others, as "blessed" or happy when she produced legitimate offspring for her husband. The principle here, however, goes beyond procreation. Giving happiness to one's spouse is one of the legitimate goals of marital sexual intercourse (5:18a).

Sixth, in marriage one can experience "joy." The word encompasses here sexual pleasure as well as all the joys of sharing life together. The expression "wife of your youth" has been taken to refer to (1) a young wife; (2) a wife chosen in one's youth; and (3) a wife to whom one has devoted the best years of his life. The sexual relationship is most fulfilling when those involved have shared the many experiences of life together (5:18).

Seventh, the man should fix his affection on his wife. He should regard her as "a lovely hind" and a "graceful doe." In the ancient world such comparisons were flattering. To compare one's wife to the graceful and beautiful wild deer of the area was the ultimate compliment. Physical attractiveness is part of the bond which holds husband and wife together (5:19a).

Eighth, the love of a wife will refresh and fully satisfy the husband. The breasts of the wife are regarded by the teacher as a source of attraction and sexual satisfaction for the husband. Probably the term "breasts" here is symbolic for the entire sexual relationship. The language clearly indicates that sex in marriage had more than procreation as its purpose. Husband and wife were to enjoy each other's bodies.

Ninth, the godly man should be "ravished" (lit. "intoxicated, reeling") always with the love of his wife. The husband is to keep his eye focused on his wife and her alone. He must determine to regard her as the most beautiful of all women. He must refuse to allow any other to capture his fancy. The point is that a healthy sexual relationship is the God-appointed way of avoiding illicit sexual entanglements (5:19b).

D. Disaster of Adultery (5:20-23).

Fidelity is not merely a duty which a man owes his spouse; marital faithfulness is a religious duty as well. That is the thesis of the closing verses of the eighth discourse. Four arguments are put forward underscoring the tragedy of adultery.

First, marital infidelity has nothing to commend it. Why would a man get involved in an adulterous affair? Why does a man become so infatuated with a strange woman? Surely it is the prompting of his lower nature, sensuality in its lowest form. No valid argument can be advanced in favor of adultery and promiscuity. Such actions defile the image of God in man (5:20).

505

Second, sexual infidelity, though often hidden from view, is known to God: "For the ways of man are before the eyes of God." The Lord "watches" (lit., "weighs") all his paths. On the basis of this divine appraisal, rewards or punishments are dispensed (5:21).

Third, the iniquities of the wicked man [here specifically the adulterer] will overtake him. Divine justice is seen in that the wicked get ensnared in their own iniquities. This general principle is especially true of adultery. One act leads to another, especially if punishment for the sin is delayed. Each repetition of sin becomes like a strand in the rope with which a sinner is held in bondage (5:22).

Fourth, the adulterer will die in his sin "without instruction," i.e., having repudiated moral guidance. Like a drunk man oblivious to the danger before him, he will stagger to his ruin. The thought is that he will die without a gleam of hope or satisfaction (5:23). While the teacher probably had in mind physical death, the New Testament paints an even more grim picture of the fate of adulterers (1 Cor 6:9; Heb 13:4).

Discourse Nine
THREATS TO MARITAL HAPPINESS
Proverbs 6:1-19

Having discussed in the previous discourse the happiness of the married life and the dangers of the promiscuous life, the teacher now speaks of certain dangers to marital bliss. He speaks of reckless pledges (vv. 1-5), sloth (vv. 6-11), mischievousness (vv. 12-15), seven vices (vv. 16-19), and adultery (vv. 20-35).

A. Warning against Reckless Pledges (6:1-5).

The teacher warned his pupil of the consequences of becoming "surety" for either a neighbor or a stranger. In such agreements one pledged to pay the debt incurred by another if he failed to repay it. "Striking the hands" was a symbolic act sealing the agreement. This was equivalent to the modern practice of shaking hands on a deal. The act no doubt was accomplished before witnesses. The hand which was stricken was that of the creditor who thereby received assurance that the responsibility of the debtor was undertaken by the surety. So the pupil is envisioned pledging himself on behalf of a neighbor, and making the pledge to a "stranger," i.e., the money lender who may have actually been a foreigner (6:1).

In agreeing to stand surety for a friend one is "snared" by the words of his own mouth. Agreeing to back the loan is fraught with danger both to the friendship and to the financial stability of one's immediate family. The phrase "with the words of your mouth" is repeated in the verse to stress that the entanglements in which the surety is involved are the result of his own indiscretion (6:2).

If he had inadvertently fallen into this trap, a person should immediately try to extricate himself. The teacher suggests a four step process. First, he should go and humble himself (lit., "trample upon himself") before the debtor to beseech him to release him from the obligation which he had assumed to back the debt. Second, if this failed, he must "urge" (lit., "beset him violently") until the surety agreement has been nullified. The Hebrew verb suggests raging at the neighbor, refusing to take "no" for an answer (6:3).

Third, the teacher advises that his student seek the release from the pledge immediately. He should not leave it to the next day. He should allow nothing to take precedence over this urgent matter. Fourth, he should struggle valiantly to free himself from his obligations as a trapped bird or deer tries desperately to tear away from a snare or trap (6:4-5).

B. Warning against Slothfulness (6:6-11).

Making stupid and unnecessary financial commitments has the potential of making one a pauper. Sloth or indolence even more surely leads to misfortune and ruin. In developing this theme, the teacher calls upon the "sluggard" ('atsel) to do two things.

First, the teacher calls upon the "sluggard" to learn a lesson from the ant. In her "ways" the ant manifests industry and foresight. From her the naive can learn wisdom. The ant is not forced to toil by ruthless rulers and cruel taskmasters to store up provisions. Yet the ant is busy throughout the summer, and especially during the harvest, gathering her "bread," i.e., food, for the winter. The point here is that the natural impulse is to care for oneself, to exercise foresight in preparing for the future. Even the humble insects have that much sense (6:6-8).

Second, the teacher called upon his student to get up and about by daybreak. Sleeping into the waking hours of the day is regarded by him as a serious character fault. Come work time, the sluggard always pleads for a little more rest, a little more "folding of the hands." Apparently the common attitude of rest was to lay on one's back with the hands folded upon the chest (6:9-10).

Why advise the student to arise early and get to work? Because poverty and want have a way of catching up to a person like a stalker or an armed man (lit., a man of shield), an invading soldier who ravages a town. Sloth increases with practice. There can be no escape from poverty for such a lazy person (6:11).

C. Warning against Mischievousness (6:12-15).

Sloth leads to the vices which are next enumerated. The sluggard often develops into a treacherous and deceitful individual. Mischievousness leads to the same end as slothfulness.

1. Basic description (6:12a). The teacher now describes the kind of person which he has in mind. First, he is "a man of Belial," i.e., a worthless or good-for-nothing person.[8] The Hebrew term always carries with it the idea of moral turpitude. In this passage the "man of Belial" is further described as a "wicked man" (*'ish 'aven*), lit., a man of vanity or iniquity. A wicked man is one who is deficient in moral consciousness, and who goes about to work wickedness and do hurt and injury to others (6:12a).

2. External characteristics (6:12b-13). The teacher now indicates several characteristics of the worthless and wicked man. First, he "walks with a false mouth," lit., perversity of mouth. The verb "walk" points to the way in which he conducts his life. His life and conduct are marked by craftiness, deceit, perversion and misrepresentation. What comes out of the mouth reveals what controls the inward thoughts (6:12b).

Second, the worthless-wicked man "winks" with the eye in order to insinuate something evil about a neighbor. Third, he "signals" (lit., "scrapes") with his feet. This may refer to some gesture by which a victim is singled out. Fourth, he "points" (lit., instructs) "with his fingers." Perhaps the thought is that he uses his fingers in mockery or derision; or alternatively, by some action with the fingers he excuses himself from telling the truth. The picture here is of one who uses all the members of his body for evil purposes (6:13).

3. *Internal disposition (6:14)*. From the external features of the worthless-wicked person, the teacher turns to the internal. First, mischief (*tahpukhot*) is in the heart of the worthless-wicked person. There he cherishes his jealousy, his hatred, his malice and his ill will. Second, in his heart or mind he is continually devising "evil," i.e., ways to harm or humiliate a neighbor. His mind is a wicked workshop. His perverse actions are the result of deliberate premeditation. Third, he "spreads strife," lit., he sends forth or foments strifes (plural). He takes delight in breaking up a friendship, a marriage, a congregation, a community. He opposes that civility which is essential to society, that harmony which is essential to individual happiness.

4. *Ultimate ruin (6:15)*. Great sins have great punishments. Retribution awaits this person of malice and deceit. It will overtake him unexpectedly, at the very time when he thinks his evil schemes are succeeding. The teacher is probably referring to sudden death. Alternatively, he may be indicating the actions of the victims once they discover the fraud and malice of the worthless-wicked man. The wicked person would thereby be "broken" like a vessel of pottery. For him there is no hope of "healing" or recovery. Either he is dead, or, if alive, never again trusted by those he had duped.

D. Warning against Seven Vices (6:16-19).

The evil qualities of deceit and malice which are disastrous to man are hateful also to God. The X+1 formula (six . . . yes seven) appears here for the first time in the book. It is a way of stating something indefinite, that is, the list is not exhaustive. Seven things follow which are regarded as "abomination" (absolutely repugnant) to the Lord, lit., "unto his soul" (6:16).

First, God hates "haughty eyes." Of course it is not merely the look which is meant, but the temperament which the look expresses. The sin of pride is placed first on the list because it is at the bottom of all disobedience and rebellion against God's moral law.

Second, God hates "a lying tongue." Lying is hateful to God because he is the God of truth (Ps 5:6; 120:3-4). Lying is the willful perversion of the truth with the intent to harm another. The sin is committed mainly with the mouth, but also when by any other means a false impression is deliberately conveyed.

Third, God hates hands that shed innocent blood. Murder is here in view. The legal execution of a person as a judicial sentence is sanctioned by the law of Moses. "Innocent" blood refers to those who have done no injury. The death of an innocent person cries to heaven for vengeance and triggers the ultimate judgment from the Lord (6:17).

Fourth, God hates "a heart which devises wicked thoughts," lit., thoughts of iniquity. The reference is to schemes which harm or humiliate another (v. 14a; 3:29). A person must not allow his mind to become the Devil's workshop. Implicit here is the doctrine of the omniscience of God. He knows those secret thoughts. In this list of seven things God hates, the heart occupies the central position. Those vices already mentioned as well as those yet to be mentioned flow from this fountain.

Fifth, God hates "feet that are swift in running [lit., hurrying to run] to evil" (cf. Isa 59:7). The language points beyond merely sliding into sin. Here is one who shows eagerness to do what is wrong. If God hates the evil plans, he hates doubly the implementation of those plans (6:18).

Sixth, God hates "a false witness who breathes out lies" (cf. Exod 20:16). Perjury may be employed to ruin the innocent or to free the guilty. Perjury destroys any possibility of justice, and thus the very foundations of society.

Seventh, God hates those that "sow discord among brethren," i.e., friends, associates, members of the same circle. The words "among brethren" underscore the diabolical nature of this sin which destroys the harmony and unity of those who ought to live together in brotherly affection. The implication is that God smiles on brotherly love and frowns on any who would disrupt it (6:19).

Discourse Ten
WARNINGS AGAINST ADULTERY
Proverbs 6:20-35

The teacher now returns to that subject which he treated in the eighth discourse. The tendency of men in general, and young men in

particular, to commit sins of impurity is no doubt the reason this subject is opened anew.

A. The Value of Wisdom (6:20-24).

The teacher eases into the main point of this discourse by extolling
the general and specific advantages of wisdom.

1. *General advantages of wisdom (6:20-23).* Again the teacher
admonishes his pupil to "keep the commandment" of his father, and
not forsake "the teaching of the mother" (cf. 1:8). Godly parents who
honored the marriage vows are cited as an encouragement for the
younger generation to resist the attraction of illicit passion. The
instructions of those godly parents should never be forgotten. A youth
should internalize that teaching ("bind them continually upon your
heart"). The "heart" suggests that this teaching should be linked to
the affections. This teaching should also be the focus of the outer
man as well ("tie them about your neck"). Godly parental teaching
should be like an ornament enhancing the beauty of one's moral life
(6:20-21; cf. Exod 13:9).

Wisdom as taught by mother and father would supply guidance for
the young man in his "walk," i.e., in the performance of his daily
tasks.[9] Thus he would not stumble or go astray. In the night when
there was danger of unexpected attack, wisdom would watch over
him. In the morning, wisdom "shall talk" to the son both advising and
encouraging. Thus will he be sustained day by day in the path of righteousness. The divine "commandment"(*mitsvah*) and "teaching"
(*torah*) illuminate the right path through life (cf. Ps 119:105). The
"reproofs of instruction" (*musar*), i.e., are the reproofs whose object
is the discipline of the soul and the moral elevation of the character.
Such reproofs are "the way of life," i.e., they lead to life; they are
conducive to the prolongation of life.[10] The warnings of Scripture
restrain a person from unwise conduct and act as a guide for the
proper way of living (6:22-23).

2. *Specific advantages of wisdom (6:24).* Godly wisdom not only
gives general guidance to a young man; if heeded, it is a hedge
against the sins of impurity, fornication and adultery. Wisdom will
keep the godly man away from "the evil woman," i.e., the woman
who has abandoned biblical morality. Such a woman lures men into

her bed with "the smoothness of the alien tongue," i.e., the language used by the alien woman. What the evil woman proposes is foreign to the righteousness of the holy covenant. The reference is to flattery, coarse speech, flirtations, invitations to enjoy illicit sex, exaggerated descriptions of the pleasure to be derived from such acts, assurances of impunity and discreetness. Godly wisdom warns of the deceitfulness of the words of such a woman (6:24).

B. Admonitions of Wisdom (6:25).

Two admonitions are now put forward by the teacher. First, the godly man is admonished not to "lust" (*chamadh*) after the beauty of the harlot in his heart (cf. Exod 20:17). The admonition is to suppress the very first inclinations to unchaste desires (cf. Matt 5:28). If a man lets his mind become engrossed with thoughts of a woman who is forbidden to him, he willfully places himself in the way of temptation. He must diligently guard his heart against ever entertaining the thought that he might under the right circumstances commit the act of adultery.

Second, the teacher admonishes the young man not to be taken in by external allurement of the immoral woman. Harlots knew the art of using their eyes seductively. Possibly there is here an allusion to the custom of Eastern women to enhance their eyes by painting the eyelids. In any case, the godly man must not be seduced by the amorous glances of a woman (6:25).

C. Arguments against Adultery (6:26-35).

In the remaining verses of chapter 6 the teacher sets forth a series of practical reasons why a young man should avoid the evil woman and the sins of fornication and adultery.

First, the promiscuous lifestyle often leads to the loss of temporal possessions. "On account of a harlot a man is brought to a loaf of bread," i.e., he is brought to poverty. When she gets through with him, all of his substance will have been exhausted, save enough for only the basic necessities of life.

Second, he who gets involved with an adulteress (lit., the wife of a man) places his life in jeopardy, since adultery was a capital crime under the law of Moses (cf. Lev 20:10; Deut 22:22). Thus the immoral woman is said to be hunting "the precious life," i.e., looking for victims whose lives might be placed in jeopardy through an affair. The phrase "precious life" (*nephesh yeqarah*) indicates the high value of life (cf. Matt 16:26). For a momentary passion one places in jeopardy his life here and, in the light of the New Testament, his life hereafter (6:26).

Third, the adulterer always gets burned. A man cannot take fire into his bosom, i.e., the folds of his garments, without burning his clothing. Nor can one walk barefoot upon hot coals without burning his feet. So one does not "go in to his neighbor's wife" with impunity. "Whoever touches her shall not go unpunished." The punishment would come (1) from the judicial officers; (2) from the husband of the woman; or (3) from God himself. The flames of lust will certainly be visited with punishment and with stings of conscience (6:27-29).

Fourth, an adulterer will find no pity from his contemporaries. Should a person steal because he is driven by sheer necessity, his fellow men may feel some sympathy for him. Still he does not escape punishment. He must restore "sevenfold," i.e., many times more than he stole.[11] The thief might end up forfeiting "all the substance of his house," i.e., all he possesses. Thus theft may reduce someone to poverty. So he who commits adultery forfeits even more, for he forfeits his own life. How stupid! For a moment of gratification he places his very life in jeopardy. If a man will not hear the teaching of wisdom with its moral and social imperatives, perhaps he would listen to this line of reasoning. It is in the self-interest of every man to avoid adulterous relationships (6:30-32).

Fifth, adulterous affairs often lead to "wounds." The reference is probably to the bodily injury inflicted by the outraged husband of the adulteress.[12] In addition, the guilty party would receive "dishonor," i.e., he would incur the censure of his fellow men. "His reproach shall not be wiped away." For the rest of his life the adulterer will bear the stigma of his sin (6:33).

Sixth, adultery unleashes a furious response from the husband of the woman involved. "Jealousy is the rage of a man." The wife's infidelity gives rise to implacable fury which relentlessly seeks revenge. "He will not spare in the day of vengeance," i.e., he will have no pity on the culprit. He would reject every appeal advanced to save him from the legal consequences of his attack upon the adulterer. Offers of monetary compensation to drop the charges of adultery would be refused. Such payments in cases of adultery were not sanctioned in the law, but no doubt were often made in actual practice. The teacher warns, however, that a man of integrity would not accept any amount of cash payment to ignore the affront to his honor (6:34-35).

ENDNOTES

1. So A. Cohen, *Proverbs* in Soncino Books of the Bible (London: Soncino, 1946), p. 21. Most moderns assume that the teacher here has assumed the role of a father as in discourses 1,3-6.

2. The term *yachidh* is used of Isaac (Gen 22:2,12) by Abraham at a time when Ishmael was still living. Bathsheba, the mother of Solomon, had other sons (2 Sam 5:14; 1 Chr 3:5). Yet Solomon was beloved by his mother as if he were an only son.

3. A "crown of glory" in the New Testament is always associated with heavenly honors. See Heb 2:9; 2 Tim 4:8; `1 Pet 5:4; Rev 2:10. Proverbs, however, seems to be anticipating temporal honors.

4. Maclaren, cited by A. Cohen, *Proverbs*, p. 23.

5. W.J. Deane holds that it is the father rather than the grandfather who is speaking in these verses. See "Proverbs" in *The Pulpit Commentary* (New York: Funk & Wagnalls, 1909), p. 90.

6. Jesus also emphasized the heart as fundamental to moral conduct: Matt 15:19; Mark 7:21-23; Luke 6:43-45.

7. The NASB regards 5:16 as two questions. In this view, the "fountains" and "rivers of water" would figuratively represent the procreative powers. The thrust then would be: Let generative power act freely within the marriage relationship, but not outside.

8. The designation "Belial" has different meanings in other passages. It may designate (1) those who have fallen into idolatry and seek to induce others to do the same (Deut 13:13); (2) those who profane sacred places (1 Sam 1:16); (3) wicked men in general (e.g., Nahum 1:11). In the New Testament the term Belial is descriptive of Satan as the representative of all that is bad (2 Cor 6:15).

9. The "going," "sleeping," and "awaking" in 6:22 occur in the same order in Deuteronomy (6:7; 11:19) from which the ideas of this and the preceding verse are derived.

10. The clause "reproofs for discipline are the way of life" has also been interpreted to mean (1) reproofs correct errors and hence enhance the happiness of life; or (2) reproofs are necessary if one is to achieve perfection in life.

11. The Mosaic law required the restoration of stolen property to be double, fourfold, or fivefold (Exod 22:1-4). Only here is a sevenfold restoration mentioned. The term here is probably to be a poetic way of saying "manifold" restoration.

12. Another view is that the "wounds" in 6:33 are scars which resulted from the scourging inflicted upon the adulterer. The Scripture, however, does not mention scourging as a punishment for adultery.

CHAPTER TWENTY-FIVE

Wisdom and Her Rival
Proverbs 7-9

Discourses eleven through thirteen place in juxtaposition two ways of life. The principles which govern these lifestyles are personified as two women: Lady Wisdom and Harlot Folly.

Discourse Eleven
WARNING AGAINST ADULTERY
Proverbs 7:1-27

Again the teacher takes up the subject of adultery. In this discourse, however, he treats the subject from a different perspective. He draws a contrast between Lady Wisdom and the adulteress.

A. Introduction (7:1-5).

The eleventh discourse is introduced by the customary exhortation (cf. 2:1; 3:1). The student is urged to "keep my words" and "lay up" as a precious treasure "my commandments." If he keeps these commandments, he will live, i.e., experience the more abundant life. The student, therefore, should regard the instruction of his teacher "as the apple of your eye," i.e., the pupil of the eye.[1] This is a proverbial expression for anything extremely precious. The sense of sight depends on the undamaged condition of the eye. Thus the thought is, Make my teaching as precious to you as your eyesight. The student also should bind those godly precepts like rings on his fingers, i.e., keep them always before his eyes. He should write them upon the table of his heart (cf. 3:3; 6:21). The instruction of godly men should be internalized, should be made the guiding principle of one's life (7:1-3).

In a more poetic vain, the teacher urges his student to embrace wisdom warmly. He should regard wisdom personified as his "sister." The brother-sister relationship expresses love, purity and confidence. A warm association with a godly sister causes a man to respect women in general and avoid harlots in particular. "Understanding," the twin sister of wisdom, should be regarded as one's "kinswoman" (moda'), i.e., familiar friend. The son should let prudence and sound sense be as dear to him as a close friend. The twin sisters of wisdom and understanding will keep the naive youth from being deceived by the alien or strange woman, i.e., the harlot. When the heart is filled with the love of something good, it is armed against the seductions which would lead one astray from the Lord (7:4-5).

B. A Street Encounter (7:6-12).

From the window of his house the teacher could look out into the street. He looked through the "lattice" which allowed him to see all that passed in the street without being himself visible from without. There he witnessed a social evil which was demoralizing the entire community. Against this evil he felt compelled to wage a vigorous battle (7:6).

First, his eyes spotted a young man who was associating with the "thoughtless ones" (peta'yim), i.e., the inexperienced or simple ones. Such are those most easily led astray. Among them the teacher discerned a young man "devoid of understanding." Without any deliberate intention of sinning, this youth had put himself in the way of temptation (7:7).

The young man was passing down the street where the harlot lived. What was his intent? Was he merely curious? Did he even know that the harlot lived on that corner? In any case, the young man was in danger. He was about to enter into a temptation with which he could not cope (7:8).

After dark, in the cool of the evening, the youth continued to "hang out" with his friends in the vicinity of the harlot's house. Had he been wise, the setting sun would have signaled him to return to his own house. About midnight[2] unexpectedly ("behold!") a harlot approached him. There could be no doubt about her intentions. First, in the East a woman who ventured out of her house into the streets after dark unattended was usually a loose woman. Second, she was dressed in the attire of a harlot (cf. Gen 38:14f.). Whatever this garb was, it was very different from the sober clothing of the pure and modest. Third, she was "cunning of heart" (*netsurath lebh*), i.e., she was acting in secretive way. While deceiving her husband with pledges of her love, she would assure her lovers of the same thing. In truth she loved no one but herself. She sought only to satisfy her evil passion (7:9-10).

The harlot is "boisterous," i.e., she lacks the refinement and dignity of a respectable woman. She is "rebellious" against all moral restraint. "Her feet abide not in her house," i.e., she is a gadabout. She is the exact opposite of the careful, modest housewife who stays at home and manages the affairs of her family. She prowls the streets of the town searching for new victims to conquer. "She lies in wait at every corner," i.e., one of her kind is readily available anywhere in the town. The woman is represented, not as a common prostitute, but as a licentious wife, who, in her unbridled lust, acts the part of a harlot (7:11-12).

C. A Harlot's Enticements (7:13-20).

The wayward wife used several enticements to lure the young man into a liaison. First, she employed bold actions. The harlot approaches the young man, takes hold of him, and kisses him. Like Potiphar's wife, she has no shame (cf. Gen 39:12). Second, she "strengthened her face," i.e., put on a bold and brazen look to correspond with what she was about to say. She then invites him to her house (7:13).

519

Third, the woman used the prospect of a wonderful meal to lure the young man to her house. She had offered "peace offerings" when she had paid her vows to the Lord that day. According to the law, part of the meat of such offerings had to be eaten by the presenter and his/her household in a religious meal. None of the meat was to be left until morning (Lev 7:15f.). The implication is that she had a good supply of meat at home that had to be consumed before daylight. The religious nature of the feast is utterly ignored or forgotten. This woman may be a "stranger" who conformed only outwardly to the law of Moses. In her heart she clung to the impure worship of her native land (7:14).

Fourth, the woman suggests that she needed someone with whom to eat this sumptuous meal. Therefore, she had come forth into the street to seek someone with whom she could party. Her words may also suggest that he was exactly the one for whom she had been looking. Thus she adds a bit of flattery to her proposal. She suggests that others had been passed by just so she might spend the evening with this young man. He was the very lover for whom she was looking (7:15).

Fifth, the harlot hints at a sexual tryst by describing her bed. It was adorned with expensive covers imported from Egypt (lit., "striped coverings, Egyptian linen"). The material must have been expensive and highly prized. The young man probably had never laid his head on more luxurious pillows. Sixth, the wayward wife had perfumed that bed with various spices in anticipation of an evening of romance. Myrrh, aloes and cinnamon were dissolved or mixed with water, and then sprinkled on the couch (7:16-17).[3]

Seventh, all subtlety is put aside as the harlot finally asks the young man to sleep with her. She promises an entire night of love-making. "Let us take our fill of love until the morning." Having promised quantity of sexual expression, she hints of its quality: "Let us enjoy ourselves with loves." The use of the plural suggests either intensity or variety in the love-making (7:18).

Eighth, she tries to eliminate any fear that the young man might have about entering the house of a married woman. "The man"—a contemptuous reference to the harlot's husband—was out of town on a trip. Therefore, there was no danger of either interruption or detec-

520

tion. Her language conveys the thought that she has no sense of obligation to her husband, and certainly no affection for him. The youth need not fear any retaliation from him, for he will never know. The husband had taken with him a large amount of cash suggesting that he would be away for some time. He would not come home until the "full moon" some days hence, since v. 9 suggests that the meeting took place on a moonless night (7:19-20).

D. A Youth's Indiscretion (7:21-22a).

The youth could not resist this frontal attack by a woman who apparently was skilled in such matters. His fall occurred in four steps. First, the youth yielded in his mind. "She caused him to yield with her persuasive words" (leqach). In 4:2 this term was used of Lady Wisdom's speech. It may have been deliberately chosen in sarcastic contrast to the true and ennobling doctrine of wisdom. The tempted youth has the choice of following virtuous or vicious leqach (7:21a).[4]

Second, she "drew him away" with her smooth talk. His body followed the lead of his blinded mind, albeit it reluctantly, no doubt, at first. The woman takes the youth by the arm and begins to lead him toward her house (7:21b). Third, the youth "goes after her suddenly." All at once his resistance gives way. He hastens after her to the house (7:22a).

Fourth, the youth meets with terrible disaster. He goes as an animal led to the slaughter, oblivious to the danger which lies ahead. He goes "as a fool," i.e., a madman, to the punishment which awaits him. He goes as a bird swooping down to take the bait in a snare. There he will remain until an arrow pierces his liver, i.e., he dies. He does not realize that he follows the harlot at the cost of his life (7:22b-23).

E. Exhortations (7:24-27).

The teacher began by addressing his words to an individual student. Now he turns to young men generally. He realizes how necessary his warning is to all who are strong in passion, weak in will and wanting in experience. Such need to listen carefully to what the teacher says. The teacher urges youth not to allow their hearts to turn to the ways of a harlot. Actions proceed from desire. Remove the desire, and the illicit action will never take place (7:24-25).

The teacher offers good reasons for his appeal. The harlot has "cast down [to Sheol] many wounded." Her course is marked with ruined souls as a ruthless conqueror leaves a field of battle strewn with corpses. A "mighty host" of men have lost their lives pursuing harlots. One should regard the harlot's house as "the ways of Sheol," i.e., at her house many paths to Sheol, the abode of the dead, have their beginning. Sexual immorality leads to other vices and crimes which have death as their end (7:26-27).

Discourse Twelve
THE EXCELLENCE OF WISDOM
Proverbs 8:1-36

The steamy scene of chapter 7 gives way in chapter 8 to a wholesome picture. In the previous chapter an impure woman entices a young man to follow the paths of immortality. In chapter 8 a more beautiful woman—Lady Wisdom—urges young men to follow paths of nobility, integrity and fidelity.

A. Wisdom's Call (8:1-5).

Wisdom calls for the attention of all young people. She selects the more conspicuous sites—"the high places by the way"—for the purpose of attracting the largest number of listeners. She stands, not on dark corners as the harlot of chapter 7, but at the crossroads (lit., the house of the paths). There Lady Wisdom takes her stand. "Beside the gates" and "doors" to the city she cries aloud where she is sure of an audience (8:1-3).

Lady Wisdom appeals to persons of all classes, both "men" (*'ishim*, the upper crust) and the sons of men (*bene 'adam*), i.e., the masses who are taken up with material interest. She addresses especially the "thoughtless," i.e., those easily influenced for good or evil and "fools" (*kesilim*), i.e., the intellectually heavy and dull (cf. 1:22). Such are desperately in need of "prudence" (cf. 1:4) and an "understanding heart" (cf. 2:2).

B. Wisdom's Worth (8:6-11).

The teacher declares that he is speaking "princely utterances." The

522

idea is that his words would proceed from his mouth with the nobility of truth and rectitude. "Wickedness" (*resha'* = the contrary of moral truth and right) is an "abomination" to the lips of this teacher, i.e., it is totally repugnant to him. He would never deliberately utter that which is wicked. His words are spoken in righteousness. There is nothing "perverse" or "crooked"—no distortion of the truth, in his words. All is straightforward and direct (8:6-8).

Wisdom's words are "plain" (lit., in front) "to him who understands." The idea is that the person who is willing to receive the truth shall be at once able to recognize it as such. Those who "find knowledge" will recognize the teacher's doctrine as "right." When one opens his heart to receive divine instruction, he is rewarded by having his understanding enlightened (8:9).

The instruction (or discipline) of the teacher is more valuable than silver. One should prefer it more than the purest gold or rubies. Nothing to which men attach value can be compared to wisdom (8:10-11).

C. Wisdom's Claims (8:12-21).

Wisdom personified now speaks for herself. She claims to "dwell" with prudence. The idea is that wisdom possesses that cleverness and tact which is needed for the practical purposes of life. Therefore, whoever associates with wisdom will become acquainted with "prudence." Wisdom possesses "knowledge of deeds of discretion" or right counsels. She presides over all well-considered designs (8:12).

1. What she hates (8:13). Wisdom now declares in its negative formulation the fundamental proposition which is the foundation of all her teaching. First, the "fear of the Lord," i.e., true faith, "is to hate evil." There can be no fellowship between light and darkness; he who serves the Lord must renounce the works of the devil. Second, true faith hates "pride and arrogance" (cf. 6:17) which are the the opposite of the virtue of humility. Third, true faith hates "the evil way," i.e., any departure from the right way of living. Fourth, true faith hates the perverse tongue, i.e., sins of speech.

2. What she is (8:14-16). Having said what she hates, wisdom now says what she is, and what she can bestow on those who follow her. Wisdom possesses "counsel," i.e., all that can help forward righteousness, and "sound wisdom" (*tushiyyah*), i.e., that which is essen-

tially good and useful to the well being of an individual. The possession of these qualities enables wisdom to give good advice to the perplexed and confused. Wisdom declares "I am understanding," i.e.,
understanding is part of her very nature. Wisdom possesses "power"
to achieve success in life. She enables kings (cf. 1 Kgs 3:9), gover-
nors, princes, nobles and judges to rule justly (8:14-16; cf. Isa 11:2).

3. *What she loves (8:17-18)*. Wisdom declares her love for all
those who love her. They who love virtue and wisdom are regarded
with special favor by God. This explains why those who diligently (lit.,
those who seek early) seek wisdom find her (cf. Matt 7:7). Furthermore, the teacher is assuring his students that the highest gift of life is
within every person's grasp. Wisdom offers to her lovers "riches and
honor," indeed "enduring riches." "Righteousness" is the last reward
that wisdom bestows on her friends. Without righteousness material
blessings would not be worth having. The teacher may have meant
for the term "righteousness" to explain what he meant by "enduring
riches" (8:17-18).

4. *What she offers (8:19-21)*. Wisdom is like a tree which yields
fruit which is better than gold or silver (cf. 3:14). "Fine gold" (*paz*)
indicates gold from which all mixture or alloy has been separated.
This is a further development of the figure of wisdom as a tree which
appeared in 3:18 (8:19).

Using an intensive verb, wisdom declares: "I walk firmly in the way
of righteousness, in the midst of the paths of justice." The idea is that
wisdom does not swerve to one side or the other (cf. 4:27). They that
love wisdom shall inherit "substance," lit., that which exists, or is real,
hence property or possessions. The idea here is that people must
pursue the accumulation of possession in worthy ways as advocated
by Lady Wisdom (8:20-21).

D. Wisdom's Origins (8:22-26).

Wisdom has made high claims for herself in chapter 8. In the verses which follow, however, those claims reach their apex. Wisdom
asserts that she existed before the foundation of the earth.

Yahweh "possessed" (*qanah*) wisdom "at the beginning of his
way," even "before his works of old," i.e., before the process of creation. The meaning of the verb in this context is hotly disputed. Some

modern versions translate the term "created." The text then would say that God created wisdom before he created the earth. In the Book of Proverbs, however, the verb *qanah* elsewhere always means "to possess" (8:22).[5]

Wisdom was "set up" (lit., poured out), i.e., appointed or established, from "everlasting," i.e., the beginning, even before the earth existed. What is here affirmed is that wisdom is superior to all earthly things. Wisdom was there "from the beginning, before the earth was" (8:23).

Using the technique of emphasis by enumeration, wisdom continues to affirm her antiquity. She existed before "the depths," i.e., the great deep of Gen 1:2, and before "the fountains," the subterranean reservoirs which feed the oceans and rivers. Before the mountains or hills "were settled," wisdom was "brought forth" (*chul*). The word figuratively indicates wisdom's conception in the mind of God, and the beginning of her operations. Before God made the earth, the fields, or even the "dust of the world," i.e., the matter of which the physical world was constructed, wisdom was there (8:24-26).

E. Wisdom's Work (8:27-31).

When God stretched out the heavens, wisdom was there. Wisdom cooperated when God "set a circle" on the face of the deep. The reference most likely is to the sky which is called a "circle" because the earth which it covers is round. When he made the skies above the earth (Gen 1:7) and the fountains of the deep below "showed their might," i.e., burst forth with power as during the Flood (Gen 7:11), wisdom was there. She was there when he "appointed the foundations of the earth," i.e., the great mountains, or set for the sea its fixed limit (cf. Gen 1:9). Wisdom was "the craftsman" at the side of God (8:27-29).

As wisdom witnessed the progressive formation of the universe, she was filled with delight. Like a young child she playfully displayed her exuberance before the creator. When the work of creation was finished, wisdom rejoiced in "the habitable world of his earth," i.e., the completed earth made fit for the habitation of living creatures. Especially did wisdom take pleasure in the sons of men (8:30-31).

F. Wisdom's Exhortation (8:32-35).

Since she takes special delight in humankind, wisdom offers herself as a guide in the discovery of true happiness in the world. Those who keep the ways of wisdom will be truly happy. Therefore wisdom pleads with men to hear her instruction (*musar*), to be wise, and to accept that which wisdom wishes to offer. "Watching daily at my gates" has been taken to refer to (1) eager students waiting at the school door for their teacher to appear; (2) clients besieging a great man's doors; (3) Levites guarding the doors of the temple; and (4) a lover at his beloved's gate. He keeps close to the entrance so as to be sure not to miss her whom he longs to see (8:32-33).

For emphasis the thought is repeated: Happy is the man who hearkens to wisdom. Such is one who watches daily at the gates and doors of the house of wisdom so as to be as close as possible to her. Since wisdom is the tree of life (cf. 3:18), whoever finds her finds life. At the same time, that person "finds favor with Yahweh," i.e., the Lord smiles on his life with blessings of various kinds. On the other hand, those who hate wisdom, love, i.e., show preference for, death because the wages of sin is death (8:34-36).

Discourse Thirteen
THE SUPERIORITY OF WISDOM
Proverbs 9:1-18

The thirteenth discourse contains in parabolic form an invitation of wisdom, and that of her rival folly. This unit is an appropriate conclusion to the first division of Proverbs because here the warnings contained in the previous discourses are summarized.

A. The House of Wisdom (9:1-3).

In contrast to the house of immorality described in chapter 7, wisdom (the Hebrew uses the plural of excellency, i.e., profound wisdom) has her own house (cf. 8:34). This house is a mansion, for it contains seven pillars hewn from stone. The reference is to the pillars of the inner court which supported the gallery of the first story. Four of these were in the corners, three in the middle of three sides, while the entrance to the court was through the fourth side of the square. The

526

number seven here may have the symbolic significance of perfection which it often has in Scripture.[6] Wisdom has made and adorned this house to which she invites her pupils (9:1).

In her lovely home Lady Wisdom prepares a banquet of meat and "mixed" drink. Wine which was too fiery to drink was made palatable by mixing water with it. The language is figurative for the food for thought which wisdom provides. The "table" which wisdom furnished was in reality nothing more than a mat spread out before the guest who sat on the ground or reclined on a low couch (9:2).

Wisdom sent forth her "maidens" as messengers to invite selected guests whose presence was particularly desired (cf. Matt 22:3). In addition, wisdom herself issues a general invitation to all who are willing to come. She stands upon the high places of the city so as to achieve maximum exposure for her invitation (9:3).

B. The Invitation of Wisdom (9:4-6).

The "simple" or thoughtless are invited to turn aside to the house of wisdom. Those who lack "understanding" (lit., heart) are those who are teachable. These are invited to partake of the banquet which Lady Wisdom has prepared. The "bread" and "wine" represent all that is needful for nourishment (9:4-5; cf. Isa 55:1).

In order to enter the house of Lady Wisdom young men must leave the ranks of the simpletons. Only then can they find "life." It is not a mere prosperous life on earth that is here envisioned, but something far higher and better (9:6).

C. The Exclusion of Wisdom (9:7-10).

Those who are deliberately evil are not invited to the house of Lady Wisdom, for they would not accept the invitation anyway. "Scorners" are those who are consciously and willfully perverse. They choose the path of evil over that of righteousness. These are prudently excluded by wisdom from the banquet. The one who tries to correct a scorner only gets insulted. "He that reproves a sinner, it is his blot." Reproof of a "wicked man" would boomerang upon the reprover. The idea is that the wicked man's blemish would attach itself to the reprover in that he would be met by the retort: "Who are you to presume to correct me? You are no better than I!" Evil men regard the reprover as a personal enemy and heap upon him abusive words and deeds (9:7).

Reproof is wasted on scorners. They "hate" anyone who would presume to reprove them. Sometimes reproof only hardens and exasperates. On the other hand, a "wise man" and a "righteous man" appreciates correction from any quarter. He grows in wisdom with each rebuke. He learns from his teachers and thus will "increase in learning." The wise are thus rewarded with ever increasing measures of wisdom because they are humble and willing to learn (9:8-9).

Reverence for Yahweh is the "beginning" (techillah), i.e., the essential prerequisite, of wisdom. One has no "understanding" of life if he does not have experiential knowledge of the "All-Holy" (qedoshim). This title for God, which appears only here, is a plural of intensity, and signifies the one who is preeminently holy (9:10).

D. The Incentive of Wisdom (9:11-12).

Wisdom claims to be able to multiply one's days and increase the years of his life. The idea is that by following the path marked out by wisdom one avoids violent and premature death which stalks those who choose the path of evil (cf. 3:2,16; 4:10). Jesus expanded and explained such promises with the concept of eternal life. Those who embrace him have already passed from death to life (9:11).

Each individual has within him the power to choose wisdom and reap the reward, or to remain a scorner and pay the price. One who is wise is wise for himself, i.e., to his own profit. Those who choose to mock godliness and virtue "shall bear it," i.e., incur the penalty for their conduct (9:12).

E. The House of Folly (9:13-15).

Folly, the rival of wisdom, is represented here under the guise of an adulteress. Folly symbolizes a life of vice and evil. The woman folly is described with three adjectives. First, she is "riotous" (homiyyah), i.e., turbulent, and controlled by passion (cf. 7:11). She is quite different from her calm, dignified rival. Second, she is "thoughtless" (petayyuth) in the worst sense of the word, i.e., without safeguard or restraint. She has no moral fiber to resist any temptation. Third, folly "knows nothing" that she ought to know. Willful and persistent ignorance accompanies folly. She goes on her way recklessly ignoring the consequences of her conduct (9:13).

Like Lady Wisdom, folly seeks to make herself known to the masses. First, she sits at the door of her house. She does not send forth her maidens, nor stand in the streets and proclaim her mission. Folly has an easier task. All she has to do is to sit and beckon seductively to her potential clients. Second, folly's house is in the highest, and thus most conspicuous, places of the city. Here again folly mimics her rival (v. 3), for wisdom too cries out in the highest places of the city (9:14).

Folly calls to those who pass by, those who "go right on their ways," without thought of deliberately indulging in unlawful pleasures. As they walk in the path of right and duty she tries to turn them aside to her house. Folly's house is no mansion supported by seven pillars. It is an ordinary habitation. That, however, does not in any way deter those who flock there, for they are drawn by the seductive charms of folly. Her victims disregard the lowliness of her habitation when they are promised uninhibited passion within (9:15).

F. The Invitation of Folly (9:16-17).

Harlot Folly utters an invitation to passers-by which consciously imitates that of Lady Wisdom: "Whoever is simple, let him turn in here" (cf. v. 4). First, folly addresses the "simple" or thoughtless. Lady Wisdom addressed the simple because they were inexperienced and undecided, and might be guided in the right direction. Harlot Folly speaks to the same group because they have not yet made their final choice. They can still be swayed by lower considerations. They can still be led astray. The simple often find it difficult to distinguish between good and evil, false and true, especially when sensual appetite has been aroused. These are easily lured into wickedness. Second, folly addresses those "who lack understanding" just as did Lady Wisdom. These are people who have not yet made a firm resolution to follow the path of virtue. They are teachable, and easily influenced (9:16).

Harlot Folly makes a strong pitch to her potential customers. "Stolen waters are sweet, and bread eaten in secret is pleasant." Here eating and drinking are metaphorical for sexual relations, and "stolen" water points to an adulterous affair. Whereas Lady Wisdom offered

529

meat and wine to her guests, Harlot Folly offers only bread and water! The life of wisdom is rich and satisfying; that of folly is beggarly. Yet Harlot Folly suggests that her bread and water has the charm of being "stolen." It is attractive because it is unlawful. The godly man is to drink water out of his own cistern, i.e., confine his sexual activity to his own wife (5:15). Harlot Folly is suggesting that illicit sexual affairs are more enjoyable than that which godly marriage offers. Furthermore, add to that the secret aspect and the danger of being exposed, and one has a more exciting experience in the house of the harlot (9:17).

G. The End of Folly (9:18).

A simpleton listens to Harlot Folly and enters her house. He soon comes to realize that there is a moral price to be paid for that stolen water and secret bread. Those he finds in that house cannot be said to be living. They are ghosts (repha'im), or perhaps demons of the nether world. Harlot Folly's house is the gateway to Sheol (cf. 2:19; 7:27). Those who enter there are already dead—morally dead, spiritually dead.

ENDNOTES

1. The Hebrew reads literally, "the little man ('ishon) of the eye." The pupil is so called from the miniature reflection of objects seen in the pupil, especially of the person who looks into another's eye.

2. The Hebrew reads literally, "in the little man ('ishon) of the night and darkness." The same expression denotes midnight in 20:20. Just as the pupil of the eye is the dark center in the iris, so is midnight the dark center of the night.

3. Myrrh was imported from Arabia and the coasts of the Red Sea and Persian Gulf. It is a gummy substance possessing an aromatic odor not particularly agreeable to modern taste. Aloes is the juice from the leaves of the aloe plant which grew in India and the Far East. The ancients used the dried root for aromatic purposes. Cinnamon is the fragrant bark of a tree growing in Ceylon and India and the east coast of Africa.

4. A. Cohen, Proverbs in Soncino Books of the Bible (London: Soncino, 1946), p. 42.

5. The modern versions render qanah (1) possessed (NIV; NASB; NKJV); (2) created (RSV; JB); (3) made (BV). The LXX supports the rendering "created." Nonetheless, in the twelve other occurrences it means "to possess."

6. Some see here a reference to the sevenfold gifts of the Holy Spirit which rested on Christ (Isa 11:2). This is not likely. Neither does the "house" have anything to do with Christ's incarnation (John 2:19) nor his work in forming the church which is his body (1 Pet 2:5).

CHAPTER TWENTY-SIX

Contrasting Lifestyles
Proverbs 10-12

At chapter 10 a new division of the Book of Proverbs begins. The text contains the title: "The proverbs of Solomon" which obviously points to the author of this material.[1] The first great collection of proverbs within the book (10:1–22:16) contains 375 maxims.[2] The sections within this block of proverbs usually commence with the phrase "a wise son."

The proverbs in chapters 10-12 are antithetical in construction. Half of the verse points to a principle in the life of wisdom, and half to the opposite principle in the life of folly. Perhaps these proverbs have been placed here in the book to illustrate in practical terms the results of the two ways of life illustrated by Lady Wisdom and Harlot Folly in the preceding chapters.

INTRODUCTION
The Choice of Wisdom
Proverbs 10:1-5

The general introduction to chapters 10-12 indicates the five contrasts which will be developed in the proverbs of this unit.

1. *Joy and grief (10:1).* "A wise son makes a glad father; but a foolish son is the grief of his mother." The terms "wise" and "foolish" here have an ethical, not an intellectual, connotation. The mother sees more of the son's conduct because she spends more time at home with him, while the father is preoccupied with business. Thus the son's conduct grieves her more deeply.

2. *Profit and loss (10:2).* "Treasures of wickedness profit nothing." Money acquired by illegal means brings no genuine happiness. Even worse, in the day of judgment those treasures will avail nothing when that person must give an account of himself in the judgment. On the other hand, "righteousness delivers from death." The term "righteousness" *(tsedaqah)* refers to moral goodness in general and charity[3] in particular.

3. *Satisfaction and frustration (10:3).* "Yahweh will not allow the soul of the righteous to famish." The term "soul" here as frequently means "life." The idea is that God will provide the necessities of life (cf. Matt 6:26,33). On the other hand, he will thrust aside the desire *(havvah)* of the wicked. When their desire appears to be within their grasp, God thrusts it away from them. The wicked are never satisfied. They experience no real enjoyment out of what they crave. The position of this Yahweh proverb at the center of this introductory unit should be noted. The author is suggesting that wisdom and folly are closely related to righteousness and wickedness.

4. *Industry and indolence (10:4).* "One becomes poor who deals with a lazy hand." The word for "hand" *(kaph)* is the open, ineffective hand or palm. Biblical ethics stress the dignity of work (cf. Exod 20:9). Proverbs focuses on the disadvantages of indolence. Here laziness results in poverty. On the other hand, "the hand of the diligent brings wealth." Here the word "hand" *(yad)* is the hand tense and braced for vigorous work.

5. *Foresight and procrastination (10:5).* "A son that acts pru-

dently gathers [crops] in summer." The introduction to the first great collection of proverbs concludes as it began, with the contrast between wise and foolish sons. The term "son" suggests that the individual is a member of a family, but it also assumes that he is an independent worker. Crops not gathered in the fair weather of summer were destined to be ruined by the heavy autumn rains. On the other hand, "one who snores (*nirdam*) in the harvest is a son that acts shamefully."

THE WISE AND THE FOOLISH
Proverbs 10:6-22

Most of the sentences in this unit state contrasting ideas. The exceptions are vv. 10,18, and 22 in which the first thought is expanded in the second.

A. Contrasting Outcomes (10:6-12).
1. Blessings vs. cursings (10:6). "Blessings are upon the head of the righteous." Either God rewards the righteous person with blessings, or others bestow their blessings upon him because of his righteousness. On the other hand, "the mouth of the wicked conceals violence," i.e., so that he may wait for the opportunity of practicing violence. The idea is that the wicked plot the ruin of their neighbors and thus incur their curses instead of their blessings. The verse indicates the contrast between the manifest blessedness of the righteous and the sinister activities of the wicked.

2. Pleasant vs. painful memories (10:7). "The memory of the righteous shall be for a blessing." After a righteous person dies, the memory of his good deeds will endure. People will recall his name with respect and gratitude. The memory of the departed one would also be a blessing by being an example to subsequent generations. On the other hand, "the name of the wicked shall rot," i.e., end quickly in complete forgetfulness. Few wish to name their children Hitler, Nero or Judas.

3. Humility vs. arrogance (10:8). "The wise in heart accepts commandments." He is not proud or conceited; he accepts the divine law with all its directions and is not above learning from others. On

535

the other hand, "the foolish of lips [NIV "chattering fool"] comes to ruin." The reference is to a person who engages in senseless talk. While he is chattering, he cannot be learning. Without the guidance of wisdom's commandments such a person comes to ruin. The contrast in the verse may be indicated this way: A wise person has a solid heart; a fool has loose lips.

4. *Security vs. insecurity (10:9).* "He who walks uprightly walks securely." Such a one walks in simplicity, having nothing to conceal or to fear. He therefore is free of danger and anxiety because the Lord is a shield to him (cf. 2:7). On the other hand, "the one who perverts his ways [i.e., deals in crooked practices] shall be known." He shall be exposed, punished, and put to open shame. Since he fears this fate, he cannot walk securely.

5. *Guilelessness vs. craftiness (10:10).* "He who winks with the eye gives pain." The winking of the eye here, as in 6:13, is a sign of craft, malice and complicity with other wicked comrades. The effect of malicious innuendo is to cause the victim mental anguish and possible material injury. Even more dangerous than the cunning plotter is the blubbering fool. "The foolish of lips shall come to ruin." The last half of the verse is repeated from v. 8 but is used in a different way. In the previous verse the reference was to the damage which chattering fools cause to themselves. Here the damage done to others by the chatterer is in view.

6. *Enlivening vs. deadly speech (10:11).* "The mouth of the righteous is a fountain of life." God himself is called "the well of life" (Ps 36:9) and "the fountain of living water" (Jer 2:13). The man of God draws from this supply and sheds life and refreshment around. His words are a source of vitality to those who listen to his exhortation and advice. On the other hand, "the mouth of the wicked conceals violence" (cf. v. 6). The words of the wicked are harmful and hypocritical. They conceal their true intent which is violence toward the innocent.

7. *Quarrelsomeness vs. amiability (10:12).* "Hatred stirs up strifes," i.e., by focusing on faults, making mountains out of molehills, and questioning motives. Hatred keeps alive the old feeling of revenge, and seeks opportunities of satisfying it. On the other hand, "love covers all transgressions." Love puts shortcomings out of sight,

enables one to overlook insults and wrongs (cf. 1 Pet 4:8). This proverb is probably intended as a comment on the last line of the previous proverb, and possibly also on v. 10. The reprehensible actions mentioned in those verses are here attributed to hatred and the desire to stir up strife.

B. The Wise and the Foolish (10:13-21).

The next series of proverbs are marked off in verses 13 and 21 by references to one who "lacks sense" (*chasar lebh*). A number of verbal links join several of the proverbs in this unit together in loose couplets.

1. Regarding wisdom (10:13-14). "In the lips of him that has understanding wisdom is found." Only from the lips of a man who has the insight to draw correct distinctions between right and wrong, truth and error, can words of wisdom be heard. The man of understanding is discreet in speech. He does not cause trouble by rash or foolish words. On the other hand, "a rod is for the back of him that is void of understanding" (lit., heart). Some people do not have the well-established principles which guide their conduct. These must forcibly be led in the right direction, like an animal upon whose back the driver's blows fall. A fool brings upon himself punishment by his ill-considered conversation (10:13).

"Wise men conceal knowledge," i.e., they are not talkative and make no show of what they have learned. When they speak it is with due deliberation. They lay up knowledge like a treasure for use on proper occasions. On the other hand, "the mouth of the foolish invites ruin." The fool does not weigh his words. He blurts out statements which may do considerable harm either to himself or to others (10:14).

2. Regarding wealth (10:15-16). "The rich man's wealth is his strong city," i.e., his protection against many troubles in life. Wealth is not evil in itself. It has distinct advantages. On the other hand, "the ruin of the poor is their poverty." The lack of wealth puts a person at a disadvantage and exposes him to even worse misfortune. The teacher does not romanticize poverty. There is nothing desirable about being poor. The term "poor" (*dal*) suggests weakness and inability to help one's self (10:15).

"The wages of the righteous are for life." Earnings from honest toil are devoted to procuring the necessities of life for a person and his family. On the other hand, "the increase of the wicked is for sin." The "increase" may suggest the more abundant income which is achieved from illicit activities. Money which is dishonestly obtained is often squandered in vice which leads only to death (10:16; Rom 6:21).

3. *Regarding witness (10:17-18).* "A path to life is the one who keeps discipline." The idea seems to be that the one who submits to personal discipline is a wholesome influence and good example to others. On the other hand, "he who forsakes reproof leads others astray." Such a one is a bad influence on others (10:17).

"He who hides hatred has lying lips." The picture is of one who professes a friendship which he does not feel. He thus becomes hypocritical in his speech. Even worse, "he that utters slander is a fool," i.e., is morally defective. Only a brainless person indulges in either hypocritical or slanderous speech because a sensible person knows that sooner or later the truth will be known (10:18).

4. *Regarding words (10:19-21).* "In a multitude of words, transgression is not lacking." The more one talks, the greater the risk of saying what is inappropriate (cf. Matt 12:36; Jas 1:26). "Loquacity leads to exaggeration and untruthfulness, slander and uncharitableness."[3] On the other hand, "the one who refrains his lips is wise." The teacher advocates keeping the tongue under wraps (10:19).

"The tongue of the righteous is as choice silver," i.e., silver free of dross. The words of a righteous man are of pure intent and without hypocrisy. On the other hand, "the heart of the wicked is of little worth," i.e., is like some common metal which has little value (10:20).

"The lips of the righteous feed many." Some take this to be a reference to the power of prayer. Because of the prayers of the righteous, God sends abundance to earth which satisfies the needs of many. More likely the reference is to the teaching of the righteous which provides nourishment to those who hear. On the other hand, "the foolish die for want of understanding." They cannot feed others because they have no spiritual depth themselves. They eventually die because of the lack of spiritual nourishment (10:21).

C. A Theological Key (10:22).

"As for the blessing of Yahweh, it makes one wealthy." The Hebrew places the emphasis on the word "blessing" by adding the pronoun "it." Real prosperity emanates from God, and he bestows it on those who are worthy. He, i.e., Yahweh, "does not add trouble with it." When one's good fortune is a blessing from God, one is free of the anxieties which ill-gotten riches create for their possessor (10:22).

The "Yahweh proverb" of v. 22 would have made an ideal chapter conclusion. This proverb is clearly intended to color the interpretation of all the preceding verses. For example, Yahweh is the source of the wealth mentioned in vv. 15-16; he is the source of the "blessing" mentioned in vv. 6-7. The diligence which "makes rich" in v. 4 will not succeed without the blessing of the Lord.

THE RIGHTEOUS AND THE WICKED
Proverbs 10:23-32

In vv. 23-32 the contrast between the righteous and the wicked with their respective fates is set forth. The words "righteous" (*tsaddiq*) and/or "wicked" (*rasha'*) occur in seven of the ten verses. In two other verses equivalent terms are used. Only v. 26 is an exception.

A. The Folly of the Wicked (10:23-26).

The first four proverbs focus on the negative actions of the wicked.

1. The wicked sin lightly (10:23). "It is like jesting to a fool to do wickedness," i.e., he finds amusement and satisfaction in that which is wrong. His moral superficiality enables him to enjoy sin. His conscience does not bother him. The text assumes that wrongdoing may become part of a person's nature, his normal and joyous activity. On the other hand, "wisdom" is the delight of "a man of discernment." The wise man finds his refreshment in living a wise and prudent life, which is as easy and as pleasant to him as evil is to the wicked.

2. The wicked worry correctly (10:24). "As for the fear of the wicked, it shall come upon him." Though the wicked lightly carries on his evil practices, he is troubled with the thought of the retribution which awaits him. On the other hand, "the desire of the righteous he shall give." The righteous desire only that which is in agreement with God's will, and this God grants, if not in this world, certainly in the life to come.

3. *The wicked are destroyed completely (10:25).* "When the whirlwind passes, the wicked person is no more." His life is like an unstable building which is swept away by a storm (cf. Matt 7:24). On the other hand, "the righteous is an everlasting foundation." Such a one survives the whirlwind because his virtue gives him resilience and power of endurance.

4. *The wicked offend constantly (10:26).* "As vinegar to the teeth, and as smoke to the eyes, so is the sluggard to them that send him." Vinegar causes irritation to the teeth just as smoke causes irritation to the eyes. Those who entrust important business to a sluggard, i.e., a lazy person, will likewise be irritated by his inability to get the job done in a timely manner.

B. The Fullness of the Righteous (10:27-32).

The last six proverbs of chapter 10 stress in their opening sentences the positive results of leading a life of righteousness or wisdom.

1. *The righteous have a glorious prospect (10:27-28).* "The fear of Yahweh prolongs days" because it is the beginning of knowledge (1:7) and of wisdom (9:10), and thus furnishes to people the correct rule of living (cf. 3:2; 9:11). The promise of long life as the reward of a believer is often found in this book, where temporal retribution is set forth. On the other hand, "the years of the wicked shall be shortened" by his lack of self-control or because he is victimized by an evil associate (10:27).

"The hope of the righteous is gladness," i.e., when their hope is realized they are glad. On the other hand, "the expectation of the wicked shall perish." That for which they eagerly hope shall not materialize (10:28).

2. *The righteous have a glorious refuge (10:29-30).* "The way of Yahweh is a stronghold to the upright." Those who walk in the way which the Lord has mapped out will find courage to face difficulties in life. On the other hand, that same way of the Lord "is a ruin to the workers of iniquity." They abandon that path and consequently incur devastating punishment (10:29).

"The righteous shall never be moved." Such are able to withstand both the vicissitudes of life and the attacks of the wicked. The context suggests that the righteous will not be uprooted from their land and driven into exile. On the other hand, "the wicked shall not inhabit the land," i.e., permanently. The Israelites were threatened with exile if they disobeyed the law of God (10:30; cf. Lev 26:33).

3. *The righteous have a glorious testimony (10:31-32).* "The mouth of the righteous brings forth wisdom" as a tree brings forth flowers and fruit. It has a positive influence on others. On the other hand, "a perverse tongue will be cut off" like a nonproductive branch of a tree. The abuse of God's great gift of speech shall be severely punished (10:31; cf. Matt 12:36f.).

"The lips of the righteous know what is proper." He speaks what will please God and edify his neighbor. On the other hand, "the mouth of the wicked is completely perverse" (10:32).

THE TREACHEROUS AND THE BLAMELESS
Proverbs 11:1-31

The various proverbs assembled in chapter 11 continue to develop the theme of the contrast between the way of God's law and the lawlessness of wicked persons. Twenty-three of the proverbs are stated in antithetical parallelism.

A. A Collage of Contrasts (11:1-11).
The first eleven verses of chapter 11 are thematically closely related. A Yahweh proverb introduces the series, and sets the tone for what follows. Thus throughout this unit the proverbs set in juxtaposition conduct which is approved by Yahweh, and that which is abhorrent to him.

1. *Honesty vs. dishonesty (11:1).* "A false balance [lit., scales of deceit] is an abomination to Yahweh" (cf. Lev 19:35f.; Deut 25:13ff.). On the other hand, "a perfect weight [lit., stone] is his delight," i.e., it has his approval. Stones were used as weights from early times. Honesty and integrity are at the foundation of social duties taught by wisdom.

2. *Humility vs. pride (11:2).* "Arrogance comes, then comes shame," i.e., contempt. No one feels compassion when an arrogant man

falls. Pride shall have a fall; arrogance in the end meets with disgrace (cf. Luke 14:11; 1 Cor 10:12). On the other hand, "with the lowly is wisdom." The lowly are those who walk humbly with God (Micah 6:8). Wisdom leaves the haughty and lodges in the humble mind. By disposition the lowly are ready to receive God's grace and gifts.

3. *Probity vs. improbity (11:3).* "The integrity of the upright guides them." Those who are upright choose integrity as their standard of conduct. It will prove a reliable guide and be a safeguard against error and danger. On the other hand, "the perverseness (*seleph*) of the faithless shall destroy them." Those who resort to dubious methods to gain their ends ultimately will be ruined by their own schemes (cf. Ps 35:8).

4. *Liberality vs. selfishness (11:4).* "Riches will not profit in the day of wrath," i.e., a time of calamity (cf. Zeph 1:15ff.). In such a time of crisis, wealth does not protect a person. On the other hand, "righteousness delivers from death." As in 10:2 "righteousness" may refer particularly to alms giving. One who has been generous with the poor will die a peaceful death content in the realization that he has done what he could to help his fellow man.

5. *Righteousness vs. wickedness (11:5-8).* "The righteousness of the blameless shall make straight his way." The "blameless" (*tamim*) are the upright and honest. Righteousness leads such a person along the safest route to his desired goal, removing obstacles from his path. On the other hand, "the wicked shall fall by his own wickedness." Such a one is led by his own evil propensities. He loses the light of conscience (John 11:10), and stumbles to his destruction.

"The righteousness of the upright shall deliver them." On the other hand, "the faithless shall be trapped by evil desires" which lead to sin. The indulgence of their passions destroys sinners. This is an emphatic reiteration of the preceding sentence (11:6).

"When a wicked man dies, his expectation perishes." The "wicked man" here is one who holds a position of authority which he abuses by acting lawlessly. Such a man sets his heart upon worldly prosperity, long life, and impunity. All these are cut off, and the moral government of God is confirmed, by his death. This is but a specific illustration of the principle that "the hope of strength perishes." The hope which is based upon a person's physical power is doomed to disappointment (11:7).

"The righteous is delivered out of trouble." God is at hand to help the righteous out of any crisis. On the other hand, "it comes on the wicked instead." The evil from which the righteous is saved falls upon the wicked (11:8; cf. Esther 7:10).

6. *Integrity vs. slander (11:9).* "With his mouth the godless person [lit., the polluted] destroys his neighbor." Such a person lacks any honor. He attacks his neighbor with false accusations and insinuations. The verse may refer specifically to courtroom action. In that case, the idea is that a godless person is unscrupulous with regard to evidence in order to win his case. On the other hand, "through knowledge shall the righteous be delivered." His integrity enables an innocent person to expose the lies of his adversary (11:9).

7. *Blessing and curse (11:10-11).* "When it goes well with the righteous, the city rejoices." Why is this so? Because the righteous share their good fortune with their fellow man. On the other hand, "when the wicked perish, there is joy" of a different kind. The community is happy that a disturbing element has been removed from the scene (11:10).

"By the blessing of the upright a city is exalted." Such bring a good influence on the life of the community through their godly counsel, prayers and righteous deeds. They lift the moral standards and bring increased harmony and contentment. On the other hand, the city "is overthrown by the mouth of the wicked." Slander and talebearing upset the harmony of the city and undermine its stability. Impious language and evil advice bring ruin to a city (11:11).

B. A Collage of Characters (11:12-21).

If verses 1-11 focus on negative practices, vv. 12-21 paint word pictures of the people who disrupt a community and offend God.

1. *The contemptuous vs. the considerate (11:12).* "He that despises his neighbor lacks understanding." The picture here is of one who shows open contempt for a neighbor. Such a one acts foolishly, because he makes an enemy of the despised person who may have an opportunity to retaliate. On the other hand, "a man of discernment

holds his peace." If he has cause to feel contempt for another, he keeps his thoughts to himself so as not to create dissension.

2. *The talebearer vs. the confidant (11:13).* "He that goes about as a talebearer reveals secrets." The reference is to those who go about chattering, gossiping, and slandering (cf. Lev 19:16). To such a person it is not safe to trust anything. On the other hand, "he that is of a faithful spirit conceals a matter." A "faithful spirit" is a right disposition, one which desires the welfare of neighbors. Such a one is able to respect confidences. He keeps confidential even the knowledge which comes to him by accident.

3. *The despot vs. the democrat (11:14).* "Where there is no wise direction (*tachbuloth*), a people falls." The Hebrew word is thought originally to have referred to rope-pulling, i.e., steering or directing a ship. A nation needs wise counselors to guide those who run the ship of state. On the other hand, "in the multitude of counselors there is safety." In English the proverb is stated: "Two heads are better than one."

4. *The irresponsible vs. the conservative (11:15).* "He that puts up security for another will surely suffer." See on 6:1. Putting up one's wealth as collateral for someone else's loan is here discouraged. Too often that results in financial harm. On the other hand, "he who refuses to strike hands in pledge is safe." Such a one is not burdened by worry or liability to pay his guarantee to his financial ruin. "Striking the hands" was the means by which such formal agreements were ratified.

5. *The virtuous woman vs. the aggressive man (11:16).* "A gracious woman gains honor." Here is depicted the quiet victories of a beautiful character. Such a woman is honored by family and community. On the other hand, "strong men obtain riches." Brute force at its best can only amass and hold wealth. This is the only place in Proverbs where a comparison of this kind is made between man and woman. Thus grace is more effective than strength, and honor is better than wealth.

6. *The sympathetic vs. the cruel (11:17).* "A kind person benefits himself." The person envisioned here is one who practices *chesed*, i.e., acts of benevolence. Such acts are a blessing to others, but also to the one who performs those acts (cf. Matt 5:7). On the other hand, "he that is cruel troubles his flesh." One who is harsh in his dealings

with others creates enmity toward himself which often is translated into violent deeds.

7. *The wicked vs. the righteous (11:18-19).* "A wicked man earns deceptive wages [lit., wages of falsehood]." Such wages have only temporary value. On the other hand, "he who sows righteousness has a sure reward [lit., a reward of truth]." To "sow righteousness" is to act righteously, to live in such a way that the result is holiness (11:18).

"That true righteousness is to life" is an oft repeated theme in the book. Genuine righteousness has the promise of this life and of that which is to come (1 Tim 4:8). On the other hand, "he who pursues evil is to death," i.e., he brings ruin eventually on himself. This proverb constitutes a climax of sorts in the listing of the respective fates of the righteous and wicked. The contrast is not merely between benefit and harm, reward and disappointment, but between life and death (11:19).

8. *Conclusion (11:20-21).* The fates of the wicked and the righteous are now accounted for theologically. "An abomination to Yahweh are those who are perverse of heart." The reference is to the wicked of mind who depart from the straight paths of moral rectitude to travel the crooked paths of moral perversity. An abomination is something which is utterly repugnant. On the other hand, "his delight is in those who are blameless of way," i.e., who follow the way appointed by God (11:20).

"The evil man shall not be unpunished." This is a cardinal teaching in Proverbs, that retribution finally overtakes the wicked. Here this observation is introduced by the solemn exclamation: "my hand upon it." This is equivalent to saying, "most assuredly." On the other hand, "the seed of the righteous shall escape" the punishment which is reserved for evil men (11:21).

UNBECOMING ATTRIBUTES
Proverbs 11:22-31

The last ten proverbs in chapter 11 differ both in form and theme from one another and from the proverbs which precede.

A. Indiscretion in a Woman (11:22).

"A gold ring in a pig's snout is a fair woman that turns aside from refinement." This is the first example of a similitude in the book. A nose-ring was a common adornment of women in that period (cf. Gen 24:22; Isa 3:21). Such a fine piece of jewelry, however, would be totally out of place in a pig's nose. The word "refinement" (*ta'am*) here literally means "taste." The word in this context embraces both good sense and good taste. The external beauty of such a woman is as incongruous as a precious ring in the snout of a pig.

B. Desire in a Wicked Man (11:23).

"The desire of the righteous is only good." Those who desire only what is proper receive for themselves "the good," namely, the favor of the Lord. On the other hand, "the expectation of the wicked—that upon which they set their hope and heart—is wrath." The immoral lifestyle only brings upon one the wrath of God.

C. Stinginess in a Person of Means (11:24-26).

"There is one who scatters, yet prospers [lit., continues to increase himself or be increased]." The idea is that the person who devotes his money to benevolence, becomes the richer for it. On the other hand, "one withholds what is appropriate but comes to poverty." That which is appropriate might be (1) a debt; or (2) a proper act of generosity. The miser only loses what he hoards (11:24).

"The generous person [lit., the soul of blessing] shall be made rich [lit., made fat]." The reference is to the kind and sympathetic person who responds to the call for help from those in need. To be made "fat" (*dusshan*) is commonly employed for the idea of prosperity (cf. 28:25). Furthermore, "he that refreshes [lit., waters] others shall himself be refreshed [lit., watered]." This metaphor is derived from agriculture. If a person irrigates his land, he has his reward in a good harvest. In a similar way those who are generous have their recompense in the divine bounty which is bestowed upon them (11:25).

"People curse one who withholds grain" in a time of scarcity so as to inflate the price. Such a practice is a sin against justice and charity. On the other hand, "a blessing shall be upon the head of the one who sells it." Such a one forgoes the opportunity of making high profits from the emergency. Yet God blesses him in abundance (11:26).

D. Trust in Riches (11:27-29).

The next three proverbs continue the theme of the misuse of wealth. Three observations are made regarding the sin of trusting in wealth.

1. Trust in riches obscures worthy goals (11:27). "The person that seeks in the morning for good seeks favor." The reference seems to be to a person who is eager to make others happy. Thereby he wins the favor and goodwill of those he seeks to help. Perhaps the favor obtained is also God's. On the other hand, "the person who seeks evil, it shall come upon him." Those who plan to harm others, the injury will recoil upon them to their own hurt.

2. Trust in riches leads to moral downfall (11:28). "The person who trusts in his riches shall fall." Wealth is of all things the most uncertain, and leads the heart astray from God (1 Tim 6:17). What is condemned here is the belief that riches can save a bad man from the consequences of his evil deeds, i.e., from divine wrath. On the other hand, "the righteous shall flourish as a leaf." The "righteous" here are those who have the godly perspective on wealth. Such grow in grace and spiritual beauty, and bring forth the fruit of good works. The idea of the leaf which shall not wither is a metaphor for prosperity (Ps 1:3). This proverb may be intended as a commentary on the preceding one.

3. Trust in riches results in oppressive greed (11:29). "The person who troubles his house shall inherit wind." The family is "troubled" when the breadwinner is miserly and denies his dependents the necessities of life. One may also trouble his family through ill-temper and bad management. The "family" here might include household servants. Such a one inherits "wind," a metaphor for that which is worthless and empty. His stinginess deprives him of a comfortable home-life. He is left only with money which has no real value because it is being hoarded. Furthermore, "a fool shall belong as a servant to the wise." The miser is practically a slave to those who will eventually inherit his wealth. Being wiser than he, they will spend that wealth liberally.

E. Conclusion (11:30-31).

The unit concludes with two proverbs setting forth the positive products of righteousness and the certain recompense of wickedness.

"The fruit of the righteous is a tree of life." The life of one who lives by the principles of wisdom has a positive effect on those around him (cf. 3:18). Furthermore, "he that is wise wins souls." He attracts people to himself and thus imparts to them sound advice (11:30).

"If a righteous man is recompensed [lit., repaid] in the land, how much more the wicked and the sinner." Even a righteous man is not perfect (Eccl 7:20). His faults are judged by God and punished during his lifetime. If that is so, God will not overlook the misdeeds of the wicked. He will exact a full penalty upon them (11:31; cf. 1 Pet 4:18).

THE RIGHTEOUS AND THE WICKED
Proverbs 12:1-14

Chapter 12 originally may have been circulated independently as instruction in proper living. This ancient tablet of instruction commences with a commendation of discipline. "Whoever loves knowledge loves correction [*musar*]." A person must be willing to accept criticism of his conduct and to benefit therefrom. On the other hand, "he that is stupid hates correction." Unwisdom rejects correction. The noun "stupid" (*ba'ar*) refers to someone who is like a beast in that he is insensible to higher aspirations, to regret for the past or to hope for improvement in life (12:1).

A. The Righteous and Wicked Contrasted (12:2-7).
1. In respect to God (12:2-3). "A good man shall obtain favor from Yahweh" and therefore is blessed with divine protection and help." On the other hand, "a crafty man [lit., a man of devices] will be condemned." The reference is to one whose thoughts are perverse but clever. God will not allow such a one to escape punishment. This Yahweh proverb offers a theological interpretation of the recommendations which precede and follow (12:2).

"A man shall not be established by wickedness." Man is metaphorically compared to a tree. Wickedness gives that person no firm hold for growth or life. On the other hand, "the root of the righteous shall never be moved." His root being well placed, this tree is safe and brings forth much fruit (12:3).

2. In respect to wives (12:4). "A virtuous woman is a crown to her husband." More literally, "a wife of strong character [*'esheth chayil*]." The language is applied to one who is powerful either in mind, or body, or both. Both virtuous disposition and sound intellectual capacity are included in the term (cf. Ruth 3:11). Such a wife is an honor to her husband. She adorns and beautifies his life. She adds to the social status of her husband and elevates him in the esteem of the community. On the other hand, "she who does shamefully is as rottenness in his bones." Such a wife is like a disease which gradually wears down and weakens the bodily frame. She poisons her husband's life and deprives him of strength and vigor.

3. In respect to thoughts (12:5). "The plans of the righteous are right." His designs are well-intentioned and morally sound because the mind of the righteous man is disciplined by wisdom. On the other hand, "the counsels of the wicked are deceit." Their warped minds invent crooked methods for reaching their goals. To them the end always justifies the means.

4. In respect to words and deeds (12:6). "The words of the wicked are a bloody ambush." The wicked conspire together and plot murder (cf. 1:11), or at least their lies, slanders, and false accusations endanger lives (cf. 1 Kgs 21:13). On the other hand, "the mouth of the upright shall deliver them," namely, the victims of the conspirators. If the righteous have the opportunity, they warn the unwary and protect them from the wicked. They plead the cause of the oppressed and use their eloquence in their behalf.

5. In respect to destinies (12:7). "The wicked are overthrown, and are not," i.e., they cease to exist in their powerful positions. Once overthrown they cannot recover (cf. 10:25). What the stroke is against the wicked is not named. It may be a just judgment by God— financial reversal, sickness, family problems. Whatever it is, the wicked cannot endure. On the other hand, "the house of the righteous shall stand." His "house" (family) can successfully withstand the assaults of misfortune and the schemes of enemies.

B. Examples of the Wicked and Righteous (12:8-12).

1. The prudent person (12:8). "A man is commended according to his intelligence," i.e., common sense, the ability to form a sound judgment in everyday matters. The reference is to a person who gives practical proof of wisdom by life and character. His words and actions show that he is motivated by high views. Such a person is praised and acknowledged by all (cf. 1 Sam 18:5). On the other hand, "he that is of a distorted understanding shall be despised." These warped minds are responsible for disastrous decisions. They have distorted views of things, judge unfairly, and have no sympathy for others.

2. *The self-sufficient person (12:9).* "Better is he that is lightly esteemed and is a servant to himself, than he that plays the man of rank and lacks bread." The first picture is of a man who performs the humble tasks of a servant in order to have the money to purchase for his family the necessities of life. The second picture is of one putting on airs, pretending to be what he is not. One should not inflict privations upon himself to preserve an outward show of affluence which does not correspond with reality.

3. *The merciful person (12:10).* "A righteous man has regard for the life [lit., knows the soul] of his beast," i.e., he pays attention to the animal's needs. He is careful to supply his beast with the food he needs. The law of God legislated kindness to animals (Exod 20:10; 23:4,5; Deut 22:6,10; 25:4). In the East generally there is a deep sense that animals are not only the slaves of man, but the creatures of God. A person's behavior toward dumb creatures is an index of character. Furthermore, using the lesser to greater argument: If one is to be merciful to beasts, how much more to one's spouse and children! On the other hand, "the tender mercies of the wicked are cruel." The idea seems to be that the kindest acts of a wicked man are still cruel by God's standards. A wicked man does not know the first thing about kindness.

4. *The diligent person (12:11).* "He that tills his ground shall have plenty of bread." This is not an admonition to follow agricultural pursuits, but an endorsement of the value of hard work. The person who follows "vain things," i.e., nonproductive pursuits, "is void of understanding," i.e., does not display wisdom and prudence. He displays moral weakness and depravity. He puts empty pursuits ahead of making his living secure and thus ultimately (so it is implied) comes to poverty.

5. *The envious person (12:12).* "The wicked man desires the stronghold [metsodah] of evil men." He wants to stabilize his position.

He longs for that which evil men regard as guaranteeing security, namely, ill-gotten gain.[4] Yet he gets small return for his labor. On the other hand, "the root of the righteous yields fruit." Without any evil devices or plotting, the righteous gain all that they want as the natural result of their high principles. While the righteous flourish, the security of the wicked man is swept away.

C. The Speech of the Wicked and Righteous (12:13-14).

"In the transgression of lips is an evil snare." False and mischievous talk, aimed at ensnaring others, results in the speaker himself being trapped by his words. By speaking unadvisedly or intemperately one brings trouble upon himself. On the other hand, "a righteous person escapes [lit., goes out of] trouble." The reference is to a person who does not offend with his lips. He avoids the snares of the wicked man. Since his lips speak only truth, the righteous person is ultimately vindicated (12:13).

"From the fruit of the lips one shall be satisfied with good." The reference is again to the righteous person. A man's words are like seeds. If they are wise, pure and kindly, they will bring forth the fruit of love, favor and respect. Furthermore, "the work of the hands of a man shall return to him." The good works of the righteous as well as his good words rebound favorably to himself both in this life and in the life to come (12:14).

WISE AND FOOLISH SPEECH
Proverbs 12:15-26

Verse 15, which begins the second half of chapter 12, strongly resembles v. 1. Both verses are concerned with the fool ('evil) and the prudent and the attitudes of both toward counsel. This verse serves as an introduction to the second half of the chapter.

"The path of a fool is straight in his own eyes." The fool consults with no one, respects no other opinion. His way is the only way of accomplishing anything. On the other hand, he that is wise listens to wise counsel." He has a healthy distrust of his own unaided judgment which might lead him astray (12:15).

That one has failed to listen to wise counsel and is therefore a fool can be seen immediately in the speech of a person. The next series of proverbs takes up and develops this topic, which was introduced in vv. 13-14.

A. The Speech of Fools (12:16-22).

The proverbs which follow enumerate five types of foolish speech.

1. Angry speech (12:16). "A fool shows his annoyance in the same day." He shows that he is upset immediately. He has no idea of controlling himself or checking the expression of his wounded ego. Lashing out in the heat of anger, he arouses contention. On the other hand, "a prudent person conceals shame." He does not make a fool out of himself by shooting off his mouth. He exercises restraint and ignores an insult. He knows that by showing his resentment he will only make matters worse. He knows that it is best to let passions cool before he attempts to set things right.

2. Perjured speech (12:17). "He that breathes [*yaphiach*][5] out truth utters righteousness." The verse relates to the testimony of a witness in a court of law. The term "righteousness" here is used in its legal sense of "justice." The idea is that a true witness supports the cause of justice by contributing to a right verdict. On the other hand, "a witness of lies [breathes out] deceit." Such a one misleads the judges and is responsible for a miscarriage of justice. By his perverted testimony he reveals his true character.

3. Inflammatory speech (12:18). "There is one who speaks thoughtlessly like the piercings of a sword." Reckless words often have a harmful, and even fatal, consequence. The edge of the sword was called "its mouth." The human mouth can do as much damage as that "mouth" of metal. On the other hand, "the tongue of the wise is health." His words soothe anguish, undo injury, and heal wounds.

4. Deceitful speech (12:19). "The lip of truth shall be established forever." Truth is consistent and invincible. It endures the test of time. On the other hand, "a lying tongue is but for a moment." Literally, it lasts "while I wink the eye," i.e., lasts as long as it takes to blink an eye. Lying is soon found out and punished.

5. Evil counsel (12:20-22). "Deceit is in the heart of them that devise evil." The reference is to those who give evil advice. Such are treacherous counselors. Their advice can only bring misfortune, not joy and comfort. On the other hand, "to counselors of peace is joy." Some people work for a harmonious society and their endeavors bring them and those they counsel a feeling of joy (12:20).

"No harm befalls the righteous." The "harm" here is not misfortune or calamity, but the evil consequences that follow doing evil. A righteous man escapes the dangers faced by the wicked. Others take the term harm ('aven) in an ethical sense. The meaning would then be that a righteous man will not commit some atrocious act because his nature will cause him to recoil from such conduct. On the other hand, "the wicked are filled with evil." They easily succumb to the lure of sin and engage in evil deeds in spite of the warnings of punishment to follow (12:21).

"Lying lips are an abomination to Yahweh." This is now the second time the teacher has uttered this truth (cf. 6:17). God hates anything that is perverse. On the other hand, "those who deal truly are his delight." God delights in what is straightforward (12:22).

B. The Speech of the Wise (12:23-26).

1. Restrained speech (12:23-24). "A prudent person conceals knowledge." The man of common sense is cautious and reserved. He is not inclined to utter unadvisedly what he knows, but waits for a fitting opportunity either because of personal humility, or wise caution. The allusion is to circumstances which demand caution (cf. 11:13). Under certain conditions, Proverbs advocates outspokenness (cf. 15:2). On the other hand, "the heart of fools proclaims foolishness." The fool rushes in to display his folly. He blurts out his opinion at the most inappropriate moments. The quick response exposes the stupid ideas which arise in his mind which he regards as wisdom.

"The hand of the diligent shall rule." Strong and active individuals rise to the surface in any organization or community. Such persons reach the position where they become the employer of others. They become the boss. On the other hand, "the slothful shall be under tribute." He will be content to remain a servant to others, an employee. If any connection exists between this and the preceding proverb it may be this: some people are all talk, while others quietly pursue their goals to the victory (12:24).

2. Encouraging speech (12:25). "Anxiety in the heart of a man shall bow him down." People who allow themselves mentally to dwell on their problems will be defeated by depression. The cares of life bring dejection and despair (cf. Matt 6:34; 1 Pet 5:7). On the other hand, "a good word makes it glad." A word of encouragement may prove a real help in a time of trouble.

3. Guiding speech (12:26). "The righteous is guided by his friend." i.e., he consults his friend for advice. He is open to the opinions of others. On the other hand, "the way of the wicked leads them astray." They are opinionated and refuse advice. Consequently they are misled.

C. Conclusion (12:27-28).

The instruction regarding the wicked and the righteous concludes with two proverbs, one humorous, the other serious.

"Laziness will not roast his game." The passage satirizes the lazy person in a somewhat humorous way. He is too lazy to cook what he has captured. He just discards the game after the thrill of the hunt. He makes no good use of it. On the other hand, "the substance of a diligent person is precious." That which an honest, industrious person acquires by his labor is stable and of real value. The contrast is between one who is wasteful and one who is frugal (12:27).

"In the path of righteousness is life." Death is the penalty for sin. As a general principle, life is prolonged for the righteous. Furthermore, "along that path [lit., in the way of a path] there is immortality [lit., no-death]." This can only be an allusion to the immortality which follows the end of a righteous life upon earth. Righteousness holds forth the prospect of life more abundant here, and life eternal as well. The life and immortality alluded to here was brought into the light through the gospel of Jesus Christ (12:28; 2 Tim 1:10).

ENDNOTES

1. The words "the proverbs of Solomon" are missing from the Septuagint.

2. Patrick Skehan has pointed out that the numerical value of the Hebrew letters of Solomon's name totals 375. "A Single Editor for the Whole Book of

Proverbs," in *Studies in Ancient Israelite Wisdom* (Washington, DC: Catholic Biblical Association of America, 1971), pp. 15-26.

3. W.J. Deane, "Proverbs" in *The Pulpit Commentary* (New York: Funk & Wagnalls, 1909), p. 197.

4. Others understand *matsod* in 12:12 to be the "net" of evil men, i.e., the devices which they use to enrich themselves.

5. The verb *yaphach* is used of giving evidence in 6:19; 14:5,25; 19:5,9).

CHAPTER TWENTY-SEVEN

True Perspectives on Life
Proverbs 13:1-15:19

The second section of the first great collection of proverbs commences, as did the first section, with the words "a wise son." For the most part this section contains antithetical parallelism, i.e., the second half of the verse presents a deliberate contrast to the first half. Again, organization is difficult to ascertain.

ACCEPTING DISCIPLINE
Proverbs 13:1-25

Chapter 13 is dominated by the theme of the need to accept instruction and discipline. This theme is explicit in six verses, and implicit in three others. The first thirteen verses are cast in the form of the advice that a father might give his son, while the last twelve verses are described as the teaching of the wise. Unlike the other chapters in the collection 10:1–22:16, chapter 13 contains no reference to God.

A. The Teaching of a Father (13:1-13).

"A wise son [is] discipline of a father." To make sense of this clause, NIV supplies the verb "heeds," NASB "accepts." The meaning is that on account of a father's discipline the son is wise. On the other hand, "a scoffer does not listen to rebuke." A scoffer here as in 1:22 is one who mocks moral principles, spiritual insights and filial duty. Such a person is hopeless, but he rebuffs any attempt to correct him (13:1; cf. 1 Sam 2:25). Having set forth the value of discipline, Solomon identifies nine areas in which the young need discipline.

1. Discipline respecting words (13:2-3). "From the fruit of the mouth of a man one shall eat good." If a righteous man's words are kindly and designed to build up others, he will "eat good," i.e., enjoy a happy and peaceful existence. Why? Because he will gain the good will of his neighbors and the blessing of God. On the other hand, "the desire of the unfaithful is violence." Treacherous men devise evil schemes to encompass the ruin of others. By hook or crook they will enhance their own well being at the expense of others. They yearn to commit deeds of violence. In the end the violence they plan for others will recoil upon themselves (13:2).

"The person who guards his mouth keeps his life." The aim here is to prevent rash talk. On the other hand, "the person who opens wide his lips shall have ruin." While such a reminder is appropriate in any age, it is particularly so in an autocratic society. An incautious word could cost a person his life (13:3).

2. Discipline respecting work (13:4). "As for the sluggard, his soul desires and has nothing." "Soul" *(nephesh)* here may mean "appetite" as in 10:3. The lazy man hungers, but will not supply his want. He has the wish but not the will. The empty wish without corresponding exertion is useless. On the other hand, "the soul of the diligent shall be gratified abundantly" (cf.11:25).

3. Discipline respecting honesty (13:5). "A righteous person hates lying" (lit., a word of falsehood). "Lying" here probably includes any deceitful or dishonest act. On the other hand, "a wicked man does smelly and shameful things." The first verb of this clause *(yabh'ish)* means literally, "cause a stench," or "stir up a foul odor." A dishonest person brings shame to himself and disgrace upon those who are associated with him.

4. *Discipline avoids disaster (13:6).* "Righteousness guards the person who is upright in the way." The idea is that righteousness is a safeguard against a person's straying from the right path of life. Those who are innocent in the walk of life are preserved from evil, moral and material. On the other hand, "wickedness overthrows sin," i.e., the one who sins.

5. *Discipline in lifestyle (13:7-9).* "One pretends to be rich, yet has nothing." Some people wish to give the impression of being rich for social reasons (Luke 12:21; Rev 3:17). On the other hand, "another pretends to be poor, yet has great wealth." Misers live as though they are poor although they are wealthy. Thus they are able to protect themselves from requests for assistance or from robbery. The proverb teaches one not to trust in appearances (13:7).

"The ransom of a person's life are his riches." This may explain why some wealthy people pretend to be poor. Governments penalize the wealthy, force them to pay exorbitant fines for infractions which would be overlooked in a poor man. Rich men are subject to frivolous lawsuits from greedy litigants spurred on by even more greedy lawyers. On the other hand, "the poor hears no threatening." Since he has nothing, no one tries to "shake him down" or blackmail him (13:8).

"The light of the righteous shines brightly [lit., rejoices]." Light (*'or*) here is the symbol of the grace and virtue which adorn the life of a good man. These qualities beam through all his actions with a cheerful, kindly radiance. On the other hand, "the lamp (*ner*) of the wicked shall be put out." The lamp of the wicked is the false show of wisdom or piety which may glimmer and deceive for a time. The pretentious light of the wicked is exposed for what it is and extinguished (13:9).

6. *Discipline respecting quarrels (13:10).* "Only through arrogance does contention last." A quarrel might easily be settled if the parties to it were reasonable. Pride, however, distorts judgment and makes arbitration difficult. One who is haughty and overbearing is sure to quarrel with others. On the other hand, "wisdom is found with those who take advice" (cf. 11:2). Those who humbly seek advice possess wisdom, and wisdom soon puts an end to a quarrel.

7. *Discipline respecting wealth (13:11).* "Wealth gotten by vanity [lit., a breath] shall be diminished." While "vanity" may include robbery and violence, the thrust here is on methods which have no real

worth. Wealth obtained without exertion, or by illegitimate and dishonest means is not blessed by God. Speculation and gambling are examples of attempts to accumulate wealth hastily and without effort. On the other hand, "the person who gathers little by little [lit., with the hand] shall increase." Patient industry, regular saving, and legitimate investment over time builds wealth steadily (13:11).

8. Discipline respecting disappointment (13:12). "Hope deferred [lit., drawn out] makes the heart sick," i.e., depresses a person and lowers his vitality. The reference is to the discouragement which sets in when one is not able to achieve goals in a timely manner. On the other hand, "desire fulfilled is a tree of life." Accomplishing a worthwhile goal invigorates and heartens (cf. 3:18). A "tree of life" in Proverbs is that which contributes to life more abundant.

9. Discipline respecting God's word (13:13). "Whoever despises the word becomes pledged[1] to it." The reference must be to the word of God. The point is that one is not exempt from obeying the commandments of God just because he willfully ignores them. In the ancient world a debtor deposited a pledge which was forfeited in the event of loan default. So every person's life is, as it were, on pledge to obey God's law. If one does not submit to the demands of that law, he forfeits his life. On the other hand, "he that fears the commandment shall be rewarded." He shows respect for the law by immediate compliance with its demands. Such a person receives his life back with a reward.

B. The Teaching of the Wise (13:14-25).

"The instruction of the wise is a fountain of life" (cf.10:11). Godly teaching points the way to life more abundant. It saves from many dangers, material and spiritual, even from "the snares of death" (cf. 5:5; 7:22f.), i.e., pitfalls which can bring a premature and godless death (13:14). The remaining proverbs of ch. 13 expand on the "life" and "snares" theme of v. 14.

1. Beautiful vs. boorish character (13:15). "Good understanding [sekhel tobh] gives grace." The Hebrew expression denotes the perception of what is right and proper. Such a quality produces "grace," i.e., beauty of character (cf. 11:16). One who possesses good understanding finds acceptance with both God and man (cf. Luke 2:52). On the other hand, "the way of the unfaithful is harsh." The "unfaithful" (*bogedim*) are those who behave boorishly. Their harsh way leads to an even harsher destiny.

2. *Circumspect vs. clown-like actions (13:16).* "Each prudent person acts with knowledge." A prudent person is one who is not easily misled. He weighs circumstances and consciously decides his course of action. On the other hand, "a fool displays [lit., spreads out] his folly" as a merchant might spread out his wares in a marketplace. He acts impetuously, and thus reveals his lack of prudence.

3. *Faithful and unfaithful ministry (13:17).* "A wicked messenger falls into evil." When he has no personal integrity, a representative may disregard his instructions and thereby do damage to the person who dispatched him. Such a messenger ultimately will be detected and punished. On the other hand, "a faithful ambassador," i.e., one of trustworthy character, "is health," i.e., is a source of health. He is a source of comfort both to his employer and to those to whom he is sent. By such a person a sound and healthy condition is reached.

4. *Honor vs. shame (13:18).* "Poverty and shame come to one who refuses instruction." In business life, a person who acts on his own opinions, rejecting the guidance of persons more experienced, probably will become impoverished. At the same time, he will earn the contempt of his associates because of his stupidity. On the other hand, "he who keeps reproof is honored." Such a person possesses humility which wins respect from others.

5. *Honest effort vs. cheating (13:19).* "A desire which has come into existence is sweet to the soul." When a worthwhile goal has been reached or a wish fulfilled an individual is full of satisfaction. On the other hand, "it is an abomination to fools to depart from evil." Fools can only achieve their goals by evil devices and means. Were they to abandon evil, they would never be able to see their wishes realized. Hence, they could never entertain the thought of departing from evil.

6. *Wise vs. foolish companions (13:20).* "He who walks with wise men shall be wise." Wise men have a positive influence on those who spend time in their presence. On the other hand, "the companion of fools suffers harm." The bad habits of the fool are quickly learned and imitated to one's detriment. Thus a person becomes like those with whom he associates.

7. Good vs. misfortune (13:21). "Misfortune pursues sinners." Eventually sinners meet with their just deserts. They suffer the natural consequences of their deeds in external injury, loss of property and reputation. They also experience the sting of conscience and remorse. On the other hand, "the righteous shall be rewarded with good." They shall have the answer of a good conscience, happiness both here and hereafter.

8. Conservation vs. waste (13:22). "A good man leaves an inheritance for his children's children." In godly families wealth is handed down through the generations because the children are wise enough to preserve the principal. On the other hand, "the wealth of the wicked is laid up for the righteous." The sinner's undisciplined children squander what is bequeathed to them. They consequently have nothing to leave their children. Another interpretation of these words is this: property unjustly acquired or wickedly used is taken from those who have it. It ultimately finds its way into better hands.

9. Honest labor vs. dishonest gain (13:23). "Abundance of food is in the field of poor people." The word "field" (*nir*) means ground worked for the first time, hence that on which much labor is bestowed. The poor, but righteous man, who industriously cultivates his little plot of ground, secures a good return on his labor. On the other hand, "there is that which is swept away by reason of injustice." Rich men are often brought to ruin by their disregard of justice (*mishpat*). The contrast is this: the righteous poor are amply supplied by honest labor while the wicked rich lose everything by wrong conduct.

10. Godly discipline vs. indifference to wrong doing (13:24). "He that spares his rod hates his son." The verb "hates" (*sana'*) sometimes is used in the sense of not loving, or not loving as much as one could (cf. Deut 21:15). The point is that a man displays no love for a child by failing to correct him. On the other hand, "he who loves him seeks him early with discipline." He does not overlook the child's faults and exercises disciplinary measures to eradicate them. The verb "seek early" (*shachar*) is derived from a noun which means "early morning." This emphatic form suggests that the discipline would come either (1) in the morning of life before the bad habits are firmly fixed; (2) immediately after the offense; or (3) diligently.

11. Satisfaction vs. lust (13:25). "The righteous eats to the satisfaction of his desire." He can find satisfaction in the meals which he eats. On the other hand, "the belly of the wicked shall want." He never has enough to satisfy him.

THE WAY OF WISDOM
Proverbs 14:1-27

The first twenty-seven proverbs of chapter 14 are designed to help one find the path of wisdom and stay on it. No single theme is treated in this chapter, and many verses appear to be unrelated to those adjacent to them.

A. Identifying the Way (14:1-7).

The first series of proverbs stresses the truth that people who pursue wisdom find joy, and those who do not experience sadness.

1. Focus on the family (14:1). "The wise ones of women [each] builds her house." The term "builds" is used figuratively for building up the prosperity of the family. On the other hand, "folly [in a woman] with her own hands tears it down." The reference is to any activity, however good in itself, which diverts a woman from her number one priority, the family. The verse underscores the tremendous influence of a woman in the home.

2. Fear of Yahweh (14:2). "He who walks in his uprightness fears Yahweh." Reverence for God motivates and characterizes the righteous lifestyle. One's holy manner of life is evidence that he has been influenced by religious motives. On the other hand, "he whose ways are perverse, despise him." Perverse ways are sinful ways. All sin is offensive to God (cf. Gen 39:9). Those who neither fear nor love the Lord make no effort to exercise self-control. Wickedness is a proof that one has lost all reverence for God and concern about pleasing him.

3. Wise speech (14:3). "In the mouth of a fool is a branch [producing] pride." Growing conceit, accompanied by insolence towards others, tends to get a person into trouble. On the other hand, "the lips of wise men preserve them." Such do not abuse speech to insult and injure others. Their words tend to conciliate others, and promote peace and good will. They speak with courtesy and caution and thus avoid potential harm.

4. Hard work (14:4). "In the absence of oxen, the crib is clean." The owner is thus spared the labor of providing food for the animals or cleaning the area where the animals are normally kept. On the other hand, "great harvests come from the strength of an ox." This animal was used for plowing and threshing the grain. Without the ox there is nothing to put in the granary. The advantages of keeping an ox far outweigh the disadvantages. An investment of time and effort is essential to an abundant harvest.

5. Honest testimony (14:5). "A faithful witness will not deceive." He cannot be induced to swerve from the truth by threat or bribe. On the other hand, "a false witness breathes forth lies," i.e., lies pour out of his mouth like breath from the nostrils (cf. 6:19).

6. Search for wisdom (14:6-7). "Should a mocker seek wisdom, then it is not," i.e., it does not exist for him. Such a one cannot find wisdom because he lacks the essential prerequisite, namely, the fear of the Lord (Ps 111:10). True wisdom is not to be attained by those who are too conceited to receive instruction, who presume to depend upon their own judgment, and who weigh everything by their own standard. But why would a mocker seek wisdom at all? Perhaps for ulterior motives. He surmises that wisdom would enhance his prestige and position. He does not love wisdom for its own sake, hence he never receives it. On the other hand, "knowledge is easy to the person of discernment." Spiritual knowledge comes easy to one who realizes that the fear of God is a necessary precondition, and who earnestly seeks it from the hand of the Lord (14:6).

"Go from the presence of a foolish man." One should not spend much time in the company of a fool. Why? Because in his presence "you will not recognize lips of knowledge." He will speak no wisdom, hence his words will not be worth hearing. When one leaves the presence of a fool he carries nothing away with him (14:7).

B. Understanding the Way (14:8-19).

"The wisdom of the prudent is to understand his way." A prudent person weighs his steps carefully. He notes the various options open to him and deliberately chooses the one he believes to be right. He considers the ultimate outcome of his actions, as well as the motives from which they spring. On the other hand, "the folly of fools [results in] misdirection." Not having the patience or prudence to consider alternatives, the fool errs from the right path. What follows are proverbs illustrating this general principle (14:8).

1. *Consider the bond (14:9-10).* "As for fools, guilt is the intermediary," i.e., the bond between them.[2] That which binds foolish men together is the guilt which they share. On the other hand, "among the upright there is good will." That is the bond which draws them to one another (14:9).

No matter how close the bond between people, there is yet a gulf between them which cannot be bridged. "A heart knows the bitterness of his soul." Nobody can make another person understand exactly how he feels in a time of bitter sorrow. The same is true of great joy. "And in its joy a stranger cannot mingle himself." The verse is not suggesting that sorrows and joys cannot be shared. Rather, the writer is affirming here that no one can share with another his feelings in the same way in which he himself experiences them (14:10).

2. *Consider the end (14:11-13).* "The house of the wicked shall be overthrown." Sinners take great pains to increase their material prosperity, and to leave heirs to carry on their name and family. Divine providence, however, overrules their plans. That house will be overthrown. On the other hand, "the tent of the upright [i.e., those who adhere to honesty] shall flourish." Good men do their duty in life. They try to please God, and treat their neighbor right. The result is that God prospers them beyond all that they thought or hoped (14:11).

"There is a way that seems right to a man, but its end is the ways of death." A traveler may imagine that he has discovered a shortcut to his desired goal of success and happiness. Too late he discovers that the path leads instead to an early grave. The plural "ways" indicates that there are many bypaths which lead to death, as compared to one straight high road that leads to life more abundant. The language may apply either (1) to a perverted conscience; (2) to an uninstructed conscience; or (3) to the blinding effects of passion and self-will which make a person think that his way is the best way (14:12).

"Even in laughter the heart may ache, and as for its end rejoicing [may turn to] heaviness." The day most illuminated by sunshine may quickly become clouded. Life is full of uncertainty. Another interpretation is that outward mirth often masks hidden sorrow. In this life sorrow follows in the steps of joy. Only by experiencing sorrow can one really come to know joy (14:13).

3. *Consider the recklessness of the foolish (14:14-17).* "One turned away of heart has satisfaction from his [own] ways." The reference is to one who deliberately has turned away from the right. Such a one has one desire: to enjoy life. He is indifferent to questions of ethics or any thought of accountability to God. On the other hand, "a good man is [apart] from him," i.e., the good man does not accept the worldview of the one who has turned his heart away. He has a higher view of life's purpose (14:14).

"A simple person believes anything." He is gullible. He believes all that he hears without proof or examination. Having no fixed principles of his own, he is at the mercy of any adviser, and is easily led astray. He lacks discernment, and hence often is led into immorality. On the other hand, "a prudent person brings understanding to his step." He investigates, plans, evaluates and weighs options. He looks before he leaps (14:15).

"A wise person fears, and turns away from misfortune." The focus here is again on caution. A wise person fears committing evil, thereby offending the God he loves. He examines and ponders actions by the standards of his faith. By exercising such caution the wise person avoids disasters caused by impulsiveness. On the other hand, "the fool is presumptuous and confident." He behaves impulsively, and becomes involved in trouble. He trusts only in himself (14:16).

"A person of quick temper acts foolishly." He injures himself physically, mentally, and spiritually. He does harm to society as a whole, and to those he loves in particular. Such a person in his haste and passion does things which in calmer moments he must see are foolish and ridiculous. On the other hand, "a person of wicked schemes is hated." This proverb contrasts hasty anger which leads to folly, and deliberate malice-provoking hatred (14:17).

4. *Consider the ultimate victory (14:18-19).* "The simple inherit folly." Lack of wisdom causes these thoughtless ones to do what is foolish. Thus folly is said to be their inheritance. On the other hand, "the prudent have knowledge as their crown." The crown is that which honors and adorns. Knowledge (= wisdom) adorns and enhances character and standing (14:18).

"Evil people bow down before good people, and wicked people at the gates of the righteous." The final victory of good over evil is here set forth. The day will come when the wicked will acknowledge their defeat. The verb is in the Hebrew perfect indicating absolute certainty with regard to this outcome. The conviction that goodness wins out in the end is the triumphant affirmation of biblical revelation (14:19).

C. Cause and Effect Principle (14:20-27).

Wisdom recognizes that there is nothing which is causeless and unaccounted for in life. Applying this principle in personal and social situations is the burden of the next series of proverbs.

1. The sources of hatred and attraction (14:20). "Even by their neighbors the poor one is hated." The "neighbors" are people with whom he makes casual contact. "Hated" here is equivalent to *shunned.* A poor person has few if any friends because he is a constant burden on others. The shunning of the poor person grows out of selfishness. On the other hand, "lovers of a rich man are many." A rich man has many friends.

2. The sources of contempt and of compassion (14:21). "The person who despises his neighbor sins." One must not assume superior airs and look down upon a neighbor regardless of his destitute condition. A person of low estate has a claim for love and pity, and it is a sin to withhold them from him for selfish reasons (Lev 19:18). On the other hand, "the one who is gracious to the humble, happy is he." The merciful disposition is an evidence of a soul's communion with the God of mercy (cf. Matt 5:7).

3. The sources of perplexity or peace (14:22). "Do not they go astray who devise evil?" Solomon uses the interrogative form emphatically to affirm that they who plan and carry out evil most assuredly go astray from the right way, i.e., the way of life. Their perspective becomes so distorted that they can no longer see the proper course. On the other hand, "mercy and truth are for those who devise good." Those who work for the welfare of the community are appreciated, honored and respected. What is more, such receive God's blessing. The graces of mercy and truth point to the graciousness of God's dealings with the righteous, and the fidelity with which he keeps his promises to them.

567

4. The causes of gain and loss (14:23-24). "In all toil there is profit." The Hebrew *'etsebh* includes the idea of what is painful. However difficult the work and small the remuneration, some advantage is derived from honest labor. On the other hand, "the talk of lips is but to poverty." The contrast here is between merely talking, and actually doing. Idle chatter accomplishes nothing and leads to poverty (14:23).

"The crown of the wise is their riches."[3] The wisdom which crowns the life of the righteous is the only riches which they crave. On the other hand, "the folly of fools is folly." Nothing good can be expected of a fool because his acts will always be characterized by folly (14:24).

5. The sources of social security (14:25). "A faithful witness delivers souls" by clearing the innocent of false charges. On the other hand, "one who breathes out lies is deceit," i.e., he is a personification of fraud. Falsehood has become his very nature.

D. Conclusion (14:26-27).

The foregoing instruction comes to an emphatic conclusion in the concept of the fear of the Lord. "In the fear of Yahweh is a strong fortress." Godly fear casts out all fear of man and makes the believer confident and bold (cf. Rom 8:31). Furthermore, "for his children there shall be a place of refuge." The children of a godly person learn to trust in God from their father (14:26; Exod 20:6).

"The fear of Yahweh is a fountain of life, to depart from the snares of death" (cf. 13:14). The fear of the Lord can be so described because it produces obedience, and thus nourishes the flowers and fruits of faith. It produces graces and virtues, and thus prepares the soul for eternity (14:27).

ADVICE FOR RULERS
Proverbs 14:28–15:4

Verses 28 and 35 are royal proverbs. The intervening verses, although individually applicable, may be intended as special advice for kings.

568

A. His General Behavior (14:28).

"In the multitude of people is the king's glory." The political standing of the king depends on the number of people who pledge him allegiance. Thus kings must behave so as to retain the loyalty of their subjects. On the other hand, "in the lack of people is the ruin of the prince." A small kingdom invites attack and conquest by more powerful neighbors.

B. His Temperament (14:29-30).

1. A cool head (14:29). "One that is slow to anger is of great understanding." A ruler's prudence and wisdom are displayed by his being slow to take offense and being patient under injury. Such a one spares himself worry, and physical repercussions. He also helps to maintain a peaceful atmosphere in the community, which is a blessing to others as well as to himself. On the other hand, "he who is hasty in spirit exalts folly," i.e., exhibits folly, flaunts it in the eyes of all people.

2. A peaceful heart (14:30). "A heart of peace is life to the body" (lit., is lives of flesh). The reference is to a ruler of even temperament, one who takes all things in stride. Such temperament affects body health positively. On the other hand, "envy is the rottenness of bones," i.e., it has a deteriorating impact upon the body (cf. 12:4). In this context the word "envy" (*qin'ah*) may have the connotation of "passion" or "hotheadedness" which is detrimental to both physical and moral health.

C. His Governance (14:31-34).

1. A fundamental premise (14:31). The rule of the king must be based on the fundamental proposition that all people are the creatures of God. "The person who oppresses the poor despises his maker." A sin against a person is a sin against God, for man is made in the image of God. The issue in this beautiful proverb is whether the possessive pronoun refers to the oppressor or to the one oppressed. If the former, then the oppressor has committed a sin by defying the will of the God who commanded that the poor should be assisted. If the latter, then the thought is that the oppressed is as much a creation of God as the oppressor. Both belong to God. No one has a right to attack someone who belongs to God. On the other hand, "he who is gracious to the needy honors him," i.e., God. Not only is the needy person to be helped, but the help is to be rendered in a gracious manner so that the needy is not humiliated in the process (cf. Matt 25:40,45).

2. A fundamental obligation (14:32). The king had the responsibility to punish those who did wrong. "In his calamity, the wicked person is thrust down" without any hope of recovery. When misfortune comes upon him, he has no defense, no hope. He utterly collapses. His friends forsake him. There is no one to comfort or uphold him. He cannot rise again. On the other hand, "there is a refuge in the day of his death for the righteous." Such a one does not abandon hope of deliverance even when he is in a life-threatening situation. In this verse there may be a hint of immortality (Job 13:15; Ps 23:4).

3. A fundamental attribute (14:33). In Proverbs wisdom is frequently listed as a requirement of kings. "In the heart of a discerning person, wisdom rests." It need not boast of its presence. The intelligent person appreciates the worth of wisdom. So wisdom quietly enters into his life and settles there. On the other hand, "in the midst of fools she is made known." Fools have no perception of the worth of wisdom. Hence wisdom must actively assert her claims in order to gain the attention of fools.[4]

4. A fundamental goal (14:34). "Righteousness exalts a nation." "Righteousness" is rendering to all their due, whether to God or to man. While the principle here would be applied by Jews to Israel, the language is such that it is transnational. The verse illustrates the universalistic character of the teaching of this book. On the other hand, "sin is a reproach to any people." The words for "nation" (*goy*) and peoples (*le'ummim*) are usually applied to foreign nations rather than to Israel. The sin of the nations contrasted with the "righteousness" of the first clause must be injustice, impiety and violence.

The word translated "reproach" ("disgrace" NIV; cf. Lev 20:17) is spelled the same as the frequently used word which means lovingkindness (*chesed*). Therefore, the line has been interpreted by some rabbis to mean that the lovingkindness of the peoples is sin. The idea would be that the virtues of the heathen are really vices. Still another worthy interpretation takes note of the fact that the word translated "sin" (*chatta't*) is the same word used for the sin offering. Thus the idea is that for the heathen, their deeds of lovingkindness act like expiatory sacrifices for them.

D. His Private Administration (14:35–15:2).

In the court and among his closest advisors the king must also manifest wise behavior.

1. *Discernment (14:35).* "The king's favor should be toward the servant who acts wisely." Both Joseph and Daniel were advanced in royal service because they acted wisely. On the other hand, "his anger should be on one who acts shamefully." Credit should be given where it is due. Failure should receive censure.

2. *Appropriate speech (15:1-2).* "A soft answer turns away wrath." One who suffers injury should give an answer to his antagonist. He should not withdraw in sullen silence. If, however, one wishes to maintain peace, he must forego the hot, loud or sarcastic retort and give a pacifying reply (cf. 1 Sam 25:24). On the other hand, "a harsh word stirs up anger." The "harsh word" (*debhar 'etsebh*) is any statement which produces pain or irritation (15:1).

"The tongue of wise people adorns knowledge" either by expressing that knowledge (1) at the right time and place; or (2) in the right manner. The wise man not only possesses knowledge, he can give it proper expession. His language is carefully crafted. He neither overstates nor understates a situation. His words are well chosen. He does not antagonize. His speech is polite, dignified and precise. On the other hand, "the mouth of fools pours forth foolishness." A fool cannot open his mouth without proving his folly. He speaks without due consideration or discretion. He is uncouth and ill-mannered. He contributes nothing of substance to a conversation. His speech is badly phrased. His misinformation and antagonistic manner drives people from the truth (15:2).

E. Conclusion (15:3-4).

A Yahweh proverb reminds the king that ultimately his activities are subject to the teaching and judgment of the Lord, from whom nothing can be hidden. "In every place are the eyes of Yahweh." The verse stresses the minute scrutiny by God with the superficial estimate made by man. The eye of God observes every place where humankind lives. The omniscience and omnipresence of God are strongly emphasized here. "In every place he detects (*tsaphah*) both evil and good men." Men tend to make hasty generalizations regarding the goodness or badness of cities and nations. The gaze of God, however, is more discriminating (15:3).

A king who always speaks as though he were in the very presence of God will be a blessing to his people. "A tongue that brings healing is a tree of life." The reference is to the "soft answer" of 15:1. It soothes the feelings of the person addressed. That kind of tongue results in a more abundant life for the speaker as well as for the person addressed. On the other hand, "perverseness in it [the tongue] is a wound to the spirit" of both parties. "Perverseness" (*seleph*) refers to twisting words with evil intent, i.e., falsehood. The word "wound" (*shebher*) is literally "breaking" in spirit. Not only do such words break the spirit of the one addressed, they recoil upon the speaker as well (15:4).

THE DISCIPLINE OF TEMPER AND TONGUE
Proverbs 15:5-19

The call for a son to pay attention to his father's instruction and to heed his admonition marks the beginning of a new body of instruction. Chapter 15 is characterized by its theological tone. Nine of the thirty-three verses here are Yahweh proverbs.

A. Introduction (15:5-7).

"A fool rejects his father's discipline." By word and action he shows disdain for the discipline (cf. 13:1). On the other hand, "he who heeds correction acts prudently." The author assumes that the correction given by godly parents is always done in the best interests of the child (15:5).

"The house of the righteous person is a treasure store." His house is full of good things, both physical and spiritual, which God's protection allows him to enjoy. His resources are not wasted or wrongly used. On the other hand, "in the income of the wicked is something troubled." The term "income" (*tebhu'ah*) is usually employed in this book for what the wicked acquire (cf. 10:16). Great gain acquired by wrong, or expended badly, brings only trouble and ruin upon a man and his family. With that income comes embarrassment and guilt which prevents the owner from enjoying his ill-gotten gain. Verse 6 is not closely related to what precedes or what follows. It may have been placed in this position to make the point that true wisdom is consonant with righteousness, and folly with wickedness (15:6).

"The lips of the wise sprinkle knowledge." Their words provide encouragement and enlightenment to all who hear them or hear of them. On the other hand, "the heart of fools is not thus." The "heart" here is parallel to "lips" because, as the seat of intelligence, it directs speech. Fools do not spread knowledge, but spiritual ignorance and misunderstanding (15:7).

B. Wisdom and Godly Fear (15:8-11).

Three of the four proverbs grouped here are Yahweh proverbs. Here wisdom is equated with righteousness, and folly with wickedness which comes under the judgment of Yahweh.

1. Pleasing Yahweh (15:8-9). "The sacrifice of the wicked is an abomination to Yahweh." The Old Testament stresses that the value of sacrifice depended upon the mind and disposition of the offerer (see 1 Sam 15:22; Isa 1:11ff.; Amos 5:22ff.). On the other hand, "the prayer of the upright is his delight." God preferred the simple prayer of an upright man who could not afford a sacrifice to the pompous rituals performed by men of wealth who were wicked (15:8).

"The way of the wicked is an abomination to Yahweh." No wonder his sacrifice is an abmonination. Everything he does displeases the Lord. On the other hand, "the one who intently pursues righteousness he loves." Solomon here underscores the essence of Old Testament faith. Rituals and ceremonies—even prayer—were not the ultimate test of a person's religion. God smiles on that one who is on the path of righteousness, and who pursues that elusive goal with all his might (15:9).

2. Rejecting the way (15:10). "Stern discipline is for the one who forsakes the path." The "path" here is that way in which the one who pursues righteousness walks (cf. 12:28). Furthermore, "he who hates reproof shall die." Such a person gives ample evidence that he has no desire to repent. He persists in his evil. His rebellious lifestyle leads to an early grave, and ultimately to the second death (cf. Rom 6:23).

3. Punishing the wicked (15:11). Yahweh controls death. "Sheol and Abaddon are before Yahweh." Sheol is the abode of dead spirits. Abaddon (lit., "place of perishing") appears to be the lowest depth of hell, the "abyss" of the New Testament (Luke 8:31; Rev 9:2; 20:1). The afterlife is full of mystery to man. To God, however, all things are known. His eye penetrates even the most secret corners of the unseen world (cf. Job 26:6). Furthermore, if God knows all there is to know about the afterlife, how much more then must he know "the hearts of the children of men." To God the human heart is an open book (cf. Jer 17:10).

C. Wisdom and Cheerfulness (15:12-17).

Four of the six proverbs in this unit are concerned with happiness or cheerfulness. Interspersed are two proverbs (vv. 12,14) which stress the importance of accepting the teaching of the wise, which v. 16 suggests is equivalent to the fear of Yahweh.

1. An implicit appeal (15:12). "A mocker does not love one to reprove him." The "mocker" *(letz)* is one who is arrogant. Mockers are free thinkers, either indifferent to religion or skeptical thereof. Such people resent the efforts of anyone to set them straight. Furthermore, "unto the wise he will not go," i.e., for the purpose of receiving instruction (cf. 1:22; 13:1).

2. Cheerfulness manifested (15:13). "A joyous heart makes for a pleasant face." The face reflects the mood of the soul. On the other hand, "by sorrow of heart the spirit is broken." Happiness is shown in the outward look, but sorrow has a deeper and more abiding influence. It touches the inner person, creating despondency and despair. The entire demeanor of a person reveals the condition of the heart.

3. An implicit appeal (15:14). "The discerning heart seeks knowledge," i.e., hungers for knowledge. The more knowledge one has, the more he desires to have. The more he learns, the more he realizes how little he knows. On the other hand, "the mouth of fools feeds on folly." Such are interested only in the temporal and sensual gratification. They have no desire to know God and his word. The fool gulps down every silly opinion he hears, and eagerly disseminates that foolishness to all who will listen.

4. The power of positive thinking (15:15). "All the days of the afflicted are evil." An "afflicted" (*'ani*) person has a gloomy view of life. He is unable to cope with his hard circumstances. He worries much about the future and always forecasts the worst. On the other hand, "the cheerful heart has a continual feast." Solomon is advocating positive thinking. Though one is poor, he can still find life enjoyable if he cultivates a cheerful spirit. The implication is that the disposition is not dictated by outward circumstances. One who rejoices in his portion, however meager, has true riches.

5. *Happiness comparisons (15.16-17)*. "Better is a little with the fear of Yahweh, than great treasure and tumult with it." What is earned "with the fear of Yahweh," i.e., in a way that is honest, affords peace of mind, a greater treasure than vast wealth. The "tumult" (*mehumah*) envisioned here is that of oppressed people who cry out because they have been defrauded. Wealth earned in that manner cannot be a blessing to the one who possesses it. Another view is that the "tumult" is the care and labor and anxiety which accompanies the preservation of wealth (15:16).

"Better is a meal of vegetables where there is love, than a fattened ox with hatred." A humble and frugal meal becomes a banquet fit for a king when love is present among those who share in it. The most sumptuous repast, however, becomes unpalatable when those about the table are filled with animosity toward each other. A dish of vegetables would be the common meal in this period, whereas meat would be reserved for festive occasions. A "fattened ox" is one which has been taken out of the pasture to be fattened in the stall especially for the table (15:17).

6. *Detriments to happiness (15:18-19)*. The theme of happiness concludes with two proverbs which discourage behavior which thwart cheerful living: anger and sloth. First, "a hot-head [lit., a man of heat] stirs up discord." The reference is to one who easily loses his temper. Such a person only inflames a situation. On the other hand, "a patient person quiets a quarrel." Strife subsides when cooler heads prevail. The term "strife" (*rib*) often means "a legal dispute." It takes two to have a quarrel. Where one keeps his temper and refuses to be provoked, anger must subside (15:18).

"The way of the sluggard is like a hedge of thorns." A lazy man fails to trim his hedges. The thorns which protrude hinder his own movements along the paths. On the other hand, "the path of upright people is a highway." Such people are not lazy. They tread their appointed path in life resolutely and trustfully. What the sluggard regarded as dangerous and impassable, becomes for this righteous man "a highway." The word "highway" means literally, that which has been cast up with earth, and then flattened evenly (15:19).

ENDNOTES

1. The verb "pledged" (chabhal) in 13:13 is rendered variously: "will pay for it" (niv); "will be in debt to it" (nasb); "will be destroyed" (nkjv).

2. The verb *litz* here seems to have the meaning "to act as an interpreter or intermediary." Others take *litz* in its more common sense of "mock." This is the basis of the following translations: "Fools mock at sin" (NASB); "fools mock at making amends for sin" (NIV). Of the major English translations, BV comes closest to that proposed here: "the bond between foolish men is guilt."

3. Another possible translation of 14:24 is: "their riches are a crown unto the wise," i.e., when the wise own wealth they use it in a manner which brings them honor; but when fools have riches their use of it reveals their folly.

4. The Septuagint and Syriac support another reading of the last line of 14:33, namely, "but in the heart of fools she is not known."

CHAPTER TWENTY-EIGHT

Making Right Choices
Proverbs 15:20-19:25

The third section of the first great collection of proverbs begins in 15:20 with the catch phrase "a wise son." The opening verse has close affinities with 10:1 and 13:1, both of which stand at the head of a distinct group of proverbs.

CONTRAST BETWEEN
THE WICKED AND RIGHTEOUS
Proverbs 15:20-33

The core of the next fourteen proverbs presents a contrast between the righteous and the wicked with a heavy emphasis on the role of Yahweh as judge and distributor of rewards and punishment (vv. 25-30). This core is sandwiched between two passages, the theme of which is the need to receive instruction and to acquire wisdom (vv. 20-24,31-33).

A. Accepting Advice (15:20-24).

1. Filial respect commended (15:20). "A wise son causes his father to rejoice." The son is a reflection of his father. A godly father especially takes pleasure in watching his son walking circumspectly. On the other hand, "a fool of a man despises his mother." Though his mother may still love him, this attitude must cause the mother the deepest grief. The purpose of this verse is clearly to stress the importance to the young of becoming wise through heeding their parents' teaching. The verses which follow elaborate on this theme.

2. Understanding commended (15:21). "Folly is joy to the one who is lacking in understanding [lit., heart]." The term "folly" (*'ivveleth*) has both an intellectual and ethical connotation. Without the ability to discern between good and bad, a person is pulled naturally in the direction of the latter. On the other hand, "a man of discernment makes his going straight." He makes a conscious choice to walk in the path which is morally right.

3. Counsel commended (15:22-23). "Where there is no counsel there is the frustrating of plans." Usually a plan has a better chance to succeed when one has discussed it with others, especially critics. To fail to submit one's plans to scrutiny by others is to court disaster. On the other hand, "in the multitude of counselors it is established." The verb suggests that each plan is made successful by submitting it in advance for review by advisers (15:22).

"In the answer (or utterance) of his mouth a person has joy." People tend to regard their own opinions as true, their arguments as sound, and their stated intentions as good. In other words, people like to hear themselves talk. On the other hand, "a word in its time, how good it is." The reference is probably to a word of criticism appropriately timed and framed (15:23).

4. The ultimate issue (15:24). "The path of life is upward for the wise." It leads away from the pitfalls which mean premature and eternal death. The path may be steep and painful, but it leads away from destruction. A wise person "turns away from Sheol beneath." Sheol is the abode of the dead which is always represented as "beneath" or "down" even as heaven is represented as "up." Primarily a long and happy life is promised (cf. 3:16) to the person who fears the Lord.

B. Weighing Wickedness (15:25-30).

1. Ultimately judged (15:25). "As for the house of the proud, Yahweh will pluck it up." The "proud" *(ge'im)* are prominent men who abuse their power. Such shall be brought low by the Lord. Furthermore, the proud are removed so that the Lord may "establish the border of the widow." God will champion the cause of the widow and protect her property rights. The "widow" is taken as the type of weakness and desolation. Here is another example where evil loses out in the end, and righteousness prevails.

2. Presently offensive (15:26). Wickedness offends God. "An abomination to Yahweh are the thoughts of the wicked person." The reference is to schemes which are designed to injure the innocent and helpless. These thoughts work their way out in deceitful words. On the other hand, "pure are pleasant words." Such are words motivated by good will. They are honest, friendly and helpful. In the sight of God such words are "pure," i.e., not only acceptable, but commendable.

3. Frequently unproductive (15:27). "A troubler of his house is one who is greedy of gain." Money gained through greed and dishonesty cannot be enjoyed. All ill-gotten gain brings sure retribution. This throws the entire family into turmoil and hardship. An avaricious man troubles his house in another sense. He harasses his family by niggardly economics. He overworks and underpays his employees. He deprives his household of all comfort, and loses the blessing of God upon a righteous use of earthly wealth. On the other hand, "one who hates bribes shall live." Those who despise dishonest gain have the promise of life more abundant. Primarily this refers to the judge or magistrate who is incorruptible, gives just judgment, and dispenses his patronage without fear or favor. Such a person shall "prolong his days" (cf. 28:16). There is perhaps here a hope for immortality to which integrity leads.

4. Publicly flouted (15:28). "The heart of a righteous person contemplates before answering." The "heart" here as elsewhere in Proverbs points to the intellectual/emotional aspect of a person. The point is that a righteous person reflects before speaking so that the words that he speaks are both sympathetic and helpful. He wishes to avoid saying anything false, or inexpedient, or injurious to his

579

neighbor. On the other hand, "the mouth of wicked people pours out evil things." Such people speak recklessly, impulsively, without any reflection. Hence they do a great deal of damage.

5. *Spiritually isolated (15:29-30).* "Yahweh is far from wicked people." When they cry out to him in some emergency, he is not available to them (cf. John 9:31). On the other hand, "the prayer of righteous people he shall hear." This proverb may be intended as a comment on the previous one which contrasts the flow of words from the wicked with the considered speech of the righteous.

"The light of eyes makes the heart rejoice." Context suggests that the reference is to the brightness which shines in the eyes when one hears good news. Furthermore, "a good report makes fat the bones." Bones full of marrow were a symbol of good health to the ancients. Thus, good tidings invigorate the body. The promise that Yahweh hears the prayer of righteous people is good news (15:30).

C. Accepting Advice (15:31-33).

"The ear that hears the reproof of life shall lodge in the midst of the wise." The ear here by synecdoche refers to the whole person. The "reproof of life" is that criticism which, if accepted, would prolong life. A person may wish to associate with wise men so that he might hear such life giving reproof (15:31).

"One who ignores discipline, despises himself [lit., his soul]." Such a one shortchanges himself. He cheats himself out of a more abundant life. The line may suggest something stronger: he throws his life away by rejecting the correction of his hurtful and harmful ways. On the other hand, one who hears correction acquires understanding [lit. heart]." Such a one comes to realize that virtue prolongs and enriches life (15:32).

"The fear of Yahweh is the instruction of wisdom." The tenets of the wisdom teachers are in accord with divine teaching. Furthermore, "before honor is humility." The fear of Yahweh leads to humility. Humility in turn permits one to receive instruction in wisdom. When one's life reflects wisdom, he receives honor from both God and man (15:33; Jas 4:6; Phil 2:5ff.).

MAN UNDER GOD
Proverbs 16:1-33

The concluding verse of chapter 15 is a bridge to the collection of proverbs in chapter 16. Its emphasis on the fear of Yahweh and humility are further amplified in this unit.

A. The Heavenly King (16:1-9).

Verses 1-9 present a comprehensive picture of Yahweh as in total control of human affairs. Verses 1 and 9 form a framework within which the intervening proverbs expound and illustrate this conviction.

1. Introduction to the theme (16:1). "To man belongs the arrangements of the heart." The reference is to the entire intellectual capacities of man. He has the power of connecting ideas, drawing conclusions, and arranging logical arguments. On the other hand, "from Yahweh is the utterance of the tongue." The ability to phrase one's ideas in convincing language is a special gift of God (cf. Matt 10:19).

2. Yahweh tests human motives (16:2-4). "All the ways of a person are clean in his own eyes." A person may be blind to his own faults or he may be following an ill-informed conscience. Yet this is no excuse in God's eyes. People try to justify their actions. In so doing, they may even engage in self-deception. On the other hand, "Yahweh weighs spirits," not just the outward life and actions only. He knows the true motivation behind each deed (Heb 4:12). He also knows secret faults, unsuspected by others, and perhaps even by one's self (16:2).

"Roll on to Yahweh your works." This admonition carries forward the thought of the preceding proverb. One should submit all his deeds to God for his assessment. Furthermore, if one heeds this admonition, his "thoughts shall be established." The very act of submitting deeds to divine appraisal is evidence that the thoughts of the heart are sincere. The plans and deliberations out of which the "works" spring shall meet with a happy fulfillment, because they are undertaken according to the will of God, and directed by his guidance (16:3).

"Everything Yahweh has worked out for his own purpose, even the wicked for the day of evil." He is the absolute creator. He is

581

sovereign over his creation. He has given purpose to everything he has made, though at times man may have difficulty discovering that purpose. Everything exhibits his goodness and wisdom, and tends to his glory. Furthermore, his purpose extends even to the wicked. God did not create any person evil, for that would conflict with the doctrine of free will articulated in other wisdom texts (cf. Eccl 7:29). Nor should this verse be forced to teach that God has willed the damnation of some (cf. 1 Tim 2:4; John 3:17). Knowing, however, that some men would choose wickedness, God arranged that the universe should include a "day of evil" or judgment in which retribution would be meted out (16:4).

3. *Yahweh acknowledges humility (16:5-6).* "An abomination of Yahweh are all who are proud of heart." Defiance of God and his word is the outward evidence of one who is proud of heart. Such "shall not be unpunished" (16:5; cf. 11:20).

On the other hand, "with mercy and faithfulness iniquity is covered." Should sinners repent and begin to practice mercy and faithfulness, whatever sin had been committed would be "covered over" or hidden from God's sight. Such graces show themselves only in one who is really devout and God-fearing; they are the fruits of a heart at peace with God and man. Solomon probably did not mean to exclude the role of sacrifice in expiation of sin, but rather meant to stress that sacrifice as mere ritual cannot atone for sin. Furthermore, "by the fear of Yahweh a man is turning from evil." Reverence for God gives a person strength to turn away from sin when tempted. The verse thus addresses two fundamental aspects of biblical religion: how to remove sin, and how to avoid it.

4. *Yahweh provides deliverance (16:7-8).* "When a person's ways please Yahweh, even his enemies shall make peace with him." A person in the right relationship with the Lord, lives a life that is winsome and attractive. The blessings which God showers on the faithful attract the worldly (16:7; Gen 26:27f.).

What kinds of ways please Yahweh? "Better is a little with righteousness, than great revenues with injustice." "Righteousness" here may mean a holy life or just dealings. "Revenues" (cf. 10:16; 15:6) means dishonest gain. "Injustice" may refer either generally to wickedness, or specially to fraud and oppression (16:8; cf. 15:16).

5. Conclusion (16:9). "The heart of a man plans his way." Freedom of will permits people to choose the course of their life. The verb "plans" is a form that points to the intensity of thought and care. On the other hand, "Yahweh determines his steps." Man prepares his plans with the utmost deliberation, but it rests with God whether or not he shall carry those plans through to completion, and what degree of difficulty will be faced in the process. If one's choice meets with approval, God will direct his steps to the desired goal.

B. The Earthly King (16:10-15).

Verses 10-15 focus on the king as God's representative. He has received from God powers which properly belong to him. The point here is this: what is required of kings is the same as what is required of ordinary men and women.

1. Divine powers of judgment (16:10). "A divine sentence is in the lips of a king." The term "divine sentence" (*qesem*) regularly refers to an act of pagan divination (cf. Deut 18:10). In the ancient world a king's word had the importance of a divine oracle in the mind of the people. His word put an end to all controversy or division of opinion. The kings of Israel were anointed with the sacred oil. Kingship was a sacred office. Hence the king must regard his pronouncements as something holy. Furthermore, "in judgment his mouth should not trespass." The word "trespass" (*ma'al*) is used in the technical sense of Lev 5:15 of putting to improper use anything which had been dedicated to the Lord. The implication is that judgment was sacred, and therefore the king must never violate justice.

2. Guardian of weights and measures (16:11). "The balance and scales of justice are Yahweh's." Even a king cannot alter weights and measures to suit his own purposes. The standards are fixed by God and delegated to the king to administer fairly. The great principles of truth and justice govern all the transactions of buying and selling. Biblical faith impinges on the world of business. Furthermore, "all the weights of the bag are his work." The weights used in the scales are made by God. The king may not provide his own. That cheating in this area was quite common is indicated by the pointed preaching of the prophets (e.g., Micah 6:11).

3. Advocate of integrity (16:12-13). "The abomination of kings is the doing of wickedness." This has been taken to mean that (1) it is an abomination for kings to commit wickedness; and (2) that kings should abhor those who commit wickedness. This is the case "because the throne is established by righteousness." He who sits on the throne must be righteous, and must use the authority of his office to encourage and enforce righteousness. Such a king will find his throne "established," i.e., made permanent. His subjects are willing to obey him, and are ready to die for him and his family. The point is that law-makers should not be law-breakers (16:12).

"Righteous lips are the delight of kings, and the one who speaks uprightly each one of them loves." The "kings" here envisioned are those who measure up to the ideal set forth for rulers in Scripture. Such rulers hate flattery and dissimulation, and encourage honest speaking. Leaders cannot properly govern when those around them speak only flattering falsehoods (16:13).

4. *Absolute power (16:14-15).* "The wrath of the king is as messengers of death." In his anger the king will utter death warrants on all who offend him. Anger the king and punishment is at hand. On the other hand, "a wise person will pacify it," i.e., the king's anger. Such a person will avoid defying the king.

"In the light of the king's countenance is life," i.e., happiness and prosperity. As the king's anger and the darkening of his countenance are death (v. 14), so, when his look is cheerful and bright, it sheds joy and life around. Furthermore, "his favor is like the cloud of latter rain" (cf. Ps 72:6). Such a cloud was a welcome sight to the inhabitants of the parched land. The latter rain fell in March or April and assured the bountiful harvest (16:15).

C. Right Choices (16:16-23).

An appeal to acquire wisdom signals the beginning of yet another collection of instructional proverbs. "To acquire wisdom, O how much better than gold." This verse is a brief summary of the thought in 3:13-18. Furthermore, "to acquire understanding is chosen more than silver" (16:16).

1. *Avoid evil (16:17).* "The highway of the upright is to depart from evil." The way trodden by the upright is compared to a properly constructed path which has been leveled and cleared of obstructions.

One who wishes to walk this path must depart from evil.[1] Furthermore, "the one who keeps his soul guards his way." He does not
walk aimlessly, but makes a conscious choice to walk on the way of
the upright.

2. *Cultivate humility (16:18-20).* "Before destruction is pride,
and before a fall a haughty spirit." Pride is an offense against God, for
it attributes success to one's own energy and effort when in fact it
should be attributed to the benevolence of God. Inevitably pride will
be humbled by God (16:18).

"Better a lowly spirit with the humble, than to divide the spoil with
the proud." The "lowly spirit" is the opposite of the feeling of self-
importance. The "humble" (poor) are the despised people who earn a
scanty living by honest means. To "divide the spoil" is a figure taken
from military life. Here the expression points to the enrichment of the
strong at the expense of the poor. To share in the fruits of the pursuits of the proud, and to enjoy their pleasures, a person must cast his
lot with them and participate in the crimes by which they gain their
wealth. It is better to be among the victims than among those who
victimize others (16:19).

Humility manifests itself in obedience to God's word. "Whoever
acts wisely in respect to a word shall find good." Acting wisely in
respect to the divine word would mean obeying it. Furthermore,
"whoever trusts in Yahweh, blessed is he." He is blessed, not only
materially, but spiritually as well. This Yahweh proverb is central in
this group. It performs the familiar function of identifying wisdom (or
instruction) with trust in the Lord.

3. *Speak wisely (16:21-24).* "One who is wise in heart is called
discerning," i.e., he becomes known in his community as an intelligent person. A "discerning" person is one who can be consulted in
times of doubt and difficulty. Furthermore, "the sweetness of the lips
increases learning." A man of discernment answers with carefully chosen words. He speaks those answers in a pleasant voice. Thus his
responses find ready acceptance in ever larger circles (16:21).

"A fountain of life is understanding to the one who has it." The
possessor of understanding has in himself a source of comfort and an
invigorating power which is as refreshing as a cool spring to a thirsty
traveler. In all troubles he can fall back upon his own good sense and

prudence, and satisfy himself therewith. On the other hand, "the chastisement of fools is folly." Folly is the scourge which punishes a fool. By refusing the teaching of wisdom, the fool makes misery for himself, deprives himself of the happiness which virtue gives, and pierces himself through with many sorrows (16:22).

"The heart of the wise gives discernment to his mouth, and increases learning upon his lips." Such people speak thoughtfully. They invest their words with insight and sagacity. The intellect and knowledge of the wise display themselves in their discourse (16:23).

"As a honeycomb are pleasant words, sweet to the soul, and health to the bones." "Pleasant words" are comforting words. Wisdom adorns words with graciousness. The happy result of such words are felt in body and soul. "Bones" here refer to the entire body (16:24).

4. *Conclusion (16:25):* The consequences of choices. "There is a way that is upright before a man, but its latter end are the ways of death." Identical with 14:12.

D. Warnings about Troublemakers (16:26-30).

Verses 26-30 form a tightly knit group of verses about different types of persons who disrupt community life. Such lists are found elsewhere in the book (e.g., 6:16-19).

1. *The hungry man (16:26).* "The appetite [lit., soul] of a laborer works for him; for his mouth compels him." Hunger is a powerful incentive to cause a person to work, but it is not the best incentive. This proverb is probably intended to suggest that hunger alone is not a sufficient motive for work. Proverbs regards work in and of itself as beneficial to mankind.

2. *The worthless man (16:27).* "A worthless man [i.e., scoundrel] digs a pit with evil." The reference is to evil words, to slander or words of enticement which are meant to ensnare the innocent. Furthermore, "his speech is like a scorching fire." The words on the lips of the worthless person harm and injure others (cf. James 3:6).

3. *The perverse man (16:28).* "A perverse person stirs up strife." The "perverse person" is literally "the person of upside down [utterances]." A person who perverts truth intentionally creates strife and discord. Furthermore, "a backbiter causes a best friend[2] to separate."

Some malicious individuals are determined by their twisted talk to turn one away from his best friend.

4. The violent man (16:29). "A violent man [i.e., career criminal] entices his neighbor, and leads him in a path that is not good." He wrongs another by fraud or oppression. He attempts to lure his friends into a "path that is not good," i.e., a life of crime.

5. The calumnious man (16:30). "One who winks his eyes is plotting perversity." He insinuates that he could say more about a person if he wished. Such is the slanderer's mode of operation. Furthermore, "who compresses his lips completes evil." This action of the mouth, like the wink of the eye, is suggestive that one knows more than he lets on. A wise person will note such body language and take warning.

E. Concluding Reminders (16:31-33).

1. The forward look (16:31). "A glorious crown is gray hair; in the way of righteousness it is found." Length of days is viewed as the crowning blessing of the Lord upon the life of one who lives by God's word. This is a cardinal doctrine of the wisdom literature. The verse also is indicative of the respect for the aged in Israelite society (cf. Lev 19:32). In pagan societies of that day one's worth in the community declined as his physical prowess waned (16:31).

2. The inward look (16:32). "Better is one who is slow to anger than a mighty warrior, and the one who rules his spirit more than one who captures a city." Self-control is superior to physical strength. Conquering one's self is the greatest battle one will ever win. The "spirit" in this verse refers to the temperament of a person.

3. The upward look (16:33). "In the lap the lot is cast; but from Yahweh is all its judgment." The lot was employed religiously in cases where other means of decision were not suitable or available; it was not to supersede common prudence or careful investigation. Pious Israelites believed that Yahweh guided the selection of the proper lot. The "lap" here is the fold in the garment in which were placed the two lots from which the choice was to be made. These lots—probably stones of various shapes or colors—were then drawn from the garment folds or shaken out on the ground (e.g., Josh 18:10; Acts 1:24-26).

THE AMBIGUITY OF HUMAN ACTIONS
Proverbs 17:1-28

Chapter 17 focuses on the ambivalence of human affairs. The same activity can sometimes be good, sometimes bad.

A. The Pursuit of Tranquility (17:1-9).

1. Domestic tranquility (17:1-3). "Better is a dry morsel along with quietness, than a house full of sacrifices of strife." A home without love, however luxurious, is a place of misery (cf. 15:16f.). Dry bread was soaked in wine or water before it was eaten (cf. Ruth 2:14). Meat was eaten at festive meals. A house with "sacrifices," i.e., the sacrificial meat, was an affluent family (17:1).

"A servant who deals wisely will rule over a son who acts shamefully, and in the midst of brothers he shall inherit a portion." In recognition of ability and loyalty a master might grant a servant his freedom and include him among his heirs (Eccl 10:7). Scripture furnishes several examples of servants who rose to prominence (17:2 ; Gen 24:2; 2 Sam 16:4).

Family life, like the other aspects of human existence, is ruled by an omniscient God. "The refining pot is for silver, and the furnace for gold; but a tester for hearts is Yahweh." That which fire does for the metals, God does for the heart. By means of sorrow, sickness and economic difficulty he purifies it from dross and brings forth the good that is in it (17:3; 1 Pet 1:7; Rev 3:18).

2. Community tranquility (17:4-5). "An evildoer inclines [the ear] to wicked lips giving ear to falsehood upon a destructive tongue." Such a-one listens with eagerness, and so encourages the scandalmonger. "Wicked lips" here point to one who slanders another. Gossip is destructive of reputation and sometimes even of life (17:4).

"One who mocks the poor shows contempt for his maker; one who rejoices at calamity shall not go unpunished." Delight in others' misfortune, even those of enemies, is a most detestable form of selfishness and malice (cf. Job 31:29). God makes poor and makes rich (1 Sam 2:7). Hence, mocking a person's poverty is blasphemy. "Calamity" is either brought about by God or permitted by him. Thus to rejoice over calamity is to show contempt for God (17:5).

3. *Geriatric tranquility (17:6).* "A crown of old men are children's children and the glory of children are their fathers." Children are one of the greatest of life's blessings. To be surrounded by a large and devoted band of grandchildren was more desired by the ancient Hebrews than a crown. A large number of children guaranteed the stability of the family. By the same token, children eagerly boast about their fathers if they have reason to. Here is a powerful incentive for a father to live honorably, so that his children should have reason to be proud of him.

4. *Judicial tranquility (17:7-8).* "Unsuited to a fool is a lip of excess, how much less a lying lip to a person of noble character." "A lip of excess" points to superior talk or overbearing speech. The "fool" (*nabhal*) is a person of depraved character. His lifestyle is nothing to brag about. Even less is a lying lip suited to a prince (*nadhibh*), one who is supposed to be of noble character (17:7; Isa 32:8).

"A precious stone is the bribe in the eyes of the one who has it: wherever he turns he shall prosper." A bribe accomplishes whatever it is intended to accomplish. It is like a jewel that dazzles the sight and affects the mind of him who receives it. This proverb does not commend taking bribes, a forbidden practice (cf. Exod 23:8; Deut 16:19). Solomon is simply stating a fact of life without indicating the morality of bribery. It is possible that the verse has a more general application, and applies to gifts given to appease anger or to prove friendship (17:8).

5. *Interpersonal tranquility (17:9).* "One who conceals a transgression is seeking love; but one who repeats the matter separates close friends." The reference is not to societal crimes, but to transgressions against individuals. If one wishes to maintain a friendship he had better overlook offenses against himself. Such restraint promotes friendship. The Mosaic law taught forbearance (Lev 19:18). If, however, the guilty party repeats the offense, then he bears the responsibility for severing the friendship because the repetition will be resented. Others take the second clause differently: He who is always dwelling on a grievance, returning to it and bringing it forward on every occasion, alienates the greatest friends.

B. Disruptions of Tranquility (17:10-15).

Certain evil characters shatter the tranquility which constitutes the ideal life. One must avoid such characters if he would have peace in his life.

1. The rebellious (17:10-11). "A rebuke descends on a person of understanding more than striking a fool a hundred times." A person of understanding responds to a mere word of constructive criticism positively and immediately. A fool is thick-headed. He pays no attention to correction no matter how severe it might be (17:10).

"Only rebellion does an evil man seek, and a cruel messenger shall be sent against him." The "rebellion" may be against God or against civil authority. In either case, such revolt does not go unpunished. The "messenger" here is the executioner of the king's wrath. He is called "cruel" because his errand is deadly, and he is pitiless in its performance (17:11).

2. The vicious (17:12). This verbless proverb literally rendered is: "The meeting of a bereaved bear with a man, and not [the meeting of] a fool in his folly." Apparently the author intended a comparison. The Syrian bear, common in Palestine in Bible times, is now all but extinct. The ferocity of a bear robbed of its young is legendary (2 Sam 17:8; Hos 13:8). Still more dangerous is a fool in his folly. Consider as examples the infanticide ordered by Herod (Matt 2:16) and the reckless language of Saul against his son Jonathan (1 Sam 20:30).

3. The ingrate (17:13). "One who returns evil for good, evil shall not depart from his house." The verse may refer to God's visitation upon the wicked. Others, however, see here the natural result of such perverted conduct (cf. 1 Sam 25:21f.). One who treats his fellow man with such contempt will not find anyone to come to his aid when he is in trouble.

4. The contentious (17:14). "He who releases water [so is] the beginning of strife; therefore before it bursts forth, abandon the contention." A quarrel begins like a small hole in a dam, letting out a tiny trickle. If it is not stopped immediately, the hole is enlarged and a flood pours forth. If one senses irritation and agitation, that is the time to break off the activity before the contention bursts forth.

5. The unjust (17:15). "The one who acquits the wicked and the one who condemns the innocent, an abomination to Yahweh are the

590

two of them." Two forms of injustice are condemned: the acquittal of a guilty person and the condemnation of an innocent one (cf. Exod 23:6f.).

C. The Keys to Tranquility (17:16-20).

1. Acquisition of wisdom (17:16). "Of what use is money in the hand of a fool to acquire wisdom when there is no understanding?" Even if a fool sought to purchase wisdom he would not be able to do so. Such a one does not possess the qualities of mind and character with which to acquire understanding.

2. Cultivation of friendships (17:17). "At all times the friend loves and a brother for adversity is born." Even in adversity, when friendship experiences the ultimate test, the friend/brother is there with support. A genuine friend is regarded as superior to a blood relative in a time of emergency (cf. 18:24; 27:10). In this verse "a brother" is a synonym for a true friend.

3. Cautious business practices (17:18). "A person lacking understanding is the one who strikes a hand guaranteeing a pledge in the presence of his neighbor." The gesture of striking hands sealed a solemn legal commitment (cf. 6:1; 11:15). The "neighbor" here is the creditor. What is censured is the weakness which, for the sake of worthless companions, lets itself be hampered and endangered by others' obligations. The modern equivalent of what is considered stupid here is the co-signing of a note.

4. Humble lifestyle (17:19). "One who loves transgression loves strife and one who exalts his gate seeks destruction." The "transgression" here is not against God, but against a neighbor. Strife leads to many breaches of the commandments. The "gate" has been taken to refer to the mouth, i.e., talking arrogantly; it has also been taken as a symbol for a house, i.e., living in an ostentatious manner. In either case, a person by such conduct invites envy, anger and ultimate ruin.

5. Consistent speech (17:20). "He who is crooked of heart does not find good," i.e., he does not prosper. A "crooked heart" is a warped mind which cannot think straight. Such a person creates hardship and misfortune for himself because he creates antagonism. He will gain no blessing in his worldly matters, much less in spiritual things. Likewise, "he who turns himself about with his tongue shall fall

591

into evil." He says one thing at one time and something quite contrary at another. This results in "evil," i.e., harm to his reputation and livelihood.

D. Parental Tranquility (17:21-25).

The similarity between vv. 21 and 25 suggests a small collection. The general theme is on the disappointment caused by children who refuse to follow wisdom. These proverbs may be intended as an appeal to the young to heed their parents' teaching.

"One begets a fool to sorrow for himself, and the father of a fool does not rejoice." Two kinds of fools are mentioned in this verse. The first "fool" (*kesil*) is a child who is bold and self-confident in his folly. He is worldly wise, but devoid of scruples. The second "fool" (*nabhal*) is one who is dull and stupid. He lacks mental powers. A son of either kind is a constant source of grief to his parents (17:21).

The sorrow of the preceding verse triggers this proverb regarding a broken spirit. "A joyous heart is good medicine." A cheerful disposition affects one's overall health. On the other hand, "a broken spirit dries up the bones." Depression affects bodily health negatively. By metonymy the bones here stand for the whole body (17:22).

"A gift from the bosom a wicked man takes to pervert the paths of justice." The "wicked man" here is either the judge or a witness willing to commit perjury for a price. The "gift" (*shochad*) is a bribe. It is taken "from the bosom," i.e., secretly from the fold of the garment, and not from the purse or bag in which money was normally carried. The wicked judge accepts a bribe from one of the litigants involved in a lawsuit. Judges had no appointed salaries; hence the unprincipled among them were open to bribery (17:23; Exod 23:8; Deut 16:19).

"With the face of a discerning man is wisdom." The idea is that an intelligent person directs his look towards wisdom, and therefore she beams upon him with all her light. Such a person concentrates all his powers on achieving wisdom. On the other hand, "the eyes of a fool are in the ends of the earth." Such a one cannot concentrate his mind, so his gaze wanders in all directions. He pursues a hundred different things as they happen to come his way, but misses the most important quest of all (17:24).

"A vexation to his father is a foolish son, and bitterness to the one who bore him." Solomon again points to the pain which foolish children bring to their parents (17:25; cf. 15:20; 17:21).

E. Proper Restraint (17:26-28).

"If to punish an innocent person is not good, [how much worse is it] to smite noble people for their integrity." The writer seems to mention first a less serious injustice, namely, fining (cf. Deut 22:19) an innocent person, and then one that is more serious, namely, scourging men of high character because they adhere to lofty principles and refuse to compromise (17:26).

"One who restrains his words has knowledge; and he who is cool of spirit is a person of understanding." The proverb is urging one to avoid reckless speech and an uncontrolled spirit which provokes enmity (17:27).

"Even a fool may be thought to be wise if he keeps silent, discerning if he restrains his lips." Silence is sometimes taken to be evidence of a profound mind (17:28).

FRIENDS AND FOES
Proverbs 18:1-24

The proverbs in chapter 18 are grouped loosely around the theme of friends and foes.

A. Speech and Friendship (18:1-8).

Solomon identifies certain types of speech which are detrimental to friendship.

1. Arrogant speech (18:1-2). "For desire one shall seek who has separated himself, and defies [lit., breaks out against] all sound wisdom." The conceited, self-willed person, sets himself against public opinion. He delights in differing from received customs, takes no counsel from others, and thinks nothing of public interests. Such a person attends only to his own private ends and fancies (18:1).

"A fool does not delight in understanding, except in the laying bare of his heart." Such a one takes no pleasure in the wisdom of others. He is self-opinionated. He does not desire to possess the ability of distinguishing between the true and the false. His only desire is to disclose his own mind and air his personal opinions, although these are based on nothing else than his stupidity. His own dogmatic views are unquestionably correct. By such he thinks he is showing himself superior to others, and benefiting the world at large (18:2).

2. *Contemptuous speech (18:3).* "When a wicked man comes, contempt also comes, and with disdain provocation." The wicked man has contempt for others, and for all that is pure, good and lovely. He heaps abuse on all who strive to impede him in his evil courses. All that he says or does brings disgrace, and he is always ready to revile any who are better than himself. This is a cause of disharmony. When one treats others with disdain he provokes hostility and sometimes violence.

3. *Imprecise speech (18:4).* "Deep waters are the words of a person's mouth, [but] a flowing brook is a well of wisdom." The reference is to an ordinary, average person.[3] "Deep waters" are those which lie far beneath the surface. Only with great effort can they be brought up. So the words of an ordinary person are obscure and imprecise. They can only be understood with difficulty. On the other hand, "a flowing brook is a well of wisdom." A wise man is a fountain of wisdom. One can drink from that water (i.e., understand what he is saying) as easily as he can drink from a flowing stream.

4. *Unjust speech (18:5).* "If to show partiality to [lit., lift up the face of] the wicked is not good, [how much less] to turn aside the innocent in judgment." The "wicked" here is the guilty party in a court case. The word translated "innocent" (*tsaddiq*) is frequently rendered "righteous." To show partiality is to be guided in judgment, not by the facts of a case, nor by the principles of right and wrong, but by extraneous considerations. For example, judgment might be rendered for-(or against) a person on the basis of his appearance, manners, fortune, or family.

5. *Contentious speech (18:6-7).* "The lips of a fool enter into strife, and his mouth calls for strokes." A fool's talk results in personal quarrels or even lawsuits. He meddles with disputes in which he is not concerned, and by his silly interference not only exposes himself to reprisals, but also exacerbates the original difficulty. At times such interference brings upon the speaker a beating. The word "strokes" (*mahalumot*) can refer to the blows delivered by an offended person, or to the scourging ordered by a court (18:6).

"The mouth of a fool is his ruin, and his lips are the snare of his soul." This proverb is a more generalized statement of the thought of the preceding verse. A fool's words get him into trouble (18:7).

6. *Gossip (18:8).* "The words of a whisperer are like choice morsels, and they go down to the depths of the belly." A "whisperer" (*nirgan*) is a gossip. The juicy tidbits of gossip are eagerly devoured by persons disposed to listen to them, as a glutton helps himself freely to tempting food. The slanderous words do not make a superficial impression, but penetrate into the innermost recesses of the listener where they are thoroughly digested. They are treasured up in memory to be used as occasion may offer.

B. Actions Conducive to Friendship (18:9-13).

1. *Be industrious (18:9).* "Even one who is slack in his work is a brother to an owner destroying [his property]." The reference is to one who does his work in some fashion, but not heartily and diligently. He does not realize that labor is not only a necessity, but a means of discipline and sanctification. Such a person is a "brother," i.e., he is in the same category, as the property owner who ruins his possession. A dilatory workman ruins his livelihood as surely as a landowner reduces himself to poverty if he neglects his property. The proverb implies that negligence in duty is as dangerous as actual destructiveness.

2. *Trust in Yahweh (18:10-11).* "The name of Yahweh is a tower of strength: the righteous person runs into it and is set on high." The "name" of Yahweh signifies all that God is in himself—his attributes, his love, mercy, power, and knowledge. He who seeks refuge in the Lord is "set on high" so that he is inaccessible to the dangers which threaten below (cf. Ps 61:3). The picture here is of a central fortress in which, at times of danger, the surrounding population could take refuge (18:10).

"The wealth of the rich person is his strong city, but like a high wall [only] in his estimation." Wealth affords protection (cf. 10:15), but if that wealth is misused the protection is illusionary. The fool imagines that his wealth is an unassailable defense which will preserve him amid all the storms of life. Such is not the case. That "high wall" would one day fall, smashed by Yahweh in the judgment (18:11).

3. Humble the heart (18:12). "Before a fall the heart of a person is haughty; before honor goes humility." The first clause is similar to 16:18. The second clause is identical to the second clause of 15:33.

4. Speak cautiously (18:13). "One who answers a word before he hears, it is folly to him and shame." One should listen carefully before answering, making sure that he understands the import of what is being said. A wise person does not interrupt the speech of his fellow, and is not hasty to respond to his proposals.

5. Bear up patiently (18:14). "The spirit of a person will sustain his infirmity." Willpower and determination can counterbalance physical weakness and enable a person to win the day. On the other hand, "a broken spirit who can bear?" If the willpower is undermined, a person cannot endure. He must surely succumb and suffer defeat. In the first clause the term "spirit" is masculine, in the second feminine. The change of gender suggests that the manly quality of the inner person has become weakened through affliction. The implication is that believers should be as reticent to wound a brother's spirit as they would be to injure his body. The latter may be healed by medical treatment; the former is more severe in its effects, and is sometimes irremediable.

C. Dealing with Disputes (18:15-24).

Verse 15, with its emphasis on acquiring knowledge, may be, like other similar verses, the beginning of a new "instruction." "The heart of the discerning person acquires knowledge, and the ear of wise people seeks knowledge." Both the inner and outer organs of perception (heart and ear) must be utilized by those who search after wisdom. The understanding of the wise person is always expanding and increasing its stores, because his ear is open to instruction (18:15).

1. Offering gifts (18:16). "A person's gift enlarges [the path] for him, and before great people it brings him." The gift (*mattan*) is not necessarily a bribe; it could be a present given to persons of influence by one who needs their help to achieve his purpose. "To enlarge the path" is an idiom meaning to make the way easier so that one may reach the goal. Such gifts often gain access to the presence of the great and influential. In view here is the oriental custom of offering suitable gifts to one in authority when a favor or an audience is desired (cf. Matt 2:11; Luke 16:9).

2. Evaluating the evidence (18:17). "The first in presenting his case seems right; his neighbor comes and searches him out." The plaintiff who states his case first puts forward the evidence which puts him in the best possible light. When he is finished, it looks as though he must be in the right. His neighbor—the defendant—comes and searches out the other's case, i.e., he brings evidence forward which places the previous testimony in question. Thus judges must not come to a conclusion until both sides are heard.

3. Casting the lot (18:18). "Strife the lot makes to cease, and separates the strong." This proverb may be related to the preceding. In cases where the evidence is not compelling in any direction, the parties to a dispute may agree to have their differences settled by means of the lot in the belief that the result will be decided by God (cf. 16:33). "The strong" are disputants who are powerful and whose cases judges might not wish to settle.

4. Offending a brother (18:19). "A brother transgressed against [is more unyielding] than a strong city; and their contentions are like the bar of a citadel." The closer the kinship the more bitter the enmity between two persons if it occurs, and the harder to reconcile them. They close the door against reconciliation, shut the heart against all feeling of tenderness. One could more easily storm a citadel with iron bars.

5. Speaking cautiously (18:20-21). "From the fruit of a person's mouth shall his belly be filled, with the increase of his lips shall he be filled." A person has to bear the responsibility for what his mouth utters. Words are viewed as something on which a person feeds. By their consequences words determine a person's position and fate (18:20).

"Death and life are in the power of the tongue, and those who love it, each one shall eat its fruit." Under certain circumstances cautious speech may preserve life just as reckless speech may imperil it. They who love to use the tongue must accept the consequences of the way in which they make use of it whether for good or evil (18:21).

D. Foundations of Friendship (18:22-24).

1. Godly marriage (18:22). "He who has found a wife has found a good thing, and has obtained favor from Yahweh." The context makes it clear that a *good* wife is meant. Such a wife is an asset, an aid to one's material and moral advancement. A godly marriage also obtains the favor of the Lord.

2. *Godly mercy (18:23).* "Entreaties the poor speak, and the rich person answers with strong words." The rich are unsympathetic toward the petitions of the poor. This proverb is designed to warn the rich not to allow wealth to suppress human compassion.

3. *Focused friendship (18:24).* "A man of friends [comes] to injure himself; but there is a lover that stays closer than a brother." A "man of friends" signifies one who indiscriminately multiplies his friends. Some of those "friends" will do him harm and bring him to ruin. It is the quality of friendship, not the quantity of "friends" which is important. The "lover" here is a special friend who can always be counted on in time of trouble.

WEALTH AND POVERTY
Proverbs 19:1-25

Wealth and poverty again form the dominant theme of the proverbs grouped in chapter 19.

A. The Problems of Poverty (19:1-7).

1. *Poverty is not the worst condition (19:1-2).* "Better is the poor person who walks in his integrity than he who is perverse in his lips and a fool at the same time." It is better to be honest and remain poor than to be one who seeks to escape poverty by a dishonest life. The latter is a fool to believe that he can prosper by evil methods. Either he will be discovered and suffer punishment, or God would thwart him in his plans (19:1).

A poor person may act through ignorance. That is not as bad as someone who deliberately sets as his goal an evil deed. "If [to act] without knowledge is not good, [how much more] does one who hastens with his feet miss the mark." The proverb draws a contrast between two reprehensible lines of action. The ignorant person has no definite purpose in view; he does not know what to do or how to act in the circumstances of his life. The second recklessly plunges forward and misses the way. Haste here is opposed to knowledge because the latter involves prudence and circumspection while the former blunders on in the direction of unintended consequences (19:2).

2. *Poverty may lead to hostility toward God (19:3).* "A man's own folly overturns his way, and against Yahweh his heart is sullen." Through his own stupid choices a person ruins his life. Then he blames God for his failure.

3. *Poverty results in friendlessness (19:4-7).* "Wealth adds many friends." People are attracted to wealth for they think that they shall derive benefit therefrom (cf. 14:20). On the other hand, "a poor man from his friend is separated." Poverty drives away even the last friend of a person (19:4).

"A witness of lies shall not be held guiltless, and he that puts [lit., breathes] forth lies shall not escape." The reference here is to one whose lies are as frequent as the breath of his nostrils. Virtually every word he speaks is false (cf. 6:19; 14:5,25). Eventually his lies are discovered and he is censured by society, and ultimately punished by God. The connection with the preceding proverb may be this: A poor and friendless man might be tempted to accept a bribe for false testimony in a court of law (19:5).

"Many shall entreat [lit., smooth the face of] the favor of the noble, and every man is a friend to a person of gift," i.e., a person who gives many gifts. The reference is probably to the wealthy politician who attempts to attach followers to his cause by the bestowal of gifts (19:6).

"All the brethren of the poor person hate him; how much more do his friends avoid him! He pursues [them with] sayings, [but] they are not." Blood relatives hate one who constantly begs for assistance. Much less are friends inclined to aid one who does not have the blood-tie. He continues to pursue both relative and friend with pleas for assistance. They, however, "are not," i.e., they are nowhere to be found (19:7).

B. Things That Are Not Fitting (19:8-15).

A proverb commending wisdom introduces another small collection focusing on things which are not fitting. "He who acquires a heart loves his soul; he who keeps understanding [loves] to find good." Acquiring a heart here is equivalent to acquiring wisdom. Such a person aims to make the most of his capabilities and get the most out of life. One who "keeps understanding" is one who lets prudence direct his actions. "To find good" is to find material prosperity. Once acquired, wisdom and prudence must be guarded like a precious jewel lest one lose them for want of care or lack of use (19:8).

1. *Perjury (19:9).* "A witness of lies shall not be held guiltless; and he that breathes out lies shall perish." Not only shall the liar not escape, he shall perish (cf. 19:5).

2. *Aggrandizement (19:10).* "Luxury is not appropriate for a fool; much less for a servant to rule over princes." A fool would abuse luxury and become the more confirmed in his folly. By unwise favoritism of a ruler, a slave of lowly birth might be raised to eminence and set above the nobles and princes of the land. A servant when invested with such power abuses it and becomes tyrannical.

3. *Rage (19:11-12).* "Intelligence of a man [is when] he restrains his anger; and his glory is to pass over transgression." An intelligent person restrains himself by overlooking the annoyances of life. "Transgression" as in 17:9 is not a social crime, but a personal offense (19:11).

"Roaring like a lion is the wrath of the king; and like dew upon vegetation is his favor." The roar of the lion inspires terror and warns of danger, even death. On the other hand, the king's favor is likened to the dew which keeps vegetation alive during the rainless seasons (19:12).

4. *Domestic disharmony (19:13-14).* "Ruins to his father is a foolish son, and a downpour which drives out are the contentions of a wife." The Hebrew plural emphasizes that time and again the foolish son brings ruin upon his father. A wife's nagging drives her husband out of the house (19:13).

"House and riches are the inheritance of fathers; but from Yahweh is an intelligent wife." House and riches are an ancestral heritage which come to the sons as a matter of course. To possess a wife of merit is not a matter of course, but a special blessing of the Lord (19:14; cf. 18:22).

5. *Laziness (19:15).* "Laziness results in deep sleep, and the idle soul shall suffer hunger." A lazy person sleeps while he should be working. "Deep sleep" *(tardemah)* implies profound insensibility, a

virtual trance. Slothfulness also enfeebles the mind, corrupts the higher faculties, and converts a rational being into a witless animal. Such a one pays the price in experiencing hunger.

C. Family Wisdom (19:16-24).

1. Obedience essential (19:16-17). "He who keeps commandment keeps his soul; he that despises his ways shall be put to death." Most likely "commandment" here has become a technical designation for the *Torah,* the law of Moses. One who keeps God's law preserves his life. One who despises God's ways will be put to death, i.e., by the sentence of the court.

Solomon now gives a concrete example of the kind of obedience commended in the preceding proverb. "A lender to Yahweh is one who is gracious to the poor; and his good deed he shall recompense to him." The word "poor" points to one who is in need of any kind of help, not necessarily money. God becomes the debtor to anyone who aids the poor because the helpful deed has his approval. The Lord always pays his debts. Thus one can expect a blessing for his kindness to the needy (19:17; cf. Matt 25:40).

2. Discipline essential (19:18). "Chasten your son, for there is hope; but to the killing of him lift not up your soul." Corporal punishment may cause a child to mend his ways and thus escape the death of a criminal. The discipline should be administered while there is "hope," i.e., while the child is still young and impressionable, and not confirmed in bad habits. The second clause has been taken to mean that the discipline must not be so severe that it places the life of the child in jeopardy (cf. Eph 6:4; Col 3:21). Others understand the meaning to be that if the parents do not administer discipline, they are choosing social, spiritual and even physical death as the end of their child. The NIV captures the meaning of the clause: "do not be a willing party to his death."

3. Self-control essential (19:19). "A man of great temper must pay the price; if you rescue him, you will have to do it again." A person rough in anger shall bear the penalty which his lack of self-control brings upon him. Though he be saved from the consequences of his intemperance once and again, while his disposition remains unchanged such efforts will prove useless. The help that is given such a person only makes him think that he may continue to indulge his anger with impunity. In some cases he may vent his wrath on his deliverer.

4. *Wisdom essential (19:20-21)*. "Hear counsel and receive instruction in order that you may be wise in your latter end." One should seek advice and even expert guidance (*musar*) before acting. The phrase "in your latter end" in Proverbs means in the future, the rest of one's life. Thus the wisdom gathered and digested in youth is the prudence and intelligence of manhood and old age (19:20).

"Many are the plans in a man's heart; but the counsel of Yahweh, it shall stand." This proverb places in juxtaposition the plans of man and the purpose of God. Man constantly changes his plans, shifting from good to better, and from bad to worse. The "counsel" or purpose of God, however, is unchanging (19:21).

5. *Honesty essential (19:22)*. "A man's desire is his kindness, but a poor man is better than a liar."[4] The intention to do good is that which gives real value to an act. A poor person's desire to aid a distressed neighbor, even if he is unable to carry out his intention, is taken for the act of mercy. A poor man who gives to one in distress his sympathy and good wishes, even if he can afford no substantial aid, is better than a rich man who promises much and does nothing, or who falsely professes that he is unable to help.

6. *Godly fear essential (19:23)*. "The fear of Yahweh is to life; and [the God-fearing] abides satisfied without being visited by calamity." Under the temporal dispensation (the Mosaic covenant), true piety was rewarded by a long and happy life in this world. The law of Moses promised a life free from calamity for the faithful (Lev 26:6; Deut 11:15; etc.). Under the dispensation of the Spirit, Christians expect not immunity from trouble, but grace sufficient for each occasion and growth in sanctification which results therefrom.

7. *Laziness condemned (19:24)*. "The lazy person buries his hand in the dish; even unto his mouth he will not put it." In the biblical period people dipped their hand into a common dish and helped themselves with their fingers (cf. Ruth 2:14; Matt 26:23). The sluggard finds it too great an exertion to feed himself. This hyperbole is intended to denote the gross laziness which recoils from the slightest labor and will not even make the least effort to secure a livelihood.

8. Discipline commended (19:25). "A scorner you smite and a simple person will become prudent; rebuke a discerning person, he will understand knowledge." This proverb contrasts two methods of instruction. The simpleton learns prudence when he has an object lesson of how the mocker suffers for his wickedness. He needs the powerful deterrent of fear of punishment (cf. 1 Tim 5:20). On the other hand, a person of intelligence only needs a word of reproof to straighten him out.

ENDNOTES

1. In 16:17 some understand "evil" to mean misfortune or calamity. The idea would then be: "the path of the upright avoids misfortune." The term "evil" here probably has its ethical sense.

2. The term "best friend" (*'alluph*) in 16:28 is used of (1) a woman's husband (2:17); and God himself (Jer 3:4).

3. Others take *'ish* in 18:4 to be the ideal man in all his wisdom and integrity. Such a man's words are deep waters which cannot be fathomed or exhausted.

4. NIV renders 19:22 "What a man desires is unfailing love." The margin offers the reading: "A man's greed is his shame." While *chesed* sometimes has the meaning "shame" (cf. 14:34), there is no reason to depart from its usual meaning of "kindness" here.

CHAPTER TWENTY-NINE

Acknowledging God in Everyday Life
Proverbs 19:26-22:16

The fourth section of the first collection of proverbs begins in 19:26 with another reference to a son. A number of allusions to Yahweh appear in this series of proverbs. The author sees the presence of God "wherever human beings come up against their own limitations, and that is frequent indeed."[1]

MOCKING AUTHORITY
Proverbs 19:26-29

The last four proverbs of chapter 19 deal with mocking what is just and right (1) in the home; and (2) in the courts.

A. Mocking Authority in the Home (19:26-27).

"One who mistreats [lit., deprives of property] a father [and] drives away a mother is a son acting vilely and shamefully." This proverb condemns a son who fails to make proper provision for his parents in their old age, so that the father is destitute and the mother has to leave her home to live with others (19:26).

"Ceasing, my son, to hear instruction is to err from the words of knowledge." The warning here is against listening to wise teaching (*musar*) with no intention of putting it into practice. If one continues to do evil, he has not really listened to his teacher. Such a one only increases his guilt by knowing the way of righteousness perfectly while refusing to walk therein (19:27).

B. Mocking Authority in the Courts (26:28-29).

"A worthless witness mocks at justice; and the mouth of the wicked devours iniquity." The "worthless witness" (*beliyya'al*) is one who is utterly depraved, one who knowingly, willingly, eagerly gives false evidence. Such a one scoffs at justice and senses no personal obligation to see that standards of society be maintained. Instead of standing with his fellow citizens against evil, he swallows iniquity as if it were some tasty beverage, i.e., he rejoices in iniquity, consumes it, embraces it. He breaks the law by giving false testimony (19:28; cf. Exod 20:16; Lev 5:1).

"For scorners judgments are established; and stripes for the backs of fools." Scofflaws eventually are brought to justice if not here, then hereafter. The scoffer may stay within the law and thus avoid civil penalties. He cannot, however, escape the judgment of God. "Stripes" refers to the corporal punishment administered under the law of Moses (19:29; cf. 18:6).

THE NEED FOR SALVATION
Proverbs 20:1-19

The first nineteen proverbs of chapter 20 speak of the general sinfulness and need of salvation on the part of all men.

A. Condemnation of Vices (20:1-4).

Four evils should be avoided by the wise student. Prudence is the safeguard against these pitfalls.

1. Intoxicating beverages. "A mocker is wine, a brawler is strong drink, and anyone who errs in it is not wise." The effects produced in the drinker are attributed to the beverage itself. An intoxicated person behaves like "a mocker," i.e., one who scoffs at what is holy, rejects censure, and ridicules all that is serious. "Strong drink" is any intoxicating drink not made from grapes. It was produced from the fermentation of certain fruit juices, e.g., pomegranate and date. Strong drink causes otherwise peaceful people to become boisterous brawlers, no longer masters of themselves or restrained by the laws of morality or society. To "err" in the use of these beverages is to overindulge. Such a person does not behave in a manner becoming a wise person (20:1).

2. *An angry king (20:2).* "A roar like a lion is the terror of the king; one who offends him sins with regard to his life." A lion roars when springing upon its prey. The roar inspires terror in the victim because he knows, at that point, no escape is possible. One who arouses the royal wrath has transgressed "with regard to his life," i.e., he has placed his life in jeopardy.

3. *Strife (20:3).* "It is an honor to a man to cease from strife; but every fool readily enters into strife." To refuse to be drawn into a quarrel brings honor to a person in that he escapes the insults and injuries which he would otherwise endure, or inflict on his neighbor. The fool recklessly takes on controversy with detriment to himself and to his family.

4. *Laziness (20:4).* "Because of winter the sluggard will not plow; therefore, in the harvest he will seek [lit., beg] and have nothing." After the harvest in the autumn the work of plowing must be done. At this time the ground in Palestine, moistened by winter rains, is most easily and profitably worked. The lazy farmer neglects this work. He puts off tilling his fields day after day so that his land is never cultivated. Consequently he has no crop to reap when autumn comes.

B. Discerning Human Character (20:5-12).

Human beings are weak creatures morally. A tendency toward sin is part of the human constitution. In the next series of proverbs the question of the discernment of character is discussed from every angle. Viewed positively, the proverbs in this unit commend one who is (1) faithful to commitments (v. 6), (2) committed to integrity (v. 7), (3) impartial in judgment (v. 8), (4) humble in self-evaluation (v. 9); and (5) honest in business (v. 10).

1. The difficulty of discernment (20:5-6). "Deep waters are the counsel in the heart of a man; but a man of understanding will draw it out." "Counsel" here is the real intention of a person as distinct from the words with which he conceals it (cf. 18:4). Like deep water in the bosom of the earth, a person's real intentions are hard to bring to the surface. By judicious questions and remarks one who understands human psychology can draw out the hidden thought (20:5).

"Many a man will announce each his enduring mercy; but a man of abundant faithfulness who can find?" The idea seems to be that many people boast of their charity (cf. Matt 6:2), but not many are faithful. The "faithfulness" intended is fidelity to promises, the practical execution of the boasted benevolence. The proverb stresses the contrast between promise and performance (20:6).[2]

2. Parental discernment (20:7). "The one who walks in his integrity is a righteous person; happy are his children after him." Walking in integrity denotes a person who is loyal to moral principles and the ordinances of God. Such a person chooses to model a moral life for his children. Hence, his children shall be happy and shall remember him with fondness even after his death.

3. Judicial discernment (20:8). "A king who sits upon a throne of judgment winnows all evil with his eyes." The king was the chief magistrate in the land. "A throne of judgment" is a throne distinguished by impartial justice. Such a king sifts the true from the false in the evidence submitted to him. As anointed ruler he was believed to have been endowed with the ability to see through any lies. Those lies and pretenses which cloak evil are scattered to the winds as the chaff flies before the winnowing fan. Nothing unrighteous can abide in his presence.

4. Personal discernment (20:9-10). "Who can say: I have made my heart clean, I am pure from my sin?" No human being is faultless (Rom 3:23; 1 John 1:8). To deceive oneself in this matter is so easy. Sins may lurk undetected, motives may be overlooked, so that no one can rightly be self-righteous or conceited, or proud of his spiritual condition (20:9).

"A stone [weight] and a stone, an ephah [measure] and an ephah, both of them alike are an abomination to Yahweh." Stones were used for weighing. Dishonest traders used two sets of measures, one for buying, and one for selling (cf. Lev 19:36; Deut 25:13). God hates such fraudulent practices. The ephah was a dry measure roughly equal to a bushel. Some connect this verse in thought with the preceding, seeing it as a warning against judging a neighbor by a standard which one is unwilling to apply to himself (20:10).

5. *The basis of discernment (20:11-12).* "Also in his deeds a lad makes himself known whether his work is pure or upright." It is only in people's actions that their character can be known. A young lad is transparent, simple, and straightforward in his actions. He has not yet learned the tactics by which adults hide their true intentions. Habits are learned early in life. The boy is the father of the man. The conduct of the lad will help one to prognosticate regarding his direction in life (20:11).

"The hearing ear and the seeing eye, Yahweh made even both of them." Yahweh has given to everyone the organs of hearing and sight, so that they may be able to judge character by what they hear and see in the speech and actions of others. Since he made both faculties, they must be used in ways which are pleasing to their maker. One would conclude that the creator must be greater than the created. Thus God hears that which escapes the ear, and sees what the human eye cannot observe (20:12).

C. Religion in the Workplace (20:13-19).

Effective involvement in the workplace requires several qualities which are recommended in the following series of proverbs.

1. *Industry (20:13).* "Do not love sleep lest you be dispossessed; open your eyes [to] fullness of bread." One should not be sleeping when there is work to be done (cf. 19:15). Only one who is energetic in his labors avoids poverty. The word "eyes" connects this verse to the preceding. God gave the faculty of sight, but man must make good use of it.

2. *Confidence (20:14).* "Bad, bad says the buyer; but going his way then praises himself." The buyer depreciates the goods which he wants in order to get the price reduced. After paying the cheaper price he departs to boast of the bargain and his shrewdness. In the marketplaces of the Near East this was (and is) an everyday occurrence. Probably here Solomon wished to warn his pupils to discount depreciatory comments, to be confident in their goods or services.

609

3. Knowledge (20:15). "There is gold, and many corals; but a precious jewel are the lips of knowledge." Lips uttering knowledge are more valuable than gold or coral.

4. Firmness (20:16). "Take his garment that is security for a stranger, and hold him in pledge that is pledge on account of alien men."[3] A garment was commonly deposited as security for a debt (Exod 22:25). The verse is not recommending harsh treatment to those who, because of inadvertent misfortune, had fallen into debt. Rather, the text speaks here of the misfortune which comes from stupidity and willful neglect of advice. Proverbs sounds many warnings against the folly of acting as security for another's debt (6:1; 11:15; 17:18; 22:26). The point here is that if a person ignores this advice, and pledges himself to back the debt of a stranger, hold him to the consequences. Take his garments, or hold him in pledge as a servant so as not to suffer loss.

5. Honesty (20:17). "Sweet to a person is the bread of falsehood; but afterward his mouth shall be filled with gravel." Dishonesty brings no lasting satisfaction. The "bread of falsehood" is food derived from fraudulent transactions. At first one feels pride in his ability to hoodwink his brother; but when the fraud is discovered, the consequences are most unpleasant for him.[4] One will find in that illicit bread, no nourishment, but rather discomfort and injury. "Gravel" is a figure for a disagreeable and injurious experience (cf. Lam 3:16).

6. Prudence (20:18). "Every plan is established by counsel, and with good advice carry on war." One should consult with experienced counselors on every issue, and especially before undertaking a war. War is a necessary evil, but it must be undertaken prudently and with due consideration of circumstances and capabilities (cf. Luke 14:31).

7. Confidentiality (20:19). "One who reveals secrets is one who goes about as a talebearer; so do not mix with one who opens wide his lips" (cf.11:13). One should not associate with a gossiper who spreads confidential information. He cannot be trusted with any secret; therefore one must exercise caution in what is said to him. One who "opens wide his lips" is one who cannot keep his mouth shut.

IMPORTANT RELATIONSHIPS
Proverbs 20:20–21:4

The fifteen proverbs in this section appear to be a thematic group. These verses contain no less than seven Yahweh proverbs. There are also three proverbs which refer directly to kings.

A. Yahweh and Mankind (20:20-25).

Proverbs 20:20-25 focuses on various aspects of Yahweh's relationship with human beings.

1. *The certainty of punishment for sin (20:20-21).* "One who curses his father or his mother his lamp shall be extinguished in the apple of the eye of darkness." Cursing one's parents was a capital crime under the law of Moses (Exod 21:17; Lev 20:9). One who abused parents would find himself surrounded on all sides by midnight darkness, without escape, with no hope of divine intervention. "Lamp" is a metaphor applied to happiness and prosperity, to a person's fame and reputation, and to his posterity. The stubborn and disobedient son or daughter would suffer in body and soul, in character, in fortune, and in his own children (20:20).

"An estate [may be] quickly acquired at the beginning, but the end thereof shall not be blessed." The "estate" here may be possessions generally. Assets acquired through get-rich-quick schemes will disappear as quickly as they were acquired. This verse also may be connected to the preceding. It may apply to a bad son who thinks his parents live too long, and by violence robs them of their possessions; or to one like the prodigal son who demanded prematurely his portion of the paternal goods (20:21).

2. *Yahweh responsible for recompense (20:22).* "Do not say, Let me recompense evil; wait for Yahweh and he will save you." To "recompense evil" means to return evil for evil (cf. 24:29). Biblical faith enjoins patient hope for the just intervention of the Lord to correct the inequities of life (Rom 12:14,17; Matt 7:12).

3. *Yahweh requires honest dealings (20:23).* "An abomination to Yahweh is a stone [weight] and a stone, and dishonest scales do not please him." On God's attitude toward diverse weights, see 20:10; on the false balance, see 11:1.

4. *Yahweh provides guidance (20:24)*. "From Yahweh are the goings of a man, and as for a man, how shall he discern his way?" The steps of a great and powerful man (*gebher*) depend, as their final cause, upon Yahweh who conditions and controls results. A man (here the word is *'adam*, a weak mortal) cannot see all sides, as God does, cannot comprehend the beginning, middle, and end in one view. How then can one of such limited purview understand his own way? Man, whether powerful or weak, needs divine revelation—the principles of wisdom—to point out the proper path of life (cf.16:9).

5. *Yahweh regards vows as irrevocable (20:25)*. "[It is] a snare to a man rashly to say 'Holy' and after he vows, to make inquiry." Under the emotion of religious fervor, a person feels the urge to express his love of God by dedicating some of his possessions to the Lord. To use the word "holy" was a formula for consecrating something to holy purposes. After one has made his vow he may begin to consider whether he can fulfill it or not. Such an impulse is a "snare" in that it strangles his conscience, and leads a person into the grievous sins of perjury and sacrilege. One should, therefore, give the fullest consideration to the matter before he utters a vow.

B. The King and His Subjects (20:26–21:4).

Proverbs 20:26–21:4 is concerned, directly or by implication, with the king: his relationship with his subjects and his subordination to Yahweh.

1. *The king's judicial function (20:26)*. "A wise king winnows the wicked, and causes the wheel to turn over them" (cf. 20:8). The king separates the wicked and the good, as the winnowing fan or shovel divides the chaff from the wheat (cf. Matt 3:12). The "wheel" is that of the threshing cart. This was a wooden frame with three or four rollers under it armed with iron teeth. It was drawn by two oxen. It crushed out the grain and cut up the straw into fodder. To cause the wheel to pass over the wicked is to suppress the evil elements in the kingdom.

2. *The king's subordination to Yahweh (20:27)*. "A lamp of Yahweh is the spirit of a person, searching all the inward parts." The "spirit" (*neshamah*) is the breath of life which God breathed into man's nostrils in the beginning (Gen 2:7). This God-given "spirit"

includes, but is not limited to, what moderns call *conscience*. This spirit is called "the lamp of Yahweh" because it is a gift from him (cf. Matt 6:23). That lamp burns brightly in the life of one who has filled his heart and mind with God's word. The "spirit" searches all the inward parts (cf. 1 Cor 2:11). So if one is to search out and discover his innermost thoughts, desires, affections, and will he must have the bright lamp of divine revelation.

3. *The king's success (20:28)*. "Mercy and truth preserve the king, and he upholds his throne in mercy." The exercise of mercy and kindness by the king make his subjects happy and content, thus reducing the potential for revolution. A just and kindhearted monarch establishes his throne and the right of his children to sit upon it.

4. *The king's wisdom (20:29)*. This proverb may have the intention of commending the old king who has profited by his long experience. "The glory of young men is their strength; and the beauty of old men is their gray head." The young take pride in their physical prowess. One does not expect from them the wisdom that comes from long experience in life. The gray hair, the symbol of old age, marks one as honored because of the accumulated wisdom which he possesses.

5. *The king's punishment (20:30)*. "Stripes of a wound cleanses away evil; so also blows of the innermost parts of the belly." The reference is to blows that cause a wound, and are not so light as to be ignored. Afflictions of this kind have the effect of halting a person who has adopted evil ways. The second clause appears to refer to the blows which fall upon the inner man, e.g., a shattering grief or overwhelming misfortune.

6. *The king's heart (21:1-2)*. "Like watercourses is the heart of the king in the hand of Yahweh: he turns it wherever he pleases." The most autocratic monarch was not free from God's jurisdiction. In the same way that an irrigator can cut a watercourse in any direction he desires, so God sways the heart of the despot. By hidden influences and providential arrangements God disposes the monarch to order his government so as to carry out the designs of the heaven's ultimate sovereign (21:1).

"Every way of a man is upright in his own eyes; but Yahweh weighs hearts." Here is a warning against self-deception and self-complacency which thinks its own ways the best (21:2; cf.16:2).

7. The king's duty (21:3). "To do righteousness and justice is more acceptable to Yahweh than sacrifice." Offerings cannot be acceptable to God from a person who indulges in wrongdoing and persists in evil ways. The combination of "righteousness" (*tsedakah*) and "justice" (*mishpat*) here as elsewhere suggests equity which is derived from the principle of love.

8. A warning for the king (21:4). "Haughty eyes and an ambitious heart, the lamp of the wicked, are sin." The reference is to pride which reveals itself in a look which implies that other people are inferior, scarcely worthy of notice (cf. 6:17). The "ambitious heart" (lit., broad of heart) has been taken by NIV and NASB as a metaphor for pride. Probably, however, the allusion is to inordinate longing for wealth and power. Such a heart, wholly filled with self, is the cause of the haughty eyes. The "lamp of the wicked" is a metaphor for the sinner's outward prosperity and inward joy. These are founded in self, and thus they are displeasing to God.

THE PROVIDENCE OF GOD
Proverbs 21:5-31

Chapter 21 begins and ends with references to the providence of God. Sandwiched in between is an assortment of proverbs which illustrate how that providence works in human affairs. The initial and final verses provide an interpretation of many of the proverbs in the chapter: those which speak of human wisdom (vv. 11,16, 20, 22) can now be seen in the light of the general principle that true wisdom can come only from Yahweh. The several proverbs which speak of the activities and fates of the righteous and wicked should be interpreted in the light of v. 3 which speaks of the judgment of Yahweh.

A. Providence and Human Vice (21:5-9).

A kinship exists between all vices just as between all virtues. Human vice springs from a disturbance of one's relationship with God.

1. Covetousness (21:5). "The plans of the diligent are only toward success; but everyone who is hasty [it is] only to want." Here diligence is contrasted with hastiness. The person who makes up his mind to work steadily will find his prosperity increasing. The get-rich-quick method ends in disaster.

2. *Dishonesty (21:6).* "Procuring treasures by a lying tongue is a vapor dispersed [by] seekers of death." The wealth accumulated by deceit melts away, its possessors derive no profit from it. Instead of riches, they in reality seek death which is the punishment of sin.

3. *Violent deeds (21:7-8).* "The violence of the wicked will drag them away because they refuse to practice justice." People who resort to violent deeds get caught in the net of their evil schemes. They are unable to break free, even if they wish. The violence with which they treat others shall rebound on themselves. Their deliberate choice of the criminal method saps their willpower to live honestly. This is a judicial retribution on them for willfully declining to do what is right (21:7).

"The way of a person is crooked and strange; but as for the pure, his work is straight." The person here described must be the criminal of the preceding verse. This person's way of life is not open and straightforward, simple and uniform, but stealthy, crooked, and perverse. On the other hand, the pure in heart will be right in action. He follows his conscience and God's word and goes direct to his course without turning or hesitation (21:8).

4. *Contentious spirit (21:9).* "Better to dwell upon the corner of a roof than [to have] a woman of contentions and a house of companionship." The flat-roofed houses of Palestine were used as apartments for many purposes. During the rainy season such an apartment would be exposed to inclement weather. It is preferable to live alone and experience discomfort than to live with a contentious woman. A "house of companionship" is a commodious house in which friends are entertained. The joys of such fellowship are more than offset by the presence of such a wife. The inclusion of this verse here in a unit describing the ways of the wicked suggests that a quarrelsome wife is evil.

B. Warnings from Life-experience (21:10-13).

In this small unit Solomon observes that (1) the covetous soul is merciless (v. 10); simpletons must learn the hard way (v. 11); God ultimately overthrows the wicked (v. 12), and the hard of heart find no sympathy (v. 13).

"A wicked soul desires evil; his neighbor finds no favor in his eyes." A wicked person cannot rest without planning for some new evil activity. He does not look with pity on friend or neighbor if they stand in the way of gratifying his desires. He will sacrifice anyone, however closely connected, so that he may work his will. Such a person is totally self-centered. He cannot experience compassion, even for a neighbor who is destitute (21:10).

"When the scoffer is punished, the simple is made wise; and when the wise is instructed, he receives knowledge." The simple person sees the fate of the scoffer and fears similar suffering (19:25). Chastisement has a deterrent effect as far as he is concerned. The wise person, however, takes advantage of every circumstance, to increase his knowledge. He learns from others and hence avoids their mistakes (21:11).

"The Righteous One takes note of the house of the wicked, overthrowing the wicked to [their] ruin." The Lord keeps sinners under his eye that he may punish them at the appropriate time (21:12).[5]

"One who shuts his ears to the cries of the weak, also he shall call, but shall not be answered." A twofold retribution is threatened on the unmerciful person. First, he himself shall fall into distress. Second, in his distress he would appeal to his neighbors for help, but his appeal would go unanswered. The callousness he displayed will be remembered against him when he is in need of help (21:13).

C. Life's Alternatives (21:14-19).

This unit indicates various alternatives with which one is faced in life with regard to lifestyle.

1. Tranquility vs. turbulence (21:14). "A gift [given] in secret pacifies anger, and a bribe in the bosom strong wrath." The verse states a fact of experience. Bribery is condemned elsewhere in Proverbs. The "bribe in the bosom" is one enfolded in the cloak, and thus secretly transported and presented.

2. Justice vs. iniquity (21:15). "Joy to the innocent is [the] doing of justice, but ruin to the workers of iniquity." The righteous feel real pleasure in doing what is right. They have the answer of a good conscience and the feeling that, as far as they can, they are making God's will their will. A stable society can exist only when justice is strictly administered.

616

3. *Wandering vs. rest (21:16).* "A person who strays out of the path of understanding, in the congregation of dead spirits he shall rest." The person described is one who forsakes the way of wisdom, the path of virtue, the religious life. The verse seems to contrast the restless wanderings of the unwise in life with the rest they will only experience in death. The sinner shall soon be with the dead spirits (*repha'im*; cf. 2:18), i.e., shall meet with a speedy death. The "rest" is viewed as penal. The hint here is that retribution follows death.

4. *Frugality vs. waste (21:17).* "A person of want is one who loves rejoicing; one who loves wine and oil shall not be rich." One who "loves rejoicing" is one who overindulgences in material comforts. Such a person becomes "a person of want" (*machsor*), a poor person. "Wine and oil" were used in luxurious banquets, the oil for cooling the person. Indulgence in such luxuries would be a token of prodigality and extravagance which are the precursors of financial ruin.

5. *The upright vs. the wicked (21:17).* "A ransom for the innocent is the wicked person; and in place of the upright are the faithless." In the end the guilty person pays the penalty for the hardships which an innocent person has to undergo if wrongly convicted. The "faithless" (*boged*) is the law-breaker. He eventually experiences the same plight as the upright who suffer without cause (21:18).

6. *Solitude vs. disruptive relationships (21:19).* "Better to dwell in a desert land, than with a contentious wife and vexation." A "desert land" is an uninhabited spot. A solitary life is to be preferred over a home that has become a war zone (cf. 21:9). "Vexation" or turbulence in the home is the result of the presence of a wife who is contentious.

D. Wealth and Greed (21:20-26).

The next series of proverbs focuses for the most part on the acquisition and preservation of wealth.

1. *The wise preserve wealth (21:20).* "There is valuable treasure and oil in the dwelling of the wise; but a fool of a person swallows it up." Through wise stewardship a godly person can accumulate a store of desirable articles. "Oil," a symbol of comforts, is an example of that treasure. A fool soon runs through and exhausts all that has been accumulated.

2. *The righteous are comfortable in life (21:21).* "One who pursues righteousness and mercy shall find life, righteousness, and honor." To "pursue" righteousness and mercy is to accept these as guiding principles of life. "Righteousness" is the virtue which renders to both God and man their due. "Mercy" (*chesed*) is brotherly love. Such a one finds "life" more abundant, i.e., a long and prosperous life in this world. He also finds "righteousness" which in the second clause may have the meaning of "blessing" as in Ps 24:5, i.e., righteous treatment from God who is faithful to reward. The "honor" is the respect and reverence among fellow men, not to mention glory in the next world.

3. *Wisdom superior to brute force (21:22).* "A wise person scales a city of mighty men and brings down the stronghold in which it trusted." Intellectual and moral power overcomes physical strength. The "stronghold" refers to the city's defenses. The courage and strength of valiant men cannot defend a city against the skillful counsel of a wise strategist. Such a person lays low the strength in which the defenders trust; he not only takes the fortress, he demolishes it.

4. *Wisdom guards the mouth (21:23-24).* "One who keeps his mouth and his tongue keeps his soul from trouble." The reference is to the potential damage of incautious speech. The person who knows when to speak and when to keep silent stays out of trouble. The "soul" here is the person (21:23).

"Presumptuous, arrogant—scoffer is his name—behaving in overbearing pride." This verse intends to cite the characteristics of one who can be called a "scoffer" (*lets*), Solomon's favorite name for the free-thinking skeptic of his day. A scoffer's contempt for revealed religion grows out of pride of intellect, which refuses instruction and blinds the eyes to the truth (21:24).

5. *Greed is fatal. (21:25-26).* First, greed is fatal to the lazy. "The craving of a sluggard will kill him, for his hands refuse to work." The sluggard always craves more sleep. His desire for idleness will be the death of him (21:25).

Second, greed is fatal to the wicked. "There is one who always desires greedily, but a righteous person gives without sparing." Some link this verse to the preceding, but it is best to regard it as a separate proverb. There are claims made on all sides, demands for help, urgent appeals such as one would think no person could satisfy. The righteous, however, has been blessed with enough and to spare. He is generous and charitable. He is industrious. He uses his stewardship well, and so arranges his expenditure that he has something to give to the needy person (21:26).

E. God's Just Judgments (21:27-31).

Solomon now sets forth in a series of proverbs the justice of God's judgments.

1. Judgment on religious acts (21:27). "The sacrifice of the wicked is an abomination; how much more so when it is brought with evil intent." The "wicked" here are those who think their sacrifice will avert divine judgment even while they continue in their sinful conduct (cf. 15:8). The sinner goes through religious ceremonies without faith or repentance. That is bad enough. Even worse, however, is the sinner who brings his sacrifice with "evil intent." He may intend to bribe God in order to achieve divine acquiescence in a sin which he has no intention of relinquishing. On the other hand, he may be attempting to impress people with his piety so as to take advantage of them more easily. Such an outrage on God's purity and justice may well be called "an abomination."

2. Judgment on judicial acts (21:28). "A false witness shall perish, and a person who hears shall speak continually." A false witness might incur the death penalty from the court (Deut 19:19), otherwise God would condemn him. The "person who hears" is one who is attentive, who listens before he speaks, and reports only what he has heard. Such a person will speak "continually," i.e., what he says is never falsified, silenced, or refuted. His truthful testimony cannot be challenged.

3. Judgment on impudent acts (21:29). "A wicked person hardens his face; but as for the upright, he establishes his ways." To "harden the face" is to act impudently. Such people shamelessly trample on the rights and feelings of others. They are insensible to rebuke or any soft feeling. This obduracy is displayed in the countenance. On the other hand, the "upright," i.e., the wise and godly person, "establishes" his ways, i.e., he directs his conduct with an understanding of the difference between right and wrong. An upright person acts only after due thought. The proverb then contrasts the opportunist and the person of principle.

4. *Judgment on futile acts (21:30-31).* "There is no wisdom, understanding or counsel in opposition to Yahweh." Man's wisdom and planning are of no avail when they are contrary to God's eternal purposes. "Wisdom" and "understanding" in this verse signify the intelligence which enables a person to think and scheme. "Counsel" refers to consultation with others for the devising and execution of a plan (21:30).

"A horse is prepared for the day of battle, but to Yahweh is the victory." The war horse is harnessed and protected with armor. It here symbolizes all the instruments of war. God decides the outcome of battles regardless of the amount of military might which the combatants array against one another. In the spiritual realm this proverb finds an echo in 1 Cor 15:57 (21:31).

A GOOD NAME
Proverbs 22:1-16

Solomon now presents a series of proverbs which are grouped loosely around the theme of the good name.

A. Defining a Good Name (22:1-6).

Verse 1 puts the acquisition of wealth in proper perspective. This observation would be especially appropriate for a young man setting out on his career. Verse 6 speaks of the "way" in which children must be trained. Hence, the first six verses seem to be intended to be instruction for the young.

1. *A good name superior to wealth (22:1).* "A name is to be chosen more than great riches, loving favor more than silver or gold." Context suggests that it is a *good* name or reputation which is to be chosen. The Old Testament regards a good reputation as one of the most valuable assets of a person. "Loving favor" (lit., good grace) refers to the kind of personality and character which create a favorable impression.

2. *Yahweh is Lord of rich and poor (22:2).* "The rich and poor have met together; Yahweh is maker of all of them." All people

620

regardless of economic circumstances are equally creatures of God. One who is truly a man recognizes everybody as his fellow man.

3. *The need for wisdom (22:3)*. "A prudent person sees danger and hides himself; but thoughtless people pass on and are made to pay the price." The prudent person (*'arum*) keeps clear of danger. His keen insight reveals to him the final destination of the various paths which one may choose in life. "Thoughtless people" (simpletons), on the other hand, do not possess such insight. They continue in the path of danger until they finally have to pay the price. The singular "prudent person" is placed in contrast with the plural "thoughtless people." For every prudent person there is a multitude of simpletons.

4. *The reward of godly fear (22:4)*. "The reward of humility is the fear of Yahweh, riches, and honor and life." Humility is the absence of pride. The feeling of dependence, the lowly opinion of self, the surrender of the will, the conviction of sin—all effects which are connected with humility—are encompassed in the term "fear of Yahweh." True piety is the source of every virtue and every blessing: riches, honor, and life (cf. 3:16).

5. *The consequences of being crooked (22:5)*. "Thorns [i.e., snares] are in the way of the perverted; one who keeps his soul stays aloof from them." Life is compared to a pathway, in places hedged by thorns, which hamper progress and harm the passerby. More specifically, the thorns are snares which lie in the way of the unwary. A wise person sees these impediments and stays away from those paths.[6] If any difference in meaning is to be ascribed to the "thorns" and "snares" it is this: the former term refers to pains and troubles, the latter to unexpected dangers and impediments.

6. *The necessity of training children (22:6)*. "Train up a lad according to his way [and] when he is old he will not turn aside from it." The verb translated "train" (*chanakh*) means "to give something into the mouth, to give to be tasted" like a mother putting baby food into the mouth of her child. The verb came to mean "to imbue" or "train." "His way" does not speak primarily of the moral and spiritual path of life, but of one's niche in life. Whatever occupation he is later to follow, it is necessary to prepare him for it in his early years. Then habits are formed which will influence his conduct in manhood. This

maxim is an injunction to parents to consider the child's nature, faculties and temperament in the education which is given him.

B. Preserving a Good Name (22:7-12).

1. Recognize the dangers of wealth (22:7-8). "The rich shall rule over the poor, and a borrower is servant to the lender." The word "rich" is singular, the word "poor" is plural, for there are many poor for one who is rich. The author faithfully depicts the facts of life, whether he approves of them or not. Wealth breeds power and preeminence. Poverty leads to trouble and servitude. A person loses his independence when he is beholden to another for assistance. A debtor loses to a certain extent his freedom. The implication is that everyone would strive and labor to master a competency, and thus avoid the evils of poverty (22:7).

Whereas wealth confers power, it does create certain dangers. "One who sows iniquity shall reap calamity; and the rod of his arrogance shall fail." The evildoer will be overtaken by misfortune (cf. Gal 6:7). Such a person will also be deprived of his ability to act lawlessly. "Rod" here is a symbol of power. The writer is thinking of the cruelty and injustice practiced on a neighbor. The violence which one intends to inflict on another shall fall harmlessly, i.e., vanish away (22:8).

2. Be generous (22:9). "[One who is] good of eye shall be blessed, for he has given of his bread to the weak." The "good of eye" are those who are disposed to be helpful and kindhearted. It is the opposite of the "evil of eye" (23:6; 28:22). The eye is the window through which a person's character may be discerned. A benefactor of the needy is blessed by God in time and eternity (cf. 11:26; 2 Cor 9:6).

3. Reject the scoffer (22:10). "Drive out the scoffer that contention may go out, and that strife and shame may cease." A person who comes within the category of scoffer has no moral or religious principles. Nor does he possess social graces. He has no respect for things human or divine. Should he have any place in the communal organization, he will be the cause of friction. For the sake of the harmony of the body such a person must be expelled.

4. Be sincere (22:11). "One who loves purity of heart, [who has] grace in his lips, his friend is the king." If one intends to climb the social ladder he must possess two qualities. First, he must possess

622

purity of heart, i.e., his motives must be sincere. Insincere flattery may succeed for a time, but in the end the king will see through that approach. Second, he must possess "grace in his lips," i.e., the ability to express his thoughts in gracious language. A person possessing these two qualities eventually attracts the king's attention and enduring friendship.

5. *Maintain God-consciousness (22:12)*. "The eyes of Yahweh preserve [him who has] knowledge, but he subverts the words of the faithless person." God watches over and protects the person who knows him and walks in his ways, and uses his abilities for the good of others.[7] On the other hand, the speech of a faithless person (*boged*)—the false, treacherous, perfidious person—does not express the truth. God frustrates the outspoken intentions of such a person which he had planned against the righteous.

C. Hindrances to a Good Name (22:13-16).

The chapter concludes with the enumeration of four common hindrances to the achievement of a good name.

1. *Laziness (22:13)*. "The sluggard says: There is a lion outside; in the midst of the streets I will be slain." This is one of several humorous jibes at the lazy person in the book (cf. 19:24). The sluggard invents a fantastic reason for not going about his business. The supposed lion is without, in the open country, and yet he professes to be in danger in the midst of the town![8] Lions, though now extinct in Palestine, seem to have lingered till the time of the Crusades.

2. *Immoral women (22:14)*. "A deep pit is the mouth of strange women; one with whom Yahweh is angry shall fall there." "Strange women" are prostitutes, who were Israelites acting contrary to the principles of the covenant (cf. 2:16). By her "mouth" is meant her wanton, seductive words, which entice a man to destruction of body and soul. The "deep pit" is a symbol of irretrievable ruin. He who has incurred the wrath of God by previous unfaithfulness and sin is left to himself to fall prey to the wiles of the wicked woman.

3. *Undisciplined childhood (22:15)*. "Foolishness is bound up in the heart of a lad; the rod of correction shall cause it to depart from him." "Foolishness" (*'ivveleth*) here is the love of mischief, the waywardness and self-will which appear to be "bound up" in a child, i.e.,

part of his very nature. Corporal punishment is necessary to remove this delinquency.

4. *Mistreating the weak (22:16)*. "One oppresses the weak [only] to increase his wealth; one gives to the rich, yet to come to want." The Hebrew is ambiguous and open to a variety of interpretations. The first clause seems to state a moral truth intimated elsewhere in this book (e.g., 13:22; 28:8), namely, that the riches extorted from the poor will in the end redound to his benefit. Under the providential control of God, the oppression and injustice from which he has suffered shall work to his ultimate good. The second clause asserts that the rich man may actually be experiencing loss while he appears to be increasing his wealth. One gives (bribes?) to a rich man to abet him in a dubious project. By adding to the wealth of the rich, the donor increases his indolence, encourages his luxury, vice, and extravagance, and thus paves the way to his ruin. Thus things are not always as they appear to be. The poor may experience great gain through the oppression inflicted on them; the rich may experience great loss through the gifts which are heaped upon them.

ENDNOTES

1. John J. Collins, *Proverbs, Ecclesiastes*, in Knox Preaching Guides (Atlanta: John Knox, 1980), p. 48.

2. Others understand 20:6 as drawing the contrast between professed friends and true friendship. The first clause is then rendered: "Most men meet a man who is gracious to them." People say nice things, and promise nice things, but never deliver on those promises.

3. NIV follows the reading suggested by the Massoretic scribes: "alien woman." This is based on the reading of 27:13 which is viewed as a verbal repetition of this verse. The *kethib* (consonantal Hebrew text) reads "alien men."

4. The Jewish commentator Rashi thought that the "bread of falsehood" in 20:17 is a euphemism for illicit intercourse with a married woman.

5. Others take 21:12 to refer to a "righteous" or innocent person who might be tempted to show pity to the house of a "wicked" or guilty man out of sympathy for his wife and family. By so doing he perverts (rather than "overthrows") wicked men in that such clemency will tempt them to initiate more evil deeds.

6. Others take the thorns and snares in 22:5 to refer to the hindrances proceeding from the wicked themselves which injuriously affect others.

7. Others take "knowledge" in 22:12 as the equivalent to divine revelation or true doctrine. All attacks upon divine revelation must fail. The second half of the verse speaks of a transgressor, suggesting that the first half of the verse speaks of the opposite of the transgressor, namely, one who possess heavenly wisdom.

8. Others think that the sluggard in 22:13 is offering two excuses: If he went into the fields he faced the danger of the lion; if he went into the streets of the town he might be attacked by ruffians.

CHAPTER THIRTY

The Words of the Wise
Proverbs 22:17-24:33

A major division of the material in Proverbs begins in 22:17. The heading here ("words of wise men") is reminiscent of 1:6. The material here differs from that which precedes in three ways. First, the style of the proverbs from here through the end of chapter 24 is very different from those that precede. Verses of two contrasting clauses for the most part disappear and are replaced by longer sentences, which as a general rule comprise two verses, sometimes three. Here the tone is hortatory as opposed the the largely descriptive style of the preceding section. The negative particle *'al* ("not") appears in this small unit seventeen times as compared to but twice in the twelve preceding chapters.

The First Appendix
INSTRUCTIONS TO A YOUNG MAN
Proverbs 22:17-23:11

Proverbs 22:17-23:11 has generally been regarded as a single instruction that has been carefully constructed. It consists of two series of admonitions concerning actions to be avoided (22:22-28; 23:4-11). Sandwiched between is advice directed to a young man about how to achieve his social and material ambitions. The entire section is preceded by an introduction. The unit contains only two direct references to Yahweh (22:19,23), although the "redeemer" in 23:11 appears to be an indirect allusion to him. In all other respects the instruction has the character of a father's instruction to his son as in the original instructions in chs. 1-9. There is here, however, no personification of wisdom such as on occasion appears in the earlier chapters. In fact, the word "wisdom" does not occur in this section at all.

A. Introduction: Appeal for Attention (22:17-21).

"Incline your ear and hear the words of the wise, and your heart apply to my knowledge." As in chapters 1-9 the wise one again addresses his disciple directly. The "words of the wise" would refer to more advanced knowledge as in 1:6. "My knowledge" is that which this teacher imparts by bringing to notice these sayings of the wise men (22:17).

As an incentive to his pupil, the teacher suggests some motivations for listening to the words of the wise. First, the consequences would be pleasant if the disciple would keep these teachings "within him," (lit., in your belly), i.e., deep in the heart. The teachings should be "established" on the lips, i.e., openly professed. They should regulate words and teach wisdom and discretion (22:18).

Second, godly wisdom would cause the student to put his trust in Yahweh. The instruction of this book is designed to teach total confidence in the Lord. This trust will lead a person, as soon as he knows and understands God's will, to do it at any cost and to leave the results to the Lord.

Third, the words of the wise have been personalized for the student. "I have made them known to you this day, even to you." Godly wisdom must be taken personally. Each individual is responsible before God to apply godly wisdom in his life. The urgency of embracing godly wisdom is underscored by the expression "this day." The student is not to remember vaguely that some time or other he received this instruction, but that on this particular day he heard it. Those who hear godly wisdom should embrace it immediately (22:19; cf. Heb 3:7,13).

Fourth, that which is being presented is a repetition of what had formerly been taught.[1] The importance of this instruction is indicated by the fact that the material is now being written down. This is the only reference to writing in the whole of the Book of Proverbs (22:20).

Fifth, the teaching of the wise emphasized the importance of being a reliable messenger. The disciple of wisdom should "bring back words which are true to those who send you." The carrying of messages necessary for the conduct of business or for family or personal reasons was a necessary and frequent practice in the ancient world. The accurate communication of messages by a young man would be a good test of his competence (22:21).

B. Admonition: Things to Avoid (22:22-28).

1. *Oppression of the poor (22:22-23).* The actual advice of the wise begins with an admonition not to wrong the poor. "Rob not the weak, because he is weak, neither crush the poor in the gate." The "weak" (*dal*) is a person who is defenseless through poverty or physical disability. One who lives by the principles of godly wisdom will not take advantage of such a person. In ancient communities justice was dispensed in a complex of buildings called "the gate." There unscrupulous judges might oppress "the afflicted," rendering decisions from which, no matter how wrong, there was no appeal. If, however, the helpless find no justice in the gate, Yahweh will "plead their cause," i.e., be their advocate and defender (cf. Exod 22:22ff.). The Lord will "despoil" those who attempt to "despoil" the poor, i.e., will bring ruin and death on the unjust judge or rich oppressor.

2. *Association with the violent (22:24-25).* A student of wisdom should not have close association with hot-tempered people. "Make no friendship with a master of anger, and with a person of wraths do

not go about." A person of "wraths" is a passionate person who easily loses his temper. Those who associate with such characters learn their ways and "get a snare" to their souls. Hotheads may get embroiled in quarrels with fatal consequences.

3. *Giving pledges (22:26-27)*. The pupil is warned not to make guarantees for other men's loans. To "strike hands" was the gesture which sealed a business transaction (cf. 6:1). If he cannot pay the debt, the creditor might seize any possession of value including even the bed on which he slept.

4. *Removing boundaries (22:28)*. Godly wisdom requires respect for the property rights of others. Hence "remove not the ancient landmark which your fathers have set." Removal of property markers was considered one of the most despicable crimes in the ancient world (cf. Deut 19:14).

C. Instruction: Ways to Advance (22:29–23:3).

1. *Diligent in labor (22:29)*. One who is diligent or skillful in any profession receives recognition and promotion. He may even come to "stand before," i.e., enter the service, of kings. A diligent, intellectual and clever laborer will not be content long to remain in the employment of obscure employers, lit., men of no importance (22:29).

2. *Master of etiquette (23:1-3)*. If the young man is going to advance in social station, he must know how to conduct himself in the presence of the king. First, the pupil is warned about gluttony. If he does not practice self-restraint, the pupil will "put a knife" to his throat, i.e., place his life in jeopardy by incurring the host's displeasure. The pupil should not be desirous of the king's dainties since "they are deceitful food" (lit., bread of lies). The ruler's hospitality may have a sinister purpose.

D. Admonition: Things to Avoid (23:4-11).

The writer now returns to admonition as he continues to list practices which should be avoided by one who pursues wisdom.

1. *Fixation with wealth (23:4-5)*. "Do not weary yourself to be rich." The advice here is not to make the acquisition of wealth the chief aim of life. A fixation on wealth leads to evildoing and neglect of all higher interests. "Cease from your own understanding." The

"understanding" (binah) is that which is necessary for the acquisition and maintenance of wealth. Godly wisdom teaches that people should not set their eyes upon riches like a ravenous bird which swoops upon its prey. Riches have a way of taking to themselves wings and flying away.

2. *Dining with misers (23:6-8)*. The disciple of wisdom should not eat a meal with "one who has an evil eye," i.e., a stingy person. Such a person may extend a cordial invitation. Throughout the whole meal, however, he is calculating what this hospitality might be costing him. Though he may invite the guest to eat and drink, his heart is not in his words because he is worried about the outlay. When the guest senses the true attitude of the host, the food grows nauseating. The vomit would cause the guest to "lose" the "sweet words" which normally a guest will bestow upon a host when he has enjoyed a fine evening.

3. *Discourse with fools (23:9)*. The disciple of wisdom should waste no words on a fool. If one has to explain the subtlety of an observation, he is wasting his time (cf. Matt 7:6). Even if a fool grasps what is said, he will not appreciate its wisdom.

4. *Moving boundaries (23:10-11)*. For the second time in this section the teacher urges his disciples to avoid moving boundary stones (cf. 22:28). This might indicate that at the time these proverbs were composed dishonest land acquisition was a major problem. One who would walk wisdom's path should respect the rights of the defenseless. He should not try to seize property by moving the ancient landmarks. He should not trespass into the fields of the fatherless for the purpose of damaging property, stealing produce or appropriating property. The redeemer (go'el) of the fatherless is none other than God himself. He (the pronoun is emphatic in the Hebrew) will "plead their cause," i.e., defend their rights against any who would attempt to injure them. Thus the motive clause in the last admonition is virtually the same as that of the first admonition in this section (cf. 22:23).

ADDITIONAL WARNINGS FOR YOUNG MEN
Proverbs 23:12-35

The proverbs in the last half of chapter 23 do not display the cohesiveness of those in the first half. These verses contain a number of short instructions, as well as material of other kinds. In this unit there is but one reference to Yahweh (v. 17) and one reference to "wisdom" (v. 23). Four passages have been identified as introductory to short collections of admonitions or observations. They serve to mark out the divisions of this material.

A. Avoid Envy (23:12-18).

1. Introduction (23:12-16). Encouragement to apply the heart to instruction and the ears to words of knowledge serves the purpose of introducing the next unit. A wise father or teacher will not withhold correction from a child (cf. 13:24; 19:18). He will not overlook the waywardness of a child using the excuse that the child will one day outgrow it. Corporal punishment on a wayward child will correct the fault and save the child "from Sheol," the abode of the dead, i.e., from capital punishment or death at the hands of an evildoer when he is an adult.[2] The Hebrew emphasizes the pronoun "you" in verse 14 as if to stress the obligation to employ corporal punishment for the ultimate good of the child. Uncorrected children grow up to be undisciplined adults (23:12-14).

The teacher's heart will rejoice whenever a pupil shows himself wise to learn and practice the instruction which is given him. The pronoun is repeated for the sake of emphasis, the speaker thus declaring his supreme interest in the moral progress of his disciple. When the student speaks "right things," his godly instructor will rejoice in his innermost being (lit., his kidneys). Right words indicate a mind that has been disciplined by morality (23:15-16).

2. The admonition (23:17-18). The student is encouraged not to envy sinners. Though they may appear to prosper for a time, the godly person will not covet their wealth and imitate their lifestyle. Rather, the teacher wants his pupil to be zealous for the fear of Yahweh.[3] The reason for this advice is that "there is a future." When his life is over the sinner receives his punishment, and the godly are rewarded. Thus the "hope" of reward for steadfastness in the things of God "shall not be cut off" at death (23:17-18).

B. Avoid Dissipation (23:19-21).

1. Introduction (23:19). The teacher now begins to warn his pupil about some of the most devastating vices. Again he addresses his student as "my son" and calls upon him to pursue the way of wisdom with his "heart," the seat of intellect and emotion.

2. Admonition (23:20-21). A student of wisdom should avoid "winebibbers" (those who gather for the express purpose of drinking) and "gluttons." The wise one regarded gluttony as evil as drunkenness. Intemperance leads to prodigality, carelessness, and ruin. Excessive indulgence makes a person drowsy and hence unfit for work. For this reason the drunkard and glutton eventually come to poverty.

C. Avoid Immorality (23:22-28).

1. Introduction (23:22-26). The teacher calls on his pupil to treat his parents with respect throughout life. He shows this respect by hearkening to the instruction and advice of his father; and by not despising his mother by losing patience with her when she is old and garrulous (23:22).

The student will honor his parents by purchasing "truth" (*'emeth*), i.e., the true principles for guidance of life. Truth is the highest value, and one should spare no pains, cost or sacrifice to obtain it and then keep it safe. A godly person will not "sell," i.e., part with truth. One must not barter it for earthly profit or sensual pleasure. One must not permit himself to be reasoned out of it or laughed out of it. One should not part with truth for any consideration.

"Truth" operates in the sphere of wisdom, understanding, and instruction. "Wisdom" (*chokhmah*) and "understanding" (*binah*) refer to the perception and practical knowledge of truth. "Instruction" (*musar*) refers to training in truth. A son who obeys the admonition of the preceding verse will be considered "righteous" and "wise." Such a son will bring joy to his father and mother (23:23-25).

In addition to heeding parental advice, the teacher appeals to the student to "give me your heart," i.e., pay attention to what I am about to say. The teacher calls upon the student to "observe" his ways. This Sage teaches by example as well as by precept (23:26).

2. Observation (2:27-28). Now comes the observation concerning the dangers of sexual misconduct. The teacher observes that "a harlot is a deep ditch." A prostitute's monetary demands can bring a man to poverty. "An alien woman is a narrow pit." The reference is probably to an adulteress. The "narrow pit" is one with a narrow mouth, from which, if one falls into it, it is difficult to extricate oneself. The expression indicates the seductive nature of the vice of unchastity: how easy it is to be led into it! How difficult to rise from it! (23:27).

The "alien woman" was not only a passive pitfall, she was an active danger. Like a robber she goes on the prowl looking for some unsuspecting victim. Her seductive ways make her more dangerous than the prostitute. She "increases the faithless among men." The harlot leads her victim to be faithless to his God, his spouse, his parents, his teachers and himself (23:28).

D. Avoid Drunkenness (23:29-35).

1. The introduction (23:29-30). The indictment of drunkenness is introduced with a riddle consisting of six questions. The questions constitute a strong indictment of alcohol. First, strong drink places one in danger: "Who cries, Woe?" Second, strong drink brings lamentation: "Who cries, Alas?" Third, strong drink often turns one who is civil into a complaining and contentious person: "Who has contentions?" The drunkard's senses are so dulled that he is under the delusion that he has been wronged. Fourth, strong drink produces self-pity: "Who has sorrowful thought?"[4] This self-pity shows itself in complaining about lost fortune, ruined health, and alienated friends. Fifth, strong drink brings "wounds without cause." With no good reason the drunkard becomes aggressive and exchanges blows with another person. Wounds "without cause" are the result of quarrels in which a sober person would never have engaged. Sixth, strong drink distorts physical features. "Redness of eyes" is a description of the inflamed condition of the eyes after excessive drinking (23:29).[5]

In 23:30 the answer to the six questions of the preceding verse is given. "They that tarry long at the wine" have all the negative experiences named above. So also do "they that go to seek mixed wine," i.e., wine mixed with certain spices or aromatic substances. The Hebrew uses two participles to indicate the frequentative action of the winebibbers. Whenever such people hear of a supply of wine being available, they rush out of their way to sample it. In spite of all its negative effects, people still are drawn to strong drink. Thus to the indictment of strong drink made by way of interrogation, the wise one adds yet another charge. Strong drink creates addiction (23:30).

2. *The admonition (23:31)*. The discussion of strong drink now turns to admonition. The teacher warns first of the attraction which wine has to the eye. "Look not on the wine when it is red," i.e., do not let yourself be attracted by its beautiful color. The wine is said to give "color [lit., eye] in the cup." It is as though the cup had an eye which glanced at the drinker with a seductive look which he could not resist. Second, the teacher warns of seduction of the taste of wine. Literally the Hebrew reads, Do not be deceived "when it goes by the right road," i.e., by the smooth taste of this beverage as it goes down the throat.

3. *The explanation (23:32)*. The so-called "motive clause" for the preceding admonition is now given: "At the last it bites like a serpent and stings like a viper." The deadly nature of strong drink is compared to the painful bite of a poisonous snake.

4. *The amplification (23:33-35)*. Verses 33-35 appear to be a continuation and amplification of the motive clause with a humorous twist. First, strong drink distorts the vision. "Your eyes shall see strange things."[6] Second, strong drink leads to perverse (lit., upside down) speech. The drunkard's notions are distorted, and his words partake of the same character; he confuses right and wrong; he says things which he would never speak if he were in full possession of his senses (23:33).

Third, strong drink deadens the brain to reality. The drunkard is "as he that lies down in the midst of the sea." The inebriated person is cut off from all his former pursuits and interests in life. He becomes unconscious of surrounding circumstances. Fourth, strong drink renders a person oblivious to danger. The drunkard will curl up to sleep on the top of a ship's mast from which he surely must fall to his death (23:34).[7]

Fifth, strong drink leads to a terrible hangover. Verse 35 vividly reveals the state of the drunkard's mind as he begins to come out of his stupor. He sees and feels the wounds of his body, but has no recollection of the fracas which caused the damage. All he desires is to throw off the effects of this hangover so he can start another round of drinking (23:35).

INVOLVEMENT WITH THE WICKED
Proverbs 24:1-22

The introductory and concluding verses of chapter 24 relate to the subject of involvement with wicked and foolish people. Most of the other proverbs in this chapter can be subsumed under this heading without doing any violence to the text. For the most part these proverbs are tetrastich in form, i.e., they consist of four lines each. Yahweh is mentioned in this unit twice by name (vv. 18,21). The Lord is alluded to in v. 12 as "he who weighs hearts" and "he who keeps watch" over his people. The unit contains three references to "wisdom" (vv. 3,7,14).

A. Warning against Evil Company (24:1-2).

The first admonition in chapter 24 lacks an introduction. Its connection with the preceding unit is found in the continuation of the theme of things to be avoided. The teacher urges his pupil not to be envious of evil men, i.e., of the wealth they gain by lawlessness. The reference is to those who make a career of crime. The pupil should never entertain even the desire "to be with them," i.e., to join their gang. The hearts of these career criminals "plot violence," i.e., acts of robbery and worse. All they can talk about is "making trouble." Their company is a pollution, and association with them makes one a partner in their sinful doings.

B. The Advantage of Wisdom (24:3-9).

1. Wisdom increases wealth (24:3-4). Instead of resorting to crime for the means to live, one can build up a comfortable and stable home by the application of wisdom. The term "wisdom" here not only embraces moral principles, but signifies shrewdness as well. The wisest of men focuses his energy on home building (cf. 9:1; 14:1). By "understanding," that home is "established," i.e., placed on a solid basis. By "knowledge," not violence, one may add to his house furnishings which are costly and comfortable.

2. Wisdom increases strength (24:5-6). A wise man does not need the reinforcement of gang association for he is, literally, "in strength." Even in circumstances where physical strength is the deciding factor, the possession of wisdom is helpful in overcoming the opponent. In fact, a person of knowledge "strengthens might," i.e., his wisdom enables him to use his strength to the fullest advantage. A specific example of this principle is found in the waging of war. A wise person will not go to war without the best advice available (cf. 20:18). He knows that in the multitude of counselors there is victory (cf. 11:14). Thus even in physical warfare, wisdom wins out (24:5-6).

3. *Wisdom increases respect (24:7-9).* "High [with respect] to the fool [are all aspects of] wisdom," i.e., wisdom is beyond a fool's reach. The terms "high" and "wisdom" are plural, indicating the many different facets of this godly grace are beyond the reach of a fool. The proverb stresses the rarity and inaccessibility of wisdom, and the refusal of fools to make any exertion in order to obtain it. A fool cannot "open his mouth in the gate," i.e., in the assembly where wise men deliberate regarding community affairs. On the other hand, the fool is one who "plots evil." People refer to such a scheming, mischief-making individual as, literally, a "lord of mischiefs." In this person misapplied cleverness abounds. One must not be misled by this person's apparent astuteness to attribute to him wisdom. He is an impostor! The plan of such foolish people is sin in the sight of God. The fool who is also a "scoffer" is "an abomination to men" because he stirs up strife and confusion.

C. The Encouragement of Boldness (24:10-12).

1. *A warning (24:10).* The student of godly wisdom should not be "slack." This admonition is probably to be connected with that which follows. One should not ignore the deadly peril into which a neighbor might be heading. Otherwise, when he faces a day of adversity (*tsarah*) his strength will be small (*tsar*) because God would withhold aid. The wise one has employed here a play on words in the Hebrew.

2. *An admonition (24:11).* The student of wisdom should "deliver" those that are "taken to death" and "rescue" those "that are tottering to the slaughter." The reference is probably to people who are in peril of death at the hands of lawless persons. Rescue is possible either by forceful intervention or the payment of a ransom. The godly person will not "withhold himself" from saving human lives unjustly imperiled.

637

3. An explanation (24:12). What is the motive for the admonition of the preceding verse? Some might be inclined to avoid involvement in such a dangerous situation. One might plead that he by himself could not effect the rescue of the doomed person. Why, then, had he not called on others to assist him? The excuse then would be ignorance of the perilous situation in which the neighbors had been placed. The one who weighs hearts will accurately evaluate such excuses as worthless. The Lord will then render "to every man according to his work."

D. Final Admonitions (24:13-22).

1. Wisdom is delightful (24:13-14). The teacher encourages those who follow wisdom to separate themselves from the wicked. As honey is beneficial and pleasant to the body, so is wisdom to the soul. One who has found wisdom has a "hope" that will not be cut off. The discovery of wisdom by a man gives him a confident outlook on life.

2. Wisdom is resilient (24:15-16). Criminals are exhorted not to waste their time in attacking the "dwelling" or "resting-place" of the righteous.[8] A righteous person may fall "seven times," i.e., often; but since he is under the power of God he is resilient. The verb "fall" *(naphal)* is not used here of moral indiscretions but of setbacks which are inflicted upon the righteous by life. In the midst of worldly cares, the righteous person never loses his trust in God. Always God's providence watches over him and delivers him out of all his afflictions. The "wicked," however, stumble under adversity. They fall without rising again. One blow is sufficient to crush them forever.

3. Wisdom is humble (24:17-18). While the overthrow of public enemies was often celebrated with festal rejoicing (cf. Exod 15), gloating over the fall of personal enemies is forbidden. Yahweh may turn his wrath away from that enemy. The point is not that God ceases to punish a wicked person because someone else is pleased at the punishment. The gloater becomes the greater sinner, and God will become more concerned to bring him down than to punish the enemy.

4. Wisdom is patient (24:19-20). The student of wisdom must guard against agitation (lit., make yourself hot) over the temporary ascendancy of evildoers. Neither should he be envious of these wicked people. The wicked have no future in this life nor the one to come. "The lamp of the wicked shall be put out," i.e, his end will come suddenly.

5. *Wisdom is respectful (24:21-22).* On the positive side, the student of wisdom should cultivate in his heart the fear of Yahweh and the king, i.e., he should be respectful of authority. The order is to be observed here: first Yahweh, then the king. Godly people obey the laws of legitimate authorities in so far as those ordinances do not contradict the higher laws of God. The godly will not "mix with" those who are committed to change, i.e., those who revolt against the laws of both God and man. Such revolutionaries will suddenly experience calamity and ruin arising from the anger of God and/or the wrath of the king.

The Second Appendix
FURTHER WORDS OF THE WISE
Proverbs 24:23-34

The heading in 24:23 "these also [belong] to the wise," i.e., the words of the wise, signals a second collection of proverbial material which was added to the original Solomonic core of the book. This appendix contains no parental introduction, nor references to Yahweh, nor to wisdom. The unit is structured thus: three admonitions are sandwiched between two series of observations.

A. Observations Regarding Impartiality (24:23-26).

Godly wisdom shows no partiality in respect to the administration of justice. Such "respect of persons" (lit., the recognition of faces) is forbidden in the law (Lev 19:15; Deut 16:19). Peoples shall "curse" officials who declare the wicked to be "righteous," i.e., innocent. Miscarriages of justice make citizens feel insecure. On the other hand, magistrates who "reprove," i.e., convict, the wicked "shall be a delight," i.e., shall fare well. "A blessing of good" fortune shall come upon those just officials (24:23-25).

Godly wisdom engages in straightforward and honest speech. Such speech is like "a kiss on the lips," i.e., a token of friendship (24:26).[9]

B. Miscellaneous Admonitions (24:27-29).

1. Prepare for marriage (24:27). Before one contemplates marriage he should be sure he can support a wife and family. He should first "establish," i.e., finish, his outside work, and make his field ready. The idea is to have the ground prepared with crops and livestock. Then the man might "build" his house, i.e., marry and rear a family. Economic viability has much more to do with a successful marriage than romantic passion.

2. Avoid frivolous testimony (24:28). "Do not be a witness without cause against your neighbor" either officiously as busybodies, or maliciously as slanderers. The idea is that one should not pretend to offer evidence in court if he has no grounds on which to do so. Such a person was in danger of becoming a deceiver. The deceit is not so much intentional falsehood as misrepresentation arising from haste consequent on eagerness to push forward testimony unsought.

3. Avoid seeking revenge (24:29). One should not plan to do to a neighbor what that neighbor has done to him. The *lex talionis* of Deut 19:21 does not apply to private wrongs. This proverb may suggest why one would be tempted to give the false testimony alluded to in the preceding verse.

C. Observations Regarding Slothfulness (24:30-34).

In the closing verses of chapter 24 the subject of slothfulness is taken up again. The form is that of a short moral tale similar to those found earlier in the book (e.g., 4:3ff.; 7:6-23). The teacher recounts his own experiences—whether real or fictional—in order to make a point.

The wise one had passed by the field of the sluggard and the vineyard of the person "without understanding." The vineyard and the field were the two chief objects of the farmer's care, which needed constant labor if they were to prove productive. The sluggard does not have the good sense to perceive that hard work is essential if a farm is to flourish. The wise one found the fields of the sluggard overgrown with thistles and nettles (weeds). The wall which protected the crops from trespassers and straying cattle had fallen into disrepair (24:30-31).

The teacher learned an important lesson at the farm of the sluggard. He saw in that field and vineyard the end result of a lazy lifestyle which craves sleep when work is necessary (cf. 6:10f.). The "poverty" and "scarcities" of that man come "marching . . . like an armed man," i.e., their coming is inevitable and irresistible (24:32-33).

ENDNOTES

1. A variation is found in the Hebrew text of 22:20. The *kethib* reading is *shiloshom* = day before yesterday, formerly. KJV and NASB follow the *qeri* reading *shalishim* = officers, hence "excellent things." NIV gives to the word a numerical sense: "thirty," with the two previous options in the footnote.

2. Others understand 23:13 to be saying that corporal punishment never killed a child. The following verse suggests the interpretation that the punishment will deliver the child from a worse fate later in life.

3. The last clause of 23:17 lacks a verb. The verb *qana'* (be jealous/zealous) appears to be used in both of its senses in this verse. One should not be *jealous* or envious of sinners but should be *zealous* for God.

4. The noun *siach* in 23:29 has been rendered "babbling" (KJV), "raving" (NIV), and "complaining" (NASB). The word properly means something like "meditation," hence the proposed rendering "sorrowful thought" for this context.

5. Others render "dullness of eyes" in 23:29, a reference to the stupor caused by alcoholic beverages.

6. "Strange things" (*zarot*) is understood by the KJV to refer to strange women, i.e., harlots. This understanding is certainly possible, and some commentators think probable. Proverbs makes repeated references to "strange women." Intemperance unbridles lust and causes the eye to rove after unchaste women.

7. Others apply the imagery of 23:34 to the wobbly legs of the drunkard which cause him to lie down. The ground under him seems to heave up and down as though he were aboard a ship.

8. The terms "dwelling" and "resting-place" in 24:15 have a pastoral association. They may suggest that the admonition is addressed to city criminals who set out to attack righteous men who live in agricultural settlements, because these were not defended.

9. Some scholars doubt that kissing the lips was customary as token of friendship in the days of Solomon. In the second century BC this practice was regarded as immodest. The verb *nashaq* in some contexts means "to equip, to arm" (cf. Ps 78:9). The suggestion has been made that the reference is to one who "equips" or "arms" the lips with knowledge.

CHAPTER THIRTY-ONE

Wisdom as the Greatest Blessing
Proverbs 25-29

Another collection of Solomonic proverbs is said to have been "copied out" by the "men of Hezekiah." Apparently King Hezekiah commanded these men of literary skill to extract from the mass of Solomonic proverbs this small selection which was then produced as a separate compilation. This collection of proverbs differs from the earlier Solomonic collection (10:1–22:16) in that it contains only six Yahweh proverbs. The former collection is notable for the frequency of its cases of imagery, expressed in similes and metaphors, while the present collection contains few examples of this.[1]

WISDOM AND THE ROYAL COURT
Proverbs 25:2-27

The proverbs in chapter 25 may have had the purpose of giving advice to courtiers or would-be courtiers.[2] The chapter consists of alternating clusters of observations and admonitions.

A. Observations Regarding Royal Policy (25:2-5).

Solomon made two observations about royal policy. First, that policy should be clear and understandable to all the subjects. The mysterious way in which God governs the world actually redounds to his glory. It points to the working of an infinite wisdom which is inscrutable by man. That which is the chief glory of God is his mysteriousness. On the other hand, kings are human beings. Unintelligible policies and ordinances are not to the credit of a king. Unfortunately often the actions of the royal mind are as difficult to comprehend as the height of the heavens or the depths of the earth. One must not flatter himself with the thought that he can always count on the favor of the king. His good disposition may only be apparent, and may at any moment be changed (25:2-3).

Second, royal policy needs to be righteous, i.e., in harmony with the principles of divine revelation. A metal worker must have refined metal in order to produce a perfect design. The dross must first be removed. So also the wicked counselor, who exercises an evil influence upon the king, must be removed if royal policy is to be formulated in righteousness (25:4-5).

B. Admonitions Regarding Court Conduct (25:6-10).

Solomon now offers three admonitions designed to indicate to would-be courtiers how they should behave in the presence of the king. First, one should know his place and not step out of it. At royal feasts the guests were seated according to rules of precedence. One should never displace "great men," i.e., dignitaries who have a superior claim to a place nearer to the king. Otherwise the courtier's inferior rank would be publicly exposed. By humility the would-be courtier can avoid the humiliation which he had observed inflicted on others. To be invited by the king to occupy a more prestigious seat is much better (25:6-7; cf. Luke 14:7ff.).

Second, a courtier should avoid being contentious. One should not bring a suit against a neighbor before he has assured himself that he has a sound case. The defendant may win the case, and thus put the plaintiff to shame (25:8).

Third, a courtier should not betray confidences. In an argument with a neighbor the temptation exists to reveal secret information about him. A person who betrays confidential information will be reviled as a talebearer by those who hear him. His bad reputation would remain with him forever (25:9-10).

C. Observations Regarding Speech (25:11-15).

The teacher first comments on appropriate speech. "A word spoken upon its revolvings," i.e., in the revolution of time or seasonably, "is like apples of gold in settings of silver." Some think the reference is to carvings of apples overlaid with gold upon a silver background. Others think the reference is to apricots rather than apples. The writer is envisioning this golden fruit against the setting of bright yet pale foliage (25:11).

Second, the text urges the value of correction. Reproof which is tactfully given and willingly received is as valuable as an ornament of fine gold (25:12).

Third, a courtier must be a faithful messenger. Such a one refreshes the one who sent him as snow would refresh hot laborers in the day of harvest (25:13).

Fourth, a courtier should make good on his promises. A "false gift" is one which does not compare with what was boastingly promised. A braggart who cannot make good on his word is like vapors or wind which disappear without being followed by the rain which they normally herald (25:14).

Fifth, a courtier must show forbearance. "Forbearance" is patience, calmness that does not break out into passion whatever be the provocation. A prince or judge (katson) is often quick-tempered, but their wrath soon subsides. Those who serve such a ruler should patiently endeavor to restore him to a more equitable frame of mind. "A soft tongue breaks the bone," i.e., gentle speech, rather than harsh words, will overcome more effectively stubborn opposition (25:15).

D. Admonition Regarding Moderation (25:16-17).

First, the courtier should possess moderation in eating. Even if one is consuming "honey" he should not overindulge lest he become sick and vomit it. "Honey" here signifies anything desirable and enjoyed. Overindulgence will cause satiety and eventual loathing (25:16).

Second, the courtier should practice moderation in associations. He should visit only occasionally (lit., make your foot rare from) in the house of his neighbor. Familiarity breeds contempt. One can quickly wear out his welcome. The neighbor may come to hate the frequent visitor (25:17).

E. Interpersonal Relationships (25:18-20).

Three comparisons are presented which contain within them implied admonitions. First, the teacher compares one who bears false witness against his neighbor to a club, a sword and a sharp arrow. False testimony can shatter, slash and pierce as surely as these weapons of war (25:18).

Second, misplaced confidence is like a broken tooth or a dislocated foot. This comparison may warn against placing confidence in someone who is unreliable. Others think the reference is to the misplaced confidence of the faithless man. In a time of trouble, that in which he trusts—wealth, friends, cunning—will prove worthless.

Third, the teacher warns against untimely cheerfulness (cf. Rom 12:15). One who tries to "sing songs" to someone with a "heavy heart" (lit., an evil heart) is compared to one who takes off a garment in cold weather, or to vinegar on soda. One who underdresses on a cold day is foolish. Placing vinegar on soda produces a sour, angry fermentation. Such will be the reaction of one who is in a foul mood when someone tries to cheer him up (25:20).

F. Disarming an Enemy (25:21-22).

The teacher admonishes his pupil to repay evil with good. Even an enemy should be fed when he is hungry and given water when he is thirsty (cf. 2 Kgs 6:22). Friendly action of this kind, so unexpected and unmerited, will have a painful effect upon that enemy, like heaping burning coals on his head. That inward pain has a beneficial effect for it leads to remorse over the enmity. Furthermore, Yahweh will reward the brotherly act by bestowing his blessing.

G. Final Observations (25:23-28).

Another series of observations closes the instruction for would-be courtiers. These observations are implied invectives against social and moral defects.

1. *Against slander (25:23).* Backbiting angers people. As surely as the north wind brings a cold rain, so will the sly tongue produce an angry countenance.

2. *Against isolationism (25:24-25).* A quarrelsome wife makes life miserable (21:9). Better to live in meager surroundings than in a spacious house with such a woman. One must not, however, choose to be a hermit. Even when separated from a loved one the news of their well-being brings refreshment like cold water refreshes a thirsty body (cf. Gen 45:27). If that is true merely of the *news* about a loved one, how much more the personal *presence* of that loved one will provide joy and satisfaction.

3. *Against cowardice (25:26).* A good person neglecting to assert himself and to hold his own in the face of sinners is useless to society. He is compared to a "trampled" fountain, i.e., one which has been polluted by trampling; or to a "polluted" well, i.e., one into which the walls have collapsed so that one is unable to draw water. The mouth of the righteous should be "a well of life" (10:11), i.e., wholesome, refreshing, helpful. His conduct should be consistent and fearless in upholding that which is right. He must be uncompromising in opposing sin. When such a person "gives way" to the wicked, compromises principle, and no longer makes a stand for truth, purity and virtue, he loses his high character, brings scandal on the faith, and lowers his own spiritual nature.

4. *Against lack of self-restraint (25:27-28).* To overindulge in honey is not good (cf. 25:16). Glory, like honey, is a good thing; but being too engrossed with one's share of glory is like eating too much honey. A person without self-restraint is like a city whose walls have been breached by an invading army. A person is defenseless against the attacks of his impulses when he is not the master of himself.

UNDERSTANDING HUMAN TYPES
Proverbs 26:1-28

Chapter 26 is much more integrated than most of the chapters in this part of the book (chs. 25–29). There are four clear sections, each having its own topic. The chapter contains no reference to Yahweh. The purpose of the chapter is to identify certain types of characters who are to be avoided.

A. The Fool (26:1-12).

In the course of life one must interact with fools. How should they be treated? This is the burden of the next series of proverbs.

First, a fool (*kesil*) should not be given a position of honor. To raise a fool to a position of honor would (1) confirm him in his folly; (2) give others a false impression of his worth; and (3) afford him increased opportunity for mischief. A fool in a post of honor is as harmful to society as unseasonable weather. Snow in summer would be harmful to the crops. Rain in harvest would prevent the housing of the produce at the proper time (26:1).

Second, a fool should not be feared. A fool might utter an undeserved curse on someone. That curse will not come, i.e., will not fall upon the person for whom it was intended.[4] Such groundless outbursts of condemnation are like the birds which aimlessly and harmlessly fly through the skies (26:2).

Third, a fool should be disciplined with force. A whip is needed to keep a horse moving in the right direction. An ass, being less willful than a horse, can be guided by means of the bridle, without recourse to a whip. So words of advice are insufficient to keep a fool on the right course. More forceful means—the rod—have to be employed (26:3; cf. 10:13; 19:29).

Fourth, a fool should not be debated on his own terms. One should not degrade himself by answering a fool "according to his folly," i.e., by stooping to his level in an exchange of recriminations; by arguing with him as if he were a sensible person (26:4).[5]

Fifth, a fool should be exposed and silenced. One should "answer a fool according to his folly," i.e., as his folly deserves. The folly needs to be exposed and shame brought upon it. Hopefully, this will bring the fool to a better state of mind. If one does not respond in this way, the fool "will be wise in his own eyes." He will think that he has said something worth hearing or that he has silenced the believer by his superior intelligence (26:5).

How are these last two proverbs, which seem to contradict each other, to be reconciled? One might ask a foolish question, but do so innocently or in the right spirit. In such a case do not give a flippant answer to the question, i.e., respond with a forthright answer. On the other hand, if one asks the same question but in an arrogant manner or in an effort to ridicule the truth, refute his error in such a powerful way that the foolishness of the questioner is made clear.

Sixth, a fool should not be trusted, at least not with a verbal message. He most likely would distort the verbal message and deliver an incorrect version. That messenger would be like "feet" to the message sender. By dispatching a fool with his message the sender, as it were, disables himself. Even worse, the wrong message may incense the recipient who, assuming its correctness, harms the sender. Thus by sending the fool the sender is "drinking violence" to himself (26:6).

Seventh, a fool should not be heeded. A parable in the mouth of a fool is as useless as the legs of a cripple. It falls lame from his mouth, affords no instruction to others, and makes no impact upon its hearers. In fact, a parable in the mouth of a fool is like a thorn-bush in the hand of a drunkard, i.e., a harmful weapon recklessly employed (26:7,9).

Eighth, a fool should not be praised. Paying honor to a fool is as futile as tying a stone in a sling. A fool cannot live up to the honor bestowed on him. That honor remains as useless to him as the stone which cannot be hurled from a sling (26:8).

Ninth, a fool should not be hired. To hire a fool or one merely passing by to perform a task is like hiring a reckless archer. That incompetent will do more harm than good. If one wants a task to be completed he must hire an expert (26:10).

Tenth, a fool should be regarded as incorrigible. A fool repeats his mistakes even though he has suffered harm from them previously. He, like a dog, ejects undigestible food only to return to his own vomit. The dog being senseless, will eat that food again and suffer for it (2 Pet 2:22). Even worse than the fool is one who is "wise in his own eyes." A fool who is conscious of unwisdom may be set right; but one who considers himself perfect, and needing no improvement, is beyond cure; his case is hopeless. Conceit closes the door on self-improvement (26:11-12).

B. The Sluggard (26:13-16).

The teacher next brings together a series of humorous sayings regarding the sluggard ('atsel). First, a slothful person is full of excuses. Such a person looks for any excuse, even the most far-fetched, to stay indoors and thus avoid work. He may justify his sloth by citing dangers ("a lion") outdoors in the street (26:13; cf. 22:13).

Second, a slothful person loves sleep. He tosses and turns on his bed like a door swinging on its hinges. The door makes no progress beyond its own confined sphere of motion. So the slothful person turns himself on his bed from side to side, but never leaves it to do any work. The door creaks when it is moved, so the lazy man groans when he is aroused (26:14).

Third, a slothful person avoids the slightest exertion. When he finally gets out of bed this bum buries his hand in the dish (cf. 19:24). He is so lazy that he cannot expend the energy to bring his hand to his mouth (26:15).

Fourth, a slothful person is arrogantly opinionated. He is too lazy to undergo the mental discipline which would enable him to give an intelligent reply in discussing issues. He considers research to be an unnecessary weariness of the flesh. He flatters himself that he is quite able without study to give a satisfactory account of any question presented to him. Yet he considers himself wiser than "seven men," i.e., a round number or several, who collectively and cautiously have rendered an opinion in the matter (26:16).

C. The Petulant (26:17-21).

The undesirable traits of a petulant person are now set forth. First, he meddles in the strife of others. He was merely passing by, yet he stops to insert himself into the quarrel. He "angers himself," or gets exercised over the situation. Such a person is courting danger. He is like one who takes a dog by the ears and gets bitten (26:17).

Second, a petulant person excuses terrible misconduct as a practical joke. He deceives his neighbor and then excuses himself by saying, "I was only joking!" When a person has injured a neighbor by lies or malice, the plea that it was only a joke is not permitted. The injury is no less real because it (allegedly) was done in jest. Such a person is like one who recklessly hurls firebrands or arrows. Someone is bound to get hurt. "Firebrands" are darts with some blazing material attached to them (26:18-19).

Third, a petulant person delights in stoking the fires of controversy. This he may do through a whispering campaign of slander, false reports and innuendo (cf. 16:28). As a fire must have fresh fuel to continue burning, so contention is kept alive by such whispering. Others are more openly "contentious," i.e., they delight in contention. Whenever they are near, new coals and wood are thrown on the fires of controversy (26:20-21).

D. The Malicious (26:22-26).

The next series of proverbs deals with malicious, especially deceitful, persons who dissimulate their hatred under a cloak of friendship. Gossips love to hear gossip. The words of a whisperer are as "dainty morsels," i.e., something delightful. They are taken into the innermost parts of the body, i.e., they are eaten and digested (26:22; cf. 18:8).

Hypocrites express friendship fervently with their lips. Yet the hearts of such people are wicked. They plot the ruin of the others who are lulled into a false sense of security by their "burning [fervent] lips." Such people are like "the silver of dross," i.e., the base metal which is left when the pure silver has been refined. This inferior silver was used to overlay earthenware and gave the vessel the appearance of being valuable. The point is that a glittering exterior often hides the reality within (26:23).

Some people are full of hatred, yet they feign friendship by friendly speech. Such a person "lays up" deceit until an opportunity occurs to vent the animosity. The teacher advises his readers to put no trust in the pleasant words of such a man. Within the heart of that man are "seven abominations," i.e., countless wickedness. Hatred is frequently concealed with deceit. Sooner or later that hatred finds expression in some vicious act. The matter is then brought before the public assembly acting in a judicial capacity. At that time the fate of the hater is made clear (26:24-26).

The person who maliciously digs a pit with the intention of injuring another, shall fall therein. Whoever attempts to roll a stone upon another shall be crushed by that same stone. This refers to rolling stones up to a height in order to hurl them down upon an enemy (26:27).

A liar selects as the objects of his slander those whom he hates. The person with a "smooth mouth" conceals his real thoughts. His intention is to bring about somebody's downfall (26:28).

INSTRUCTIONS REGARDING
FRIENDS AND FAMILY
Proverbs 27:1-27

Like chapter 26, this chapter contains no Yahweh proverb. The structural unity is hard to discern. In the first ten verses the topic of friendship plays a dominant, though not an exclusive, role. Verses 11-27 may once have constituted a loose compendium of parental teaching.[6]

A. Focus on Friendship (27:1-10).

1. Detriments to friendship (27:1-4). Arrogant boasting is an enemy of friendship. Boasting takes two forms, equally evil. First, a person should not boast about the future. "Do not praise yourself in respect to tomorrow," i.e., boast about what you will accomplish. One boasts of tomorrow who counts upon it presumptuously and who settles on what he will accomplish during that tomorrow. "For you do not know what a day will bring forth." If man is ignorant of what will happen today, how can he anticipate what will happen the next day? Second, a person should not boast about the past or the present. "Let another person praise you, and not your own mouth," i.e., leave any praise to others (John 8:54; 2 Cor 10:18). Those who "toot their own horn" will have few friends in this world (27:1-2).

Anger is another enemy of friendship. A fool does not know how to express anger appropriately. He flies into a rage. For those around him this is a heavy burden to bear, like the weight of sand or a stone (27:3).

Another enemy of friendship is jealousy. "Wrath is cruel, and anger is overwhelming, but who is able to stand before jealousy." A jealous wrath is the worst kind. It destroys marriages, families and friendships. The reference here is not so much to the general feeling of jealousy as to the outraged love in the relationship between a husband and wife. Such jealousy does not blaze forth in some sudden outbreak, and then die away; it lives and broods and feeds itself hourly. It is ready to act at any moment. It stops at nothing to be rid of the latest provocateur (27:4).

2. The values of friendship (27:5-10). From the negative, the teacher proceeds to the positive. Friendship cannot exist without honest, loving criticism. One does not truly love another who conceals a rebuke. "Faithful are the wounds of a friend." Though painful, they are administered in love (Eph 4:15). The verbal chastisement hurts deeply, but only thus will faults be corrected. On the other hand, "the kisses of an enemy are profuse." The enemy repeatedly may offer expressions of friendship—Judas kisses—but he has an ulterior motive (27:5-6).

"The satisfied soul tramples upon a honeycomb," i.e., he rejects it with disdain. Honey normally would be regarded as a welcome and wholesome article of food. On the other hand, "to the hungry person every bitter thing is sweet." The husks in the hog pen looked appealing to the Prodigal. Perhaps the thought is this: One who is surrounded with friends often takes them for granted and treats them with disdain. Those without sweet friendship will not be discriminating in their choice of companions (27:7).

A bird that wanders from its nest is in danger. So is a person who wanders from his place. Surrounded by friends and family one has the benefit of wise counsel and corrective rebuke. To walk away from that "nest" is to expose oneself to danger (27:8).

The advice of a friend is a valuable possession. "Hearty counsel" is literally "advice of the soul," i.e., advice given with a genuine desire to be helpful. Such advice from a friend is compared to perfume and incense. It has a sweet aroma which gives pleasure to those who receive it. In a time of calamity one would be better off turning to a tried and true family friend than to a "brother," i.e., a kinsman. In an emergency a neighbor who is near may be of more benefit than a kinsman at a distance. For this reason one should cultivate friendship with those who live in close proximity. One has no control over the circumstances of birth and blood-relatedness; a friend, however, is chosen (27:9-10).

B. Family Instruction (27:11-22).

Again the teacher addresses his pupil as "my son" as he does at least twenty-three times in the book. He urges his student to "be wise," i.e., act in conformity with the teachings of wisdom. He offers three reasons: First, such conduct would make the heart of the teacher glad, i.e., it would give him personal satisfaction. Second, wise conduct on the part of the "son" would also serve to silence critics who might question the qualifications and ability of the teacher. Third, wisdom teaches prudence and prudence avoids dangers (cf. 22:3) in the path of life (27:11-12).

The compendium of parental instruction directs the "son" to hold a foolish man to his obligations. See comments on 20:16 (27:13).

The "son" is warned about insincere greetings. The teacher pictures one who rises early to bless his friend in a loud voice, i.e., he heartily wishes the neighbor well. He feigns interest in the well-being of his friend. "It shall be counted a curse to him." The reference is probably to the man who was greeted. He should not be deceived by the words, but assess them as no better than a curse (27:14).

Next the "son" is warned about a quarrelsome wife. Such a wife is compared to a downpour which comes through the roof of a house and drives everyone outside (cf. 19:13). The roofs of homes in the east were ill-constructed. Being flat and porous they were subject to severe leakage. The nagging woman drives the family away. The character of such a woman cannot be hidden from neighbors any more than the wind can be confined or the smell of ointment camouflaged. This woman would only raise her voice the louder if she thought that her husband was anxious for others not to hear her (27:15-16).

If a nagging spouse drives one out of the house, one should not thereafter become a recluse. "Iron sharpens iron, and a man sharpens the countenance of his friend." Knowledge is more accurately acquired by studying in the company of others. Social interaction has a decisive effect upon the formation of the character of a young person (27:17).

Next the teacher sets forth the reward of industry. A farmer is able to eat the fruit of the fig tree he has labored to cultivate. The abundance of the produce of this tree makes it a good figure of the reward of faithful services. So also those who labor in the service sector will be rewarded for their diligent labor on behalf of their masters. If this is true of earthly masters, how much more is it true of the heavenly master (27:18; cf. Matt 25:21).

The language of 27:19 is concise, almost cryptic, and consequently is very difficult. Literally the verse reads: "As water to the face, so the heart of man to man." A person sees a true reflection of himself in a still pool of water. So truly does the heart of one person discern in others his own character. A liar thinks all others to be liars. A thief projects his greed on his neighbors. A fornicator assumes that everyone else is involved in immorality.[7]

Next the teacher warns against greed. Sheol and Destruction—the abode of departed spirits—are never satisfied. Despite the multitudes that descend into the grave, death clamors for more. So the eye, the organ which arouses lust (1 John 2:16), is never satisfied. Unless controlled by the principles of wisdom, the eye will continually find more things to crave. What is said here of the eye is true of all the senses: the craving for their gratification grows as it is fed. Therefore the senses should be guarded carefully, lest they lead to excess and transgression (27:20).

The teacher sets forth a principle by which the character of a person can be tested: "A person is tested by his praise." Does he mean, "by the things he praises"? or "by the praise that others bestow on him"? Either interpretation presents a profound truth. In the former case, the test of a person is the kind of person or deed which he commends. If he idolizes a criminal or whoremonger, for example, that probably indicates that he has tendencies in these directions. The second interpretation warns young people not to believe all the flatteries which might be heaped upon them in life. Many people are ruined by praise. If a person comes forth from it without injury, not rendered vain, or blind to his defects, or not disdainful of others, his disposition is good. The commendation lavished upon him may be morally and spiritually beneficial (27:21).

Though one grind a fool in a mortar, the folly will not be removed from him. Separating the husks from the grain by the use of pestle and mortar is much more delicate and careful than threshing in the usual clumsy manner. The figure is used here to symbolize the most elaborate pains which are wasted on the incorrigible fool. An obstinate, self-willed, unprincipled person cannot be reformed by any means; his folly has become a second nature and cannot be eliminated by any teaching or discipline however severe.

C. Commendation of Diligence (27:23-27).

The teacher now sings an ode in praise of a pastoral and agricultural life. Some view these verses as a call to return to the pastoral life of the patriarchs. Probably, however, the teacher intended here only a commendation of diligence and prudence.

The "son" is urged to "be diligent to know the state" (lit., face), i.e., appearance or condition, of his flock. "Riches" derived from business transactions are unstable. The "crown" or honor heaped upon those who reside in cities is not an enduring heritage. It cannot be passed on to descendants like land. Once the harvest is over, the lambs can be sheared. Their wool provides clothing. The milk of the goats—a fundamental in the diet of the period—provides food for the entire household and resources for additional land acquisition.

INSTRUCTION IN PROPER BEHAVIOR
Proverbs 28:1-28

The theme of chapter 28 is instruction. This is indicated by (1) the quadruple use of the term *torah* (teaching) in the first nine verses; and (2) the similarity of the terms used in these verses with those used in the instructions of chapters 1-9.

A. The Importance of Instruction (28:1-9).

"The wicked flee when no one is pursuing." The conscience of a wicked person makes him insecure. On the other hand, the righteous are confident "as a young lion." They are undismayed in the presence of danger, because their conscience is at rest, and they know that God is on their side. Whatever happens, they are safe in the everlasting arms (28:1).

Frequent turnover in the leadership of a country creates political instability. Such a condition is a punishment for the transgression of that land. On the other hand, "a man of understanding and knowledge" in a position of leadership enables "right," i.e., justice, to live long in the land. The taxes imposed by a wealthy ruler are bad enough, but they become much more severe when a poor man grasps power which he uses for self-enrichment. Such a ruler is compared to a "rain" which sweeps away everything—even food stores—before it. A greedy ruler strips citizens of their wealth (28:2-3).

Some people forsake the law (*torah*), i.e., instruction of the wise because they reject its morality. They therefore approve of the way of life led by the wicked. They love iniquity and want to see it extend its influence, and arm itself against good men, who are a standing reproach to them. On the other hand, those who keep the law "contend with them," i.e., feel resentment against those who forsake the law. They are filled with righteous indignation; they cannot hold their peace when they see God's law outraged. They demand that the offenders be punished (28:4).

Those who follow evil do not distinguish between justice and its opposite. An evil person's moral conception is perverted; he cannot distinguish between right and wrong. Whatever light was in him has become darkness. By giving themselves over to wickedness, such persons are judicially blinded (John 12:39f.). On the other hand, those who seek to know and obey Yahweh "understand it completely," i.e., they are sensitive to the distinction between right and wrong (28:5).

"Better is the poor person who walks in his integrity, than he who is perverse of two ways, though he is rich." Honest poverty is preferable to dishonest wealth. The "two ways" are the evil way, which he is actually pursuing, and the good way which he pretends to follow. Such a double-dealing deceiver puts on religion to mask wicked designs—in this case in order to gain wealth (28:6).

"He who observes instruction (torah) is an understanding son." Such a son discerns his obligation to gladden his parents' heart by good conduct. He is obedient both to the law of God and to the instruction of his parents. On the other hand, "he that is a companion of gluttons" shames his father. Gluttons were bad companions. Association with them leads to riotous living and reckless spending. Such a lifestyle holds the instruction of God and family in contempt (28:7).

He who increases his wealth by exorbitant interest[8] amasses it for another who will give it to the poor. Enriching oneself through interest on loans to poor Israelites was strictly forbidden in the law (Lev 25:36f.). God will not allow such a person to retain the profit. He will divert this wealth into the possession of one more worthy to have it, namely, one who is gracious to the poor (28:8).

One who deliberately refuses to listen to torah (instruction) will have no access to God through prayer. "Even his prayer is an abomination." This person refuses to abandon his favorite sin even while engaging in worship to the God whose law he breaks. Such a person's prayer lacks the ingredients of sincerity, unselfishness, submissiveness and faith. If man is deaf to God's instruction, God will be deaf to man's supplication (28:9).

B. Wicked vs. Righteous (28:10-28).

Almost every verse contrasts the behavior of the wicked and the righteous.

1. The backslider and the faithful (28:10). One who leads astray an upright person into "an evil way," i.e., the path of wickedness, shall fall into his own pit. The upright person may rise from that temporary lapse. The one who deceived him, however, sinks ever deeper and becomes twofold more the child of hell for playing the devil's part. On the other hand, "the whole-hearted," i.e., steadfast in loyalty to God, "shall inherit good," i.e., be blessed of God. He will be abundantly rewarded by God's grace and protection, by the comfort of a conscience at rest, and often by prosperity in his worldly concerns, not to mention his eternal reward (28:10).

2. The rich and the poor (28:11). "The rich person is wise in his own eyes." He has been successful in business. Therefore, he assumes he is clever in all matters. This purse-proud person expects others to show deference to his views on subjects far removed from his field of expertise. On the other hand, "the poor that possesses understanding sees through him," i.e., correctly evaluates his mental capacity.

3. Righteous vs. wicked rulers (28:12). "When the righteous exult, there is great glory." The righteous exult when the land is administered justly, when good has triumphed over evil. Under just rule taxation is not oppressive and the citizens have money to spend on personal adornment and a comfortable home. On the other hand, "when the wicked rise [to power], men must be sought for," i.e., they go into hiding. They know that a wicked ruler will confiscate through the mechanism of taxation all of their possessions. In a worst case scenario, the life of a righteous person may be in jeopardy when the wicked are in power.

4. Impenitent vs. penitent (28:13). "He that covers his transgression shall not prosper." Such a person refuses to admit his guilt. He either denies his involvement, denies that the action itself is sin, or makes excuses to justify his conduct. Such a person, however, is never free from a burden of guilt (cf. Ps 32:3). On the other hand, "whoever confesses and forsakes them shall obtain mercy." Confession without repentance is worthless. One must determine not to repeat the offense. God pardons one who sincerely renounces his transgression. The confession is made to God, against whom all sin is committed, and to man, if one has transgressed against him. God can heal the heart of that believer who honestly confesses his sin before him (cf. 1 John 1:9).

5. *Godly fear vs. hardness (28:14).* "Happy is the person who fears always." Fears what? This is not the verb used for reverencing God. The verb here (*pachad*) signifies apprehension of sin and its consequences. One who fears sin is one who prepares for temptation that he might resist it (1 Cor 10:12; Phil 2:12). On the other hand, "he who hardens his heart shall fall into evil." He scoffs at such fear and disregards the thought of God's punishment. Such a one scorns the grace of God. He must ultimately experience "evil," i.e., calamity, the manifestation of divine judgment.

6. *Ruthless vs. compassionate rulers (28:15-16).* "A wicked ruler over the poor people," i.e., a people weak and resourceless, is likened unto a "roaring lion" or a "ravenous bear" (lit., a bear roaming). To helpless people a powerful tyrant is as fatal as a vicious beast. Such rulers are like lions in strength and cruelty, like bears in craft and ferocity. Lack of intelligence makes a prince cruel and callous to suffering. Not possessing the wisdom and prudence necessary for right government, such a ruler defrauds his subjects, treats them unjustly, and causes great misery. On the other hand, he who "hates covetousness shall prolong his days." Why? Because only a ruler who deals with his subjects liberally and equitably can attain to old age. Greed leads to a ruler's tyranny in the form of heavy exactions from the people. When this vice is absent, both the ruler and his people are happy. The expression "prolong his days" is a Hebrew idiom for "live a long, happy and secure life" (28:15-16).

7. *Lawbreakers vs. the law-abiding (28:17).* "A person that is oppressed because of the blood of any person, unto a pit he shall flee." The reference seems to be to a person who is guilty of homicide.[9] He is "oppressed" either (1) by his guilty conscience; or (2) by the authorities who hunt him from place to place. The "pit" to which he flees is either

(1) a hiding place; or (2) the grave. The idea seems to be that this murderer will remain a fugitive until he dies. "Let none support him," the sage urges. No one should attempt to save him from the punishment which he had incurred or to comfort him under the remorse which he suffers. Let him be left alone to meet the fate which he deserves. Citizens must line up with law enforcement and against those who violate the laws of God and man.

8. *The blameless vs. hypocrites (28:18).* One who walks uprightly (*tamim*), i.e., innocently, blamelessly, shall be saved from the calamities, temporal and spiritual, which befall the wicked. On the other hand, "one who is perverse in respect to two ways, shall fall in one." The reference is to a person who is not straightforward, one who vacillates between right and wrong or pretends to be pursuing one path while he is really taking another. Such a person shall fall "all at once" or "once for all" (lit., "in one"), i.e., suddenly and without warning.

C. Wisdom in Respect to Wealth (28:19-22).

One who tills his field will have plenty of bread. On the other hand, one who follows after "vain things" shall have his fill of poverty (28:19).

"A faithful person," i.e., one who shows fidelity in his transactions, "shall abound with blessings." The verse teaches that "honesty is the best policy." On the other hand, one who is eager to get rich "shall not be free of guilt." His eagerness to accumulate wealth quickly will tempt him to commit fraud or theft (28:20).

Showing partiality in courts of law is not good. "For a person will transgress for a piece of bread." A judge might think himself justified in departing from strict justice in the case of a person driven by hunger to steal a piece of bread. Even in this circumstance, however, there should be no "respecting of persons." The law must be upheld (28:21; cf. Exod 23:3; Lev 19:15).

One who has "an evil eye," i.e., envies the possessions of others, "hastens after riches." Such a person does not realize that "poverty awaits him." His grasping greed brings no blessing with it. It stirs others to defraud him. In the end this greed consigns him to merited poverty. The idea is that God will punish him by bringing him to a state of destitution (28:22).

660

D. Wisdom and Self-centeredness (28:23-27).

Reproof is to be preferred to flattery. One who rebukes another shall in the end find more favor than one that flatters with the tongue. A person may be taken in by flattery for a time, but eventually he comes to realize that he who corrects his faults is his real friend (28:23).

Robbing parents is viewed as a terrible crime. The sage describes a person who robs his parents but refuses to admit he has done anything wrong. The proverb has in view the attempt (legal or otherwise) to get control of the property of parents and thus diminish their resources. The thief feels his actions are proper since he stands to inherit his parents' possessions. Such a person "is the companion of a destroyer," i.e., he allies himself with those who undermine the social order. He is a thief, and fails in the simplest duty (28:24).

Greed causes much harm. "One who has a greedy spirit [lit., is wide of soul or desire] stirs up strife." One who has a grasping disposition is liable to encroach upon a neighbor's rights and so become a cause of contention. The person of insatiable desire excites quarrels and mars all peace (cf. James 4:1). In the end such a one destroys himself. On the other hand, "one who puts his trust in Yahweh shall prosper" (lit., shall be made fat), i.e., shall have what he needs and more. The person in view here is the patient, God-fearing man, who is content to do his duty, and leave the result in the Lord's hands (28:25).

Overconfidence should be avoided. "One who trusts in his own heart is a fool." Such a person relies on his own understanding and is not guided by competent teachers and advisers. He also neglects the principles of godly wisdom and follows the course of least resistance. On the other hand, "one who walks in wisdom, he shall escape." This person looks outside himself for direction; he trusts in the wisdom which is from above; he walks in the fear of the Lord, and is spared from the dangers to which self-confidence exposes the fool (28:26).

Charity is to be encouraged. "One who gives to the poor shall not lack" because he is actually lending money to the Lord (cf. 19:17). Since God will be no man's debtor, the benefactor of the poor will receive divine blessing. On the other hand, "one who hides his eyes from the poor receives many curses" hurled at him by those upon whom he has no compassion. He either turns away his eyes that he may not see the misery around him or pretends not to notice it, lest his compassion should be claimed (28:27; cf. Deut 15:9).

E. Summary (28:28).

Verse 28 sums up the whole chapter. When wicked men rise to power, people hide themselves from fear of oppression. When those wicked rulers perish, the righteous "increase." Some take this to refer to increase in power and influence. Others see here a reference to the increase in numbers. The righteous come into the open and their presence is more noticeable.

MORE INSTRUCTION FOR THE WISE
Proverbs 29:1-27

Chapter 29 is similar to chapter 28 both in form and, to some extent, in content. Here again the antithetical form of the proverb is predominant.

A. Private Morality and Public Good (29:1-7).

"A man of reproofs," i.e., a man who had been frequently cautioned, "who hardens his neck, shall suddenly be broken." To "harden the neck" is an idiom derived from obstinate draught animals which will not submit to the yoke. Thus one who has hardened the neck has refused to bend the neck in submission to authority. Such a person will be broken. Though retribution be delayed, those who refuse correction will come to a fearful and sudden end. He is "without remedy," i.e., without hope of recovery. Despising all correction, he has no possibility of restoration (29:1).

When righteous people are able to assert themselves and take charge of society, "the people rejoice." When society is governed by the high standards of the righteous, there is general happiness, prosperity abounds, and voices ring cheerfully. On the other hand, when a wicked man takes over "the people groan." They have bitter cause for complaint because of oppression and injustice. The proverb paints the contrast between good and bad government (29:2).

"A man who loves wisdom makes his father rejoice." Ordinarily the word "son" is used in such verses. The substitution of "man" may signify an adult whose father is advanced in years and so dependent upon him. One who loves wisdom is one whose life is disciplined by moral principles, especially as they relate to sexuality. Such a man would bring joy to his father because he has the wherewithal to maintain his elderly parents in comfort. On the other hand, "he who keeps company with harlots wastes his substance." Thus both he and his father are reduced to poverty (29:3).

"A king by justice causes the land to stand." By governing with justice he stabilizes the land and brings prosperity to its citizens. On the other hand, "a man of extractions," i.e., one who is greedy for bribes, "tears it down," i.e., destroys the land (29:4).

"A person who flatters his neighbor spreads a net for his steps." In Hebrew the word "flatter" (machaliq) means literally "to make smooth," i.e., his words so as to deceive. Who falls into the net, the flatterer, or the one being flattered? Probably the "net" is the punishment upon the deceiver (cf. 26:27; 28:10). God punishes those who attempt to get ahead by using hypocritical deception (29:5).

"In the transgression of an evil person there is a snare." The snare is intended for the ruin of another, but the schemer is himself caught up in it. On the other hand, "the righteous sings and rejoices." He does not plot against others, and fall into the snare of divine retribution. Therefore he can go on his way rejoicing (29:6).

"A righteous person knows the cause [lit., judgment, just rights] of the poor," i.e. he understands their plight and is sympathetic to their needs. On the other hand, "the wicked person" does not understand knowledge," i.e., pays no attention to the rights of the weak. He can daily look on the plight of a Lazarus at his gate and hear no call to pity and charity (29:7).

B. Dishonorable Passions (29:8-9).

"Men of scorn blow [the flame of] a city," i.e., they take delight in exploiting the differences within the population in order to arouse disorder (cf. 22:10). "Men of derision" are those who despise and scoff at all things great and high, even the sacred. These are the persons who raise rebellion in a country and excite opposition to the authorities. On the other hand, "wise people turn aside wrath," i.e., they are peacemakers. They try to smooth out differences so that a peaceful atmosphere is created (29:8).

"If a wise person contends with a foolish person, whether he gets angry or laughs, there is no quietness." To try to argue with a fool is futile. He will either laugh off the arguments, or he will get angry. In either case the discussion leads nowhere. The issue will not be resolved (29:9).

C. Righteous Government (29:10-17).

Righteous government is concerned to hold in check violence in society. "Men of blood," i.e., violent men, "hate one who is sincere," i.e., one who recoils from a wrong act when it is to his advantage to do wrong. Strict principles earn the hatred of the unscrupulous. The righteous life is a tacit reproach to men of blood, robbers, murderers and the like. "And as for the upright, they seek [the well-being of] his life."[10] Whereas evil persons hate a sincere man and desire to harm him, the upright appreciate his qualities and wish to do him good (29:10).

Righteous government does not render decisions out of anger. "A fool sends forth all his spirit," i.e., his anger (cf. 16:32; 25:28). He gives full vent to his temper and fails to exercise any restraint. On the other hand, "a wise person in respect to afterwards stills it." Another difficult expression. Does he still his own anger, or that of the fool? If the former, a wise person takes thought of the consequences of his action and so restrains his anger. He does not wish to do anything which would lead to more serious trouble. If it is the anger of the fool which is stilled, then the proverb is saying that a wise man knows how to apply soothing remedies to the angry man, and in the end renders him calm and amenable to reason (29:11).

Fair judgment is a primary responsibility of government. In order to render fair judgment the ruler must be able to distinguish between true and false evidence or reports. "If a ruler listens to falsehood," i.e., false accusations, "all his servants are wicked." They will be tempted to take advantage of the ruler's weakness and bring lying charges against others. A ruler sets the moral tone for his servants. The proverb alludes to the fact that some rulers do not care to hear the truth. The result is that his servants flatter and lie to him. His court is charged with unreality and deceit (29:12).

Righteous government must recognize that all people are created equal, i.e. with equal standing before the bar of justice. "The poor person and the man of oppressions meet together; Yahweh gives light to the eyes of them both." The oppressor here is a rich man. The rich in Proverbs are characterized as a class which oppresses the poor. "Light to the eyes" is a metaphor for life itself. Both the oppressed and the oppressor owe their light and life to God. The former should therefore be respectful of the latter, and the latter should not be resentful of the former. Here is comfort for the poor, that he has a tender Father who watches over him; here is a warning for the rich, that he will have to give an account of his stewardship (29:13).

Righteous government must defend the rights of the poor. "A king who faithfully judges the poor, his throne shall be established forever." The monarch was the supreme judge in the land. To secure the rights of the helpless was the highest priority of government. "Forever" here indicates "indefinitely." Inflexible fidelity to duty is taught in this proverb—that perfect impartiality which dispenses justice alike to rich and poor, uninfluenced by personal or social considerations (29:14; cf. 16:12; 20:28; 25:5).

Righteous government must deal with juvenile transgression. Two methods are available for training a child in wisdom: "the rod [corporal punishment] and reproof," i.e., verbal admonition. On the other hand, "a lad let go," i.e., allowed to run wild and unchecked, "brings shame to his mother." The proverb suggests that the mother's love may have degenerated into overindulgence, that her weakness may have been responsible for the lack of discipline. A spoiled child brings shame even to a mother who is generally more sympathetic and patient than a father (29:15; cf. 10:1).

Righteous government must restrain the lawless. "When the wicked are increased," i.e., when they are able to take charge of society, "transgression increases," i.e., injustice and general lawlessness. Their evil example is copied, and a lowering of moral tone and a general laxity in conduct prevail. "But the righteous shall gaze [with satisfaction] upon their fall." In a moral universe the wicked ultimately lose their positions of power. Righteous people will rejoice in the downfall of wicked men (29:16).

Righteous government begins in the home. "Correct your son and he will give you rest, yes, he will give delights to your soul." A disciplined son will relieve parents of anxiety. The "delights" may be a reference to the physical comforts which parents enjoy in their later years when their son lives a steady life (29:17).

D. Hindrances to Social Harmony (29:18-23).

"Where there is no revelation a people is let loose," i.e., lacks restraint. Vision (*chazon*) was a medium of divine communication to prophets. The strong teaching of the prophets was the moral compass of ancient Israel. This is the only passage in the book which acknowledges the importance of prophecy in regulating the life and religion of the people. Without that teaching the people show no moral restraint (cf. Exod 32:25). Confusion, disorder and rebellion are the result when the high standards of divine revelation no longer restrain the excesses of the people. If immorality results where there is no divine revelation, "happy is he who keeps the law," i.e., the written revelation communicated through Moses (29:18).

"With words [alone] a servant will not be corrected, for though he understands, he will not respond." The reluctant slave thoroughly understands the order given, but he pays no heed to it. Brutality toward servants was forbidden under the law of Moses (Exod 21:20,26f.). Mere words, however, often will not correct a moral defect. More drastic forms of punishment will be necessary (29:19; cf. Luke 12:47).

"Do you see a man who is hasty in his words? There is more hope for a fool than for him." To be "hasty" in words is to talk rashly without consideration of what one says. That person ultimately makes a devastating mistake. A fool has more hope of escaping danger than he. The dull, stupid person (*kesil*) may be instructed and made to listen to reason; the hasty and ill-advised speaker consults no one, takes no thought before he speaks, nor reflects on the effect of his words. Such a person is almost impossible to reform. For this reason Scripture cautions believers to be "slow to speak" (29:20; cf. 26:12; James 1:19).

"One pampers his servant from his youth and at the end he will be a son."[11] The verb "pampers" (panak) refers the spoiling of a person by overindulgence and luxury. Such treatment is particularly unsuitable for a bond-servant, for it tends to make him forget his dependent position. A pampered slave who reaches adulthood will claim the privileges of a son, perhaps ousting the legitimate children from their inheritance (29:21).

"A man of anger stirs up strife, and a master of wrath abounds in transgression." A man of anger is one who is given to passionate outbursts of violence. Such a man both makes enemies by his conduct and falls into manifold excesses of word and deed while under the influence of his wrath. This is the case because in his rage his moral sense becomes clouded by the fumes of anger (29:22).

"The pride of a person shall bring him low, but a lowly spirit shall attain honor." Pride is devastating (cf. 11:2; 16:18). The humble person does not seek honor, but by his life and action unconsciously attains it (29:23; cf. 15:33; 18:12).

E. The Necessity of Prudence (29:24-27).

"The one who is a partner of a thief hates his own soul." Such a person is his own worst enemy since he contributes to his own undoing. That pitiful person is further described as "one who is put under oath and declares nothing." The accessory may not have actually committed the theft, but he has knowledge of it and is in a position to give evidence. He refuses to testify in the case lest he implicate himself. Thus does he bring upon himself the curse which is pronounced upon all those who withhold evidence (29:24).

"The fear of man brings a snare." Fear of repercussions often paralyzes a person's efforts when confronted by an emergency. The fear hinders his action and prevents him from putting forth his maximum effort. On the other hand, "one who trusts in Yahweh shall be exalted," i.e., set above the dangers that threaten him (29:25).

"Many are seeking the favor [lit., face] of a ruler, but from Yahweh is the judgment of a person." People would turn to the supreme judge in the land when they were involved in a suit in an attempt to secure a favorable verdict. By bribery, flattery or self-humiliation the plaintiff attempted to make the face of the king smile upon his case. The real and only reliable judgment comes, not from an earthly prince (who may be prejudiced and is certainly fallible), but from the Lord. His approval or disapproval is final and indisputable. One should seek to please him rather than any man, however great and powerful (29:26).

"An abomination to righteous people is a person of iniquity, and an abomination to a wicked person is one who is upright in the way." An "abomination" (*toebhah*) is an object of loathing. The term is used more than twenty times in Proverbs. Throughout the ages the war between godliness and wickedness has been raging. The upright refuse to compromise with the wicked and look upon evil with revulsion. On the other hand, wrongdoers regard the righteous person with contempt because he is a standing reproach to them. By every look and action the righteous person seems to express his condemnation on the lifestyle of the wicked. With a reminder that the Genesis 3:15 conflict must continue through the generations, the Book of Proverbs proper comes to an end (29:27).

ENDNOTES

1. R.N. Whybray, *The Composition of the Book of Proverbs* (Sheffield, England: JSOT, 1994), p. 120.

2. See G.E. Bryce, "Another Wisdom 'Book' in Proverbs," JBL 91 (1972), 145-157; and R.C. Van Leeuwen, *Context and Meaning in Proverbs 25–27* (Atlanta: Scholars Press, 1988).

3. Whybray, *Composition*, pp. 91f.

4. The literal reading of 26:2 is: "a curse without cause shall not come." Another reading—the so-called *qere* reading—is: "a curse without cause shall come to him," i.e., to the fool who uttered it.

5. Examples of Jesus carrying out the admonition of 26:4 are found in Matt 21:23; 22:21f; Luke 13:23; John 21:21.

6. Whybray, *Composition*, p. 125.

7. Others take 27:19 to mean that it is only in frank and sympathetic intercourse of friendship that a person really gets to know himself, and to realize what is in him.

8. Two words for interest are used in 28:8: *neshech* (lit., bite) was interest bitten off (deducted) before the loan was made. *Tarbith* is always found with *neshech*. It is a fixed rate of interest for a small loan of money or grain to be paid together with the principal after the harvest.

9. For inadvertent manslaughter one might flee for safety and sympathy to one of six cities of refuge (Num 35:11ff.).

10. The second half of 29:10 is difficult. The expression "seek the life" usually means "to plot one's death." This would make upright men plot the death of the sincere. NIV forces the Hebrew to say that that bloodthirsty men of the first half of the verse seek to kill the upright. NASB has followed Jewish commentators in assigning to the verb "seek" (*bikkesh*) the idea of "seek the well-being."

11. The Hebrew *magon* in 29:21 is of uncertain meaning. Recent translations render *magon* as "grief" (NIV); "son" (ASV; NASB; BV); and "heir" (RSV).

CHAPTER THIRTY-TWO

Final Words of the Wise
Proverbs 30-31

The headings over chapters 30 and 31 set these two chapters off from the rest of the book as a kind of appendix. Difference of style, language and content in these chapters confirms that the material has been appended to the Solomonic collections. Neither Agur nor King Lemuel can be identified with certainty.

THE REFLECTIONS OF AGUR
Proverbs 30:1-33

Agur was a poet or moralist, well known in Solomon's time. He was probably one of the wise men alluded to in 24:23. In two ways Agur claims that his words are a divinely revealed prophetic utterance. First, he refers to his writing as a "burden" (*ham-massa'*), a term used in the Old Testament for a prophetic declaration (e.g., Isa 13:1). Second, he employs the term "oracle" (*ne'um*) which is common in prophetic literature as the most solemn claim for divine inspiration.

Agur addressed his message to two men: Ithiel and Ucal. The name Ithiel appears elsewhere in Nehemiah 11:7, but Ucal only here. Neither man can be identified. They obviously were friends or disciples of Agur. The opening sentence of the burden itself in the Hebrew suggests that these two may have put some questions before Agur regarding divine providence. The compiler of Proverbs thought the instruction for these men was worthy of wider publication.

A. The Prologue (30:2-6).

Agur begins with a humble confession. He is incapable of understanding the mind of a human being, so how much less would he presume to comprehend the mind of God. All of his study of wisdom has made him feel that he lacked wisdom. If he could not profess to be an expert in wisdom, how much less could he pretend to be an expert on the knowledge of God? The more he learned about God, the less he really knew God. For Agur God was the "Holy One." The basic idea in the concept of holiness is "separateness." Morally God transcends man to such a degree that no mortal can fully understand him (30:2-3).

Agur raises a series of five questions which point to the impossibility of any person having perfect knowledge of God (cf. Job 38). First, "Who has ascended up into heaven and descended?" To fully understand God one would have to ascend into heaven. No person had done this. None had descended from heaven at this time save God himself (Gen 11:7; Exod 19:18).

Second, "Who has gathered the wind in his fists?" Obviously man cannot gather up the invisible wind so as to restrain it or to release it at his pleasure. That is an act of God (Amos 4:13; Ps 135:7). Third, "Who has bound the waters in his garment?" This question is clarified by Job 26:8, "He [God] binds up the waters in his thick clouds." God stores up waters to provide the rain without which existence on earth is impossible. Obviously man cannot do this. Fourth, "Who has established all the ends of the earth?" The reference is to the fixing of the boundaries of the earth as the habitation of the human race, across which the ocean does not trespass. Obviously man had nothing to do with this. The answer to the first four questions is the same: Almighty God!

Fifth, "What is his name, and what is his son's name, if you know?" If someone asserts that any person possesses these qualifications, then he should name that person. Obviously the question is sarcastic. If such a person existed at any time in the past, then what is the name of his son or descendant? (30:4).

Philosophy cannot lead to the creator. Ultimately, man must be satisfied with that which God has revealed to man in his word. "Every word of God is "tried," i.e., tested and proved to be true. This sentence uses two words which are found nowhere else in Proverbs: "word" ('imrah) and "God" ('eloah). The reference is to the declarations of God in the inspired record, the Torah. Those who take refuge in the God of the Bible find him to be a shield against assaults by the unbelieving. Thus the second half of the verse indicates a second way in which the knowledge of God is obtained, namely, through the experiences of those who trust in the Lord (30:5).

Beyond that word, man dare not tread with speculation about the heavenly mysteries which baffle human comprehension. "Do not add unto his words." No attempt should be made to supplement the divine revelation with one's own ideas (cf. Deut 4:2). God's will, as announced in revelation, is to be simply accepted and acted upon, not watered down, not overstrained. The one who is guilty of this faces "rebuke" in the form of some misfortune which would reveal the divine displeasure. Events would prove the pretender to be a "liar," i.e., the falsity of his unfounded opinion would be made obvious (30:6).

B. Agur's Prayer (30:7-9).

In this humble prayer, Agur models the reliance upon God which he has just advocated. In the first of his numerical sayings he asks but two things of God before he leaves this world. First, he asks that God will remove from him all that is false (lit., vanity), i.e., that which is hollow or worthless, and "lies." To live aright, one must be a lover of truth and integrity. He must not be contaminated by that which is false.

Second, he asks that the Lord will give him "neither poverty nor riches." Both extremes in life subject one to a whole series of special and powerful temptations. Agur wants only "the bread of my portion," his allotted share of bread. His needs are small, and he begs to be granted a sufficiency to avoid being lured into sin (30:7-8).

Agur now explains the rationale for his prayer. Should he become rich and have more than he really needs he might be tempted to say in his heart, "Who is Yahweh?" i.e., Who needs him? (Deut 8:11ff.; 32:15). On the other hand, should he come to poverty he might commit the sin of theft in order to survive. Being then accused of theft he might "lay hold of the name of my God." This has been taken to mean that he would (1) swear falsely in God's name to his innocence; or (2) blame his sin on God for having reduced him to a state of poverty. In the light of the proverbs which follow it is best to take this expression as referring to the blasphemy which often follows impatience and lack of resignation to God's will (30:9).

C. Agur's Aphorisms (30:10-14).

1. Regarding slander (30:10). Slandering any person is a reprehensible act. This sin is especially vile when the victim is a slave who will not be believed when he denies the accusation. The slander would make the master suspicious of his slave. The slave could only utter a curse upon his slanderer. Since the curse is uttered against one who is guilty, that curse would not fall harmlessly to the ground. Thus Agur is urging his student to maintain a kindly feeling for those in lowly condition.

2. Four wicked types (30:11-14). The Hebrew uses the term "generation" (*dor*) in the sense of "group" or "class." First, some people are so wicked that they curse their father and do not bless their mother. Not to bless the mother is a litotes and is equivalent to "to curse." This sin violates the commandment to honor and obey parents. Cursing parents was a capital crime under the law of Moses (30:11; Exod 21:17).

Second, some are "pure in their own eyes" because they observe certain conventional or ritual proprieties. The sin here is hypocrisy and Pharisaical self-righteousness. In their heart "they are not washed from their filthiness." They have not cleansed their heart by complete repentance, either because they have not examined themselves and know nothing of the real state of their conscience, or because they care nothing about it and will not regard it in its true light (30:12).

Third, some are proud, even haughty. Their "eyelids are lifted up" in contempt upon their fellows (30:13). Fourth, some have teeth like swords and knives which they use to devour the poor and needy (Amos 8:4). They use their power mercilessly to destroy the helpless (30:14).

D. Numerical Sayings (30:15-31).

A distinctive feature of Agur's teaching is his use of the numerical saying. Earlier in the book Solomon constructed a similar type of proverb (cf. 6:16-19). Four of the examples belong to a particular class known as the "graded numerical proverb."[1]

Scholars disagree as to the purpose of such proverbs. Perhaps the most attractive suggestion is that they are based on riddles in which the audience is required, simply as a game, to guess which phenomena fit a particular stated category. Signs of humor which can be seen in some of them may point to their entertainment value (e.g., the things which make the earth totter in vv. 21-23). This explanation would give them a common purpose and at the same time account for their random and miscellaneous character; but there is no evidence that this was the intention.

1. The insatiable (30:15-16). The horse leech, a common blood-sucking pest in Palestine, is used here as a symbol for that which has an insatiable appetite. There are two, three, even four things which, like the horse leech, never have enough: (1) Sheol, the abode of the dead, which can never be filled with its victims; (2) the barren womb (lit., the closing of the womb), i.e., the burning desire for children characteristic of an Israelite wife; (3) the earth, in that its soil must yearn for water for its fertility; and (4) fire, which greedily seizes upon any fuel available to keep burning.

2. The impious (30:17). This is an independent proverb only connected with the preceding by being founded on an allusion to an animal. Agur depicts a son arrogantly mocking the advice of his fathers. "The eye that mocks at his father" will be plucked out by "the ravens of the valley." The "eye" here is the mind's instrument for expressing scorn and insubordination; it is the index to the inner feeling. One who disobeys his mother is equally as guilty and will receive the same treatment. So the punishment here implies that the rebellious son will meet with a violent death and his body will be left unburied.

3. The incomprehensible (30:18-20). Agur states that there were four things which he could not comprehend because they were too "wonderful," i.e., mysterious, for him. First, "the way of an eagle [vulture] in the air," i.e., how can such a heavy bird keep flying and not fall to the ground. Others suggest that the mystery is that the bird leaves no outward sign in the sky where he has passed.

Second, "the way of a serpent upon a rock," i.e., how can this creature move along without feet? Others think the mystery is the tracklessness of the snake's course. Third, "the way of a ship in the midst of the sea," i.e., how does it remain afloat? Or how can one track the ship through the ocean. Fourth, "the way of a man with a young woman," i.e., a sexual affair. The sin of unchastity demands secrecy and affords no token of its commission. This interpretation is exemplified and confirmed in the following verse (30:18-19).

"So is the way of an adulterous woman." What Agur had said of a man in the preceding verse, he now applies to the adulteress. Once committed, her sinful act cannot be traced. The adulteress is so degraded as not to feel anything sinful in her act of infidelity. To her, adultery is nothing more than a physical satisfaction, like eating food. The phrase "she eats" is a euphemism for the sin which she commits (cf. 9:17; 5:15). She "wipes her mouth" as if to leave no trace of her illicit repast; i.e., she cleans herself after the encounter. She says to herself: "I have done no wickedness." She forgets him who sees in secret. She is content only to escape detection by men's eyes, and to assume the character of a virtuous wife (30:20).

4. The intolerable (30:21-23). Agur humorously depicts the earth tottering under the burden of four kinds of persons. The four evils he names destroy the comfort of social life, uproot the bonds of society, and endanger the safety of a nation. He selects two illustrations from each sex. First, the earth totters under "a servant when he becomes king" (cf. 19:10).

Second, the earth totters under "a fool when he is filled with food." The "fool" (*nabal*) is a low, profligate fellow, who is rich and without care. When such a one rises to high position, or has power over others, he becomes arrogant, selfish, unbearable. Such a person also may come to deny the role of the Lord in his life (cf. vv. 8-9; 28:12; 29:2).

Third, the earth totters under "an unloved woman who is married." The reference could be to a woman who had a long wait to secure a husband. If such a one eventually does win a husband, she uses her new position to vex those who formerly depreciated her, and to make them as miserable as she can. Fourth, the earth totters under "a handmaid who is heir to her mistress." The reference may be to a servant who displaces her mistress in the husband's affections and takes her place as his wife. Such a one tends to become conceited, arrogant, and odious to all around her.

5. *The insignificant (30:24-28).* Agur directs attention to the animal kingdom from which his students can learn useful lessons. There are four things which are little upon the earth, but which are exceedingly wise. Bigness is not necessarily the same as greatness. First, "the ants" are named. They are a "people," because they live in a community, and have authorities which they obey. Their actions are regulated by certain definite laws. Ants are "not strong." Yet they are wise enough to lay in store during the summer months the food which they will need during the winter. The ant already has been proposed as an example to the sluggard (cf. 6:6). Here foresight is commended.

Second, the feeble rock-badgers (lit., hiders) show wisdom by making their houses in the crags of the rocks. These inaccessible places provide protection from predators. Here the safety of a sound shelter is commended. Third, the locusts, which have no king, "go forth all of them by bands." They appear to divide themselves into companies like an army (cf. Joel 2:7). Unity and discipline in their ranks make these insignificant creatures a formidable pest. Here the triumph of organization is commended. Fourth, the "lizard" or "spider"—the Hebrew word has both meanings—is so small that it can be crushed in the hand. Yet that small creature can gain admission to the grandest type of building. Here the success of persistency is commended.

6. *The imposing (30:29-31).* Agur now mentions four creatures which are imposing in appearance. First, he mentions the lion "which is mightiest among the beasts." Because of his might the lion does not turn away in fear from any other animal as it goes its way.

Second, the *zarzir motnayim*—lit., "girt of loins"—has been identified as a strutting "rooster" (NIV) or "cock" (NASB), greyhound, warhorse, and zebra. It is impossible to decide with certainty. Third, the

677

he-goat is named. Agur has in mind the stately march of the he-goat before the herd. The animal has an arrogant bearing; he scrutinizes strangers with a dauntless stare. Fourth, Agur names "a king with his army around him" as an illustration of stateliness.

E. Final Advice (30:32-33).

Agur advises his students to exercise restraint. A student should put his hand to his mouth, i.e., check himself, if he contemplates acting in a foolish manner. Churning milk makes butter, and wringing a nose causes a flow of blood. So strife is often deliberately created. A quarrel need not happen and can be averted. "Wrath" is "wrung out" of a person just as blood is "wrung out" of the nose.

A MOTHER'S ADVICE TO HER ROYAL SON
Proverbs 31:1-9

Nothing is known of a king by the name of Lemuel. He most likely is an unidentified foreign king.

What is written here is called a "burden." See comments on 30:1. This heading applies specifically to verses 1-9. His "mother" is said to have taught Lemuel with the words which follow. The genre of royal instruction was current in the Near East over a very long period of time.[2] This mother's advice, however, is the only example of royal instruction of which the author is a woman.[3] The mother of a reigning king was always regarded with the utmost respect, taking precedence over the king's wife. Many wise women are mentioned in Scripture, so there is nothing incongruous with Lemuel's mother giving him instruction (31:1).

A. Pursue Chastity (31:2-3).

The mother opens her remarks to her son by three times asking "What?" This is probably abbreviated for "What am I to say unto you?" The repetition enforces attention of the son. It expresses the mother's anxious care for his well-being. She describes Lemuel as "my son," "son of my womb," and "son of my vows."[4] Like Hannah (1 Sam 1:11), this mother had made vows to God prior to the birth (31:2).

She advises the king not to give his "strength" unto women. "Strength" (chayil) is "vigor," the bodily powers which are sapped by sensuality. She feared he would exhaust his physical energies in the harem and thus be unable to discharge the duties of his office. Perhaps she was thinking that a multitude of women occasion sensuality, provoke quarrels, and use their wiles to influence government policy. Often such women have been known to ruin kings and states. He should avoid conducting the affairs of state in a way which leads to revolts among the populace (31:3).

B. Avoid Debauchery (31:4-7).

This wise mother urged her son to realize that it was not fitting for a king to be intoxicated. Wine dulls the judgment in the exercise of royal functions. The evils of drunkenness are bad enough in a private citizen; they are greatly magnified in the case of a king whose misdeeds may affect an entire nation. Strong drink causes leaders to act in undignified ways, and causes them to lose the respect of their subjects. The spelling of the name of the king here is *Lemoel* which points more specifically to the derivation of this word. Perhaps the mother was suggesting that the use of the wine was particularly inappropriate to one who bore the name "[dedicated] to God" (31:4).

Intemperance leads to selfish disregard of others' claims, an inability to examine questions impartially, and consequent perversion of justice. Under the influence of alcohol, princes might "forget that which is decreed," i.e., render judgments which were not in harmony with the decrees of previous kings, and even of God himself. Thus would justice be perverted for "all the sons of affliction," i.e., those who looked to the king to uphold their rights (31:5).

The king should practice abstinence in respect to wine. He should be prepared, however, to give strong drink to one who might need it, e.g., one who was ready to perish. Strong drink might provide a jolt which would have a restorative effect on one who was languishing near death. Wine might also aid one who was "bitter in soul," i.e., suffering mental anguish (cf. Ps 104:15). The wine would help that man to forget the misery of his poverty (31:6-7).

C. Rule Justly (31:8-9).

The king should be active in matters of justice. He should speak for the "dumb," i.e., the person who for any reason is unable to plead

679

his own cause. Such people are described as "those appointed to destruction," lit., the sons of passing away. The reference is to any who might be in imminent danger of perishing if left unaided. By so doing he will be fulfilling his responsibility to minister justice to the poor and needy.

THE IDEAL WIFE
Proverbs 31:10-31

Proverbs has devoted much space to the unfaithful wife. The book concludes with a lengthy and glowing description of the good wife. These verses originally formed an independent unit.[5] The unit is a complete alphabetic acrostic, with the initial letters of its twenty-two verses forming the Hebrew alphabet. Some critics regard the acrostic as a late development in Old Testament literature. In the literature of the region, however, acrostics can be documented to at least 1000 BC.[6]

On the surface this poem seems to have been intended as a handbook for young people of marriageable age. For the young men it would have served as a checklist of qualities to look for in a prospective bride. For the young ladies it would serve as a kind of handbook to give them the ideal for which they should strive if they were to obtain a husband. Modern scholars see something more. They see in the ideal wife personified wisdom. Thus the poem makes a fitting climax to the entire book.

Aleph: "A wife of noble character who can find?" The expression combines the ideas of moral goodness and bodily vigor and activity. The representation in this chapter is that of the ideal woman—the perfect housewife, the chaste helpmate of her husband, upright, God-fearing, economical, and wise. Whoever has married such a woman knows from his experience how priceless is her worth. She is far more valuable than rubies or corals (31:10).

Bet: Her husband has full confidence in her management of the domestic economy. He knows that she will act discreetly, and promote his interests while he is absent. His confidence in her is profitably rewarded. Because of her labors the husband has no lack of "gain" (lit., spoils). Here the term must refer to the wealth which accrues to the man from his wife's enterprise (31:11).

Gimel: The wife is consistent in her conduct toward her husband, always pursuing his best interests. The noble wife does her husband good "all the days of her life," i.e., in good times or bad, in the springtime of youthful romance, and in the waning years of declining age. Her love, based on high principles, knows no change or diminution. She fully justifies the confidence he placed in her when he chose her to be his bride (31:12).

Dalet: "She seeks wool and flax," i.e., she sees that there is an ample supply of material from which to make the necessary clothing for the family. "She makes according to the pleasure of her hands," i.e., she works the material into the best garments. In this labor she takes great pleasure because she considers this labor as her responsibility, and she regards idleness as a serious moral defect (31:13).

Hey: Like merchant-ships, the noble wife travels far and wide without regard to distance to procure the food for the household in the best markets and for the best prices (31:14).

Vav: She arises before sunrise to prepare the food for the day. Even the maidservants of the household are the objects of her industrious care (31:15).

Zayin: The noble wife identifies a certain field, the possession of which is for some reason desirable. After due examination and consideration, she buys it. "With the fruit of her hands," i.e., money accumulated from her skillful management, she is able to pay for the planting of a vineyard. An ideal estate had its own vineyard (31:16).

Chet: This ideal wife undertakes all her tasks with vigor. "She girds her loins with strength," i.e., she tackles difficult tasks which required her to fix her skirt firmly round her waist so that she would not be impeded in her work. "She makes strong her arms" through daily exercise. Thus she is capable of great and sustained exertion (31:17).

Tet: From experience this wife knows that her "merchandise" is "good," i.e., profitable. Her prudence and economy leave her a large surplus profit, which she contemplates with satisfaction. "Her lamp does not go out by night." She is not idle even when night falls and outdoor occupations are terminated (31:18).

Yod: When her other work is finished, she spends her leisure in spinning and making garments for her own family (31:19). The "spindle" is the cylindrical wood (later the wheel) on which the thread winds itself as it is is spun. The "distaff" is that to which the bunch of flax is tied. From this flax the spinning wheel draws the thread (31:19).

Kaph: This ideal wife is not impelled by selfish greed to improve her means and enlarge her revenues. She is sympathetic for the poor. "She stretches out her palm (*kaph*) to the poor." Hers is an open-handed policy of liberality. "She reaches out her hand (*yad*) to the needy." She is not satisfied with merely dispensing charity. She is personally involved in aiding the poor (31:20).

Lamed: This wife was not afraid of the coming "snow." Her family ordinarily is dressed in "scarlet," i.e., warm and stately garments. They will be prepared for the cold weather (31:21).

Mem: "She makes coverings for her bed." The reference is to pillows or cushions. Her business acumen enables the wife herself to dress in "fine linen and purple," i.e., costly garments (31:22).

Nun: Her husband is known "in the gates" for the excellence of his clothing. Her industry enabled her husband to participate in civil affairs as one of the elders of the land (31:23).

Samech: The noble wife makes and sells commercially "linen garments" and "girdles," i.e., sashes or belts which were worn around the waist (31:24).

Ayin: The ideal wife is clothed with "strength and dignity." She is invested with a moral force and dignity which arm her against care and worry. The power of a righteous purpose and strong will reveals itself in her carriage and demeanor. This enables her to "laugh at the time to come," i.e., the future causes her no anxiety because she knows the one in whom she trusts (31:25).

Pey: This woman is not merely a good housewife, attending diligently to material interests; she guides her family with words of wisdom. When she opens her mouth it is not gossip, or slander, or idle talk that she utters. Her words are distinguished by good sense and discretion. "The law of kindness is on her tongue," i.e., she lovingly instructs those around her. She gives her directions to children and servants in sympathetic language and not in a domineering tone of voice (31:26).

Tsade: The noble wife exercises careful surveillance over all that goes on in the family. She "looks well to the ways of her household." In addition to giving orders, she sees that they are duly carried out and supervises every detail of the home. She "does not eat the bread of idleness" but bread earned by diligence and hard labor. She is full of energy and always well occupied (31:27).

Qoph: The children of the noble wife "rise up and call her blessed," lit., make her happy, with the evidence of their appreciation and love. Her husband also rises up and "praises her." Those who know her best appreciate her most (31:28).

Resh: The husband publicly says concerning his spouse: "Many daughters have done valiantly, but you excel them all." Such may (and should) be said of any Christian matron who loves husband and children, guides the house, is discreet, chaste, enterprising, and good (31:29).

Shin: The poet now reflects upon the picture he has painted of the noble wife. He does not decry feminine beauty, but it is not the essential or most important qualification in a wife; character is the true criterion. "Grace is deceitful." A graceful exterior is no index of a woman's nature. "Beauty is vain," (lit., a breath). It does not endure. What is most important is that a wife be one who "fears Yahweh." A god-fearing woman shall find praise. Thus the Book of Proverbs returns to the maxim with which it began (cf. 1:7), namely, that the foundation of all excellence is the fear of Yahweh (31:30).

Verse 30 contains the only reference to God or religious matters in the poem. The verse, however, draws attention to itself by its length. The poet may have used that device to signal the climax in the catalog of virtues.

Tav: The poet urges his students to give the virtuous woman full credit for all that she is and does. Though her activities are mainly centered on the home, yet she should be praised "in the gates," i.e., in public places, because of the vital contribution she makes to the whole community. She needs no far-fetched adulation; her lifelong actions speak for themselves. The unanimous verdict of all in official places is to assign to this mother and wife the highest honor (31:31).

The description of the virtuous woman serves (1) as a challenge to young women; (2) a hallowing of domestic life; and (3) a guide to young men of what they should seek in a wife.

ENDNOTES

1. On the graded numerical proverb, see W.M.W. Roth, "The Numerical Sequence x/x + 1 in the Old Testament," *Vetus Testamentum* 12 (1962): 300-311; *Numerical Sayings in the Old Testament*, VTSup, 13 (Leiden: Brill, 1965); M. Haran, "The Graded Numerical Sequence and the Phenomenon of 'Automatism' in Biblical Poetry," in G.W. Anderson et al. (eds.), *Congress Volume: Uppsala 1971*, VTSup, 22 (Leiden: Brill, 1972): 238-267.

2. R.N. Whybray, *The Composition of the Book of Proverbs* (Sheffield, England: Sheffield Academic Press, 1994), p. 152.

3. Examples of the royal instruction genre are the Egyptian Instruction for King Merikare (ca. 2100 BC) and the Akkadian Advice to a Prince (ca. 800 BC). English translation of the former can be found in ANET, pp. 414-418; and the latter in W.G. Lambert, *Babylonian Wisdom Literature* (Oxford: Clarendon, 1960), pp. 110-115.

4. The term "son" in 31:2 is *bar*, one of the Aramaic forms found in these last two chapters.

5. The Septuagint recognized vv. 1-9 and 10-31 as independent entities, separating them by five whole chapters.

6. The so-called Babylonian Theodicy (ca. 1000 BC) is a well-known example of the use of the acrostic format in the ancient Near East. English translation in Lambert, *Babylonian*, pp. 71-89.

A BASIC TOPICAL INDEX TO
THE BOOK OF PROVERBS

An excellent topical index to Proverbs can be found in Donald Hunt, *Pondering the Proverbs*, Bible Study Textbook (Joplin: College Press, 1974), pp. 437-504.

DEATH:
1. Sheol: 1:12; 5:5; 7:27; 9:18; 15:11,24; 23:14; 27:20; 30:16.
2. Abaddon: 15:11; 27:20.
3. Pit: 1:12; 28:17.
4. Rephaim: 2:18; 9:18; 21:16.
5. General: 5:23; 8:36; 9:18; 11:7; 14:32; 23:13f.

FAMILY:
1. Husband/wife: 1:8f.; 2:17; 5:19; 6:20; 12:4; 14:1; 18:22; 19:14; 31:11,23.
2. Parents/children: 1:9f.; 2:1ff.; 3:1,23; 4:3ff.,8f.,12; 5:11f.; 10:1,5; 13:1,24; 15:20,32f.; 17:6; 19:26; 20:20; 22:6,15; 23:14; 28:24; 29:3,15; 30:11,17; 31:1-9.
3. Brothers: 6:19; 17:17; 18:19,24; 19:7; 27:10.

FOOLS:
1. The simple (gullible): 1:32; 12:11; 14:15; 15:21; 19:25; ch. 7.
2. Fool: 1:29,32; 10:1,23; 13:16,20; 15:2,7,20; 17:7,10,12,21, 24f.,28; 18:6; 19:13; 20:3; 24:7; 26:6; 27:3; 29:9,11; 30:22.
3. Scoffer: 3:34; 9:7f.; 13:1; 14:6; 15:12; 19:25,29; 21:11,24; 22:10; 24:9; 29:8.

FRIENDS:
1. Constancy: 14:20; 17:17; 18:24; 19:4,6f.; 27:10.
2. Candor: 27:6; 29:5.
3. Counsel: 27:9,17.
4. Tact: 25:17,20; 26:18f.; 27:14.
5. Vulnerability: 2:17; 16:28; 17:9.

GOD:
1. Fear of God: 2:5; 3:7; 9:10.
2. God weighs the heart: 24:11f.
3. No evasion of sin: 15:8; 21:3,27; 28:9.
4. Getting rid of sin: 16:6; 28:13.
5. Faith and trust: 3:5,7; 22:19; 29:25.
6. God's sovereign will: 19:21; 21:31.
7. Divine discipline: 3:12.
8. Revelation: 28:4; 29:18.

LIFE: 3:22; 4:10; 6:23; 8:35; 10:16; 11:7; 13:12; 14:30,32; 15:4, 24,27; 16:15; 19:23; 21:21.

NEIGHBORS: 3:27-29; 6:1-5; 11:12; 12:26; 14:20f.; 17:17; 18:17,24; 21:10; 22:24f.; 24:17,19; 25:8f.; 27:6.

SEXUAL SINS: 2:18f.; 5:9-23; 6:26-35; 23:27f.; 29:3.

SLUGGARD: 6:6-10; 10:26; 12:27; 13:4; 15:19; 18:9; 19:24; 21:25f.; 22:13; 24:30f.; 26:13-16.

WISDOM, Attainment of:
1. Available: 9:4,16.
2. Costly: 2:7-9.
3. Revelation: 2:6; 30:6.
4. Discipline: 2:1-6; 3:11ff.
5. Conversion: 8:13; 9:4-6; 14:12.
6. Devotion: 8:34; 9:9; 10:8; 26:12.
7. Advice and criticism: 13:10; 17:10.

WISDOM, Dimensions of:
1. Instruction: 1:2f.; 3:11; 9:1; 23:13; 24:32.
2. Reproof or correction: 1:23; 3:11.
3. Understanding or insight: 1:2; 2:2; 6:32; 10:13.
4. Wise dealing: 1:3; 2:7; 8:14; 10:5; 12:8.
5. Shrewdness: 1:4f.; 12:2; 22:3.
6. Knowledge and learning: 1:5; 2:5; 3:6.

WORDS:
1. Power: 10:21; 11:9; 12:18,25; 16:24; 18:14,18,21; 29:5.
2. Spread: 6:12-14; 10:10f.; 12:14; 15:4; 16:27-30.
3. Weakness: 14:23; 26:23-28; 28:4,12; 29:19.
4. Honesty: 16:13; 25:12; 27:5f.; 28:23.
5. Sparse: 10:14,19; 11:12f.; 13:3; 17:28.
6. Calm: 15:1; 17:27; 18:13; 25:15.
7. Apt: 2:6; 10:20,32; 15:2,23,28; 16:1; 22:11; 25:11f.
8. Character: 4:23; 10:20; 12:17; 14:5.

ECCLESIASTES

CHAPTER THIRTY-THREE

Getting Acquainted with Ecclesiastes
Faith the Key to Meaning

Biblical faith does not try to stifle tough questions. Experience demonstrates that doubt drives an intellectually honest person to investigation, and investigation leads to greater faith. Christianity is a thinking person's religion. Ecclesiastes may serve as a stepping stone to those who find biblical faith to be intellectually unacceptable.

Ecclesiastes contains twelve chapters, 222 verses and 5,584 words. In the case of this particular book there is evidence that the original was organized into verses.[1] Though the book is relatively small, it bristles with difficulties for the interpreter.

TITLE OF THE BOOK

The term *Ecclesiastes* is derived from the title of the book in the Septuagint. The term refers to one who addresses the assembly of citizens. It is closely related to the Hebrew title *Koheleth* (*Qoheleth*). This term is a feminine singular participle from a root meaning "to assemble, gather." The name appears seven times in the book. Modern English versions generally translate the word "Preacher."

The author obviously wishes to portray himself as a teacher addressing a body of disciples. While "Preacher" is not an inappropriate translation of either the Hebrew or the Greek, the word might be a little misleading. Koheleth was not a preacher in the modern sense. He took his texts, not from the law and prophets, but from personal observation.

THE AUTHORSHIP OF THE BOOK

The writer of Ecclesiastes writes under the pseudonym *Koheleth*. No unanimity exists among scholars as to the identity of Koheleth.

A. Solomonic View.

From the earliest times this book has been attributed to Solomon, although his name does not appear anywhere in it. The traditional view of the synagogue is that Koheleth was a nickname for Solomon. Until the time of Luther, Solomonic authorship was also generally assumed in Christian circles.

Several facts point toward Solomon as the author. First, the root of the name Koheleth is used in 1 Kgs 8 when Solomon gathers the people for the dedication of the temple. Second, Koheleth identifies himself as a king and a son of David (1:1-2). That this phrase points to the direct successor of David, not some distant descendant, is a fair assumption. Third, Koheleth's claim of great wisdom (1:16) and great works (2:4-11) certainly fits the career of Solomon.

The Jewish tradition expressed in the Talmud (*Baba Bathra* 15a) that "Hezekiah and his company wrote Ecclesiastes" probably means no more than that this group of scribes edited and published the book. Certainly Jewish tradition elsewhere is quite explicit in naming Solomon as the author of Ecclesiastes (*Megilla* 7a; *Shabbath* 30a)

The majority of conservative scholars have joined liberals in regarding this book as postexilic and therefore non-Solomonic.[2] In some conservative works Solomonic authorship is not even discussed as a serious option. The traditional view of Solomonic authorship, however, is not without its defenders.[3]

B. Alternative Views.

Scholars who deny Solomonic authorship insist that the author of this book did not pretend to be Solomon so as to deceive his audience. His literary intent, they say, is plain. He does not mention Solomon nor carry the disguise beyond the first two chapters. His strategies were to capture his readers' attention and to use the circumstances of Solomon to prove ironically the weaknesses in his fellow sages' teachings; he then sets aside Solomon's garb and presses his arguments home. In effect, he is using Solomon to judge the opinions of those who claimed to be disciples of Solomon's wisdom.[4]

Critics, of course, have no idea who actually penned the words of this book. They generally portray the writer as a radically unorthodox Jew whose shocking statements were later mitigated by the insertion of more orthodox material by some editor(s). An appreciation for the structure of the book renders such an hypothesis totally unnecessary. Increasingly the literary unity of Ecclesiastes is being recognized by scholars.[5]

Another view is that the author intended for Koheleth to represent Solomon, but that Koheleth is not the author of the book.[6] A second voice is identified in chapter 12, one who speaks in the third person to evaluate the words of Koheleth for his son. This anonymous wise man is the author of the book. There is, however, no good reason for assuming that the author could not at times refer to himself in the third person just like the prophets sometimes did. The words "says the Preacher" and the third person reference in 12:9-10 are just as much Koheleth as the first person passages.

OBJECTIONS TO SOLOMONIC AUTHORSHIP

Critics have raised five major objections to the traditional view of Solomonic authorship.

1. The author seems to speak, at least occasionally, from the standpoint of a third party observer, even critic of kings rather than as the king himself (8:1-9; 10:17,20). Answer: Solomon donned his philosopher's hat when he wrote this book. Surely he was aware of many kings of his day who were tyrannical, gluttonous, and autocratic. Surely he was not unaware of the corruption which permeated the bureaucratic machinery which monarchs set up. Perhaps in some instances

the aging Solomon was preaching to himself (4:13). Solomon would not be the last writer to step out of his role as ruler to discourse on philosophical issues related to governing. Archer calls attention to the *Meditations* of the emperor Marcus Aurelius as an example of a ruler who could write as a philosopher.[7]

2. Ecclesiastes supposedly betrays the influence of Greek Stoic and Epicurean philosophy; therefore it could not have been written by Solomon. Answer: Actually Koheleth's viewpoint is fundamentally at odds with that of the Stoics.[8] The so-called Epicurean admonition to enjoy eating and drinking was common in the ancient east centuries before Solomon.[9] In general scholars are retreating from the insistence upon the Greek influences on the book.[10]

3. Ecclesiastes supposedly contains various telltale anachronisms which point to post-Solomonic authorship. For example 1:16 is taken to mean that Koheleth was comparing himself with all the *kings* who were before him in Jerusalem. That indeed would be a strange statement for Solomon to make since only one Israelite king preceded him on the Jerusalem throne. Jerusalem, however, had been a royal city for centuries before it fell into Israelite hands. Many kings must have ruled there, including the mysterious Melchizedek. Then again, perhaps Koheleth was comparing himself with Jerusalem's earlier sages, some of whom may be named in 1 Kgs 4:31.

Another often cited anachronism is alleged to be in 1:12. "I *was* king in Jerusalem." This surely means that the writer was no longer king, and hence could not be Solomon. This is supposed to be a clever clue left by Koheleth to tell his readers that he really was not Solomon. Answer: The verb in 1:12 more properly should be rendered "I became king." That a king in his old age should look back on the commencement of his reign using the Hebrew perfect tense would be appropriate.

Still another alleged anachronism is the phrase "king in Jerusalem" which does not occur elsewhere as a designation for Solomon. Usually he is called "king of Israel." The importance of this fact, however, has been greatly exaggerated. Solomon is said to have "reigned in Jerusalem over all Israel" (1 Kgs 11:42). In any case, statements in the historical books characterizing the reign of Solomon are comparatively few in number and are certainly not exhaustive.

4. The major argument against the Solomonic authorship is the language and style of the book. Scholars have pronounced the Hebrew used in this book as "late." It contains Aramaic words which most critics regard as proof positive that the book comes from no earlier than the postexilic period. Gleason Archer, however, has effectively neutralized this argument. The language of Ecclesiastes was influenced by the type of writing which it is, namely, a philosophical discourse. There is nothing in the language of the book which, on linguistic grounds, can be used to disqualify Solomonic authorship.[11]

The fact is that the text of Ecclesiastes fits into no known period in the history of the Hebrew language. (1) It is quite dissimilar to the Hebrew of the acknowledged postexilic books (Malachi, Nehemiah, Esther). If Ecclesiastes came from this period, as some conservative scholars argue, how can its language be so dissimilar? (2) The language of Ecclesiastes does not match up with Daniel or Zechariah 9-14 which the radical critics assign to the intertestamental period (mid 2nd cent BC). (3) The Hebrew of Ecclesiastes cannot be matched up with the sectarian documents of the Qumran community (4) nor the still later rabbinic writings.[12] The language of this book is dictated not as much by its genre as by its age. No other book of this type has survived, hence there is no reasonable way to reconstruct a history of this genre. At present there is no sure foundation upon which to date this book on linguistic grounds.

Some scholars have detected a Phoenician or even an Aramaic influence upon this book.[13] Neither influence would necessarily preclude Solomonic authorship. The Phoenician and Aramaic commercial ties of Solomon are well documented in the historical books of the Old Testament.

5. The times reflected in Ecclesiastes are characterized by misery and oppression (e.g., 4:3; 7:10). That does not seem to fit the description of the Solomonic age as it appears in the historical books (1 Kgs 4:25). Answer: In such passages Solomon is describing the problems which life can present to an individual even when there may be prosperity all about. The lives of individuals and even nations alternate between good times and bad. Solomon addresses in this book the human situation divorced from any particular geographical or chronological setting.

BACKGROUND OF THE BOOK

The Jewish tradition is that Solomon wrote the Song of Songs in his youth, Proverbs in his maturity, and Ecclesiastes toward the end of his reign of forty years. In spite of the great prosperity which characterized his reign, the people were gradually drifting away from the Lord. Solomon could see evil days ahead for his people because of their apostasy which he himself had to some degree encouraged. Ecclesiastes is at the same time the evidence of the personal repentance of Solomon, and an exhortation to his subjects to reassess the meaning of their lives.

The historical books give only an outline of Solomon's career. In his early reign he had a close walk with the Lord. He received a special gift of wisdom from above. He was responsible for constructing the first temple of the Lord in Jerusalem. At some point in his reign, however, his numerous wives led him into apostasy. So far as the historical record is concerned, Solomon never returned to a strong relationship with the Lord.

CANONICITY OF THE BOOK

Ecclesiastes was one of the five Antilegomena—the books spoken against—in rabbinic circles. Differing attitudes toward Ecclesiastes emerged during the intertestamental period. As noted above, Ben Sirach, who wrote his work Ecclesiasticus perhaps as early as 280 BC, indicates by his usage that he regarded Koheleth as canonical.[14] A century or so later, however, another Jewish philosopher writing under the name of "Solomon" seems to take exception to some of the teaching of Ecclesiastes.[15]

The Mishnah records a dispute between two major Pharisaic teachers over Ecclesiastes. The disciples of Shammai did not accept the canonicity of Ecclesiastes, while the more influential school of Hillel defended it (M. *Eduyoth* 5:3; *Yadaim* 3:5). In the rabbinic literature two reasons are given for opposition to the canonicity of the book: (1) the book was "written in Solomon's own wisdom" (T. *Meg.* 7a); and (2) "its words are self contradictory" (T. *Sabbath* 30b). Prob-

ably behind these allegations were the (alleged) pessimism, Epicureanism, skepticism and annihilationism of the book.

In the rabbinic literature two defenses of the canonicity of Ecclesiastes are offered. First, in the Talmud (*Meg.* 7a) a rabbi cites Proverbs
30:6 "Do not add to his words." This shows, said the rabbi, that
whatever Solomon wrote down was inspired. Why? Because one
should never add to an inspired book. Thus what Solomon wrote
down should be distinguished from the three thousand proverbs which
he did not write down. Therefore, the contention that Ecclesiastes
was "written in his own wisdom" is not sufficient to remove this book
from the sacred collection. The argument then is: whatever Solomon
wrote was inspired and therefore canonical.

Another rabbi made an argument based on the content of the
book. "The sages wished to hide[16] the book of Ecclesiastes. . . . Yet
why did they not hide it? Because its beginning is religious teaching
and its end is religious teaching." (T. *Sabbath* 30b).

Ecclesiastes was clearly one of the four "books of hymns to God
and precepts for the conduct of human life" which were part of the
Scriptures employed by Josephus (*Against Apion* 1.8). Josephus'
Bible was no doubt the same Bible employed by Jesus and the
apostles.

No direct quotes from Ecclesiastes appear in the New Testament
although there may be allusions to it in Romans 8:20 and James
4:14. Several of the Church Fathers quote the book as Scripture.
Nonetheless, Theodore of Mopsuestia (ca. AD 400) did question
Koheleth's right to be included among the holy books.[17]

PLACEMENT OF THE BOOK

In the Hebrew Bible Koheleth is usually grouped with Ruth, Song,
Lamentations, and Esther as part of the grouping known as the
Megilloth ("rolls") within the third great division of the Hebrew Bible,
the *Kethubhim* ("Writings"). Its position in respect to the other four
members of the *Megilloth* is not uniform.

In the Septuagint and Latin Vulgate the three books attributed to
Solomon follow upon Psalms which was attributed to Solomon's
father David. The English Bible has followed this arrangement.

UNITY OF THE BOOK

Scholars frequently have suggested that the original book of Koheleth was so repulsive, so blasphemous, that orthodox editors inserted material here and there to mitigate his radical statements.[18] In fact, several hands may have been at work in producing the book. This approach now, however, is gradually being abandoned. Wisdom literature from Babylonia and Egypt indicates a similar tendency to combine conventional and unconventional wisdom, and to embed traditional proverbs in original material. The so-called contradictions within the book indicate that Koheleth was wrestling with the complexities of life. The number of "contradictions" is greatly exaggerated. Some apparent contradictions can readily be resolved when one recognizes that the author often quoted material in order to refute it (cf. 4:5,6).

The strongest argument against multiple authorship is that of motive. If the original book caused so many theological problems, why was it not simply rejected? Why would editors try to salvage a work which they deemed to be at variance with the fundamentals of their faith?[19]

TEXT OF THE BOOK

Some scholars have proposed that the book of Ecclesiastes was originally written in Aramaic.[20] This theory, however, has not gained wide support. Among the manuscript fragments from Qumran Cave IV were three from Ecclesiastes. Parts of seventeen verses appear here. The fragments have been dated to the middle of the second century BC. Based on this meager evidence, scholars concluded (1) that Ecclesiastes had canonical status in Qumran; and (2) that these manuscripts indicate that they had been copied from earlier Hebrew manuscripts rather than having been translated from an Aramaic original.[21]

STRUCTURE OF THE BOOK

A. General Structure.

A general structure of this book is rather clear. It begins with a short prologue which introduces some of the themes of Koheleth's thought. The bulk of the book (1:12–12:8) is a long monologue which consists primarily of autobiographical reflections on the meaning of life. The book concludes with a brief epilogue (12:8-14). The prologue and epilogue are distinguished from the main body of the book by the use of third-person references to Koheleth. In this respect the book reflects the same overall structure as the Book of Job.

Many attempts have been made to identify the sequential structure of the lengthy speech of Koheleth which forms the centerpiece of the book.[22] Unable to find clearly marked units arranged in a meaningful order, most commentators have opted for viewing the book as a miscellaneous collection of proverbs. They view the book as more of a notebook containing random and disjointed notes, rather than a carefully crafted essay. The book is said to have a unity of style, topic, and theme, but not a logical progression of thought. Gordis found nineteen units in the book, while Scott discusses it in twenty-four sections.[23]

B. Thought Sequence.

Throughout the book the author shows two opposite views of life. First, he views things around him as the natural man would do, without the light of divine revelation. In these sections Koheleth is pessimistic and skeptical. "All is vanity." At other times, however, he writes as one to whom God has revealed himself. Here the observations and conclusions have the ring of surety and hope. For example: "Everything God does will remain forever" (3:14). This pattern of alternating perspectives continues throughout the book.

The writer himself furnishes the clue in 12:11 to how he has written this book. He speaks of the two types of passages found in the book—the negative and the positive—under the metaphors of "the goads" and "the nails." The goads (the passages which view life negatively) are those which prod the reader to think, to evaluate. The "nails" (the positive, God-centered passages) are the fixed points of reference in the quest for meaning.

A few writers see a more formal arrangement of material. They divide the book into two main sections, namely, a theoretical foundation based on observation of life (chs. 1–6) and practical conclusion based on those observations (chs. 7–12). Ginsburg, on the other

hand, opted for four broader divisions flanked on either side by a prologue and epilogue.[24] On the pages to follow the analysis of A.S.
Wright has been followed.[25] His analysis has the advantage of demonstrating the book's subtle inner unity.

CHARACTERISTICS OF THE BOOK

Thus far no exact parallels to the Book of Ecclesiastes have been
discovered in the ancient Near East. Some of the same issues are discussed in texts from Babylon, Egypt and Greece. One text from
Mesopotamia has even been dubbed "A Babylonian Qoheleth."[26]
Recently the book has been classified as "a framed autobiography"
and has been compared to the wisdom biographies which have been
discovered in Mesopotamia.[27]

Ecclesiastes belongs to the domain of biblical poetry. The fact is
concealed by the prose format in which most of the book is printed in
English versions. But even the prose sections are so saturated with
parallelism that many of them meet the criteria of Hebrew poetry and
could easily be printed in verse form. The writer relies on imagery. He
demonstrates skill with metaphor. Futility, for example, is like trying
to catch the wind.

Ecclesiastes contains a number of different literary forms. Some of
these are: (1) general reflections (e.g., 1:2-11); (2) personal or first
person reflections (e.g., 1:12-18); (3) exhortations (e.g., 4:17-5:8);
and (4) individual wisdom sayings or proverbs (9:17-10:20). In the
final chapter of the book Koheleth has used an allegory to enforce his
admonition to remember the creator in the days of youth (12:2-7).
The first person reflections are the backbone of the book. The
proverbs function to reinforce or summarize conclusions and to suggest practical ways of dealing with life's difficulties. Sometimes
proverbs are quoted so that Koheleth can take issue with them.

This collection of poetic units has been assembled under the over-
arching theme of a quest. The writer has undertaken a journey of
mind and soul, a journey to find meaning and satisfaction in life. From
the beginning the reader senses that the material is presented from
the standpoint of one who was successful in his quest. This impression is confirmed by the final paragraphs where the writer states that

he has reached "the end of the matter" (12:13). He is sharing, as it were, the mistakes of direction which had sidetracked his pursuit of the goal during his lifetime. Here then are warnings to fellow travelers of byways and dead end alleys that lead nowhere and accomplish nothing of significance. The passages bemoaning the futility of life under the sun reflect his former despair while the quest was in progress, before he reached the goal.

PURPOSE OF THE BOOK

A. Negative Purpose.

The author utilized the traditional tools of wisdom to refute and revise worldly wisdom's traditional conclusions.[28] Like Job he protested the simple answers, the broad generalizations which his fellow teachers put forth. In a world beset by tremendous problems, the rules of the simplistic teachers served more to frustrate than to illuminate.

Koheleth's purpose was to convince his readers of the uselessness of any worldview which does not rise above the level of himself. He demonstrates the vanity of living for worldly goals. God himself is the ultimate good. He alone gives meaning to life. Happiness is not a goal to be pursued, but a by-product of the right relationship with the creator.

B. Positive Purpose.

Ecclesiastes contains several—by one count thirteen—positive affirmations about life. While it is true that the negative passages dominate the harsh landscape of the book, it also is true that the one who travels this terrain can find rich oases at which to refresh himself scattered throughout.

The positive passages are usually much briefer than the negative ones. They are single focus, giving the impression that they are pointing out a straight path which leads quickly to the goal of satisfaction. The longer negative passages are suggestive of indecision and confusion, as though one were trapped in a maze without a clue as to what path he should follow. Thus the brevity of the positive passages does not indicate that they are unimportant in the book. Quite the contrary. These passages decisively cut through the maze of frustration which characterizes life outside of God, "under the sun."

Ecclesiastes has been called the sphinx of Hebrew literature with its unsolved riddles of history and life. Such an evaluation, however, is not fair. The book does not just state difficulties; it offers positive suggestions for coping with those difficulties. By pronouncing the book problematical the scholars have also rendered it inaccessible to modern readers.

To summarize, the immediate purpose of the book is to testify to Koheleth's personal reassessment of life's priorities, and to call upon his countrymen to do the same. The ultimate purpose of Ecclesiastes is to demonstrate that faith is the key to meaning in life.

TEACHING OF THE BOOK

Koheleth was not the skeptic which critics often allege. Nor was he a pessimist. He offered to his contemporaries positive suggestions regarding their relationship with the Lord.

A. About God.

Like all wisdom literature, Ecclesiastes builds upon the foundation of the fear of God which is the beginning of wisdom. The book stresses the doctrine of God's sovereignty and sagacity. Human beings are limited by the way in which God has determined the events of their lives. They have little power to change the course of history. Furthermore, people are limited by their inability to discover God's ways. They innately recognize that God is in charge, but they cannot understand his ways of dealing with them. He therefore counsels caution in prayer (5:2).

God's grace is seen in that he provides his people with some measure of-joy as they proceed through life (2:24f.; 3:13). Some twelve times he uses the verb "give" (natan) with God as its subject. Much about God baffled Koheleth, but he was firmly committed to the fundamental goodness of God. The Lord does not give to man everything, but he assigns him his "portion" (e.g., 2:10).

When Koheleth writes about God it is not as one who knows God from full revelation. He views life as a man does who knows and worships God primarily as creator. This is confirmed by the fact that he always refers to God as 'Elohim. He never uses the name Yahweh, the equivalent of redeemer-savior.

The theological emphasis of the book is on the providence of God. No matter what happens, the Lord still reigns. Both the good and bad times of life play a role in his sovereign will for mankind. His plan and pleasure is that man should enjoy his brief stay in this world and make use of all the bounty which God showers upon him (2:24).

B. About Death.

For Koheleth life is short and death is sure. The shadow of death falls on everything man does. The worldly person must be haunted by the specter of death, the "fly in the ointment" (10:1) of all that he accomplishes. Man knows he will die, but he does not know when. Death reverses the creative process of Gen 2. The spirit leaves the body to return to the creator while the body returns to the dust from which it came (12:7).

C. About Life.

Life is hard and unfair. Koheleth uses the term "toil" (*'amal*) to describe the rigors and harshness of life (e.g., 2:10,21). Yet life is not without its joy (e.g., 2:24f.; 3:12). One finds this joy in the simple gifts which God has given: food, drink, work, and love. Human achievement produced as much pain as joy. God did not want his people to be sour about life.

The philosophical issue in the book is this: What is the supreme good? In what does man find satisfaction and happiness? For Koheleth life "under the sun" (on earth) was really life in the dark if no ray of revelation was allowed to shine on the question. All was "vanity," i.e., emptiness and despair without God. Baxter has identified ten vanities of life which are mentioned in Ecclesiastes.[29] These are displayed in Chart No. 3 on the next page.

The ethical emphasis of Ecclesiastes is on the golden mean of conduct. Koheleth did not want his readers to go to seed, to become fanatics, to become so narrowly focused that they could not appreciate all that life has to offer. Moderation in all things was his motto. In his view one could be too religious and too righteous and thus fall into what later would be called the Pharisaical attitude.

703

Chart No. 3

THE TEN VANITIES		
1. 2:15-16	Human Wisdom	
2. 2:19-21	Human Labor	
3. 2:26	Human Purpose	
4. 4:4	Human Rivalry	
5. 4:7	Human Avarice	
6. 4:16	Human Fame	
7. 5:10	Human Insatiety	
8. 6:9	Human Coveting	
9. 7:6	Human Frivolity	
10. 8:10,14	Human Awards	

D. About Christ.

The book contains no direct messianic prophecy. Nonetheless, the person of Christ stands out in two significant ways. First, Christ is the greatest good, the ultimate satisfaction for which the believer aspires (cf. John 4:13,14). He is the water of life which quenches the human thirst for happiness. Second, Christ is the "one shepherd" or teacher from whom the wisdom of this book comes (12:11; cf. John 10:11; Col 2:3). He is the wisdom of God that satisfies the desire for knowledge.[30] By exposing the limitations of human wisdom, Koheleth prepared in his own way for the one who was greater than Solomon.

THE INTERPRETATION OF THE BOOK

Without question, Ecclesiastes contains many jarring passages. It seems, at times, to contradict the teaching of other biblical books, especially Proverbs. Various views have been expressed regarding how this book is to be interpreted and integrated into biblical theology in general.

Some see positive teaching only in the epilogue. Here the penitent Solomon is giving the final verdict on his godless wanderings which have been chronicled in the preceding chapters. What appears before 12:8 in the book represents the period of Solomon's rebellion against God. Thus nothing said in the book prior to 12:8 needs to be regarded as normative for biblical teaching.

Others argue that there is nothing unorthodox or pessimistic in Koheleth's teaching anywhere in the book.[31] This book celebrates the joy that should characterize the life of the believer. Those who take this approach are accused of twisting many of the statements of the book in order to support their view.[32]

Another approach is to hear in this book two voices, Koheleth's and that of the unnamed wisdom teacher who introduces and concludes the book. Not everything said by Koheleth is wrong (in the light of biblical theology), but nearly so. Like the Book of Job, the positive teaching comes at the conclusion of the book.

The key verse in this book must surely be 2:11: "Thus I considered all my activities which my hands had done and the labor which I had exerted, and behold all was vanity and striving after wind, and there was no profit under the sun."

The phrase "under the sun," which is used some thirty times, indicates the perspective of the writer at various points in the book. "Under the sun" means viewing life at ground level without any thought of higher values, omitting any light from revelation, and any notion of God. The phrase "vanity of vanities" expresses the general futility of activity done on earth. The phrase "vexation of spirit" describes the subjective psychological reaction to the intellectual realization that life under the sun is indeed empty and futile.

VALUE OF THE BOOK

This book has been much misunderstood. Pessimists have found here material to bolster their doleful outlook on life. Skeptics have claimed support from it for their contention of nonsurvival after death. Others quote Koheleth to confirm the theory of soul-sleeping between the death of the body and the final resurrection. Besides these, many sound and sincere believers have felt the book to be an unspiritual, uninspired and uninspiring composition which contradicts the principles of the New Testament.

Ecclesiastes is the most contemporary book in the Bible.[33] The so-called negative sections of the book amount to an exposé of the very things which dominate modern culture: sex, work, education, fame, drink. The writer creates a rogue's gallery of satirical portraits of the hedonist (2:1-11), the workaholic (2:18-23), the plutocrat (5:8-17), the fool (7:1-8), and the unfaithful woman (7:26-29). Ecclesiastes stands as the ultimate critique of secular humanism.

Some dismiss Ecclesiastes because they think the book teaches the Greek philosophy of Epicureanism which holds that pleasure is the highest good. People should eat, drink and be merry. Personal pleasure is what life is all about. Such, of course, most definitely is not the teaching of this book. There is nothing unwholesome here. The tradition of Hebrew and Christian religion has in fact laid too much stress on the sterner side of things; it is good that at least one book of the sacred canon should be found to remind believers that one duty of life is happiness. Herman Melville called Ecclesiastes "the truest of all books." Another American novelist, Thomas Wolfe, described it as "the highest flower of poetry, eloquence, and truth, . . . the greatest single piece of writing I have known."[34]

ENDNOTES

1. A.S. Wright, "The Riddle of the Sphinx Revisited: Numerical Patterns in the Book of Qoheleth," *Catholic Biblical Quarterly* 42 (1980): pp. 38-51.

2. Examples of conservative scholars who reject the Solomonic authorship of Ecclesiastes are: Stuart, Hengstenberg, Delitzsch, Young, Kidner.

3. Defenders of Solomonic authorship are G. Archer (Evangelical); A. Cohen (Jew); and Gietmann (Catholic).

4. W.S. LaSor, D. Hubbard, F. Bush, *Old Testament Survey* (Grand Rapids: Eerdmans, 1982), p. 589.

5. R. Gordis, *Koheleth: The Man and His World*. 2nd ed. (New York: Schocken, 1968), pp. 69-74.

6. R. Dillard and T. Longman III, *An Introduction to the Old Testament* (Grand Rapids: Zondervan, 1994), p. 250.

7. G. Archer, *A Survey of Old Testament Introduction*, pb. ed. (Chicago: Moody, 1985), p. 492.

8. G.A. Barton, *A Critical and Exegetical Commentary on the Book of Ecclesiastes*. The International Critical Commentary. (Edinburgh: T. & T. Clark, 1959), pp. 34-40.

9. Barton, *Ecclesiastes*, cites passages in the Gilgamesh Epic which commend the enjoyment of eating and drinking.

10. For citations, see Archer, *Introduction*, pp. 492f.

11. D.C. Fredericks, *Qoheleth's Language: Reevaluating Its Nature and Date* (Lewiston: Edwin Mellon, 1988); and Archer, *Introduction*, pp. 487-492.

12. Archer, *Introduction,* p. 489.

13. Dahood and Margoliouth see a Phoenician influence; Torrey and Ginsberg argue for an Aramaic influence.

14. C.H.H. Wright lists a number of aphorisms of Ben Sirach which are found in the biblical book. *The Book of Koheleth* (London: Hodder & Stoughton, 1883), pp. 41-46.

15. Ibid., pp. 55-76.

16. To hide the book (*ganaz*) in rabbinic circles would mean to remove it from circulation or from the curriculum of rabbinic schools. The action implied a question about the canonicity of the book.

17. Among the church fathers who quote Ecclesiastes as Scripture are these: Justin Martyr (*Dialogue* 6); Clement of Alexandria (*Stromata* 1:13); Tertullian (e.g., *Against Marcion* 5:4) and Origen (several times).

18. Barton, *Ecclesiastes,* pp. 43-46.

19. Gordis, *Koheleth,* p. 71.

20. H.L. Ginsburg, *Studies in Koheleth* (New York: Jewish Theological Seminary of America, 1950), pp. 16-39; F. Zimmerman, *The Inner World of Qoheleth* (New York: Ktav, 1973), pp. 98-122.

21. James Muilenburg, "A Qoheleth Scroll from Qumran," BASOR 135 (1954): 20-28.

22. For a survey of various attempts to find structure in Ecclesiastes see A.S. Wright "The Riddle of the Sphinx: The Structure of the Book of Qoheleth," *Catholic Biblical Quarterly* 42 (1980): 313-334.

23. Gordis, *Koheleth,* p. 252; and R.B.Y. Scott, *Proverbs, Ecclesiastes* in Anchor Bible (Garden City, NY: Doubleday, 1965).

24. Ginsburg, *Studies,* pp. 17-21.

25. Wright "Riddle," 313-334.

26. ANET, pp. 438-440.

27. Dillard and Longman III, *Introduction,* p. 252.

28. LaSor, Hubbard, Bush, *Survey,* pp. 591f.

29. J. Sidlow Baxter, *Explore the Book* (Grand Rapids: Zondervan, 1960), 3:163.

30. N. Geisler, *A Popular Survey of the Old Testament* (Grand Rapids: Baker, 1977), p. 215.

31. W.C. Kaiser, Jr., *Ecclesiastes: Total Life* (Chicago: Moody, 1979).

32. Dillard and Longman III, *Introduction,* p. 253.

33. Leland Ryken, "Ecclesiastes" in *A Complete Literary Guide to the Bible,* ed. Leland Ryken and Tremper Longman III (Grand Rapids: Zondervan, 1993), p. 274.

34. Ryken, "Ecclesiastes," p. 268.

BIBLIOGRAPHY

Barton, G.A. *Ecclesiastes*. International Critical Commentary. Edinburgh: T. & T. Clark, 1908.

Crenshaw, J.L. *Ecclesiastes*. Old Testament Library. Philadelphia: Westminster, 1987.

Eaton, M.A. *Ecclesiastes*. Tyndale Old Testament Commentary. Downers Grove, IL: InterVarsity, 1983.

Fox, M.V. *Qohelet and His Contradictions*. Sheffield: Almond, 1989.

Ginsburg, H.L. *Studies in Koheleth*. New York: Jewish Theological Seminary, 1950.

Gordis, R. *Koheleth: The Man and His World*. pb. Northvale, NJ: Aronson, Jason Inc., 1995.

Hengstenberg, Ernest W. *A Commentary on Ecclesiastes*. 1869. Reprint. Minneapolis: James and Klock, 1977.

Kidner, D. *A Time to Mourn and a Time to Dance*. Downers Grove, IL: InterVarsity, 1976.

Longman III, Tremper. *Ecclesiastes*. New International Commentary on the Old Testament. Grand Rapids: Eerdmans, 1995.

Plumptre, E.H. *Ecclesiastes; or, the Preacher*. The Cambridge Bible for Schools and Colleges. Cambridge: Cambridge University, 1907.

Reichert, Victor E. and A. Cohen. "Ecclesiastes." In *The Five Megilloth*. The Soncino Books of the Bible. London: Soncino, 1952.

Scott, R.B.Y. *Proverbs, Ecclesiastes*. Anchor Bible. Garden City, N.Y.: Doubleday, 1965.

Whybray, R.N. *Ecclesiastes*. New Century Bible. Grand Rapids: Eerdmans, 1989.

Wright, C.H.H. *The Book of Koheleth*. London: Hodder & Stoughton, 1883.

Wright, J.S. "The Interpretation of Ecclesiastes" (1945). In *Classical Evangelical Essays*. Ed. W.C. Kaiser, Jr. Grand Rapids: Baker, 1972.

Zimmerman, Frank. *The Inner World of Qoheleth*. New York: Ktav, 1973.

CHAPTER THIRTY-FOUR

The Vanity of All Things
Ecclesiastes 1:1-2:23

"Koheleth" is commonly accepted to mean "Preacher." The term signifies one who calls or addresses a public assembly. The form is a feminine participle which points to an office. The one who assumes the office of a public instructor calls himself "the son of David, king in Jerusalem." Though Solomon is not directly mentioned, the words clearly refer to him.

PROLOGUE
The Vanity of Earthly Things
Ecclesiastes 1:2-11

Koheleth begins with the assertion of his grand theme. He then illustrates this assertion and applies it to the human circumstance.

A. The Assertion (1:2-3).

"Vanity of vanities, says the Preacher, vanity of vanities; all is vanity." The writer twice uses what is equivalent to a superlative which means, everything in life is to the greatest degree vanity. The word "vanity" (*hebhel*) is used thirty-nine times in the book. The word means primarily "a breath" or "vapor" such as one might see when exhaled breath condenses on a cold day. The word is used poetically of all that is fleeting, perishable, transitory, frail and unsatisfying.[1] In this context the word suggests the futility of human effort. The rest of the book is a commentary on this verse. In asserting that "all is vanity" the writer is referring to things mundane and human. Man's works, not God's works, are vain (1:2).[2]

The assertion of v. 2 is sharpened and focused in v. 3. The writer uses a rhetorical question to express a negative opinion: "What does a man profit through all his labor in which he labors under the sun?" Life is full of toil, and the reward for that toil is not commensurate with the effort expended. Man gets precious little out of his labors in this sin-cursed world. The point is the fruitlessness of man's ceaseless activity.

The term "profit" (*yithron*) appears nowhere else in the Old Testament, but ten times in this book. It literally means "that which remains." The word seems to come from the business community. It may have been used to describe the surplus which remained on the balance sheet after all the assets and liabilities where taken into account. The point is that when all the pluses and minuses are taken into account, the balance sheet of life indicates a dismal zero, or perhaps even a negative figure.

The term "man" (*'adam*) refers to the natural man, unenlightened by the grace of God. Every son of Adam, whether Israelite or Gentile, has experienced the emptiness of life when he refuses to recognize any spiritual values.

The phrase "under the sun" is another key concept in the book. A proper understanding of this phrase safeguards the message of the entire book. The phrase is used some twenty-nine times by this author. The thought is that Koheleth is evaluating life at ground level, without any thought of God. "Under the sun" refers to life here and now, life on earth, life without any light of revelation. Where this phrase appears the writer is saying, in effect, "If one leaves out any thought of heavenly (spiritual) things, what does he have left in life?" (1:3).

B. The Illustrations (1:4-8).

Koheleth offers four illustrations of ceaseless, but futile activity. Here in this life things are in a perpetual flux. Like the movements of a carousel, there is much noise and movement, but no real progress.

1. *The succession of generations (1:4).* While man appears to be lord of the earth, in reality he is but a stranger passing through. "A generation goes, a generation comes; but the earth forever stands." Man soon passes from the scene only to be replaced by others. While this constant succession of generations of men goes on, the earth remains unchanged and immovable. The term "forever" (*le'olam*) does not necessarily imply eternity. It often denotes limited or conditional duration (e.g., Exod 21:6). What is depicted here is ever recurring change against the backdrop of enduring sameness. The verse is full of pathos. Man, who was given dominion over the earth, passes away while the earth remains. One generation is continually passing from the scene, even while its successor is starting to appear (1:4).

2. *The movements of the sun (1:5).* A second example of ever-recurring sameness is now cited. "The sun arises, and the sun goes down, and hastens [lit., pants] to its place, arising there." The picture here is of the sun setting in the west and then eagerly returning through the night to the east to begin the journey across the skies anew. The "panting" is not that of fatigue, but of eagerness. The thought here is that the sun makes no real progress; its eager panting merely brings it to the same old place, there to resume its monotonous routine.

3. *The circuits of the wind (1:6).* Koheleth next turns to the wind for an example of purposeless activity. "Going to the south and circling to the north, circling, circling goes the wind; and on its circlings returns the wind." The wind appears to be the freest of all created things. Nonetheless, the wind too exhibits ceaseless, but predictable, activity which accomplishes nothing. It is always turning back to the circuits or rounds that have been planned for it.

4. *The flow of streams (1:7).* The streams of the earth continue to empty water into the sea, but the sea is never full. Koheleth is not attempting here to discuss the water cycle. He is simply further underscoring his picture of life in this world as one of monotonous sameness and purposelessness.

711

The ceaseless and purposeless motion in the world is tiresome to observers. The writer cannot even verbalize just how tiresome it all is. Wherever his eyes turn the same sad situation can be observed. Listen though he may to the instructions of professed teachers, man makes no real advance in knowledge of the mysteries in which he is caught up. No one can really explain why the world seems filled with such frantic, yet fruitless action (1:8).

C. The Application (1:9-11).

What has been asserted regarding phenomena in the physical world is now affirmed of the events in human history. The more things change, the more things are monotonously the same. "There is nothing new under the sun" (1:9).

From time to time something appears which some might claim is fundamentally new. Not so, says Koheleth. It existed already "long ago" in some previous generation (1:10).

Human beings tend to have short memories. They have forgotten much of what went before. They fail to pass on to younger generations the information which would prevent them from repeating the mistakes of the past. The discoveries of earlier times are forgotten, and seem quite new when revived; but closer investigation proves their previous existence. What now looms large in importance will likewise be forgotten by future generations. The incomplete and selective memory of man is what makes possible the assertion that something new has appeared in human history (1:11).

Koheleth should not be viewed as an unhappy soul who has been beaten down by circumstances. He is not some gloomy pessimist. He is viewing, for the moment, life at ground level—"under the sun"—without thought to spiritual values. Man's activity is but another reflection of the ceaseless round of purposeless motion which is exhibited in nature. Without God, human activity is futile. This negative assessment of life "under the sun" indirectly calls for mankind to focus on higher values. That enables man to look at life from a different perspective.

THE VANITY OF STRIVING
AFTER WISDOM
Ecclesiastes 1:12-18

Koheleth now begins to explore three areas of life which demonstrate the vanity which he has asserted in generalities in the prologue of the book. The first is in the area of striving after earthly wisdom. In this endeavor man has attempted to break away from regimentation. Yet the attempt has been futile. Koheleth gives a personal illustration of that futility.

A. The Initial Quest (1:12-13).

The author again identifies himself as king of Israel residing in the city of Jerusalem. On this point, see the discussion in the previous chapter (1:12).

Koheleth was determined in his quest for wisdom. He "set" or fixed his "heart." In Hebrew psychology the heart was the seat, not only of affections, but of the understanding and intellectual faculties generally. To set the heart would be equivalent to setting the mind to the task.

The task at hand was "to seek" (*darash*) and "to search out" (*tur*) the mysteries of life. The first verb implies penetrating into the depth of an object; the second, taking a comprehensive survey of matters further away. The terms do not refer so much to the gathering of data as to a careful analysis of existing facts. The instrument by which these researches would be conducted was "wisdom." He would not be content merely to collect facts; he wished to investigate the causes and conditions of things of the world.

The scope of the quest was "all things that are done under heaven." Thus his investigation was sociological and psychological more than physical. He was concerned with men's actions and conduct, not with material things. He set out to explore what moderns may call the human predicament. In his quest for wisdom he left no relevant area untouched.

The investigation of life is said to be "a grievous task" (*'inyan*). This word occurs often in this book, but nowhere else in the Old Testament. It implies distracting business, engrossing occupation. The

713

quest for wisdom is an undertaking which is enough to drive almost any person to despair. Men feel a compulsion to undertake this laborious investigation, yet the result is most unsatisfactory, as the following verses explain.

This grievous task has been given to the sons of men by *'Elohim*, the creator. In this book the covenant name *Yahweh* is not used by design. Koheleth is concerned about man in his relationship to divine providence. For this reason he uses a name for God which was common among the ancient peoples. The design of this book is to set forth the condition of all men, not just the covenant people.

The creator has instilled in every human being the desire to know the answers to life's ultimate questions. Part of that which distinguishes humans from animals is the desire to know origin, destiny and purpose; to understand the why and how of all things. Even those who have no walk with the Lord feel this compulsion to discover the truth. Though this compulsion to know is God-given, the effort to know is full of frustration. The enigmas of life do not fit snugly into paradigms and syllogisms (1:13).

B. Preliminary Conclusions (1:14-16).

Koheleth now states the results of his investigation of human behavior. He claims that in his varied experience nothing had escaped his notice. His shocking ("Behold!") discovery was that "all is vanity and striving after wind." The thrust of these words is that all human endeavor is unsubstantial and ultimately unsatisfying. No matter how thoroughly a person investigates, how broad the area is that is taken in hand, it is found to be a rather fruitless endeavor (1:14).

One specific example of the frustrations of the quest for wisdom is pointed out in v. 15. Man cannot change the course of events by the utmost exercise of his powers and faculties. Life presents many problems which the keenest intellect cannot explain nor rectify. "What is crooked cannot be straightened." The reference is not to man's sinful actions, but to the perplexities in which all men find themselves. "What is lacking cannot be counted." The greatest mathematician cannot add figures which do not exist. So the wisdom of man cannot supply the defects which come to notice when he examines life (1:15).

Koheleth engaged in an internal dialogue. He reflected on the amount of wisdom which he had accumulated. "Behold, I have magnified and increased wisdom more than all who were over Jerusalem before me." To whom did Koheleth refer? Solomon was but the second Israelite king to rule over Jerusalem. He must refer to the Canaanite rulers of the city, and to sages like Ethan, Heman, Chalcol and Darda (1 Kgs 4:31). Koheleth claims that his mind (lit., heart) had seen "wisdom [*chokmah*] and knowledge [*da'ath*]." The former word refers to ethics and good behavior, the latter to the factual basis of the former. He was satisfied that he had done the utmost to acquire wisdom, yet he was still unable to explain the anomalies of life (1:16).

C. The Intensified Quest (1:17-18).

To stress his determination to acquire wisdom, Koheleth refers again to his mindset (cf. v. 13). His earnestness in the pursuit of wisdom was matched by his effort. He left no stone unturned. He even explored the opposite of wisdom in order to learn the truth by contrasting it with error. Thus he learned "madnesses" (*holeloth*) and "folly" (*sikhluth*). The former word refers to a confusion of thought, an unwisdom which deranges all ideas of order and propriety. The latter word is identified in the wisdom books with vice and wickedness. This effort to see the other side of all issues also proved to be a striving after wind, i.e., it yielded precious little of lasting value.

What Koheleth describes here is the equivalent of making an honest attempt to solve all problems and to attain to all knowledge by the processes of rational thinking. It is the effort of a philosopher to plumb the depths of every issue unaided and unenlightened by divine revelation. Candid men must admit that such efforts produce very meager results. Even with all his wisdom and knowledge man cannot control the issues of life (1:17).

Increased wisdom is frustrating. The more one knows of men's lives, the greater is the cause of grief over the incomplete and unsatisfactory nature of all human endeavors. "He who increases knowledge increases sorrow," not in others, but in himself. Exploratory surgery often reveals the most unpleasant realities. So increased knowledge leads a person to find out many disturbing things that may produce "vexation" or irritation (*ka'as*), i.e., may disturb his peace of mind. "Sorrow" also grows out of getting more knowledge, for knowledge

715

brings with it a realization that many things in the world are hopelessly bent out of shape. The wise man becomes ever more conscious of the scope of his ignorance and impotence, of the uncontrollable power of nature, of great evils which he is powerless to remedy. To a certain extent, ignorance is bliss (1:18).

THE VANITY OF PLEASURE
Ecclesiastes 2:1-11

Koheleth was dissatisfied with the result of the pursuit of wisdom. He resolves to experiment with a series of activities which delight the human senses. All turned out to be blind alleys.

A. Whimsy (2:1-2).

Again Koheleth addresses his "heart," the seat of the emotions and and intellect: "I said in my heart." The language is similar to that used by the rich fool in Jesus' parable (Luke 12:20). He urges himself to embark on a course of sensual pleasure, i.e., that which delights the senses without being necessarily sinful. The term "mirth" (simchah) refers to harmless amusements and delights. Perhaps this avenue would yield some more substantial and permanent result.

Koheleth ordered his soul, i.e., himself, to "enjoy pleasure," (lit., "see good"). The verb "see" is often used in the sense of "to experience or enjoy." Would the supreme good be found in selfish enjoyment without thought of others? No, for this new experiment yielded the same results as before: "Behold this also is vanity!" (2:1).

The result of this pursuit of mirth is underscored by the personification of "laughter" and "mirth." Koheleth evaluated "laughter" as "mad," i.e., as totally irrational. Of "mirth" he said, "What does it do?" What does mirth contribute toward the goal of real happiness and contentment? Does it fill the void in one's soul? Does it give lasting satisfaction? (2:2). Israel's wise men were quite aware of the fact that a jolly exterior can mask a heavy heart (cf. Prov 14:13).

B. Wine (2:3).

Koheleth next experimented with wine. "I sought in my heart" is literally, "I spied out in my heart." The thought is that he investigated, he made another experiment in a philosophical spirit. He determined that he would nourish himself with wine, lit., make strong my flesh with wine. Becoming a drunkard is plainly not in view here. He aspired to be what might be called a connoisseur of wine. Excessive drinking is excluded by the phrase "yet acquainting my heart with wisdom."

While experimenting with pleasure Koheleth still retained sufficient control over his passions as not to be wholly given over to vice. Though he was embarking on dangerous waters, wisdom gave him power of stopping his course before it proved fatal to him. Such is the attitude of all those who pursue vice. They wish to believe that they are in control even when the vice has become their master. Few there are who quit such conduct when it is within their power to do so.

Koheleth determined to "lay hold on folly [sikhluth]." The term includes all those harmless and enjoyable forms of nonsense. Apparently he regarded dalliance with wine as foolish, but so many had pursued that path that he felt compelled to see where it might lead. His purpose was to discover by personal experience if there was in these things any real good which might satisfy men's cravings and be a worthy object for them to pursue all the days of their life. Wine and other forms of folly are not very substantial, for their pleasures are as brief as is every man's life (2:3).

C. Work (2:4-6).

In pursuit of the supreme good, Koheleth now turned to work: "I made great my works." The little expression "for myself" indicates that these projects were not humanitarian or philanthropic in nature. They were not for the good of the kingdom, but rather for the personal satisfaction of the builder.

He first mentions architectural works. Solomon had a passion for erecting "houses." He was thirteen years in building a huge palace for himself. He also built (1) the "house of the forest of Lebanon," a splendid hall constructed with pillars of cedar; (2) the porch of pillars; (3) the hall of judgment; (4) the harem for the daughter of Pharaoh; (5) fortresses; (6) store-cities; (7) chariot-cities; and (8) cities in distant lands such as Tadmor in the wilderness (1 Kgs 7; 9; 2 Chr 8). The temple is not specifically mentioned because Solomon built that building under divine mandate and for the glory of God, not for personal glory (2:4).

Next Solomon mentions horticultural works. Like his father David (1 Chr 27:27f.), he planted (1) "vineyards." One of them was in Baal-hamon (Song 8:11). (2) He planted "gardens." The king's garden mentioned in 2 Kgs 25:4 may have been one such garden. Solomon also planted (3) "orchards" full of all types of fruit trees. For the trees in such parks see Song 4:13f. (2:5).

Solomon was also concerned about hydrological works. Providing water for his growing capital was a great concern. Vast operations were undertaken for this purpose. "The king's pool" of Neh 2:14 may have been built by him. The most celebrated water work ascribed to Solomon, however, was the aqueduct connecting three large pools west of Bethlehem with the temple mount in Jerusalem.[3] Some of Solomon's water works were used to irrigate "the growing trees of the grove," lit., to irrigate a wood sprouting forth trees, i.e., a nursery of saplings.

D. Wealth (2:7-8a).

Royal servants were one measure of the wealth of an oriental king. Solomon procured many such servants to supplement those which were born in his house. The latter were much more esteemed by their masters because their attachment to the family was greater than that of bought slaves or those captured in war. The Queen of Sheba marveled at the number of Solomon's attendants (1 Kgs 10:5).

Wealth was also measured in terms of flocks and herds. Solomon had more livestock than any inhabitant of Jerusalem before him (cf. 1:16). The enormous size of Solomon's herds and flocks is proved by the extraordinary multitude of the sacrifices which he provided at the consecration of the temple (1 Kgs 8:63), and the lavish provision made daily for the needs of the royal table (2:7; 1 Kgs 4:22f.).

Solomon also gathered for himself silver and gold in great abundance. All the vessels of his table are said to have been gold. His bodyguards were armed with golden shields. The king himself sat on an ivory throne overlaid with gold. He received from distant lands "the special treasure of kings," i.e., annual tribute. He sent his navies to ever more distant lands to import precious metals. Silver became as common in Jerusalem as stones (1 Kgs 9:28; 10:14-27; 2 Chr 1:15; 9:20-27).

Next Koheleth mentions the acquisition of male and female singers. The reference is to the musicians who were introduced at banquets and festivals to enhance the pleasure of the scene. Such exhibitions were probably accompanied by sensuous dances on the part of the female "singers."

E. Women (2:8b).

Solomon multiplied "concubines"[4] which he describes euphemistically as "the delights of the sons of men," i.e., they provide the sensual pleasures which men enjoy. The wives and concubines of Solomon numbered a thousand (1 Kgs 11:3). Fortunately this phase of the search for meaning is only briefly treated (2:8).

F. Summary and Conclusion (2:9-11).

Koheleth now summarizes the results of the five experiments which he made in an endeavor to find the supreme good. Chapter 1 underscored the superiority of Koheleth in wisdom (cf. 1:16). Here he asserts his superiority in the magnificence and extent of his possessions and luxury. The various accomplishments enumerated above made him great. He excelled all who were before him in Jerusalem (cf. 1:16; 2:7). The expression "I became great" has an interesting force in the Hebrew: "I became great, and I added," i.e., he went beyond greatness.

The writer reiterates (cf. 2:3) that his wisdom remained with him throughout his search for the supreme good. Some would limit this statement to the early part of Solomon's reign before his wives led him astray (1 Kgs 11:4ff.). Be that as it may, the point is that he retained control of himself during his exploration. He studied philosophically the effects and nature of the pleasures of which he partook. He kept always in mind the object of his pursuit. What Koheleth calls "wisdom" here is not that wisdom which comes from above, but an earthly prudence and self-restraint (2:9).

Koheleth undertook his investigation in a thoroughgoing manner. He denied himself no gratification, however foolish. He enjoyed all his labor, and all which his labor procured for him. This was the reason he did not withhold his heart from joy. He was ready to taste any pleasure which his exertions might obtain. He regarded such joy his "portion," i.e., the reward of his labor. Each new experiment was exciting for a time. His pleasure, however, lasted only as long as the project lasted and the novelty of it had not yet worn off (2:10).

Then Koheleth looked back to contemplate and evaluate "all the works which my hands had wrought." He examined carefully the effects of the conduct and proceedings mentioned in the preceding verses. Now he gives his mature judgment concerning them. His various experiments had contributed nothing to his anxious inquiry for man's real good. His sorrowful conclusion again is that "all was vanity, a grasping after wind." In all the pursuits and labors that men undertake there is no real profit, no lasting happiness, nothing to satisfy the cravings of the spirit "under the sun," i.e., in this world without light from above. Purely earthly values eventually and abruptly let one down (2:11).

THE VANITY OF WISDOM
Ecclesiastes 2:12-17

Koheleth now turned his attention to "wisdom, madness, and folly" (cf. 1:17). He studied the three in their relationship to one another and in their effects on man's nature and life. On one side of the scale he set "wisdom," in the other, those actions and habits which he rightly calls "madness and folly." He mentally weighs the benefits of these two lifestyles. He is convinced that his investigation is so thorough, so extensive, that anyone coming after him would only repeat his experiment and reach the same conclusion (2:12).[5]

A. Wisdom Superior to Folly (2:13-14a).

Koheleth reached the conclusion that wisdom outweighed folly, i.e., earthly wisdom had a certain value. It was as superior to folly as light is more beneficial than darkness. The metaphor here is found throughout Scripture: spiritual and intellectual development is represented as "light" while mental and moral depravity are represented as "darkness" (2:13).

How is wisdom superior to folly? The person who possesses true wisdom has the eyes of his heart or understanding enlightened; he looks into the nature of things; he focuses on what is most important;

he sees where to go. The fool, on the other hand, walks on still in darkness, stumbling as he goes, knowing not where his road will take him.

B. Wisdom Not Superior to Folly (2:14b-16).

Though wisdom is superior to folly in life, in two respects the wise and the foolish are equal.

1. Both the wise and the foolish are doomed to death (2:14b-15). While Koheleth cheerfully concedes the superior lifestyle of wisdom, he[6] perceived that one "event" *(miqreh)* happens to both the fool and the wise one, i.e., the final event, death. Koheleth saw this with his own eyes. He needed no instructor to teach him that both wise and foolish must succumb to death, the universal leveler (2:14).

Some might expect that God would exempt one who had cultivated wisdom from the testing of death. Such was not the case. Koheleth knew that the end which eventually overtakes the fool will one day overtake him as well. Why then had he been so "extremely wise," i.e., striven so strenuously to achieve wisdom? The thought is not that he had too much wisdom, but that he tried hard to exceed others in that area. His wisdom, however, had backfired on him. It had taught him much, but did not give contentment; it enabled him to see the emptiness of human striving, but it did not satisfy his cravings. The similar fate of both philosopher and philanderer makes life vain and worthless (2:15).

2. Both the wise and the foolish are forgotten (2:16). After death, the wise are no more remembered than fools: "for of the wise man, even as of the fool, there is no remembrance forever." Koheleth states a general truth. Some men's names are part of the fabric of history and they are remembered for generations. What this wise man has observed is that posterity soon forgets the wisdom of one and the folly of another. "All that now is will be forgotten in the days to come." Viewed from ground level, without any light of immortality, the wise man and fool die the same death.

Koheleth could have named a number of other ways in which the death of the wise and the foolish are similar. From the outward form and attendant circumstances of the physical event of death one cannot draw any conclusions about whether or not the deceased had governed his life by wise principles.

721

C. Conclusion (2:17).

If life leads only to the grave and is then forgotten, then Koheleth suggests that life itself is a burden and hateful: "I hated life; for evil unto me is the work which is done under the sun." The toil and exertions of men pressed upon him like a burden too heavy to bear. The verb "hated" might be more properly represented in the modern idiom by the word "disgusted." The more wisdom one acquires the more he becomes aware of the injustice, inequality and unfairness of life. Koheleth speaks here honestly and autobiographically. His strong revulsion at life may not be shared by everyone who reviews the facts about life and death previously set forth.

The phrase "under the sun" reminds the reader that Koheleth is considering human labor only in its earthly aspect, undertaken and executed for temporal and selfish considerations alone. Again Koheleth comes back to his miserable conclusion: All that man accomplishes in this world is "vanity and grasping after the wind."

THE VANITY OF LABOR
Ecclesiastes 2:18-23

Work is a blessing, a virtual necessity, if one is to feel a sense of fulfillment in life. From another point of view, however, daily chores fall under the label of "vanity." In this unit Koheleth speaks of that kind of labor which confines itself to earthly pursuits and ambitions and leaves out of consideration heavenly and spiritual values. Three times in this unit the writer uses the phrase "under the sun" which indicates the perspective from which he is evaluating labor. In particular Koheleth is thinking of what happens to noble efforts after one is dead. Too often it is the case that the successors of diligent workers dismantle grand programs, destroy great structures, squander enormous wealth and otherwise ruin what the previous generation sacrificed to achieve.

A. His First Complaint about Labor (2:18-20).

Koheleth declares: "I hated all my labor which I had done under the sun." He is disgusted to reflect upon all the efforts he has put forth in life, when he thinks of what will become of the productions of his genius and the treasures he has amassed. He must eventually die and leave it all behind "to the man that shall be after me." Perhaps Solomon is thinking of the foolish son Rehoboam who would be his successor on the throne (2:18).

The bitter thought that he must leave all the fruits of his labors to another is aggravated by the thought that he does not know the character of his successor. Will he be a worthy successor? Only time will tell. Whatever his character, he will rule. He will have free use and control of all that Koheleth had gathered and administered through his wisdom (2:19).

Because of his assessment of the value of earthly labor, Koheleth "turned" his heart," i.e., he broke off his addiction to work. He gave himself up to despair. Worldly work no longer had allure for him (2:20).

B. His Second Complaint about Labor (2:21-23).

Now another complaint is raised. Koheleth had amassed his wealth because he labored "with wisdom, knowledge and skill." One might have reason to hope that such labor might have greater longevity than that which is haphazardly done. Yet his successor would come into possession of that for which he had exerted no effort. "This is also vanity and a great evil" (2:21).

What does a man get for all his toil under the sun? Some pleasure accompanies the effort to reach goals; but this is poor, unsubstantial and embittered. One might strive, i.e., work tirelessly, to achieve noble goals. What does all this effort produce? The answer intended is, "Nothing." This striving, with all its wisdom, knowledge and skill, is for the laborer fruitless (2:22).

The real result of a lifelong effort is "sorrow." All one's work is "grievous." This man cannot sleep when he begins to reflect at night about who and what his successor shall be. Each night is a torment when he sees reasons for believing that his successor will be a bumbling incompetent. This also is vanity (2:23).

ENDNOTES

1. The Hebrew word translated here "vanity" appears first in the name of Abel (Gen 4:2), one whose life was cut short by the murderous deed of his brother.

2. Paul (Rom 8:20) seems to have had Ecclesiastes in mind when he spoke of the creation being subjected to vanity as a consequence of the Fall of man.

3. Some archaeologists date these Bethlehem water works only to Roman times.

4. The term translated "concubines" (*shiddah veshiddoth*) in NASB and "harem" in NIV is of uncertain meaning. The whole expression indicates multiplicity, something like "concubine and concubines."

5. Another interpretation of 2:12 is that Koheleth realized that thinkers who come after him might do what men have always done, namely, not deal with the matter exhaustively and bring it to a clean-cut conclusion as he proposes to do.

6. The Hebrew reads: "I knew, also I." The use of *gam* (also) with the personal pronoun to indicate an adversative is the way Koheleth signals an objection to a view that was currently popular.

CHAPTER THIRTY-FIVE

The Secret of Satisfaction
Ecclesiastes 2:24-3:22

Koheleth has explored all avenues in seeking true satisfaction in life. He has found all that the world offers to be vanity and striving after wind. No real satisfaction can be found "under the sun." Now he presents his first "nail," i.e., that truth upon which people can hang their hopes. He insists that only when God is reckoned in life's equation can mankind find true joy in life. For the first time he reaches beyond the level of the things under the sun and introduces the higher values which make true joy possible.

THE GIFT OF GOD
Ecclesiastes 2:24-26

Koheleth concludes that man may indeed enjoy the good things of life, but only according to God's will and permission. Satisfaction is a divine gift, not an entitlement. He then offers proof of this assertion.

A. The Assertion (2:24).

The standard versions have not translated 2:24 properly because the translators perceived that a literal translation would be at variance with what the book later declares in 3:12-13 and 8:15. The text literally says: "It is not good in man that he can eat and drink." What the verse is asserting is that it is not in the power of a person to enjoy himself simply at his own will. His ability to enjoy life proceeds wholly from God. The phrase "to eat and drink" is merely a periphrasis for living in comfort, peace, and affluence. The phrase refers to the simplest forms of enjoyment.

Koheleth also asserts that man cannot find "good" or pleasure in his labor without the blessing of God. "This also I saw that it was from the hand of God." This is the point: the power of enjoyment depends on the will of God (2:24).

B. The Proof (2:25-26).

Koheleth now offers two lines of evidence as the proof for his assertion. The first, in the form of a question, refers to his qualifications to make such an assertion. The second, invokes the sovereign justice of God.

Who had better opportunity than Koheleth for verifying the principle that all depends upon the gift of God? Who could "eat," i.e., enjoy oneself, more than this writer? Who was in a position to pursue pleasure more than he?[1] Solomon was in a position to try every avenue of human endeavor in his search for true satisfaction. In the previous verses he has delivered strong testimony of the emptiness of every human endeavor under the sun. By personal experience he had discovered that life has no substantial satisfaction to offer without God in the picture (2:25).

God rewards those who please him, and thwarts those who displease him. That is the thrust of 2:26. While the word "God" does not appear in the Hebrew of this verse, it is clear that the pronoun refers to the Lord. The person who is "good" in his sight is that one who pleases him. To that person God gives the blessings of "wisdom and knowledge and joy." The linkage of wisdom and knowledge with joy indicates that Koheleth is not speaking of the "wisdom and knowledge" which are previously labeled as "vanity." The terms here must refer to a wisdom and a knowledge which enable a person to derive joy from the things in life. The only true wisdom which is not grief, the only true knowledge which is not sorrow (cf. 1:18), and the only joy in life, are the gifts of God to those he regards as "good."

On the other hand, God gives to habitual sinners[2] "travail, to gather and to heap up." The sinner takes great pains, expends continuous labor, that he may amass wealth. God disposes of what the wicked gather in such a way that they themselves may be said to give it to him to whom God pleases to have it given. That wealth, however, passes "to him that is good before God," i.e., more worthy hands (cf. Prov 28:8).

Koheleth regards "this" also as vanity and grasping after wind. But what does he mean by "this"? Here is the central idea of the passage. The moral government of God places restrictions upon the ability of a person to enjoy the fruit of his toil. For a sinner to labor and toil to amass wealth when the disposition of that wealth is in the hands of God is nothing but striving after wind on the part of that sinner (2:26).

THE RHYTHM OF GOD
Ecclesiastes 3:1-9

Koheleth now further demonstrates how man's happiness depends upon the will of God. He shows in this unit how divine providence arranges even the most minute concerns over which man has no control.

A. The General Assertion (3:1).

Koheleth first states the following general proposition: The providence of God disposes and arranges *every* detail of man's life. He then emphasizes this proposition with a series of antithetical sentences.

"To everything there is a season, and a time to every purpose under heaven" (3:1). If any distinction is to be made between "season" and "time" it is this: A season (*zeman*) is a fixed, definite portion of time; a "time" (*'eth*) is the beginning of a period. "Everything" refers particularly to man's movements and actions, and to what concerns them. "Purpose" (*chephets*) sometimes means "delight" or "pleasure;" but here the term has the meaning of "business," "thing," or "matter." Koheleth is affirming that divine providence arranges the moment when everything shall happen, and assigns the duration of that event. His main purpose here is to confirm the conclusion he reached in the previous chapter, namely, that wisdom, wealth, success, happiness, etc., are not in man's hands. By his own efforts he can secure none of these priceless treasures; they are distributed at the will of God.

B. The Specific Illustrations (3:2-8).

In Hebrew manuscripts and in most printed texts verses 2-8 are printed in two parallel columns so that the contrasting times are clearly juxtaposed. The list contains fourteen pairs of contrasts, ranging from external circumstances to the inner affections of a person's being.

The catalog begins with the contrast between the entrance into life and the departure therefrom. "There is a time to give birth, and a time to die." Those who at one time give life to others must inevitably yield to the law of death, namely, "It is appointed unto men once to die" (Heb 9:27). The same principle is true in the vegetable realm. "There is a time to plant, and a time to uproot that which is planted." Trees planted by one generation are cut down by another. This is the final end for which trees are planted (3:2).

"There is a time to kill, and a time to heal." Most likely Koheleth had in mind either the execution of criminals, or justifiable homicide in self-defense or in the defense of the oppressed. Such emergencies occur providentially; they cannot be anticipated (cf. Deut 32:39). On the other hand, sometimes in the course of events one receives wounds which need the healing arts. Taking a life and preserving a life are events which may be forced on a person in the course of his life. The same is true in the material realm. "There is a time to break down, and a time to build up." Unsuitable, old or dangerous structures will be removed to be replaced by new and improved buildings (3:3).

Moments of extreme joy and extreme sadness come suddenly and unexpectedly. "There is a time to weep, and a time to laugh." Here is contrasted the spontaneous manifestations of the inner feelings of the heart. Such inward feelings are given full expression at funerals and weddings: "There is a time to mourn, and a time to dance." The hired mourners and the wedding guests are set in contrast to one another (3:4).

The next couplet has occasioned many interpretations: "A time to cast away stones, and a time to gather stones together." That the text refers to demolishing houses is not likely because that has already been mentioned. The practice in war of marring an enemy's field may be in view (2 Kgs 3:19,25), but that must have been a rare occurrence, too rare to merit inclusion in this list. Probably the reference is to tearing down and building stone walls, winepresses, guard towers, and roads.

Next Koheleth mentions "a time to embrace, and a time to refrain from embracing." The connection between this couplet and the preceding one is not clear. Perhaps the connection is this: one embraces a field by moving a wall. In any case, clearly there are times when the expression of affection is appropriate, and times when such displays would be inappropriate. One should not, for example, give himself over to the delights of love and friendship during penitential occasions or in worship settings (3:5).

In life there is "a time to seek, and a time give up as lost." The reference is probably to property. There is a proper pursuit of wealth, and there is a wise and prudent submission to its inevitable loss. A wise businessman knows when to pour additional resources into a concern, and when to write off that concern. There is "a time to keep, and a time to cast away." Prudence will preserve assets until that day comes when those assets are liquidated in the interest of some more important end. An extreme example would be the jettisoning of cargo by the crew of a ship which is in danger of sinking (3:6).

Koheleth next notes that there is "a time to rend, and a time to sew." Again wide-ranging explanations of this couplet have been offered. He appears to be saying simply that there are times when it is natural to tear clothes to pieces, whether from grief, or anger, or any other cause, e.g., as being old and worthless. On the other hand, there are times when it is equally natural to mend them, and to make them serviceable by timely repairs.

Koheleth adds, there is "a time to keep silence, and a time to speak." Wisdom literature has much to say on the matter of the appropriate use of the tongue. He may be referring to the expression of sorrow. Deep sorrow sometimes should remain silent rather than express itself in tears or garment tearing. An example would be sympathizing silence (Job 2:13). On the other hand, there are occasions when the sorrow of the heart should find utterance. David's lament over Saul and Jonathan (2 Sam 1:17) would be an example. The couplet, however, is capable of wider application. The young should hold their peace in the presence of their elders (Job 32:4). A person should withhold his comment when he is not knowledgeable in a certain area (Prov. 17:28). Yet wise counsel must not be withheld at the right moment (3:7; Prov 15:23; 25:11).

The wise one notes, finally, that there is "a time to love and a time to hate." On the personal level men should love righteousness, goodness, and mercy. They should hate every appearance of immorality, injustice and oppression. On the national level there is "a time of war, and a time of peace." Statesmanship discovers the necessity or the opportuneness of war and peace, and acts accordingly (3:8).

C. Conclusion (3:9).

The enumeration of fourteen contrasting conditions and events leads up to this conclusion: "What profit is there to the worker from that in which he toils?" This repeats essentially the same despondent question already asked in 1:3. The answer which Koheleth would give is "None!" In all of man's actions and under all circumstances he depends upon times and seasons which are beyond his control. He cannot count on reaping any benefit from his labor (3:9).

THE PURPOSE OF GOD
Ecclesiastes 3:10-15

Koheleth draws three conclusions based on his observations regarding God's supreme rule over all things.

A. Contemplation of God's Works (3:10-11).

Koheleth has observed the task which God has given to the sons of men, i.e., that with which they must concern themselves. Men plan, prepare and struggle to fulfill their task. All their efforts, however, are controlled by a higher law. Results occur along the way at the time arranged by divine providence. Human labor is appointed by God; it is part of man's heritage. That labor, however, cannot bring contentment or satisfy the cravings of man's spirit. Rather the fruitless struggle is intended to bring man to the realization of his own limitations and of God's supreme control (3:10).

God has ordained and designed the human experience. There is nothing wrong in any respect as far as God's administration of affairs is concerned. In fact, because of his accurate timing of constructive seasons over against seasons of dismay, everything is actually "beautiful in its own time." All the issues of life are marked by harmony of purpose and beneficent oversight by God. When men see the big picture, they surely must marvel at the way God has arranged life.

In their labors men unwittingly carry forward the purposes of divine providence. God has placed "eternity" (ha'olam) in the heart of man. Man can appreciate the lasting import of things. He can look back to the distant past and forward to the distant future. He senses that he is not just a creature of time. He has a deep-seated sense of purpose and destiny. Yet this sense of eternity does not solve all his problems nor answer all his questions. He often is at a loss to trace through in detail God's power and purpose in daily events. Occasionally he may catch a glimpse of God's lofty purposes. For the rest, man must be content to wait and hope (3:11).

B. Enjoyment of God's Gifts (3:12-13).

Koheleth concluded that man should trust God and "rejoice," i.e., make the best of life such as he finds it. He should resolve to "do good" in his lifetime. This expression is best taken in a moral sense. Virtue is essential to happiness, contentment and peace. This verse does not advocate Epicureanism. The enjoyment alluded to here is not licentiousness, but that happy appreciation of the innocent pleasures which the love of God offers to those who live in accordance with his standards of goodness. Worrying about the future serves no useful purpose. Trying to rectify what is above his power to set right can only serve to embitter a person's life (3:12).

731

Those who do good can "eat and drink," i.e., enjoy life. Such a one can "see good" in his labor, i.e., he can take delight in the material gifts that God permits to pass through his hands. This satisfaction with life is the gift of God to those who make virtue a priority. Godly joy is an outgrowth of godliness, the recognition that every good and perfect gift comes from above (3:13).

3. Contentment within God's Will (3:14-15).

Behind man's free action and volition stands the will of God. "Whatever God does shall remain for ever." His will is immutable. Man can alter nothing of this providential arrangement. He cannot hasten or retard God's designs; he cannot add to nor curtail divine plans. The awareness that God holds the world in his hands creates in man a reverential awe for the righteous government of which he is subject. This is also a ground of hope and confidence amid the sometimes jarring vicissitudes of life (3:14).

A certain orderliness is apparent in God's providential government of the world. "That which is has been already, and that which will be has already been." In 1:9 a similar thought was used to bewail the vanity of life. Here Koheleth argues that the orderly and appointed succession of events is evidence of the moral government of God. From time to time "God seeks what has passed by," i.e., he recalls again into being that which has passed from the scene and disappeared from sight and mind. This is Koheleth's way of saying that history repeats itself, but not randomly. God is sovereign over history (3:15).

THE JUSTICE OF GOD
Ecclesiastes 3:16-22

If God's providence overrules all of man's existence, how can one account for all the wickedness and injustice in the world which oppose all plans for peaceful enjoyment of life? Does not the presence of evil in the world argue against the sovereign rule of God? Koheleth now addresses this issue, especially as it bears on corruption in the courts.

A. The Problem Observed (3:16).

Koheleth records a new and disturbing observation made in everyday life. "The place of judgment" is that place where justice should be administered. Yet on the judicial seat "wickedness" sat enthroned instead of justice. The judge himself should be a righteous, i.e., a fairminded, person; but in "the place of righteousness" that same wickedness had reared its ugly head (3:16).[3] In the verses which follow Koheleth addresses this difficulty in a twofold way.

B. God's Ultimate Judgment (3:17).

The first solution to the problem of judicial injustice is the belief that God will ultimately take matters into his own hands. Faced with widespread corruption in the courts, Koheleth takes comfort in the thought that ultimately the divine judge will mete out retribution to every sinner, and reward those who are innocent. The righteous judge of all the earth shall surely do what is right in that day. His decisions are infallible. Yet his readjustments of the judicial wrongs of earthly courts come only in God's own time and season: "for there will be a time for every purpose and a time for every work."

The doctrine of future judgment offers solace to the believer among the jarring inequities and injustices of life. "There" with God, i.e., in his counsels, or in heaven, there is a time of judgment and retribution for every act of man. "There" at his judgment bar all the anomalies of life will be rectified, injustice will be punished, and virtue rewarded (3:17).

C. God's Preliminary Purpose (3:18-19).

Koheleth now argues that God has a purpose in permitting injustice to exist in this world. God allows events to take place, disorders to continue, for the ultimate profit of men. He does not at once redress grievous wrongs in this world for two reasons.

1. Injustice is a means of testing (3:18a). The problems of life serve as a means of testing or purifying men. The Hebrew uses the infinitive *lebharam* (from *barar*) which means to "separate," to "winnow," to "prove." People are certainly tested when they suffer injustice. What is in the heart quickly is made manifest. Injustices give men the opportunity of making good or bad use of them. While God's forbearance sometimes hardens sinners in impenitence (cf. 8:11), it nourishes the faith of the righteous, and helps them to persevere.

2. *Injustice is a means of humbling (3:18b)*. God tolerates life's injustices "in order that they might see that they themselves are beasts." The text does not say, "as beasts," but uses the stronger expression: "They *are* beasts." Yet this harsh language is immediately qualified by the expression "they themselves," i.e., by themselves, apart from any higher position to which they have been assigned by God. The point is that men are humbled by their inability to straighten out the inequities of life. They learn their powerlessness, if they regard merely their own animal life. Apart from their relation to God and hope of the future, they are no better than the lower creatures.

D. Man's Acknowledged Impotence (3:19-20).

Honesty requires the acknowledgment that there are disorders in the world which men cannot remedy, and which God permits in order to demonstrate that men have no more power over events than do beasts of the earth. In what specific respects are men like beasts?

1. *Their limited control over events (3:19a)*. Life consists, to a very large extent, of events over which beasts have no control and man only limited control. The occurrence of many events is totally unforeseen by man. The Hebrew expresses this thought most forcefully: "For a chance are the sons of men, and a chance are the cattle; and one chance is to them both."[4] The word "chance" (*miqreh*) refers to that which happens to a person. Thus the rendering "fate" (NASB; NIV). The NKJV comes closest to giving the intent of the verse: "For what happens to the sons of men also happens to beasts; one thing befalls them . . . ."

2. *Their manner of death (3:19b)*. Koheleth argues that man is like the beasts in that neither are able to rise above the law that controls their natural life. Both must face death. In the matter of succumbing to the law of death man has no superiority over other creatures. Both beast and man "have all one breath," i.e., both are animated by the breath (*ruach*) which is the gift of God; and death is the withdrawal of that breath. In regard to suffering and death, "man has no preeminence over a beast." The distinction between man and beast is annulled by death. Thus man's superiority, his power of con-

ceiving and planning, his greatness, skill, strength, and wisdom, all come under the category of "vanity," as they cannot ward off the inevitable blow of death. Koheleth has intentionally excluded all consideration of higher values here; he has confined himself to the sphere of the things that are "under the sun" (cf. v. 16). When one leaves out the spiritual dimension, man is absolutely in the same category of the beast as far as death is concerned.

3. *Their physical destiny (3:20)*. Both man and beast "go to the same place." The physical remains of men and beasts decay into the dust. Koheleth is not thinking of Sheol, the abode of departed spirits, but merely regarding earth as the universal tomb of all living creatures. "All are of the dust" and to that dust the material part of all creatures returns (cf. Gen 3:19; Pss 104:29; 146:4). This verse does not deny any of the deeper truths of Scripture concerning the future of man. The following verses indicate that there is a distinction at death in man and beast. The physical destiny of the two, however, should serve to humble any exalted thoughts which man may have about himself.

E. Man's Willful Ignorance (3:21).[5]

Verse 21 is intended to be a corrective to the potential misinterpretation of the preceding verse. The Hebrew text does not support the opinion of most modern commentators that Koheleth is expressing some doubt about a distinction in the destiny of the spirit of man and beast. A literal translation of the text is this: "Who knows the spirit [*ruach*] of the sons of man that goes upward and the spirit [*ruach*] of the beast that goes downward to the earth?" His point is that not many people take to heart as they ought that the destinies of the spirit of man and the spirit of the beast are totally different. In the previous verses Koheleth has demonstrated how far man and beast are alike. Now he produces the ultimate evidence of the fact that man and beast are different. Willfully ignoring the ultimate destiny of the spirit of man dooms one to a futile and fruitless existence in this world. One who has "eternity" in his heart cannot ignore the higher purpose of life and still find satisfaction in this world.

What does Koheleth mean by "upward" and "downward" with respect to the spirit of man and beast? Sheol seems to be regarded as a place of punishment by Israel's wise men. To go "upward" is to escape the shadowy existence in Sheol (Prov 15:24; Ps 49:14f.); it is to be in the presence of the creator. To go "downward" is stipulated to mean "to the earth." The spirit of the beast does not survive death nor escape the earth. It is, as it were, absorbed back into the earth. The spirit of the beast is merely a life force. It is then qualitatively inferior to that of man. The verse is not intended to be a definitive statement of personal eschatology; but it does set forth the ultimate hope of eternal life with the creator (3:21).

F. Conclusion (3:22).

Koheleth brings this discussion of how to find satisfaction in life to a conclusion with an observation and an explanation.

1. His concluding observation (3:22a). The preliminary conclusion of v. 12 is now appropriately reiterated. Man is not master of his own lot. He cannot order events as he would like. He is powerless to control the forces of nature and the providential arrangements of the world. Therefore, man's duty and his happiness consist in enjoying the present, in making the best of life, and availing himself of the bounties which the mercy of God places before him. There is no Epicureanism here, no recommendation of sensual enjoyment; the author simply advises men to make a thankful use of the blessings which God provides for them.

2. His concluding explanation (3:22b). Man must free himself from anxieties and content himself with the performance of present labors. Man must use the present, for he cannot be sure what the future may hold: "for who shall bring him to see what shall occur after him?" The passage does not refer to the uncertainties after death, but to man's future life under the sun (cf. 6:12). Koheleth is exhorting his readers to cease tormenting themselves with hopes and fears, with labors that may be useless and preparations that may never be needed. They cannot foresee the future. For all they know, their worries and labors may be utterly wasted.

The course of the argument since v. 16 runs something like this: There are injustices and anomalies in the life of men and in the course of this world's events which man cannot control or alter; these will be righted and compensated hereafter by God himself. Meanwhile, man's happiness is to make the best of the present, and cheerfully to enjoy what divine providence offers, without anxious care for the future.

ENDNOTES

1. The received text of 2:25 reads literally, "Who makes haste [besides] more than me?" The verb *chush* seems to suggest the enjoyment of the pleasures of life. NASB renders "Who can have enjoyment without Him?" NIV renders "Without him, who can eat or find enjoyment?"

2. In 2:26 the word for "sinners" is a participle which indicates continuous action.

3. This criticism of the judicial apparatus here as well as in 4:1; 5:8; 8:9f. is viewed as decisive evidence against Solomonic authorship of the book. Since the king was the chief judicial officer, Solomon would be criticizing himself. The genius of this book, however, is to view the world as it usually was, not as it was at any given place or time. The fact is that the court system in the ancient world was often corrupt.

4. All the ancient versions preferred to read *miqreh* in 3:19 as a construct rather than an absolute as it appears in the standard Hebrew text. This would read something like this: "For the lot of the children of men and the lot of the beast—one lot is theirs."

5. The comments on 3:21 follow the discussion of H.C. Leupold, *Exposition of Ecclesiastes* (Grand Rapids: Baker, 1966), pp. 97-100.

CHAPTER THIRTY-SIX

More Vanity in the World
Ecclesiastes 4:1-6:9

The theme of the vanity of all things of this world is further developed in chapter 4. This sets the stage for a warning (ch. 5) that believers not permit themselves to become vain in the midst of all this vanity.

VANITY IN EARTHLY ENDEAVOR
Ecclesiastes 4:1-16

Koheleth continues to demonstrate that man cannot be the architect of his own happiness. The happiness the world offers depends on external circumstances. There are several things which can interrupt or destroy that kind of happiness.

A. The Suffering of the Oppressed (4:1-3).

Koheleth returned to his investigation of the vanity of earthly things: "I returned and saw" means "I saw again." The verb "saw" has been used repeatedly to introduce a new phase of Koheleth's subject (cf. 2:9,16). "Under the sun," in this old sinful world, man's inhumanity to his fellow man is a terrible evil.

Koheleth looked first at the "oppressed" (ha'ashuqim).[1] The oppressions no doubt included high-handed injustice, offensive selfishness, and hindrances to one's well-being caused by a neighbor's selfish unconcern for anything except his own interests (cf. Job 35:9; Amos 3:9).

Next Koheleth mentions the effects which the oppression had on the victims: "Behold the tears of such as were oppressed." These words hint at his own sympathy for the victims of oppression. Twice he notes that the victims of oppression "had no comforter." They had no sympathizing friends to soothe their hurt. They had no champion to redress their wrongs. The point is the powerlessness of man in the face of these disorders, his inability to deal with oppressors, the incompetence of others to aid him.

Koheleth noted that on the side of the oppressors there was "power" (koach). The term here seems to be used in a negative sense and is roughly equivalent to "violence." These words are used to impeach Solomonic authorship of the book, since that monarch was noted for "judgment and justice" (1 Kgs 10:9). Such an argument, however, misses the point of wisdom literature which deals with the general human condition, not the specific conditions of a particular time and place (4:1).

As he contemplated the prevalence of oppression, Koheleth lost all enjoyment of life. He did not consider a life filled with oppression and injustice as worth much. He thought that those who had died long ago were to be "praised" or "congratulated" (NASB). They had escaped the miseries which were prevalent in modern society. The living had before them the prospect of a lifetime of oppression and suffering. This is not cynicism but realism. Life "under the sun" is hard. The point is that there are some things worse than death (4:2).

Oppression is so severe that Koheleth regards the unborn as better off than either the dead or the living: "Yet better than both is he who never existed." The unborn are better off because until existence begins one does not have to experience the miseries of life without God, without hope under the sun. Such a one would not have to observe "the evil work which is done under the sun" (4:3).

B. The Pressures on the Successful (4:4-6).

Koheleth next turns to consider another discouraging aspect of labor. He notes that "toil" and "competence" or "skill" are required to achieve anything worthwhile. He envisions a hard worker and one skilled in his craft. Unusual skill and success, however, expose a worker to envy and ill will, which rob labor of all enjoyment. Furthermore, such toil is often the outgrowth of "rivalry," i.e., the desire to be distinguished above others by such a piece of work. If the motive be tainted, how can that which results from the effort be satisfying? Thus success itself is no guarantee of happiness; the malice and ill feeling which it invariably occasions are necessarily a source of pain and distress. All things that men admire in human achievements are in reality displays of human selfishness. Koheleth would call such effort "vanity and striving after wind" (4:4).

Because diligent labor often destroys social relationships, should one become apathetic in his labor? No, says Koheleth. None but a fool (*kesil*) would do this. This man is the exact opposite of the zealous craftsman of the preceding verse. He "folds his hands together" in a gesture of laziness and disinterest in active labor (cf. Prov 6:10). The fool "eats his own flesh," i.e., he destroys himself (cf. Ps 27:2; Micah 3:3). The sluggard commits, as it were, moral suicide. He makes no effort to provide for his daily needs, and suffers extremities in consequence. He has no achievements on his record. He is completely noncompetitive (4:5).

The fool defends his lethargy with a clever proverb: "Better a handful of quietness, than two hands full of travail." He argues that at least he experiences a measure of peaceful rest. He would rather have his ease and possess but little than acquire more things with all the attendant vexation (4:6).

C. The Loneliness of the Wealthy (4:7-12).

Verse 7 begins with the customary formula: "Then I returned and I saw," i.e., "I again saw." Another subject is taken up. Most people view riches as the end all and be all of life. Not Koheleth. Those who are wealthy crave more wealth. Their striving for increased affluence— avarice—also is attended by negative consequences which Koheleth labels as "vanity under the sun" (4:7).

741

Wealth is supposed to bring happiness and make friends, such as they are; but miserliness and greed separate a man from his fellows, make him suspicious of everyone, and drive him to live alone: "There is one alone without a second." He has neither child nor brother with whom to enjoy his wealth, or for whom to save and amass riches. He has no real friends. If one allows material advantage to isolate him from friend and relative then truly it must be a sorry thing to acquire wealth.

In spite of this loneliness and isolation this miser continues to push himself to hoard more wealth. "Neither is his eye satisfied with riches," i.e., he is never content with what he has. He always wants more.

At some point the miser must wonder within himself: "For whom am I toiling?" He realizes that no one is profiting from that which he has acquired through such painful efforts. On the other hand, he himself is practicing self-denial so that he is depriving himself of "good," i.e., pleasure or the enjoyment which wealth might afford. The miser will not share with others; yet he himself can find no enjoyment since his eyes can never be satisfied. The miserly acquisition of wealth must then be considered "vanity;" it is "sore travail," i.e., a sad business (4:8).

Koheleth next places in juxtaposition the evils of isolation and the comforts of companionship. "Better the two than the one," i.e., the two and the one mentioned in the preceding verse. The reason this is true is "because they have a good reward for their labor." Their joint efforts have greater effect than the efforts of a solitary worker. Such "reward" as men have "for their toil" is in a large measure denied the man 'that stands alone. Companionship is at once helpful, profitable, and enjoyable (4:9).

Koheleth defends his assertion about the benefits of companionship with some illustrations. First, he alludes to the aid and support which companionship affords: "For if they fall, the one will lift up his companion." The picture here is of two travelers making their way over rough terrain. Should one experience trouble, the other is there to help. On the other hand, "woe to him that is alone." The word "woe" connotes sorrow. It is sad to see someone trying to make it on his own. The principle set forth in this verse could refer to moral as well as physical falls. Many have fallen into sin who would have manfully withstood temptation if they had experienced the support of others (4:10).

Second, he mentions the comfort of companionship: "If two lie together, then they have heat." Winter nights in Palestine can be very cold. The only blanket possessed by many was the outer garment worn by day. It was a comfort to have the additional warmth of a friend lying under the same blanket (4:11).

Third, companionship offers the value of protection in dangerous circumstances: "If a man overpowers the solitary one, the two will withstand him." Here the traveler is accosted by robbers. If he were alone, he would easily be overpowered by them. Two comrades, however, might be successful in repelling the assault. If the companionship of two is advantageous, much more is this the case when more combine. "A threefold cord is not quickly broken." A cord of three strands was the strongest made in the ancient world. Three is the number of completeness and perfection (4:12).

D. The Insecurity of High Position (4:13-16).

High position offers no assurance of security. It affords no satisfaction to those who make it the chief object of their life. "Better is a poor and wise youth than an old and foolish king who does not know how to receive admonition any more." Though he was once open to advice and hearkened to reproof, the old king has fossilized his self-will and obstinacy. He now will brook no contradiction. He regards himself as the sole repository of wisdom. Such a ruler was in grave danger from some ambitious youth who may have arisen from lowly origins (4:13).

The youth "goes out of the house of prisoners to reign, though even in his kingdom he was born poor." The point of the verse is the insecurity of the king. His throne might be taken from him by the most unlikely challenger. The longer one has held a position of power, the greater the disappointment when the inevitable fall from power occurs. Often men cling to leadership positions long after their effectiveness has eroded. Their selfishness sometimes forces those who once loved and admired them to take drastic action to remove them from office (4:14).

Koheleth noted that the population quickly rallied to the support of the youthful usurper. "All the living which walk under the sun" is hyperbolic for the entire population of the realm. He noted "that they were with the youth, the second, that stood up in his stead." The youth who is called "the second" is the youth who was spoken of in the preceding verses. He is raised to high office while the old king is dethroned and humiliated. The youth is designated as the "second" because he was the successor of the old king. He was the man of the hour (4:15).

Throngs flock about the new young king: "Numberless were the people, all, at whose head he stood." The masses have a new favorite. Those who entirely pin their hopes on the new king are persons "under the sun," i.e., those who do not recognize the higher values in life.

The popularity of the new king was not lasting and his influence was not permanent: "They also that come after shall not rejoice in him." A new generation will treat this king as the previous generation had treated the old king. The implication is that the new administration did no more for the people than the old had done. Surely the fickleness of citizens and the perpetual failure of their leaders "is vanity and vexation of spirit" (4:16).

VANITY IN WORLDLY WORSHIP
Ecclesiastes 5:1-9

Koheleth has demonstrated that man's outward and secular life is unable to secure happiness and satisfaction. What about popular religion? Can religious exercises bring the joy which the human spirit craves? He now has four admonitions for his readers.

A. Admonition Regarding Reverence (5:1).
The unit begins with a warning: "Keep your foot when you go to the house of God." From this it would appear that temple attendance was being strictly observed. Unfortunately regularity of worship does not always mean sincerity in worship. For hypocrites and formalists the road to God's house is like a rocky road that might cause men to fall. To "keep the foot" is equivalent to the modern "Watch your

step!" Worshipers must be careful of their conduct; they must remember where they are going. The "house of God" is the Jerusalem temple. The text certainly encourages reverence with respect to buildings dedicated to the service of God.

The second principle of reverence is this: "To approach in order to hear is better than to give the sacrifice of fools." The same thought appears throughout the Old Testament (e.g., 1 Sam 15:22). Where God's word is read and explained it is to be heard and obeyed. Drawing near to hear implies being "ready to hear," i.e., eager to hear. Such an attitude is the exact opposite of formalistic rituals which are often substituted for obedience to God's word.

Sacrifice offered by a godless man is called "the sacrifice of fools." Individuals who sink to the level of religious formalism are acting like "fools" (kesilim), i.e., stupid fellows. Such worshipers think that they are doing good and pleasing God. In reality they "know not so that they do evil," i.e., their ignorance predisposes them to err in this matter of sacrifice. They do not know how to worship God properly. They intend to please him by formal acts of devotion. These formalists fall into grievous sin. God prefers worshipers to "hear" (with a view to obeying) his law rather than to indulge in empty ritualism. The text suggests that the reading of the law was part of temple worship in the days of Koheleth (5:1).[2]

B. Admonition Regarding Prayer (5:2-3).

In respect to prayer, Koheleth admonishes: "Do not be rash with your words." The warning is against hasty and thoughtless words in prayer, words which go forth from the lips but not from the heart. Vain repetition may be one manifestation of insincere prayer. Hypocrites sense the emptiness of their prayers. They seek to make up for the deficiency in the quality of their prayer life with the quantity. In the preceding paragraph, Koheleth gave warning to guard the foot; now he urges his readers to be careful about their mouth.

On the other hand, prayer may come from the heart, but still be inappropriate. Prayers can be sinful or selfish. Koheleth urges: "Let not your heart be hasty to utter a word before God." The singular "word" makes the warning as strong as possible. One must be careful about bringing even one word before the Lord. The petitioner should weigh his wishes and ponder whether they are worthy of petition. This admonition is grounded in the nature of God: "God is in heaven, and you are on earth." The infinite distance between the holy God and sinful man is thus indicated. His exalted position demands the deepest reverence. "Therefore, let your words be few" as becomes one who speaks in the presence of the king of kings. Presumptuous chatter shows disrespect for his majesty (5:2).

The theme of babbling in prayer is further developed. "For a dream comes through the multitude of business." Cares and anxieties in business or other matters occasion disturbed sleep and produce all kinds of improper fancies and imaginations. "And the voice of a fool [comes] in consequence of many words." The thought is that as surely as excess of business produces fevered dreams, so excess of words, especially in addresses to God, eventually produces foolish speech (5:3).

C. Admonition Regarding Vows (5:4-7).

Vows were not a major component of Israelite worship. They were never commanded. Decadent religion majors in minors. Apparently vows had become very important in the religion of the day. Unfortunately they were the occasion of much irreverence and profanity. They were being rashly made, and rashly broken.

The general advice set forth by Koheleth is this: "When you make a vow unto God, defer not to pay it" (cf. Deut 23:21-23). Vows were voluntary, but once made they were to be strictly performed. A vow might dedicate certain objects or even persons to the Lord (cf. Gen 28:20); or the vow might be an act of self-denial as in the Nazirite vow.

Vows should be fulfilled because "there is no pleasure in fools." Neither God nor man has any delight in men who make solemn promises but never fulfill them. Failing to fulfill a vow would prove a person to be impious or "a fool." As such, God would regard him with displeasure. Therefore, Koheleth exhorts his readers: "Pay that which you have vowed" (5:4).

To be on the safe side, one might refrain from making vows. "Better is it that you should not vow, than that you vow and not pay" (5:5). Once made a vow partakes of the nature of an oath, and its nonperformance is a sin and sacrilege. A broken vow incurs the same punishment as false swearing.

Koheleth goes on: "Do not permit your mouth to cause your flesh to be guilty." The "flesh" here is equivalent to the whole person. A person might attempt to cover the deficiency of an unfulfilled vow by offering a sacrifice. The ploy would not work. By avoiding the fulfillment of rash or inconsiderate vows a person brings "guilt" upon himself. The necessary outcome of guilt is "punishment" and some prefer to translate the term *lechati'* in this manner here.

"Neither say before the angel, that it was an error," i.e., the rash vow was a mistake. Who is the angel? Probably the priest[3] who is called the "angel" = "messenger" of God in Mal 2:7f. No evidence exists that any temple officer had the authority to release one from the obligation of a vow. What the negligent worshiper hopes is that the priest will offer on his behalf a "trespass" or "error" offering. He confidently approaches the priest and explains: "It was an error (*sheghaghah*) that I made this vow." Trifling with vows in this way angers God. Koheleth assures the hypocrite that God would "destroy the work of your hands." The faithless worshiper would be visited with calamity in his life. Anything he attempted would be rendered unsuccessful. God cannot bless the life of one who flippantly tries to dispose of religious obligations (5:6).

Koheleth sums up his teaching regarding popular religion with these words: "In the multitude of dreams are also vanities, and [in] many words [as well]." The religion that emphasizes dreams, verbosity and vows is vanity; it has in it nothing substantial and comforting. The superstitious person who puts his faith in dreams is impractical; the garrulous person who makes rash vows and thinks his prayers will be heard because of much speaking displeases God and incurs his wrath.

The antidote to religious formalism and hypocrisy is found in setting oneself squarely in the right relationship with God. Koheleth calls his readers to the old paths: "But fear God." The name *'Elohim* stresses the power and magnificence of the Lord. The creature must always display proper reverence for the creator. A God-fearing person performs vows, relies on written revelation rather than dreams, and worships God from the heart in humble submission (5:7).

D. Admonition Regarding Faith (5:8-9).

Injustice and oppression can cause believers to become discouraged and even to surrender their faith. Koheleth envisions a situation in which a believer sees "the oppression of the poor." That is common enough, for the poor man being devoid of resources is helpless to defend himself from those who would prey upon him. The believer sees the violent "perversion [lit., robbery] of justice and righteousness." "Justice" refers to just decision by those in judicial authority. "Righteousness" is a personal quality of fairness. Both are hard to find in dark days.

Such social breakdown was especially obvious "in the province." Perhaps Koheleth means to suggest that in areas more remote from the central authority unscrupulous rulers would ruthlessly govern the people. "Marvel not at the matter," i.e., do not be surprised or dismayed at such evil doings. The existence of such conduct might cause one to question the moral government of God.

Why should the observer not marvel over the corruption and oppression at the local level? Because "a high official watches over a high official." The verb "watches" (*shamar*) means to observe in a hostile sense, to watch for occasions of reprisal (cf. 1 Sam 19:11). The idea is that in the province there were endless plottings and counterplottings, mutual denunciations and recriminations. The entire system was rotten. Those very officials who mistreat the common man are themselves mistreated by their superiors. There is some consolation in this thought. But there is more: "The highest one [plural of majesty] is over them." Over the highest of earthly rulers is God himself who governs the course of this world.[4] To him man can leave the final adjustment of all that is crooked in this world (5:8).

That God is watching over all officials is an "advantage" or "profit" in every way in the land: "It is an advantage for a land on the whole that there is a king over the cultivated field." That "king" is the Lord God. Wherever men labor to grow their crops, the best advantage of all is that there is one supreme ruler over all.[5] To him all the corrupt officials at any level must ultimately give account (5:9).

VANITY IN WORLDLY WEALTH
Ecclesiastes 5:10-20

The acts of injustice and oppression mentioned in the preceding unit spring from the craving after wealth. Koheleth now addresses the evils that accompany the pursuit and possession of wealth which, in his opinion, gives no real satisfaction. He has addressed this subject before. He does so again because (1) there are so many aspects of wealth; and (2) because wealth is especially seductive and many are entangled in its allurements.

A. Riches Cannot Satisfy (5:10-12).

Koheleth begins with an observation which one can duplicate in almost any culture: "He who loves silver shall not be satisfied with silver." One who devotes his life to gathering riches is here designated as a "lover" of them. In this context "silver" is the generic name for money or wealth. The more one has, the more one craves (5:10).

The increase of wealth can be a great inconvenience. "When goods increase, they are increased that eat them." The more riches a man possesses, the greater are the claims upon him. He increases his household, retainers, and dependents, and is really none the better off for all his wealth. The only pleasure which amassed wealth afforded the owner was that of gazing upon it. "What good is there to the owners thereof, except the beholding of it with the eyes?" What a hollow accomplishment is this! (5:11).

Great wealth also tends to rob one of sleep. "The sleep of a laboring man is sweet, whether he eats little or much." Such a person earns and enjoys his night's rest. "But the abundance of the rich will not permit him to sleep." The allusion is not to overeating which may occasion sleeplessness, but to the cares and anxieties which wealth brings. Poets of many cultures have developed the theme of the grateful sleep of the tired worker and the disturbed rest of the greedy (5:12).

B. Riches Can Be Harmful (5:13-17).

The person who strives after wealth considers it good. Not so, says Koheleth. The hoarding of riches is a "grievous evil" which he had seen "under the sun." Riches are preserved by the possessors thereof "to their hurt." Such riches only bring added grief to the miserly owner (5:13).

Riches often "perish through misfortune." The reference could be to bad business investments, natural disasters, robbery or lawsuit. Koheleth imagines that this once wealthy man had fathered a son. After his financial loss, the father has nothing to leave his son. He [the son] has "nothing in his hand," i.e., he has no possessions under his control. The son is left a pauper. Better never to have had wealth, than once having had it to lose it, for the loss of it brings much distress and disappointment which otherwise would never have been experienced (5:14).

Riches can never be a permanent possession. In one sense all rich men die poor for they must leave their wealth behind. "As he came forth of his mother's womb, naked shall he return to go as he came" (cf. Job 1:21). "He shall take nothing from his labor which he may carry away in his hand." He gets nothing for his long toil in amassing wealth (5:15).

Koheleth repeats the thought of v. 15: "This also is a grievous evil, that exactly as he came, so shall he go." He came into the world naked and helpless; he leaves in the same condition (cf. 1 Tim 6:7). "And what profit has he who has labored for the wind?" The answer is emphatically, None! To labor for the wind is to toil with no result, like "feeding on the wind." The wind is the figure of all that is empty, delusive, unsubstantial (5:16).

The misery that accompanies the loss of earthly fortune is summarized in these words: "All his days also he eats in darkness." Perhaps the meagerness of his present meals is a painful reminder of the days when he fared sumptuously. The idea is that he spends his days in gloom and cheerlessness. He also experiences "much vexation, and sickness, and wrath." The person experiences all kinds of vexation when his plans fail or involve him in trouble and privation. He may become morbid and diseased in mind and body. He is filled with anger when others succeed better than himself (cf. 1 Tim 6:9). The anger may be directed against himself as he thinks of his folly in taking on all this trouble for nothing; or it may be directed against those who are perceived to have cheated him out of his wealth; or it may be directed against God himself for allowing him to fall from such a pinnacle (5:17).

C. Riches Can Be Enjoyed (5:18-20).

The inconveniences of wealth bring Koheleth back to his old conclusion. In the light of the forgoing critique of the inadequacies of wealth his conclusion is somewhat shocking, so he introduces it with "Behold!" He describes the course he is about to recommend as "good," i.e., morally unobjectionable, and "a very fine thing" (*yapheh*, lit., beautiful), i.e., a wise path to follow.

So what is this counsel of Koheleth? He urges people to "eat and drink," i.e., to enjoy life; to use the common blessings which God bestows on mankind with thankfulness and contentment (cf. 1 Tim 6:8). People should make the best of life, and enjoy all the good things that God gives them. Furthermore he urges his reader "to enjoy the good of all his labor in which he toils under the sun." Yes, labor is toilsome "under the sun." That is the down side. But there is an up side to earthly toil. Inherent in labor are pleasant features and rewards, and especially when one sees labor as part of a God ordained scheme.

Man engages in labor, but it is the Lord who gives the increase. Both the labor itself and that which is produced by that labor are gifts of God. Temporal blessings should never be considered a natural and assured result of man's own strivings. The calm enjoyment of life is allotted to man by God: "For it is his portion." Nothing more should be expected. The point is: one should not attempt to squeeze out of labor and wealth more than either is capable of delivering (5:18).

Building on the thought of v. 18, Koheleth now stresses that, not only the riches, but the enjoyment of such is the gift of God. The term "riches" ('*osher*) is a general term for wealth of any kind; the term "wealth" (*nekhasim*) refers specifically to wealth in cattle. Not only does God supply the gifts, he also gives "the power to eat thereof." Abundance is useless without the power to enjoy it. Those who have accumulated wealth are too often the slaves of their own possessions. Only God can liberate the soul from such slavery and enable one truly to enjoy his wealth: "This is the gift of God." For all the bounty of life God is to receive the praise (5:19).

The person who has learned the lesson of calm enjoyment of material things does not much concern himself with the shortness, uncertainty, or possible trouble of life: "For he shall not much remember the days of his life" (cf. Matt 6:34). He is not inclined to anxiety "because God answers him in the joy of his heart." He experiences contentment because the tranquil joy shed abroad in his heart makes him realize that God is pleased with his life (5:20).

OTHER VANITIES ASSOCIATED WITH WEALTH
Ecclesiastes 6:1-9

In the previous chapter Koheleth set forth some of failings of wealth. He closed the chapter with some positive observations regarding the enjoyment of wealth. Now Koheleth further amplifies the subject of the failures of wealth.

A. Wealth and Happiness (6:1-6).

Koheleth begins with his personal experience, that which has fallen under his own observation (cf. 5:13; 10:5). What he has observed "is great," i.e., lies heavy, "upon men." Basically the expression refers to what is common or prevalent in society. The phrase "under the sun" is inserted to keep the orientation of the passage before the reader. Only a person who makes money his god can have the experience about to be described (6:1).

1. A rich man with no enjoyment (6:2a). The case presented is that of a person who is able to procure for himself great substance. His " riches" and "wealth" are a gift from God, for in no case is the acquisition of wealth merely an outright achievement of man. A person can acquire nothing unless God permits him to do so. Besides this wealth, this person has "honor," i.e., a good reputation.

To this individual "there is not lacking to his soul anything that he desires." He has it all! The Hebrew participle indicates that this is the usual state of affairs in his life. He never lacks for anything. Something, however, is still lacking. "God does not give him the power to eat thereof," i.e., he cannot really enjoy that which he has, he cannot take advantage of it, he cannot make proper use of it. He only knows the struggle of acquisition. The ability to enjoy good things is lacking here, possibly because of discontent, or sickness, or punishment of secret sin.

2. *A rich man without an heir (6:2b).* Before this rich man learns to enjoy his wealth, a calamity strikes. "A stranger eats it," i.e., acquires and makes use of his wealth. The term "stranger" (*nokhri*) usually refers to a foreigner. Obviously this "stranger" is not the legal heir; he is neither relative nor friend. That one cannot enjoy his wealth is said to be "vanity." That he must then surrender that wealth, probably because of war, to a total stranger is said to be a "grievous disease," i.e., as painful as the worst disease (6:2).

3. *A rich man without a tomb (6:3-5).* Koheleth envisions now a wealthy man who has a large family. The term "hundred" is obviously an exaggeration meaning "many," although some kings came close to having a hundred children.[6] Those who fathered large families in ancient society were considered extremely blessed. This fellow also lived "many years, so that the days of his years be many." Long life was also deemed a special blessing (cf. Exod 20:12). Yet though he had the external blessings, "his soul is not filled with good," i.e., he does not satisfy himself with the enjoyment of all the good things which he possesses.

This rich man's miserable life is followed by an even more miserable death. When he dies, "he has no burial." No doubt Koheleth is here depicting the result of war. The corpse of the once rich man would then be left for bird and beast to devour (cf. 1 Sam 17:46). To be left unburied after death was considered the worst fate which could befall a person. In Koheleth's opinion "an untimely birth," i.e., a fetus expelled before its time through miscarriage, was better off than one who experienced such misery (cf. Job 3:16; Ps 58:8). Such is the value of a life without God, however rich in worldly goods. While it is true that this fetus had missed the pleasures of life, he had also escaped the miseries just outlined in the preceding verses. On this point the following verses elaborate (6:3).

The miscarried fetus "comes in vanity," i.e., the baby was not capable of independent life or being. This miscarried fetus "goes in darkness," i.e., the remains are taken away and put out of sight. That miscarried fetus "shall be covered with darkness," i.e., his name would be unrecorded and therefore unremembered (6:4).

The dead infant has two advantages over the troubled rich man. First, "he has not seen the sun," i.e., he has seen nothing of life. The metaphor implies activity and work, the contrary of rest. Second, that baby has "known nothing" of life with its joys and sorrows. Third, the infant has rest: "There is rest to this more than to that." The word "rest" sums up what the ancients deemed as the most desirable thing, i.e., a life free of cares and concerns. Even leisure and sleep are troubled times for the rich man (6:5).

4. A rich man without hope (6:6). Would not the long life of the hypothetical rich man be superior to the nonexistence of the miscarried fetus? No! What Koheleth says about the rich man would still be true even if he were to live to be two thousand years old. Even in the longest possible life that man would see no "good," i.e., the enjoyment of life mentioned in v. 3. The verb "see" suggests that Koheleth is envisioning a person whose life is totally devoid of any happiness. The miscarried fetus is better off than he.

In the end "all go to one place," i.e., to Sheol, the abode of the dead. The miscarried fetus and the rich man wind up in Sheol. The point of this passage is not to speak to the whereabouts of people after death, or their rewards or punishments. The point is that in Sheol no one has anything of this world's goods. No one there can make up for missed opportunities. The hypothetical rich man experienced no good in life, and in Sheol he will have no opportunity to make up for this loss.

If a long life were spent in calm enjoyment, it might be preferable to a short one; but when it is passed amid care and annoyance and discontent, it is no better than that which begins and ends in nothingness. Sheol receives both, and there is nothing to distinguish between them there. Koheleth here is viewing life as the troubled rich man might view it. At this point he is not bringing to bear any higher values (6:6).

B. Wealth and Man's Desire (6:7-9).

Koheleth continues to deal with the matter of riches and their vanity. Within the human psyche is a fatal flaw which makes satisfaction utterly impossible without, of course, divine assistance. "All the labor of mankind is for his mouth." The natural man's labor is for his mouth, i.e., for self-preservation and enjoyment. Eating and drinking are regarded here as a figure for the proper use of earthly blessings (cf. 2:24; 3:13). Yet strive as he may, "the appetite [lit., soul] is not filled." The desires of the heart are never satisfied (cf. 1:8). Morbid insatiability possesses the soul of man. He is always striving after enjoyment, but he never gains his wish completely.

Here is a hint of what ethicists call the "hedonistic paradox." The more people pursue pleasure, the more elusive the goal becomes. Yet something within drives worldly man to continue the fruitless and draining effort to achieve satisfaction. With each new disappointment he mutters to himself, "There must be more to life than this!" He tries multiple sex partners, and the latest drugs. He accumulates more of the toys and trinkets which he thinks will quell the gnawing hunger of his soul. Nothing works. Without God his life is completely empty. He must learn through revelation that "he who finds his life shall lose it, and he who loses his life for my sake shall find it" (6:7; Matt 10:39).

Does wisdom make a difference in the equation? (cf. 2:15f.). He speaks, of course of worldly wisdom, and that kind of wisdom does nothing to quiet the restless spirit. "For what does the wise one have more than the fool?" i.e., what advantage does the wise man have over the fool. Both must labor for bodily sustenance. The same unsatisfied desires belong to both wise and foolish. In this respect intellectual gifts have no superiority.

Does a prudent poor man have any advantage in respect to desire than a fool? Koheleth speaks of a poor man who knows "how to walk before the living." The "living" signifies people in general (cf. 4:15). The expression "knowing how to walk" means to understand and to follow the correct path of life; to know how to behave properly and uprightly in his social relationships. The poor man, in his poverty, has learned to accommodate himself to his circumstances and to make the best of his lot. The fool, on the other hand, is afflicted by an insatiable hunger for more than he has. Nevertheless, the poor man and the fool are similar in that they both lead cheerless lives because their appetites remain unsatisfied.

The contrast here is between the rich wise man and the prudent poor man. Koheleth argues that both fail at enjoying life, because their desires are insatiable. What is true of these two extremes of the social spectrum is also true of all who fall in between (6:8).

Koheleth has a word of wisdom for all the sons of men. "Better is the sight of the eyes than the wandering of the desire." The "sight of the eyes" means the enjoyment of the present, that which lies before one. The "wandering of the desire" (lit., the soul) refers to the restless craving for what is distant, uncertain and out of reach. Koheleth encourages his readers to make the most of existing opportunities, to enjoy the present (6:9).

ENDNOTES

1. The form is a *qal* masculine passive participle. Thus the word is inappropriately rendered "acts of oppression" in NASB and "oppression" in NIV.

2. Some have called attention to the verb "give" in reference to sacrifice in 5:1. The verb is not the usual expression for offering sacrifice. It may possibly refer to the feast which accompanied such sacrifices and which may have frequently degenerated into excess.

3. Another view of 5:6 is this: The angel is that angel of Yahweh, that divine personage, who watched over all the affairs of Israel.

4. A more common understanding is that this last phrase should be rendered: "there are higher officials over them" (NASB; and essentially NIV and NKJV). The point would then be that the government was corrupt from bottom to top.

5. Another view is that 5:9 is praising a king who devotes himself to agriculture.

6. Ahab had seventy sons (2 Kgs 10:1), and Rehoboam had 88 children (2 Chr 11:21).

CHAPTER THIRTY-SEVEN

Counsel for Troubled Times
Ecclesiastes 6:10-8:17

The second main division of Ecclesiastes begins in 6:10. In the second half of the book Koheleth makes deductions based on the experiences set forth in the earlier chapters. These logical deductions are interspersed with warnings and rules for daily living. This half of the book is introduced by three verses which outline the issues to be discussed in the remaining chapters.

INTRODUCTION
Ecclesiastes 6:10-12

The true nature of man was revealed in the name given to him long ago: "Whatever a *man* may be, his name was given long ago." Everyone knows what that name is. In the beginning God called him "man" (*ha-'adham*). According to Gen 2:7, this name he received because he was taken from the earth (*ha'adhamah*). Man's name puts him in his proper place. What humble origins he has. What a puny creature he is.

Man therefore cannot "contend with him that is mightier than he," i.e., with God. It is useless for feeble man to rebel against his circumstances in life. The clay cannot criticize the potter for the way it is shaped. God has supreme control of things. He is the one who exalts or brings down men. If he has not willed to give riches to a man, then that man labors in vain to achieve wealth (6:10; cf. Isa 45:9).

A. Man's Ignorance Regarding Conduct (6:11).

The rebellion against God's providence often takes the form of "words" (*debharim*)[1] of impatience, doubt and unbelief. Such words "increase vanity," i.e., they only increase the perplexity in which all men are involved. "What is the advantage to a man" to engage in such undisciplined and irreverent talk? (6:11).

Such discussions about the human predicament are profitless because man does not know what is in his best interest: "For who knows what is good for man in this life?" Man cannot see beyond the bend in life's road; he cannot reliably forecast outcomes. He must therefore experience a certain amount of perplexity "during the number of the days of the life of his vanity." Such a life is one that yields no good result. It is full of empty aims, unsatisfied wishes, unfulfilled purposes.

Part of the reason man's life is so vain is because it is so short: "And he passes them [his days] as a shadow." It is the man who is here compared to the shadow, not his life. The point is that he soon passes away, and leaves no trace behind him (cf. James 4:14). Verse 11 sets forth the conclusion which is developed in 7:1–8:17, namely, *Man cannot know what is good for him to do.*

B. Man's Ignorance Regarding the Future (6:12).

Another reason man's life is so vain is because of the uncertainties of what will happen in the future: "Who can tell a man what shall be after him under the sun?" This does not refer to the life beyond the grave, but to the future in the present world, as is indicated by the expression "under the sun." To properly order his present life, a man needs to know what is to be after him. Who will be his heir to inherit his property? What kind of person will he be? Will he have children to carry on his name? Yet the answers to all of these questions, and others like them, are hidden from his view. Man's duty and happiness, therefore, are to acquiesce in the divine government. Then he can enjoy with moderation the goods of life, and the modest satisfaction which is accorded to him by the goodness of God (6:12). Here then is the conclusion to be addressed in 9:1-11:6, namely, *Man cannot know what will come after him.*

THE VALUE OF SERIOUSNESS
Ecclesiastes 7:1-7

The final verse of chapter 6 stated that no man knows for certain what is best. Yet there are some practical rules for the conduct of life which godly wisdom gives. Some of these Koheleth now sets forth in proverbial form. He first commends a serious, earnest life in preference to one of gaiety and frivolity.

A. The Value of a Good Name (7:1).

"Better is a name than good oil." The Hebrew has a paronomasia not observable in the English. The term "name" (*shem*) otherwise unqualified is sometimes used to signify a celebrated name, a good name, a good reputation. After describing all else as "vanity" Koheleth discovers one aim to be worthwhile, namely, to have the esteem of one's fellows.

That good name is compared to fragrant (lit., good) oil which was very precious in the ancient world. Perfumed oil was profusely employed to overcome the odor of perspiration. It was considered a great luxury. Such oil was abundantly dispensed at feasts and other joyous occasions (cf. Amos 6:6). A man's most cherished ambition was to leave a good reputation, and hand down to future generations an honorable remembrance.

For one who has so lived that he gained for himself a good name, the day of death is more desirable than the day of birth. For him death means the victorious end of the adventure which is life. He is in a better state than at the time of his birth when he started out on his adventure not knowing what would be in store for him. At birth the man had nothing before him but labor, trouble and uncertainty. In death, however, the anxieties are past, the storms are all over. As far as earthly values are concerned, death confers a benefit on those who suffer by releasing them from their misery. When a believer dies, all should rejoice that he reached his haven with a good name and in peace (7:1).

In what sense and to what limited degree is the day of death better than the day of birth? The proper limitation of the general statement of v. 1 is now stated, namely, death is a powerful teacher. In this one particular respect there is an advantage in death.

B. The Value of Mourning (7:2-4).

"Better to go to the house of mourning, than to go to the house of feasting." Koheleth is recommending the sober, earnest life. Wiser, more enduring lessons can be learned where grief reigns than in the empty and momentary excitement of mirth and frivolity. The "house of mourning" is one in which a death is being mourned. The practice among Jews, to observe mourning for seven days after the burial of a near relative, dates from early times (cf. Gen 50:10). Visits of condolence and periodical pilgrimages to graves of departed relatives were considered meritorious acts. On the other hand, "the house of feasting [lit., drinking]," where all that is serious is put aside, offers no opportunity for wise teaching. Such occasions, if anything, contribute only to selfishness, heartlessness, and thoughtlessness. Revelry never actually betters a person.

This proverb in no way contradicts what Koheleth said in 2:24, that a man should eat and drink and enjoy himself. In the earlier passage Koheleth was not speaking of unrestrained sensualism, but of the moderate enjoyment of the good things of life circumscribed by the fear of God. Here the "house of feasting" is one where reckless frivolity is the order of the day.

Why is the visit to the house of mourning more beneficial? Because there one will give serious consideration to this solemn truth: "that is the end of all men." Life will end. One day the visitors will be mourned, and their houses will be turned into houses of mourning. "The living will lay it to his heart." One who has witnessed the scene in the house of mourning will consider it seriously. He will draw from that experience proper conclusions concerning the brevity of life and the necessity of redeeming the time (7:2).

The previous thought is now further expanded: "Thoughtful vexation (ka'as) is better than laughter." The "vexation" caused by the visit to the house of mourning may refer to one's personal displeasure over sin in his own life; his recollection of wasted opportunities for betterment. Godly sorrow can lead to life-changing repentance (2 Cor 7:10). This is more wholesome and elevating than thoughtless mirth. "Laughter" here indicates a frivolous frame of mind. His point is that only when one is in a serious mood does he feel disposed to think seriously about life.

Why is this so? "For by the sadness of the countenance the heart is made better." A brooding mind is reflected in a troubled look. That feeling which is reflected in the face and demeanor has a purifying effect upon the heart. The expression "the heart is made better" or improved in this context has a moral connotation; confronting death helps to shape character (7:3).

The superiority of the house of mourning over the house of mirth reaches its climax in v. 4. "The heart of the wise is in the house of mourning." Their thoughts are upon the day of death. Their mind is attuned to the seriousness which is natural in a house of bereavement and it influences their way of living. On the other hand, "the heart of fools is in the house of mirth." The fool is one who thinks only of the present; he lives for the hour. He shuns places of sadness and death, because they contradict his lifestyle. Such a one is concerned only about getting all the gusto he can out of every day.

The term "heart" here suggests that the choice of houses—mourning or mirth—is prompted by one's inmost being. People "hang out" where they prefer, and what one prefers indicates his character. The wisdom of the wise is revealed by their vexation over sin as occasioned by consideration of death; folly manifests itself in the lifestyle of the party animal (7:4).

Here it becomes clear what Koheleth means when elsewhere he exhorts his readers to enjoy life. Those exhortations never mean that one should give himself over to a boisterous revelry and undisciplined indulgence. Koheleth's idea of enjoying life is a grateful use of all the good things with which God has blessed one's life. This kind of enjoyment is possible only when one squarely faces death and his personal accountability before God.

C. The Value of Rebuke (7:5-7).

Koheleth has just alluded to the silent reproof which contact with death administers to a wise person. Now he moves on to consider a more direct form of reproof.

Solemn rebuke is not pleasant. No one likes to hear it. Yet Koheleth argues that "it is better to hear the rebuke of the wise than for a man to hear the song of fools." A wise man is one who is at home in divine revelation. Many beneficial effects may be gained by listening to a sage's admonition. The prophets of the Old Testament dispensation would be an illustration of the "wise." Those who have been sobered and softened by the confrontation with death and its implications are ready to receive the seed of the word of God.

The word "rebuke" (ge'arah) is the same word used in Proverbs (13:1; 17:10) for that grave admonition which heals and strengthens even while it wounds. The wise man knows how and when to admonish to secure the most positive results.

Some might try to drown out the voice of reason and revelation with loud and loose music. The "song of fools" probably refers to the boisterous, reckless, often immodest drinking songs heard in the house of revelry (cf. Amos 6:5). Ungodly music does not edify. At the least such music distracts from sound teaching; in the extreme it subverts the mind and blinds the eyes to the truth (7:5).

The song of fools cannot profit "for like the noise of the nettles under the kettles, so is the laughter of the fool." This translation preserves the word play of the Hebrew. In that region where wood was scarce, thorns, hay and stubble were used for fuel. Such materials are quickly kindled, blaze up for a time with much noise, and soon die away. The song of fools is like that. It is loud, but of short duration and small results. The fool's mirth comes to a speedy end, and is spent to no good purpose. It is therefore "vanity" (7:6).

How does a person become foolish? The song and laughter of fools, i.e., evildoers, lead to selfish luxury, and eventually to all forms of unjust gains. Koheleth wraps up this phase of his discussion by mention of two ways in which a wise man may become foolish. First, "oppression makes a wise man foolish." The "oppression" here is the exercise of irresponsible power, that which the powerful inflict on others. Power goes to a man's head; it destroys his reason. For the moment he ceases to be directed by principle. The once wise man begins to behave like a fool.

Second, having resorted to oppression, men often give in to the acceptance of bribery: "And a gift destroys the heart," i.e., it corrupts the understanding, deprives a person of wisdom, makes him no better than a fool. Deliberate acts of wickedness destroy the moral fiber of a person. If one who is oppressed adjudges the powerful to be fools, would he wish to change places with them? Who would cast an envious eye upon an apparently successful and joyous official who was in fact a fool in need of rebuke (7:7).

THE VALUE OF PATIENCE
Ecclesiastes 7:8-14

Koheleth now commends patience, and points out the folly of impatience in dealing with life's varied circumstances.

A. Impatience Condemned by Reason (7:8).

"Better is the end of something[2] than its beginning." The end is better because then one is in a better position to form a right opinion about the matter. Was it purposeful? Was it advantageous? A hasty and superficial evaluation might conclude that an empty-headed fool is successful in life. Before the final outcome much may change. A believer should not conclude that his own life has been a failure. Such a judgment is quite premature and improper. Life is full of unexpected surprises, dramatic turns, last second victories. One should wait until the verdict of the heavenly judge has been presented to draw his conclusions about success and failure. The person who can do this can weather any storm which life may present. The point of the proverb is to stress patience. One should not be hasty in evaluating a program, plan or activity.

Why is patience commended? Because "the patient in spirit is better than the proud in spirit." To be "patient" is literally "to be long of spirit," the opposite of being "short of spirit" or quick tempered (cf. Prov 14:29). When provoked, such a person avoids making a rash retort for which he later will be sorry. Even more serious, the patient person does not call divine providence into question. The proud and conceited person, on the other hand, treats his fellow man with contempt and does not weigh his words. He thinks that all must meet his approval and operate on his time schedule. He is never content with the outworkings of providence. He rebels against the ordained course of events. Pride of spirit, though flamboyant and dramatic, cannot sustain a person through difficult times (7:8).

B. Impatience Leads to Skepticism (7:9).

Koheleth adds a further warning against the arrogance which murmurs against divine providence: "Be not hasty in your spirit to be angry." Being "hasty in spirit" is akin to experiencing vexation within. The admonition refers to that haughty indignation which a proud man feels when things do not go the way he perceives they should go. Such an attitude involves a person in difficulties with others. Even worse, it induces rash thoughts in reference to God. The heart of the prideful person imagines that he could manage things much more satisfactorily than the Lord has done.

Such unreasonable displeasure is the mark of a foolish or skeptical mind: "For vexation finds a resting place in the bosom of fools." Wise men banish such emotions from their hearts; fools nurture them. One who entertains such arrogant thoughts and allows them to rest in his heart has taken a giant leap toward atheism (7:9).

C. Impatience Leads to Negativism (7:10).

The same impatience leads a person to disparage the present in comparison with some imaginary golden age of the past. "What is the cause that the former days were better than these?" Here is the picture of someone who lives in the past, a not uncommon practice when times are bad. Is this person looking back to ancient times? Or is he thinking about the earlier days of his own life? If the former, his opinions are not founded upon adequate information. He has no objective way of knowing that past ages were in any way superior to the present. Yet he lives in the past and disparages the present. Wherever he does not live is better than where he lives. Whenever he did not live is better than the times in which he lives.

If the negative thinker has in view his own personal life, then the meaning would be this: When troubles come, one should not imagine that his past life was free of these trials. The earlier years were probably no better than the present, so one should not give in to vexation.

By asking such a question about the past, the impatient person shows that he had not reflected wisely on the matter: "For you do not inquire wisely concerning this." Every age has its light and dark side. The "good old days" were not always so good, and the present is not so bad. The Israelites who yearned for the onions, garlic and meat of Egypt had blotted from their memories the bondage, toil and misery (Num 11:5). Difficult times call for believers to look forward to the Promised Land, not back to Egypt. The future ultimately will be better than any past or any present, however good (7:10).

D. Impatience Is Incompatible with Wisdom (7:11-12).

Such negative comparisons between the past and the present are incompatible with true wisdom: "Wisdom is good, as well as an inheritance." Both wisdom and inherited wealth are good, but the advantages of the former far outweigh those of the latter as the next verse will argue.

Wisdom is "an advantage in respect to those who see the sun," i.e., in the opinion of living persons (cf. 6:5). Such as have wisdom along with wealth are honored in the community (7:11).

Both wisdom and wealth serve as a protection in life: "For in the shade is wisdom, in the shade is money." He who has wisdom and he who has wealth rest under a tree, as it were, i.e., they have protection from the hot rays of adversity. "Shade" is a common metaphor for a place of shelter from danger (cf. Isa 32:2). The Book of Proverbs speaks about the power of money to ransom a life (13:8); wisdom also can deliver a city (Eccl 9:15). Thus both are valuable assets; both have the power of deliverance.

Yet wisdom is superior to wealth: "But the advantage of knowledge is that wisdom gives life to them that have it." The terms "knowledge" (da'ath) and "wisdom" (chokhmah) are here practically identical. The terms have been varied for the sake of Hebrew parallelism. At the very least the verse is stating that wisdom secures a person from the vices and passions which tend to shorten life. More than mere physical life, however, is in view here. Wisdom in the highest sense is godliness, piety and faith. This kind of wisdom is a tree of life

765

which restores to a person that which was lost at the Fall in the garden (Prov 8:35). In wisdom is found the more abundant life (7:12).

E. Impatience Is Ultimately Ineffective (7:13-14).
Koheleth invites his readers to "consider the work of God," i.e., to employ the "knowledge" which wisdom supplies. In all that happens, wisdom discerns the hand of God. Every day the happenings of life reinforce God's omnipotence and man's impotence: "For who can make that straight which he has made crooked?" Koheleth acknowledges that some things in life are "crooked," i.e., tangled, sadly disorganized, out of alignment. These are the difficulties, the problems which one encounters in his earthly pilgrimage.

The writer encourages his readers not to perplex themselves too much about the mysteries of the universe. Man should concentrate on reflecting on God's will and how he may bring his life into conformity with that divine will. The thought that there are "crooked" things implies no actual criticism; it merely describes life as nearsighted men might describe it. From one point of view, to attempt to straighten out such things is to assume divine prerogatives, to tamper with God's government. The thought goes back to what was said in 1:15, "That which is crooked cannot be made straight." Man cannot arrange events according to his wishes. One must patiently endure whatever difficulties come his way. The wise person will endeavor to accommodate himself to existing circumstances (7:13).

The fact that man cannot remove from life all that he perceives to be crooked does not mean that he should resort to stoic resignation or apathy. Everything comes into clearer focus with the recognition that God is still on his throne no matter what may occur. Difficult days call for greater trust in God's providence and sovereign rule. Both good and bad days serve the higher purposes of God.

The inward patience will manifest itself in the outward disposition: "in the day of good, be in good," i.e., when things go well with you, be cheerful; accept the situation and enjoy it. The consistent advice of this book is that a person should make the best of the present. So far the advice is not hard to implement. Now comes the tough part: "in the evil day, consider," i.e., use the times of adversity for solemn reflection.

What is one to consider in the evil day? That "God has made the one corresponding to the other," i.e., God has made the bad days as well as the good days. Both the light and the shade in one's life are equally under the control of God. The chords of sorrow and joy, prosperity and adversity blend together under the direction of the master performer to produce a glorious harmony.

Why does God blend this good and bad? "To the end that man should find nothing after him." God intermingles good and evil in men's lives according to laws with which they are unacquainted. The attempt to forecast the future is a disquieting futility. Man seems never able to discern the good that comes from evil days. That inability continually reminds him that he cannot see what will come next upon the earth. People must learn to cast their care upon God, knowing that he cares for them (1 Pet 5:7). One cheats himself of a day of joyous living by fretting about the past or worrying about the future.

THE VALUE OF MODERATION
Ecclesiastes 7:15-18

Koheleth introduces the next unit with another reference to his own search for meaning in life: "All things have I seen in the days of my vanity." The term "all" here has the article, so the reference must be to a particular "all," namely, that which he has already mentioned or is about to mention. His statement is equivalent in meaning to the modern "Now I have seen it all!" The phrase "the days of vanity" refers either (1) to the emptiness or transitoriness of his life; or (2) to his vain efforts to solve the problem of the meaning of life.[3]

The particular problem which Koheleth focuses on here is this: "There is a righteous man who perishes in his righteousness." Righteousness has the promise of long life and prosperity. Yet here one who is attempting to do right meets disaster and early death. On the other hand, "there is a wicked person who prolongs his life in spite of his wickedness." The Hebrews expected sinners to suffer calamity and be cut off prematurely. Here is a difficulty which has perplexed thoughtful individuals almost since the beginning of time. This inversion of moral order leads to a further reflection in the following verse (7:15).

A. The Overly Wise (7:16).

Since it is a fact that righteous men perish in their righteousness, Koheleth draws the conclusion that excessive piety is not a means for securing a long and happy life. The exhortation "Be not righteous over much" has been interpreted in several ways. Is Koheleth advising that one not be too scrupulous in the observation of religious ritual? Is he suggesting that one can be so caught up in heavenly things that he is good for nothing on earth? Is it the judgmental Pharisaical spirit which is being condemned? Probably it is some incipient asceticism which Koheleth is condemning—that attitude that equates righteousness with a rigid and rigorous lifestyle. Such religion makes piety offensive, and really does not promote true righteousness.

The second exhortation is equally perplexing: "Show not yourself overly wise." Koheleth has admitted that wisdom has advantages over folly; he has also proved by experience that wisdom is ultimately a vanity because wisdom will never be able to answer all life's questions. This seems to be a warning against indulging in speculation about God's dealings or questioning the wisdom of his moral government (cf. Rom 9:19-21). A good principle carried to excess brings evil results. Consequently he advises against devoting too much effort to becoming wise.

To be overly righteous or overly wise is dangerous: "Why should you destroy yourself?" The verb "destroy" (*tisshomem*) means literally "to confound or confuse oneself."[4] A person who professes to be wiser than others, and indeed wiser than God, incurs the animosity of his fellow men. He will certainly be punished by God for his arrogance and presumption (7:16).

B. The Overly Wicked (7:17).

Along similar lines Koheleth advises: "Be not overly wicked, neither be foolish." Despite the truth that wicked men sometimes live long, it is nevertheless a fact that evil may be the cause of a premature death. Does he here sanction some wickedness provided it does not exceed a certain limit? No, his point is quite different. He warns here against the deliberate and abominable wickedness which is calculated to take advantage of God's patience. The word "wicked" (*tirsha'*) may refer here to the willful rejection of the many regulations of the law of Moses. The idea would then be, Do not cast off the restraints of the law too much.

One might conclude from certain experiences in life that God is totally indifferent to sin. Because he perceives that God is not concerned with moral matters, he plunges headlong into vice and immorality. Such conduct may well be called "foolish" because it is the fool who thinks God does not see (Ps 10:11), or does not even exist (Ps 14:1). Even if wisdom can bring one disappointment, it is true that through folly a person may take a dangerous course with fatal consequences. Vice shortens life.

Such a reckless plunge into foolish sin is dangerous: "Why should you die not in your time?" His attitude and action tempt God (1) to punish him by retributive judgment; or (2) to allow him to destroy his own life through his excesses. Sometimes, as observed in v. 15, the life of the wicked is prolonged; but this is not the norm. In the usual course of events impiety and immorality have a tendency to shorten life (7:17).

C. Avoiding Excesses (7:18).

Koheleth advises his readers to lay to heart the two admonitions he has just given: "It is good that you should take hold of this; yea, also from this withdraw not your hand." The reference is to the two contrasting rules regarding being overly righteous or overly wicked. By accepting only one of these rules, harmful consequences will ensue. If one becomes overly righteous, i.e., he trusts in his own righteousness, his trust in divine providence may be undermined, especially in bad times. If he is overly wicked, he will bring upon himself the penalty of sin. He must cling to both principles.

The god-fearing person escapes both of the extremes mentioned in the preceding verses along with the evil results associated with them. On the one hand, he will be deterred from total rejection of God's law; on the other hand, he will avoid the menace to his faith if ill-fortune comes upon him. Reverence for God will keep a person from all excesses. The godly life is a balanced life.

Koheleth was convinced that the person who balanced his life between the extremes of being overly righteous and overly wicked would "go forth with all of them," i.e., by means of both rules he would fulfill his duty in the matter of righteousness and wickedness in a proper manner (7:18).

THE VALUE OF SELF-RESTRAINT
Ecclesiastes 7:19-22

Wisdom teaches self-restraint, and wisdom is also an ally in the struggle to master oneself. Koheleth here urges restraint regarding sin and criticism.

A. Restraint Regarding Sin (7:19-20).

"For wisdom provides strength to the wise man." Here Koheleth distinguishes godly wisdom from the over-wisdom he condemned in v. 16. Like a mighty hero wisdom places itself at a man's side to help him in combat against the temptations of the world. The metaphor dropped, the verse suggests that the rules of wise conduct he has just expounded will afford protection to a person.

The aid which wisdom supplies is stronger "than ten rulers which are in the city," i.e., superior to the aid which these rulers can supply. The number "ten" signifies completeness, and is often used in Scripture for an indefinite multitude (cf. Job 19:3). The ten "rulers" (shallitim) are those who are known for their sagacity. That they are "in the city" indicates that they are superior rulers such as the larger population of a city may produce. Consultations between such wise leaders increased the chance of safety when a city was threatened by attack. Nevertheless, wisdom stands a person in even better stead when he is assailed by the difficulties of life (7:19).

Godly wisdom is absolutely necessary if one is to escape the consequences of his own inborn tendency to transgress against God. Despite the fact that a person fears God, he is certain to fall into sin during his lifetime. For that reason he requires the protection which wisdom provides. Wisdom shows the sinner the error of his way, and the way out of that error. Wisdom leads him back into fellowship with God in which alone there is moral security. Man is not, nor can he be, perfect. Even a just person sins, and therefore needs the guidance of godly wisdom (7:20; cf. 1 John 1:8).

770

B. Restraint Regarding Criticism (7:21-22).

Koheleth now mentions another area in which godly wisdom supplies strength. "Give not your heart unto all words that are spoken." The reader is encouraged not to pay attention to public or private opinions which have been expressed about him. Why is this a good principle? First, listening to the evaluations of others is usually disappointing. A person's faults, rather than his good deeds, are generally the topic of such talk. He will hear censure far more often than commendation. Second, trying to measure up to the expectations of others is practically impossible. Not all the criticism is the same. When he pleases one group, he offends another. Third, surveying the opinions of acquaintances is ego shattering. One who constantly conducts a referendum on himself will eventually find that others do not see him as he sees himself. In fact, he will find others quite ready to censure his conduct and condemn his opinions.

One should pay little attention to what others are saying "lest you hear your servant curse you." A servant would be acquainted with his master's faults. Criticism from that quarter would be intolerable. A relationship could be totally ruined by accidentally hearing what the servant truly thinks. Hence one should not try too hard to overhear what others are whispering around him (7:21).

Koheleth now appeals to the conscience of his readers. "Often also your own heart knows that you yourself likewise have cursed others." If one has spoken ill of others, he should expect unfavorable comments about himself from time to time. Thus he should not be overly upset when that verbal criticism is hurled his way. Jesus warned that one will be subject to criticism in the same way in which they have criticized others (7:22; Matt 7:1-2).

THE VALUE OF WISDOM
Ecclesiastes 7:23-29

A. The Difficulty of the Search (7:23-24).

Koheleth attributes to wisdom the practical conclusions which he has set forth in the preceding verses: "All this have I put to the test by wisdom." Would wisdom solve deeper questions? "I said, I will be wise." This was his resolve. He desired to grow in wisdom, to use it in order to unfold mysteries and explain problems. It takes wisdom to search for wisdom. Hitherto he had been content to watch the course of men's lives, and find by experience what was good and what was evil for them; now he craves for an insight into the secret laws that regulate those external circumstances. The verb "put to the test" (*nasah*) implies making a careful trial of something.

Even while he was conducting his search for answers, he made a sad discovery. One can never achieve wisdom perfectly. Koheleth says that the deeper wisdom "was far from me," i.e., it remained out of reach for him. When he sought to comprehend the grand scheme of the universe and God's government thereof he was seeking to reach out to the unattainable. Practical rules of life he had mastered; but essential, absolute wisdom was beyond mortal grasp. Man's knowledge and capacity for knowledge are limited (7:23).

Koheleth now expands on the thought of the unreachableness of ultimate wisdom. His effort was focused on "what is," i.e., the actual essence of things. "Far off is that which is, and deep, deep: who can discover it?" Here he identifies two factors which make ultimate wisdom unattainable. First, the final answers to the great questions of life are "far off," i.e., either in the remote past, even the great past beyond creation; or in the unattainable heavens beyond. One would have to have been present before the world began to see how all the elements which make up experience in this world relate to one another. Second, even when that wisdom seems to be within his grasp he finds it to be "deep, deep," i.e., utterly mysterious and beyond the grasp of the mind of man. Man is helpless before the infinite greatness of the universe (7:24; cf. Job 11:7f.).

B. The Goal of the Search (7:25).

Koheleth realized the hopelessness of his search to understand the ultimate perplexities of the universe, so he turned again to the problems of life which have been occupying his attention: "I turned myself, and my heart was [set] to know." The expression "turned myself" refers to the undertaking of a new effort in the quest for knowledge (cf. 2:20, et al.). Koheleth devoted himself with the utmost earnestness to the pursuit, but he turned his inquiry in another direction. Here he hoped to meet with better results. First, he made every effort "to search, and to seek out wisdom." The infinitives "know, explore, seek" indicate careful study from every angle. He is turning from profitless theoretical speculation about issues in life, to a practical inquiry. Second, he seeks now to explain "the reason of things." The term *cheshbon* means "account" or "reckoning." In NASB it is rendered "an explanation;" in NIV "the scheme of things." He is not going to explain the causes of all things, but rather present a summary of his conclusions about how life works.

Third, Koheleth's inquiry is centered on knowing "wickedness as folly, and foolishness as madness." His investigation led him to this conclusion, that all violations of God's laws are a willful desertion of the requirements of right reason, i.e., folly. In the final analysis, "wickedness" is "stupidity," for that is the fundamental meaning of the word "folly" *(kesel)*. This "foolishness" *(sikhluth)* is further defined as "madness" *(holeloth)*, or self-delusion. Men are beguiled into placing value in that which has only outward glamor. This is not the ultimate wisdom which is beyond the reach of man, but it nonetheless is an important discovery of those who pursue wisdom (7:25).

C. The Result of the Search (7:26-27).

One shocking result of his investigation is mentioned, almost as an aside. It was a disappointment that he found "more bitter than death." When he traces men's folly and madness to its roots, he finds that they arise generally from the seductions of "the woman." The account of the first sin in the Garden illustrates what Koheleth is here saying. The women in Solomon's life led him astray and were the source of much of his personal misery. But who is "the woman"? She has been taken to be (1) any woman; (2) an evil woman (cf. Prov 2:18f.; 7:25ff.); or (3) the Lady Folly of Prov 9, i.e., false philosophy, worldly outlook. Either (2) or (3) must be the proper identification, or maybe both. After all, an immoral woman is but one potent manifestation of Lady Folly.

So Koheleth here is not making a wholesale condemnation of the female sex. That interpretation contradicts the plain statement of the text and his recommendation in 9:9. The good woman is frequently praised in the wisdom literature (cf. e.g., Prov 11:16; 12:4; 18:22; 19:14; 31:10ff.).

That Koheleth is speaking of an evil woman appears from the next clause: "who is snares, and nets in her heart." The thoughts of the wicked woman are "nets," i.e., she occupies her mind with planning how she might entrap and retain victims. Her outward look and words are "snares" that captivate the foolish. "Her hands as bands" wrap about her victims with a powerful embrace. That embrace is stronger than the chains which bind the criminal.

Is there no escape from the entrapment of the wicked woman? Koheleth offers this hope: "he who is good before God shall escape from her." He who is "good" is one who aims to act with God's approval. The Lord will give that man the grace to resist the seductive charms of this wicked woman. "But the sinner shall be taken in her," i.e., in the snare which she in fact is. Since like is attracted to like, only an evildoer will be attracted by a debased woman. The "sinner" is one whom God punishes by letting him fall into further sins (7:26).

Koheleth assures his readers that his investigation has forced the conclusion which he has just announced in the preceding verse: "Behold! This have I found, says[5] the Preacher." He has carefully examined the character and conduct of the loose woman, and is therefore constrained to make that shocking ("Behold") evaluation. He has been "adding one by one," i.e., he has been adding one thing to another, putting together fact after fact in order to reach his conclusion. This he did in order "to find out the account," i.e., to arrive at the reckoning, the desired result (7:27).

D. The Disappointment in the Search (7:28-29).

Koheleth had reached certain conclusions based on his observation and powers of deduction. Still he continued the search. He now shares with the reader what he found and what he did not find in his disappointing search.

1. That which he found (7:28a). Koheleth found "one man among a thousand" who lived by the principles of godly wisdom, i.e., who lived a godly and upright life. The times were bad, and the men were generally evil. The term "thousand" is not to be taken arithmetically, but stands for a large number.

2. That which he did not find (7:28b). The situation with women was even worse: "but a woman among all those have I not found." Not one woman among a thousand who was living by the principles of wisdom, i.e., was living an upright life. Perhaps the allusion is to the thousand wives and concubines which Solomon had married. None of them measured up to what he thought a woman ought to be. Koheleth does not say that no upright women exist, but only that they were a greater rarity than upright men.[6] The Book of Proverbs suggests that the times were licentious and the general standard of morality was low among women of the day (7:28).

Whose fault is it that more do not reach the goal of upright living according to the principles of godly wisdom? Koheleth may not have understood everything he desired to know. He did, however, reach this rather shocking conclusion: "Only see! This have I found." His words alert the reader for a shocking statement. Universal corruption was what he found throughout the land. This was not the fault of God, for "God has made man upright." "Man" here means the human species. God created both man and woman "upright" or "straight" (yashar). The original pair not only had the capacity for being good; they were in fact morally good when God created them. Through revelation Koheleth knew this to be true. The blame for not living an upright life is placed squarely on man's doorstep.

By experience, however, Koheleth knows that man no longer manifests that original righteousness: "they have sought out many inventions," i.e., devices, ways of going astray and deviating from original righteousness. Man has corrupted his freedom of will. He has used his intellectual endowments to create new ways of violating God's righteous standards (7:29).

THE VALUE OF SUBMISSION
To the King
Ecclesiastes 8:1-8

True wisdom counsels obedience to the king. Is Koheleth referring to heaven's king? Or to the ruler on earth? Possibly he is being deliberately ambiguous. If pragmatism demands that one submit to an earthly ruler, how much more to God? On the other hand, if one for good reason should submit to heaven's king, should he not submit to those who exercise power as God's viceroys on earth? The quality which is being commended here is the submissive spirit.

A. Submission Recommended (8:1-5).

In the preceding paragraph Koheleth had undertaken a search for wisdom. He now asks: "Who is as the wise man?" i.e., who is like, or equal to a man of wisdom. The wise man has no peer. "And who [like him] knows the interpretation of a thing?" No one is so able to explain events or understand the affairs of man as well as a wise man. Indeed "a man's wisdom makes his face to shine." His contentment, cheerfulness and confidence are revealed in his demeanor. It "causes his stern face to shine." Ignorance and lack of culture reveal themselves in coarseness and impudence. When wisdom fills the heart, the face reflects a gentle and congenial look which inspires confidence in others and wins friends (8:1).

Koheleth offers this counsel to his readers: "Keep the king's commandment." Such conduct is the duty of believers in any generation. Civil government, whether monarchy or democracy, is ordained of God. The head of the government is God's agent to punish evildoers (cf. Rom 13:1). This allegiance is owed to the king "because of the oath before God." In solemn covenant the subjects would pledge their loyalty to the king (2 Kgs 11:17; cf. 2 Chr 36:13) in a coronation oath. To disobey the king was to violate a solemn oath taken in God's name. Hence obedience to civil authority became a religious duty. If the king here is God, then the oath would be that covenant which is made with him to walk by his commands (8:2; Neh 10:29).

Koheleth advises that the king's subjects "be not hasty to go out of his sight," i.e., in some rash moment to cast off allegiance to the king. "To go away" here is used in the sense of quitting the service of the crown and deserting one's assigned post. Solomon may have given this advice as he sensed the discontent of the northern tribes in the latter years of his reign. Koheleth further advises: "Do not stand in an evil matter," i.e., do not join in civil insurrection. Why? Because the king will "do whatever pleases him." He has the power to deal swiftly and harshly with rebels. If the king is God, then Koheleth is warning against apostasy when God does not at once do what the believer would have done (8:3).

The thought of the king's authority is now amplified: "inasmuch as the word of the king is powerful." The subject may have right on his side, but the king wields autocratic power. He can do as he pleases because his mandate is all-powerful, and must be obeyed. "And who may say unto him, What are you doing?" No citizen will be in a position to hold the king to account for his actions. If these observations are true with regard to earthly kings, how much more of the heavenly king (8:4)?

To encourage obedience to royal authority, Koheleth makes this observation: "Whoever keeps the commandment shall know no evil thing." Quiet submission to the civil authorities usually results in a happy and peaceful life at least in terms of freedom from government interference. The word "know" here means "to experience." Koheleth is not thinking of the exceptional times when earthly monarchs attempt to compel believers to disobey the Lord. A wise man "knows in his heart both time and judgment." If the king's rule becomes too oppressive, the wise man will know how to bide his time and resort to appropriate measures for the purpose of escaping its harsh restrictions. He can remain calm even in the most oppressive times because he knows that a day of judgment is coming. He need not resort to violence to rectify the wrongs of society because he knows that God will take care of that (8:5).

B. Submission Defended (8:6-8).

Koheleth now argues the wisdom of keeping calm during evil days. First, "to every purpose there is time and judgment." Everything has its appointed time of duration. In due course it will be brought to judgment. Second, "the evil of man is heavy upon him." A person has enough troubles without deliberately adding to them by open revolt against the king (8:6).[7]

Third, "he does not know that which shall be." Here is another reason for the submission to the king. Political circumstances change unexpectedly. One should therefore, be patient. Fourth, "who can tell him how it shall be." One cannot foresee what event will occur which might end the tyrant's rule and bring relief from oppression (8:7).[8]

The line of argument of the preceding verses reaches its conclusion with the identifications of four impossible things: (1) "there is no man that has power over the spirit to retain the spirit." No one, not even the great king, can keep back the spirit that is about to depart from the earthly tabernacle of this body. (2) "Neither has he power over the day of death." That tyrant king cannot avert the hour of death. It may come by sickness or accident or in regicide. In any case, the despot must succumb; he can neither see it nor ward it off (cf. 1 Sam 26:11). (3) The law of death is likened to a military obligation: "and there is no discharge in war." (4) "Neither shall wickedness deliver those that are given to it." No evil despot, however reckless and imperious, can go long unpunished. Certain retribution awaits (8:8).

THE VALUE OF SUBMISSION
To Providence
Ecclesiastes 8:9-15

"All of this I have seen and given my heart to every work under the sun." "All this" points forward to the problem that is about to be stated and about to be solved. Koheleth recognized that, while he may have disposed of some problems, others remained to be addressed. Now he gave his mind "to all the work that is done under the sun." He is determined to investigate every possible activity or circumstance which might become a problem of faith. The phrase "under the sun" here again indicates that the problems which he is addressing are only such because God has been left out of the picture.

A. Oppression of the Righteous (8:9b-10).

What does one discover when he lets all things pass in review before his eyes? He discovers that "man rules over man to his hurt." The "hurt" is that which a wicked ruler inflicts upon his innocent subjects (8:9b).

Sometimes those who inflict the hurt on others do not apparently experience any retribution, at least in this life. Koheleth notes: "And so I saw the wicked buried." The reference is especially to the despots of the preceding verses. These are carried to their graves with every outward honor and respect. Had they received their due reward, they would not have received such a pompous and magnificent funeral. These sinners "came" to their rest, i.e., they died a natural death.

The death of the tyrant is next described as being a removal from the holy land: "And they went out from the holy place," i.e., by death they were removed from the holy land, the holy city Jerusalem and the holy temple. Perhaps the thought is also that by death the tyrant was removed from the presence of the holy people he oppressed. Eventually, however, such oppressors would be "forgotten in the city where they had so [wickedly] acted."[9] Their name would not be preserved through their offspring or in the minds of the members of the community as a pious memory. This they deserve because "they had done thus," i.e., perverted justice. God curbs their evil by taking them in death. The power of the mighty fades with death. Their works, and even their memory, perish. Here is another example of that "vanity" which pervades all earthly circumstances (8:10).

B. Delayed Retribution (8:11-13).

What happens when evil tyrants are not dealt a death blow by the Lord? One of the results of God's forbearance with regard to the wicked is now set forth: "Because sentence against an evil work is not executed speedily, therefore the heart of the sons of men is full in them to do evil." The perception—and that is all it is—that God is doing nothing about evil men fuels skepticism about the moral government of God. The "heart," i.e., the seat of thought and will, of the sons of men becomes filled with thoughts which are directed to evil. Sometimes the longsuffering of God actually emboldens the wicked to continue even deeper into sin. On the other hand, those he oppressed may be filled with the spirit of revenge or with the wicked attitude expressed in the cliche "if you can't beat 'em, join 'em" (10:11).

Because he is not punished, the sinner might "do evil a hundred times," i.e., repeatedly. He "prolongs his days for it," i.e., for the practice of evil. He gains some kind of satisfaction and contentment in his wickedness. Contrary to the usual course of temporal retribution, the sinner often lives to old age. Even so "I for my part know it shall be well with them that fear God, who fear before him." Though he has seen sinners prosper, still he holds to the conviction that God's moral government will vindicate itself at some point in the future. Would the inequities be straightened out in this life? Or in the life to come? Koheleth does not say. In spite of all appearances to the contrary, he holds firm to his faith that it will be well with the righteous in the long run (10:12).

Koheleth was equally convinced that the wicked would one day taste the wrath of God: "But good will not be for the wicked." In the face of empirical evidence to the contrary, Koheleth's faith in the retributive judgment of God was unshaken. "Neither shall he prolong his days, which are as a shadow." As noted above, sometimes sinners live long, untroubled lives; but most often they do not. No one can fully explain why in certain cases the judgment is delayed. The "shadow" is a symbol of that which is short-lived; but even the long life of a sinner is not necessarily a blessing. The reason the wicked one shall not live out his days is "because he does not fear before God." Only fear of God can make life of any length worth living (8:13).

C. Inappropriate Outcomes (8:14-15).

Sometimes the law of retribution seems to be working in reverse: "There is a vanity which is done upon the earth: there be just men unto whom it happens according to the work of the wicked." The sad fact is that sometimes the righteous experience that fate with which the wicked are threatened. "On the other hand, there are wicked to whom it happens according to the work of the righteous." Sometimes the wicked are blessed with that prosperity which should have been the reward of those who serve God. Koheleth ends by repeating his melancholy refrain: "I said that this indeed is vanity" (8:14).

The perception of unfair treatment can lead to a bitter spirit. Koheleth commends a different coping mechanism to deal with inappropriate outcomes: "And I commended pleasure, for there is nothing good for a man under the sun except to eat and to drink and to be merry." One must not let perplexity over the moral discrepancies in the world sour his whole life. The advice here is to calmly enjoy such blessings and comforts as one possesses (cf. 2:24; 3:12,22; 5:18).

This is no invitation to live a greedy and gluttonous life (cf. 1 Kgs 4:20). "Under the sun" again indicates that Koheleth is limiting his view to man's earthly existence. If the advice here is followed, then "this should accompany him in his labor," i.e., he will be able to take with him in all his work a cheerful and contented heart. Furthermore, nothing said here in any way contradicts the sentiments expressed in

7:1ff. which urged a spirit of earnestness and sobriety. Taking life seriously does not rule out the harmless good cheer that Koheleth here recommends (8:15).

CONCLUSION
The Unfathomable Purposes of God
Ecclesiastes 8:16-17

Koheleth had spent many a sleepless night when he applied his heart to know wisdom. This was the first investigation which he made (cf. 1:16). He endeavored to acquire wisdom which might enable him to investigate God's doings. His second business was "to see the business that is done upon the earth," i.e., to learn what men do in their various stations and callings, but likewise to understand what all this means, its object and result (8:16).

In his search Koheleth "saw every work of God," i.e., men's actions and the providential ordering thereof. He concluded "that man cannot discover the work which has been done under the sun." The finite mind of man cannot understand nor explain the workings of divine providence. "Even though a man should vigorously seek, he will not discover; and though the wise man should say, I know, he cannot find it." Wisdom endeavors to know all that can be known. Nonetheless, when it comes to the things of God, there are limits to what a person can discover (8:17).

ENDNOTES

1. Another interpretation of 6:11 is this: "If things are increased, vanity is increased by them," i.e., the more wealth a person acquires, the more problems he will have.

2. Others prefer to render the Hebrew *dabhar* as "word" in 7:8. The meaning would then be: One is unable to judge the ultimate effect of any remark. One may make a perfectly innocuous observation which can nevertheless have serious consequences. The lesson would then be to exercise extreme caution in one's speech.

3. Another interpretation of "in the days of my vanity" in 7:15 is "in my vain days," i.e., my swiftly passing days.

4. Another interpretation of the verb *tisshomem* is that it means "to be amazed or astonished." The clause would then read: "Why should you be overcome with amazement?" i.e., when you receive no tangible results of your zealous pursuit of righteousness and wisdom.

5. Some have found significance in the fact that the verb here is feminine. In 12:8 the masculine form of the same verb is used. Such interchange in gender is not uncommon in Hebrew, and probably has no special significance in 7:27.

6. Another view is that 7:28 speaks of the attainment of ultimate wisdom. Few men had attained it, not even Koheleth himself, and even fewer if any women. See H.C. Leupold, *Exposition of Ecclesiastes* (Grand Rapids: Baker, 1966), pp. 176f.

7. Others take the last clause in 8:6 to mean (1) that the evil of the king will press down upon him until it brings him to the ground; or (2) when men can no longer bear up under the heavy oppression, God will intervene.

8. Others take the reference in 8:7 to be to the tyrant king. The despot cannot foresee the consequences of his ruthless policy, so he goes on blindly filling up the measure of his iniquity.

9. Others see 8:10 as making a contrast between the pompous burial of the wicked and the fate of the righteous whose very name is cast out as pollution and soon forgotten.

CHAPTER THIRTY-EIGHT

Ignorance of the Future
Ecclesiastes 9:1-11:6

The introduction to the second half of the book (6:10-12) indicated two main conclusions to which Koheleth had come through his philosophical investigations: (1) man is ignorant concerning God's dealings in the present; and (2) man is ignorant about what will take place in the future. The first of these conclusions was developed in 7:1-8:17. Now Koheleth presents the second of his conclusions.

MAN DOES NOT KNOW HIS STANDING WITH GOD
Ecclesiastes 9:1-6

The new aspect of the argument is introduced, but it is closely connected with the preceding chapter as is indicated by the opening word. "For all this I laid in my heart and all this I have sought to clear up." Koheleth has omitted no means of arriving at a conclusion which he now sets forth: "The righteous and the wise and their works are in the hand of God," i.e., in his power, under his direction. They are subject to the divine will, but in a manner which is unintelligible to the human mind. Here again the sovereignty of God is stressed. Men of faith do not rebel against such a circumstance, but rather rejoice in it. They know the heavenly Father is just, loving and compassionate (9:1a).

A. What the Living Do Not Know (9:1b-2).

What view does God take of a person's life? "No man knows either love or hatred." These terms are sometimes employed in Hebrew to express nothing more than preference and its opposite (cf. Deut 21:15; Mal 1:2f.). The idea is that one cannot judge from what befalls a person what view God might have of his character. Does God "love" (approve of) him, or "hate" (disapprove of) him? Under the sun, without revelation, it is impossible to tell what one's standing with the Lord might be. Calamities do not necessarily indicate that a person is some great sinner. Neither does material prosperity indicate necessarily that one is a child of God. Outward circumstances are no criterion of inward dispositon or of final judgment. "All is before them," i.e., practically anything may happen to a person. The idea is that all that shall happen, all that shall shape their destiny in the future, is obscure and unknown, and beyond their control (9:1b).

"All things [are] like that which [happens] to all persons." All people experience the whole range of events in their lives: sunshine and shade, calm and storm, prosperity and adversity, joy and sorrow. Apparently there is no discrimination in the distribution of good and evil. Earthquakes, pestilences, and tempests make no discrimination between good people and evil. "There is one event to the righteous and to the wicked." All people have the same lot whether it be death or any other contingency, without regard to their moral condition.

Koheleth next resorts to emphasis by enumeration to underscore the word "all" in this proposition. The "all" who experience the same fate are (1) "the righteous and the wicked," i.e., those who treat their fellow man right, and those who do not; (2) "the good," i.e., those who have no moral defilement; (3) "the clean and the unclean," i.e., those who keep the ceremonial standards of the law and those who do not; (4) "the man who offers a sacrifice and the one who does not"; (5) "the good person and the sinner," i.e., those who discharge their responsibilities to God and those who do not; (6) "the swearer and the one who is afraid to swear." The last contrast is between one who takes an oath lightly, carelessly, or falsely and one who regards it as a holy thing, or shrinks in awe from invoking God's name in any way (9:2).

B. What the Living Know (9:3-5a).

While men, unaided by revelation, cannot know their standing with God, they do know this: all people share in "one event," i.e., death (cf. 2:14-16; 3:19; 5:15; 6:12). Koheleth regards this common fate of all men as "an evil among all things that are done under the sun." Why is this considered an evil? Because it has a harmful effect upon the human temperament. Worldly men reason that all efforts at righteousness seem to produce no results. What then is the advantage of being good? Therefore, "the heart of the sons of men is full of evil." In consequence of the indiscriminating destiny, men sin recklessly; they are encouraged in their wickedness. Koheleth regards such an attitude as madness: "Madness is in their heart while they live," i.e., conduct opposed to the dictates of wisdom and reason (cf. 1:17; 2:2,12). The term "madness" (holeloth) embraces the idea of being blind to the real issues, spiritually deluded.

All their life people tend to follow their own lusts and passions. They care little for the things of God. "And after that—to the dead." The structure of this clause sounds like a terse military command which must immediately be obeyed. Alike in the circumstances they share in life, the righteous and the wicked proceed to the same goal— union with the dead. The perspective here again is "under the sun," i.e., he is speaking here of worldly people who assess life without the benefit of the light of God's revelation (9:3).

Now Koheleth adds a further reason why people live reckless, godless lives: "For one who is joined to all the living, he has hope." The attitude of hope is characteristic of people. They go on hoping that all will work out in the end, but they do nothing to foster spiritual growth. Wicked men see no reason to make any change in their lives.

The idea that the living are in respect to hope better off than the dead is now stated in a proverb: "For a living dog is better than a dead lion." The wild dog in Palestine was regarded with the greatest disdain (cf. 1 Sam 17:43; 2 Sam 3:8). The lion, on the other hand, was regarded as the most noble of beasts. The point is that the vilest creature is better off alive than the most noble is dead.

Some accuse Koheleth of inconsistency here. Has not this writer claimed a preference for death in earlier passages (cf. 4:2; 7:1)? The key here is the perspective of those passages and this one. In those earlier passages Koheleth was considering all the sorrows which one experiences in life. Death ends that sorrow and misery. Here he is thinking about the potential in life to experience joy. Death cuts one off from pleasure and "hope," i.e., earthly desire for something better. The thought could be paraphrased this way: Things can never get better for a person in this world if he is dead (9:4).

The living have still another advantage over the dead. Not only do they have hope, "the living know that they shall die." Since they know this for certain, they can make the necessary material and spiritual preparations for the inevitable. The certain knowledge of death should act like a goad to prod people to work while it is day, to employ their faculties worthily, to make use of opportunities, to enjoy and profit by the present. They cannot stand idle, lamenting their fate, but their duty is to accept the inevitable and make the best of it (9:5a).

C. What the Dead Know (9:5b-6).

On the other hand, "the dead know not anything." They are cut off from the active, bustling world; their work is done; they have nothing to expect, nothing to labor for. "Neither do they have any more a reward," i.e., no fruit for the labor they have done. Every opportunity for action or achievement of any sort is a thing of the past.

On the surface this verse seems to be a flat denial of life in the hereafter. An interpreter is not justified in considering this statement the definitive opinion of Koheleth regarding the state of the dead for two reasons. First, he is only depicting the state of the dead in relation to this world. Second, he is expressing the opinion that one would be forced to hold "under the sun" if he viewed the entire issue without the benefit of divine revelation on the subject. He is emphasizing here that one cannot take any part of this world with him when he departs. In any case, this verse must be interpreted in the light of 12:7 and the rest of the Scriptures on the subject.

Not only are the dead totally cut off from this world, even "the memory of them is forgotten." A living person is a somebody; a dead person is less than a nobody; he is not even a memory. The dead have not even this poor reward of being remembered by loving posterity, which in the mind of an Oriental was a much desired blessing (9:5).

Since their memory is forgotten, it would also be true of the dead that "they are neither loved nor hated nor envied any more."[1] With the passing of time attitudes of the living toward the dead, positive or negative, change, fade, and disappear.

The whole point of this gloomy paragraph is this: "Neither do they (the dead) have any more a portion forever in anything that is done under the sun." While he is on earth, the human being participates in the scene around him; he is an actor upon the stage of life. With death, the curtain falls, his role here ends (9:6)

Between the dead and the living there is an impassable gulf. Such is the conclusion which Koheleth reached when analyzing death "under the sun" without the benefit of revelation. Nonbelievers would be forced to say that Koheleth has accurately painted the portrait of death, for nonbelievers refuse to let the light from the empty tomb illuminate the darkness of death. The gospel brought life and immortality to light (2 Tim 1:10).

COPING WITH THE PROBLEM
Ecclesiastes 9:7-10

So how does one cope with the inscrutable providence of God, with the inevitability of death, and with the disparities he observes in life? Koheleth now suggests the spirit in which these difficulties should be met. The unit begins with the words "Come now," i.e., be up and doing. Koheleth did not want his readers to sit around brooding about life's inequities and vexations. They should stop worrying about problems which cannot be solved. He advises his readers to do three things to cope with the perplexities of life.

A. Be Festive in Spirit (9:7-8).

First, he urges his readers to enjoy life: "Eat your bread with joy." This is not an injunction to lead a selfish life of Epicurean pleasure.

Rather it is an exhortation to look on the bright side, to make the best of things. The counsel here given is wise indeed. It is a much better policy to enjoy what may be enjoyed than to brood over what cannot be understood. This advice is so simple that it might be ignored as being simplistic. The more one considers it, however, the more it commends itself to the mind. So Koheleth keeps hammering away on this point.

"Drink your wine with a merry heart." Bread and wine formed a large part of the popular diet (Gen 27:28; 1 Sam 16:20). One should not partake of these products of nature just to maintain life, but with joy and a merry heart. An ascetic way of living would only intensify the gloom which arises from contemplation of the problems of life. That gloom, however, can be dispelled by resolving to enjoy all the gifts of God.

Nothing in the Old Testament forbids the use of wine in moderation, although certain groups (Nazirites; Rechabites) took voluntary vows of abstinence in order to set a higher standard for the community at large. The same Sage warns against looking on the wine when it is "red," i.e., when it has the greater potential to intoxicate (Prov 23:31; 20:1).

This same counsel to enjoy the fruits of life has already appeared a number of times in the book (e.g., 2:24; 3:12). Koheleth adds an explanation: "For God has already approved your works." The "works" here refers to the eating and drinking just mentioned.[2] By giving man the capacity for enjoying food and drink, God has already approved such activity. God means for his good gifts to be received with reverence and thanksgiving, and that they be enjoyed. One who utilizes these gifts in this way is pleasing to the Lord (9:7).

Not only should people eat happy, they should dress happy. "Let your garments be always white." A white garment has always symbolized purity; but in the East it was also a symbol of joy. Such a garment was worn at the great annual festivals. His point is that one's clothing should convey joy. One who dresses for an occasion feels good about himself, and that feeling is conveyed to others in his demeanor.

One should also smell happy. "Let your head lack no ointment." In the heat of the East oil was poured on the head to cool it and the effect was refreshing. Perfumed oils were used on festive occasions as a symbol of joy. A pleasant aroma creates a positive mood. It expresses one's positive self-image. It makes a statement, and that statement is good. Grief causes people to go about with hair unkempt and face unwashed. Joy was expressed in a shining countenance, which was effected by pouring oil over the head. The hair could then also be smoothed and arranged. To summarize, the double counsel of this verse suggests that one should always be happy and cheerful (9:8).

B. Be Joyous in Marriage (9:9).

Koheleth advises his reader to "see life with a wife whom you love." This verse puts the negative comment about women in 7:26 in proper perspective. Men are now cheerfully bidden to enter upon the estate of matrimony. The advice is directed to the unmarried, and for this reason the text reads "a wife," not "your wife." Koheleth is encouraging his male students to choose a wife. That is the best way to "see life," i.e., experience life. The one who is to be chosen is the one that is loved. This may be a hint that the arranged marriages of early years produced many unhappy relationships. The best way to travel on the pilgrim's highway is in the company of a beloved spouse.

Koheleth here recognizes the happiness of a home where is found a helpmate beloved and worthy of love.[3] This relationship is viewed as lifelong: "All the days of the life of your vanity," i.e., throughout the time of your quickly passing life. This phrase is repeated in the verse to emphasize the transitoriness of the present, and the consequent wisdom of enjoying it while it lasts. God has given to man this short life span as a gift: "which he has given you under the sun." The enjoyment of life with a good wife is man's "portion in this life." Such moderate enjoyment is the recompense allowed by God for the toil that accompanies the earthly pilgrimage.

C. Be Energetic in Labor (9:10).

Another principle for getting the maximum enjoyment out of life is this: "Whatever your hand finds to do by the use of your strength, do it." Man's God-given strength is to be used at every opportunity. Honest labor leads to self-respect. Kingdom work is even more gratifying. Time, however, is of the essence. The hour will come when no man can work (John 9:4). Every opportunity to do good must be seized (Gal 6:10): "For there is no work, nor devising, nor knowledge, nor wisdom in Sheol where you are going." Sheol is the abode of the dead. Severed from the body, the spirit of man can no longer engage in the activities which are a normal part of living in this world. Those who are dead have no more work which they can do, no plans or calculations to make; their knowledge is strictly limited, their wisdom has come to an end.

This verse is the strongest of Koheleth's statements about the absence of physical or mental toil or progress after death. Yet it is hardly enough to warrant scholars saying that he expected annihilation or even mere semiconscious existence after death. The verse makes it clear that Koheleth believed in the continued existence of the soul/spirit after death. He differentiates life here from what it would be in Sheol. The point is that life as man has known it ceases at death.

MAN DOES NOT KNOW HIS TIME
Ecclesiastes 9:11-12

Man must work; he ought to work; but the results are uncertain and beyond his control. One's own efforts do not guarantee success in life. Koheleth now reverts to his own personal experience. "I returned, and saw under the sun." The language points to a new point of view. Again he makes his perspective clear. He is at ground level.

When leaving God's principles out of the equation he made the following observations: (1) "the race is not to the swift." One may be a fleet runner, and yet, because of some untoward accident or disturbing circumstance, not be the first to cross the finish line. (2) "The battle is not to the strong." Victory is not always achieved by the mighty men. David's defeat of Goliath is the prime illustration of this principle. (3) "Neither is bread to the wise." Wisdom does not necessarily ensure competence. Many a person of cultivated intellect and high mental power cannot find gainful employment. (4) "Nor is wealth to the discerning." The smartest of men may wind up a pauper. (5) "Nor is favor to men of ability." Reputation and influence are not necessarily accompanied by the possession of knowledge and learning. The point in all this is that human ability and resources do not guarantee success.

So why does not success come to those who most merit it? Koheleth explains that "time and chance overtake them all." Two of the factors which lead to success or failure are indicated. (1) "Time" seems to indicate that it is an element in deciding whether a person succeeds or fails in what he attempts. He may be out of form and unable to put forth his best effort. (2) The term "chance" (*pega'*) here refers to unforeseen occurrences. The term usually connotes an *evil* occurrence (cf. 1 Kgs 5:4). Some mishap may rob the better person of the prize which he deserves.

God may allow things to transpire that frustrate those who apparently have all resources and gifts at their disposal. He may allow their efforts to be thwarted. All human efforts are liable to be changed or controlled by circumstances beyond man's power. A hand higher than man's disposes events, and success is conditioned by superior laws which work unexpected results (9:11).

Not only are results out of man's control, but his life is in higher hands as well: "Man does not know his time." Certainly he does not know the time of his death. More, however, is meant. The language may include any misfortune or accident. These unexpected and unhappy incidents are compared (1) to fish that are taken in "an evil net;" or (2) to birds trapped in a snare. These similes stress that disaster may come unexpectedly. They also emphasize how insignificant the mightiest of men are in the sight of God. "So are the sons of men snared in an evil time." Calamity suddenly overtakes them which they are totally unable to foresee or provide against. The word "time" here refers to the time of judgment as it did in the preceding verse (9:12).

MAN DOES NOT KNOW WHAT WILL BE
Ecclesiastes 9:13–10:15

In this unit the poet creates a picture of the uncertainty of the future. The unit is developed in four parts.

A. Wisdom Is Vulnerable (9:13-10:1).

Koheleth now makes an observation about how wisdom is rewarded "under the sun": "This also I saw to be wisdom under the sun." He speaks, of course, of worldly wisdom. He then relates a fictitious story, but one which has close similarities to the account related in 2 Sam 20:15-22. He regarded this incident as "great," i.e., as an important illustration (9:13).

The illustration is this: A "small city" was besieged by a "great king." Great mounds or embankments were raised high enough to overtop the walls of the town. The fall of the town was all but certain. In that city the great king encounters a poor wise man. "He by his wisdom delivered the city" by his wise counsel. Probably the reference is to some timely negotiations which this wise man conducted. In spite of the great deliverance which this man effected, "yet no man remembered that same poor man." He fell back into his insignificance, and was thought of no more (9:14-15).

The story just narrated leads Koheleth to make this observation: "Then I said, Wisdom is better than strength." Wisdom can accomplish what physical strength and resources cannot effect (cf. 7:19). In spite of this demonstrable benefit of wisdom, "nevertheless the poor man's wisdom is despised." Though perhaps in an emergency situation citizens might turn to such an insignificant person, yet as a rule, in ordinary times, the counsel emanating from such a lowly source is disregarded (9:16).

Koheleth now gathers some proverbial sayings concerning wisdom and its opposite, which draw the moral from the story cited above. First, "the words of the wise in quiet are heard better than the shout of a chief among fools." A wise man offers his counsel quietly, calmly, deliberately and humbly. On the other hand, with his bluster a fool attempts to force acceptance of his folly by loudness and swagger. While the multitude turns a deaf ear to a wise man's counsel, yet there are always some teachable persons who will sit at his feet to learn from him (9:17).

Second, "wisdom is better than weapons of war." Such is the moral which Koheleth draws from the little story which he has just told. Wisdom can do what no material force can effect. It often produces results which all the implements of war could not command. On the other hand, "one sinner destroys much good." All the good which the counsel of the wise man might accomplish may be quickly overthrown by the villainy and perversity of one bad man (9:18).

Third, "dead flies cause the ointment of the perfumer to send forth a stinking savor." This is a metaphorical restatement of the principle stated in the previous verse. The point is the comparative insignificance of the cause which spoils a costly substance compounded with care and skill. Thus little faults mar great characters and reputations: "More weighty than wisdom, than honor, is a little folly." It is a sad fact of life that one foolish act will suffice to impair the real value of a person's wisdom and the estimation in which he is held. This little fault, like the dead flies, obscures the real excellence of the man, and deprives him of the honor that is really his due (10:1).

B. Impediments to Wisdom (10:2-7).

"A wise man's heart is at his right hand; but a fool's is at his left." To the ancients the right hand was the place of honor, the left of inferiority. The idea is that the wise man's heart leads him to what is right and proper; the fool's heart leads him astray, in the wrong direction. The wise person's mind, like a guardian, helps him to escape snares and dangers in his daily life. The fool has no such help (10:2).

As soon as the fool sets his feet outside the house, and mixes with other men, he exhibits his folly: "Yea, also, when he that is a fool walks by the way, his wisdom [lit., heart] fails him." Had he stayed at home, he might have been able to keep his ineptitude concealed; but such persons as he are unaware of their stupidity. They go wherever their foolish hearts prompt them. The lack of "heart" in the wisdom literature is equivalent to lacking any common sense. By his actions "he says to everyone that he is a fool."[4] As soon as he goes abroad, his words and actions display his real character; he betrays himself to all as a fool (10:3).

How should wisdom act in the face of anger and resentment? "If the anger [lit., spirit] of the ruler rise up against you, do not leave your place." The picture here is of a monarch who becomes angry at the advice of his counselor and shows his resentment by scorn and reproach. The natural reaction would be a hasty resignation from the court or an intemperate outburst against the king. But wisdom encourages restraint because "composure pacifies great offenses." The quiet resignation saves this counselor from conspiracy, rebellion, or treason into which a rash response might lead him (10:4).

Koheleth now gives his personal observation regarding the apparent confusion which often prevails in the government. "There is an evil which I have seen under the sun." Power gets into the hands of an unwise person, and then that ruler makes a grave error, i.e., a mistake of some kind. The idea here is that the evil is one not produced by any intentional action of the ruler, but resulting from human imperfection (10:5).

The error of the ruler is further described: "Folly is set in great dignity, and the rich sit in low place." A foolish ruler exalts incompetent persons to high positions. "Folly" here is abstract for "fools." The "rich" are not simply those who have wealth, however obtained, but men of noble birth and ancestral wealth. Such men often are motivated by honorable ambition to seek high positions. They are often feared by insecure rulers and kept in lowly position (10:6).

Koheleth further develops the picture of the ill-advised appointments of the foolish ruler. "I have seen servants upon horses, princes walking as servants upon the earth." By the time of Solomon the horse had come to be recognized as the animal of honor (10:7).

C. Expecting the Unexpected (10:8-11).

Koheleth next produces several proverbs which express the benefit of prudence and caution, and the danger of folly. The reference may again be to the wise man who has incurred the resentment of a ruler, and who might be inclined to follow the path of rebellion.

"He who digs a pit shall fall into it, and whoever breaks a wall, a serpent shall bite him." This proverb is repeated in Prov 26:27 where it suggests the retribution which awaits evildoers. Here the proverb is intended to inspire caution before undertaking rebellion against the crown. Koheleth envisions poisonous snakes making their abode in the crevices of a wall. Demolition of the wall would disturb those serpents. The removal of the wall may be necessary, but it is also dangerous. Caution is in order. Metaphorically, the pulling down of the wall may refer to the removal of evil institutions in a state, which exposes the reformer to many perils (10:8).

"Whoever removes stones shall be hurt thereby; he that cuts wood shall be endangered thereby." The work of a quarry man is in view (cf. 1 Kgs 5:17). The dangers to which such laborers are exposed are well known. Cutting up logs of wood, a worker may cut himself with axe or saw. Some take the idea to be that of felling trees, in which

794

case the falling timber could crush the worker, or he could be injured by a flying axe head. Metaphorically there may be a warning here about trying to dismantle time-honored institutions or customs (10:9).

In cutting wood one needs a sharp axe: "If the iron be blunt, and one does not whet the edge, then must he put to [it] more strength." More force must be put into the blows if the axe is not sharp. On the other hand, "the advantage of setting right is [on the side of] wisdom." Wisdom teaches how to conduct matters to a successful termination; for instance, in this case, wisdom would prompt the worker to first sharpen his axe. This proverb applies to all of the previously named situations. Wisdom alone enables a person to meet and overcome the dangers and difficulties which beset his social and political life. If one is bent on pressing his disaffection with the ruler, let him first be sure that his resources are adequate to ensure success (10:10).

Finally, Koheleth sets forth a proverb designed to show the necessity of seizing the right opportunity: "If the serpent bites before being charmed, then there is no use in the charmer." Snake charming is attested in Scripture (e.g., Exod 7:11). The custom still survives to this day. If the charmer is bitten before he can employ his skills, then the charming skill is of no value to him. The greatest skill is useless unless it is applied at the right moment (10:11).

D. The Futility of Words (10:12-15).

The mention of "the master of the tongue" in v. 11 leads the author to introduce some maxims contrasting the words and works of the wise on the one hand, and the worthless babbling and labors of the fool.

"The words of a wise man's mouth are gracious [lit., grace]." His words are pleasing and persuasive. Unlike the unfortunate snake charmer of the preceding verse, the wise man speaks opportunely and to good purpose. Jesus is the perfect illustration of this truth (Luke 4:22). On the other hand, "the lips of the fool will swallow up himself." He speaks before he thinks, and consequently has to subsequently withdraw the remarks he has made. Thus he brings reproach upon himself. His words are the cause of his own undoing (10:12).

The problem with the fool (kesil = dull, stupid) is that "the beginning of the words of his mouth is foolishness." He no more than opens his mouth and out pours stupidity and folly. But he does not stop there. "The end of his talk is wicked madness." By the time he is finished he has committed himself to statements that are worse than silly; they are presumptuous, and indicative of mental and moral depravity. His intemperate language may be about God's providence; or he may be lashing out against the king (10:13; cf. 10:4).

"Moreover the fool (*sakhal* = dense, confused) multiplies words." He not only speaks foolishly, he talks too much. What is still worse, he babbles on about things of which he knows nothing. "A man cannot tell what shall be [in the immediate future]." That, however, does not stop the fool. He speaks confidently of such things, thereby underscoring his stupidity. "And what shall be after him, who can tell?" He does not realize (1) that his speech may have lasting consequences; or (2) that his sins may be visited upon his offspring; or (3) that he faces bleak prospects after death. The uncertainty of the future is a constant theme in this section (10:14).

Now Koheleth turns to the work of fools, although he may be referring to the vain speculations about providence as being fools' work. "The work of fools wearies him that does not know how to go to the city." Not knowing the way to the city probably is proverbial for gross ignorance concerning the most obvious matters. The fool toils until his strength is exhausted without accomplishing anything. The point is that there is a common-sense method of accomplishing a task which only a fool fails to see and so spends his efforts to no avail (10:15).

MAN DOES NOT KNOW
WHAT EVIL WILL COME
Ecclesiastes 10:16–11:2

The consequences of wisdom and folly in the life of the common people have a parallel in wise and foolish civil rulers. Koheleth now returns to the theme of 10:4-7, namely, folly in one who holds the office of king. He emphasizes again the need for wisdom and prudence on the part of the subjects of such a king.

A. Evil In High Places (10:16-17).
"Woe to you, O land, when your king is a boy." The term "boy" (*na'ar*) includes any age up to manhood. The case envisions a youthful,

inexperienced king who is the tool of evil advisers. Many expositors think the childish Rehoboam, son and successor of Solomon, is in view. Though he was forty when he assumed office, he acted like a spoiled child (1 Kgs 12:1-14). A land is also in bad shape when its "princes eat in the morning," i.e., they take the heavy meal of the day at a time when they should be attending to the affairs of state. None but profligates would so spend the early morning (10:16; cf. Isa 5:11).

"Blessed are you, O land, when your king is the son of nobles." Koheleth has already expressed his disgust at the exaltation of unworthy slaves to high positions; here he intimates that those who descend from noble stock, and have been educated in the higher ranks of society, are more likely to prove a blessing to their land than upstarts who have achieved their position through graft or cronyism. Koheleth is here speaking of what is generally true, not what is always true. Princes of noble birth "eat in due season," i.e., they do not feast while they should be governing. They eat "for strength, and not for drunkenness," i.e., for sustenance, not for sensuality. They would not let their meals degenerate into drunken carousal (10:17).

B. Disaster in the Land (10:18-19).

Koheleth now uses the image of a house to symbolize the state. With incompetent and indolent rulers the house of state deteriorates: "Through indolence the rafters sag, and through slackness the house leaks." Good rulers would have alertly made those house repairs before the entire structure became unsalvagable (10:18).

Now Koheleth explains how the old house of state got to be in such bad shape: "For merriment they make bread, and wine [that] cheers life." The rulers spent too much time in revelry and debauchery. They have too little time and energy to devote to the affairs of state. They have used God's good gifts intemperately and for thoughtless pleasure. For these worthless rulers "money is the answer to everything." It takes money to finance their lavish lifestyle. This they possess, and they are thus able to indulge their appetites to the utmost. No doubt much of their money was acquired by extortion and bribery as well as through exorbitant taxation. They use their high office to enhance their personal wealth (10:19).

C. Caution for Desperate Times (10:20).

Under the circumstances described above, a person might be tempted to abuse and curse these terrible national leaders. Koheleth warns: "Curse not the king, no not in your thought," i.e., do not even think about cursing the king. It is dangerous to give in to this impulse. In 8:2 Koheleth offered piety as the grounds for submission to the king; here the ground is prudence, i.e., regard for personal safety. Such unscrupulous princes would stop at nothing to retain their power.

Furthermore, Koheleth advises: "Curse not the rich in your bed chamber." The "rich" are the wealthy families who govern the country. The situation envisioned is of one conversing with another person in a remote part of the house. This is like saying, "the walls have ears." Servants might be quite willing to report their master to the authorities for a price. "For a bird of the air shall carry the voice, and the winged creature will make the matter known." This is equivalent to the modern "a little bird told me." No matter how careful one might be, treasonous words would wing their way quickly to the ruthless princes. An autocrat spreads spies throughout the land to report on his subjects (10:20).

D. Actions for Desperate Times (11:1-2).

When living under political duress one had best heed this advice: "Cast your bread upon the waters." The text has nothing to do with the sowing of seed, as some claim, for the Hebrew verb *shalach* is not used of sowing or scattering seed. Who in their right mind would hurl cakes of bread into a stream of water? This seems to be a metaphor for engaging in thankless toil. The proverb then urges the wise person to do good without hope of return.[5] "You shall find it after many days." This is not to be the motive for the good deeds, but it will in the course of time be the result (11:1).

The metaphor of bread on water is now dropped, and the advice is put in plain language: "Give a portion to seven, and also to eight," i.e., give a portion of your bread to any number of those who might need it. Koheleth is recommending unlimited benevolence. The X + 1 formula is common in Proverbs, and is a way of indicating an indefinite number. The motive for this generosity is this: "For you do not know what calamity shall be upon the earth." A time may come when the benefactor may need help; he may no longer be in a position to help others. The idea is to make friends now as insurance against the day the help of others will be needed (cf. Luke 16:9). This is not the highest possible motive for giving, but wisdom books are practical. Here the practicality of benevolence is being argued (11:2).

MAN DOES NOT KNOW
WHAT GOOD WILL COME
Ecclesiastes 11:3-6

A. The Certainty about the Future (11:3).

Misfortune may come at any minute: "If the clouds be full of rain, they empty themselves upon the earth." The misfortune anticipated in the previous paragraph is as certain as the laws of nature; it is unforeseen and uncontrollable. When the clouds are overcharged with moisture, they deliver their burden upon the earth, according to laws which man cannot alter. "And whether a tree falls to the south or to the north, wherever the tree falls there will it lie." This is another illustration of man's helplessness in the face of the forces of nature, and man must accept things as they are. When the tempest overthrows the tree, it lies where it has fallen. When the evil day comes, people must bend to the blow. Men are powerless to avert it. The future can be neither calculated nor controlled (11:3).

B. The Danger of Over Caution (11:4).

Though the future is uncertain and immutable, this ought not to crush from men all diligence and activity: "He who observes the wind shall not sow." The picture is of a farmer who watches the winds waiting for the opportune time to sow his seed. If he occupies his mind with the possibility of violent winds which will blow away the seed he sows, he will be reduced to inaction. The point is that one who tries to foresee the future and prepare for every contingency will miss golden opportunities.

The same is true of the time of harvest. Here the absence of rain was the desirable thing. "He that regards the clouds shall not reap." Storms in harvest were devastating. One who feared every indication of such bad weather and altered his plans at every change in the sky, might easily put off reaping his fields till either the crops were spoiled or the rainy season had set in. The point again is that nothing in life is certain. There are no guarantees. Probability girded with prayer must be the rule for every venture. The only one who never fails is the person who never attempts anything; and that is the greatest failure of all (11:4).

C. Ignorance of Potential Good (11:5-6).

Man is ignorant of basic facts in the physical realm; how much more in the spiritual realm, the mysteries of God's moral government. Two examples of man's ignorance are noted: "You do not know the way of the wind," i.e., the changes in the directions of the wind. Who is able to predict them?[6] Second, man is ignorant of how a child grows in the womb: "as [you know not] the bones in a womb which is filled." The growth of an infant in his mother's womb is a marvel even to this day. Who really understands it?

Equally mysterious in its general scope and in its details is the working of God's providence: "Even so you know not the works of God who makes all." As everything lies in God's hands, it must needs be secret and beyond human purview. The God of creation is the God who holds the future in his hand (11:5).

Again Koheleth warns against indolence and apathy based on ignorance of the future and the inscrutability of God's dealings: "In the morning sow your seed, and in the evening do not withhold your hand." The point is that one should be about his daily business; be active and diligent in his calling. The labor of the farmer is taken as a type of business generally. A person should be up and at his business early in the morning; he should work till evening. This is a call to spend the entire day in active labor. Work undertaken in the right spirit is a blessing. It shuts out many temptations, and encourages many virtues.

So why labor morning till evening? The motive for this injunction is this: "For you do not know whether morning or evening sowing will prosper, or whether they both alike shall be good." If one fails, the other may take. At least one would have something for his labor, and possibly even double produce of both sowings. The point is: When there is work to be done, do it diligently and exhaustively, and do not be concerned with the factors which are beyond the understanding.

ENDNOTES

1. Others take 9:6 to be saying the the emotions of love, hatred and jealousy are no longer experienced by the dead.

2. Others think that the works of which God approves in 9:7 are works that are done in righteousness.

3. The word for wife or woman does not have the definite article in the Hebrew. For this reason, some scholars have proposed that Koheleth is recommending free sexual indulgence with any woman. The best commentators, however, agree that the married state is meant in the text, not mere sensual enjoyment.

4. Another view of 10:3 is that the fool regards everyone he meets to be a fool.

5. Another, but less likely, interpretation of 11:1 is that it is a commercial maxim, urging men to make ventures in trade that they may receive a good return for their expenditure. Casting seed on the water would then refer to sending merchandise across the sea to distant lands.

6. The Hebrew word can also be translated "spirit." For this reason some scholars think that only one illustration of man's ignorance is being given in 11:5, namely, the formation of the embryo and the implantation within it of the spirit of life.

CHAPTER THIRTY-NINE

The Conclusion of the Matter
Ecclesiastes 11:7-12:14

After pursuing many tortuous paths, Koheleth comes to his final conclusion regarding the meaning of life. This closing division of the book contains a poem and an epilogue in the third person.

A PROSE INTRODUCTION
Ecclesiastes 11:7-8

A prose introduction summarizes the final section of the book. Armed with cheerfulness, the believer can meet and conquer all the perplexities of life. This is the spirit that enjoys the present, but which also has an eye to the future.

A. The Joy of Life (11:7).

"And truly the light is sweet." The copula *vav* ("and") here merely notes transition. One should not become perplexed, or despondent, or paralyzed in his work, by the difficulties that meet him. "The light" here may be taken literally, or as equivalent to life. If the former, the idea is that all that the light reveals, all that it beautifies, all that it awakens, is a pleasure. When one acts benevolently and works diligently as Koheleth has previously advised, life is worth living, and affords continuous enjoyment for the faithful worker. "A pleasant thing it is for the eyes to behold the sun." To "behold the sun" is to be alive (11:7).

B. The Duty of Joy (11:8).

"For if a man lives many years, he ought to rejoice in them all." Life is sweet and pleasant; it is man's duty to enjoy it. God has ordained for him to do so whether his days on earth be many or few.

At the same time he needs to "remember the days of darkness." The reference is to death, and the life in Sheol, far from life under the sun.[1] The thought that the night comes when no man can work (John 9:4) should stir mankind to make the best of every day of life, to be content and cheerful, to perform daily duties with the consciousness that this is the day of labor and joy.

What specifically is one to remember about the day of darkness? Koheleth answers: "That they shall be many." The time in Sheol will be long. He says nothing about how those days will be passed or when those days would end. He therefore bids men to use the present which is all they can claim.

"All that comes is vanity." This may mean: To live in the future is vanity. It may never come. Death may cut it off. The present is the substance of life. Make the best of it. On the other hand, the coming vanity may refer to old age in which the faculties have lost their power. This latter explanation fits well with what follows in chapter 12 (11:8).

In the poem proper Koheleth begins by urging youth (1) to enjoy their youth; and (2) to remember the grave.

THE TIME OF YOUTH
Ecclesiastes 11:9-10

Koheleth now develops his thesis that youth is meant to be enjoyed. He does so by stating his admonition positively, and then negatively.

A. A Positive Admonition (11:9).

Koheleth opens his final poem with a call for the rational enjoyment of life. In v. 8 he called upon people to rejoice. Here the thought broadens out to the point where it bids a person in a general way to cultivate the spirit of true cheerfulness.

"Rejoice, O young man, in your youth," i.e., to begin cultivating the virtue of joy during youth. Even while young, believers should set their hearts to enjoy the blessings with which God surrounds them. Youth is the season of innocence, of unalloyed pleasure. If any can cast away tormenting anxiety concerning the future, it is young people. The joyful life begins in the heart, with attitude and resolve. It does not depend on external circumstances. "Let your heart cheer you in the days of your youth." The lightness of the heart should show itself in one's bearing and manner.

Two principles should guide the youth in his "walk" or daily life. First, he should walk in the ways of his "heart," i.e., satisfy the longings of the heart. One may follow the inclinations of a heart which is rooted in the fear of God for it will assuredly desire what is right. The form of the statement emphasizes, not the restrictions which godly morality places upon the life, but the broad areas which are thrown open for human enjoyment. Second, he should walk in the sight of his "eyes," i.e., follow after that on which he has fixed his eyes.

Koheleth is not here recommending unbridled lust or thoughtless pleasure. He adds a thought, a solemn reflection which points to the conclusion to which the book has been building: "But know that for all these things God will bring you into judgment." Does he mean judgment in this world? Does he refer to scourges, poverty, sickness, a miserable old age and the like? Such often come as natural consequences of youthful excess. Is he referring to the reproach of men? Surely the passage points to something more grave than any of these temporal experiences. Nothing satisfies the expected conclusion but a reference to the eternal judgment in the world beyond the grave.

In earlier passages Koheleth spoke of temporal judgments of various kinds (e.g., 2:26; 3:17; 7:17f.). Here he rises to a higher level. Yet he has also recognized that temporal reward and punishment fail in many cases. This fact has set the stage for this revelation that this life is not the end of everything. There is another existence in which actions will be tried, justice done, and retribution administered. He says but little about this final judgment. His previous references to Sheol lead one to think that he thought of this judgment being beyond Sheol.

B. A Negative Admonition (11:10).

In order to enjoy life the youth must remove all those things which might interfere with legitimate joy. First, he must "remove fretfulness" from his "heart." The term "fretfulness" (ka'as) refers to low spirits or discontent with existing circumstances. These feelings are to be put away from the mind by a deliberate act of the will. One must force himself to think positively. Second, he must "put away" evil from his "flesh." The ancient versions translate the word in such a way as to indicate that it is moral evil[2] which is in view here. In his enjoyment of life the youth must not defile his body with carnal sins which bring decay and sickness, and which arouse God's anger.

So why does Koheleth encourage a circumspect enjoyment of life during youth? Because "youth and manhood are vanity." This time of youth soon passes away; the capacity for enjoyment is soon curtailed. Therefore one should use these years aright, remembering the end. The word for "youth" (shacharuth) is related to a word meaning "black." Youth is the time of black hair, in contrast to the time when the hair has become gray. "Vanity" here means "fleeting" as in 7:15 and 9:9.

C. The Fundamental Admonition (12:1a).

For young people Koheleth has this exhortation: "Remember now your creator in the days of your youth." Here is the deep root which alone can make true joy possible. To "remember" certainly implies more than to recall that there is a creator. It surely means to let that remembrance shape conduct. He is to be remembered as creator, i.e., that he has complete and absolute claims upon every person. This remembrance is indicated by obedience to his revealed will. The term "creator" is a plural of excellence or majesty. Some commentators think that plurals like this are divinely intended to foreshadow the mystery of the pluralistic unity of the Godhead (Trinity) which would be further revealed in the New Covenant revelation.

Young people need to constantly remember who made them, and the purpose for which they were made. They were not put on this planet for self-gratification, not to gratify the passions of the flesh which are particularly strong in the time of youth. They were placed here to use their powers and energy in accordance with the laws of the creator. They are responsible to him for the use of the faculties and capacities with which they have been endowed. They need to acknowledge cheerfully that all they are and all they have come from God.

THE TIME OF OLD AGE
Ecclesiastes 12:1b-7

In contrast to the period of youth, when people are in the prime of life, old age is a difficult and increasingly debilitating time. The senior years are described in the verses which follow in a highly metaphorical, even allegorical, manner. This difficult passage proceeds from a general description of old age (v. 2), to the infirmates of that period of life (vv. 3-4), and the painful struggle to the grave itself (vv. 5-7).

A. General Description of Old Age (12:1b-2).

Youth need to devote their energies to the service of the creator "while the evil days come not," i.e., before those evil days creep up on them. The reference is to the grievances, inconveniences and afflictions of old age. As time marches on the bad days outnumber the good days. In contrast to the shortened periods ("days") when afflictions are dominant, are the longer periods ("years") in which older people take no pleasure. When those years draw near, one might be inclined to say, "I have no pleasure in them," i.e., life no longer offers any pleasures. The aged Barzillai (2 Sam 19:35) is the prime biblical example of this attitude. He describes his sense of discernment as diminished, his taste dull, his hearing impaired (12:1b).

Youth is the period of life during which "the sun, or the light, or the moon, or the stars, be not darkened." Light in Scripture is quite generally a symbol of joy and a token of divine favor. Here the approach of old age, the winter of life, is likened to the rainy season in Palestine, when the sun is obscured by clouds, and the light of

807

heaven is darkened by the withdrawal of the luminaries. All joys are dimmed significantly in old age. That is the time of life when "the clouds return after the rain," i.e., one storm follows on the heels of another. This imagery is intended to represent the abiding and increasing inconveniences of old age. In youth, sunshine follows times of storm; in old age, one gloomy experience follows another. The darkening of the light is a common metaphor for sadness (12:2).

B. The Infirmities of Old Age (12:3-4).

Koheleth now employs a metaphor of a dilapidated house to illustrate the deterioration which sets in during old age. Likening a person to a house is not uncommon in Scripture (e.g., Job 4:19; 2 Cor 5:1f.; 2 Pet 1:13ff.).[3]

In old age (1) "the keepers of the house shall tremble." These have been taken to be a metaphor for the hands and arms which one uses in youth to defend himself in various ways. In old age they tremble with palsy. (2) "The men of power shall bow themselves." These are a metaphor for the legs which in old age become feeble and bent. (3) "The grinders cease because they are few." These are the teeth which can no longer perform their function of grinding the food. (4) "Those that look out of the windows be darkened." These would be the eyes which are impaired with age. The eyes are said to be darkened because the clear images that should be seen have grown indistinct or dark (12:3).

(5) "The doors shall be shut in the streets." The reference is probably to the ears. They are shut to the outside world. Even the common sound of the grinding of grain, which was heard daily about the home, is scarcely perceived by the unfortunate old man. (6) The old man "rises to the bird's voice." This is usually taken to be a reference to the light sleep of the old man. He wakes up at the mere chirp of a bird. The reference, however, probably is to the voice of the old man. It becomes like the piping of a little bird. The relaxation of the muscles of the larynx and other vocal organs occasions a great difference in the pitch or power of tone of the voice. (7) The next clause probably also refers to the organs of speech: "And the daughters of music shall be brought low." The old man cannot sing a note (12:4).

C. En Route to the Grave (12:5).

Briefly the metaphor is dropped in v. 5, but the discouraging description of old age continues. First, "also they fear on high," i.e., they find difficulty mounting an ascent. Shortness of breath and failure of muscular power make such an exertion arduous and burdensome. Second, "all sorts of fears are in the path," i.e., the ordinary road. In his infirm condition he can walk nowhere without danger of meeting with some accident.

Third, "the almond tree is in blossom." Koheleth has now reverted to metaphor. The almond tree blossoms in winter upon a leafless stem. Its flowers, first pink, turn snowy white as they drop from the branches. The tree thus becomes an appropriate figure for an old man with his white hair. The white hair is an adornment to the head of an aging person, but at the same time that white hair is a sign of physical decay.

Fourth, Koheleth uses another metaphor for the walk of the aged person: "and the grasshopper crawls along." The locust just hatched in early spring as yet has no wings. It makes its way clumsily and slowly. The crippled, dragging gait of the locust when it walks is an image of the ungainly and stiff gait that is characteristic of advanced age.

Fifth, "and the caperberry shall fail." The exact translation is uncertain, but the meaning is clear. The term caperberry ('abhiyyonah) appears only here in the Hebrew Bible. The translation "caperberry" (NASB) is based on the Septuagint. The word is closely related to the Hebrew word for "desire" and that is how NIV renders it. The caperberry was used as a stimulant of appetite. Its failure to have any effect points to the failure of all physical appetites and desires. The simple meaning of the text is that all desires, physical and mental, die down, literally "break" (tapher). This occurs because the bodily needs and functions are failing, and life is ebbing away. The old man can no longer enjoy his food.

Koheleth now inserts a parenthetical statement which explains his sense of urgency in this passage: "Because man goes to his long home." The previous clauses have painted a graphic picture of the symptoms of approaching decay and death, the process of the "going." All these things happen, all these signs meet the eye, at such a period. Man's "long home" or everlasting habitation is death itself, a state of being. From these words nothing can be deduced concerning Koheleth's eschatological views. He is speaking here phenomenally. Men live their little span upon the earth, and then go to what in comparison with this is an eternity. When man goes to his long home, "the mourners go about the streets." The professional mourners are preparing to ply their trade, expecting hourly the death of the old man.

Koheleth has made his point. Young people should remember their creator before the "evil days" of old age come upon them and they no longer have the energy and zeal to demonstrate their commitment to the Lord.

D. The Finality of Death (12:6).

Having presented a poetic picture of the aging process, Koheleth now presents an equally poetic picture of death itself. The conjunction "before" connects vv. 6-7 with v. 1. Youth should remember their creator before the final stroke of death. Here he uses four brilliant figures for death.

The first two figures belong together. He mentions the loosing of the silver cord and consequent smashing of the golden bowl. The "bowl" (*gullah*) is the reservoir of oil in a lamp which supplies nourishment to the flame. When this is broken or damaged so as to be useless, the light is extinguished. The silver cord is the thread of life, the living power which keeps the body from falling into ruin. The bowl is the body itself. Gold and silver denote the preciousness of man's life and nature. The first two figures depict the separation of soul and body.

The third figure is that of the broken pitcher. This earthen vessel, if it but once strikes the stones at the well, would smash into pieces. Man's life is not only precious, it is fragile. The fourth figure is that of the broken wheel at the cistern. The picture here is of a deep well or cistern with an apparatus for drawing water. This apparatus consists of a wheel (windlass) with a rope upon it, to which was attached a bucket. The wheel fails and falls into the well, the bucket is dashed to pieces, and no water can be drawn. Perhaps the motion by which the water was drawn from the well is an emblem of the movements of the heart and the organs of respiration. When these cease to act, life is extinct. Thus the figure portrays the overthrow of the bodily organs which keep man alive (12:6).

E. The Result of Death (12:7).

The figures pointing to death are now explained: "And the dust return to the earth as it was." The body of man returns at death to the matter out of which it was originally made (Gen 2:7; 3:19). On the other hand, "the spirit shall return unto God who gave it." One who evaluates death from ground level, without the light of revelation, cannot know whether or not the spirit of man goes upward at death (3:21). Here Koheleth comes to the firm conclusion that there is a future for the individual soul, and that it shall be brought into immediate presence of a personal God after death. If this statement is viewed in the light of the preceding utterances on the part of Koheleth, then the reference must be to the final judgment in God's presence of which he has spoken before (cf. 3:17). Thus the argument is that the time to remember the creator is before the hour has come to go to him as judge for the final reckoning. The very thought of judgment denotes a personal responsibility of the spirit that returns to God.[4]

EPILOGUE: KOHELETH'S CLAIMS
Ecclesiastes 12:8-11

Koheleth brings his work to a close by restating his basic thesis regarding life, by presenting his credentials to speak, and by recommending serious study of what he has written.

A. His Basic Thesis Regarding Life (12:8).

Koheleth does not follow the destiny of man's immortal spirit; it is not his purpose to do so. His theme is the fragility of mortal things, their unsatisfying nature, and the impossibility of their securing man's true happiness. So he concludes this section with the repetition of his thesis: "Vanity of vanities, says the Preacher, all is vanity." The term "Koheleth" here has the definite article as if some special reference is being made to the meaning of the name. He who has been debating and discussing various points of view now states his final verdict. Yes,

811

all on earth is vanity. But behind all is a God of inflexible justice, who must do right. To this God men may trust their cares and perplexities.

B. His Credentials to Speak (12:9).

In the final paragraphs the author defends his work and presents his credentials to speak. First, he claims the gift of wisdom. "Besides that, the Preacher was wise." He was regarded by his contemporaries as a sage. More than that, however, is embraced in this claim. The term wisdom (*chakham*) implies that wisdom which is from above, taught by God, and rooted in the fear of God. That he uses the third person in reference to himself is nothing uncommon in Old Testament literature. Daniel did the same thing. In the New Testament, the Gospel of John concludes with a third-person epilogue intended, like this one, to confirm the authority of the writer. Second, Koheleth was a teacher as well as a sage. Even before this book was written "he continually taught the people knowledge." He had given public proof of his willingness and his ability to function as a leader of godly thought.

Third, he was a careful scholar: "Yes, he weighed, searched out, and set in order many proverbs." The first term denotes the careful examination of every fact and argument before it was presented to the public. The term "searched out" implies an attempt to delve even deeper into the issues than his previous instruction had led him to do. This weighing and the investigation issued in the composition of proverbs. The term "proverbs" includes not only the wit and wisdom of past ages in the form of pithy sayings, but also parables, truths in metaphorical guise, riddles, instruction, allegories, and the like—the kind of material that appears in this book and in the Book of Proverbs (12:9).

C. His Claims about His Book (12:10-11).

In his book Koheleth had attempted to present his thought in the most appealing manner: "The Preacher sought to find out words of delight," i.e., he wanted his written material to be pleasing and attractive as well as accurate. He carefully sought for the most acceptable terms for conveying his message.

Koheleth was absolutely sincere in what he wrote: "And that which was written was upright." The word "upright" (*yosher*) suggests that he personally believed all that he wrote. His arguments here were the conviction of his heart. Even more important, Koheleth claims that what he wrote consisted of "words of truth," i.e., it was objectively true (12:10).

Koheleth classifies his book with other wisdom books as being "the words of the wise." Such words are designed by their creators to serve two purposes. First, they are "goads." The goad was a rod with an iron spike, or sharpened at the end, used in driving oxen. Words of wisdom are called goads because they rouse to exertion, promote reflection and action, restrain from error and urge in the right direction. If such words hurt and sting, the pain which they inflict is healthful, for good and not for evil. Second, the teachings of the wise as they are assembled in masterful collections[5] "are like nails fastened." Such words give a person something to hold on to. They furnish an anchor for the soul.

All of the words of the wise proceed from "one shepherd," i.e., they have one source. That one shepherd without question is Yahweh (cf. Gen 48:15; Ps 23:1). This is an important claim to inspiration. All these varied utterances, whatever form they take, are outcomes of wisdom, and proceed from him who is all wise, even almighty God. The writer is certainly aware that God is using him to add to the collection of sacred Scriptures.

D. His Admonition Regarding Study (12:12).

Since his book is inspired of God, Koheleth recommends it for serious study. First, however, he warns against profitless study: "And what is more than these, be warned." Besides all that has been said, take this additional and important caution. "Of making many books there is no end." The subjects treated in Ecclesiastes had been treated by various authors in many different ways. The warning here is against the unprofitable reading of these contradictory and confusing works of men which were not built upon the foundation of the fear of Yahweh. The practical thrust of this passage is that believers should make the word of God the chief object of their study. "Much study is a weariness of the flesh." The thought is that one may weary the brain and exhaust the strength by protracted study on many books, but still not necessarily thereby gain any insight into the problems of the universe or guidance for daily living (12:12).

EPILOGUE: KOHELETH'S CONCLUSION
Ecclesiastes 12:13-14

Koheleth next recommends his book by giving the substance and chief point of it: "The end (sum or conclusion) of the matter when all is heard is this . . . ." The teaching of the whole book of Ecclesiastes is now gathered up in two powerful sentences. In the Hebrew text the word *soph* ("end") is printed in large characters, in order to draw attention to the importance of what is coming. The next two sentences guard against possible misconceptions and give the author's real and mature conclusion.

A. The Fear of God (12:13).
First, "Fear God and keep his commandments." This injunction is the practical result of the whole discussion which precedes. Amid the difficulties of the moral government of the world, amid the complications of society, varying and opposing interests and claims, one duty remains plain and unchanging: the duty of piety and submission to the will of the creator. "Fear" here is of course that reverent awe which grows out of the faith which the frail creature should have toward the holy God. It manifests itself in obedience to divine commands. The reason for this injunction translated literally is this: "For this is every man." This is what it means to be a man; this is the object, the chief good which man is to seek. This is the course in life which alone will give to man contentment and happiness. The obligation here set forth is put in the broadest possible terms for it is applicable to the whole human family (12:13).

B. The Final Judgment (12:14).
Second, the great duty just named is grounded upon the solemn fact of the future judgment: "For God shall bring every work into judgment." At that time and place it will be determined whether or not man has fulfilled his basic obligation to fear God and keep his commandments. This judgment has already been mentioned (11:9); but it

is here more emphatically set forth as a certain fact and a strong incentive for piety. The old theory of earthly retribution had been shown here, and in the Book of Job, to break down in too many cases. The inequities of life can only be resolved and remedied by that final judgment under the eye of the omniscient and unerring God. There "every secret thing" will be exposed (12:14).

ENDNOTES

1. Some take the "days of darkness" in 11:8 to refer to the twilight years of life when it becomes increasingly difficult to enjoy life.

2. Some consider the "evil" in 11:10 to be physical, not moral. The author would then be enjoining young people to take proper care of the body, not to weaken it on the one hand by asceticism, nor on the other by indulgence in youthful lust.

3. Some think that 12:3-5 sets forth the threatening approach of death under the image of a tempest. The commentators who support this viewpoint point to the word "rain" in v. 2. This word (*geshem*), however, never refers to a "storm."

4. Some take 12:7 to say only that the vital breath which God gave to man at creation returns to him at death. Surely, however, this would be a feeble conclusion to the intellectual wanderings of Koheleth.

5. The phrase "masters of assemblies" in 12:11 is difficult. It seems best to regard these "assemblies" as collections of proverbs rather than of people. The whole phrase would then refer to proverbs of an excellent character, the best of their sort, gathered together in writing.

THE SONG OF SONGS

CHAPTER FORTY

Getting Acquainted with the Song
Faith Expressed in Love

If Psalms is worship literature, and Job, Proverbs and Ecclesiastes are wisdom literature, what is the Song of Songs? It offers no direct instruction, or debate. Some think it is a category all its own, perhaps to be designated "wedding literature." In recent years, however, scholars have begun to recognize this book as a further example of wisdom literature. Love is a basic human experience, and human experience is what wisdom literature is all about. Like Proverbs this book does not speak of Israel's unique relationship with Yahweh. Yet this book of eight chapters (117 verses; 2,661 words) celebrates one of God's greatest gifts to man: human sexuality.

TITLE OF THE BOOK

The fifth of the poetic books is known in English Bibles by three names. Most recent English versions title the book "The Song of Songs," which is a literal translation of the Hebrew title. This title means, "the song *par excellence*." Both the Latin and the Greek versions also translated the Hebrew title literally into their respective languages. In Latin this became *Canticles Canticorum*, from which some English versions, particularly those within the Roman Catholic tradition, get the second English title for the book, namely, Canticles. Older non-Catholic translations in English use the title Song of Solomon.

The designation of the book as the Song of Songs is most fitting for two reasons. First, this book deals with the theme of themes: love. Second, its literary excellence is such as to make it well worthy of the gifted king to whom it is attributed.

AUTHORSHIP OF THE BOOK

The opening verse of the book appears to attribute authorship to Solomon by using the formula "which is to Solomon" (*'asher li-shelo-moh*). Some scholars have suggested that this is a formula of dedication rather than an attribution of authorship. The use of the preposition *lamed* ("to"), however, is the most convenient way of expressing possession or authorship in Hebrew where the same author may have composed many other works.[1]

The claim of Solomonic authorship is supported by the following facts: (1) the interest in flora and fauna fits Solomon (cf. 1 Kgs 4:33); (2) the geographical references favor a date prior to the division of the kingdom;[2] and (3) the uniform tradition within the Jewish and Christian communities.[3] Even several scholars who deny Solomonic authorship of Ecclesiastes (e.g., E.J. Young) defend the traditional view here. This is somewhat strange in view of the considerable similarity in vocabulary and syntax between the two books.[4]

Solomon is mentioned in the book seven times. This would seem to support the claims of the heading. Nonetheless, Solomonic authorship does present some problems. How does the love described in this book fit the picture presented in the historical books of a Solomon with many wives? Why does the book seem to look at Solomon at a distance? (cf. 3:6-11; 8:11-12). How is the rebuff of Solomon in 8:11-12 to be explained? These problems have caused some conservative scholars to argue for only a partial Solomonic authorship as in Proverbs.[5] Other conservatives think the book is anonymous, but comes from the Solomonic period or shortly thereafter.[6]

THE DATE OF THE BOOK

Those who see Solomon as the author of the book would date the Song early in his reign, perhaps ca. 965 BC. The lack of historical references in the book makes dating difficult. Those who reject Solomonic authorship point to (alleged) Persian and Greek words in the book, to certain features of the Hebrew syntax, and to words and phrases reflecting Aramaic influence. This evidence supposedly points to the Persian, perhaps even the Greek period, for the date of the book.

In response to this late dating of the book, these points can be made: (1) Ample evidence exists both for the intercourse between Ionia and Canaan, and for Aramaic impact on Hebrew literature from the early centuries of the monarchy. (2) The geographical references seem to point to a time when all the land—Israel, Judah and Transjordan—were part of the kingdom. (3) The witness of archaeology to Solomon's splendid reign seems to render it unnecessary to assign the book to the pomp and circumstances of the Persian Empire. (4) The Song's lavish setting accurately reflects Solomon's glory.[7]

There is no sufficient reason to deny that this book in its entirety was written by Solomon himself. The number of the so-called signs of lateness in the text has been shrinking of late with the discovery of contemporary extrabiblical poetic materials. Certain features of the text which once were regarded as a sure sign of a postexilic date are now known to have been common features of poetry at least as old as Solomon.[8] For example, the forms indicating Aramaic influence have traditionally been assigned to the postexilic period when Aramaic was the international language. Now, however, scholars realize that Aramaic influences on the Israelites predate Solomon by centuries.[9]

BACKGROUND OF THE BOOK

Solomon ascended the throne in ca. 970 BC. He was famous, among other things, for his many wives and concubines (1 Kgs 11:3). Most of these marriages were political alliances. On a trip to the northern part of his land, the king met and fell in love with a beautiful maiden. She was given by her brothers in marriage to Solomon. The Shulamite maiden, however, loved a shepherd back in the country. The book is the story of Solomon's struggle to woo this maiden to true love, and her steadfast determination to reman faithful to her beloved.

The setting for the dialogue is, for the most part, Solomon's Jerusalem palace. The Song, however, mentions a number of places, most of which are located in northern Israel, Transjordan, and Syria. Among these are Bether (2:17); Mount Gilead (4:1); Tirzah (6:4); Mahanaim (6:13); En-gedi (1:14); Lebanon, Amana, Shenir, Hermon (4:8); Heshbon (7:4); Damascus (7:4); Carmel (7:5); and Baal-hamon (8:11).

THE NATURE OF THE BOOK

If Ecclesiastes focused on man's intellect, this book is about his emotions, especially the emotion of love. The Song has been described as "a hymn in praise of sensual love with no minor strains of prudery or shame to mar its melody."[10]

A. A Collection.

Love poems found in the literature of the ancient Near East have fueled the view that the Song of Songs is really a collection of songs. Scholars have demonstrated numerous parallels between the language of this book and Egyptian love poetry.[11] Others have pointed out parallels with the songs that were sung during wedding ceremonies among the Arabs where bride and groom were made "king" and "queen" for a day. These songs extolled the physical beauty of the marriage couple.[12]

Internal analysis led Maria Falk to conclude that the book consists of thirty-one poems connected only by thematic considerations.[13] Eissfeldt found twenty-five poems.[14] J.B. White has made a classification of the various forms of love poetry which are found in the book.[15] He lists and describes, for example, (1) descriptive songs (e.g., 4:1-7); (2) songs of admiration (e.g., 1:9-11); and (3) songs of yearning (e.g., 1:2-4). These "forms," however, may simply be descriptive of various creative aspects of one brilliant composition rather than indications of the utilization of separate poems.

A very strong case can be made that the Song was written as one poem. Individual units can stand alone, that is true; but these units have been very carefully arranged in a way that precludes regarding them as a haphazard collection. This book gives every indication of a single hand at work, and that was the hand of a master craftsman.[16]

The unity of the book is evidenced in (1) the continuity of theme; (2) a chainlike structure binding one part to the preceding;[17] (3) the title, which though perhaps not originally part of the book, nonetheless gives an ancient view that this book was a single composition and not a composite; (4) the absence of any headings to mark off the individual units; (5) the appearance of the same adjuration formula three times (cf. 2:7; 3:5; 8:4); and (6) the appearance of the same leading characters throughout.

B. A Drama.

Another approach to this book suggests that it is a drama. Those who hold this view do not refer to theatrical drama, because that was nonexistent in ancient Israel. Rather they mean something like a dramatic reading with identifiable speaking parts for various characters. Some modern versions add notes to the margins indicating the speakers. This approach to the book is very ancient. Codex Sinaiticus (ca. AD 400), one of the earliest Greek manuscripts of the Bible, contains speaker notes in the margin of the text.

Origen (c. AD 250) first suggested that the Song should be interpreted as a marriage song in the form of a drama. Franz Delitzsch gave strong support to this view in the mid-1800s. A number of interpreters have endorsed this approach to the book. The problem, however, is that the various speakers are not clearly indentified in the text.

The problem of the identification of speaking parts cannot be underestimated; but this same phenomenon appears elsewhere in the Hebrew Bible. In Micah 2 and 6, for example, different characters are speaking, but sorting it all out is difficult. Some of the Psalms seem to reflect speaking parts of various groups (e.g., Ps 24).

Another problem with the dramatic view is the (alleged) lack of plot structure. If there is no plot structure in the Song, then it is no more than a collection of secular love songs. Why would such a collection be deemed appropriate for inclusion in the canon? That a collection of praise and prayer material like the Book of Psalms was canonized is not hard to understand. But how can one explain the presence of a collection of purely secular love songs? The canonical inclusion of the Song might suggest that early scholars saw in this book some unfolding narrative with an important moral.

Any lyric ballad presupposes a story that is not told in full. This poem moves from scene to scene without filling in the connecting links. Perhaps the original readers of this book knew the entire story which modern scholars strive so desperately to reconstruct.[18]

THE SPIRIT OF THE BOOK

Some see the Song as a satire on the age and ideals of Solomon.[19] The book supposedly was northern kingdom propaganda against the Solomonic kingdom. It celebrates one of the rare occasions when Solomon's amorous intentions were frustrated and that by a simple country girl from the Plain of Esdraelon. Such an interpretation makes the book humorous in a sense. The rich and eloquent king is the butt of the humor.

If Solomon is the author of the book, then satire would not be the appropriate designation of the spirit of the book. One does not satirize himself as a rule. If the author intended to put Solomon in a bad light, he surely could have done a better job. Is it wrong for a man to try to woo a maiden with gifts and flattery? Is not the maiden permitted to rejoin her beloved in the concluding chapter? Could not the rejected suitor, the powerful king, have forced himself upon the Shulamite had he so chosen?

If the spirit of the book is not satire, then what is it? Why would Solomon write an account of one of his romantic failures? Perhaps he learned from this maiden what true love is all about. Perhaps this is the kind of love to which he aspired and which he meant to encourage in his readers. Perhaps the book, like Ecclesiastes, recognizes that wealth and power have their limitations. Both were defeated by the power of the love of a maid for the man of her choice. That lesson is worthy of publication by a wise man like Solomon even if, to a certain extent, he was forced to portray himself as a rejected lover.

CANONICITY OF THE BOOK

What factors led the people of God to recognize the Song as part of the sacred Scriptures are not clear. Certainly wisdom was regarded as a gift from God (1 Kgs 3:28; 4:29), and Solomon was known to have received that gift through a dream revelation. So the connection of this song with the name of Solomon and its preservation through the vicissitudes of Israel's history are the two key factors which led to the recognition of this book as Scripture.

Most scholars assume that only after Israel learned to allegorize the Song was it embraced as part of the sacred canon. This is far from clear. While the explicit sexual references may have been a problem to later generations of Jews, there is no indication that early on the book was regarded as in any way inappropriate. The Song celebrates the mysteries of human love. It may have been used in the celebration of marriage festivals. Thus the content as well as the connection with Solomon commended this book to the scribes who first assembled the books of Scripture.

The Song of Songs was one of the five antilegomena in the rabbinic discussions regarding canonicity. The Mishnah (*Yadaim* 3:5) records the fact that there was discussion over whether Song "renders the hands unclean." This is a technical expression in rabbinic literature which refers to canonicity. The exact background of the expression is unclear, but the intent is very clear. The basis of opposition to the book is not stated, but it probably revolved around (1) the passages which speak of attractiveness of the physical body; and (2) the absence of the name of God. The spiritual value of the book must have been questioned by some.

The Jewish philosopher Philo, who quoted so extensively from the Old Testament, never mentions Song in any of his extant writings. The New Testament contains no direct reference to this book. The book, however, was among the four books of "hymns to God and precepts for the conduct of human life" which were part of the Bible of Josephus. This historian represents his opinions to be that of the majority of Palestinian Jews of his day (*Against Apion* 1.8). This in turn seems to indicate that the Song was also part of the Scriptures which Jesus and the apostles embraced and loved.

A reference in the Mishnah (*Ta'anith* 4:8) indicates that certain portions of Song were used in festivals celebrated in the temple prior to AD 70. The earliest identifiable citation from the book is found in IV Esdras 5:24-26; 7:26 (ca. AD 70-130)

By adopting the allegorical method of interpretation the defenders of the book were able to win the day. The great Rabbi Akiba seems to be deliberately overstating the case to silence all potential opponents when he says: ". . . all the ages are not worthy of the day on which the Song of Songs was given to Israel; for all the Writings are holy, but the Song of Songs is the Holy of Holies." (*Yadaim* 3:5). After the time of Rabbi Akiba the issue seems to have been settled. Song appears in the list of the canonical books in the Talmud (*Baba Bathra* 14).

In the Hebrew Bible, Song is normally placed first in the collection of five small scrolls called *Megilloth* ("Scrolls") and is followed by Ruth. The *Megilloth* are part of the *Kethubhim* ("Writings"), the third great division of the Hebrew Bible. The five *Megilloth* were read during the year at special festivals. Song was assigned to be read at Passover.

INTERPRETATION OF THE BOOK

The Song is the most obscure book in the Hebrew Bible. More than two hundred commentaries or extensive treatments of this book have been published during the long history of its interpretation.[20] This little book has been the object of a whole range of interpretations. Whether the book is a collection of love poems or a unified drama, does not fully decide the issue of how it should be interpreted. Without question the key verse in the book is 6:3a: "I am my beloved's and my beloved is mine." The question is, Who is the beloved?

A. Allegorical Interpretation.

Since shortly after the time of the New Testament, by far the most common approach to the Song among both Christians and Jews was the allegorical. Jews saw here an allegory of (1) God and Israel; (2) the history of Israel from the Exodus to the age of Messiah (Targum); or

(3) the desirability of wisdom. Christians baptized the book into Christ and found here expressions of love and commitment between Christ and the church. Interpreted in this fashion the book furnished the texts for countless homilies extolling Christ and the Church.[21]

A few examples of this approach will suffice. "My beloved is to me a bag of myrrh, that lies between my breasts (1:13) is said by the Jewish commentators Rashi and Ibn Ezra to represent the Shekinah glory of Yahweh that stood between the cherubim in the Holy of Holies. The interpretation of 1:13 in Christian circles was that the bag of myrrh is Christ, and the woman's breasts are the Old and New Testament.

Another classic example of allegory is 7:2a which reads "Your navel is a rounded bowl that never lacks mixed wine." According to some allegorists, this represents the sanctuary of a church where the communion "wine" is always present. A glance at the page headings in an older edition of the King James Version reflects this approach with its references to Christ's love for the church and vice versa.

The rabbis uttered strong warnings concerning the use of this book. Rabbi Akiba is reported to have said: "He who trills his voice in chanting of the Song of Songs in the banquet-halls and makes it a secular song has no share in the world to come."[22] Jerome reported a rabbinic tradition that a person was not permitted to read the book until he had reached the age of thirty.

The early Christians considered this book dangerous. Jerome once wrote a letter to his disciple Paula to give her a Bible reading plan for her daughter's proper education. She should start with the Psalter, then proceed to Proverbs, Ecclesiastes and Job. The Gospels should come next, then Acts and the Epistles. She should then study the prophets, the Pentateuch and Old Testament historical books. "When she has done all these she may safely read the Song of Songs but not before: for, were she to read it at the beginning, she would fail to perceive that, though it is written in fleshly words, it is a marriage song of a spiritual bridal. And not understanding this she would suffer from it."[23]

Nothing in the book suggests that it should be spiritualized in this way. So why did this system of interpretion arise? Jewish and Christian interpreters inherited from certain Greek thinkers the notion that the body was inherently evil. Sexual abstinence was viewed as a virtue. The celebration of sexual attraction in this book could not be squared with these philosophical notions.

The allegorical method of interpreting the book reigned supreme until the middle of the nineteenth century. Then the tide began to turn, primarily due to two reasons. First, a more sophisticated and biblical attitude toward human sexuality began to emerge. Second, the discovery of similar love poems in the countries surrounding Israel has _caused scholars to realize that this type of literature was common to the region and the time. This diminished the likelihood that some special system of interpretation was intended for this particular love book. Third, the increasing realization that this method was totally subjective. Interpreters were more apt to find their own idea in the text than to discern the author's intent.

B. Typological Method.

The line between allegory and typology is not always clear.[24] Essentially, allegory is deliberately written. All the details of the composition have symbolic meaning. Typology rests on an historical or real foundation. Yet God intends for his people to see within those real events spiritual significance. More specifically, the Song may celebrate an actual relationship between Solomon and a maiden. Because, however, Solomon is a type of Christ, this marriage must have been intended by God to be typical of the relationship between Christ and his church. Among those who contend for the typical view of Song are Archer, Unger, and Raven.

It is certainly true that Solomon in his office as *king* was typical of Christ. Does that, however, indicate that in all respects he previewed Christ? Certainly not. Furthermore, in the Song a marriage never actually takes place. The true beloved of the maiden in this book was a shepherd, not the king (1:7).

C. Cultic Method.

Some have proposed that Song should be understood as the liturgy used in the Tammuz-Ishtar cult.[25] The two "lovers" in the book were actually assuming the roles of the god Tammuz and his consort Ishtar. Thus the book does not celebrate human love, but the love between a god and goddess. In its overall structure and content the Song resembles to some extent the love poems which can be traced back to ancient Sumer (c. 2500 BC). Babylon (ca. 500 BC) also has yielded collections of love poems. These poems, however, have cultic overtones. They appear to have been used in temple rituals celebrating the copulation of various deities.

Another scholar associates the Song with an ancient cultic funeral feast. He speculates that on such occasions life was reaffirmed through lavish feasts and even sexual orgies. The evidence for this view is found in 8:6 which stresses the power of love even over death.[26]

Certainly a Tammuz cult did flourish in Judah (Ezek 8:14) prior to the fall of Jerusalem in 586 BC. This cult, however, was considered an abomination. That the Jews would incorporate into their sacred literature a composition with such unsavory connections is most unlikely. The vocabulary of the Song reflects the whole love-song tradition of the ancient Near East. It lacks, however, any specific reference to religious terminology including even the name of God.[27] There is no hint in the text itself that suggests any sort of cultic or religious application for this material.

D. The Literal Method.

Generally speaking the literal method of interpreting the Song is the most popular today. Often the book is called "an epithalamium," i.e., a song celebrating, in the view of most scholars, one of Solomon's weddings.

The closest parallels to the Song come from Egypt (ca. 1100 BC) (nine collections) which for the most part are simple exchanges between lovers. These collections of poems share with the Song nature motifs, vivid depiction of the physical attractiveness of the lovers, perfumes, ornaments and royal terminology. Of course the dominant theme in love poetry is the desire of the lovers to move to more intimate union.

THE MORAL ISSUE IN THE SONG

The impact of Song lies in the warmth and intensity of the love depicted, especially in the rich and graphic imagery. These qualities, which are the real strength of the book, are also a source of problems for western readers. The vivid descriptions of the lovers' bodies and their frank acknowledgment of passionate desire is too spicy for some. The Song, however, is the product of a distant time and place. While these descriptions are vivid, they are not lurid.

Some have alleged that the Song approves of premarital sexual encounters of the most intimate kind. According to Carr[28] a marriage between Solomon and the Shulamite is described in 4:16–5:1. Yet the language used in the first three chapters supposedly makes it clear that these two lovers were already sexually involved (cf. 1:12-17; 2:3-6). To avoid such an implication Carr has argued that the Song has a chiastic arrangment in which chronology gives way to topical considerations. The book reveals an orderly progression of themes and ideas in the first four chapters, pivots at 4:16–5:1, and then presents the same themes and ideas in reverse order through the last four chapters.[29] Recognizing that the whole book is a chiasmus solves the "chronological problem." The events described so graphically are not intended to be understood sequentially. Such a literary approach to the problem, however, is unnecessary.

In response to the view that Song endorses premarital sex, these points can be made. First, nowhere does the text actually say that the lovers were married. The Song, then, must be interpreted within the law of God which prohibits any pre- or extramarital intercourse.[30]

Second, the passages which allegedly indicate premarital sex between Solomon and the Shulamite have been misinterpreted. The Shulamite's love was reserved for her beloved shepherd, not Solomon. The most one could say is that these passages reflect sexual *longing*.

Third, the Shulamite regards herself as a model of chastity and virtue (8:8-10). Fourth, certain passages in the book reflect a chaste relationship between the Shulamite and her shepherd (3:4; 5:3). Fifth, the metaphors used of the Shulamite in the book point to her virtue and chastity. She is, for example, a tower (4:4; 7:4f.), a wall (8:10) or Mt. Carmel (7:5). These are figures for her purity, her inaccessibility as a chaste and sheltered virgin aloof from the temptations of those who would seek to seduce her. References to her dovelike qualities (1:15; 2:14; 4:1) are also descriptive of her purity.

CHARACTERISTICS OF THE BOOK

The text of Song is difficult. It contains in its 117 verses forty-nine words which appear nowhere else in Old Testament Hebrew, the highest percentage of *hapax legomena* of any book in the Bible. In addition, it contains many other unusual words. It reflects at points an odd syntax.

Song contains all the characteristics of Hebrew poetry—parallelism, chiasmus, assonance and occasionally even paronomasia.

The Song consists of direct discourse, for the most part in the form of poetic dialogue. Generally the reader is not told who is speaking, and sometimes the contents of the speech itself are not decisive in determining the speaker.

PURPOSE OF THE BOOK

The Song contains no preaching. No morals are drawn. There is no nationalism in the book. One theme is found throughout: love—pure, sensuous, youthful, passionate love. The immediate purpose of the Song is to bear testimony to, and thereby applaud, the steadfast loyalty of one maiden for her beloved. The ultimate purpose is to put God's seal of approval upon the genuine love between the sexes.

The literal purpose of the book has often been twisted by those who are not prepared to read frank and intimate expressions of love. This book undercuts the two main perversions of biblical sexuality: asceticism and lust. Asceticism views sexuality as an evil to be avoided; lust makes it the hub of life. Song pronounces the divine "it is good" upon sexual attraction which leads to lifelong commitment and fidelity.

The aim of the book is to glorify true love which remains steadfast even in the most dangerous and seductive situations.[31] If God created sexuality, why should the church stumble at the presence in her inspired canon of a song extolling the dignity and beauty of human love and sexual attraction?

831

THEOLOGY OF THE BOOK

The Song is not heavy in theology. Nonetheless, what this book indicates about physical love teaches believers something about the proper relationship of God and man. Belief in God in the biblical sense, is like a commitment of the whole self to another. The prophets of Israel—Hosea and Jeremiah in particular—used the tender, passionate, and powerful forces of sexual love as the basic analogy in their teachings about the ties that bind a person to God.[32]

Paul develops this figure of the relationship between God and man in Eph 5:28-33. He speaks of the relationship between Christ and the church as a "great mystery." He seems to be suggesting that all love is a mystery which foreshadows the love of Christ. This love lifts the believer upward toward the union of the soul with Christ. Thus the earthly love becomes a stepping stone to the heavenly.[33] Christians should love their Lord with the same intensity and loyalty as the Shulamite loved her shepherd.

ENDNOTES

1. Gleason Archer, *A Survey of Old Testament Introduction*, pb. ed. (Chicago: Moody, 1985), p. 497.

2. E.g., the mention of Tirzah in 6:4 suggests that it had not yet become capital of the northern kingdom. A later Jew would not have lauded the glory of Tirzah and Jerusalem in the same verse.

3. Detailed arguments for dating the book to the Solomonic age are found in M.H. Segal, "The Song of Songs," *Vetus Testamentum* 12 (1973): 470-490. Segal, however, does not think Solomon was the writer.

4. Thus (1) a significant number of words occur only in these two books; and (2) neither contains the name Yahweh for God.

5. R. Dillard and T. Longman III, for example, hold that only "a few" of "thirty-odd poems" in the book are from Solomon. *An Introduction to the Old Testament* (Grand Rapids: Zondervan, 1994), p. 264.

6. Hassell Bullock, *An Introduction to the Old Testament Poetic Books* (Chicago: Moody, 1979), p. 241. Bullock bases his position on the unfavorable light in which he perceives Solomon to be portrayed in the book.

7. W.S. LaSor, David Hubbard, Frederic Bush, *Old Testament Survey* (Grand Rapids: Eerdmans,1982), pp. 602f.

8. See M.H. Pope, *Song of Songs*, Anchor Bible (Garden City, NY: Doubleday, 1977), p. 33.

9. K.A. Kitchen, "Aram," in *The New Bible Dictionary,* ed. J.D. Douglas (Grand Rapids: Eerdmans, 1965), p. 55.

10. W.G. Cole, *Sex and Love in the Bible* (New York: Association, 1959), p. 87.

11. One such interesting parallel is the reference to the beloved as "my sister, my bride." J.B. White, *A Study of the Language of Love in the Song of Songs and Ancient Egyptian Poetry* (Atlanta: Scholars, 1978).

12. Wetzstein's findings regarding Arab wedding songs is reported and illustrated in Keil and Delitzsch, *Old Testament Commentaries: Psalm LXXVIII to Isaiah XIV* (Grand Rapids: Associated Publishers and Authors, n.d.), pp. 1271-1282.

13. Maria Falk, *Love Lyrics from the Bible* (Sheffield: Almond, 1982).

14. Otto Eissfeldt, *The Old Testament: An Introduction* (New York: Harper, 1965), pp. 489-490.

15. White, *Language of Love,* pp. 50-55. Some conservative writers (e.g., Dillard and Longman III) have endorsed this understanding of the book.

16. G. Lloyd Carr, "Song of Songs," in *A Complete Literary Guide to the Bible,* ed. Leland Ryken and Tremper Longman III (Grand Rapids: Zondervan, 1993), p. 291.

17. F. Landsberger, "Poetic Units within the Song of Songs," *Journal of Biblical Literature* 73 (1951): 203-216. Landsberger argues that each succeeding unit of the poem stems from a word, phrase or thought in the previous unit.

18. Bullock, *Introduction,* p. 235.

19. Ibid., p. 236.

20. An excellent survey can be found in H.H. Rowley, "The Interpretation of the Song of Songs," pp. 195-245, in *The Servant of the Lord.* For a more extensive treatment of the subject, see M. Pope, *Song of Songs,* Anchor Bible (Garden City: Doubleday, 1977), pp. 89-229.

21. In Medieval Europe Bernard of Clairvaux preached eighty-six sermons on the Song.

22. Tosefta, *Sanhedrin* 12:10. Cited in *Encyclopedia Judaica,* s.v. "Song of Songs" 15:147.

23. Reproduced by M.H. Pope, *Song of Songs,* in Anchor Bible (Garden City, NY: Doubleday, 1977), p. 119.

24. Helpful guidelines in differentiating between the allegory and typology can be found in A. Berkeley Mickelsen, *Interpreting the Bible* (Grand Rapids: Eerdmans, 1963), pp. 236-264.

25. T.J. Meek "The Song of Songs and the Fertility Cult," in *The Song of Songs, A Symposium,* ed. Wilfred Schoff (Philadelphia: Commercial Museum, 1924), pp. 48-69.

26. Pope, *Song,* p. 229.

27. The translation of 8:6 in JB and ASV "the flame of Yahweh" depends on taking the last syllable of the Hebrew word here as *yah,* an abbreviated form of the tetragrammaton. This is technically possible, but it is more likely that the syllable is functioning here, as it often does, to indicate a superlative. The RSV "a most vehement flame" correctly catches the force of the phrase.

28. Carr, "Song," p. 293.

29. Carr, "Song," p. 291. William H. Shea, "The Chiastic Structure of the Song of Songs," in *Zeitschrift für die alttestamentliche Wissenschaft* 92 (1980): 396.

30. Dillard and Longman III, *Introduction*, p. 263.

31. Frederick C. Eiselen, *The Christian View of the Old Testament* (New York: Methodist Book Concern, 1912), p. 253.

32. S. Stevenson, *Preaching on the Books of the Old Testament* (New York: Harper, 1961), p. 120.

33. J.L. Eason, *The New Bible Survey* (Grand Rapids: Zondervan, 1963), p. 255.

BIBLIOGRAPHY

Carr, G. Lloyd. *Song of Solomon.* Tyndale Old Testament Commentaries. Downers Grove, IL: InterVarsity, 1984.

Delitzsch, F. *Proverbs, Ecclesiastes, Song of Songs.* Orig. ET 1885. Trans. J. Martin. Grand Rapids: Eerdmans, 1975.

Falk, M. *Love Lyrics from the Bible.* Sheffield: Almond, 1982.

Ginsburg, C.D. *The Song of Songs and Coheleth.* (1857). New York: Ktav, 1970.

Glickman, S.C. *A Song for Lovers.* Downers Grove, IL: InterVarsity, 1976.

Gordis, R. *The Song of Songs and Lamentations,* rev. ed. New York: Ktav, 1974.

Goulder, M.D. *The Song of Fourteen Songs.* JSOTS 36; Sheffield: Almond, 1986.

Murphy, R.E. *The Song of Songs.* Hermeneia. Philadelphia: Fortress, 1990.

Pope, M.H. *Song of Songs.* Anchor Bible. Garden City, NY: Doubleday, 1977.

Segal, M.H. "The Song of Songs." In *Vetus Testamentum* 12 (1973): 470-490.

Snaith, J.G. *The Song of Songs.* New Century Bible. Grand Rapids: Eerdmans, 1993.

CHAPTER FORTY-ONE

The Shulamite in the Palace
Song 1:2-3:5

The setting for the first scene is the royal palace in Jerusalem, or perhaps a royal tent pitched in a favorite summer resort of Solomon. In this setting the heroine of the book pines for her true love, a shepherd from whom she has been forcibly separated. Her strong love for the shepherd is assaulted by the ridicule of the harem girls and by the flattery of King Solomon who is determined to win her affection.

THE SHULAMITE AND THE HAREM
Song 1:2-8

The problem of the identification of the speaker faces the interpreter immediately in v. 2. The speaker is obviously female. Most commentators think that in verses 2-7 the Shulamite is expressing her love either for the king or for her distant shepherd. The Shulamite, however, never in the poem clearly expresses her love for the king. It is best to regard verses 2-8 as an interchange between the Shulamite and the harem girls with the latter opening the conversation.

A. The Appeal of the King (1:2-3).

The harem girls open the book with expressions of longing for the attentions and affections of King Solomon. One of them says: "Let him kiss me with one of the kisses of his mouth." The anticipated sweetness of his lips is such that one kiss would be rapture. The harem girls then begin to list the reasons in the second person why the king's love is so desirable.

The other harem girls join the one who is so outspoken. They too desire the affection of the king. They address him, though he clearly is not present. First, they cite the multiple facets of his love: "Your love is better than wine." The word "love" (*dodhim*) is plural, perhaps to suggest the manifestation of love with many caresses; or perhaps the many ways in which the king showed his love for those who struck his fancy. The comparison to wine may suggest that a banquet was in progress at which wine was flowing (1:2).

Second, they cite the pleasant aroma of the king: "Your oils have a goodly fragrance." Third, they regard the very name of the king as even more pleasant than the perfumes which he wore. They took delight in merely uttering his name. The "name" here stands for the entire person. The king is the sweetest of persons. Fourth, the king is desirable because "the virgins love you." The term "virgin" (*'almah*) refers to a young woman of marriageable age, but never to a married woman. The competition for the affections of Solomon among the harem girls made him all the more desirable (1:3).

B. The Appeal to the King (1:4).

One of the harem girls expresses the desire that the king will "draw me," i.e., take me by the hand and lead me to his private dwelling. The other girls, perhaps jokingly, declare: "We will run [after you]," i.e., after the couple which is leaving the harem chambers for the king's private quarters.

Another harem girl imagines herself being brought into the king's chambers: "the king has brought me into his chambers." The other girls respond: "We will be glad and rejoice in you." They are happy over the fortunes of the one who has been selected by the king. They continue to speak of the love of the king around the banquet table: "We will make mention of your love more than of wine."

Someone there at the harem banquet—perhaps the Shulamite—comments on the enthusiasm of the girls over the king: "rightly do they love you." The handsome, wealthy king was a good "catch." To become the bride of this man would be a worthy ambition (1:4).

C. The Appeal by the Shulamite (1:5-7).

The Shulamite protests her presence in the harem of the king. She describes herself as "black, but comely." The word "black" indicates that she was tanned by her exposure to the sun. The rest of the poem indicates that the Shulamite was from the rural regions of the north. She received her dark complexion from working in the fields. Some think these words are called forth by the critical glances of those who viewed themselves as competitors for the attentions of the king. In the culture of the day, lily white was the attractive complexion for a court lady. The Shulamite, however, was as black "as the tents of Kedar, as the curtains of Solomon." The phrase "tents of Kedar" refers to the black tents of the Bedouin Arabs which still to this day dot the countryside. The "curtains of Solomon" refer to his traveling tent (1:5).

The Shulamite asks her antagonists not to stare at her with such scorn: "Do not see me that I am dark, because the sun has scorched me." The dark-skinned Shulamite felt self-conscious amidst the fair maidens of the harem. These words point to a modest self-deprecation on her part.

How did this young lady become exposed to the sun? She explains: "My mother's sons were incensed against me; they made me keeper of the vineyards." This is a poetic reference to her brothers, not stepbrothers as some have alleged. The mother may have been a widow, since no father is mentioned in the entire book. For reasons unexplained, the brothers were incensed against her. They would not allow her to spend her days in the family home to take care of her complexion. They made her the vineyard keeper.

Because of this family responsibility assigned by her brothers, the Shulamite was not able to take care of her own "vineyard." No doubt she refers to her complexion. She had not been able to preserve the delicacy of her skin or take any other special cares with her personal beauty (1:6).

The Shulamite longs for her beloved: "Tell me, O thou whom my soul loves, where you feed your flock, where you make it to rest at noon." Her beloved is a shepherd. Surely it would be a stretch of this term to apply it to Solomon. Mention of the vineyard and her home life caused her to long for her country beau. She obviously does not desire to be in the king's harem; she does not share the harem girls' enthusiasm for becoming the bride of Solomon.

Being modest, she wishes to meet her beloved "at noon," not like the wanton ladies of the court who seek their lovers at night. In the heat of the midday shepherds would lead their flocks under shady trees near a stream.[1]

The Shulamite feels keenly her estrangement from her beloved. She compares herself to "one that is veiled beside the flock of your companions." In the presence of other men she is veiled. Only her beloved would be permitted to gaze upon her face. She anxiously longs for her beloved shepherd to bring the flock in at the end of the day. Perhaps she had been in that position many times before. The flocks of other shepherds had come home, but where was her beloved? That same anxious feeling now smites her (1:7).

D. The Rebuke of the Harem (1:8).

The harem girls reject the Shulamite's evaluation of her own appearance. They address her as "the fairest among women." They then rebuke her for longing for prior country life. "If you know not," i.e., if she does not appreciate the privilege and opportunity to which she has been exposed there in the palace, then she had better return to her rural home: "Go your way by the paths of the flock, and feed your goats beside the shepherds' tents." There she eventually will be reunited with her beloved, her shepherd.

LOVE TESTED AND TRIUMPHANT
Song 1:9–2:7

Having withstood the scorn of the harem girls, the Shulamite now comes face to face with the dashing young prince. Sensing that the

Shulamite did not share the enthusiasm of the harem for his attentions, the king was determined all the more to woo her and win her
affection.

A. The Suitor's Charm (1:9-11).

Solomon now enters the chamber of the harem. He addresses the
Shulamite and pays his tribute of admiration to her beauty. He
intends with his flattery to dazzle the simple country girl. "I have compared you, O my love, to a mare in Pharaoh's chariots." Solomon
had imported Pharaoh-chariots from Egypt (1 Kgs 10:28f.; 2 Chr
9:28). The horses of Egypt were noted for their stately beauty and
graceful movements (1:9). Such a comparison, while strange to western minds, is frequent in eastern poetry.

The trappings of the mare may have stimulated this further description of the Shulamite: "Your cheeks are comely with plaits of
hair, your neck with strings of jewels." The horse's bridle was frequently adorned with silken tassels, fringes, and other ornaments of
silver. The strings of jewels about her neck were like the pearls which
hung down across the forehead of the animal (1:10).

Using the majestic plural, the king promises to further bedeck his
future bride with even more beautiful and costly jewels: "We will make
for you ornaments of gold with beads of silver" (1:11).

B. The Maiden's Resolve (1:12-14).

"While the king was at his table, my spikenard sends forth its fragrance." Apparently King Solomon sits in the harem apartment for a
banquet with those who were his prospective brides. No doubt he was
reclining at a low table, which was the custom of the day. To fortify
herself against the charm of the king the Shulamite focuses on her
spikenard, a powerful perfume of Indian origin. This was a very expensive fragrance which was worn in a little pouch around the neck (1:12).

The Shulamite lets that pouch of myrrh between her breasts
remind her of her beloved: "My beloved is to me a pouch of myrrh
which lies all night between my breasts." The Hebrew women were
accustomed to carry little bags of myrrh suspended from their necks
and hanging down between the breasts under the dress, diffusing an
attractive fragrance round them. Her point is this: her beloved is at

her heart. He is as delightful to all her thoughts as the fragrance was to her senses. Her love for him is constant and uninterrupted. Thoughts of him are with her night and day. The language here in no way hints at premarital sexual intimacy (1:13).

A second figure advances the figure of pleasant fragrance: "My beloved is to me a cluster of henna blossoms in the vineyards of En-gedi." The henna comes from a tall shrub of the cypress family reaching to eight or ten feet. It is exceedingly beautiful in appearance, and gives forth a delightful odor. En-gedi is a lovely district on the west of the Dead Sea where Solomon made terraces on the hillsides and covered them with gardens and vineyards. The figure is, perhaps, intended to be an advance in rhetorical force upon that which preceded— the fragrance diffused and almost overpowering, as of a blossoming tree (1:14).

C. The Suitor's Charm Continued (1:15).

The king continues to address the maiden with flattering words: "Behold, you are fair, my love; behold you are fair." The repetition of the interjection "behold" suggests that the king was smitten by the charms of this maiden. She is very sweet and fair to him. His attention is focused on her eyes: "Your eyes are doves." The dove is a natural symbol of love. He gazes into those eyes and sees only purity and innocence. To the ancients, the eyes were an index to character.

D. The Maiden's Resolve Continued (1:16-2:1).

The Shulamite ignores Solomon's wooing and addresses (in her mind and fantasy) her beloved: "Behold, you are fair, my beloved, yes, pleasant." She uses some of the same words which Solomon addressed to her to describe her beloved shepherd (1:16).

She then begins to describe the field in which their love was first aroused. The maiden imagines herself transported to the side of her beloved: "Our couch is green. The beams of our houses are cedar, and our rafters of fir." The two would meet, not in a luxurious palace, but in a wooded glen. The green grass would be their couch; the leafy and fragrant cypress trees would be the beams of their outdoor palace. The use of the plural "houses" is significant. In the forest glens the lovers had many palaces, not just one (1:17).

Why does the maiden long for this rural retreat? She was not at
ease in Solomon's palatial splendor. She was by nature "a rose of
Sharon, a lily of the valley." The term "rose" (*chabhatsseleth*) can
refer to any wild flower. The crocus is probably the nearest to the root
meaning of the word. "Sharon" here probably refers to an open field
or plain, although there was a district called Sharon in the coastal
plains as well as another Sharon across Jordan (1 Chr 5:16). The "lily"
(*shoshannah*) was abundant in Palestine. Both red and white varieties
are known there. The point is, the Shulamite is a country girl; her
beauty is the beauty of nature. She longs for her rural home (2:1).

On the assumption that the maiden speaks only to Solomon and
about him in the book, this sudden transition to a rural setting is
inexplicable.

E. The Suitor's Charm Continued (2:2).

The king takes up the metaphor which the Shulamite uses of her
self. "As a lily among thorns, so is my love among the daughters."
The interpreter is left to ponder whether (1) her last words were audi-
ble; or (2) the author intends for Solomon here to appear ridiculous.
Even as she pines for her beloved in her imagination, he is using her
very language in an (hopeless) effort to win her affection. In any case,
Solomon here confesses that he is captivated by her rustic beauty.
The Shulamite stands out among all the lovely ladies of the palace. All
around her are not worthy of notice beside her. They are prickly
thorn plants; she is a delicate and beautiful lily. The term "daughters"
is not otherwise qualified. Probably he means the young women who
were there in the palace awaiting the judgment of the king as to
whether or not he would marry them.

F. The Maiden's Resolve Continued (2:3).

Again the Shulamite turns the flattery of Solomon into even
greater flattery for her beloved. "As the apple tree among the trees of
the wood so is my beloved among the sons." The apple tree is noted
for the fragrance of its blossom and the sweetness of its fruit. "Trees
of the wood" would be those which are wild, their fruit sour and
rough. Many of the wild trees had neither flower nor fruit. The
thought is that, compared to other men—Solomon included—her

beloved is sweet and fragrant. He stands out like an apple tree among the fruitless trees.

The maiden goes on to recall how she "sat down under his shadow with great delight." The Hebrew verb form suggests the intensity of the feeling of delight which she experienced. The "shadow" here signifies both protection and refreshment. A woman finds both in the presence of her beloved.

She goes on to assert: "his fruit was sweet to my taste." The apple tree metaphor is here being further developed. She may be referring to the kisses of the beloved; or more generally, simply to the enjoyment which she had in his company (2:3).

G. A Fortifying Fantasy (2:4-7).

Thoughts of the delight which she had in the presence of her beloved sends the maiden into a virtual trance. She detaches herself entirely from her surroundings and imagines herself with him again in places where the young lovers had frequented in the past.

"He brought me to the banqueting house [lit., the house of wine]." Probably the reference is to their outdoor hideaway mentioned in 1:16f. There the two would enjoy their private banquets. A picnic shared by lovers is better than any banquet. At such times the maiden declares "his banner over me was love." The "banner" is a military one. His love for her protected her, caused her bashfulness to give way to boldness. At the same time, that banner warned away rivals. As a victorious commander plants his standard over the conquered territory, so the shepherd's love had conquered her heart. Furthermore, his love was the banner to which her loyalty was pledged. She would no more desert that banner than a soldier would abandon the colors of his regiment (2:4).

These thoughts of her beloved make the Shulamite physically weak. She is overcome by her emotion; she is in a state of ecstasy. She needs sustenance quickly. So she asks the palace maidens: "Sustain me with raisin cakes, refresh me with apples." The food for which she longs is the grape-cakes—the grapes sufficiently dried to be pressed together as cakes, which was very refreshing and reviving. Such cakes were moist, not dry like raisins as they are known in this country. The "apples" as well as the grape cakes would supply quick energy and prevent the maiden from passing out. She has been made "sick" of love, i.e., she is desperately love sick (2:5).

What has triggered her love sickness? Memory of what happened in that outdoor banquet hall. "His left hand is under my head, and his right hand embraces me." Just to think about his strong arms around her makes the Shulamite quiver with excitement and grow faint. Such memories fortify her against the seductive charms of the royal suitor. Verse 6 could also be rendered as a wish (NASB). In this case the maiden is expressing a need for her beloved's support in this hour of trial, when attempts are being made to alienate her affections (2:6; cf. 8:3).

Having vowed her loyalty to her beloved, the Shulamite pleads that the harem girls desist from trying to turn her affections to Solomon. She invokes the shy and timid "roes" and "hinds of the field" in her appeal. Being graceful, these animals were symbols of feminine beauty. Perhaps she means to suggest that she is shy and timid like those lovely animals. She, like they, desires only to be left alone.

The daughters of Jerusalem should not "stir up" nor "awaken" love until she pleases to do so. The point is that true love needs no arousing from without. It should be as free and unfettered as the gazelles and hinds (2:7).[2]

FOND MEMORIES OF COURTSHIP
Song 2:8–3:5

The king and court ladies have failed to persuade the Shulamite to abandon her beloved. The scene now shifts to the rural area from which she hailed. The maiden reveals how she came to be taken into Solomon's palace.

A. An Invitation Declined (2:8-17).

The Shulamite here goes back in thought to the scenes of her home-life, and the sweet days of first love. She is longingly looking for the arrival of her shepherd lover. At last she hears him. Excitement mounts: "Behold! he comes!" at least in her imagination. He is as anxious to be with her, as she is to be with him. He comes "leaping upon the mountains, skipping upon the hills." She must be alluding to her shepherd, since the language would hardly be appropriate to Solomon (2:8).

The maiden describes her beloved as "a roe or a young hart." Both animals are shy. She is within the house when the beloved arrives. "Behold, he stands behind our wall, he looks in at the windows, he shows himself through the lattice." He stands behind the wall outside the house. He playfully looks through the windows, now through one and now through another, seeking her with his longing eyes. The "windows" (lit., the openings) probably refers to a lattice window, a pierced wooden structure (2:9).

At last the shepherd speaks: "My beloved spoke, and said unto me, Rise up, my love, my fair one and come away." These are the first words attributed to the shepherd in the book. He asked the young lady to leave the house and accompany him on a walk (2:10).

It was a beautiful day for a lovers' walk. The winter rains were over. Flowers were appearing throughout the land. The air was again filled with the songs of birds, especially that of the turtledove. Vines and fig trees were blossoming and filling the air with fragrant aroma. The shepherd's invitation was to fellowship in the midst of the pure loveliness of nature, when all was suitable to sustain the initial feelings of awakened love: "Arise, my love, my fair one, and come away" (2:11-13).

For a time the bashful maiden refused to join the young man outside the house. Therefore he compares her to a "dove" that is in the clefts of the rock. Though she had shown herself briefly at the window, she was inaccessible to him. He wants to see her countenance, and hear her voice for "sweet is your voice, and your countenance is lovely" (2:14).

The maiden offers an excuse for not joining the young man for the spring walk: "Take us the foxes, the little foxes, that spoil the vineyards; for our vineyards are in blossom." This may be an excerpt from a folk-song sung at harvest. She had responsibilities in the vineyard (cf. 1:6). The "foxes" (shu'alim) or little jackals (cf. Judg 15:4) were very numerous in Palestine (2:15).

The Shulamite was not able to enjoy the company of her beloved that day. Yet she was confident of the bond of love that existed between them: "My beloved is mine, and I am his." She must go out to the vineyard; he would be spending that time "feeding [his flock] among the lilies." Apparently the lovely pastures were filled at this time of year with the lilies of the field (Matt 6:28). Perhaps the Shulamite addresses these words parenthetically to the palace women. She may have been separate from her beloved, but she was still united to him in love (2:16).

At the end of the day the two lovers could be reunited. Meanwhile, he needs to be about his work as well as she. "Until the day be cool, and the shadows flee away, turn, my beloved, and be like a roe or a young hart upon the mountains of Bether." Some urgency seems to be conveyed in these words. Perhaps she feared what her brothers might do to him if they found him at the house. The separation is only until sunset when she will expect him back. No place called "Bether" is known. The word means separation. Hence while he feeds his flock the mountains will separate him from the maiden. At the end of the day she encourages him to bound over those mountains like the roe or hart to get back to her as soon as possible (2:17).

B. A Desperate Search (3:1-5).

The evening had come; the beloved had not made his appearance. The Shulamite went to bed, but she could not sleep. "By night on my bed I sought him whom my soul loved." She kept getting up and peering out the window to see if she could see any sign of the beloved: "I sought him but I found him not." The word "night" is plural, suggesting that this sleepless worry may have continued for more than one night. On the other hand, the plural may be a poetic way of indicating that that night seemed like several nights. The verse suggests that the maiden is suffering from self-reproach in having grieved her lover and having kept him away from her earlier that day (3:1).

At some point during the night the Shulamite determined that she would venture out to look for her beloved: "I will rise now, and go about the city, in the streets and in the broad ways; I will seek him whom my soul loves." Shepherds often would bring their flocks back into the towns to spend the night in public pens. She knew her beloved most likely would be there with his sheep. Yet for a single maiden to venture forth into the night would be a risk which only the greatest love would undertake. To make matters worse, the search was initially fruitless.

The term "city" ('ir) refers to a permanent settlement without reference to size. To argue from the use of this word that Jerusalem must be the city, and that the term excludes a shepherd lover is ridiculous. The city probably was Shulam from which the lovers came (3:2).

The solitary maiden stalking the streets of the city was intercepted by the watchmen: "The watchmen that go about the city found me." She immediately asked them: "Have you seen him whom my soul loves?" On this occasion the maiden escaped unharmed by the watchmen, but probably not without a stern lecture on the dangers of being alone at night in the streets of the city. Perhaps the kindly policemen even directed her to where her shepherd was sleeping (3:3).

Shortly after leaving the watchmen the Shulamite found her man: "It was but a little that I passed from them, but I found him whom my soul loves. I held him and would not let him go, until I had brought him into my mother's house, and into the chamber of her that conceived me." The modesty of the last clause is indeed beautiful. The mother would, of course, at that time be in her sleeping chamber. There alone would the maiden receive her lover at such a time. The mother obviously approved of the young man. The text also suggests that the mother was understanding of the strong emotion of her daughter and was sympathetic for her plight of growing up in a household dominated by harsh brothers. Thus the poet emphasizes that the love which the Shulamite expresses is set upon the ground of perfect chastity and purity.

What a contrast this scene presents to that with which the book opens. The earlier scene was one of harem lust and opportunism; but here is innocent love and chaste affection. No wonder Solomon tried so desperately to win the affection of this jewel among maidens! (3:4).

Needless to say, the whole scene just described makes no sense on the hypothesis that Solomon himself is poetically called the shepherd. Those who hold that view sense the difficulty here and explain it away as being only a dream in which all kinds of unlikely things can occur. If anything is clear, the maiden was not dreaming that night, for there is nothing to indicate that she ever went to sleep. It is far better to view this as the memory of an actual event which transpired before the Shulamite ever came to Solomon's palace. She recalls it here to fortify herself against the onslaught of Solomon's verbal flattery.

The memory of that blissful night in the company of her beloved sends the Shulamite again into ecstatic happiness. She again addresses the young maidens around her in the palace and beseeches them not to pry her away from this blissful memory. She repeats the refrain of 2:7: "I charge you, O daughters of Jerusalem, by the roes and by the hinds of the field, that you stir not up, nor awake my love, till she pleases." This verse indicates that the whole of the preceding passage was uttered by the maiden in the presence of the king's harem. This refrain seems to be a general note of praise, celebrating the preciousness of pure, spontaneous affection (3:5).

ENDNOTES

1. S.M. Lehrman, "The Song of Songs," in *The Five Megilloth* (London: Soncino, 1961), p. 3.
2. Ibid., p. 7.

CHAPTER FORTY-TWO

Love Wins Out
Song 3:6-6:3

The trial of the Shulamite's love intensifies in the second phase of the poem. The scenes here correspond almost exactly with those in the first division.

THE ARRIVAL OF THE SHULAMITE
Song 3:6-11

Having piqued the curiosity of his readers, at last the poet tells the story of how the Shulamite came to be in Solomon's palace.

The inhabitants of Jerusalem express their surprise and admiration at the sight of the procession as it approaches the city: "Who is this [lady] that comes out of the wilderness like pillars of smoke, perfumed with myrrh and frankincense, with all powders of the merchant?" What a splendid sight that must have been! Everyone in Jerusalem was interested in seeing who the latest of Solomon's female acquisitions might be. Rumors about the city must have provoked curiosity for days.

A maiden from Galilee was being conducted to Jerusalem in royal splendor. The procession apparently took the Jordan valley route south, because as it approached Jerusalem it is said to come "out of the wilderness." Moving up the steep hills from the Jordan valley to Jerusalem the procession would of necessity pass through the wilderness of Judea. Censers of frankincense were being swung to and fro filling the air with fragrant smoke. Columns of dust and smoke from the burning incense rose up to heaven and marked the progress of the procession (3:6).

The question posed by the curious crowd is soon answered as the procession moves closer: "Behold, it is the palanquin of Solomon." The word "palanquin" (*mittah*) refers to a portable bed, or sitting cushion, hung around with curtains. This one was royal, belonging to Solomon. It was easily recognizable because of its magnificence.

Solomon had made every effort to secure the safety of his prospective bride as well as her comfort on the long, dangerous, and dusty trip from Galilee. The palanquin was guarded by "sixty mighty men of the mighty men of Israel." It would appear that Solomon had sent one tenth of his personal bodyguard to escort his future bride (cf. 1 Sam 27:2; 30:9) The guard of warriors round the litter secured the bride from any sudden alarm as she traveled through the wilderness which was infested with bandits and outlaws. The journey from Shulam to Jerusalem would be about fifty miles. It would have been necessary to spend at least two nights *en route*. So the escort consisted of soldiers who were skilled in the use of the sword: "They all handle the sword, and are experts in war; every man has his sword upon his thigh because of fear of the night" (3:7-8).

The palanquin is further described as it comes closer into view: "King Solomon made himself a palanquin of the wood of Lebanon. He made the pillars thereof of silver, the bottom thereof of gold, the seats of it of purple." The frame was of imported wood—"wood of Lebanon"—i.e., the cedar or cypress (cf. 1 Kgs 5:10). The precious metals and royal colors added to the wonder of this vehicle. The interior of the palanquin was "lovingly fitted out by the daughters of Jerusalem." The ladies of the court, in their affection for the king, had prepared or procured costly tapestries to spread over the purple cushion (3:9-10).

The "daughters of Zion" are urged to go forth to greet their king. Apparently the king accompanied the Shulamite back to Jerusalem, or at least went forth to meet her. The term "daughters of Jerusalem" probably refers to the women of the city in general as opposed to the ladies of the royal harem who probably never were permitted to leave their quarters in the palace. The "daughters of Zion" represent all the people. The occasion of the marriage of the king was a day of celebration, and the celebration was apparently led by the women of the city.

The daughters of Zion would be witnesses of the marriage ceremony. They would see "King Solomon, with the crown with which his mother has crowned him on the day of his wedding." Custom called for the mother of the groom to adorn the head of her son with a wedding coronet. No doubt that crown would be a wreath of interlaced gold and silver strands. This is a crown of joy, not royalty. According to the Talmud, such a custom continued for many years. This was a happy day for the king, for his family and for all his subjects. No mention is made here, however, of the happiness of the Shulamite. One can only imagine the sadness that filled her heart as she approached marriage with a man she did not love. The greatest sadness is that which is kindled by the joy of others (3:11).

THE WOOING BY SOLOMON
Song 4:1–5:1

All is ready for the joyous wedding celebration, all that is except the bride. Solomon makes another attempt to win her affection with a barrage of verbal flattery.[1]

A. The Beauty of the Bride (4:1-5).

Where the king and the Shulamite were when he addressed the following words to her is not stated. Some imagine they are traveling in the wedding procession. Others suggest that the conversation took place in the palace. The wedding may have been put on hold while Solomon attempted one last time to get the maiden to commit to true love. On the other hand, it was an old custom to sing praises to the bride at her wedding.

The king begins with a general description of the beauty of the bride: "Behold, you are fair, my love; behold, you are fair." The loveliness of the bride is set forth in seven comparisons. Seven is the number of completeness and perfection.

First, he speaks of her eyes. The praise of the eyes is common in Eastern love poetry. Her eyes gleam in color, motion and luster like a pair of doves from behind the veil which covers her face.

Second, her hair was long and dark, and lay down the shoulders uncovered and free. Her locks are like "a flock of goats that have descended Mount Gilead." The goats of the region were mostly black. When the sun shone upon the goat, its hair glistened with a beautiful sheen. The reference is to the luxuriance and rich color of the hair. "Gilead" is a chain of mountains beyond Jordan renowned for its rich pasture and abundant flocks (4:1).

Third, the suitor focuses on the teeth of his bride. They are compared to "a flock of ewes that are newly shorn, which are come up from the washing." Her teeth were perfectly smooth, regular, white and moist. "Every one has twins, and none is bereaved among them." The upper set correspond exactly to the lower set. The newly shorn sheep would first be washed, probably in pairs. They then would go up side by side from the water. Each keeps its mate as they come up from the pool. Since dental hygiene was practically nonexistent in the ancient world, a woman with perfect teeth would indeed stand out above others (4:2).

Fourth, her lips are praised: "Your lips are like a thread of scarlet, and your mouth is lovely." The term scarlet refers to a glistening red color. "The mouth" may refer to her speech or conversation. Fifth, Solomon mentions her temples or perhaps cheeks. "Your temples are like a piece of a pomegranate behind your veil." The inside of a pomegranate is of a red color mixed and tempered with ruby color. Is he referring to some ornaments which appear through the veil? Some think the reference is to her rosy cheeks (4:3).

Sixth, the king praises the majesty as well as the beauty of his bride: "Your neck is like the tower of David, built for an armory upon which there hang a thousand bucklers, all the shields of the mighty men." The Shulamite has a queenly bearing about her. She was full of dignity and grace in her bearing. The exact building to which

Solomon compares her neck is disputed. It must have been a tall building which was used as an armory. Surrounded with ornaments the maiden's stately neck reminded the king of this building (4:4).

Finally, having described the maiden's facial features and neck, the king now focuses on her breasts. "Your two breasts are like two fawns that are twins of a gazelle, which feed among the lilies." This is a beautiful and yet perfectly delicate figure. It stresses the lovely equality, perfect shape and sweet freshness of the maiden's bosom. The meadow covered with lilies suggests beauty and fragrance. The two young deer lying in a bed covered with lilies represents the fragrant delicacy of a chaste virgin bosom, veiled by the folds of a dress redolent of sweet odor (4:5).

B. The Desire of the Shulamite (4:6).

The Shulamite interrupts Solomon as she had done before (cf. 1:12,16). "Until the day be cool, and the shadows flee away, I will go my way to the mountain of myrrh and to the hill of frankincense." She has used this language previously (cf. 2:17). The maiden shrinks away from such praise as Solomon has heaped upon her. She desires to be left alone. But what specifically does she desire to do? The verse could be interpreted in more than one way. Perhaps she has resigned herself to the inevitable marriage with the king. She only wishes to be left alone to walk in the palace gardens until that night when the marriage would be consummated. On the other hand, those fragrant hills are where her beloved shepherds his sheep. She may be expressing her desire to spend her last day of maidenhood revisiting those hills in memory where once she roamed with her beloved.

C. Intensified Wooing (4:7-15).

What interpretation Solomon gave to the response of his bride cannot be ascertained. This much is certain: he tries all the harder to win her affection. Again he praises her perfect beauty: "You are altogether lovely, my love; and there is no spot in you" (4:7).

Solomon invites her to give herself fully unto him. "Come with me from Lebanon, my bride, with me from Lebanon." Perhaps he senses that her heart is still back home in "Lebanon," i.e., in the mountains of the north. She should look away from the past and embrace the future—her future as a member of the royal harem. She is, after all, his "bride," i.e., she is betrothed to him, she is destined to become his bride. Three peaks in the Lebanon range are named: Amana, Senir and Hermon. Those were rough places, he intimates. They were inhabited by lions and leopards. As fortune would have it, the king has now rescued this maiden from that rough country and brought her to the luxury of his palace (4:8).

The king now begins to confess how he has been smitten in the heart by this maiden. "You have captured my heart [lit., hearted], my sister, my bride." She has made his heart to "beat faster" (NASB). The use of the term "sister" may hark back to the times when the sister relationship was on a higher plane than the wife relationship. Thus to call his bride his "sister" was the highest compliment the suitor can bestow. The term suggests that his attraction for the Shulamite is not based solely on physical attraction; he shares with her a kinship of interest.

The Shulamite has captured the king's heart with but one of her eyes and but one strand of her necklace. It was customary for eastern women to unveil one of her eyes when addressing someone. This would render visible some of the ornaments worn about the neck.[2] The idea is that only a portion of her beauty has overpowered him. He cannot even imagine what effect the whole blaze of her perfection will have upon him (4:9).

The king yearns for his love to be reciprocated. "How beautiful is your love, my sister, my bride! How much better is your love than wine, and the fragrance of your oils than all manner of spices." Her fragrance beckons him. He longs to know her intimately (4:10).

The very sound of her voice arouses his passion. "Your lips, O bride, drip honey; honey and milk are under your tongue." Her voice is soft and gentle, her words sweet. As milk and honey strengthen the physical body, so the sound of her voice strengthens Solomon's ardor. He also is attracted by her fragrant garments: "and the fragrance of your garments is like the fragrance of Lebanon." The reference is to the custom of perfuming garments. The girl must have donned some splendid garment for her wedding (4:11).

There is yet another feature of this Shulamite maiden which attracts the king, namely, her virginity. Two figures are used for her virginity: the garden and the fountain. "A garden shut up is my sister, my bride." She is a virgin. She is chaste and modest, just like a garden walled up to prevent intrusion by strangers (cf. Isa 5:5). She is like "a spring shut up, a fountain sealed." Water was scarce in the area. Owners of fountains sealed them with clay which quickly hardened in the sun. Thus sealed, they became private property. So the Shulamite has saved herself for her husband, and Solomon was about to become her husband. He anticipated entering that garden of delight, of refreshing himself in that fountain which had hitherto been inaccessible to any man (4:12).

While the garden itself is as yet inaccessible, what he can know of this maiden is attractive enough. "Your shoots are an orchard of pomegranates, with precious fruits, henna with nard plants." The "shoots" of the garden represent that part of herself—her person and personality—which are visible. Plants growing over the wall of an enclosed garden give evidence of the beauty within. So what the king knows of his bride makes him desire to know her in the intimacy of marriage. Seven spices are mentioned as growing in that garden, spices such as Solomon would import from the far East in his celebrated ships. She is not like an ordinary garden, but an orchard full of the most delicious fruits, so many and so rare are her charms. The point is that perfect sweetness and attractiveness combine in this fair maiden (4:13-14).

This country maiden is a refreshing sight to one who was accustomed to the pampered palace women. "You are a fountain of gardens, a well of living waters, and flowing streams from Lebanon." The allusion is to the clear, cool streams coming down from the snowy heights of the Lebanon mountains. The sweet freshness of the country maiden suggested this figure (4:15).

D. The Longing of the Maiden (4:16).

The Shulamite's passions have been stirred by the flattery of the suitor, but not for him. She longs to give herself to her beloved: "Awake, O north wind, and come wind of the south; blow upon my garden, that the spices thereof may flow out. Let my beloved come into his garden, and eat his precious fruits." She longs that the wind may carry fragrance to her beloved in the distant north. She longs to give herself to him, to allow him to find fulfillment in intimate union with her. To him alone would she willingly and lovingly unlock that garden of delight.

E. The King's Heightened Longing (5:1).

Solomon, in his excitement, takes courage and dares to apply the Shulamite's invitation to himself: "I have come to my garden, my sister, my bride; I have gathered my myrrh along with my balsam. I have eaten my honeycomb and my honey; I have drunk my wine and my milk." He anticipated entering her garden, i.e., making love with her. This he compares to gathering spices within a garden, and eating honey, wine and milk. Her love would sustain him even as food sustains the body. In his mind he has already imagined how that night of love will be. The verb tenses express certainty of what he longed would happened.

The king is so certain of making the Shulamite his own, that he calls upon the young people around him to share his joy: "Eat, O friends; drink, yes drink abundantly." A celebration is in order. The marriage union is about to take place.

LOVE FORTIFIED THROUGH MEMORY
Song 5:2-7

Solomon's amorous advances and verbal flattery are deflected through a swoon. She falls into a trance to escape the consummation of a marriage with a man she does not love. His second attempt to woo the maiden had ended just like the first (cf. 2:8–3:5). She tells Solomon this: "I sleep, but my heart is awake" (5:2a). Before Solomon she is a lifeless body, but in her mind she is focusing on earlier experiences with her beloved. By this means she maintains her virginity, and focuses her resolve to be faithful to her beloved.

In her trance-like state the Shulamite hears the voice of her beloved shepherd: "A voice! My beloved was knocking: Open to me . . . for my head is drenched with dew, my locks with the damp of the night." During certain months, dew falls so plentifully in the region that it saturates clothes like rain. There is a resemblance between this scene and the one related in 3:1-4; but the difference is very clear. In the former case the beloved is represented as dismissed for a season, and then the relenting heart of the maiden sought after him and found him. In this case he "stands at the door and knocks." He has come from a long journey over the mountains, and he arrives at her house in the middle of the night.

The shepherd also was skilled in verbal expressions of love. He addressed the maiden with four epithets. (1) "My sister" indicates that he treats her as his equal. Her attraction to him is more than sexual. (2) "My darling" is a term of endearment indicating free choice. (3) "My dove" points to purity, simplicity, and loveliness. (4) "My perfect one" indicates perfect devotion, undoubting trust (5:2).

The Shulamite replied with modesty: "I have taken off my dress; how shall I put it on? I have washed my feet; how shall I defile them?" She had retired for the night; she did not wish to be disturbed. It would not be appropriate for her to allow him to enter under the circumstances. Furthermore, it would be too much trouble to prepare herself to greet him properly (5:3).

Then she relates how she saw him put his hand through the hole in the door, attempting to reach the latch: "My beloved put in his hand by the hole of the door, and my heart was moved for him." He failed in his attempt to unlatch the door. How much he loved her! How hard he had tried to come to her! The thought moved her heart (lit., her bowels), the seat of emotions. She must admit him. The Hebrew word translated "moved" means literally "to make a noise." It is frequently used to describe the sounds of roaring waves of the sea. Her agitated heart was moved like storm tossed waves (5:4).

The Shulamite hastily prepared herself, and hastened to the door: "I rose up to open to my beloved." She found the parts of the door which he had touched dripping with fragrant myrrh: "And my hands dripped with myrrh, and my fingers with liquid myrrh, upon the handles of the bolt." This may mean (1) that the innate personal sweetness of the shepherd's presence left its fragrance on that which he touched; or (2) that the shepherd had come to the door perfumed as if for a festival. Myrrh was a costly ointment. Some have argued that it would be unlikely that a shepherd would have access to such expensive ointment. Yet even more unlikely is the notion that the lover at the door was Solomon (5:5).

The maiden then opened the door, only to find that her beloved had disappeared: "I opened to my beloved; but my beloved had withdrawn himself and was gone." She felt compelled to seek him out. She had to explain why she had not answered his call immediately: "My heart had gone out as he spoke." She loved him more than she knew. His pitiful appeal at the door had made her realize how much she did love him. "I searched for him, but I did not find him; I called him, but he did not answer me." She wants desperately to tell him how she feels. Off into the night she goes, as in 3:2 (5:6).

On this trip through the city, the Shulamite was not as fortunate as she had been in her earlier search for her beloved (cf. 3:3). Then the watchmen had allowed her to pass unmolested, had even indicated to her where her beloved could be found. This time the story is different: "The watchmen that go about the city found me, they smote me, they wounded me; the keepers of the walls took away my mantle from me." Apparently they mistake her for a thief or spy. Perhaps she had been warned of such a fate during her first midnight foray into the city. Now she is smitten and wounded with reproaches and false accusations, as though she were a guilty and evil-minded woman. She was subjected to abuse and ill treatment from those who should have been her guardians. Worse might have befallen her had she not escaped, leaving her robe behind her (5:7).

This trance-like recollection was exceedingly painful to the Shulamite. She had turned away from her beloved. She had failed to respond to his request to be at her side. Sorry for how she had treated him, she had risked life and limb to find him that night, to tell him how much she loved him. She never saw her beloved again. She never got to express to him the feelings of her heart. The king had taken her away to be his bride. She had little hope at this point that she would ever be reunited with her shepherd.

LOVE FORTIFIED THROUGH DECLARATION
Song 5:8–6:3

A. An Appeal to Her Friends (5:8).

The trance ends. Again the Shulamite addresses the "daughters of Jerusalem." She is desperate that her shepherd know how much she loves him. She pleads with these ladies to tell him, if they should ever see him: "I adjure you, O daughters of Jerusalem, if you find my beloved, that you tell him that I am love sick." They must tell him, for she cannot. Once married to Solomon, her contact with the world outside the palace would be over (5:8).

B. An Inquiry about Her Beloved (5:9).

The palace ladies were stunned by the continuing loyalty of this maiden to her shepherd. What kind of person must he be to hold her affections captive even while she is surrounded by the temptation to become the wife of Solomon? "What kind of beloved is your beloved, O most lovely among women? What kind of beloved is your beloved, that you adjure us so?" The tone here may be mocking as in the response of these same women in 1:8. In any case, their inquiry presents the bride an opportunity to enter into a glowing description of the object of her love. In her eyes, the beloved shepherd is perfect in every way. He is everything he can and should be.

C. A Description of the Shepherd (5:10-16).

The Shulamite is only too happy to describe her wonderful lover. "My beloved is dazzling and ruddy, the chief among ten thousand." The term "dazzling" (tsach) means a bright, shining clearness. The term "ruddy" ('adhom) is dark red, no doubt indicating health and vigor. Unlike the nobility of the palace who displayed aristocratic paleness, the shepherd had the rugged good looks of an outdoorsman. He was a man's man. He was the kind of fellow who would stand out even in the largest crowd (5:10).

The maiden now enumerates ten excellent features of this young man. First, "his head is like gold, pure gold," i.e., his head is exquisite. Second, "his locks are wavy [lit., heaps upon heaps], black as a raven." The idea is that his hair hangs in wavy curls from his head (5:11).

Third, "his eyes are like doves beside the water; washed with milk and fitly set." His eyes are pure and clear. Their moistness expresses devotion and feeling. The pureness of the white of the eye is represented in the bathing or washing in milk. Doves are fond of bathing, and usually choose the vicinity of streams for their abode. The eyes are full and large. The phrase "fitly set" (lit., sitting in fullness), compares his eyes to precious stones set in a ring. The figure refers, no doubt, to the steady, strong look of those eyes (5:12).

Fourth, "his cheeks are like a bed of balsam, banks of sweet-scented herbs." The bearded cheek is compared to towers of aromatic plants. Perhaps the beard was perfumed. Fifth, "his lips are lilies, dripping with liquid myrrh." The lips are soft, lovely, and inviting. They drop words like liquid fragrance, i.e., he was gracious and tender in his speech (5:13).

Sixth, "his hands are rods of gold set with beryl." The outstretched hands are meant. The fingers are full, round, and fleshy like bars of gold. They are delicately rounded fingers, tipped with well-shaped nails, as if inlaid with precious stones. "Beryl" (tarshish) is chrysolite. In color it is yellow, and pellucid, thus suggesting that the nails are transparently pink.

Seventh, "his abdomen is carved ivory inlaid with sapphires." She speaks of the perfect smoothness and symmetry of his abdomen, like that of a beautiful ivory statue, the work of the highest artistic excellence. The sapphire inlay refers to the beautiful blue veins which appear through the skin and give a lovely tint to the body. The point is that every inch of his body is more precious to her than all the wealth of Solomon (5:14).

Eighth, "his legs are pillars of alabaster set on pedestals of pure gold." The white alabaster is a figure for greatness and purity; the gold points to sublimity and nobleness. Ninth, "his appearance is like Lebanon, excellent as the cedars." He may not be a king, but he has a kingly bearing. His height was awe-inspiring and delightful, his posture impeccable. As the cedars tower above other trees, so he is outstanding among men (5:15).

Tenth, "his mouth is full of sweetness." When he speaks his words are full of winning love. In every way the shepherd was appealing and attractive: "And he is wholly desirable." This is the man for which she pines. This is the man with whom she longs to spend her life: "This is my beloved, and this is my friend, O daughters of Jerusalem" (5:16).

D. An Inquiry by the Friends (6:1).

The Jerusalem maidens are bemused[3] by the description of the perfect man which they have just heard. They mock her love by sarcastically saying: "Where has your beloved gone, O most beautiful among women? Where has your beloved turned aside, that we may seek him with you." They feign interest in locating such a "catch." The Shulamite interprets their jesting seriously. She continues to pour out her heart (6:1).

E. A Declaration of Love (6:2-3).

"My beloved has gone down to his garden, to the beds of spices, to feed in the gardens, and to gather lilies." The shepherd no doubt returned to the beautiful and fragrant grass lands to pasture his sheep. She imagines him gathering a bouquet of lilies to bring to her (6:2).

Though separated by distance and circumstances, the Shulamite is confident of two things: She loves this shepherd, and he loves her: "I am my beloved's and my beloved is mine." Though other women may choose to chase after him, she was confident in her relationship to him. These harem girls are not to search him out; that was the Shulamite's responsibility (6:3).

ENDNOTES

1. S.M. Lehrman thinks that the shepherd is speaking after the arrival of the king to claim his bride. "The Song of Songs," in *The Five Megilloth* (London: Soncino, 1961), p. 13. One would think that it would be extremely dangerous for a man to talk this way to the bride of the king, even if he could have access to her presence.

2. Ibid., p. 15. Another interpretation is that she has captured his love with but one glance of her eyes.

3. Others interpret the verse to mean that the women were so moved by her description as to want to help her find him.

CHAPTER FORTY-THREE

Back with the Beloved
Song 6:4-8:14

To conclude his poem, the writer brings back to the stage the characters connected with the Shulamite. Each utters, or at least listens to, words which sum up the true condition of the maiden.

SOLOMON'S FINAL WOOING
Song 6:4-13

Solomon reappears on stage, as it were. He makes his last effort to win the affection of the maiden. He renews his flatteries emphatically.

A. The King's Flatteries (6:4-10).

Solomon begins his final effort by comparing the Shulamite to lovely cities: "You are beautiful, O my darling, as Tirzah, as lovely as Jerusalem." Tirzah and Jerusalem were regarded by Israelites as the two most beautiful cities of the land. They are used here as symbols of the surpassing beauty of the Shulamite. Yes, and her beauty is yet greater: It is "as awesome as an army with banners." Her beauty is overwhelming, it is subduing and all-conquering, like a warrior-host with flying banners going forth to victory. Solomon, the famous ladies' man, confesses that he had been vanquished by this sweet and unpretentious country girl (6:4).

The smitten king begs the maiden to look away from him: "Turn away your eyes from me, for they have overcome me." He feels helpless to withstand the gaze of her eyes. Her looks melt him, and make it impossible for him to speak coherently to her.

Yet Solomon continues: "Your hair is like a flock of goats that have descended from Gilead." This is a repetition of the comparison made in 4:1. He goes on to repeat the comparison of her teeth to newly washed twin ewes, and her temples [or cheeks] to a slice of pomegranate (6:5-7; cf. 4:2f.).

Solomon now compares his bride to the other members of the harem. "There are sixty queens and eighty concubines, and virgins without number." The setting of this love story is in the early reign of Solomon before he reached the three hundred wives and seven hundred concubines of 1 Kings 11:3. The Shulamite exceeded all these women in beauty and purity: "My dove, my perfect one is unique. She is her mother's only one; she is the pure child of the one who bore her." Just as the maiden stood out in her family as the favorite of her mother, so she stands out as unique among the women of the palace. Emphasis here is on the purity of the maiden. Her innocence, modesty and purity were qualities which attracted Solomon to her.

Because of her stunning beauty and excellent moral qualities, the Shulamite was admired by all the women of the harem: "The daughters saw her, and called her blessed; the queens and the concubines, and they praised her" (6:8-9).

Verse 10 is praise directed toward the Shulamite. Solomon is speaking, but he is citing the reactions of the court ladies when they first laid eyes on the Shulamite. "Who is this that bends forward like the morning, fair as the moon." The first figure seems to refer to the rising sun, breaking through the shades of night on the eastern horizon. She is fair (lit., white) as the moon. The figure refers to her true womanly delicacy and fairness.

The remaining figures in v. 10 remove any thought of mere weakness: She is "clear as the sun, awesome as an army with banners?" The word for "sun" is not the usual *shemesh*, but *chammah*, "heat." The fierce rays of the Eastern sun are terrible to those who encounter them. This woman has power to captivate and conquer. She is as awesome as an army (6:10).

B. The Maiden's Predicament (6:11-13).

Now at last the poet reveals how the Shulamite came to be headed for marriage with the king: "I went down into the garden of nuts to see the green plants of the valley, to see whether the vine budded and the pomegranates had blossomed." She had been busy with her country chores that fateful day, checking on the family gardens and vineyards (6:11).

Suddenly she found herself swept away by a royal entourage which was passing by: "Before I was aware, my soul set me over the chariots of my noble people." She seems to be reproaching herself for having allowed her curiosity to draw her too near the escort of the young king, who with his court, was on an outing in the neighborhood of the place where she lived. She acknowledges that she had brought her predicament upon herself. She does not seem to have been taken violently. She had been overawed by the spectacle and momentarily charmed by the attentions of the king (6:12).

It is clear that the Shulamite attempted to flee, but when? At the time when she first was noticed by the king and his attendants back in the country? Or was she attempting now in the palace to flee reality, to flee the presence of the palace women who attended to her? Though the second alternative is more difficult to comprehend, the dialogue which follows supports it.

In her state of trance, the maiden rises and endeavors to escape the palace. The women shout after her: "Return, return, O Shulamite; return, return, that we may look upon you." That beautiful women want to gaze on the loveliness of the maiden is another way of underscoring her superior beauty. For the first time in the poem the maiden is identified regionally as the "Shulamite," i.e., one from Shulam or Shunem.

The Shulamite responds with charming modesty: "What will you

see in the Shulamite as at the dance of Mahanaim?" She has no realization of how beautiful she really is. The "dance of Mahanaim" (lit.,
two companies) has been interpreted several ways. Was it a dance in
which the inhabitants of Mahanaim excelled? Was it metaphoric for
an angelic dance, since angels once appeared at Mahanaim? Was it
the name of one of the sacred dances alluded to in Scripture? Did the
Shulamite begin to dance before the harem girls? This much is clear:
The timid country maiden did not wish to be a spectacle (6:13).

PRAISE FOR THE SHULAMITE'S BEAUTY
Song 7:1–8:4

A. Praise by the Court Ladies (7:1-5).

To the ladies of the palace, the Shulamite appears noble, royal and
beautiful beyond description. For this reason they address her, not as
Shulamite (i.e., country girl) but as "prince's daughter" (nadhibh). The
term connotes "noble in disposition." The women start with her feet
and praise her beauty to her head.

First, "how beautiful are your feet in sandals." Does this suggest
that before coming to the palace she had gone barefoot? The beautiful footwear added to the loveliness of her feet. Second, "the curves
of your hips are like jewels, the work of the hands of an artist." Like a
beautiful dancer, her movements were full of grace. They are compared to the swinging to and fro of jeweled ornaments made in
chains. The skilled craftsman is an artist who is master of that work
which remains beautiful (7:1).

Third, "your navel is like a round goblet which never lacks mixed
wine." The ladies are in the privacy of their apartment in the palace.
There is nothing indelicate in this description, though it is scarcely
Western. "Mixed wine" is wine with water mixed with it. The "round
goblet" is intended to convey the shape of the lovely body. The flesh
color appears through the semitransparent clothing. The belly moves
gracefully as in dance like the diluted wine in the goblet. The "navel"
is here regarded as the center of the body.

Fourth, "your belly is a heap of wheat set about with lilies." The
great heaps of wheat were symmetrically arranged in the field. On top
of the heaps objects which moved in the wind were placed so as to

discourage hungry birds. Such would be regarded as a beautiful sight in an agricultural society. The smooth, round, fair body of the maiden is seen to advantage in the varied movements of her dance (7:2).

Fifth, "your two breasts are like two fawns that are twins of a roe." Earlier Solomon had used similar language (4:5). This praise comes from the lips of the palace ladies (7:3).

Sixth, "your neck is like the tower of ivory." The palace ladies echo the previous praise of Solomon (4:4). The ivory tower was probably a well known landmark of the area. It probably got its name because it was decorated with inlaid ivory panels. The comparison is obvious: her neck is slender, dazzlingly white in appearance, imposing and captivating.

Seventh, "your eyes are as the pools in Heshbon, by the gate of Bath-rabbim." Heshbon is located in Transjordan in the region known as Moab. Her eyes were moist, inviting and clear as spring water.

Eighth, "your nose[1] is like the tower of Lebanon which looks toward Damascus." The nose formed a straight line down from the forehead, conveying the impression of symmetry. At the same time it conveyed a dignity and majesty inspiring with awe like the tower of Lebanon. The reference is perhaps to a particular tower. The language does not necessitate that this tower be located in Lebanon. It may have been built with cedars from Lebanon. This tower could have been within sight of the palace. That it faced toward Damascus would mean that the tower was in the northeastern wall of the city (7:4).

Ninth, "your head upon you is like Carmel." Carmel was considered the most beautiful area of Canaan. The meaning is the exquisite fitness of the head upon the neck, which is one of the most lovely traits of personal beauty. Tenth, "the hair of your head [is] like purple." The purple shellfish is found near Carmel. The thought is that the locks of her hair are a glistening purple color, i.e., their black is purple as they catch the lights.

B. Praise by the Suitor (7:6-9).

The young king is excited to rapture by the sight of his bride. He gives vent without restraint to his passion. He addresses the Shulamite directly.

First, he expresses his general delight with her. "How beautiful and how delightful you are, my love, with all your charms" (7:6). Second, he commends her stature: "your stature is like a palm tree, and your breasts are like its clusters." The palm tree may be selected on account of its elegance. It is commonly employed in Eastern poetry as the emblem of love. Beautiful dark brown or golden-yellow clusters of fruit crown the summit of the stem. Such clusters impart beauty to the tree, especially when seen in the evening twilight (7:7).

Her breasts stimulate his desire. "I said, I will climb the palm tree, I will take hold of its fruit stalks." The king tells her to what heights he would go to obtain her love. "Oh, may your breasts be like clusters of the vine, and the fragrance of your breath like apples, and your mouth like the best wine!" Her speech was sweeter to him than the choicest wine (7:8-9a).

C. Response of the Shulamite (7:9b-10).

The Shulamite interrupts the flatteries of Solomon as she did earlier in the poem. Her lips may be like the best wine, but only her beloved would know their full impact: "It goes down smoothly for my beloved, flowing gently through the lips of those who fall asleep." Just as much wine causes deep sleep, colored by pleasant dreams, so would her speech stir his pleasant emotions (7:9b).

The reference to sleep suggests that the maiden enters her trance-like state. Here she can address her beloved freely. It is as though he is present with her at that moment.

First, she expresses her love for him and her confidence in his love for her: "I am my beloved's, and his desire is for me." This is a forthright and final rejection of the wooing of the king (cf. 6:3). None can separate her from her beloved (7:10).

Second, she invites her beloved on an excursion to the country: "Come, my beloved, let us go out into the country, let us spend the night in the villages." She would rather go to the villages with her beloved than to go to Tirzah or Jerusalem with Solomon.

Third, she imagines that he will join her in her daily responsibilities: "Let us rise early and go to the vineyards; let us see whether the vine has budded, and its blossoms have opened, and whether the pomegranates have bloomed."

Fourth, she longs to rejoin her beloved in the country so that she might give him her love: "There I will give you my love." There in the country she would serve him with the fruits new and old which she had been keeping for him: "The mandrakes have given forth fragrance; and over our doors are all choice fruits, both new and old, which I have saved up for you, my beloved." Fruits were stored on shelves or cupboards above doorways where they were left to dry and be out of reach. She assures her lover that she has put away all the good things for him only to enjoy (7:13).[2]

Fifth, she expresses the wish that her beloved were her brother. "Oh that you were like a brother to me who nursed at my mother's breasts. If I found you outdoors, I would kiss you; no one would despise me, either." Apparently in her home the course of true love did not run smoothly. There were too many prying eyes, too many restrictions. If the beloved had been her brother, their companionship would have been freer and less restricted. This has received three interpretations. First, she refers to a blood brother. She wants her relationship to her beloved to be the highest and the purest and the most permanent possible. Whereas marital bonds may be broken, nothing can destroy the bond of blood.

The second view is that the Shulamite refers to a "milk brother," i.e., an unrelated child suckled by her mother. At least then she would live with him, and express her love for him without anyone having a right to condemn her. The third view is that the Shulamite is longing for a marriage of the highest sort with her beloved. There is some indication that the brother-sister relationship was regarded as higher than that of the husband-wife. Thus a wife of exceptional quality might be called "sister" or even adopted as one's sister (8:1).

Were he her "brother" she could sit at his feet in her mother's house, and let him teach her all she does not know;[3] none would question her bringing him home. Then she in turn would offer him spiced wine and the fruit juice: "I would lead you and bring you into the house of my mother, who used to instruct me; I would give you spiced wine to drink from the juice of my pomegranates." This "juice" ('asis) was a fermented juice obtained from crushing fruit in a winepress. She stresses *my* pomegranates because she herself had prepared the beverage for him (8:2).

She longs to sink into his arms, and be held by him: "Let his left hand be under my head, and his right hand embrace me" (8:3).

What ecstasy she experiences in the arms of her beloved. She does not wish this fantasy to be disturbed. For the third time (cf. 2:7; 3:5) she reminds the daughters of Jerusalem that true love cannot be aroused by others: "I want you to swear, O daughters of Jerusalem, Do not arouse or awaken love, until she pleases" (8:4).

THE SHULAMITE AND HER BELOVED
Song 8:5-7

The scene is introduced by the collective voice of a choir: "Who is this coming up from the wilderness, leaning on her beloved?" The chorus sees in the distance two personages approaching—a youth with a maiden who is leaning upon him in trustfulness and tenderness. What a contrast to her arrival in Jerusalem carried in the magnificent royal palanquin, and surrounded by the royal bodyguard. Now she has regained her liberty, and has hastened home to seek her friend. The question here is clearly intended to be parallel to that of 3:6.

The Shulamite found her beloved taking a nap under a tree which, during their courtship, had been their special place: "Beneath the apple tree I awakened you."[4] That tree was near the house where he had been born: "There your mother was in labor with you, there she was in labor and gave you birth." In the East, childbirth in the open air was not uncommon (8:5).

Now that she has found him, her sole wish is to be forever with him: "Set me like a seal over your heart, like a seal on your arm." The literature of love contains no marriage proposal which exceeds this one in passion. She longs to be constantly near him, never to be parted. Seals were suspended from the neck of a woman with a cord. Men generally wore a signet ring on the right hand.

The Shulamite celebrates the strength of the love which has made her victorious: "For love is as strong as death." Love is as irresistible as death, which none can overcome. Its "ardor" (NASB margin; NIV) is "as cruel as the grave." Love excites a zeal which completely enslaves one. It is as powerful as fire which flashes forth to consume all before it. Indeed, true love is like "a most vehement flame" (RSV).

Only the power of death and the insatiableness of Sheol (the abode of the dead) can equal the overpowering, all-consuming power of true love (8:6).

The flame of true love cannot be extinguished by external forces: "Many waters cannot quench love, nor will rivers overflow it." True love cannot be purchased: "If a man were to give all the riches of his house for love, it would be utterly despised." Thus true love is unconquerable and unpurchasable. This verse is the climax of the book. In her own experience the Shulamite has demonstrated the truth here stated (8:7).

THE SHULAMITE AND HER BROTHERS
Song 8:8-10

At her mother's house the Shulamite speaks with her brothers who had been responsible for raising her. Apparently her father was dead.[5] She reminds them of what they had said about her when she was approaching puberty: "We have a little sister, and she has no breasts, What shall we do for our sister on the day when she is spoken for?" On her wedding day, they stipulated that their generosity would depend on her virtue. When they first discussed this matter, she was not yet of marriageable age. To be "spoken for" means that a marriage request had been received (8:8).

The family resolves to adjust their actions to the character of the girl: "If she is a wall, we will build on her a battlement of silver." The thought is that the young lady would be crowned with honor, if not wealth, if she maintains her virginity. On the other hand, "if she is a door, we shall barricade her with planks of cedar," i.e., solitary confinement for her own protection. A "door" is a female who is flirtatious and improper in her relations with men. Should their sister go that direction, she would face family shame and even servitude (8:9).

The Shulamite now claims moral excellence: "I was a wall, and my breasts were like towers; then I became in his eyes as one who finds peace." She was now mature, ready for marriage. She is past the stage of life indicated in v. 8. She had been like a city besieged by the suitor. Yet she never gave in to the allurements of wine and wealth, fame and flattery. Her resolute love, chastity, and fidelity had forced the suitor

871

who besieged that wall to sue for peace. She can now claim that which the brothers had stipulated as the reward for her chastity (8:10).⁶

THE SHULAMITE AND SOLOMON
Song 8:11-12

The Shulamite finally settles her account with Solomon, the persistent suitor. The king owned a large vineyard in a place called Baalhamon. The place name means "master of a multitude." The exact location is unknown. "He entrusted the vineyard to caretakers," i.e., he let it out to tenants. It brought the king large revenues. Each tenant was to pay him a thousand shekels for the fruit of the vineyard. This valuable vineyard is cited as an example of the enormous wealth which had been used to tempt the Shulamite to yield to Solomon. Perhaps it had been offered to her family as the *mohar* (bride gift) in exchange for the Shulamite's hand in marriage (8:11).

The Shulamite had spurned the offer of the vineyard. It had been returned to Solomon. The king could continue to extract from it those huge revenues. The Shulamite had her own vineyard: "My very own vineyard is at my disposal." She refers to her own person figuratively as a vineyard. Though modest in comparison with that of Solomon, it was entirely hers. It had not been rented out to others. The point is that her love was not for sale. She had remained loyal to her shepherd despite the glittering temptations to become Solomon's bride.

THE SHULAMITE AND THE SHEPHERD
Song 8:13-14

The shepherd now speaks. He addresses the Shulamite as "you who sit in the gardens." The term "gardens" here symbolizes social life with its restraints in contrast to the open pasturelands which symbolize freedom. He refers to certain companions who had accompanied him from the pastures. On behalf of these friends and himself, he asks the Shulamite for a song: "My companions are listening for your voice—Let me hear it." Perhaps they have gathered to hear of some of her experiences in the palace (8:13).

The Shulamite responds to this request for a song with these mys-

872

terious words: "Flee, my beloved, and be like a young stag on the mountains of spices." She is urging her beloved to hurry to her, as though fleeing, to come to her. Are these the words of some love song which she had sung to her beloved and about him throughout the days of their courtship? If so, she sings it now again to the delight of their many friends who have come to wish them well. On the other hand, the thought may be that she will sing to him when they are alone. The rugged heights which once separated them are no longer barriers between them (cf. 2:8,17), but delightful, like mounds of spices (8:14).

ENDNOTES

1. Some think the "nose" in 7:4 refers to the face as a whole.

2. S.M. Lehrman, "The Song of Songs," in *The Five Megilloth* (London: Soncino, 1961), p. 28.

3. The Hebrew is ambiguous. It could read, "that she [the mother] might teach me." Her mother would teach her to prepare spiced wine, or, if the spiced wine be euphemistic, teach her the secrets of love. So Lehrman, *Song*, p. 29.

4. Another interpretation: As the two make their way to her house, they pass by places which had special meaning to their relationship.

5. Another interpretation: She reminds them how unnecessary had been their fear for her chastity when tested by temptation.

6. Another interpretation of 8:8-10: The Shulamite is speaking to the brothers regarding a younger sister. This interpretation is difficult to reconcile with 6:9 which hints that the Shulamite was the only daughter of her mother.